Access 2003
ALL-IN-ONE DESK REFERENCE
FOR
DUMMIES®

Access 2003
ALL-IN-ONE DESK REFERENCE
FOR
DUMMIES®

by Alan Simpson, Margaret Levine Young,
Alison Barrows

WILEY

Wiley Publishing, Inc.

Access 2003 All-in-One Desk Reference For Dummies®
Published by
Wiley Publishing, Inc.
111 River Street
Hoboken, NJ 07030
www.wiley.com

Copyright © 2003 by Wiley Publishing, Inc., Indianapolis, Indiana

Published by Wiley Publishing, Inc., Indianapolis, Indiana

Published simultaneously in Canada

For general information on our other products and services or to obtain technical support, please contact our Customer Care Department within the U.S. at 800-762-2974, outside the U.S. at 317-572-3993, or fax 317-572-4002.

Wiley also publishes its books in a variety of electronic formats. Some content that appears in print may not be available in electronic books.

Library of Congress Control Number: 2003105629

ISBN: 0-7645-3988-4

1B/RZ/QZ/QT/IN

Manufactured in the United States of America

10 9 8 7 6 5

About the Authors

Alan Simpson is the author of over 80 computer books on all sorts of topics: Windows, databases, Web site design and development, programming, and network administration. His books are published throughout the world in over a dozen languages and have millions of copies. When not building computers or writing books about them, Alan eats or sleeps. He doesn't have a fancy job title, because he's never had a real job, and still doesn't know how to tie a tie.

Margaret Levine Young has co-authored several dozen computer books about the Internet, UNIX, WordPerfect, Access, and (stab from the past) PC-File and Javelin, including *The Internet For Dummies* (published by Wiley Publishing, Inc.) and *Windows XP Home Edition: The Complete Reference* (published by Osborne/McGraw-Hill). She met her future husband Jordan in the R.E.S.I.S.T.O.R.S., a high-school computer club before there were high school computer clubs. Her other passions are her children, music, Unitarian Universalism (www.uua.org), reading, and anything to do with cooking or eating.

Alison Barrows has authored or co-authored books on Windows, the Internet, Microsoft Access, WordPerfect, Lotus 1-2-3, and other topics. In addition to writing books, Alison writes and edits technical documentation and training material. She holds a B.A. in International Relations from Wellesley College and an M.P.P. from Harvard University. In real life she hangs out with her "guys" — Parker, 3, and Mason, 1, and tries to carve out some time to practice yoga. Alison lives with her family in central Massachusetts.

Dedication

To Susan, Ashley, and Alec, as always. (AS)

To Jordan, Meg, and Zac, with love. (MLY)

To Matt, Parker, and Mason. (AB)

Authors' Acknowledgments

We would like to acknowledge the care of Paul Levesque, Nicole Haims, Terry Varveris, Rebecca Senninger, Greg Guntle and all the others who shepherded this book through the editing and production process, as well as all the folks listed on the Publisher's Acknowledgements page who worked on this book.

Alison thanks Colleen, Jessica, Lizzie, Matt, and Dotty for taking great care of my little guys so I can get work done. Matt (also known as honey) gets special thanks as my hardware guru. Alison would also like to thank Margy and Alan — I'm honored to be involved in such a great team.

Publisher's Acknowledgments

We're proud of this book; please send us your comments through our online registration form located at www.dummies.com/register/.

Some of the people who helped bring this book to market include the following:

Acquisitions, Editorial, and Media Development

Project Editor: Paul Levesque

Acquisitions Editor: Terri Varveris

Copy Editor: Rebecca Senninger

Technical Editor: Greg Guntle

Editorial Managers: Leah Cameron, Kevin Kirschner

Editorial Assistant: Amanda Foxworth

Cartoons: Rich Tennant (www.the5thwave.com)

Production

Project Coordinator: Ryan Steffen

Layout and Graphics: Amanda Carter, Seth Conley, Carrie Foster, Stephanie D. Jumper, Jacque Schneider, Julie Trippetti

Proofreaders: Debbye Butler, John Tyler Connoley, Kathy Simpson, Brian H. Walls

Indexer: Sharon Hilgenberg

Special Help: Teresa Artman, Barry Childs-Helton, Jean Rogers, Virginia Sanders

Publishing and Editorial for Technology Dummies

Richard Swadley, Vice President and Executive Group Publisher

Andy Cummings, Vice President and Publisher

Mary C. Corder, Editorial Director

Publishing for Consumer Dummies

Diane Graves Steele, Vice President and Publisher

Joyce Pepple, Acquisitions Director

Composition Services

Gerry Fahey, Vice President of Production Services

Debbie Stailey, Director of Composition Services

Contents at a Glance

Table of Contents

Introduction

*N*o sooner are we used to Access 2002 when all of a sudden, here's Access 2003 to worry about. Of course, if you never used Access before in your life, then you're starting fresh, so never mind. Whether you never used any version of Microsoft Access, and aren't even sure what a "version" is, or you're upgrading from a previous version, you've come to the right book.

The basic idea behind Microsoft Access is to allow individuals and small businesses to manage large amounts of information the way the big corporations do — with relational databases. The difference is that while the big boys spend millions on computer hardware, software, and staffs of nerdy database administrator types, Access allows you do it all yourself with a run-of-the-mill PC and a realistic software budget.

Microsoft Access 2003 is the latest-and-greatest version of a long line of Access versions, starting (not surprisingly) with Version 1. Not that it's the 2,003rd version. Somewhere along the way Microsoft switched from using sequential numbers for versions to using years. An idea first pioneered by the automotive industry, who sells things like "2003 Ford Mustangs" as opposed to "Mustang 11s." In fact, Microsoft Access 2003 is Microsoft Access Version 11.

Without going into boring detail about what's new in Access 2003, you find the usual kind of stuff you find in new versions these days — more power, more flexibility, more Web-based features, more things you can do with it. And of course, along the lines of the holy grail of everything computerish these days, more taking advantage of everything the Internet has to offer.

Luckily, Access has been very stable for the last three versions. The menus and toolbars are almost identical in Access 2000, 2002, and 2003, except that each new version has a few new commands. If you use an older version of Access, this book is still useful. Almost everything we describe is the same in the latest three Access versions, and where there are differences, we make a note.

About Access 2003 All-in-One Desk Reference For Dummies

If you ever have the misfortune of trying to read anything written by one of the aforementioned database administrator types, you know all about being faced with a decision among the lesser of evils. Option 1) Try to figure out what on earth these database nerds are talking about. Option 2) Part with your hard-earned money to hire someone to do the work for you, only to have someone with poor taste in clothing look at you like you're an idiot every time you open your mouth. Or Option 3) Forget computers altogether and stick with index cards.

Option 1 is probably the least of the evils, but potentially the most difficult to achieve. Figuring out what someone is talking about when they assume that everyone on the planet was born already knowing what terms like *third normal form* and *Transact-SQL* mean is tough. Option 2 is too odious to warrant serious consideration. Which leaves Option 3, or a new Option 4 — this book.

The nerds who wrote this book are aware of the fact that *nobody* on the planet was *ever* born knowing what *any* technical term means. In fact, if at all possible, we avoid technical terms like a root canal. But because you are probably faced with technical terms outside this book, we do explain what they mean along the way.

As a rule, big fat computer books aren't such a great option. For that reason, this isn't really a big fat computer book. It's nine small computer books combined into one. Each small book represents a single topic that you can pursue, or ignore, as your personal tastes and immediate needs dictate.

The idea here is definitely *not* to try to read the book cover-to-cover, unless you're desperately seeking a cure for insomnia. Rather, use the Table of Contents up front, or the Index out back, to look up information when trying to figure it out by guessing just isn't cutting it.

To prevent this book from topping 3,000 pages, we don't explain every possible way to do every possible thing in Access. Instead, we chose what we think are the most important database management tasks, and we show you the best way to do each one.

Conventions

Speaking of insomnia, this book, like most books, follows certain conventions to alert you to different kinds of stuff, as follows:

Boldface: Stuff you actually *do* while sitting at your computer is shown in boldface, to distinguish it from boring information you probably don't care about anyway.

Italics: When reality rears its ugly head and we're forced to use a technical term, we always show that term in italics the first time it's used. Then we define that term, right there on the spot. Of course, that doesn't mean you won't forget the definition two minutes later. But you can easily flip back a few pages and locate the definition amidst all the other words on the page.

`Monospace`: Monospace text (text in that typeface right back there) represents *code,* instructions that are written for computers, rather than people, to follow. Computers are so stupid, the term "stupid" is a compliment. Unconscious, non-thinking, non-beings (a.k.a. *machines*) is more like it. Anyway, when writing instructions for a computer, you *really* have to spell it out for them, right down to the blank spaces between words. Monospace text makes seeing where you have to put the blank spaces to avoid making Access say "Huh?" easier. (Actually, it can't even say "Huh?" More likely it says something really stupid like "Syntax error in *something or other.*")

Foolish Assumptions

Despite the fact that the word "Dummies" is clearly emblazoned on this book's cover and elsewhere, we don't presume you're a complete idiot. (The machine you're working with, yes. You, no.) We do assume that you already know how to do some things, such as turn on your computer and click and double-click things with your mouse. Maybe type with at least one finger.

We also assume you know what those *key+key* symbols, such as "Ctrl+Esc," mean. But just in case you don't, they always mean "Hold down the first key, tap the second key, and then release the first key." Also, we always use the term "press" when referring to something you do with the keyboard. For example, the instruction "Press Ctrl+Esc" means "Hold down the Ctrl key on your keyboard, tap the Esc key, and then release the Ctrl key." Click, on the other hand, is something you do with the mouse pointer on your computer screen and the buttons on your mouse.

We also assume (perhaps foolishly) that you know how to work menus. So when telling you some sequence of commands from a menu, we use the word "Choose" followed by the commands to choose separated by an ⇨ symbol. For example, when we say "Choose Start⇨All Programs⇨Microsoft Office⇨Microsoft Access Office 2003" that's short for "Click the Start button, click All Programs on the Start menu that appears, click Microsoft Office on the All Programs menu that appears, and then click Microsoft Office 2003 on the last menu that appears." Click, of course, means, "rest the mouse pointer on the item, and then press and release the left mouse button." When we tell you to *drag* something, we mean to move your mouse pointer to the item, and hold down the left mouse button while moving the mouse. To *drop* the item, just release the mouse button after dragging it.

Access has smart menus that try to show only the commands that you used recently. If a command is mysteriously missing from a menu, click the double-V button at the bottom of the menu (or just wait a few seconds) for Access to show you the less popular commands on the menu.

We also show things like Web site URLs (addresses) — those www.*whatever*.com things you see all over the place. We may even throw in an occasional e-mail address (the *somebody@somewhere*.com things) without explaining how to use them. Hopefully these assumptions on our part aren't too foolish. But if we had to explain *all* that stuff here, there wouldn't be much space left for talking about Microsoft Access 2003.

What You Don't Have to Read

Because reading the instructions is something we all resort to only when guessing just won't work, we try to point out things you really don't have to read. For examples, sidebars (which have a gray background) are little chunks of text with their own titles. If the title looks boring, skip the whole thing.

We also put little *icons* (pictures) in the left margin to point out text that you can maybe skip over. Or in some cases, really shouldn't skip over. The icons are pretty self-explanatory. So if you want to skip the next section, that's fine by us.

Icons

As far as those presumably self-explanatory icons go, here are the explanations you can probably skip over or, at best, glance at:

This is stuff you probably don't want to ignore. Because if you do, you may well regret it. Not that you're gonna blow up your computer or the Internet or anything if you do. But the consequences may be inconvenient or unpleasant enough to justify spending a few seconds to read what it says.

May be worth reading if you're looking for a shortcut, or a better way to do things. Not as important as a warning. But probably worth a few seconds of your time.

Either stuff we already told you and you probably forgot, or something that's at least worth trying to keep in the back of your mind. Even if it's way back there. Kinda like where you parked your car when you go to the mall.

This *is* a reference book, and we certainly don't expect anyone to read it cover to cover. But sometimes, you just have to know "Subject x" before "Subject y" even comes close to making any sense. So when we're forced to talk about a "Subject y" kind of thing, we use this icon to point out where "Subject x" is covered.

Stuff that definitely falls into the "insomnia cure" category.

Organization

If you already looked at the Contents at a Glance up near the front of this book, or the Table of Contents right after it, you already know how stuff is organized here. In that case, you may now skip to the "Where to Go from Here" section. But because showing the contents a third time is customary (albeit kinda dumb), without the benefit of page numbers, we follow suit here. This book is actually nine little books organized as follows:

Book I: Essential Concepts: If this is your first time using Microsoft Access, and you really don't know where else to go, starting here is a good idea. This is the stuff you really need to know to get anything done with Access.

Book II: Tables: Everything in Access centers around *data* (information) stored in tables (not the coffee kind, the columns-and-rows kind). You can't do much of anything with Access until you have some information stored in tables. This book is a good second stop for you *newbies* (beginners).

Book III: Queries: Data stored in tables tends to be pretty random and, eventually, pretty plentiful. This book shows you how to pick and choose the information you want to see, and how to organize it in a way that's more useful, such as alphabetically.

Book IV: Forms: You can definitely get away without making forms in your Access database. But if you get tired of looking at information stored in rows and columns, and are up for being creative, forms are definitely worth getting into.

Book V: Reports: Whereas forms are a way to get creative with stuff on your screen, reports are a way to get creative with stuff you print on your computer's printer. Here's where you can do things, for example, printing form letters, mailing labels, numbers with totals and subtotals, and stuff like that.

Book VI: Macros: Automating Stuff in Access: There's a technical term for you — *macros*. Nothing to be intimidated by, though. They're just a way of writing simple instructions that tell Access how to do something you're sick of doing yourself. Optional, but more fun than the name implies.

Book VII: Database Administration: Sounds like a real yawn, we know. Sometimes you just gotta do things such as make backup copies of your information, or get other people to help you with boring stuff such as typing information into your tables. This is the place where we cover those kinds of things.

Book VIII: Programming in VBA: For the aspiring mega-nerd, we didn't let this topic slide. This is where the techno-geeks make their money. Though you can skip it if you have no such aspirations. The first chapter is titled "What the Heck Is VBA?," so you don't need to feel intimidated.

Book IX: Access on the Web: Don't be misled by this title. It isn't about wandering around the Internet and looking for yet more information about Microsoft Access. It's about such thrilling topics as using Access on a home or small business network. If Access helps your business grow to where you have to hire employees, and you prefer to hire ones who know less about computers than you, this book makes that possible.

After that comes an appendix on how to install Microsoft Access 2003, in case you haven't gotten that far. If Access is already on your computer, there's nothing noteworthy here. If you do need to install Access, and don't feel like looking there, here's the condensed version of the appendix: Insert your Microsoft Office or Microsoft Access CD into your computer's CD drive, wait a few seconds, and then follow the instructions that appear on-screen.

Web Site for the Book

Before writing this book, we created a fully functioning mail order management database, named MOM 2003, to use as examples throughout. This probably won't be obvious, especially if you skip around through chapters. But that's what we did.

Anyway, you're welcome to download and use that database if you're interested. You can find two versions available online:

✦ **MOM 2003 (Sample Data):** The sample database with some bogus samples typed in for you to play around with.

✦ **MOM 2003:** The same as the first database, but without phony sample data. Use this one if you prefer to type in your own data.

To download the database, and to find links to other Access-related Web sites, check out this book's Web site at `www.dummies.com./go/access03_ allinone`.

We love to hear from you readers, just to tell us what you thought of the book. Our address is `access-aio@gurus.com`. Don't ask zillions of Access questions, though — if we spent time doing free consulting for people, we wouldn't have any time to write books! If you have Access questions that this book doesn't answer, see the book's Web site for more sources of information, including online Access discussion groups.

Where to Go from Here

If you patiently read the preceding "Organization" section, you probably know where you need to go next. If not, you beginners should head straight to Book I, Chapter 1 to get your bearings. For the rest of you who already know some of the basics of Access, just pick whatever book or chapter talks about what you're struggling with right now.

And by the way, thanks for buying (begging, borrowing, or stealing) this book. We hope it serves you well. For those of you who bought, an extra thanks for helping us pay down our credit cards a little.

Book I

Essential Concepts

The 5th Wave   By Rich Tennant

"The new technology has really helped me get organized. I keep my project reports under the PC, budgets under my laptop, and memos under my pager."

Contents at a Glance

Chapter 1: Introducing Access 2003

In This Chapter

✓ Getting a handle on Microsoft Access

✓ Listing the eight types of Access objects

✓ Laying out some essential database concepts

Access is the Microsoft database management program, part of the Microsoft Office suite of programs. A database management program enables you to maintain *databases* — collections of data arranged according to a fixed structure. The structure makes the information easy to select, sort, display, and print in a variety of formats. With Access, you can create and maintain as many databases as you need — you can even share them with other people over a local area network or the Internet.

Access is a general-purpose program that works with almost any kind of information. A database can be as simple as a list of addresses to replace your card file. Or you can create a wine cellar database with information about each bottle in your cellar or a bookstore inventory database with information about books, publishers, customers, and special orders. Access can also handle complex databases that contain lots of types of information and lots of customized programming.

An Access database can contain lists of records about almost anything, from sales to sports scores. Unlike a spreadsheet program, Access makes displaying your information in lots of different formats easy, including alphabetical listings, formatted reports, mailing labels, and fill-in-the-blank forms.

Access 2003 comes with Microsoft Office 11. Previous versions of Access have also been part of the Office suite — Access 2002 in Office XP, Access 2000 in Office 2000, and Access 97 in Office 97. Because Access is part of Microsoft Office, sharing information with Word documents and Excel spreadsheets is easy. This book describes Access 2003, but except where noted, everything we say is true for Access 2000 and 2002, too.

Access includes a powerful programming language (VBA, described in the section, "Modules for writing your own programs," later in this chapter).

And you can use Access to work with data stored in large corporate databases. These features make Access a great choice for creating *front ends* for corporate databases — which means you can use Access to edit, display, and print data from larger, shared databases, without having to do any programming.

The Eight Types of Access Objects

Access databases are made up of *objects* — things you can create, edit, and delete, with names and settings. *Object-oriented* systems allow you to create things one piece at a time, using pieces that fit together.

Access contains various kinds of objects, including objects for storing, displaying, and printing your data, as well as objects that contain programs that you write. At first, you'll probably use only a few types of objects, but as you customize your database, you may end up using them all. You start with *tables* for storing data, *forms* for editing data on-screen, *reports* for printing data, and *queries* for selecting and combining data. Later, you may create *macros* and *modules,* which contain programs that you write; *projects,* which work with corporate data; and *data access pages,* which allow you to edit Access data via a Web browser.

In this section, we cover each of the main types of Access objects: tables, queries, forms, reports, macros, modules, projects, and data access pages.

Tables for storing your data

Tables are where you put your data. A table is an Access object that is made up of a series of *records,* which are like the index cards that make up an address list. Each record contains information in the same format. In an address list, each record contains information about one person: name, address, and other facts. Each individual piece of information — such as the first name, the last name, or the street address — is called a *field*.

Your database can contain many tables. A bookstore database can contain a table of books (with title, publisher, price, and other information about each book), a table of vendors from whom you buy books (with company name, address, discount terms, and other information about each vendor), and maybe a table of your regular customers (with name, address, and other information). Figure 1-1 shows a table of names and addresses. Each row is a record, and the fields are shown in columns.

After you set up tables in your database and type in (or import) information, you can sort the records, select records that match a criterion, and then display and print the records.

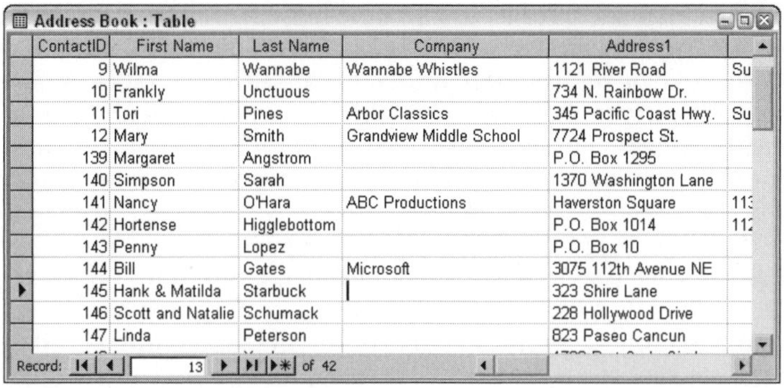

Address Book : Table

ContactID	First Name	Last Name	Company	Address1	
9	Wilma	Wannabe	Wannabe Whistles	1121 River Road	Su
10	Frankly	Unctuous		734 N. Rainbow Dr.	
11	Tori	Pines	Arbor Classics	345 Pacific Coast Hwy.	Su
12	Mary	Smith	Grandview Middle School	7724 Prospect St.	
139	Margaret	Angstrom		P.O. Box 1295	
140	Simpson	Sarah		1370 Washington Lane	
141	Nancy	O'Hara	ABC Productions	Haverston Square	11
142	Hortense	Higglebottom		P.O. Box 1014	11
143	Penny	Lopez		P.O. Box 10	
144	Bill	Gates	Microsoft	3075 112th Avenue NE	
145	Hank & Matilda	Starbuck		323 Shire Lane	
146	Scott and Natalie	Schumack		228 Hollywood Drive	
147	Linda	Peterson		823 Paseo Cancun	

Record: 13 of 42

Figure 1-1: A table contains a list of records, and each record is made up of fields.

Proper design of your tables — choosing how many tables to create and which fields are stored in which table — is key to creating a usable and flexible database. Chapter 3 of this book includes a step-by-step procedure for designing your database, and Book II explains how to create tables and fill them with data.

Queries for selecting your data

Queries are a means to slice and dice your data. The most commonly used type of query helps you select data from a table, perhaps to select which records you want to include in a report. You can create a query that shows you all the people in your address book who live in Vermont, or all those for whom you don't have a phone number. When you create this type of query, you enter *criteria* that specify what values you want to match in specific fields in the tables (for example, **VT** in the State field, or nothing in the Phone Number field, or both).

Is a spreadsheet a database?

Many people use spreadsheet programs, such as Microsoft Excel or Lotus 1-2-3, to store lists of records. Some spreadsheet programs have limited database capabilities, but they aren't designed to do as much as a database program. You can use a spreadsheet to store an address list, and you can enter, edit, delete, and sort the addresses (one per row on the spreadsheet), but printing mailing labels or form letters is a major chore. Spreadsheets do not think of your data in terms of tables, records, and fields, but rather in terms of cells (the basic unit of a spreadsheet) in rows and columns. We bet you're glad you're using Access for your database work!

You can also use queries to combine information from several tables. A bookstore database may store book author names in the Books table and book ordering information in the Purchase Orders table. A query can pull information from both of these tables — you can create a query to show all the Terry Pratchett novels that you ordered for the last month, for example. Queries can also create calculated fields, including totals, counts, and averages.

Another type of query is the *action query,* a query that does something to the records that you select. You can create action queries to copy records from one table to another, to make a change to all the records you select, or to delete records you select. *Crosstab queries* help you analyze the information in your tables, by summarizing how many records contain specific combinations of values.

Queries are the way that you get useful information out of your tables, and you'll probably create zillions of them as you play with your database. Book III explains how to create and use queries of all kinds.

Forms for editing and displaying your data

An easy way to do data entry, especially if you enter data into more than one related table, is to use a *form.* A form displays the information from one or more tables on-screen. You can edit the data or type in new records. You can choose the layout of the table's information on the form — you can specify the order in which the items appear, you can group items together with lines and boxes, and you can use pull-down lists, radio buttons, and other types of on-screen controls for entering and editing data. The form in Figure 1-2 shows information from the Product table of an online store.

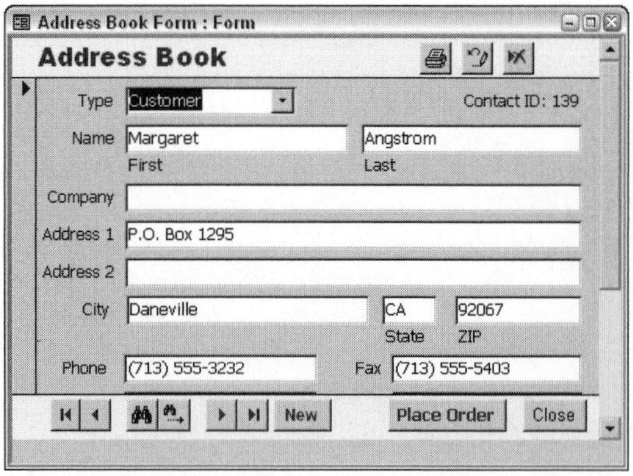

Figure 1-2:
A form shows information stored in one or more tables, for data entry and editing.

Address Book Form : Form

Address Book

Type: Customer · Contact ID: 139

Name: Margaret / Angstrom
First / Last

Company:

Address 1: P.O. Box 1295

Address 2:

City: Daneville / CA / 92067
State / ZIP

Phone: (713) 555-3232 / Fax: (713) 555-5403

New   Place Order   Close

You can build intelligence into forms, too — you can program boxes that automatically capitalize what you type in, or that check your entry against a table of valid values.

After your database goes into production — you use it for its intended application — forms are the most-used Access object. Book IV explains how to design, create, modify, and use forms.

Reports for printing your data

Forms are primarily designed to appear on-screen; *reports* are designed for printing, as shown in Figure 1-3. Like forms, reports display information from tables, and you can choose the layout of the information. Most reports are based on queries; you use a query to choose the information to appear in the report. The report design defines the order in which records appear, which fields appear where, fonts, font sizes, lines, and spacing.

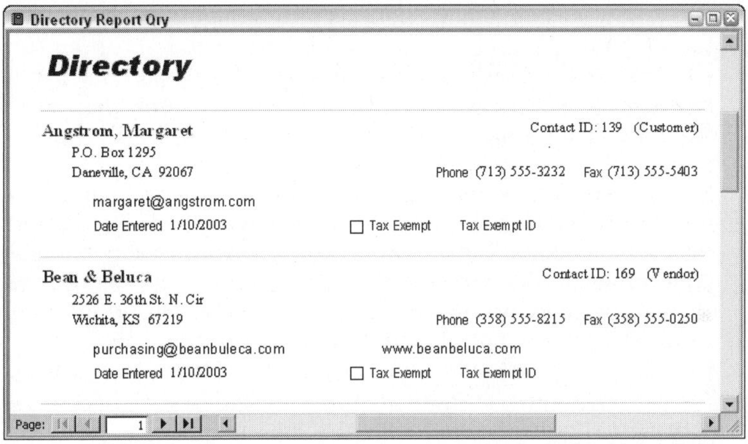

Figure 1-3:
A report
displays
information
from one or
more tables,
for printing.

In addition to reports on normal paper, you can create reports for printing on envelopes, labels, or other printed forms. Access comes with report wizards that make creating fancy reports easy. It can also print charts and cross-tabulations (*crosstabs*) based on the data in your database.

Book V covers how to create and print reports, charts, and crosstabs.

Macros for saving keystrokes

Access includes two separate programming languages: macros and VBA. *Macros* are programs that automate commands you give when you use Access. For example, you can write a macro that moves the cursor to the last record in the Orders table whenever you open the Order Entry form. (What are the chances that you want to edit your very first order? More likely, you want to edit the last order or enter a new order.) Or you can write a macro that moves your cursor to the next applicable blank in a form, based on the entries you made so far.

After you know how to create macros, you can create buttons on your forms that run the macros with a quick click. You can also tell your form to run a macro automatically whenever you move to a field on the form, or enter data into the field — handy!

You don't have to be a programmer to create macros. Access helps you write them by providing menus of commands. Book VI explains how to create nifty and useful macros to clean up your data entry and a number of items automatically.

Modules for writing your own programs

Okay, now we come to the serious programming stuff: *modules* — another term for VBA programs. *VBA* (Visual Basic for Applications) is a programming language based on the age-old BASIC language. Macros are fine for saving a few keystrokes or cleaning up the data you enter in a field, but when the going gets complex, you can use VBA.

Say you receive orders for your online store via e-mail messages in a specific format. You can write a VBA program to read these e-mail messages from your e-mail mailbox and create records in your Orders table. Why cut and paste when a VBA program can do the job? Or you could write a VBA program to be called when you click the Ship This Order button on your Orders form: The program prints a packing slip, prints a mailing label, updates your inventory numbers, and generates an e-mail message to the customer. Why should you remember to do all those tasks when a VBA program can do them all?

Programming isn't for the faint of heart, but when you have the rest of your database up and running, take a look at Book VIII for an introduction to VBA programming. Writing small programs is not hard, and after you get used to programming, who knows what you'll end up creating!

Projects for accessing shared databases

If you're not a corporate user (or part of some large organization), skip this one — you'll never use the special databases called *projects*. Still here? Fine. An Access project is a special type of database in which the actual data you normally store in your Access tables goes to a large corporate database, to be stored there instead. Your Access project file contains only your tools — the forms, reports, pages, macros, and VBA modules you need for creating or modifying projects. You connect to the corporate database to get your data from the corporate database's tables and queries.

The great thing about Access projects is that they give you a consistent way to use Access effectively when you work with corporate data. Instead of having to learn the ins and outs of database programming with some large, scary program, you can use Access forms and pages to look at the data and reports to print it out.

Book IX, Chapter 2 walks you through creating an Access project. You need to get information about your organization's database from your Information Services department, including a password to give you permission to use the files.

Pages for editing data in your Web browser

Forms are great for entering and editing data, but you have to be running Access to use them. What if you want non-Access folk to work with the information in your database? *Pages* (or *data access pages*) enable you to create Web pages containing forms, so anyone with the Internet Explorer browser can edit records in the tables in your database. Anyone, that is, with permission to do so — you need to set up the security features to control who can look at and change your information.

Book IX, Chapter 1 talks about pages and how to make them. After you create pages for use with your database, you also find out how to upload them to your Web server so that other people can use the pages. Book VII, Chapter 3 describes the Access security features to control who has permission to see or change each field in each table.

Essential Database Concepts

Here are the Four Commandments of databases. (Aren't you relieved there aren't 10?). You'll find lots more important rules and guidelines throughout this book as you discover how to work with various Access objects, but here are some that apply right from the start, no matter what kind of database you are using.

✦ **Store information where it belongs, not where it appears.** Where you store information has nothing to do with where it appears. In a database, you store information in tables based on the structure of the information. (Don't worry — Chapter 3 of this book explains how to figure out the structure of your data.) Each piece of information likely appears in lots of different places. For example, in a database for an online bookstore, book titles and authors' names appear on your invoices, purchase orders, and sales receipts. But the right place to *store* those book titles and author names is in the Books table, not in the Sales table or the Purchase Orders table.

✦ **Garbage in, garbage out (GIGO).** If you don't bother to create a good, sensible design for your database, and if you aren't careful to enter correct, clean data, your database ends up full of garbage. A well-designed database is easier to maintain than a badly designed one, because each piece of information is stored only once, in a clearly named field in a clearly named table, with the proper validation rules in place. Yes, it sounds like a lot of work, but cleaning up a database of 10,000 incorrect records is (pardon the understatement) even more work. See Book II, Chapter 5 for ways to avoid GIGO.

✦ **Separate your data from your programs.** If you create a database to be shared with or distributed to other people, store all the tables in one database (the *back end*) and all the other objects in another database (the *front end*). Then you link these two databases together to make everything work. Separating the tables from everything else makes updating queries, forms, reports, or other stuff later without disturbing the data in the tables easy. (See Book VII, Chapter 1 for how to separate a database into a front end and back end.)

✦ **Back up early and often.** Make a backup of your database every day. With luck, your office already has a system of regular (probably nightly) backups that includes your database. If not, make a backup copy of your database at regular intervals, and certainly before making any major changes. (See Book VII, Chapter 1 for how to make backups.)

Chapter 2: Getting Started, Getting Around

In This Chapter

↙ **Understanding the Access window**

↙ **Using the Database window**

↙ **Using other Access window elements**

↙ **Working with Access objects and wizards**

↙ **Playing with Access's sample databases**

↙ **Saving keystrokes with keyboard shortcuts**

*B*efore you can do much with Access, you have to get it installed and running. If Access isn't already installed on your computer, see Appendix A for what to do. Then come back to this chapter for how to run it and understand the stuff you see in the Access window.

Running Access

Windows usually provides more than one way to perform a task, and starting Access is no exception. The most popular way to start Access is to click Start and choose All Programs⇨Microsoft Office Access 2003. (You may need to choose All Programs⇨Microsoft Office⇨Microsoft Office Access 2003.) If you have an earlier version of Access, click Start and look around for it — be sure to try choosing Programs or All Programs, and then Microsoft Office.

Another way to get the program started is by double-clicking the name or icon of an Access database in Windows Explorer or My Computer (this method both starts Access and opens the database you double-click). Or double-click the Access icon if it appears on your Windows desktop.

When you start Access without opening a database, the Access 2003 window looks like Figure 2-1.

Toolbar   Task pane

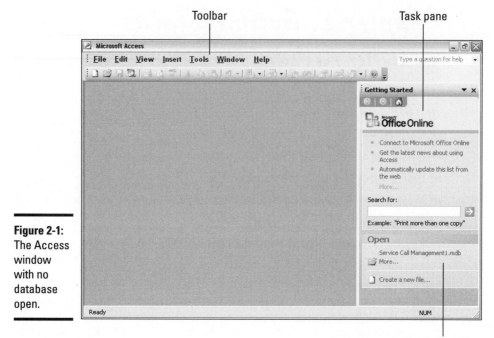

Figure 2-1:
The Access
window
with no
database
open.

Recently opened database files

The Access Task Pane, Toolbar, and Menus

The Access window includes the usual Windows elements — the title bar
and menu of commands across the top of the Access window — along with
something new to Access 2003: the task pane. The *task pane* shows information and links for tasks that Access thinks you may want to do. If you don't
see it, you can turn it on and off by choosing View➪Task Pane. You can
change what the task pane displays by clicking its title bar (which starts out
saying Getting Started) and choosing one of these options:

Task Pane	Contents
Getting Started	Links for opening and creating a database, plus Microsoft Online links
Help	On-screen help from your hard-disk files and from the Microsoft Web site
Search Results	Results of searching for a file
File Search	A basic file search, enabling you to search your computer for files

Task Pane	Contents
Clipboard	A list of the last 24 items you copy or cut to the Office Clipboard to choose one to paste
New File	Options for creating a new database
Template Help	Information about database templates (sample databases you can tailor for your use)
Object Dependencies	Displays the objects in your database that depend on the selected object (see Book VII, Chapter 1 for how this works)

Like the toolbars in other Windows programs, the Access toolbar contains buttons for tasks that Microsoft thinks you do frequently, as shown in Figure 2-2. The buttons on the toolbar change depending on what you are doing: When you create a query, the toolbar includes buttons for configuring your query. Sometimes some buttons are unavailable (nothing happens if you click one), because it applies only in specific situations. (You can't click the Save button if nothing is open.) When a button is unavailable, its icon appears pale and ghostly.

Table 2-1 shows what the most commonly used buttons do. These buttons don't all appear on any one toolbar — we harvested the most useful buttons from toolbars that appear throughout Access. You find detailed explanations of what these and other buttons do throughout this book.

Figure 2-2:
The Access
toolbar.

Table 2-1   **Frequently Used Toolbar Buttons**

Button	Name	Shortcut or Key	What It Does
	New	Ctrl+N	Creates a new database
	Open	Ctrl+O	Opens an existing database (and closes the currently open database)
	Save	Ctrl+S	Saves the selected object

(continued)

Table 2-1 *(continued)*

Button	Name	Shortcut or Key	What It Does
	File Search	none	Displays the Basic File Search task pane (new in Access 2003)
	Print	Ctrl+P	Prints the selected object
	Print Preview	none	Displays the selected object as it will look when printed
	Spelling	F7	Checks the spelling in the selected object
	Cut	Ctrl+X	Deletes the selected text or object and saves it in the Clipboard
	Copy	Ctrl+C	Copies the selected text or object to the Clipboard
	Paste	Ctrl+V	Pastes the contents of the Clipboard to the active window
	Undo	Ctrl+Z	Undoes the last undoable action
	Properties	Alt+Enter	Displays the properties of the selected object
	OfficeLinks: Word	none	Opens the active object in another Microsoft Office application (click the down arrow for other OfficeLinks options)
	Relationships	none	Displays the Relationships window
	New Object: AutoForm	none	Creates a new form using a wizard (click the down arrow for other types of objects)

Button	Name	Shortcut or Key	What It Does
	Microsoft Access Help	F1	Displays the Help window
	Database Window	F11	Opens the Database window
	Find	Ctrl+F	Finds text (with the option to replace it) in the open table, query, or form
	Delete	Del	Deletes the selected object
	Analyze	none	Analyzes table design, improves database performance, or documents database objects
	Sort	none	(Ascending or Descending) Sorts the records in the current datasheet or form
	Filter by Selection	none	Restricts your view to records that match the selected entry
	Filter by Form	none	Displays a form with which you can restrict your view to specified records
	Design View	none	Displays the Design view of the selected or open object
	Field List	none	Displays a list of field names for inclusion on a form or report
	Toolbox	none	Displays a palette of tools for designing a form or report
	Code	Alt+F11	Displays the VBA Editor with VBA code for the current form or report

To see what a toolbar button does, move your mouse there but don't click. In about a second, a little box appears (a *ToolTip*, if you must know) with the name of the button.

Everyone knows how to choose commands from menus — just click a word on the menu, which expands so you can click a word on the next menu, and so forth. However, sometimes the command you want is mysteriously missing from a menu. Here's why: Access remembers which commands you usually use, and hides the ones you haven't used in a while (along with obscure commands you probably never use). If a command is missing from a menu, click the double-chevron button at the bottom of the menu to reveal the entire list of commands. Or just wait a few seconds — Access figures that you are looking for more commands and displays the rest of the commands on the menu.

Opening a Database

Before you can work on a database, you have to open it in Access. In fact, before you can open it, you have to create it! If you want to try Access but you don't have a database to work with, skip ahead to the "Playing with the Access Sample Databases" section, later in this chapter, for how to try out the Access sample databases.

To open an existing database, follow these steps:

1. **Click the Open button on the toolbar.**

   Alternatively, you can choose File➪Open or press Ctrl+O.

2. **Choose the file name from the Open dialog box that appears.**

   You may need to browse to it. Use the icons on the left side of the Open dialog box to see different folders.

3. **Click the Open button or double-click the file name.**

   Access opens the database. If you see an alarming security message, see the sidebar, "What's this weird security error message?"

If you want to open a database that you used recently, you can choose File and choose the file name from the bottom of the File menu, or look in the Open section of the task pane for the file name. From the My Computer or Windows Explorer window, you can double-click the file name of an existing database to open it. To start Access *and* open a recently used file, choose Start➪My Recent Documents and choose the file.

What's this weird security error message?

If you try to open a database containing any programming (in the form of macros, VBA procedures, or action queries, which we explain in later books), Microsoft wants you to know that you are taking a chance. Programming can include viruses that could infect your computer. Access 2003 shows the warning message in the following figure.

Before you panic, you need to understand some things. First, unlike in the real world, in the computer world viruses don't just happen. A *virus* is a program that must be written by a human. In nature, viruses exist because they're living beings (sort of) that can reproduce themselves. In a computer, viruses are programs, created by humans, intentionally written to do bad things and also to make copies of themselves.

So why the warning? The warning is just a general disclaimer that appears whenever you open *any* document that contains any macros, VBA procedures, or action queries. The message doesn't know if the database contains viruses or not. The message is just telling you that programs — not viruses — are in the database.

If the database you open when you see this message is something you downloaded from the Internet from some unknown, dubious source, then you may want to click the Cancel button to skip opening the database. Instead, create a new, blank database and import the tables, queries, forms, and reports into it (but no macros or VBA code). If the database comes from someone within your organization whom you trust not to accidentally infect it with a virus, click the Open button. If you created the database and it's *supposed* to contain macros, VBA procedures, or action queries, you can prevent Access from displaying the message when you open it. See Book VI, Chapter 1.

If you have antivirus software, you'd do well to scan any and all files you download from the Internet for viruses before actually opening those files. These days, most viruses spread through e-mail attachments. Virtually all antivirus programs automatically scan all incoming e-mail attachments for viruses before allowing you to open them.

When you work with a database, additional windows appear within the Access window. Exactly what you see depends on the database. A simple database displays the Database window, described later in this chapter. Some databases include macros or VBA modules that display a form and hide the Database window. The database can also be programmed to hide the toolbar, menu, and other standard Access components entirely.

Opening oldies

Access 2003 can open databases created in previous versions of Access. Here's the scoop on what happens when you open such old Access files:

✦ **Access 2002 (Office XP):** It just opens. Access 2003 uses the same file format as 2002. (If you have Access 2000, it can't open Access 2002 or 2003 files.)

✦ **Access 2000:** It just opens, even though the file format is slightly different. The Access title bar says "Access 2000 file format" but everything should work fine. If you create any new objects in that old file while it's open in Access 2003, they won't work if you open the database file later in Access 2000, but everything else should work.

✦ **Access 2.0, Access 95, or Access 97:** When you first open one of these older-format database files, Access gives you two choices:

  • You can *enable* the database, which means that Access 2003 keeps the file in its usual elderly format so you can reopen it later in the older version of Access.

  • You can *convert* the old database to Access 2003 format. It's your choice: make it based on whether you or other people need to open this database in older Access versions. See Book VII, Chapter 1 for more information about converting database from one Access version to another.

When you open an enabled database in Access 2003, you work only with the data: You can't create or modify database objects, such as forms and reports. Some older VBA modules won't run in Access 2003, either.

I have that open already!

Access is a *multi-user database*, which means that more than one person can open an Access database at the same time. The usual way that this works is that several computers on a network (usually a local area network in an office) run Access, and all can open the same database at the same time. Access keeps track of who is doing what, and prevents the users from crashing into each other. Two people trying to edit the same thing at the same time can be tricky — Access locks out the second person until the first person is done with the edit.

For more information, see Book VII, Chapter 2.

Playing with the Access Sample Databases

Access comes with some databases to give you something to play with while you find out how the program works. They can even help spark ideas for your own databases. When you install the Access program, you may have installed the sample databases; if not, you can install them now.

Installing the sample databases

To install the sample databases, take a look at Appendix A, which tells you how to run the Access installation program. When you start the installation program, follow these steps:

1. **Choose the Add or Remove Features option and click Next.**

   The installation program shows you a list of Office programs. Access should be selected.

2. **Click the Choose Advanced Customization of Applications check box. (It doesn't appear in earlier versions of Access.) Click Next.**

3. **Click the plus box (little plus sign) to the left of the Microsoft Access For Windows option from the list of Office programs.**

   A list appears, showing entries such as Help, Typical Wizards, Additional Wizards, and Sample Databases.

4. **Click the Sample Databases button and choose the Run From My Computer option.**

   This option tells the installation program to install the sample databases on your hard disk.

5. **Click the Update button.**

   The installation program installs the sample databases. If you made any other changes to your Office configuration, it makes those changes, too.

Access installs your sample databases. If Windows is installed on drive C, then the sample databases take up residence at the following place:

```
C:\Program Files\Microsoft Office\Office\Samples
```

Taking Northwind for a spin

The Northwind sample database is an order-entry system that an imaginary mail-order gourmet food company uses for tracking orders, customers, suppliers, and products. To open the Northwind database, choose Help➪ Sample Databases➪Northwind Sample Database. Or, if you're especially brave, click the Open button on the toolbar, navigate to

```
C:\Program Files\Microsoft Office\Office\Samples
```

and choose `Northwind.mdb`. You see an introductory screen (actually, a form); click OK after you read it.

Okay, the database opens — you can tell because a window has appeared with the name of the database as its title. So what can you do with it? How can you see what's in it? The next section describes this window, and how to get it to display all the stuff in the database.

Mission Control: The Database Window

The Database window (shown in Figure 2-3) is the table of contents for your database. From it, you can access any table, query, form, report, data access page, macro, or VBA module in the database. From the Database window you can also create new objects, view relationships in the database, change the name of an object, copy an object, or delete an object.

Objects list   Objects of the selected type

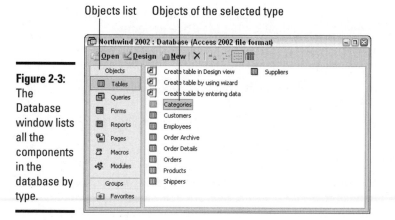

Figure 2-3:
The Database window lists all the components in the database by type.

You can display the Database window any time by pressing F11.

The Database window has its own little toolbar, with buttons for opening the selected object, opening the object in Design view, creating a new object, deleting the object, or choosing how to view the list of objects. The right-most button displays your objects in Details view, so you can see when each object was originally created and when it was last modified. In Details view, adjust the column widths (so you can see the full names of things with long names) by clicking and dragging the right edge of the column heading.

To see a database object, first choose the object type from the list at the left side of the Database window: Tables, Queries, Forms, Reports, Pages, Macros, or Modules. Then choose the specific object (you may need to scroll the object list to the right to find the object you want) and click the Open button on the toolbar (or double-click the object name).

If you're wondering about the Groups button in the lower-left corner in the Objects list of the Database window, see Book VII, Chapter 2, which explains how you can put shortcuts to frequently used objects into *groups*.

Creating, Deleting, Renaming, Copying, and Printing Objects

Throughout this book, you hear about how to create and modify tables, forms, reports, and other Access objects using the Database window. A couple of tasks that work the same way for all Access objects crop up time and again, so you may as well find out about them right here. Before you try any of these tasks, click the type of object you want to work with (such as tables or forms) so you see a list of the existing objects of that type.

✦ **Creating an object:** Click the New button on the Database window toolbar. What happens next depends on the type of object: You usually get a chance to create the object by either running a wizard to step you through the process or by using Design view — a window with commands for designing the object. If Access decides that you want to make a new database, you see the New File task pane.

See Book II, Chapter 1 for creating tables; Book III, Chapter 1 for queries; Book IV, Chapter 1 for forms; Book V, Chapter 1 for reports; Book VI, Chapter 1 for macros; Book VIII, Chapter 2 for VBA modules (Ha! It wasn't Chapter 1 this time!); and Book IX, Chapter 1 for data access pages.

✦ **Deleting an object:** Select the object and press the Delete key. Simple enough! Clicking the Delete icon on the toolbar works, too. Access asks if you are really, truly sure, before blowing the object away. Just remember that when you delete a table, you delete all its data, too.

✦ **Renaming an object:** Click the name of the object and press F2. Or click the name once, pause, and click again. Either way, a box appears around the object's name. Type a new name and press Enter.

✦ **Copying an object:** Select the object you want to copy, press Ctrl+C, and press Ctrl+V. (The Copy and Paste buttons on the toolbar work, too.) Access pops up a Paste As dialog box asking for the name to use for the copy. Type it in and click OK. When you are creating a form or report, starting with a copy of an existing report rather than starting one from scratch is faster!

✦ **Printing an object:** Select or open the object you want to print and then press Ctrl+P, click the Print button on the toolbar (shown on the left in the margin), or choose File➪Print. If you want to see what you get before you waste paper on it, click the Print Preview button on the toolbar (shown on the right in the margin) or choose File➪Print Preview before printing.

✦ **Creating a shortcut to an object:** If you frequently want to start Access, open your database, and immediately open a specific object, you can create a Windows shortcut to the object. The shortcut can live on your Windows desktop or on your Start menu. Just drag the object from the Database window to your Windows desktop — Windows creates the shortcut. You can then drag this shortcut to the Start menu.

You can find lots more about printing in Book V, Chapter 2, which talks about making and printing reports.

Using Wizards

Years ago, in a land far, far away (Washington state, actually), Microsoft invented *wizards,* programs that step you through the process of executing a commonly used command. Instead of presenting you with a big, hairy-looking dialog box with zillions of options, a wizard asks you one or two questions at a time, and uses the information you already provided before asking for more input. All programs in Microsoft Office, including Access, come with wizards.

Wizards appear in dialog boxes that pop up in response to a command. For example, in the Database window, click the Forms button, and then double-click the Create Form by Using Wizard option. The Form Wizard pops up, as shown in Figure 2-4.

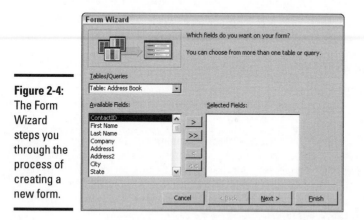

Figure 2-4:
The Form Wizard steps you through the process of creating a new form.

All of the Microsoft wizards follow the same pattern of asking a series of questions. Answer each question and click the Next button at the bottom of the dialog box. If you want to go back and change the answer you gave on a previous window, click the Back button. You can bag the whole thing by clicking Cancel. The Finish button is grayed out (and unclickable) until you provide enough information for the wizard to complete his (her? its?) task.

Getting Help

Access offers some online help, though our experience suggests that what you get isn't always helpful. As Microsoft tries to make online help friendlier and friendlier, it seems to contain less and less useful information. Maybe you'll have better luck than we do!

To ask the Access Help system a question, type a question or some words in the Help box in the upper-right corner of the Access window. When you press Enter, Access first searches its Help system for matches and then displays any search results in the window. Click a topic to see more information.

 If the task pane is displayed, you can see helpful information by clicking the task pane's title bar and choosing the Help option from the shortcut menu, or press the Help button on the toolbar. Click the Assistance link in the Office Online section of the task pane to search the Microsoft Access Web site for information. Your browser runs and you see a Web page with search information.

The Help box in the upper-right corner and the Help task pane are both new in Access 2003: If you have an older version of Access, choose Help⇨Microsoft Access Help from the menu or press F1.

The following Web sites we find useful for getting answers to Access questions:

✦ **The Access Web:** www.mvps.org/access

✦ **Microsoft Support:** support.microsoft.com

✦ **The MSDN Library (Microsoft Developers' Network):** msdn.microsoft.com/access

✦ **TechNet Online:** www.microsoft.com/technet

Saving Time with Keyboard Shortcuts

Some people like to keep their hands on the keyboard as much as possible. For a fast typist, pressing keys is quicker and more efficient than pointing and clicking with the mouse. For you folks, Access (like most other Windows programs) includes keyboard shortcuts — key combinations that issue the same commands you normally choose from the menu or toolbar. Table 2-2 shows a list of our favorite shortcuts.

Some of these keystrokes only work in specific situations — for example, when you edit something or work in a particular kind of window. Throughout this book, we tell you which keys do what and when.

Table 2-2	Shortcut Keys in Access
Key Combination	*Action*
F1	Displays the Help task pane
Ctrl+F1	Opens the task pane
F5	Goes to the record with the record number you type
F7	Checks the spelling in the selected object
F11	Opens the Database window
Del	Deletes the selected object
Alt+Enter	Displays the properties of the selected object
Ctrl+C	Copies the selected text or objects to the Clipboard
Ctrl+F	Finds text (with the option to replace it) in the open table, query, or form
Ctrl+N	New database
Ctrl+O	Opens a database
Ctrl+P	Prints the selected object
Ctrl+S	Saves the selected object
Ctrl+V	Pastes the contents of the Clipboard to the active window
Ctrl+X	Deletes the selected text or object and saves it in the Clipboard
Ctrl+Z	Undoes the last undoable action (our all-time favorite!)
Ctrl+;	Types today's date
Ctrl+"	Duplicates the entry from the same field in the previous record

Customizing Your Toolbar

Toolbars are great — clicking a single button is a convenient way to do lots of Access tasks. However, most people find that they never use some toolbar buttons, while other important commands aren't on the toolbar. If this is the case with you, consider customizing the toolbars that Access displays.

If you want to change the buttons that appear on a toolbar, follow these steps:

1. **Choose Tools⇨Customize. Click the Toolbars tab if it's not already selected.**

You see the Customize dialog box shown in Figure 2-5.

Figure 2-5:
The Toolbars tab of the Customize toolbar allows you to choose which toolbars appear on-screen.

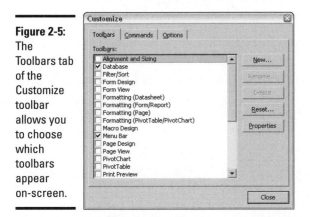

2. **If the toolbar that you want to customize doesn't appear on-screen, click its check box in the list of toolbars on the Toolbars tab.**

As soon as you select a toolbar, it appears.

3. **Click the Commands tab.**

You see a list of the categories of Access commands, and the names and icons for each command, as shown in Figure 2-6.

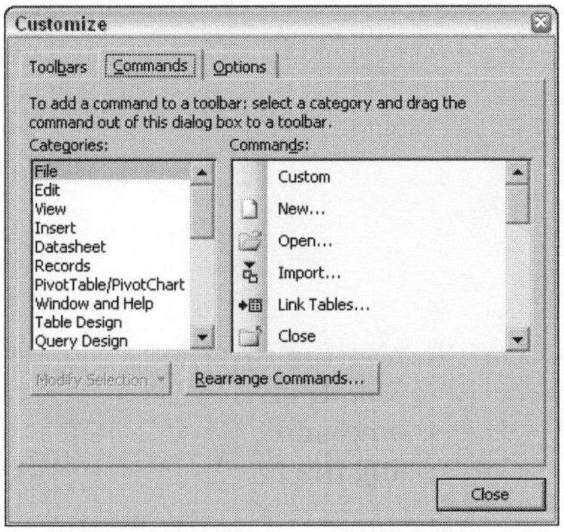

Figure 2-6:
Commands that you can add to your toolbars.

4. **To add a button to a toolbar, click the category that contains the command, find the command, and drag it to the toolbar.**

   If you're not sure what category a command is in (we never are), just look around. When you drag the button to a toolbar, a little I-bar appears to show you where Access plans on inserting the new button.

5. **To remove a button from a toolbar, just drag it off the toolbar.**

   Poof! It's gone.

6. **To rearrange the buttons on a toolbar, drag the button to where you want it to appear.**

7. **When the toolbar looks right, click Close in the Customize dialog box.**

   Don't worry about getting the toolbar exactly right the first time. As you use Access, you'll notice buttons that you never use, and you'll get ideas for buttons you wish were there. You can always make more changes later.

Changes you make to most toolbars affect Access all the time, not just when this particular database is open.

While you are customizing your toolbar, you can customize your menu, too. However, we don't recommend it — eliminating a command you really need is too easy. If you make unintended changes to a toolbar or the menu, select it in the Customize dialog box and click the Reset button to return it to its normal self.

You're not stuck with only the toolbars that come with Access. You can create your own toolbar and put only your favorite buttons on it. See Book VII, Chapter 3.

Chapter 3: Designing Your Database the Relational Way

Relational database design? Yikes! Sounds like a serious programming project. But what is it, exactly? Designing a database means figuring out how the information is stored — which information Access stores in each table of the database, and how it all connects together. Unlike working with a spreadsheet or word processor, you need to design a database first — you can't just start typing information in. (Well, sure, you can, but we don't recommend it — the result is usually a mess.) How easy it is later to enter and edit information and create useful queries, forms, and reports depends on how well your database is designed. A good database design can stream-line your work in Access.

This chapter takes you through the process of designing the table(s) you need in your database, including the relationships between them. Book II, Chapter 1 contains the instructions for creating the tables in Access.

What Are Tables, Fields, and Keys?

In Access, you store your data in *tables*, which are lists of records like the index cards that make up an address list. Each record contains information in the same format, in *fields*, which are individual pieces of information.

If you want to keep track of the customers of your store, you make a table of customers, with one record per customer. Each record is made up of the same set of fields, which could be the customer's last name, first name, street address, city, state or province, zip or post code, country, and phone number as shown in Figure 3-1.

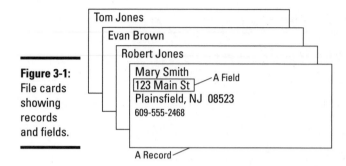

Figure 3-1:
File cards
showing
records
and fields.

After you use Access to create a table, you can enter, edit, delete, and sort the records in various ways, and print many types of reports, including columnar reports, forms, summaries, mailing labels, and form letters. Access allows you to create as many tables as you need in your database.

Designing a database includes deciding what tables your database includes, and what fields are in each table. This is the computer equivalent of designing the form or file card onto which you write the data, with blanks to be filled in.

Data types

Fields can be different *data types*. Some fields contain textual alphanumeric information, such as a last name or street address. Other fields contain numbers, such as someone's age. Others contain logical information — yes or no. And others contain dates or times, such as the date that the record was added to the database. Table 3-1 contains a list of the most commonly used Access data types.

Table 3-1	Commonly Used Data Types for Fields
Data Type	*What It Holds*
Text	Short chunks of text up to 255 characters, or special codes that contain non-numeric characters, such as phone numbers (xxx)xxx-xxxx and zip codes (xxxxx-xxxx) that require parentheses and hyphens, which aren't allowed in numbers.
Memo	The same information as a Text field, but more of them — up to 65,536 characters.
Number	Only numbers. You may use + or − before the number, and a decimal point. You can use Number fields in numeric calculations. Number fields come in a bunch of different sizes, depending on how large the numbers are and how many decimal places you want to store. See Book II, Chapter 1.
Currency	Numbers with a currency sign in front of them ($, ¥, and so on). You can do numeric calculations with these fields.

What Are Relationships? **37**

Book I
Chapter 3

Designing Your
Database the
Relational Way

Data Type	What It Holds
AutoNumber	Numbers unique to each record and assigned by Access as you add records, starting at 1.
Date/Time	Dates and times (what else?). You can do date and time calculations with these fields.
Yes/No	Yes or no or other two-word sets, such as True/False, On/Off, Male/Female, and so on.

Primary key fields for your tables

A *primary key field* (or just *key*) is a field that uniquely identifies each record in a table. If each product in a Products table has a different product code, then the Product Code field uniquely identifies a record in this table. If you search the Products table for a product code, you come up with at most one record.

However, not all tables have an obvious key field. You may have to combine two or three fields to come up with values that are different for each record in the table. In a Books table, for instance, you may have several books with the same title. If you assume that an author never writes more than one book with the same title, a combination of the Title and Author fields may work as a key field.

For an address list, you may think that the combination of first and last name would do the trick, but it doesn't take long before you realize that you know two Jim Smiths. You could use a combination of first name, last name, and phone number, but you have another alternative: have Access issue each record a unique number, and use that number as the key field. If you can't figure out a good set of keys to use for a table, add an AutoNumber field, and Access automatically numbers the records as you add them.

Access doesn't absolutely require every table to have a primary key field (or fields), but if you plan to set up relationships between your tables, some tables definitely need them. Also, key fields speed up a search for records; Access creates an index for each primary key field and can zero in quickly on any record by using those primary key values.

What Are Relationships?

Some projects (most projects) require more than one table. For example, a database for a store has to handle lists of customers, lists of products, and lists of vendors, for a start.

A *relational database* is a database that contains tables that are related — well, no, not as cousins or sisters-in-law. Two tables are *related* if they contain fields that match. If you have an online video store, a relational database system probably includes related Products and Vendors tables:

✦ **The Products table:** This is a list of the videos and other products you sell, containing one record for each product. Each record for a product includes a field that identifies the vendor from whom you buy your stock.

✦ **The Vendors table:** This list includes name, address, and other information about each vendor.

The Products table and the Vendors table are related because the record for each video includes the name of a vendor. Figure 3-2 shows how this relationship works.

Figure 3-2:
A one-to-many relationship links the Products and Vendors tables — three videos come from one vendor.

Products

Title	Vendor
Six Stories about Little Heroes	ART
Adventures in Asia-National Geographi	ROU
The Adventures of Curious George	ROU
I've Always Loved Airplanes	CHB
Aladdin and the Magic Lamp	EBA
Aladdin and the Magic Lamp	PV
The Alamo	COL
Amahl and the Night Visitors	MOV
The Amazing Bone and Other Stories	ROU

Vendors

Vendor Code	Company	Address1
PV	Palace Video	
REE	Reel.com	1250 45th Street
ROB	Robert's Hard to Find	
ROU	Rounder Kids	1263 Lower Road
SCH	Schunick Productions	2 Winton Court
SHM	Shmoo Patties	Bram Layman
SKI	Skinnyguy.com	

Well, sure, you *could* store product information and vendor information in one big table, but you'd soon be sorry. You may want to add fields to the Products table to contain the address of the vendor from which you bought the video. But here's the problem: Whenever a vendor's address changes, you have to make that change in the record for *every item* you buy from that vendor. What a pain!

A key principle of database design is: *Store each piece of information once.* If you store information more than once, then you have to update it more than once. (In real life — trust us on this one — if you update it in some places but not in others, you end up with a mess.)

How relationships work

Sorry, no advice for the lovelorn here — luckily, relationships between tables are much simpler than relationships between people. For two tables to be related, you specify one or more fields in one table that match the same number of fields in the other table. In Figure 3-2, the Product table relates to the Vendors table because the Vendor field in the Products table contains values that match the Vendor Code field in the Vendors table. When you look at a video in the Products field, you can find information about the product's vendor by finding the record in the Vendors table that has the same value in the matching field.

Relationships, also called (less romantically) *joins*, come in several flavors:

✦ **One-to-many:** One record in one table matches no, one, or many records in the other table. The relationship in Figure 3-2 works this way because one vendor can sell many videos.

✦ **One-to-one:** One record in one table matches exactly one record in the other table — no more and no less.

✦ **Many-to-many:** Zero, one, or many records in one table match zero, one, or many records in the other table.

The next three sections explain these three types of joins.

One-to-many relationships

This type of relationship is the most common among tables (by analogy, think of one person with a circle of friends). In a one-to-many relationship, many records in one table can match one record in another table. Here are some examples of one-to-many relationships:

✦ **Items in customer orders:** If you run a store, customers frequently buy several items at the same time. One record in the Orders table could match several records in the Products table.

✦ **Vendors and invoices:** If your company buys many items from another company, you end up with a bunch of invoices from (and payments to) that company. The relationship between the Vendors table and the Invoices table in an accounting database is one-to-many.

✦ **People living in states or provinces:** The United States and Canada use standard two-letter state and province abbreviations, and if you have an address list, these codes should be correct. (Quick — is Quebec "QU" or "PQ"? No peeking.) To make sure you type in the valid state and province codes for the United States and Canada, you can create a State/Province Codes table against which you can validate entries in the State field of your Addresses table. One record in the State/Province Codes table can match many records in the Addresses table.

You use a one-to-many relationship to avoid storing information from the "one" table multiple times in the "many" table. For example, you don't want to store all the information about each student in the record for every class — unless you want to hear the groan of an overloaded drive. Storing each student's information in one place (the Students table), and storing only the student's name and/or student ID in the Classes table is more efficient (and easier to maintain).

Many database designers call the "one" table the *master* table and the "many" table the *detail* table. In Access, *primary key* means the matching field(s) in the master table; *foreign key* means the corresponding field(s) in the detail table. In Figure 3-2, the Vendors table is the master table and the Products table is the detail table. The primary key (in Vendors) is the Vendor Code field; the foreign key (in Products) is the Vendor field.

One-to-one relationships

This type of relationship — where one record in one table matches exactly one record in another table — is much less common in database design. However, you may have reasons (perhaps security reasons) for separating information into two tables. You may store information about the employees of your company. The Employees table contains the basic information about each employee (name, address, phone, and other personal information). The Employee Health table contains information about each employee's health insurance policy (in your company, all employees have insurance). Each record in the Employees table matches exactly one record in the Employee Health table, and vice versa.

The question is: If you have exactly the same number of records in the two tables, and they match exactly, why not just combine them into one table? Most of the time, that's exactly what you should do. In the employee-database example, you can just add the health insurance information to the Employees table and do away with the Employee Health table.

However, occasionally you have a good reason to separate information into two tables connected by a one-to-one relationship. We came up with two scenarios:

✦ **Security:** One of the tables contains much more sensitive information than the other, and you want to restrict who can see the information in that table. Store the sensitive information in a separate table.

See Book VII, Chapter 3 for how to set up security for a database.

✦ **Subset of records:** Maybe only some of the employees in your company have health insurance. (This is the real world, after all.) Rather than leaving a lot of fields blank in the Employees table, storing insurance data in a separate, related table is more efficient.

✦ **Multiple databases:** Some information is stored in a separate database. When you use one database, you can *link* to a table in another database to work with the information in that table as if it were stored in your own database. If someone else's database has information you need and you link to it, you can't combine the two tables into one table, but you can set up a relationship.

Don't be surprised if you almost never create one-to-one relationships between database tables; *we* hardly ever do.

For a one-to-one relationship, you need one or more fields that link the two tables. Make sure that both tables have the same primary key field(s).

Many-to-many relationships

Many-to-many relationships are more complicated than either one-to-one or one-to-many relationships, because a many-to-many is really two relationships in one. Here are some examples of tables in which zero, one, or many records in one table can match zero, one, or many records in the other:

✦ **Students in courses:** If you create a database to keep track of students in a school, many students are in each class, and each student takes many classes. You have many records in the Students table matching one record in the Courses table. You also have many records in the Classes table matching one record in the Students table.

✦ **Committees:** If you set up a database for a club or religious group, you may want to keep track of who is on what committee. One person can be on lots of committees, and one committee can have lots of members. The relationship between the People table and the Committees table is many-to-many.

✦ **Books and authors:** One book can be written by a group of authors (such as this book). And one author can write many books. The relationship between the Books table and the Authors table in a bookstore inventory database can be many-to-many.

Figure 3-3 shows a many-to-many relationship between students and courses. Each student is in several classes; each course has its own bunch of students.

The problem is that Access (and most other relational-database programs) can't handle many-to-many relationships. Access refuses to accept that these relationships exist. (Don't we all know people like that?) But don't worry — you can work around this problem. You can create an additional table that saves the day. The new table records the *connections* between the two tables.

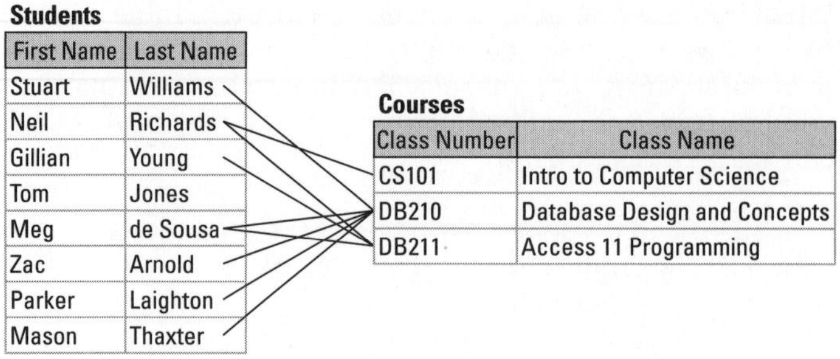

Figure 3-3:
Many
students
can be
in each
course,
and each
student can
take many
courses.

Students

First Name	Last Name
Stuart	Williams
Neil	Richards
Gillian	Young
Tom	Jones
Meg	de Sousa
Zac	Arnold
Parker	Laighton
Mason	Thaxter

Courses

Class Number	Class Name
CS101	Intro to Computer Science
DB210	Database Design and Concepts
DB211	Access 11 Programming

In the students and courses example, you can make a new table called
Course Registrations. This new table is called a *junction table*. Each record in
the Course Registration table assigns one student to one course. The
Students table and the Course Relationship table have a one-to-many relationship: The Students table is the master table and Course Registrations is
the detail table. The Courses table and the Course Registrations table also
have a one-to-many relationship: Again, the Courses table is the master
table. In fact, you probably want that table anyway, because you need somewhere to record the student's grade in that course. (We frequently find that
the new junction table is useful anyway.)

Figure 3-4 shows the relationships among the three tables: Students, Course
Registrations, and Courses. To provide a single primary key field that
uniquely identifies each student, we added a Student ID field to the Students
table. Each record in the Course Registrations connects one student (by
Student ID) to one course (by Class number). In real life, we'd add fields for
the student's grade, payment date, and other information about the student's enrollment in the course.

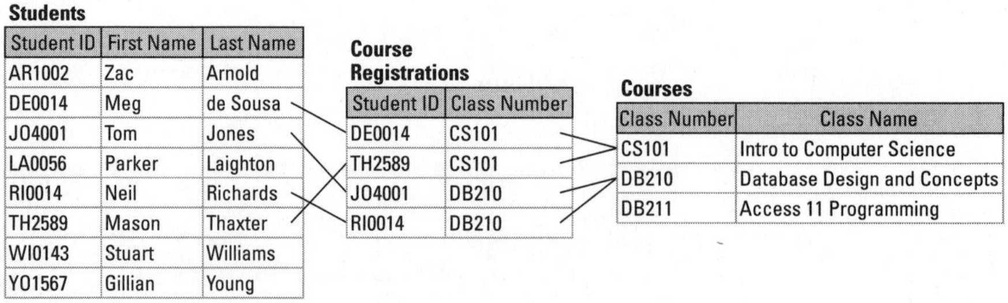

Figure 3-4:
To store
a many-to-
many
relationship,
create a
junction
table that
connects
the two
tables.

Students

Student ID	First Name	Last Name
AR1002	Zac	Arnold
DE0014	Meg	de Sousa
JO4001	Tom	Jones
LA0056	Parker	Laighton
RI0014	Neil	Richards
TH2589	Mason	Thaxter
WI0143	Stuart	Williams
YO1567	Gillian	Young

Course Registrations

Student ID	Class Number
DE0014	CS101
TH2589	CS101
JO4001	DB210
RI0014	DB210

Courses

Class Number	Class Name
CS101	Intro to Computer Science
DB210	Database Design and Concepts
DB211	Access 11 Programming

Designing a Database

When you feel at ease with the concepts of tables, fields, and relationships, you're ready to design your own relational database. The rest of this chapter walks you through designing your database tables so your database is easy to use, flexible, and efficient. We use the example of a bookstore as we go through the steps to show you how designing works.

Identifying your data

Find out what information is available, who maintains it, what it looks like, and how it is used. Make a list of the possible fields (don't worry yet about which fields end up in which tables). For example, a bookstore needs to track product descriptions, prices, purchase dates, customer names, who bought what, shipment dates (for online orders), and other information.

Eliminating redundant fields

Look over the fields you identified — make sure they're all actually *needed* for your application. Is each piece of information something that may appear on a form or report later, or be needed to calculate something? If not, throw it out.

In this case, it's worth repeating: Don't store the same information in more than one place. Redundant information makes double work when updating the information. Instead, figure out the right place to store the information, and store it once. If you can calculate one field from another field, store only one. For example, storing both age *and* birth date is pointless; a person's age changes — the birth date doesn't. Store the birth date; you can always get Access to do the math for you.

The same is true for information that you can look up. For codes of all types (such as state and province codes, product codes, and the like), make a table for the code that includes a field for the code and a field for its meaning. Then all the other tables in your database store only the code, and Access looks up the code's meaning when you need it to appear in a form or report. For the online bookstore, you don't need to store the title and author of each item that a customer buys; instead you can just store the ISBN (unique book number) of each book.

On the other hand, sometimes you can't avoid redundancy. For example, an item of information may change in one place but not in another, so you may have to store it in more than one place. In the bookstore system, when the price of a book changes, the amount that the previous customers paid for the book hasn't changed. In addition to storing the book's current selling price, you may want to store the book's price in the record for each sale.

Organizing fields into tables

You have a bunch of fields. Are they all in one table, or should you set up multiple tables?

One way to tell whether your system needs multiple tables is to check whether you have different numbers of values for different fields. Say the bookstore carries 200 different products (mainly books, we assume) and you have about 1,600 customers. You have 200 different product names, prices, and descriptions, while you have 1,600 different customer names, addresses, and credit card information. Guess what — you have two different tables: a Products table with 200 records and a Customers table with 1,600 records.

You could start out with a design like this:

Products	*Customers*
ISBN or Product Code	First Name
Title	Last Name
Author	Street Address
Publisher	City
Pub. Year	State/Province
Price	ZIP or Postcode
Cover Photo	Payment Method
Taxable (Yes/No)	Credit Card Number
Shipping Weight	Credit Card Exp. Date
Vendor Name	Check Number
Discontinued?	Tax Exempt (Yes/No)
Product Type	Book 1
Product Notes	Book 2
	Book 3
	Shipping Cost
	Sales Tax
	Total Price
	Purchase Date

You'd soon realize, however, that one customer can make more than one purchase. Combining customer information with purchase information won't work — what happens when a customer buys something else? So you leave information about the customer in the Customers table — all the facts about the customer that don't change from one purchase to the next — and move information about a specific purchase into a separate Orders table, like this:

Customers	*Orders*
First Name	Customer First Name
Last Name	Customer Last Name
Street Address	Purchase Date
City	Book 1
State/Province	Book 2
ZIP or Postcode	Book 3
Phone Number	Shipping Cost
Tax Exempt (Yes/No)	Sales Tax
	Total Price
	Payment Method
	Credit Card Number
	Credit Card Exp. Date
	Check Number

But wait — what if the customer buys more than three books at a time? (We usually do.) And if you own the bookstore, you don't want to put an arbitrary limit on how many items your customer can buy. (Limit your profit for the sake of your database? In a word, nope.) Any time your database design includes a bunch of fields that store essentially the same kind of information (for example, Book 1, Book 2, and Book 3), something is wrong. An order can consist of zero, one, or many books — does that sound familiar? Yes, a one-to-many relationship exists between an order and the items in that order, so you need to make a separate table for the individual items, like this:

Orders	*Order Details*
Customer First Name	ISBN
Customer Last Name	Quantity

Orders

Purchase Date

Total Product Cost

Shipping Cost

Sales Tax

Total Price

Payment Method

Credit Card Number

Credit Card Exp. Date

Check Number

Order Details

Price Each

Each time a customer places an order (or comes into your store to make a purchase), you create one record in the Orders table, along with one record for each item purchased in the Order Details table. The Order Details table has room to store the quantity of that item, in case the customer wants more than one of something. (We're sure that you want to buy a copy of this book for everyone you know, right?) You should also store the selling price of the book. Access can calculate the cost of that quantity of each book (price × quantity), so you don't need to store that information.

The following reasons are why not to store multiple fields (such as Book 1, Book 2, and Book 3) in one table, and to create a separate table instead:

✦ **You can't anticipate the right number of fields.** If someone buys more than three things (as in this example), you have to create a separate order and enter everything twice.

✦ **You can't analyze the information later.** What if you want to see a list of everyone who bought the last *Harry Potter* book, so you can notify them that the next one is coming out? If you have multiple fields for this information, your query needs to look for orders that contain a *Harry Potter* book in Book 1 or Book 2 or Book 3. What a pain.

We don't want to drive this into the ground, but creating multiple, identical fields is a problem that many first-time database designers make. Be good to yourself and don't do it!

Add tables for codes and abbreviations

Look at your tables to see whether the fields contain any standard codes, such as two-letter state and province codes, zip codes, or other codes. For example, the bookstore's Customers table includes a State/Province field and a Zip/Postcode field. The Products table contains a Product Type field so the bookstore can track sales of books (type B) versus other types of stuff (such as, F for food or A for audiotapes). Determine whether your system needs to do one of these tasks with the codes:

✦ **Validate the codes.** Wrong codes cause trouble later: Validate the codes when you type them in is always best. If someone types **VR** for Vermont, the post office may not deliver your package. And later, when you analyze your sales by state, you have some Vermonters with the right code (VT) and some with the wrong code.

✦ **Look up the meaning of the code.** Codes usually stand for something. Should your system print or display the meaning of the code? If you have a report showing total sales of products by type, printing "Books," "Food," and "Audiotapes," rather than "B," "F," and "A" is nice.

If you want to either validate or look up the codes you store, create a separate table to hold a list of your codes and their meanings. For example, you could add the following two tables to the bookstore database:

States	*Product Types*
State Code	Product Type Code
State Name	Product Type Description

Although zip codes and postcodes are codes (well, yeah), most databases don't include tables that list them. The reason is simple: Pretty soon your system would be overstuffed with them (about 100,000 zip codes exist, for openers). Plus you have to update the table constantly as the post offices issue — and change — zip and postcodes. If you *really* want to validate your zip codes, you can buy a zip code database from the U.S. Postal Service at www.usps.com.

Choosing keys for each table

The next step in designing your database is to make sure each table has its own primary key field(s). Each table needs one or more fields that uniquely identify each record in the table. Look for a field in the table that has a different value in each record. For example, in the Products table, each book has a unique ISBN (International Standard Book Number) — for a convenient example, look on the back of this book and you can find its ISBN just above the bar code. If your bookstore sells stuff other than books — say, bookmarks, espresso, and expensive little pastries — then you can make up codes for them. If one field is different for every record in the table, you found your primary key field. For lists of codes, the code field is the key.

Autonumbering your records

Well, okay, you may not find a unique field. It happens — tables that list people (such as the Customers table) can pose such a problem. Some people have the same name; family members or roommates can share an address and phone number. Most businesses end up creating and assigning unique numbers to people to avoid this problem. (For privacy reasons, don't even *think* of asking for anyone's Social Security number. Make up your own customer number!)

Access makes assigning each record in a table a unique number easy. Just add an AutoNumber field to the table, and Access numbers the records as you enter them. In your bookstore system, you can add a Customer Number field to the Customers table.

The advantage of using an AutoNumber key as the primary key field is that you can't change its values. After you relate two tables by using an AutoNumber field as the primary key, breaking the relationship between the tables if you have to edit the value of the AutoNumber field later is impossible.

For the Orders table, you can use the Customer Number (instead of the customer's name) to identify who places the order. However, because one customer may make several purchases, you still don't have a unique key for the Orders table. One solution is to use a combination of fields as the primary key. How about using the Customer Number and Purchase Date fields together as the primary key? This solution works fine as long as a customer doesn't make two orders in the same day. (Hmm, that may not work — people sometimes forget to buy everything they needed, and come back for one or two more items. Instead, you can add an AutoNumber field to this table to provide a unique Order Number.)

Two key fields are sometimes better than one

Sometimes using a combination of fields works fine. In the Order Details table, you'd better add a field for the Order Number, so you can get immediate access to whatever order contains these items. You don't need to add a Customer Number field in this case; after you identify the Order Number, Access can look up the Customer Number and other customer information.

The Order Number doesn't uniquely identify records in the Order Details table because one order can (and a bookseller would really love it to) include lots and lots of books. Use a combination of the Order Number and the ISBN as the primary key for the table — that way one order includes one entry for each book purchased.

A sample order-entry database design

Here is the new, improved table design for a bookstore system, with asterisks by the primary key fields:

Products

* Product Code (ISBN)
Title
Author
Publisher
Publication Year
Price
Cover Photo
Taxable (Yes/No)
Shipping Weight
Vendor Name
Discontinued (Yes/No)
Product Type
Product Notes

Customers

* Customer Number
First Name
Last Name
Street Address
City
State/Province
Zip or Postcode
Phone Number
Tax Exempt (Yes/No)

Orders

* Order Number
Customer Number
Purchase Date
Total Product Cost
Shipping Cost
Sales Tax
Total Price
Payment Method
Credit Card Number
Credit Card Exp. Date
Check Number

Order Details

* Order Number
* Product Code (ISBN)
Quantity
Price Each

States	*Product Types*
* State Code	* Product Type Code
State Name	Product Type Description

Linking your tables

If you end up with only one table, you can skip this step — but that situation is fairly rare. Almost every database ends up with a second table at the very least — to contain those pesky codes.

Look at the tables in your database and see which tables contain fields that match fields in other tables. Determine whether there's a one-to-one, one-to-many, or many-to-many relationship between the two tables (as described in the section "What Are Relationships?" earlier in this chapter). For each pair of related tables, you can determine which fields actually relate the tables by following these guidelines:

✦ **One-to-many relationships:** Figure out which is the "one" (master) and which is the "many" (detail) table in this relationship. Make sure that the detail table has a foreign key field (or fields) to match the primary key field(s) in the master table. The Customers and Orders tables have a one-to-many relationship in the bookstore example, because a customer may have no, one, or many orders. (Okay, someone is technically not a customer if they have no orders at all, but still counts as a one-to-many relationship.) The primary key field in the master table (Customers) is Customer Number. To relate the tables, the Orders table has to have a Customer Number field as the foreign key.

✦ **One-to-one relationships:** Make sure both tables have the same primary key field(s).

✦ **Many-to-many relationships:** Access can't store a many-to-many relationship directly. Set up a junction table to connect the two tables, containing the primary keys of the two tables. In the bookstore example, the Orders and Products tables have a many-to-many relationship: One order can have many products and one product can occur in many orders. The Order Details table provides the junction table, containing the primary key of the Orders table (Order Number) and the primary key of the Products table (Product Code or ISBN). This junction table can also include additional information (the Order Details table includes the quantity of the book that's ordered as well as the price of each book).

 The related fields don't need to have the same name in the two related tables. But the types, lengths, and contents of the fields have to match. (We usually find the two fields having the same names less confusing — preserving sanity is also good for business.)

Refining your links

The relationships between your tables can be a bit more complex — what relationship isn't? — so you may need to make a few more decisions about how your table relationships work:

+ **Referential integrity:** This nifty feature means you can tell Access not to allow a record to exist in a detail table unless it has a matching record in the master record. For example, if you turn on referential-integrity-checking for the relationship between the Customers and States fields, Access won't allow you to enter a record with a State/Province code if the code doesn't exist in the State Code field of the States table. It's a "No bogus codes!" rule, and doesn't require any programming (as you find out in Book II, Chapter 6).

+ **Cascading updates:** Another way-cool Access feature updates detail records automatically when you change the matching master record. For example, if you find out that you have the wrong ISBN for a book and you change it in the Product Code field in the Products table, you can configure Access to update the code automagically in the Order Details table.

+ **Cascading deletes:** As with cascading updates, this feature deletes detail records when you delete the master record.

This feature is a bit more dangerous than cascading updates, and you may not want to use cascading deletes for most related tables. If a book goes out of print and you stop carrying it, deleting it from the Products table is a bad idea. What is supposed to happen to all those matching records in the Order Details table (assuming that you sold some copies of the book)? Don't delete the Order Details records, because then it looks like you never sold those books. Instead, mark the book as unavailable (in our example, set the Discontinued field to yes) and leave the records in the tables.

Now you have a fully relational database design. The last step is to clean up the loose ends.

Cleaning up the design

You have tables, you have fields, and you have relationships. What more could you want in a database design? You're almost done. Look at each field in each of your tables and decide on the following for each field:

+ **Data types:** The section, "Data types," earlier in this chapter describes the types of information you can store in Access fields. Decide what kinds of information each field contains, how large your Text fields need to be, and what kinds of numbers your Number fields hold. (Book II, Chapter 1 explains the sizes of Number fields.) Make sure to use the same data type and length for related fields. For example, if Product Code is a Text field that is 10 characters long in the Products table, make it the same length in the Order Details table.

If you use an AutoNumber field as the primary key in a master table, use a Long Integer Number field for the foreign key in related tables.

✦ **Validation:** You can set up validation rules for Text, Number, and Date/Time fields, as described in Book II, Chapter 5. Think about limits on the legal values for the field. For example, you may want to specify that the Price field in the Products table can't be over $200, or that the Publication Year field must be between 1500 and 2100. (This rule should work unless you run the bookstore for Hogwarts Academy.)

✦ **Defaults:** Some fields have the same value for most records. For example, the Discontinued field in the Products table will be NO for most records. (How often would you type in an item that's already discontinued?) You can set the default value — the value that the field starts out with — to the most common value; you have to change it only for the records that have a different value.

✦ **Indexes:** If you plan to sort your table or search for records based on the values in a field, tell Access to maintain an index for the field. Like the index of a book, an index helps you (or Access) find information; Access stores information about the field to speed up searches. Access automatically indexes on primary key fields and foreign key fields, but you can designate additional fields to be indexes.

That's it! You're done designing your database!

Tips for Choosing Field Types

Here are some guidelines for choosing field types.

Choosing between Text and Yes/No fields

Fields that can have only two values (such as *Yes* and *No*, *True* and *False*, or *On* and *Off*) are also called *Boolean* or *logical* values. You can store Boolean information in a one-letter Text field, using Y and N. But if you use a Yes/No field, Access can display the information on forms as a check box, option button, or toggle button.

Another advantage of going the Yes/No field route is that you can easily switch between displaying the field as Yes and No, True and False, or On and Off by changing the Format property for the field. Using a custom format, you can choose any two text values to display instead of *Yes* and *No*. You can display the values Discontinued and Available for a Yes/No Field.

Choosing between Text and Memo fields

Text fields are limited to 255 characters — if you need more than that, use a Memo field. An Access Memo field can contain over 65,000 characters of textual information — but the extra elbow room costs you some versatility. You can't index Memo fields — and they can't serve as primary or foreign keys. If you plan to sort or search your records on the contents of this field, or use the information in it to relate one table to another, a Text field is usually your best bet. So is brevity.

Some database designers avoid the Memo field altogether, because they find that databases with Memo fields are more likely to get corrupted (unreadable by Access). The same is true of OLE Object fields (used for storing pictures, spreadsheets, documents, and other large objects) — your database may get indigestion.

Choosing between Text and Number (Or Currency) fields

Access displays and sorts Number and Currency fields differently from Text fields. Here are the differences:

✦ When displaying a Number or Currency field, Access drops any leading zeros (for example, 08540 becomes 8540 or $8,540).

✦ You can format Number and Currency fields in many ways, giving you control over the number of decimal places, specified currency symbols, and the use of commas. Access can vertically align these fields on the decimal points, which makes columns of numbers easier to read.

✦ Access can calculate totals, subtotals, and averages for Number and Currency fields, as well as doing other numeric calculations.

✦ When sorting a Number or Currency field, values sort from smallest to largest (at least they do when you are sorting in ascending order). But when you sort a Text field, values are sorted alphabetically, starting at the left end of the field. This difference means that in a Text field, Access sorts 55 before 6, because the 5 character comes before the 6 character. The following tables shows how Access sorts the same list of numbers in Number and Text fields.

Number Sort	Text Sort
1	1
2	11
5	2
11	21
21	44
44	5

Use Number fields for all numbers except numeric codes (such as zip codes or phone numbers), which are described in the next section. Store any number you may want to add to a total in a Number or Currency field. Choose a Currency field for money values.

Storing names, money, codes, and other stuff

Now that you know the concepts and procedure for designing a relational database, here are a few suggestions for choosing field types for your information:

+ **People's names:** For lists of people, creating a Name field and putting full names into it is tempting. Don't do it: You'll want to sort records by last name, or create listings with last name first, or otherwise fool with the format of people's names. Create separate First Name and Last Name fields.

+ **Phone numbers and postcodes:** Use Text fields rather than Number fields, even if you plan to type only digits into the field. The test to use is this: Is there any chance that you'd ever want to do math with this information? If the answer is no, then use a Text field.

+ **Money:** Use a Currency field rather than a Number field. Calculations with Currency fields are faster than those with most Number fields.

+ **Percentages:** To store percentages, such as a discount, create a Number field and enter decimal numbers between 0 and 1 (inclusive) for percentages between 0 and 100. When you create the table, you can format the Number field as a percent. Then, if you enter a value and habit makes you type **33%**, Access converts the value automatically to 0.33.

+ **Pictures:** Access allows you to store pictures in a field — specifically, you use an OLE Object field — but unless the pictures are small, doing so turns out to be a bad idea. The database reacts to a large OLE object like an anaconda trying to swallow a rhino — its size balloons. If the pictures are small, go ahead and store them in OLE Object fields, so that everything that makes up the database is in one file. If your pictures are large, if they change frequently, or if you use them for other purposes and need to store them as separate files anyway, store the pathname that leads to the files that contain the pictures. In the bookstore example earlier in this chapter, the Products table includes a Cover Photo field. Instead of making that field into an OLE Object field, you can store all the cover pictures in a separate folder on the hard disk — and store file names for each picture in a Text field. If the pictures are in various folders, store the entire pathname in the field, as in the following example:

```
D:\Bookstore\Database\Products\Iliad.jpg
```

✦ **Calculations:** Don't create a field that stores the results of calculations that use other fields in the same table. Fields should contain only raw data — Access can do the calculations later. The problem with storing calculated values (other than just plain wasting storage space) is that if the numbers on which the calculation was based happen to change, the calculation is then wrong — and fouls up any calculations or reports based on it. In the bookstore database example, in the Order Details table, you may want to add a Total Cost field to contain the Quantity field multiplied by the Price Each field. However, if the customer decides to change the quantity of items purchased, the calculated amount is then wrong. A better approach is to allow Access to do the work at the last minute — Access can multiply, apply discounts, and sum up totals when you display information or print reports.

✦ **Codes:** Decide on the formats to use for phone numbers, invoice numbers, credit card numbers, purchase order numbers, and other codes. Decide whether to use all capital letters, and whether to include or omit dashes and spaces. If you ask Access to search for someone with a credit card number 9999-8888-7777-6666 and the card number is stored as 9999888877776666, the search won't find the record.

Secret keys

The primary key field for a table doesn't have to be information that the user sees. In fact, many programmers prefer to use a primary key field that has no other use than to uniquely identify records. If you create an AutoNumber field to act as a primary key field, the user of your database never has to see or type the values of this field.

When you sign in to the Amazon Web site to order a book, you never have to type in your customer number. Instead, you sign in with your e-mail address and Amazon looks up your customer number automatically. Similarly, when you order a book or other merchandise, you never have to type the item number. You just find the item you want and click the Add This Item To My Cart button.

Storing Single Facts

Some pieces of information exist all by themselves. They aren't part of a list — there's just one item. For example, the name of your organization is a single piece of information, and so is the pathname to the location of your database. If you want these pieces of information to appear on any reports, forms, or queries or used in calculations or importing, typing them willy-nilly into said reports, queries, or other Access objects is tempting — but in practice this turns out to be a lousy idea.

Here's the problem: What happens when one of these facts changes? Suppose that your organization's name or address changes, or you move your database's location to another folder on another computer. You sure don't want to have to root around your database looking for the places where such information appears.

Instead, create a table called Constants or Facts (or any name you like) *with just one record in it.* Create a field for each piece of information you need to store: maybe your table contains Our Name, Our Address, Our City, Our State, Our ZIP, and Our Phone Number fields. Wherever you want this information to appear (reports, mainly), Access can look it up in your table. Then, if something changes (your telephone area code, most likely), you have to update it in only one place!

Creating a Database

Okay, if you faithfully read this book every night before bedtime — doesn't everybody? — you're 50 pages or so in by now. If you still haven't created your database, enough, already! You're armed with your database design and you're ready to start. (If you haven't been following along, then maybe you'd better review those 50 pages *before* you start.)

When you set out to create a new Access database, you have two options: create it from scratch or use a template.

Starting with a blank slate

After you have a beautiful database design (allow us to recommend the — ahem — stellar example in this chapter), you can start with a blank database and create the tables, fields, and relationships. That means running Access without opening an existing database. Follow these steps:

1. **Click the New Database button on the toolbar.**

   The New File task pane appears, with links for various ways to create a new database, as shown in Figure 3-5. (Access 2000 and 2002 display a New dialog box instead; select the Database option and OK.)

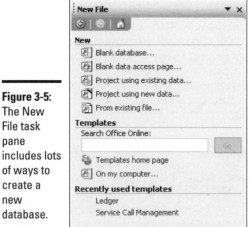

Figure 3-5:
The New
File task
pane
includes lots
of ways to
create a
new
database.

2. **Click the Blank Database link.**

   You see the File New Database dialog box, in which Access asks for a file name for the new database. (If you are running Access 2000 or 2002, select the Database option and OK.)

3. **Navigate to the folder where you want to store the new database, and type the file name into the File Name box. Then click Create.**

   If you are just trying this out, you can use the file name Test. Access automatically adds the extension .mdb to Access database files. Then you see the Database window, as described in Chapter 2 of this book.

4. **Create your tables.**

   Book II, Chapter 1 tells you how. (You tell it about each of the fields in the database, including the field name, data type, and field length.)

5. **Create relationships between the tables.**

   You find out how to do this in Book II, Chapter 6. Access displays a Relationships window that draws lines between related tables.

You can always rename the database later. Close the database, and run Windows Explorer by double-clicking My Computer on the desktop or choosing Start⇨All Programs⇨Accessories⇨Windows Explorer. Navigate to the folder that contains the database and find its file name. Then click the file name, press F2, and type a new name for the database file.

Using database templates

Lots of databases serve similar functions. Imagine how many address-book databases actually exist in this world, add order-entry databases, and club-membership databases, and you may start to see a pattern emerge. In fact, if you create one of these common database applications, Microsoft may have a pre-designed database you can start with. Chances are you want to make some changes, but starting with a *template* — a canned Access database — is easier than starting from scratch.

Analyzing your table design

Access comes with a wizard that can eyeball your database design, looking at the way that you divide your information up into related tables. Specifically, it helps you fix a table that contains repeated values in some fields, splitting the table into two or more related tables.

The Table Analyzer Wizard (shown in the following figure) walks you through the process, creating the new tables and moving the fields and values. To run the Wizard, choose Tools⇨ Analyze⇨Table.

Table Analyzer Wizard

Products and Suppliers

Product	Supplier ID	Supplier	Address
Ravioli Angelo	PAST	Pasta Buttini s.r	Via dei Gelsomir
Gnocchi di nonr	PAST	Pasta Buttini s.r	Via dei Gelsomir
Carnarvon Tige	PAVL	Pavlova, Ltd.	74 Rose St.
Outback Lager	PAVL	Pavlova, Ltd.	74 Rose St.
Pavlova	PAVL	Pavlova, Ltd.	74 Rose St.,
Vegie-spread	PAVL	Pav, Ltd.	74 Rose St.

Supplier name is misspelled.

Supplier information is repeated.

**The Table Analyzer:
Looking At the Problem**

Your table or spreadsheet may store the same information many times. Duplicating information can cause problems.

First, duplicating information wastes space.

» Show me an example.

Second, duplicating information can lead to mistakes.

» Show me an example.

Cancel | < Back | Next > | Finish

To create a database using a template, follow these steps to see whether a useful template is available:

1. **Display the New File task pane by clicking the New button on the toolbar.**

   Refer to Figure 3-5.

2. **Select the Templates Home Page option in the Templates section of the task pane.**

   You have to be connected to the Internet for this command to work; the pages are displayed from the Microsoft Web site. The Templates Home Web page appears in your Web browser, including a long list of template categories for all the programs in Microsoft Office (Word, Excel, Outlook, PowerPoint, and Access). The exact appearance and workings of this page may have changed since this book was written — Web pages can change at any time, and usually do!

3. **Click a likely looking template type, such as the Employee Management or Monthly Calendars templates.**

   You see a list of template files of that type. Note, however, that they may not be Access databases: Access databases have a little key icon to the left of the template description. We find most of the available templates to be Word documents (showing a little *W* icon) or Excel spreadsheets (showing a little *X* icon); Access database templates aren't exactly hen's teeth, but they are fairly scarce.

   Browse around the Templates Web site. If you don't find a template that sounds similar to your application, then partner, you're on your own — roll up your sleeves and create your database from scratch, as described in the previous section.

4. **If you find a template that looks useful, click its file name.**

   You see a form from the database appear in your browser.

5. **To download the template file, follow the directions on the Web page.**

   Access downloads the template file and stores it in your My Documents folder. (You can move and rename it afterward if you like.) You see the template database open in your Access window.

6. **Look around the database, and then make changes to the tables, fields, and relationships.**

   Book II, Chapters 1 and 6 tell you how to tweak 'em like a pro.

Older versions of Access come with some templates, but don't provide a link to the Microsoft online library. In the New dialog box, click the Databases tab to see some templates.

Choosing Access 2000 or 2002 File Format

Different versions of Access use different file formats. When Microsoft adds new features to Access, sometimes it needs to add information to the database files that those new Access versions create — which means that older versions of Access may not be able to read the files.

Luckily, Access 2003 uses the same file format as Access 2002 (the version that came with Office XP). Normally, when you create a new database using Access 2003, the database is in Access 2002/2003 format.

Naming things (for *serious* database designers)

If you create a database that is used with larger database systems — such as those running on SQL Server or Oracle — you may want to use a systematic approach to naming the objects in your database. First, omit all spaces in your table and field names, because some database systems can't handle them. Even in Access, avoiding spaces means less typing later on when you create queries, forms, reports, macros, and VBA modules. That's because you won't have to enclose your table and field names in square brackets ([ ]).

Also, don't use words that have specialized meanings to Access, including these words: *Name, Date, Word, Value, Table, Field,* and *Form.* You can actually confuse Access. It's not a pretty sight.

If you really want to impress your programming friends, consider using prefixes on all your object names to show what kind of object you are naming. Here's a set of commonly used prefixes:

tbl	Table
qry	Query
frm	Form
rpt	Report
mcr	Macro
bas	Module
dap	Data access page

For example, a serious programmer might rename the Products table as tblProducts.

Fewer programmers use prefixes for fields, to show the data type of each field. If you want to, and if you want to read more about the Reddick VBA Naming Conventions from which these prefixes come, go to the www.xoc.net Web site and click the links for RVBA Conventions.

However, what if you are creating a database that you plan to use with ear-lier versions of Access? For example, some people in your office may still be using Access 2000 or Access 97. Will they be able to use your shiny new Access 2003 database? To answer this burning question, consult the follow-ing handy guidelines:

✦ **Access 2000:** Access 2003 (and 2002) can also create and work with databases in Access 2000 format. Choose Tools➪Database Utilities➪ Convert Database➪To Access 2000 File Format. When you provide a new name for the database and click the Save button, Access creates a new, Access-2000-format version of the database. You can open and maintain this database later in Access 2000, 2002, or 2003.

✦ **Access 97:** Access 2003 (along with Access 2002 and 2000) can also create Access-97-format databases. Choose Tools➪Database Utilities➪ Convert Database➪To Access 97 File Format, type a file name, and click the Save button. However, if you want to open this file later in Access 2003, your options are limited. You can either *enable* the database so you can work with its data — but not change objects such as forms and queries — or you can convert it back.

See Chapter 2 of this book for what happens when you open older Access databases in Access 2003. Note that Access 2000 can't open Access 2002/2003 format databases — you just get an error message.

Book II

Tables

The 5th Wave By Rich Tennant

"Your database is beyond repair, but before I tell you our backup recommendation, let me ask you a question. How many index cards do you think will fit on the walls of your computer room?"

Contents at a Glance

Chapter 1: Creating and Modifying Tables

In This Chapter

✓ **Making tables using the Datasheet view, Design view, and the Table Wizard**

✓ **Fine-tuning fields using Design view**

✓ **Defining a primary key**

✓ **Printing your raw data**

Tables are the most basic building block in your database — they hold the data that you need to save and to analyze. Creating tables and entering data may not be the most glamorous thing you do with your database, but having well-designed tables and correctly entered data makes your database as useful as possible. Before you begin putting data in tables you need to consider the design of your database. Book I, Chapter 3 describes how to design a database — read it before you create a bunch of tables that you then have to reorganize!

This chapter guides you through creating tables and defining fields in Design view. Chapter 2 of this book goes into the details you need to know about entering and editing data. The other chapters in this book cover all the other important details that keep your tables — and the data in them — in good shape for use in queries, forms, reports, and the other objects in your database.

If you are not sure what fields and records are, refer to Book I, Chapter 3.

About Table Views

When you look at a table, you probably look at it in one of two views — Datasheet view or Design view. Datasheet view is used for entering and viewing data, and Design view is used for refining field definitions and table properties.

Two Pivot views are also available — PivotTable view (covered in Book III, Chapter 4) and PivotChart view (covered in Book V, Chapter 3) — for when you're ready to analyze your data.

Before we start talking about using each view, we want to give you a brief tour, so that you can recognize the elements of each view. To switch between Design view and Datasheet view click the View button, the first button on the toolbar. The button changes depending on the view you're using.

Datasheet view

A datasheet shows you data. Similar to a spreadsheet, Datasheet view displays your data in rows and columns. Rows are the records; columns are the fields. In Figure 1-1 you see a datasheet with all the parts labeled.

Use a datasheet to view, enter, edit, and delete data. In Datasheet view, you can also create and delete fields, sort and filter data, check spelling, and find data. Datasheet view is covered in more detail in Chapter 2 of this book.

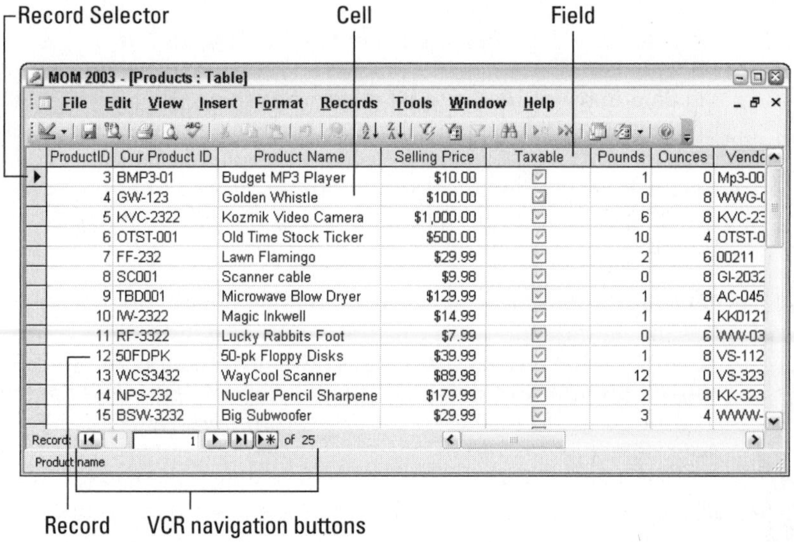

Figure 1-1:
Datasheet
view.

Design view

In Design view, you don't see any data; instead, you define and edit field names and the type of data each field holds. You can also provide a field description. Design view also contains field properties — more advanced ways to define fields and help make sure that data entry is accurate. In Figure 1-2 you see a table in Design view, with its various parts labeled.

Data type drop-down list

Record Selector   Fields   Field description

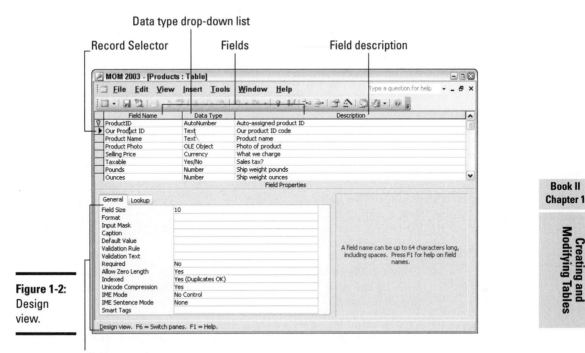

Figure 1-2:
Design
view.

Field properties

Saving Your Table

As soon as you enter data, Access saves it. Why do you need to save your tables? In order to save the table and field definitions. What you save when you save a table is the table definition, which includes how the table looks in Datasheet view (such as the size and order of the columns) and the information in Design view (the field names, data types, descriptions, and field properties).

Save a table design by clicking the Save button, pressing Ctrl+S, or closing Design view and clicking the Yes button when Access asks you if you want to save the table. Provide a name that describes the data stored in the datasheet in the Save As dialog box — chances are you will use any table when you create other database objects, and naming the table descriptively saves you time when you are looking for the data you need later.

Creating Tables for Your Data

Before you create a table to hold your data, take some time to consider the design of your database — that is, what fields and tables you need so that your data is well organized and easy to analyze. Book I, Chapter 3 has all the information you need to know before you sit down and design your tables.

After you figure out how to organize your data, you're ready to sit down with Access and create tables.

You may need to create a database to hold your tables. Book I, Chapter 3 covers how to create a brand new database. To create a table, first open the database that you want to hold the table. If you don't see the Database window, click F11 to display it. Click the Tables button in the Objects list on the left side of the Database window. Three options display — your choices for creating a new table:

✦ **Create Table in Design View:** Design the table by naming fields and defining the type of data the field will hold, and perhaps using field properties to further define the field.

✦ **Create Table by Entering Data:** Open a datasheet and begin entering data. You name your fields and define any field properties later.

✦ **Create Table by Using Wizard:** Use the Table Wizard to create a table with pre-defined fields. The Table Wizard has business and personal tables available, for example, Contacts, Customers, Employees, Products, Addresses, Household Inventory, and others, and you can refine every table as you need.

Don't stress too much about deciding whether you want to create a table in Design view or by entering data in Datasheet view. Switching back and forth between Datasheet and Design view in order to define the tables and fields exactly the way you want them is easy.

Creating a new table using Datasheet view

Of the three methods available for creating tables, the most straightforward is creating a datasheet and begin entering data. A datasheet looks like a spreadsheet; if you're familiar with Excel or another spreadsheet program, creating a table by entering data into a datasheet may be a good place to start. In a datasheet, fields are columns, and records are rows. (If you're confused by this talk of fields and records, go to Book I, Chapter 3!)

Follow these steps to create a new table in Datasheet view:

1. **Open your database.**

If you haven't created a database yet, open Access and click the Create a New File option in the Getting Started pane that appears on the right side of the Access window. Then click the Blank Database option in the New File pane to display the File New Database dialog box. Give your database a name and click the Create button. For more on creating a new database see Book I, Chapter 3.

You should see the Database window. If you don't see the Database window, press F11.

2. **Click the Tables button in the Objects list to see the options for creating a table, as shown in Figure 1-3.**

Figure 1-3:
The
Database
window.

3. **Double-click the Create Table by Entering Data option.**

You see a blank datasheet in Datasheet view, as shown in Figure 1-4. Access names it Table1 (you can change that when you save the table).

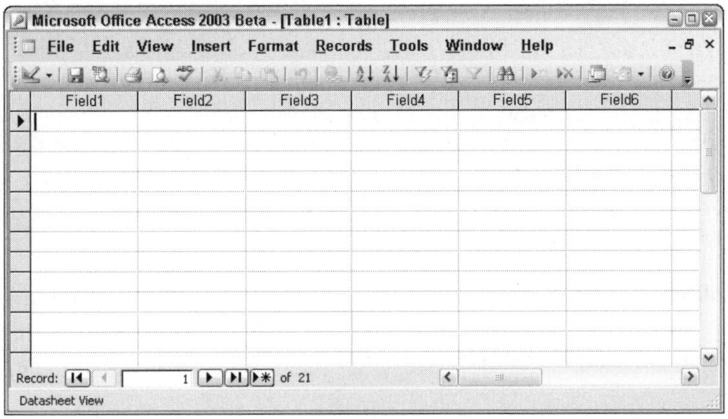

Figure 1-4:
A nice blank
datasheet,
ready for
data.

4. **Enter one record of data (fill the first row).**

For example, enter a first name, last name, street address, city, state, and zip code, pressing Tab between each entry to move to a new field. Figure 1-5 shows a table with one record (row) of data entered.

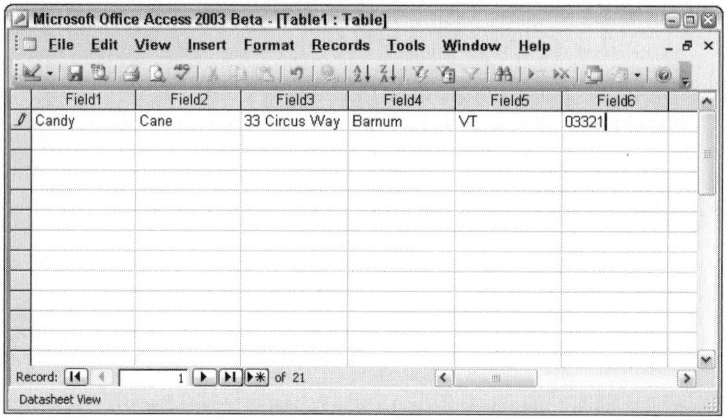

Figure 1-5:
Start entering data, pressing Tab between each field.

Access uses the Pencil icon in the left border of the row (also called the record selector) to indicate that you are "writing" data — that is, entering or editing data. Enter data in as many columns as you think you need in the table.

5. **Save the table by pressing Ctrl+S.**

Access displays the Save As dialog box.

6. **Type a name for the table in the Name field and press Enter.**

Use a descriptive name so that you can find the table in the future.

7. **When Access asks whether you want to define a primary key, choose Yes or No.**

Don't worry; whatever you choose, you can change later. If you feel the need to make an informed decision now, skip ahead to "Defining the Primary Key," later in this chapter. If you choose to create a primary key now, Access creates a new, numbered field that gives each record a unique number. If you want to skip this step, you define a primary key manually when you know which field or fields you want to use to uniquely identify each record.

When Access saves the table, it removes extra columns (fields) that you haven't used. If you need more, find out how to add them later in this chapter in the section "Adding a field."

Now that you have a table you may want to:

+ **Rename fields**: Double-click the field name, type a new name, and press Enter.

+ **Enter data**: Press Tab to move from cell to cell. Access automatically saves the data when you move to the next cell.

See Chapter 2 of this book for more information about what you can do in a datasheet.

Creating tables using Design view

Design view is a good place to create a table if you know a lot about the type of data you put in the table and you want the fields you create to be designed for the data you have to put in them. If you're creating the table but don't yet have any data, Design view is the perfect place to start. Of course, you can always switch to Datasheet view by clicking the View button on the toolbar to enter data at any time.

Follow these steps to create a table in Design view:

1. **Click the Tables button in the Objects list on the left side of the Database window to display the table options and then double-click the Create Table in Design View option.**

Access opens a blank table in Design view. Notice the flashing cursor in the first row of the Field Name column.

2. **Type the name of the first field. Press Tab to move to the Data Type column.**

The field properties for the field fill in automatically, and the data type is set to the Text option.

3. **Select a data type from the Data Type drop-down list.**

Choices include Text, Memo, Number, Date/Time, and Currency.

4. **Type a description of the field in the Description column. (This is optional, but we recommend it.)**

The description can be especially useful if many people use the database, or if you may not use the database for a while. Use the Description column to explain exactly what you intend the field to be used for.

5. **Define additional fields in the table by repeating Steps 2 through 4.**

6. **Click the Save button or press Ctrl+S to save the table. Type a descriptive name in the Name field and press Enter.**

7. **When Access asks whether you want to define a primary key, choose Yes or No.**

   Don't worry; whatever you choose, you can change later. If you feel the need to make an informed decision now, skip ahead to the section, "Defining the Primary Key," later in this chapter. If you choose to create a primary key now, Access creates a new, numbered field that gives each record a unique number. If you want to skip this step, you define a primary key manually when you know which field or fields you want to use to uniquely identify each record.

Creating tables using the Table Wizard

The Table Wizard provides a bunch of commonly used tables with predefined fields. You can select the table that meets your needs, and choose only the fields that you need. If the Table Wizard has the right table for your purpose, using the wizard can be a good way to get started. You can customize a table made by the Table Wizard using the table's Design and Datasheet views.

See Book I, Chapter 2 for more information on using wizards.

Follow these steps to create a table with the Table Wizard:

1. **Click the Tables button in the Objects list on the left side of the Database window (refer to Figure 1-3) and double-click the Create Table by Using Wizard option in the list of options that appear on the right.**

   The Table Wizard appears, as shown in Figure 1-6.

Figure 1-6:
The Table Wizard.

2. **Decide whether your table has personal data or business data and select the appropriate radio button.**

   Access displays a list of sample tables for the category you select.

3. **Select a sample table by clicking it.**

   The available fields for that sample table show up in the Sample Fields list.

4. **Select sample fields that you want to include in the new table from the Sample Fields list by highlighting the field and clicking the right arrow button.**

   The field you select moves from the Sample Fields list to the Fields in My New Table list.

   If you change your mind about a field, simply highlight it in the Fields in My New Table list and click the left arrow button. The field moves back to the Sample Fields list.

   You can use the double arrows to move all fields into or out of the Fields in My New Table list.

5. **Repeat Steps 3 and 4 until you select all the fields you want in your table and click the Next button.**

   You can select fields from multiple tables if you like.

6. **Name your table.**

7. **Tell Access whether you want a primary key field created for you, or if you want to select the primary key field yourself and click Next.**

8. **Choose whether you want to see the table in Design view, in Datasheet view (the Enter Data Directly Into the Table option), or if you want Access to create a simple form from the fields in the table where you can enter data.**

9. **Click Finish.**

If you don't want to use the Table Wizard because you already started creating a table, but you want a field with some pre-defined field properties, use the Field Builder. The Field Builder lists fields from the Table Wizard sample tables. When you use the Field Builder, you get a field with the data type and field properties that are appropriate.

Use the Field Builder to define a field by following these steps:

1. **Display the table in Design view.**

2. **Place the cursor in the Field Name column.**

3. **Click the Build button on the Design View toolbar to see the Field Builder.**

   As with the Table Wizard, you choose the table that contains the field you want (use the Business and Personal buttons to see a different list of tables), and then select the field. Click OK to add the field to your table.

Refining Your Table Using Design View

Design view is the place to go when you want to be really specific about what you want a field to hold. Design view also provides some tools you use to make sure that the data entered in a field is what you want it to be — that's covered in more detail in Chapter 5 of this book.

The top part of the Design View window lists the fields in the table, their data type, and a description, if one has been added.

The bottom part of the Design View window displays *field properties* — configuration information about the current field. If you're a novice Access user, don't worry about field properties. You don't have to do anything with them at all; if you do need them at some point, however, we tell you exactly how to use them.

Many (but not all!) of the tasks you do with Design view can also be done in Datasheet view. Datasheet view is covered in more detail in Chapter 2 of this book.

Table 1-1 lists buttons that are important in Design view.

Table 1-1		Design View Buttons and Their Functions
Button	*Name*	*What It Does*
	View	Displays the table in Datasheet view.
	Primary Key	Makes the selected field the primary key field for the table.
	Indexes	Displays the Indexes window with the indexed fields in the table and their index properties.
	Insert Rows	Adds a row (field) to the table design where the cursor is, or inserts as many rows as are selected.

Button	Name	What It Does
	Delete Rows	Deletes the selected row (field).
	Properties	Displays the Properties sheet.
	Build	Displays a dialog box to help you build a field or expression. Available when cursor is in Field Name, Default Value, Validation Rule, or Smart Tags.

Choosing field names

When you create fields, give at least a couple of seconds of thought to the name you give them. Although you can change a field name, thinking of the name as permanent is safer. Pick a name that is descriptive, not too long, and easy to figure out. You often see the name without the description when you are building other objects, so naming fields well now saves you time later.

Some fields are used to connect tables — for instance, in your Holiday Gifts database you may have a person's name (or some other unique identifier) in the table for listing addresses as well as the table for listing the gift(s) you give them each year. Try to use the same name for fields that appear in multiple tables when the field is, in fact, the same. If the field is similar but not identical, give it a different name.

Starting every name with a number or a letter, and keeping names to 64 characters or less is a good idea.

If you are even thinking of using your database in a real SQL environment, don't use spaces in your field names. SQL does not like spaces at all.

Changing a field name

If, despite our carping about choosing good field names the first time around, you find that you want to rename a field, you need to turn on the Name AutoCorrect feature. The Name AutoCorrect feature finds all the times you use the field name in other objects in the database and changes the field name appropriately. The feature does work, but we don't trust it entirely. Changing field names in the database building process sooner rather than later is easier, before you use the field name a zillion times in tables, queries, forms, reports, and in code. Keep a table of old and new names in case any problems crop up.

You can rename a field in a single table, but if you use the field in other places in the database, be sure the Name AutoCorrect feature is on by choosing Tools⇨Options and clicking the General tab. The Name AutoCorrect box has three check boxes — be sure the second (Perform Name AutoCorrect) is selected.

To change a field name in Design view, right-click the current name, select Rename from the shortcut menu, type a new name, and press Enter.

Copying a field

You can copy a field definition easily — be aware that you only copy the definition, though, and not the data. You can even copy a field definition from one table to another — this is an easy way to be sure that related fields have the same definition (usually only one field needs the primary key designation, though, so be sure to remove it from the other field).

To copy a field, follow these steps:

1. **Click the record selector (the gray box to the left of the field name) to select the field.**

2. **Press Ctrl+C or click the Copy button on the toolbar.**

3. **Move the cursor to an empty row in the table where you want to copy the field.**

4. **Press Ctrl+V or click the Paste button on the toolbar.**

5. **Type a new name in the Field Name field, if necessary, and press Enter.**

    The field title is highlighted, so when you type a new name, you replace the old name.

Moving a field

To move a field, select the row by clicking the record selector — you can select multiple rows by dragging the row selectors. Then drag the record selector up or down to where you want to drop it. As you move the mouse, a dark horizontal line shows where the row moves when you release the mouse button.

Adding a field

If you want to add a field in the middle of a table in Design view, place the cursor where you want the new field to appear (or select the row) and click the Insert Rows button. Rows at and below the cursor are pushed down to make room for the new field.

Deleting a field

You can delete a field in Design view. Deleting a field deletes the field definition and all the data stored in the field.

Follow these steps to delete a field:

1. **Select the field by clicking the record selector (the gray box to the left of the field name).**

2. **Press the Delete key.**

   If the field has no data, Access deletes it. If the field has data, you see a dialog box asking you to confirm that you do, indeed, want to permanently delete the field and its data.

Choosing a data type

Access provides nine data types for you to choose from. Choose the data type that best describes the data you want to store in the field and that works with the type of analysis you need to use the field for. For instance, storing phone numbers in a text field works fine because you probably never need to add or subtract numbers. Prices, however, should be stored in a number or currency field so that you can add, subtract, or even multiply them by the number of units ordered and create an invoice.

A few fields need data type that may not be obvious, mainly telephone numbers and zip codes and other such fields. Generally, even though these fields store numbers, you want to set these fields to text data type. Doing so allows you to store leading zeros (so that 01505 doesn't appear as 1505) and add characters such as dashes and parentheses. The Input Mask Wizard, covered in Chapter 5 of this book, helps you define fields for phone numbers, zip codes, social security numbers, and dates. The Input Mask Wizard is also useful for any codes you may use in your database, or other types of fields that may sometimes appear with spaces or dashes or other punctuation (such as a credit card number) so that the data is always entered consistently, and you can find data when you need it.

Table 1-2 lists the data types and describes the type of data to choose each for.

Table 1-2	Data Types	
Data Type	*What It Holds*	*When to Use It*
Text	Numbers, letters, punctuation, spaces, and special characters up to 255 characters.	All text fields except really long ones. Also good for zip codes and phone numbers. You can't do number type calculations with a text field.
Memo	Text, and lots of it — up to 65,536 characters.	When you have lots of text, such as comments. Can't be indexed, and can't be a key field.
Number	Numbers. When you select Number type, you may want to change the Field Size property to the option that best fits the field. Field sizes are explained in Table 1-3.	For numbers that you may want to add and multiply and do other calculations with. You can also use decimal points, +, and - in a Number field (to designate positive and negative numbers).
Date/Time	Dates and times.	For dates and times. You can do calculations such as finding the number of days between two dates and adding hours to a time to calculate a new time with date/time fields.
Currency	Numbers with a currency sign in front of them.	When you store currency data, such as prices. You can do calculations with currency fields as with number fields. Holds monetary values. Calculations with Currency fields are faster than those with Single or Double Numbers field sizes (the kinds of numbers that can include fractions for cents). Single and Double field sizes for number fields are explained in Table 1-3.
AutoNumber	A unique number generated by Access for each record.	When you want each record to have a unique value that you don't have to type in. The value starts at one and is incremented for each record.
Yes/No	Binary data such as Yes/No, Male/Female, True/False, and so on.	When you have a field that can only have two entries. Appears as a check box on the datasheet and can appear as a check box, option button, or toggle button on forms and can be either "on" or "off." Use the Format field property to define the values — for instance, true/false, male/female, available/discontinued.

Data Type	What It Holds	When to Use It
OLE Object	An electronic object such as a picture, a sound, or another object created with OLE-compatible software.	When you want to store something in Access or link to something created and opened with another application.
Hyperlink	URLs, e-mail addresses, and other types of links.	When you want to link to a Web page, e-mail address, or file. See more about hyperlinks in Chapter 2 of this book.
Lookup Wizard	Not really a data type — this option runs the Lookup Wizard.	When you want to select a table or a list to use as a drop-down list for the field.

Some database designers avoid the Memo field altogether, because they find that databases with Memo fields are more likely to get corrupted (unreadable by Access). The same is true of OLE Object fields, which are used for storing pictures, spreadsheets, documents, and other large objects.

When to use AutoNumber fields

AutoNumber fields have one and only one purpose: to act as the primary key field for tables that don't have an existing field that uniquely identifies each record. Don't use AutoNumber fields for anything else. In fact, most Access database designers use AutoNumber fields to create primary key fields and then make sure those key fields never appear on forms and reports.

Here's why: You have no control over the numbers that Access issues when numbering your records. If you start adding a record and then cancel it, Access may decide that the number is used and skip it the next time you add a record. You can't change the AutoNumber field's value. If you need a series of numbers to not end up with holes (skipped numbers), then don't use an AutoNumber field.

If you use an AutoNumber field to keep track of invoices, and it issues your invoice numbers, you end up with skipped invoice numbers. If this isn't a problem for you, fine — make the Invoice Number category an AutoNumber field and print it on your invoices. But if missing invoice numbers is a problem, use a regular Number field for your invoice numbers and don't use the unique AutoNumber field on forms and reports.

If you want to start numbering invoices at 1001 rather than 1, create an Invoice Number field. If you want to get fancy, create a macro that automatically fills in the next invoice number in the sequence. But in the event of a mistake where you enter an incorrect check number, you can go back and make changes without changing the value of the primary key field.

Choosing whether to embed pictures and other external information

You may have information stored in other files — pictures, PowerPoint presentations, Web pages, or whatever — that relates to records in your database. For example, you may have a Windows folder with a digital photo of each product in your database, or each vendor may have a Web site.

If you want to connect this external information with records in a table, you have two options: Store it right in the database (embed it), or store a link in your database to the external file. We don't recommend embedding a lot of graphical information in your database. Link it instead. Chapter 4 of this book provides more information on linking data.

Linking works for all kinds of external information, including all types of files, as well as files that live out on the Web.

If you link to pictures (or other files) rather than embedding them, you may have a problem if you move your database file to another computer. You may need to move the other files, too. If the link is to a URL (Web address) or UNC (LAN address), the address may continue to work. But if the link is a pathname on your local computer, you need to move the linked files to a folder with the same pathname that they used to be at.

Formatting Fields with Field Properties

Field properties are generally used for formatting fields. They can also be used to validate data, which we cover in Chapter 5 of this book.

Field properties are defined for each field (not surprisingly!). You can only see the field properties for one field at a time. To see the field properties for a field, select the field in the top half of the Design View window. You can select the field by clicking the record selector (the gray box to the left of the row) or by clicking anywhere in the row. The selected field has a triangle arrow to its left. Select a new field to see a whole different set of field properties. The field properties you see depend on the data type of the field — for instance, you won't see the Decimal Places property for a Text field.

Click a field property to see a short description to the right — that tells you if it's a formatting property or a data validation property (some can be used in both ways).

How do you use field properties to format a field? For number fields, you can define the number of decimal places you want to display. For text fields, you can tell Access to change the text to all capital letters or all lowercase. You can even use the Format property to add extra characters to a Text or Memo field (although for most applications the Input Mask Wizard is easier to use than the Format property — see more about input masks in Chapter 5 of this book).

Formatting Number and Currency fields

You can use the Field Size and Format properties together to define how fields display. The common formats for Number and Currency fields are built right into Access — you can choose from those listed in Table 1-3.

Table 1-3	Number Formats
Number Format	*How It Works*
General Number	Displays numbers without commas and with as many decimal places as the user enters
Currency	Displays numbers with the local currency symbol (determined by the Regional settings found in the Windows Control Panel), commas as thousands separators, and two decimal places
Euro	Displays numbers with the Euro symbol, commas as thousands separators, and two decimal places
Fixed	Displays numbers with the number of decimal places specified in the Decimal Places property (immediately after the Format property; the default is 2)
Standard	Displays numbers with commas as thousands separators and the number of decimal places specified in the Decimal Places property
Percent	Displays numbers as percentages — that is, multiplied by 100 and followed by a percent sign
Scientific	Displays numbers in scientific notation

The Field Size property can affect the format.

You can define your own number format using the following symbols:

#	Displays a value if one is entered for that place
0	Displays a 0 if no value appears in that place

.	Displays a decimal point
,	Displays a comma
$ (or other currency symbol)	Displays the currency symbol
%	Displays the number in percent format
E+00	Displays the number in scientific notation

To create a number format with comma separators and three decimal places, type the following: ###,##0.000

You can define a numeric format so the value is different from the format. You can define formats for positive and negative numbers, for zero, and for null values (when no value is entered). To use this feature, enter a four-part format into the Format property separated by commas. The first part is for positive numbers, the second for negatives, the third if the value is 0 and the fourth if the value is null (for example, #, ##0;(#,##0);"—";"none"). Using this type of format you can display positive and negative numbers in different colors, if you like, such as positive in green and negative in red.

To store percentages, such as a discount, create a Number field with a Single field size (to keep the size of the field small — see the next section) and enter numbers between 0 and 1 (inclusive) for percentages between 0 and 100. When you create the table, you can format the Number field as a percent. When you enter a value, you type **33%** and Access converts the value to 0.33.

Setting the field size

Using the Field Size property correctly keeps your database efficient — doing so keeps the field size as small as is practical, thus making for a smaller, more compact database. For Text fields, the Field Size property can also help you screen out incorrect data — if you know that you only need four characters in a certain field, then set the field size to 4. Anything longer produces an error message. (For more about screening out incorrect data, see Chapter 5 of this book.)

Using the Field Size property for any of your Number fields is a little more complicated, but again, using the shortest practical field size makes your database more efficient. Table 1-4 shows your choices for the field size of a Number field (these are listed from the smallest amount of space required to store each value to the largest).

Table 1-4	Field Sizes for Number Fields	
Setting	*What It Can Hold*	*When to Use It*
Byte	Integers from 0 to 255.	Use if values are small integers less than 256.
Integer	Integers from -32,768 to 32,767.	Use for most fields needing integers, unless you need to store values more than 32,768.
Long Integer	Integers from -2,147,483,648 to 2,147,483,647.	Use when the Integer setting isn't enough.
Single	Numbers from about -3.4E38 to -1.4E-45 for negative numbers and from about 1.4E-45 to 3.4E38 for positive values. Decimal precision to 7 places.	Use for numbers with decimal values. Holds big numbers and lots of decimal places — Double holds even more. Generally speaking, Single is sufficient, but you can change the setting to Double without losing data.
Double	Numbers from about -1.7E308 to -4.9E-324 for negative numbers and from about 4.9E-324 to 1.8E308 for positive values. Decimal precision to 15 places.	Any values that Single won't hold.
Decimal	Numbers from -10^28-1 through 10^28-1 in .mdb (Access database) files. Numbers from -10^38-1 through 10^38-1 in .adp (Access project) files. Decimal precision to 28 places.	Use for values with lots and lots of decimal places.
Replication ID	Globally unique identifier (GUID) used for replication.	Use for an AutoNumber field that is the primary key when you replicate the database and add more than 100 records between replication. (Not a common choice!)

Book II
Chapter 1

Creating and
Modifying Tables

The default field size for Text fields is 50; for Number fields, it's Long Integer. You can change the default size by choosing Tools⇨Options, clicking the Tables/Queries tab, and changing the Default Field Sizes settings.

You can change a field size after you entered data, but if you shrink the size, any Text data longer than the new setting is truncated and any Number data that doesn't meet the requirements is rounded (if you choose an integer setting) or converted to a `Null` setting if the value is too large or small for the new setting.

Formatting Date/Time fields

Access provides the most common formats for dates and times — click the down arrow to see the formats. You can also create your own Date/Time format — for online help, press F1 or use the Help button on the toolbar — that provides all the codes you need. Combine them in the same way that you combine the text or number codes to define a format.

Formatting text fields

Use the `Field Size` and `Format` properties together to format text fields. The `Field Size` property limits each entry to the number of characters you specify. You can change the field size from a smaller size to a larger size with no problems. If you change a larger size (say 20) to a smaller size (say 10), you lose characters past the 10th character.

You enter symbols into the `Format` property in a kind of code:

For This Format	Type This Format Property
Display text all uppercase	>
Display text all lowercase	<
Display text left-aligned	!
Specify a color	Enter one of the following colors between [] square brackets: black, blue, green, cyan, magenta, yellow, white
Specify a certain number of characters	Enter @ for each required character (see also Chapter 5 of this book)
Specify that no character is required	&
Display pre-defined text	/text (the `Default Value` property may also be useful). For instance, enter /NA to display the text NA. Appears in all records until another value is entered.

Defining the Primary Key

The *primary key* is a field in each table that is used to uniquely identify each record in the field. (Primary keys are described in Book I, Chapter 3, including how to choose which field or fields to use for your primary key.) The simplest primary key field is a counter with a value of one for the first record, two for the second record, and so on. You can create a counter field by using an AutoNumber field. If you allow Access to create a primary key for you when you save a table, it creates an AutoNumber field.

Another example of a primary key is a social security number in a table where each record contains information about a single person and each person is listed only once in the table. Sometimes each record may be uniquely identified by the combination of two fields, such as an item number and the manufacturer. Note that using first and last name may not always be unique!

After you define a field as a primary key, Access prevents you from entering a new record with the same primary key value. When in doubt, an AutoNumber field is a good bet for a primary key, but the AutoNumber field doesn't allow Access to help you avoid repeating data as another field does.

Follow these steps to create a primary key:

1. **Display the table in Design view.**

2. **Click in the row containing the primary key field, or select the row by clicking the record selector.**

To select multiple rows to create a multiple field primary key, click the first record selector, and then Ctrl+click the record selectors you want for any additional fields.

 3. **Click the Primary Key button on the toolbar.**

Access displays the key symbol in the record selector for the field.

If you already have data in the field and two records have the same value, you cannot make the field the primary key for the table. ***Remember:*** The primary key field has to uniquely identify each record.

Indexing Fields

When you index a field, Access sorts and finds records faster using the Index field. An index can be based on a single field, or on multiple fields. The primary key field in a table automatically gets indexed, and you can choose other fields to index also.

Although indexing speeds up many operations, it slows down some action queries because Access may need to update the indexes as the action is performed.

To index a field, choose one of the Yes values for the field's `Indexed` property. Three values for the `Indexed` property are available:

✦ **No:** Doesn't index the field.

✦ **Yes (Duplicates OK):** Indexes the field, and allows you to input the same value for multiple records.

✦ **Yes (No Duplicates):** Indexes the field and doesn't allow you to input the same value for more than one record. The primary key automatically gets this value.

You can see details on the indexed fields by clicking the Indexes button to see the Indexes window, shown in Figure 1-7.

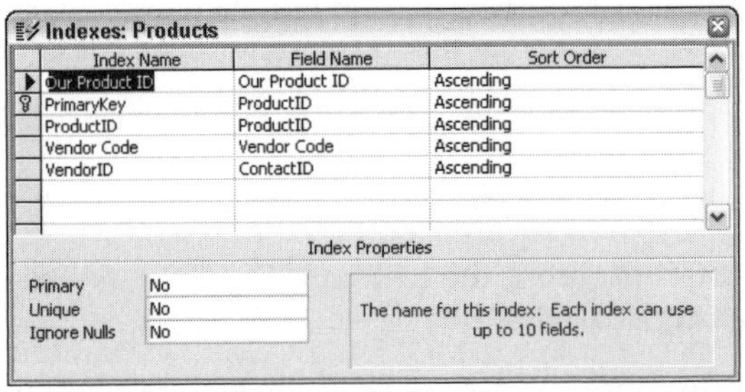

Index Name	Field Name	Sort Order
Our Product ID	Our Product ID	Ascending
PrimaryKey	ProductID	Ascending
ProductID	ProductID	Ascending
Vendor Code	Vendor Code	Ascending
VendorID	ContactID	Ascending

Index Properties

Primary	No
Unique	No
Ignore Nulls	No

The name for this index. Each index can use up to 10 fields.

Figure 1-7:
The Indexes window.

The Indexes window displays all the fields in the table that are indexes, their default sort order (which you can change), and their index properties. The index properties are as follows:

✦ **Primary:** Yes when the field is the primary key for the table, No otherwise.

✦ **Unique:** Yes when the value of the field for each needs to be unique, No otherwise.

✦ **Ignore Nulls:** Yes when nulls (blanks) is excluded from the index, No when nulls is included in the index.

Printing Table Designs

Printing the Design view of your table is not as easy as clicking the Print button — you may have noticed that the Print button is not available when Design view is displayed. Luckily, Access includes a cool feature called the *Documenter dialog box* to help you document your database. To print your field definitions with field properties, follow these steps:

1. Choose Tools⇨Analyze⇨Documenter from the menu.

Access displays the Documenter dialog box, as shown in Figure 1-8. Of course, your Documenter dialog box has different objects in it.

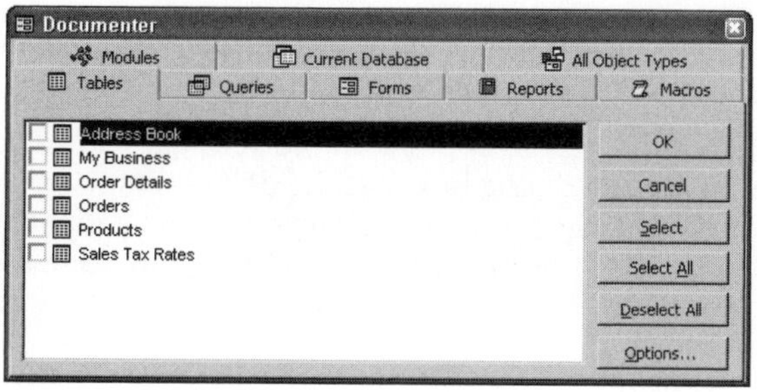

Figure 1-8:
The
Documenter
dialog box
displays a
tab for each
type of
object in the
database.

2. Click the Tables tab to display a list of tables in your database.

3. Select the table(s) you want to print by clicking the check box in front of the table name.

Or use the Select button to select the highlighted table(s) or just click the Select All button to get the whole enchilada — all the tables.

4. Click the Options button to display the Print Table Definition dialog box, as shown in Figure 1-9.

Use the Print Table Definition dialog box to choose those aspects of the table definition you want to print.

5. When done, click OK to close the Print Table Definition dialog box.

The Documenter dialog box makes its return.

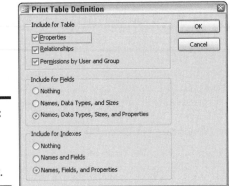

Figure 1-9:
The Print
Table
Definition
dialog box.

6. **Click OK in the Documenter dialog box to display the object definition report in a form that can be printed.**

The contents of the report depend on the settings you selected in the
Print Table Definition dialog box, but the default displays properties for
the table at the top, the name of each field with its properties, how the
table is related to other tables in the database, and table index fields
and the primary key. A portion of a report is shown in Figure 1-10.

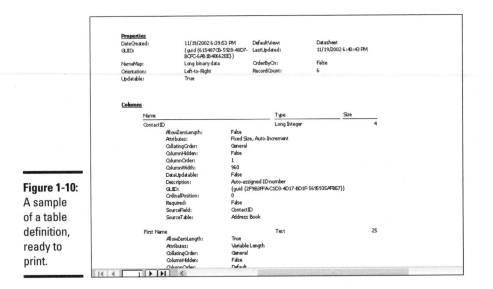

Figure 1-10:
A sample
of a table
definition,
ready to
print.

7. **Click the Print button on the toolbar to print the report.**

Chapter 2: Entering and Editing Data in Datasheets

In This Chapter

✔ Using datasheets to enter and view data

✔ Navigating a datasheet

✔ Checking spelling in your datasheet

✔ Viewing and using related data

*A*ll the data in your database is stored in tables, probably in more than one of them. Tables have two views: Design view, which is covered in Chapter 1 of this book, and Datasheet view, where you see the data in the table. Although you can work in Access without ever looking at a boring datasheet, you should know your way around one, just in case you need to look at one.

Not only do datasheets provide an unadorned view of the data in your table, you can do quite a lot of work in a datasheet. If you enter a lot of data, you may find that you like entering it into a datasheet (although you may prefer a form). You can also modify and delete data using a datasheet. You can change the look of a datasheet by moving columns around, changing column width and row height, and freezing rows. This chapter covers the basics of working with data in a datasheet. Later chapters in this book cover even more analysis that you can do just by using the datasheet.

Datasheets are one way to view tables. You can also view queries with datasheets — you see the result of a query in a datasheet. Everything you can do with a table you can also do with a query in Datasheet view.

You can easily view the contents of a table, add new records to the table, and make changes to the data using Datasheet view. *Datasheet view* shows data exactly as it is stored — in rows (records) and columns (fields). Opening a table in Datasheet view is easy. Just double-click the table's name in the Database window. Or click the View button on the toolbar of a table that's in Design view.

Looking at a Datasheet

A datasheet displays data in a table — it has rows (records), columns (fields), and cells that hold individual pieces of data. Figure 2-1 shows an example of an Access datasheet.

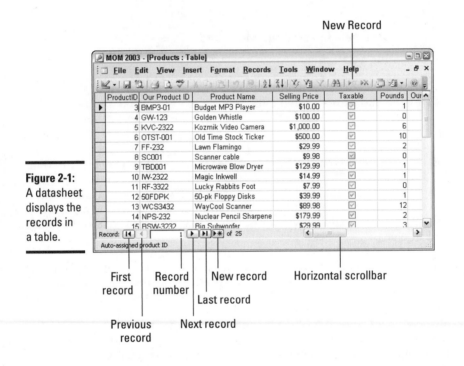

New Record

First record

Record number

New record

Last record

Horizontal scrollbar

Previous record

Next record

Figure 2-1:
A datasheet displays the records in a table.

Table 2-1 lists the important buttons on the toolbar in Datasheet view.

Table 2-1	Standard Toolbar Buttons in Datasheet View	
Button	*Name*	*What It Does*
	View	Displays the views for a table
	Save	Saves the table configuration
	Print	Prints the datasheet (doesn't display the Print dialog box)

Button	Name	What It Does
	Print Preview	Displays a print preview of the datasheet
	Spelling	Begins spell check of data in the datasheet
	Cut	Cuts selected data to the clipboard
	Copy	Copies selected data to the clipboard
	Paste	Pastes data from the clipboard
	Undo	Undoes the last action
	Insert Hyperlink	Displays the Insert Hyperlink dialog box to allow you to browse to a hyperlink (for Hyperlink data type fields only)
	Sort Ascending	Sorts records from A to Z and small values to large values using the selected field
	Sort Descending	Sorts records from Z to A and large values to small values using the selected field
	Filter by Selection	Filters the table by selection (see Chapter 3 of this book for more information on filtering by selection)
	Filter by Form	Filters the table by form (see Chapter 3 of this book for more information on filtering by form)
	Apply Filter	Filters the table (see Chapter 3 of this book for more information on applying filters)
	Find	Displays the Find and Replace dialog box so that you can search for data
	New Record	Moves to the end of the datasheet to enter new data

**Book II
Chapter 2**

**Entering and Editing
Data in Datasheets**

(continued)

Table 2-1 *(continued)*

Button	Name	What It Does
	Delete Record	Deletes the current record, or the selected records, after checking that you actually want to delete the data
	Database Window	Displays the Database window
	New Object: Autoform	Creates a new object — use the drop-down list to choose the object you want to create based on the displayed table. Some of the choices allow you to easily create a new object based on the current datasheet
	Help	Opens the Help pane

To see a table in Datasheet view, double-click a table name in the Database window. If you look at a table in Design view, click the View button, the first button on the toolbar, to see it in Datasheet view. The View button allows you to switch between Design and Datasheet views.

Navigating the Data

Moving around in a datasheet is pretty straightforward. Use the vertical scrollbar (refer to Figure 2-1) or the Page Up and Page Down keys to move quickly up and down the datasheet (from record to record). Use the horizontal scrollbar to move from left to right, and press Enter or Tab to move the cursor from field to field.

If you know the number of the record you want (for example, the fourth record in the table), type the record number into the Record Number box at the bottom-left of the datasheet (refer to Figure 2-1) to jump straight to the fourth record. Record numbers are relative — records are not assigned a permanent record number. But when you want to go to the fourth record listed on the page, type **4** in the Record Number box and then press Enter. Sorting the datasheet so that records appear in a different order means that the record that is fourth changes.

You can move around in a datasheet three different ways:

✦ **Mouse:** Click a cell or use the scrollbars.

✦ **Keys:** Use Page Up and Page Down and the other keys in Table 2-2.

✦ **Buttons:** Click the VCR-like record navigation buttons at the bottom-left of the datasheet (refer to Figure 2-1), or you can click the New Record button in the toolbar to jump to the end of your listings.

Table 2-2	Datasheet Navigation Keystrokes
Key	*Where It Takes You*
Page Down	Down a page
Page Up	Up a page
Tab	The next cell
Shift+Tab	The previous cell
Home	The first field of the current record
End	The last field of the current record
Ctrl+↑	First record of the current field
Ctrl+↓	Last record of the current field
Ctrl+Home	First record of the first field (top-left corner of the datasheet)
F5	Puts the cursor in the Record Number box — type a record number and press enter to go to that record

Adding and Editing Records

To create a new record, start typing in a blank row. To move to a blank row, click one of the two New Record buttons — you find one nestled with the record navigation buttons at the bottom-left of the datasheet and one on the toolbar. Type your data and press Enter or Tab to move to the next field. When you get to the last field of a record and press Tab or Enter, Access automatically moves you to the first field of a new record.

As you enter data, you may come across fields that are check boxes or drop-down lists. You can easily use the mouse to change a check box setting or select from a list, but you can also use the keyboard. Press the Space bar to change a check box setting from checked to unchecked, for example. Or press F4 to see a drop-down list, press the ↓ key to select your choice, and then press Enter.

If you change your mind about your entry, press the Escape key to cancel it. If you already pressed Enter, you can undo the last entry by clicking the Undo button or by pressing Ctrl+Z. Another useful keystroke to know is Ctrl+' — it repeats the value in the record immediately above the cursor.

Table 2-3 lists all the keystrokes you ever want to use as you enter and edit data.

Table 2-3	Keystrokes in Datasheet View
Keystroke	*What It Does*
Ctrl++	Moves the cursor to a new record
Enter or Tab	Enters the data and moves to the next cell (to the right, or to the first field of the next record)
Escape	Cancels the current entry
Undo or Ctrl+Z	Undoes the last entry
F4	Displays a drop-down list (if present) in the current cell
Ctrl+C	Copies the selected data
Ctrl+X	Cuts the selected data
Ctrl+V	Pastes data from the Clipboard
Delete	Deletes the selected data
Ctrl+Enter	Enters a line break within an entry
Ctrl+(+)	Moves to a new record
Ctrl+(-)	Deletes the current record
Space	Switches between the values in a check box or option button

Keystrokes that enter data

Access has a few extremely convenient keystrokes that enter data for you, which are listed in Table 2-4. You can also use the Windows cut-and-paste shortcut keys. (Ctrl+C to copy the selected information to the Clipboard, Ctrl+X to cut the selected information and move it to the Clipboard, and Ctrl+V to paste the information from the Clipboard at the current cursor location.)

Table 2-4	Entering Data with Keys
Keystroke	*Data It Enters*
Ctrl+'	Repeats the entry for the field from the previous record
Ctrl+;	Inserts the current date
Ctrl+Shift+ :	Inserts the current time
Ctrl+Alt+Space	Inserts the default value for a field

Editing the data you have

Editing is pretty straightforward. To edit data, simply place your cursor in the cell containing the data you want to change, use the Backspace or Delete keys to get rid of unwanted stuff and then type in your replacement stuff. Or, if you already selected (highlighted) the text or a value, whatever you type replaces the selection. If you don't want to replace a selection, press → or F2 or click in the cell to deselect and display the cursor.

Use these tricks when selecting text:

✦ To replace the entire value, move the pointer to the left of the field until it changes into a big plus sign, and then click to select the whole cell.

✦ Double-click to select a word or value.

✦ Click at the beginning of what you want to select, press the Shift key, and then click at the end of what you want to select.

If you have lots of text in a cell and want to see it all at once, select the cell and press Shift+F2 to see the cell in a Zoom box (shown in Figure 2-2). You can make any changes, and then press Enter or click OK to return to the datasheet. Use the Font button in the Zoom box to change the font, and perhaps more importantly, the font size. Any changes you make are retained — the next time you display the Zoom box, you see the data with the new font settings.

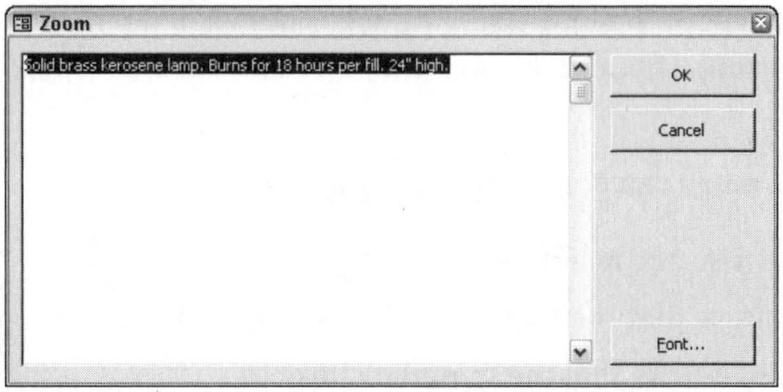

Figure 2-2:
Press Shift+F2 to see the Zoom dialog box.

Table 2-5 lists keystrokes that you can use while in editing mode.

Table 2-5	Keystrokes to Use While Editing
Keystroke	*What It Does*
Home	Moves to the beginning of the entry
End	Moves to the end of the entry

(continued)

Table 2-5 *(continued)*

Keystroke	What It Does
← or →	Moves one character to the left or right
Ctrl+← or Ctrl+→	Moves one word to the left or right
Shift+Home	Selects from the insertion point to the beginning of the entry
Shift+End	Selects from the insertion point to the end of the entry
Shift+←	Selects one character to the left
Shift+→	Selects one character to the right
Ctrl+Shift+←	Selects one word to the left
Ctrl+Shift+→	Selects one word to the right

Entering and editing hyperlinks

Working with fields with the Hyperlink data type can be a little tricky (but doesn't have to be). Fields are defined as hyperlink fields in one of two ways: If you create a table in Datasheet view, and type in hyperlink data, Access may define the field as a hyperlink field (start Web links with http:// to have Access recognize them as hyperlinks); alternatively, if you define the field in Design view with the Hyperlink data type, then the field is a hyperlink field.

When you type something into a hyperlink field in a datasheet, the text you type instantly turns to a hyperlink — blue, underlined text that you click to go to whatever site the link refers to. You can't click the hyperlinks to edit them — clicking a hyperlink takes you to the linked file, which can prove tricky.

A hyperlink entry can consist of four different parts:

+ The text you see in a datasheet or form

+ The address that the hyperlink links to (the only required part)

+ The sub-address that the hyperlink links to

+ A screen tip — text that you see when the cursor hovers above the hyperlink

Because the full hyperlink entry consists of four parts, you may find the Edit Hyperlink dialog box easier to enter and edit hyperlinks.

Entering hyperlinks

The most common types of hyperlinks are links to Web pages or to files on your PC or LAN. You can enter those kinds of addresses by simply typing the address or path of the page or file you want to link to (or paste it from your Web browser or Windows Explorer for an even easier method).

However, you may choose to enter a hyperlink using the Edit Hyperlink dialog box (shown in Figure 2-3) in order to take advantage of the extra features found in this dialog box. To display the Edit Hyperlink dialog box, do one of the following:

✦ Right-click the hyperlink field and choose Hyperlink⇨Edit Hyperlink from the shortcut menu.

✦ Click in the field (if empty) and press Ctrl+K.

If a hyperlink is in the field, you can't click it without opening the hyperlink — instead, use the Tab key to move the cursor to that cell or right-click to see the shortcut menu.

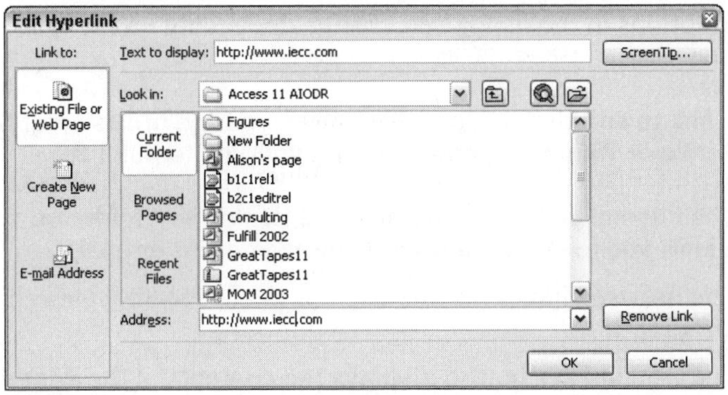

Book II
Chapter 2

Entering and Editing Data in Datasheets

Figure 2-3:
Press Ctrl+K
to enter or
edit a
hyperlink in
the Edit
Hyperlink
dialog box.

Edit Hyperlink	✕
Link to:	Text to display: http://www.iecc.com ScreenTip...
	Look in: 📁 Access 11 AIODR
Existing File or Web Page	Current Folder: 📁 Figures, 📁 New Folder, Alison's page, b1c1rel1
Create New Page	Browsed Pages: b2c1editrel, Consulting, Fulfill 2002, GreatTapes11
E-mail Address	Recent Files: GreatTapes11, MOM 2003
	Address: http://www.iecc.com Remove Link
	OK Cancel

If you enter an e-mail address in a hyperlink field, use the Edit Hyperlink dialog box — otherwise Access puts http:// in front of the text that you type as the hyperlink text. And that, as you may guess, does not open a new e-mail message window; e-mail addresses need to be prefixed with mailto:.

The Edit Hyperlink dialog box provides different options depending on the type of link you are creating. You can create a link to open any of the following:

✦ An existing file or Web page.

✦ An object in the current database.

✦ A data access page — a Web page made by Access to display database data without using Access — that you haven't yet created. (For more on data access pages, see Book IX, Chapter 1.)

✦ An e-mail address.

Use the buttons on the left side of the dialog box — the ones under the Link To heading — to select the type of link before you enter any additional information about the hyperlink.

The following options always appear in the Edit Hyperlink dialog box, no matter what you end up linking to:

✦ **Text to Display:** The text that displays as a hyperlink.

✦ **Some way to define the object that you're linking to:** The address or name of the object.

✦ **Screen Tip:** Click this button to enter text that appears when the cursor hovers over the hyperlink text.

✦ **Remove Link:** Deletes the hyperlink.

Other options in the dialog box change depending on the type of link you're creating.

If you link to an existing file or Web page, you see browsing options for finding the file or Web page you want the hyperlink to point to:

✦ The Current Folder button displays the current folder on your PC and allows you to enter a path or browse your PC or LAN.

✦ The Browsed Pages button displays pages recently viewed with your browser.

✦ The Recent Files button displays the contents of the Windows Recent Documents folder.

✦ The Browse the Web button opens your browser.

✦ The Browse for File button opens the Link to File dialog box, where you can browse to a file.

✦ Displays a list of bookmarks marked with the HTML code `href="#bookmark"` on the page or in the file so that you can select a sub-address.

✦ The Address option displays the URL of the file or page. Access fills this in automatically as you type, or you can type the address in manually. The drop-down list displays recently used files and URLs.

If you link to an object in the database, you see a list of types of database objects. Click the + (plus) sign next to the type of object you want to link to, and then click the name of the object.

If you create a new data access page, type the name of the new document, click the Change button to change the path, if necessary, and choose whether you want to edit the document now or later. Access creates a new data access page in the current database with the name you specified and the extension .htm.

If you link to an e-mail address, specify the e-mail address and the subject of the e-mail message that is created when the user clicks the hyperlink.

Editing hyperlinks

Editing hyperlinks can be a bit tricky. Unlike other types of fields, clicking a hyperlink doesn't put the cursor into the field so that you can make changes. Instead, clicking a hyperlink takes you to whatever the hyperlink points to. You can't move the cursor around with the mouse! You have to use one of these methods instead:

✦ Tab to the hyperlink and press Ctrl+K to display the Edit Hyperlink dialog box.

✦ Right-click the hyperlink and choose Hyperlink➪Edit Hyperlink from the shortcut menu to display the Edit Hyperlink dialog box.

Using the Edit Hperlink dialog box, you can either change the text to display or change the address that the hyperlink points to (near the bottom of the dialog box).

You can also edit a hyperlink by tabbing to it and pressing F2, but you see the multi-part hyperlink separated by # — a bit messy to deal with, to be honest — and you can't use the mouse to move the cursor. The dialog box method is a more surefire method!

You can remove a hyperlink by right-clicking and choosing Hyperlink➪ Remove Hyperlink from the shortcut menu. The hyperlink text remains, but the link is broken.

Deleting records

Warning: Deleted data cannot be recovered using the Undo button! But sometimes you want to delete data. Delete a record (remember that a record is a whole row of data) by selecting it (by clicking the record selector to the left of the record), or by putting the cursor anywhere in the record.

Then press the Delete key or click the Delete Record button. Access asks you if you are sure you want to delete the data. Click the Yes button to delete. The row you select is deleted, and the data below the deleted row moves up to fill the space.

Entering special characters

Occasionally you may need to enter characters that aren't on your keyboard. Access doesn't provide an easy way to do this, but you can do it. If you know how to find your special character in another program, you may want to create it in that program and cut and paste it into Access. Otherwise, follow these steps:

1. **Choose Start⇨All Programs⇨Accessories⇨System Tools⇨ Character Map.**

   The Character Map appears. You see a grid of characters. The drop-down list at the top of the box lists the fonts. The box at the top is where the characters you select (in Step 3) appear.

2. **Browse to find the character you need.**

   Each font has a different set of characters, so you may need to browse through the fonts to find the character you need. Use the vertical scrollbar to see all the characters within a font.

3. **Double-click the character or select it and click the Select button to display it in the Characters to Copy box.**

   Repeat Step 3 until you have all the characters you need.

4. **Click the Copy button.**

   The contents of the Characters to Copy box copy to the Windows Clipboard.

5. **Return to Access and click the Paste button or press Ctrl+V.**

   If you don't see the character you copied, you may have to format it with the font you selected in Character Map.

Checking Your Spelling

 You can check your spelling in a datasheet or form by clicking the Spelling button on the toolbar. You can easily skip some fields that may have words that Access doesn't recognize, especially if they are full of codes or abbreviations. (See Table 2-6 on exactly how to do that.) You may also find selecting a field or two to run a spell check on rather than checking the whole datasheet makes sense. (You can select a field by clicking the field name; select several consecutive fields by selecting the first field and, while holding the Shift key, clicking the last record.)

When you spell check, Access compares the words in the datasheet to the words in its own dictionary. Anything not found in the dictionary is "misspelled." Of course, plenty of words that you use may not be in the dictionary, such as technical terms or unique product names. Don't assume that the Spelling dialog box is always right — your spelling may be just fine.

A routine spell check goes like this:

1. **Click the Spelling button on the toolbar to open the Spelling dialog box (shown in Figure 2-4).**

Access finds the first word that is not in its dictionary, and displays it in the Not In Dictionary box. In the Suggestions box, Access lists possible correct spellings of the word.

2. **You decide how to deal with the word:**

- Double-click a word from the Suggestions list to replace the misspelled word, or click the correctly spelled word once and then click the Change button.

- Click the Ignore button to ignore the word and find the next misspelled word.

- Click the Cancel button to exit the spell check and correct the word in the datasheet manually.

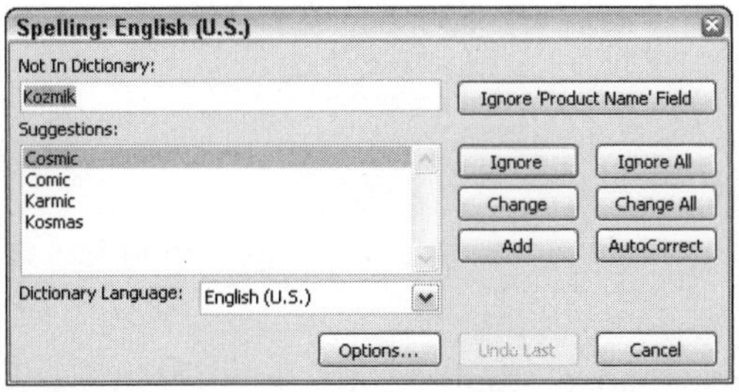

**Book II
Chapter 2**

Entering and Editing
Data in Datasheets

Figure 2-4:
The Spelling dialog box can find and correct potentially embarrassing typos.

You may want to use the options in the Spelling dialog box listed in Table 2-6 as you check spelling.

Table 2-6	Buttons in the Spelling Dialog Box
Button	*What It Does*
Ignore "Field name" field	Tells Access not to check spelling in the field where it has found the latest misspelled word.
Ignore	Skips the current word and finds the next misspelled word.
Ignore All	Skips all instances of the word when it's found.
Change	Changes the misspelled word to the word selected in the Suggestions box.
Change All	Changes all instances of the word to the word selected in the Suggestions box.
Add	Adds the word to the dictionary. Use this carefully as it's difficult to undo! Access uses main and custom dictionaries that are shared by all the Microsoft Office applications. You can use Microsoft Word to remove words from a custom dictionary — check Word's online help for details.
AutoCorrect	Adds the misspelled word and the correctly spelled word selected in the Suggestions box to the AutoCorrect list. AutoCorrect automatically replaces words when you enter them or press the Space bar.
Options	Displays the Options dialog box where you can tell Access whether to suggest words, whether to ignore certain words, and which dictionary to use (you can specify a foreign language by using the Dictionary option).
Undo Last	Undoes the last change made by the Spelling dialog box.
Cancel	Closes the Spelling dialog box and retains any changes made.

Using AutoCorrect for Faster Data Entry

AutoCorrect helps you in two distinct ways:

✦ It corrects misspelled words as you type.

✦ It replaces an abbreviation you type with more complete text, saving you time.

To turn on AutoCorrect, choose Tools➪AutoCorrect Options to display the AutoCorrect dialog box, shown in Figure 2-5. Check that the Replace Text as You Type option is selected.

To add a common abbreviation to the AutoCorrect list, display the AutoCorrect dialog box and follow these steps:

1. **Enter the abbreviation in the Replace box.**

2. **Enter the full term in the With box.**

3. **Click the Add button.**

4. **Check that the Replace Text as You Type option is checked.**

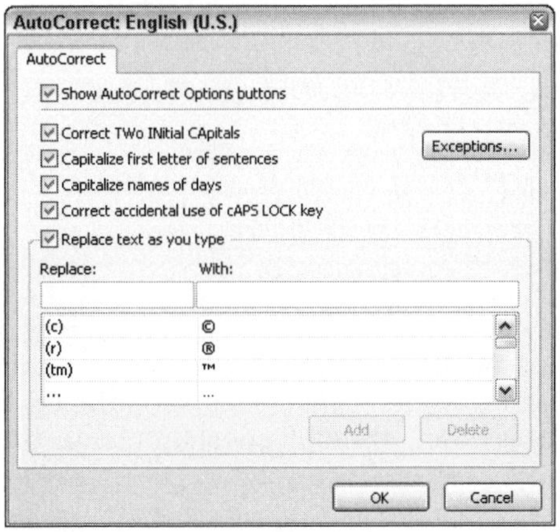

Figure 2-5:
The
AutoCorrect
dialog box
helps you
set up
abbrevia-
tions for
faster data
entry.

You can delete an AutoCorrect entry by selecting it in the list and clicking the Delete button.

By default all the options in the AutoCorrect dialog box are on (checked). You may want to turn some or all of them off (unchecked) if Access is making corrections that you don't want it to make.

The Exceptions button displays the AutoCorrect Exceptions dialog box (shown in Figure 2-6) where you can tell Access not to capitalize after a period that ends an abbreviation (on the First Letter tab), and when you want two or more initial caps to stay the way you enter them (on the INitial CAps tab).

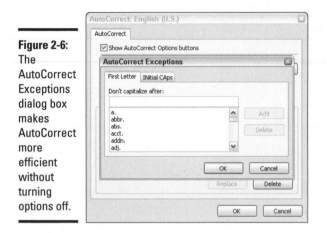

Figure 2-6:
The
AutoCorrect
Exceptions
dialog box
makes
AutoCorrect
more
efficient
without
turning
options off.

Formatting a Datasheet

Datasheets can't provide the good-looking output you get with a report or a form, but you can make some changes to make a datasheet more readable and attractive. The formatting options are available on the Format menu, although we generally access them through shortcut menus or with clicking or dragging.

Format changes usually cannot be undone using the Undo button or Ctrl+Z. You can undo changes by closing the table without saving, but of course you lose all the formatting and design changes you made since the last time you saved the table.

Changing the font

In an Access datasheet the font and font size of all the data are the same — you can't change the font for just some of the data.

Change the font by choosing Format⇨Font to display the Font dialog box (shown in Figure 2-7).

Select to change the font, font style, and font size. You can underline text by using the Underline check box in the Effects box. The Color option changes the color of the data in the datasheet.

Changing gridlines and background color

Gridlines are the gray horizontal and vertical lines that separate cells in a datasheet. You can change the color of the gridlines or choose not to display the gridlines at all. You can even choose a special gridline effect other than plain lines.

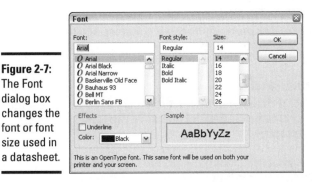

Figure 2-7:
The Font dialog box changes the font or font size used in a datasheet.

Display the Datasheet Formatting dialog box (shown in Figure 2-8) by choosing Format➪Datasheet. Make any changes (changes reflect in the Sample box), and click OK. You have the option of making the datasheet work from right to left instead of the usual left to right — not an option often used, but if you need it, you can find it here.

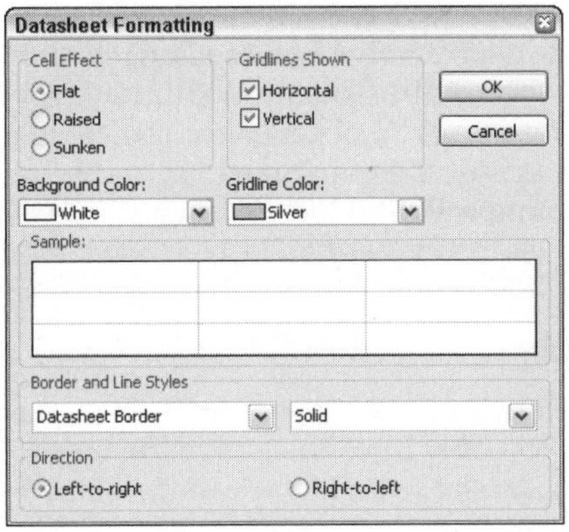

Figure 2-8:
The Datasheet Formatting dialog box changes gridlines, cell effects, or the background color of the datasheet.

Rearranging columns in a datasheet

You can rearrange the order of fields in the datasheet in either Datasheet or Design view. Follow these steps, in Datasheet view, to move columns:

1. **Select the column you want to move by clicking the field name.**

   You may want to select a block of columns by then Shift+clicking the last field name in the block.

2. **Drag the column(s) to their new position.**

   As you move the mouse, a dark vertical line shows where the columns move to when you release the mouse button.

If you can't move a column, it's probably frozen. Choose Format⇨Unfreeze All Columns to unfreeze it. For more on freezing columns, see the aptly named section "Freezing columns," later in this chapter.

Changing column width

When you initially create a datasheet, all the columns have the same width. But columns are easy to change, and when you save the table, the new column widths are saved too.

To change the width of a column, move the pointer to the bar separating the field names at the top of the column. The mouse pointer changes into a double-headed arrow (shown in the margin). Drag the bar to the appropriate width, or you can double-click to size the column for the widest data in the column.

You can change the width of several adjacent columns at the same time by selecting them (click the field name of the first column, and then Shift+click the field name of the last column), and then changing the width of one column. All the selected columns have the same (new) width.

If you prefer, use the Column Width dialog box to change column width — right-click a field name and choose the Column Width option from the short-cut menu. Enter the width in number of characters. You can use the Standard Width check box to reset the column width to the standard, or the Best Fit button to fit the column width to its contents. Click OK to close the dialog box.

Changing row height

You change the row height in one of two ways — with the mouse or with the Row Height dialog box. You only have to change the height of one row — all the rest change to match. All the rows change to the same height; you can't just change one.

Changing row height with the mouse is very similar to changing column width: Move the mouse pointer to the record selectors until the pointer turns into a double-headed arrow (shown in the margin). Then drag up (to make the row shorter) or down (to make the row taller).

Alternatively, right-click a record selector and select the Row Height option from the shortcut menu to display the Row Height dialog box (shown in Figure 2-9). Enter the row height in points (there are 72 points in an inch). The Standard Height check box formats the row height at the standard height for the font size that you have chosen (the point size of the font, plus a cushion for the top and the bottom of the row).

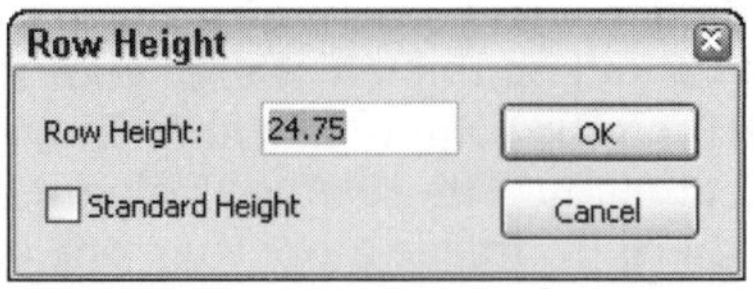

Figure 2-9:
Use the
Row Height
dialog box
when you
know how
many points
high your
row should
be, or when
you want to
reset to the
standard
height.

Row Height

Row Height: 24.75   OK

☐ Standard Height   Cancel

Inserting and deleting columns

Remember, columns are fields, so when you insert a column you are adding a new field, and when you delete a column you delete the field and all its data. You can add and remove fields in Design view — that's covered in Chapter 1 of this book.

To insert a field in Datasheet view, follow these steps:

1. **Right-click the field name of the column where you want the new, blank column.**

2. **Choose the Insert Column option from the shortcut menu.**

   A column with the name Field 1 (or some other number) is added. The selected columns and all the columns to the right move to make room.

3. **Rename the field name by right-clicking it and choosing the Rename Column option from the shortcut menu.**

4. **Type the new name and press Enter.**

   The new field also appears in Design view.

To delete a field and all its data, right-click the field name and choose the Delete Column option from the shortcut menu. Click the Yes button to permanently delete the field and its data.

Hiding columns

If you want to hide a column in a datasheet (perhaps the data is sensitive), select the column or columns and choose Format➪Hide Columns. To display hidden columns, choose Format⇨Unhide Columns. A dialog box appears, where you can choose which columns to redisplay.

Freezing columns

When you're working with a wide datasheet, you may want to freeze one or more columns so that they don't scroll off the left side of your screen. To freeze one column, first select it, and then right-click and choose the Freeze Columns option from the shortcut menu. The selected column pops to the left of the datasheet, and stays there. To freeze more than one column, select them and then choose Format⇨Freeze Columns. To unfreeze columns, right-click the field name and choose the Unfreeze All Columns option from the shortcut menu.

Changing default formatting for new tables

Access allows you to change default formatting for tables using the Datasheet tab of the Options dialog box. Any changes you make only affect new datasheets, and not tables and queries already created.

Display the Options dialog box by choosing Tools⇨Options from the menu. Click the Datasheet tab. Use the dialog box to change colors, font, gridline, and cell effect options.

Most of the options in this dialog box (default colors, default font, gridlines, and cell effects) have already been discussed in this chapter. The Show Animations feature sounds like more fun than it is — chances are you already see animation, such as the way that columns slip to the right when a new column is inserted in a datasheet (we know you have to go try it now!). Smart Tags are little tags (they appear as small triangles in a field) with actions defined for them. Using the Options dialog box, you can turn them off in datasheets so that they don't appear (they won't anyway, unless you define them).

Taking Advantage of Subdatasheets

For a couple of versions now, Access has had a nifty feature that allows you to display data from related tables in your datasheet. This feature makes viewing and entering related data without using a form easy.

Access automatically creates subdatasheets in a datasheet if you create a one-to-one relationship with another table, or if the datasheet is on the one side of a one-to-many relationship with another table. (You need to define a relationship in the Relationship window, or use the Lookup Wizard that creates a relationship as the wizard creates a drop-down list.) Queries may have subdatasheets also. (See Book I, Chapter 3 and Chapter 6 of this book for more information on relationships.)

When a subdatasheet is available, you see a + (plus) sign in the first column of the table. Click the + sign to see the subdatasheet. When the sub-datasheet displays, the + sign changes to a - (minus) sign. Click the - sign to remove the subdatasheet. By default, subdatasheets display one record at a time. To display all subdatasheets, choose Format⇨Subdatasheets⇨ Expand All. To remove all subdatasheets, choose Format⇨Subdatasheets⇨ Collapse All.

Figure 2-10 shows a datasheet with two levels of subdatasheets. The main datasheet shows names and addresses of customers. The first level datasheet lists order information, and the second level subdatasheet lists order details (items ordered).

When a subdatasheet displays, you can use it as you can use a table — to view, format, enter, edit, or delete data.

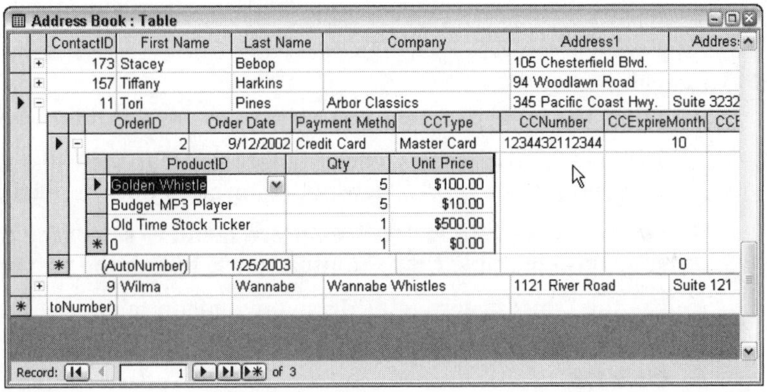

Book II
Chapter 2

Entering and Editing
Data in Datasheets

Address Book : Table

	ContactID	First Name	Last Name	Company	Address1	Addres:
+	173	Stacey	Bebop		105 Chesterfield Blvd.	
+	157	Tiffany	Harkins		94 Woodlawn Road	
-	11	Tori	Pines	Arbor Classics	345 Pacific Coast Hwy.	Suite 3232

	OrderID	Order Date	Payment Metho	CCType	CCNumber	CCExpireMonth	CCE
-	2	9/12/2002	Credit Card	Master Card	1234432112344	10	

	ProductID	Qty	Unit Price
▶	Golden Whistle	5	$100.00
	Budget MP3 Player	5	$10.00
	Old Time Stock Ticker	1	$500.00
*	0	1	$0.00

| * | (AutoNumber) | 1/25/2003 | | | | 0 | |

| + | 9 | Wilma | Wannabe | Wannabe Whistles | 1121 River Road | Suite 121 |
| * | | toNumber) | | | | |

Record: ⏮ ◀ [1] ▶ ⏭ ▶* of 3

Figure 2-10: This table displays two levels of sub-datasheets.

Access determines which table to display as a subdatasheet based on the relationships you define in the database. However, you can select a table or query to be used as a subdatasheet. Choose Insert⇨Subdatasheet for the easiest way, but you may prefer to use the Properties sheet. (Display the table in Design view and click the Properties button.)

TIP

You can use a query as a subdatasheet — doing so allows you to filter the data displayed in the subdatasheet using criteria defined in the query.

When you select a subdatasheet manually, you need to know the name of the table or query you use as the subdatasheet, as well as the names of the two related fields — one in the parent table and the other in the subdatasheet table. The two fields need to meet the requirements of related fields (see Chapter 6 of this book). Follow these steps to select a table or query to be used as a subdatasheet:

1. **Choose Insert⇨Subdatasheet to display the Insert Subdatasheet dialog box shown in Figure 2-11.**

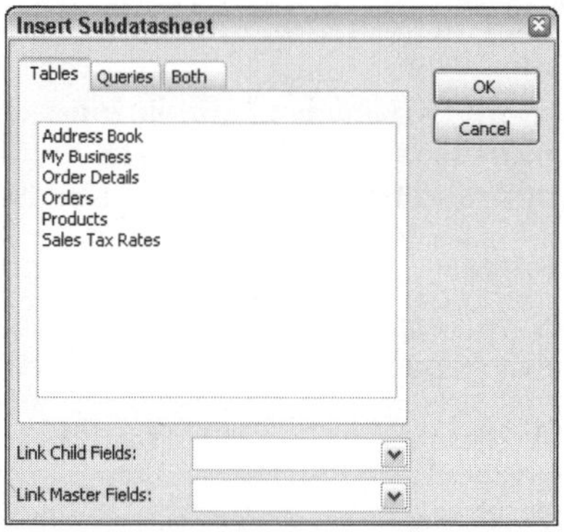

Figure 2-11:
Use the
Insert
Subdata-
sheet dialog
box when
you want to
specify the
subdata-
sheet.

Insert Subdatasheet	
Tables Queries Both	OK
	Cancel
Address Book	
My Business	
Order Details	
Orders	
Products	
Sales Tax Rates	
Link Child Fields:	
Link Master Fields:	

2. **Select the table or query you want to use as a subdatasheet.**

To view just your tables, click the Tables tab; to view just your queries, click the Queries tab; to view both tables and queries, click the Both tab.

3. **Use the Link Child Fields drop-down menu to select the field from the subdatasheet table that you want to use to link the two tables.**

4. **Use the Link Master Fields drop-down menu to choose the field from the parent table that you want to use to link the two tables.**

5. **Click OK.**

Subdatasheets aren't available in Access Projects. See Book IX for more information about Access Projects.

Chapter 3: Sorting, Finding, and Filtering Data

In This Chapter

✔ Sorting data in a datasheet

✔ Finding a specific record

✔ Using filters to find a subset of a datasheet

A datasheet is a good place to start analyzing your data, especially if you only need to look at the data in one table. Within a datasheet, you can sort (alphabetize) using any field and filter to find records that are alike or that meet a simple criteria. And if you're looking at a datasheet generated by a query, these datasheet tools may be just what you need to find the data you want without redefining the query.

Sorting the Rows of a Datasheet

You may enter data randomly, but it doesn't have to stay that way. Use the Sort buttons to sort the records (rows) into an order that makes sense.

Before you sort, decide which field you want to sort, and then place your cursor somewhere in that field. Then use one of the two Sort buttons on the toolbar to sort the datasheet.

Sort Button	Sort Order
A Z ↓	Sorts from smaller to larger and A to Z
Z A ↓	Sorts from larger to smaller and Z to A

Sort order oddities

When sorting a Number or Currency field, values sort from smallest to largest (at least, they do when you are sorting in ascending order). But when you sort a Text field, values are sorted alphabetically, starting at the left end of the field. This difference between the two fields means that in a Text field, Access sorts 55 before 6, because the 5 character comes before the 6 character. For example, Access sorts the same list of numbers in Number and Text fields like this:

Number Sort	Text Sort
1	1
2	11
5	2
11	21
21	44
44	5

Sometimes you need to know exactly how Access sorts blanks and special characters. The sort order, in ascending order, is the following:

- blanks (null)
- space
- special characters like !, ", #, %, &, (, comma, period, [, ^, `, ~ (in that order, incidentally)
- letters (Access does not distinguish between uppercase and lowercase letters when sorting)
- numbers

If you need to know how Access sorts some characters that aren't listed here, make a test table with the characters you need to sort, and sort them!

When you sort a Number field in ascending order, Access lists records from the smallest number to the largest. When you sort a Text field in ascending order, records are alphabetized, from A to Z. When you sort a date field into ascending order, records are listed from oldest date to most recent date. Descending order is the opposite in all three cases; largest-to-smallest number, Z to A, or most recent to oldest date.

Finding (And Replacing) Data

If you're looking for a specific piece of data in a datasheet, use the Find button to display the Find and Replace dialog box. For example, you're sure that someone from your hometown ordered something recently — where's that order?

If you want to look within a single field, put the cursor anywhere in that field's column before you begin the search.

Display the Find and Replace dialog box (shown in Figure 3-1) by pressing Ctrl+F or by clicking the Find button on the toolbar.

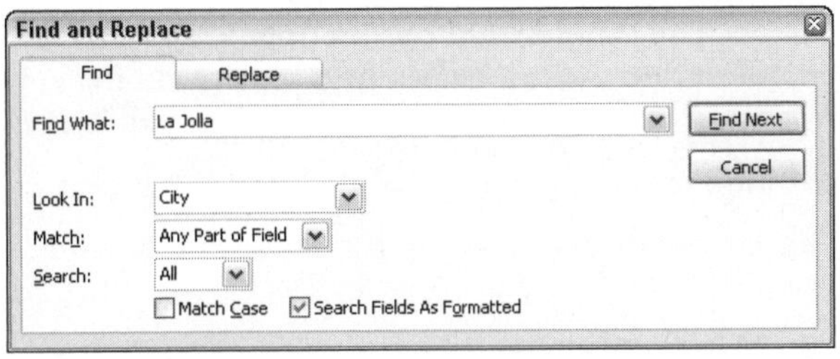

Figure 3-1:
Press Ctrl+F
to see the
Find and
Replace
dialog box.

Find and Replace

Find | Replace

Fi_n_d What: | La Jolla | ▾ | Find Next

Cancel

_L_ook In: | City | ▾

Mat_c_h: | Any Part of Field | ▾

_S_earch: | All | ▾

☐ Match _C_ase   ☑ Search Fields As F_o_rmatted

Using the Find and Replace dialog box for quick and dirty searches is as easy as 1-2-3:

1. **Press Ctrl+F to display the Find and Replace dialog box.**

2. **Type what you're looking for in the Find What box.**

3. **Press Enter or click the Find Next button.**

Access highlights the first instance of the Find What text.

Quick and dirty may work just fine for you, but you need to know about a few Find and Replace dialog box refinements — such as telling Access to limit its search to particular places. The default settings on the Find and Replace dialog box tell Access to search the field the cursor is in and to match your search term word for word. You may find, however, that other options in the dialog box make finding exactly what you're looking for easier. Keep reading to find out more!

The Find and Replace dialog box options

If you don't know how to use the options in the Find and Replace dialog box, you may not find what you're looking for.

The Find and Replace dialog box has the following options:

✦ **Find What:** Type the text of the value that you are looking for.

✦ **Look In:** Tell Access where to look — the field the cursor is in, a series of fields, or the whole table. If you select a bunch of fields or records before displaying the Find and Replace dialog box, Access searches the selected cells and you can't change the Look In option. (Select contiguous fields by clicking the first field name and then Shift+clicking the last field name.)

✦ **Match:** Choose how the search results match the Find What text. You can choose from the following options: Any Part of Field, Whole Field, or Start of Field. The Any Part of Field option finds the most instances. If you search for *Flamingo* using the Any Part of Field option, Access finds *Lawn Flamingo*. The Whole Field option only finds cells that matches the whole word, *Flamingo* — it does not find Lawn Flamingo. The Start of Field option finds cells that begin with Flamingo, such as *Flamingos*.

✦ **Find Next:** Finds the next instance of the Find What text.

✦ **Search:** Choose the direction (from the cursor) to search: Up, Down, or All.

✦ **Match Case:** Match the case of the text — if you want to find THIS but not This, use the Match Case option.

✦ **Search Fields as Formatted:** Finds data according to how it looks, rather than how it was entered. If you use an input mask on a telephone number field, you may input ten digits but they appear with parentheses around the area code and a hyphen after the exchange. If you use the Search Fields as Formatted option, you can search for (508) to find phone numbers in the 508 area code.

The broadest search uses the following options: Look In *Tablename* : Table (the whole table), Match Any Part of Field, Search All, and deselect Match Case. Other choices in the Look In, Match, and Search options narrow the search and may miss particular instances of the Find What text — not necessarily a bad thing, by the way, especially if you have a very clear idea of where you want to find what you're looking for.

Replacing the data you find

To replace data with new data, first define what you're looking for using the Find tab, as described in the previous section, and then use the Replace With option on the Replace tab to define how you want to replace it.

You can replace instances one at a time by using the Replace (to replace) and Find Next (to skip that instance) buttons. Or you can replace all instances using the Replace All button.

The Undo button can only undo the last replacement made — it won't undo a whole slew of them, so use the Replace All button carefully.

If the Find and Replace dialog box isn't quite what you need, you may want to filter your datasheet and then make replacements, or you may want to try out some action queries. For more on filters, see the next section; for more on action queries, check out Book III.

Filtering a Datasheet

Filtering a datasheet is a way to focus on specific records, rather than all the records in a table. You can filter out records that aren't relevant to what you're trying to do at the moment.

When you filter data, you use criteria to tell Access what you want to see. A *criterion* is a test that the data passes in order to display after the filter applies. For example, you may ask Access to show you the records with an order date of 5/1/03. A more advanced criterion is orders with a date on or after 5/1/03.

You can use five types of filters in a table. Table 3-1 tells you how to use each filter.

Table 3-1	Types of Datasheet Filters
Type of Filter	*When You Should Use It*
Filter by Selection	You have a record with a certain value in a field, and you want to find all the other records that have the same value in that field.
Filter by Form	You have more than one criterion; for instance, you want to find orders placed before 6/1/03 paid for by credit card.
Filter for Input	You want to type the value or values that you're looking for in a particular field, or you want to use an expression as your criterion.
Filter Excluding Selection	You can find a record with a certain value in a field, and you want to exclude all the records that have the same value in that field.
Advanced Filter/Sort	You want to do more than the other filters allow, such as sorting and applying criteria to multiple fields. Advanced Filter/Sort creates a query using only one table.

Filtering basics

If you want to get a handle on the whole filtering concept, start out by taking a look at the parts of a datasheet that relate to filters. Figure 3-2 shows a datasheet with the filter buttons and indicators marked. This datasheet has a filter applied — you can tell because of the Filtered datasheet indicators at the bottom of the datasheet. Also, the Apply/Remove Filter button is highlighted — if it's clicked again, the filter is removed and all the records in the datasheet display.

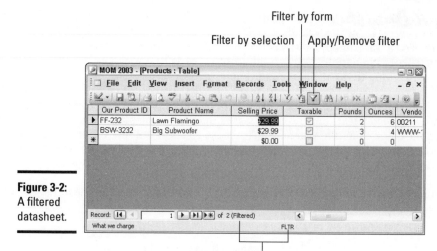

Figure 3-2:
A filtered
datasheet.

Filtered datasheet indicators

You can apply a filter to any datasheet — that includes a table, of course, but also subdatasheets and datasheets generated by queries. You can enter and edit data in a filtered datasheet. Just be aware that the filter is not applied to any new records until you re-apply the filter (by choosing Records➪Apply Filter/Sort).

You may filter using the Filter by Selection or Filter by Form buttons, or you can use the menu. Display the Records menu to see the filtering options, including those that don't have buttons (some are on the Records menu, and some in the Filter sub-menu).

To re-apply the last filter you applied, choose Records➪Apply Filter/Sort.

To remove a filter, click the Apply Filter button or choose Records➪Remove Filter/Sort.

A filter runs a simple query on one table — a good way to start analyzing your data. Filtering can help you warm up to creating more complex queries. If you're confused about queries, creating a filter can help you figure out how to write criteria for a query (and so can Book III!). When you create the filter, choose Records➪Filter➪Advanced Filter/Sort to see it in the design grid. Look at the Criteria row to see what the criteria look like. To close the design grid, click the Close button on the toolbar.

Filters appear in the `Filter` property of the Properties sheet. You can filter a table by entering an expression there, but almost no one does that because the filter stays applied, and some records may be filtered out the moment you open the table.

The next sections detail how to use each type of filter.

Filtering by selection

Filtering by selection is the simplest kind of filter — it finds records with matching values in one field. To filter by selection, follow these steps:

Book II
Chapter 3

Sorting, Finding,
and Filtering Data

1. **Find a record with the value or text you want to match and then place your cursor in that cell to match the whole value.**

   - To find all products with the price of 29.99, place the cursor in a Price cell with the value 29.99.

   - To match the beginning of the value, select the first character and as many thereafter as you want to match. To find all entries in the field that start with La, highlight the La in Lawn Flamingo before filtering.

   - To match part of the value, select the characters in the middle of a value that you want to match. Select 99 to find all values that contain 99, such as 499.

2. **Click the Filter by Selection button on the toolbar.**

   Access filters the datasheet to display only records that have the same value in that field.

To see the entire table, click the Remove Filter button (which is the flip side of the Apply Filter button; the same button on the toolbar toggles between the Apply Filter button and the Remove Filter button).

Filtering by exclusion

Filtering by exclusion is very similar to filtering by selection, except that rather than seeing only records that match your criteria, all the records that match are excluded from the datasheet.

To filter by exclusion, select a value to exclude in the same way that you select a value to match when filtering by selection:

✦ Place the cursor anywhere in the cell to exclude values that match the whole value. For instance, place the cursor in a cell with the value ME to exclude all addresses in the state of Maine.

✦ Select the beginning of the value and as many characters thereafter as you want to match to exclude all records with matching beginning values.

✦ Select the characters in the middle of a value to exclude all records containing the selection anywhere in the field.

To filter by exclusion after you select the values you want to exclude, choose Records➪Filter➪Filter Excluding Selection. (This type of filter isn't on the toolbar.)

Filtering by form

When you have multiple criteria, you can use the Filter by Form feature to find the records you need. Clicking the Filter by Form button displays a form that looks like a single row of the table you're filtering. Use the form, shown in Figure 3-3, to specify the criteria you want to use to filter your data.

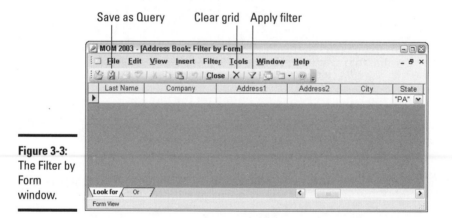

Figure 3-3:
The Filter by Form window.

When you filter by form, you not only get to use multiple criteria, you also get to choose how the data filters through whatever multiple criteria you set up. Do you want a record to meet all the criteria in order to display? Or is just meeting one criterion enough to display on the filtered datasheet? The following two operators are what you use to tell your critera how they should act together:

✦ **And:** The criteria act together hand in glove — a record has to pass all criteria in order to display on the filtered datasheet.

✦ **Or:** A record has to pass only one criterion in order for it to display on the filtered datasheet.

You may use more than two criteria using both the Or and And operators. The way you put criteria in the form defines how multiple criteria act together. Criteria on a single tab act as if they are joined by the And operator. Criteria on separate tabs act as if they are joined by the Or operator.

Follow these steps to filter a datasheet by form:

1. Click the Filter by Form button or choose Records⇨Filter⇨Filter by Form.

Access displays the Filter by Form window, which looks like an empty datasheet with different buttons on the toolbar. Some menu choices are also different than those you see when you look at a datasheet.

2. Move the cursor to a field you have a criterion for.

For instance, if you only want to see addresses from Pennsylvania, move the cursor to the State field. A drop-down list arrow appears in the field.

3. Click the arrow to see the list of entries in the field.

You may want to type the first letter or digit of your criteria to move to that point in the drop-down list.

4. Select the value in the drop-down list that you want the filtered records to match.

Access displays text that the filter is looking for inside quotation marks.

If you aren't looking to match the entire field but are looking for a match in part of the field, type **LIKE** *"value that you're looking for"*. For example, type **LIKE "new"** in the City field to find all records with *new* in the city name. You can use more complex criteria too — for more information, see Book III, Chapter 3.

5. If you have criteria for another field that needs to be applied at the same time as the criterion you set in Step 4, repeat Steps 2 through 4 for the additional field.

Setting up criteria to work together illustrates the usefulness of the And operator. If you want to find addresses in San Francisco, CA, set the State field to CA *and* the City field to San Francisco.

6. If you have a completely different set of rules to filter records by, click the Or tab at the bottom-left of the Filter by Form window.

Access displays a blank Filter by Form tab. When you set criteria on more than one tab, a record only has to meet all the criteria on any one tab to display on the filtered datasheet.

7. Choose the criteria on the second tab in the same way that you chose those on the first — click the field and choose the value that you want to match.

If, in addition to all the addresses in San Francisco, you want to see all the addresses from Boston, MA, set the State field on the Or tab to MA and the City field to Boston.

When you use an Or tab, another Or tab appears, allowing you to continue adding as many sets of Or criteria as you need.

8. Click the Apply Filter button on the toolbar to see the filtered table.

Table 3-2 lists some other options you have in the Filter by Form window.

Table 3-2	Using the Filter by Form Window	
Button (If Applicable)	*If You Want To . . .*	*Here's How To do It*
	Delete a tab's worth of criteria	Click the tab and choose Edit⇨Delete Tab.
⊠	Delete all criteria	Click the Clear Grid button on the toolbar.
💾	Save the filter as a query, so that you can use it later	Click the Save As Query button, give the new query a name, and click the OK button. To see the query, click the Queries button in the Database window.
▽	See the original (unfiltered) table	Re-click the (depressed) Apply Filter button to return to the original table.
▽	Re-filter the same table	Click the (undepressed) Apply Filter button to use the last filter defined.
	Use an expression as a criterion	Type the expression in the field to which it applies. See more about expressions as criteria in Book III, Chapter 3.

Filtering Using Advanced Filter/Sort

The Advanced Filter/Sort feature in Access is really a query — the simplest kind of query. It allows you to find and sort information from one table in the database. This option is available from a datasheet by choosing Records⇨Filter⇨Advanced Filter/Sort.

Use Advanced Filter/Sort when you want to use the more familiar Query by Example (QBE) grid to sort and filter a table.

Figure 3-4 shows the Advanced Filter Sort window.

Field names   Table name

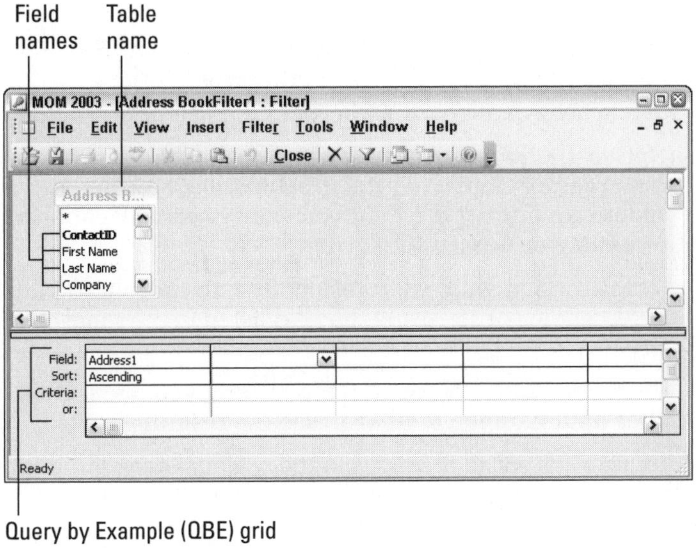

Figure 3-4:
The
Advanced
Filter Sort
window.

Query by Example (QBE) grid

This section gives you the basics of performing an advanced filter and sort, but because the features of the Advanced Filter/Sort window are nearly identical to the features of queries, you may want to read Book III, Chapter 1 for more details.

Follow these steps to sort and filter a table using the Advanced Filter/Sort feature:

1. **Open the table you want to filter in Datasheet view.**

2. **Choose Records➪Filter➪Advanced Filter/Sort.**

Access displays the Filter window, which has two parts, just like Design view for queries.

3. **In the top half of the window you see a box with the table name and all the fields in the table listed. Double-click the first field you want to use to filter the table.**

The field displays in the Field row of the first column of the QBE grid in the bottom half of the window.

Instead of double-clicking a field, you can choose a field from the Field drop-down list in the QBE grid. Click in the Field row of the grid to see the arrow for the drop-down list.

4. **Click the Criteria row in the first column and type the criteria to limit the records you see.**

   If you want to see only items that cost more than $10, select the Selling Price field as the field you want to use as your filter and then type **>10** in the Criteria row of the same column of the QBE grid.

5. **Repeat Steps 3 and 4 to add other fields and criteria to the grid.**

6. **(Optional) Choose a field by which to sort the resulting table. Set a sort order by displaying the drop-down list for the Sort row in the column containing the field you want to sort by choosing the Ascending or Descending order.**

   Access sorts the table that results from the advanced filter in ascending or descending order, using the field listed in the same column as the sort key.

7. **When you finish creating all the criteria you need, click the Apply Filter button on the toolbar to see the resulting table.**

   Access displays all the fields in the original table, but it filters the records and displays only those that meet the criteria.

You can do several things with the resulting filtered table:

✦ **Filter it again:** Use the filter buttons and Records➪Filter to filter the table even more.

✦ **Print it:** Click the Print button.

✦ **Sort it:** The best way to sort is to use the Sort row in the design grid (choose Records➪Filter➪Advanced Filter/Sort to display the Filter window again). But you can use the Sort Ascending or Sort Descending buttons to sort the table by the field that the cursor is in.

✦ **Fix it:** Choose Records➪Filter➪Advanced Filter/Sort to display the Filter window again to fix the criteria or other information in the grid.

✦ **Add data to it:** Add data to the table by clicking the New Record button and typing the data.

✦ **Edit data:** Edit data the same way that you do in the datasheet and press F2. When you look at the unfiltered table, you see any changes you made in the filtered table.

✦ **Delete records:** You can delete entire records if you want — click the record you want to delete and click the Delete Record button.

✦ **Toggle between the filtered table and the full table:** Click the Apply Filter button. If you're looking at the full table, clicking the Apply Filter button displays the filtered table (according to the last filter that you applied). If you're looking at the filtered table, clicking the Apply Filter button displays the full table.

If you want to save your advanced filter, you have to save it in Design view. After you apply the filter, return to Design view by choosing Records⇨ Filter⇨Advanced Filter/Sort and click the Save as Query button to save the advanced filter. You can find the filter, after it's saved, through the Queries button in the Database window.

Creating a report or form with a filter

Now that you know how to filter a datasheet, you may realize that what you really want to do is create a form or report with the same filter that you have just applied to a datasheet. You can, and quite easily, by using the New Object button (the second to last button on the toolbar). First filter the datasheet, and then select the type of object you want to create from the New Object button drop-down list. Access prompts you to save the table, and then either display the new object (if you select AutoForm or AutoReport) or display the New Form or New Report dialog box. You can find the filter you created in the Filter property of the Properties sheet for the new object.

Chapter 4: Importing and Exporting Data

In This Chapter

✔ Importing data from other programs into Access

✔ Linking data from other programs into Access

✔ Cleaning up your imported data

✔ Exporting data from Access

*E*ven if you love Access, you may not use it for every single data-oriented task you need to do. And because of that, you may find that you need to get data from another format (such as an Excel spreadsheet) into Access. Or you may want to take data from an Access database and use it elsewhere — say a statistical, spreadsheet, or word processing package.

But never fear — you can get data from other applications into Access. Or, if you prefer, you can leave your data in other applications and have Access link to it (although you should have a good reason to do that). Access provides a number of ways to import and export data.

The rest of this chapter covers different methods of getting data into and out of Access, starting with the easiest method — cutting and pasting.

Cutting, Copying, and Pasting

The most basic way to move information is cutting and pasting (or copying and pasting) using the Windows Clipboard or the Office Clipboard. Cutting and pasting is a straightforward and relatively simple way to move or copy information into or out of Access, or from one place to another within Access.

You can use the Cut, Copy, and Paste commands in three ways: by clicking buttons in the toolbar, by choosing commands from the Edit menu, or by pressing shortcut keys. Table 4-1 lists buttons, menu options, and keystrokes for cutting, copying, and pasting.

Button	Menu Option	Keystroke	What It Does
Table 4-1	**Cutting, Pasting, and Copying Options**		
✂	Edit⇨Cut	Ctrl+X	Cuts the selection and stores it on the Clipboard
🗐	Edit⇨Copy	Ctrl+C	Copies the selection to the Clipboard
📋	Edit⇨Paste	Ctrl+V	Pastes the contents of the Clipboard

To copy or cut and paste data, follow these steps:

1. **Select the data or object that you want to cut or copy.**

2. **Choose your favorite method (menu, toolbar button, hot key) to cut or copy what you selected.**

   When you cut something, it disappears from the screen and is stored on the Windows Clipboard. When you copy something, it stays where it is, and Access also places a copy in the Windows Clipboard.

3. **Move the cursor to the place where you want the item to appear.**

4. **Choose your favorite method (menu, toolbar button, hot key) to paste the item.**

The Office Clipboard

Using the Windows Clipboard works the same as using the Office Clipboard, except that the Office Clipboard has more features — mainly, it stores up to 24 clips. The Windows Clipboard stores only one clip. You can use the Office Clipboard when cutting and pasting within Office applications. You can use the Windows clipboard for copying and pasting in any Windows application that supports its use. When you cut or copy something to the Clipboard, it is saved on both the Windows and Office Clipboards. When you paste from the Clipboard using a keystroke or a button, you get the most recent thing you put on the Clipboard, which is also the top item on the Office Clipboard.

If you always get the most recently copied item, what's the point of the Office Clipboard storing up to 24 of your recent clips? If you cut or copy more than one item without pasting, Access displays the Clipboard task pane (shown in Figure 4-1), which shows the list of items on the Office Clipboard. The Office Clipboard stores items from all Office applications — Access, Excel, Word, Outlook, and PowerPoint. If you have clips on the

Office Clipboard, but don't see the Clipboard anywhere, choose View⇨ Toolbars⇨Task Pane and choose the Clipboard option from the task pane drop-down list (at the top of the task pane).

Figure 4-1:
The Office Clipboard.

The Clipboard task pane displays the clips that you cut or copy, along with an icon to show you what type of clip it is (from Access, Excel, Word, and so on). Paste any clip — not just the most recent one — at the cursor's position by clicking the clip. Delete a clip from the Clipboard by right-clicking the icon and choosing the Delete option from the shortcut menu. The Paste All button pastes all the stored items at the cursor's position.

Close the Clipboard task pane by clicking the Close button in the pane's upper-right corner.

Cutting and pasting small to medium-ish amounts of data

Cutting and pasting is most useful for small pieces of data, but you may also use it for a number of fields and records worth of data. If you move lots and lots of data, look at the import and linking options covered later in this chapter, but if you're copying small or medium amounts of data, copying and pasting may work just fine. Access gets picky when you paste more than one piece of data into a datasheet; to help make pasting work, follow these guidelines:

✦ Fields (columns) need to be in the same order in the source document as in Access. You may need to rearrange columns in either Access or the source document.

✦ You need to select multiple cells (fields, records, or both) if you want to paste into multiple cells. You don't have to select the exact number of cells that you're copying into — if you don't know the exact number of rows or columns that you want to copy data into, select more than you think the data will fill. One easy way to select cells in a worksheet is to click the first cell (in the upper-left corner of the range), and then Shift+click the last cell (in the lower-right corner of the range).

✦ If you are adding data into a datasheet that already has data, you may want to paste data into a temporary datasheet before pasting it into the permanent datasheet.

✦ You can't copy data into an AutoNumber field. Access generates AutoNumber values for copied records.

✦ The data type needs to match the data type of the field you're pasting into. The exceptions are Text and Memo data types, which can accept any type of data.

✦ You can't paste a duplicate value into the primary key field (just like you can't type a duplicate value into a primary key field).

✦ You can't paste into a hidden field. Unhide all the fields that you are pasting data into before pasting (choose Format➪Unhide Columns).

✦ Data you paste must meet any validation rules and work with any input masks.

✦ If you want to paste data based on field names rather than order, paste into a form, not a datasheet.

✦ To append entire records (with the exception of any AutoNumber fields), choose Edit➪Paste Append.

✦ You can't copy into subdatasheets as you copy into the main datasheet. Copy into one table at a time.

Moving data from Excel to Access

Do you have a relatively small amount of data you want to copy and paste from Excel to Access? Follow these steps for a very convenient way to copy and paste:

1. **In Access, press F11 and click the Tables button in the Objects list to display the Tables list in the Database window.**

2. **In Excel, open the workbook and display the worksheet that contains your data.**

Make sure that the first row of data makes adequate field names (you can always change them later).

3. **Select the data in Excel and press Ctrl+C to copy the data to the Clipboard.**

4. **Return to the Table list in the Database window in Access and press Ctrl+V to paste the data into a new table.**

5. **When Access asks if the first row of your data contains column headings, click the Yes button.**

   Access creates a new table from the Excel data with the same name of the Excel worksheet that contained the data. You may need to rename your table, but wasn't that easy?

Alternatively, you open a new or existing table, arrange your windows so that you can see both the data in Excel and the table where you want to put the data, and drag the data from Excel to Access.

If you have large amounts of data, try the Import Spreadsheet Wizard, explained later in this chapter.

Importing or Linking to Data

If you have large quantities of data that you want to use in your Access database, or if you want to take advantage of the features offered by the Link or Import Wizards, you can import or link to the data.

What applications are compatible with Access?

Here's the scenario: You were lucky enough to find the data you need in your database, and it's even in electronic form, but it's in dBASE, Excel, Word, another Access database, or some other file format — what do you do? In most cases, Access either imports the data directly or creates a link to the data. Currently, you can import or link to files in the following formats:

✦ Microsoft Access databases (versions 2.0, 7.0/95, 8.0/97, 9.0/2000, 10.0/Access 2002, 11/Access 2003) and Projects (versions 9.0/2000, 10.0/Access 2002, 11.0/Access 2003)

✦ dBASE versions III, IV, 5, and 7 (linking requires updated ISAM drivers available from Microsoft Technical Support, www.microsoft.com)

✦ Paradox, Paradox for Microsoft Windows 3.*x*, 4.*x*, 5.0, and 8.0 (linking requires updated ISAM drivers available from Microsoft Technical Support, www.microsoft.com)

✦ Microsoft Excel spreadsheets versions 3.0, 4.0, 5.0, 7.0/95, 8.0/97, 9.0/2000, 10.0/ 2002, and 11/2003

+ Lotus 1-2-3 spreadsheets (linking is read-only) .wks, .wk1, .wk3, and .wk4 formats

+ Microsoft Exchange

+ Delimited text files

+ Fixed-width text files

+ HTML versions1.0 (if a list), 2.0, 3.*x* (if a table or list)

+ XML documents

+ SQL tables, Microsoft Visual FoxPro2.*x*, 3.0, 5.0, and 6.*x* (import only), and data from other programs and databases that support the ODBC protocol (an updated list of supported ODBC drivers is available from the Microsoft Knowledge Base, www.microsoft.com)

If you have data in a format that your version of Access can't use, you may be able to download updated drivers from the Microsoft Web site at www.microsoft.com. Or you can see if the application allows you to export the data to one of the accepted formats. Then you can import it into Access.

To link or to import, that is the question

You have a number of choices about how to make your data available in Access. You must choose whether you want to actually store the data in Access (import the data) or create a link to the data:

+ **Import:** Make a copy of the data in Access. (Copying and pasting is the simplest form of importing.)

+ **Link:** Keep the data in another file and tell Access to get the data each time it is needed.

Some factors to consider when deciding whether to import or link include the following:

+ **Storage:** When you import data, you may be doubling the storage required because you are storing the data in Access as well as its original format.

+ **Customization:** If the data is stored in a format other than Access and you want to define a primary key, enforce referential integrity, change field names, and/or customize field and table properties, you should import the data.

+ **Maintenance:** Does the data get updated, and if so, how? If a system is in place to update data in another format, leaving the data where it is and linking to it makes sense, unless you're prepared to create a system to update it in Access. However, if the data is not analyzed in its current format, moving the data to Access and creating a system makes sense for updating it there.

✦ **Accessibility:** If you're leaning towards linking to the data, will the data always be available when you need it? Is it likely to move, or will you need it when you are traveling or not on your usual LAN? If the data is not accessible, Access will not be able to use that data for queries, reports, and forms.

Getting external data

After you decide whether to import or link to your data, you're ready for the next step. If you can, look at the data you want to import. Look for the following factors:

✦ **Are fields stored in columns and records in rows?** This is relevant to text and spreadsheet files.

✦ **Does the data you need begin at the top of the file?** For text and spreadsheets, Access expects to see one row of names and then the data.

✦ **Is all data within a field of the same type?** If not, the field imports as a Text or Memo field, which can't be used in mathematical equations.

✦ **Is the number of fields in each row the same?** This is of particular concern in a text file. If necessary, add null values to make your data line up.

✦ **Are the field names in the data you are importing identical to the field names in the Access table?** When you append data, the field names you're importing must be identical to the file you're appending to.

Are you importing the data into a new table, or do you want to append the data to an existing table? Appending can be tricky — you may want to first import into a new table in Access and then use an append query. (You find more on appending in general later in this chapter; for more on the append query in particular, see Book III, Chapter 3.)

When your data source is ready, you're ready to either import or link. The following are general instructions — they are followed by some particulars for specific file formats.

1. **In Access, open the database that you want to add the imported or linked data to.**

2. **Choose File⇨Get External Data⇨Import or choose File⇨Get External Data⇨Link Tables.**

Alternatively, click the Tables button in the Database window, click the New button, and choose the Import Table option or the Link Table option from the New Table dialog box.

Access displays either the Import dialog box or the Link dialog box, where you specify the name of the file that contains the data you're importing or linking to.

3. **Use the Files of Type drop-down menu to choose the file type that you're importing from.**

   For example, if you're importing data from an Excel file, choose Microsoft Excel. Access then displays the Excel files in the current folder.

4. **Navigate through the folders (if necessary) to find the file that contains the data you want to use. Click the file name so that it appears in the File Name box of either the Import or the Link dialog box.**

   If you are linking, and the file that you are linking to is not on your computer (it is on a LAN or another remote computer), use the universal naming convention (UNC) path for the file rather than using a drive letter that is mapped. The UNC path is a more reliable way for Access to locate the data. A UNC path looks like the following: *server**directory**file* — you need to know the server name to type the UNC.

5. **Click either the Import button in the Import dialog box or the Link button in the Link dialog box.**

   You see the Import button if you're importing data; the Link button if you're linking data. (The name of the button depends on whether you chose to import or link your table in Step 2.)

6. **Depending on the type of file you're working with, you may see a wizard that guides you through the process of choosing the data you want to import or link to.**

   The windows you see depend on the type of file that contains the data you're importing or linking to. The following sections guide you through the text and spreadsheet wizards.

   Other data types (including .dbf) immediately import and are ready for use, and the Import or Link dialog box remains open so that you can choose another file to import or link to.

When the import or link is complete, you see a new table listed in the Database window. Imported tables appear just like other tables, and you use them like any other table — you can change field names and properties, create relationships, enter and edit data. Linked tables appear with an arrow and, an icon indicating the type of file that the link is to (such as dB for dBASE, X for Excel, and a fox for FoxPro). You can use most linked tables like any table in the database — some types, however, are read-only, and you can't enter and edit data. You cannot change field properties or enforce referential integrity for linked tables.

The following sections provide details on using the Import and Link Wizards for text and spreadsheet files. You may see Import Wizards for other types of files too, that are similar to the text and spreadsheet files in the information they need — Access wants to know how to get to and use the file, and how to break the data into fields.

Importing text or spreadsheet data

If you import or link a text file, the Import Text Wizard or Link Text Wizard starts when you select the appropriate file using the Import (or Link) dialog box and click the Import (or Link) button in the Import (or Link) dialog box. The two wizards are very similar, but the Link Text Wizard has fewer steps. Follow these steps to complete the Text Wizards:

1. **In the first wizard window (shown in Figure 4-2), select the Delimited option or the Fixed Width option to describe how your data is divided up and then click the Next button.**

The Delimited option is for situations where commas, tabs, or another character separate each field, whereas the Fixed Width option is for situations where spaces make the columns line up.

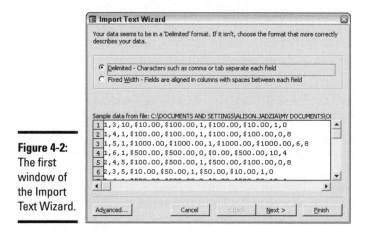

Figure 4-2:
The first
window of
the Import
Text Wizard.

2. **Further define where one field ends and the next begins in the second window. When done choosing your options, click the Next button.**

   If you choose the Delimited option in Step 1, you see Figure 4-3, which asks you what character separates your fields (choose from the options or use the Other option to specify the character used). Also specify whether the first row contains field names, and if a text qualifier is used (symbols that surround text, such as double or single quotation). Your data is shown with vertical lines to separate fields.

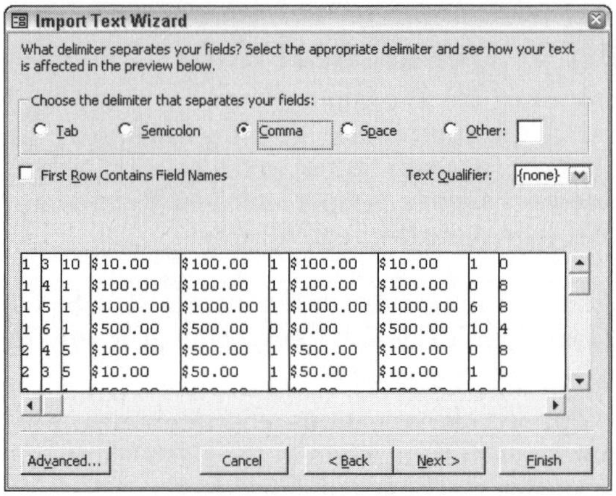

Figure 4-3:
Help
Access
figure out
where each
field in your
delimited
text file
begins and
ends.

   If you choose the Fixed Width option, you see Figure 4-4, which shows you where Access guesses the field breaks go. Create a break by clicking, delete a break by double-clicking, or move a break by dragging.

   If you are linking to a text file, skip to Step 6.

3. **In the new window that appears, specify whether you want to store the imported data in a new table or add it to an existing table (pick the table from the drop-down list). Click the Next button.**

   If you choose an existing table, your imported fields need to match the fields in the existing table exactly — they need to be in the same order, and of the same data type.

4. **In the next window that appears, click a column in the displayed data to change properties for that field and then click the Next button.**

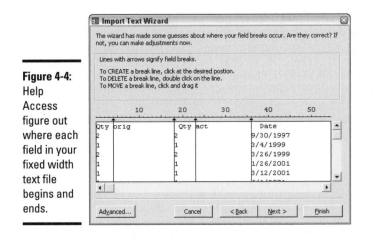

Figure 4-4:
Help
Access
figure out
where each
field in your
fixed width
text file
begins and
ends.

For example, you can further define each field by typing a field name; and you can choose the data type, whether or not to index the field, and whether to skip importing or linking to this particular field.

You don't have to complete this information for each field — you can go with the choices Access made.

5. **In the next window that appears, either select a primary key field, let Access create a new AutoNumber field as the primary key, or specify that the field doesn't have a primary key field. When finished with your selections, click the Next button.**

6. **In the last window that appears, name the table by typing a name in the Table Name box and then click the Finish button.**

The last window of the Import Text Wizard contains a check box that runs the Table Analyzer Wizard. If you choose to have a wizard analyze the table, the Table Analyzer Wizard looks for duplicated data and recommends how to create multiple related tables that don't contain repeated data. You may also choose to display the Access Help system when the wizard is done.

After you click Finish, Access creates the new table, and lists it in the Database window.

Click the Advanced button in the last window of the wizard to display the Import Specification or Link Specification dialog box again. If this is an import or link that you may want to repeat, save the specs using the Save As button.

The Import Specification dialog box, shown in Figure 4-5, displays all the specifications for the text file import. You can edit these specs, save them, or import specs that you created and saved when you did another text file import. This dialog box has options that you've seen before in the wizard (such as the file format, field delimiter, and text qualifier) as well as the following options:

✦ **Language:** Select the language for the text in your table.

✦ **Code Page:** Select a code page. Just keep the default selection unless you know for certain that the imported data is using one of the other available options.

✦ **Date Order:** MDY (month/day/year) is standard, but you can select another option as needed to match your date data.

✦ **Date Delimiter:** Type in the character used to separate month, day, and year.

✦ **Time Delimiter:** For typing in the character used to separate hours and minutes.

✦ **Four Digit Years:** Deselect this option if your data has only two digits used to designate the year.

✦ **Leading Zeros in Dates:** Select this option if your data has zeros before single digit months (for example, 02 for February).

✦ **Decimal Symbol:** Type in the character used as a decimal point. In the United States, the decimal symbol is a period, but in many European countries, the decimal is a comma.

✦ **Field Information:** List the field name in the file you are importing or linking (click to edit), the data type that Access has chosen (change by choosing from the drop-down list), whether the field is indexed (change by choosing from the drop-down list), and a check box if you want to skip the field.

✦ **Save As:** Save the Import Specifications settings (or Link Specifications) for use with a later import or link.

✦ **Specs:** Lists saved specs that you can select from.

When done setting your options, click the OK button.

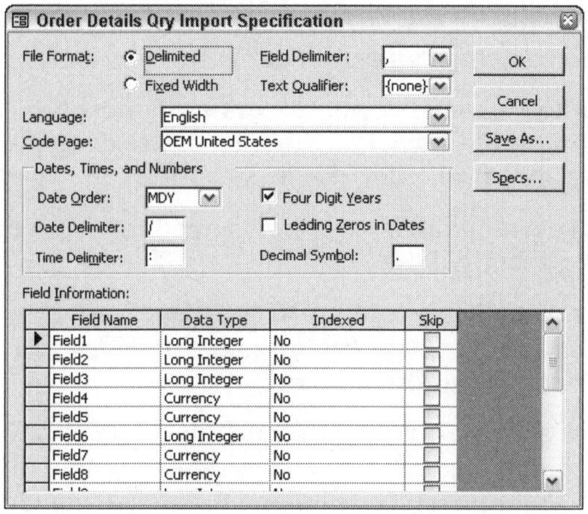

Figure 4-5:
The Import
Specifica-
tion dialog
box gives
you lots of
options on
how to
import your
text file.

The Import Spreadsheet and Link Spreadsheet Wizards

If you import or link a spreadsheet file, the Import Spreadsheet Wizard or Link Spreadsheet Wizard starts when you select the appropriate file using the Import (or Link) dialog box and click the Import (or Link) button in the Import (or Link) dialog box. Follow these steps to complete the Spreadsheet Wizards:

1. **Select the sheet that contains your data in the first window that appears, as shown in Figure 4-6, and then click the Next button.**

   You can only import or link to data on one sheet at a time. Use the Show Named Ranges option to see named ranges in the spreadsheet.

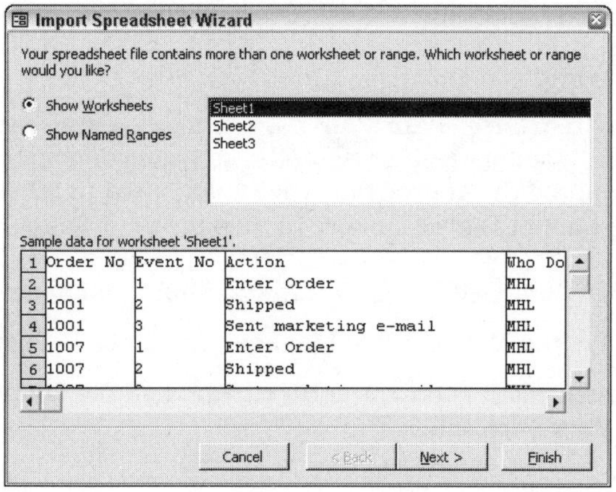

Figure 4-6:
The Import
Spreadsheet
Wizard.

**Book II
Chapter 4**

Importing and
Exporting Data

2. **In the second window of the wizard, tell Access whether the first row contains column headings and then click the Next button.**

3. **In the next window, choose to put the data in a new table or add the data to an existing table (pick the table from the drop-down list). Make a selection and then click the Next button.**

   If you choose an existing table, your fields need to match the fields in the existing table exactly.

4. **In the next window, click a column in the displayed data and change properties for that field. Click the Next button when you are happy with the properties for all the fields.**

   The next window allows you to further define each field by typing a field name, choosing data type, choosing whether or not to index the field, and choosing to skip importing or linking to this particular field. You don't have to complete this information for each field — you can go with the choices Access made.

5. **In the next window, either select a primary key field, let Access create a new AutoNumber field as the primary key, or specify that the table doesn't have a primary key field. When you finish your selections, click the Next button.**

6. **In the last window, name the table and then click the Finish button.**

   The last window of the wizard contains a check box that runs the Table Analyzer Wizard. If you choose to have the wizard analyze the table, the Table Analyzer Wizard looks for duplicated data and recommends how to create multiple related tables that don't contain repeated data. You may also choose to display the Access Help system when the wizard is done.

   When the wizard finishes, you see the database window with your new table listed.

Managing links

If you create links to external data sources, you may need to manage those links. For instance, when data changes in the source, you can tell Access to get the new data, and if the source file moves, you need to tell Access where to find it. Use the Linked Table Manager to manage your links:

1. **Choose Tools⇨Database Utilities⇨Linked Table Manager.**

   Access displays the Linked Table Manager, as shown in Figure 4-7.

2. **Select the check box(es) for the table(s) whose links you want to refresh and then click OK.**

Access refreshes the data in the selected tables using the external file listed in the table. If the external file isn't found, you see the Select New Location Of dialog box, where you can specify the new location. If more than one table was not found, Access searches the new location for all the missing tables.

If you want Access to always ask you where the files are, select the Always Prompt for New Location check box before you click OK to update your data.

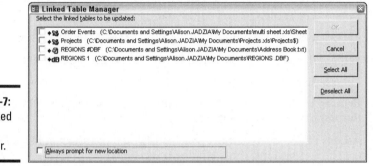

Figure 4-7:
The Linked
Table
Manager.

Cleaning up your imported data

If you import large amounts of data, you may need to clean it up a bit to make it efficient for use in Access. If you have any doubt about what clean data looks like, review Book I, Chapter 3 on designing databases.

One useful tool for cleaning up imported data is the Table Analyzer Wizard. This wizard looks for repeated data to determine if the table should be broken into two or more tables. The various Import Wizards offer to run the Table Analyzer Wizard. You can also run it by selecting the table you want to analyze in the Database window and choosing Tools➪Analyze➪Table (you can also open the table and run the Table Analyzer).

If you decide not to use the Table Analyzer Wizard, you may want to inspect your data for duplicate data. Remember that the primary key field cannot have duplicate data.

Your new table may need relationships defined with other tables in the database (see Chapter 6 of this book, for more on relationships). You may also want to edit the table name or field names, and fields may need some fine-tuning — you can use the Design view to edit data type and properties (Chapter 1 of this book).

Getting Data from Another Access Database

If the data you need is already in an Access database, decide whether you want to import it or link to it.

If you want to import (or link to) a table and all its data from another Access database, the process is simple — follow these steps:

1. **Open the database where you want to use the data.**

2. **Choose File⇨Get External Data⇨Import. (Choose File⇨Get External Data⇨Link Tables to link to the data.)**

Access displays the Import dialog box (or the Link dialog box).

3. **Select Microsoft Access in the Files of Type drop-down list.**

Access displays the Access databases in the current folder.

4. **Browse to the database that has the table you need. Select it and click the Import (or Link) button.**

Access displays the Import Objects dialog box shown in Figure 4-8 (or the similar Link Tables dialog box).

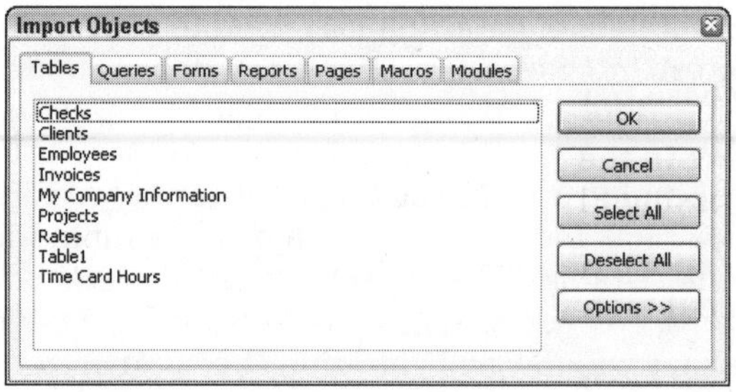

Figure 4-8:
The Import Objects dialog box allows you to import database objects from another Access database.

5. **Select the table you want from the Tables tab.**

To select multiple objects, use Ctrl+click and/or Shift+click. Click the Select All button to select all objects displayed on the current tab (for instance, all tables). Click the Deselect All button to deselect all objects on the current tab.

Click the Options button and choose the Definition Only option if you don't want to import the data, just the table definition (table properties and field definitions).

6. **Click OK to import the objects (or create the link).**

   The new objects appear in the Database window. You can view and edit them like any other database object.

You can use this method to import any database object — not just tables.

Getting Data Out of Access

Another way to go about moving data from one Access database to another is to export the table from one database into the database where you need it. This is similar to importing — the difference is which database you have open when you start.

Using the same technique you use to export a table, you can export any object from an Access database to another Access database, or to a file that isn't an Access file — a dBase or Excel file, for example. You can also use this technique to create a static HTML file. (To create a dynamic HTML page that reflects the current contents of the database, create a data access page. For more on data access pages, see Book IX.)

To export an object, follow these steps:

1. **Open the database that contains the object.**

2. **Select the object in the Database window (display the Database window by pressing F11).**

3. **Choose File⇨Export, or right-click the object and then choose Export from the shortcut menu.**

   Access displays the Export dialog box.

4. **Select the file type that you want to export to using the Save as Type drop-down list.**

   This list includes options for Microsoft Access, different versions of Excel, dBase, Lotus 1-2-3, and Paradox; SharePoint Team Services, Microsoft Active Server Pages, Microsoft IIS 1-2, Rich Text, HTML, Text Files, Microsoft Word Merge, XML, and ODBC Databases.

5. **Select the file to which you want to save the object by typing the name in the File Name box.**

   You can export to an existing Access database, but when you export to other file types, you create a new file (which you can then import into an existing file, if needed).

6. **Click the Export button.**

If you're exporting to a file type other than an Access database, the object is exported.

If you're exporting to an existing Access file, you see the Export dialog box, where you can rename the object (if you want to) and tell Access whether you want to export all the data or just the object definition (field names, format, and any expressions).

When you save a report to HTML, Access asks you for the name of the HTML template file. You can find out about HTML template files from the Access Help system.

Access quietly completes the export process.

To see whether the operation worked, open the file to which you exported the object.

Exporting to Word and Excel with OfficeLinks

A shortcut to exporting data to Word or Excel is to use the OfficeLinks button on the Database window toolbar. Select the object you want to export, and then choose the appropriate type of OfficeLinks. OfficeLinks offers three choices:

✔ **Merge It with Microsoft Word:** Uses the selected table or query as the data source for a Microsoft Word mail merge. By using mail merge you can create a basic document, which is customized with specific data. A form letter is an example — the basic letter is the same for everyone, but each letter has a customized name and address. The names and addresses can come from an Access table or query. The Merge It option runs the Microsoft Word Mail Merge Wizard, which guides you through creating a new document (such as a letter) and personalizing the letter with data in your database (such as adding names and addresses from the Addresses table).

✔ **Publish It with Microsoft Word:** Exports the object to Word.

✔ **Analyze It with Microsoft Excel:** Exports the object to Excel.

Chapter 5: Avoiding "Garbage In, Garbage Out"

In This Chapter

✔ Using field properties to get the right data in the right fields

✔ Creating drop-down lists with lookup fields to provide choices during data entry

✔ Defining how data in a field looks with input masks

✔ Filtering data with validation rules

*I*f the data that goes into your database is garbage, then any output or analysis you do with queries and reports is garbage too. Fortunately, Access offers lots of tools to help you make sure that the data that goes in each field is the data that's supposed to go in that field.

Access provides a number of tools that help ensure that correct data gets put in your database. Of course, we're talking about avoiding mistakes as data is entered — if someone is purposefully entering erroneous data, these tools may not help much! Some of these Access features are described in other chapters, but they deserve a mention here, too. The rest are exclusive to this chapter.

Finding the Right Tool to Keep Garbage Out

You can find many of the tools to keep garbage out in Design view. You can use the data type to keep inappropriate data out of field, as you can many field properties. *Remember:* Field properties appear in the bottom half of Design view — make sure you're viewing the field properties for the field you're working with by clicking the field name in the top half of Design view. Field properties are also covered in Chapter 1 of this book.

As you define a field in Design view you can use the following field properties to make sure that the right data gets in the right field:

✦ **Data type:** Use the correct data type to eliminate data of the wrong type. Text and Memo field types accept just about any input, so use the Number, Date/Time, or Currency field types to screen out data of a different type whenever appropriate. (See Chapter 1 of this book for more about choosing data types.)

Although data type is technically not a field property, it appears in Design view and is the first line of defense against incorrect data.

✦ `Field Size`: Limits the number of characters. For instance, if you know that a field should never exceed four characters, set the field size to 4 characters. (See Chapter 1 of this book for more about field size.)

✦ `Format`: Makes the data look right. For instance, you can change text to all caps or all lowercase. Input masks, explained later in this chapter, work with the `Format` field property. (See Chapter 1 of this book for more about the `Format` field property.)

✦ `Input Mask`: An *input mask* limits the information allowed in a field by specifying what characters you can enter. Use an input mask when you know the form the data should take — for instance, if an order number has two letters followed by four digits. Phone numbers and zip codes are other examples of fields where input masks are useful. You find out lots more about input masks later in this chapter.

✦ `Default Value`: Defines a value that appears by default if no other value is entered. The default value appears in the field until another value is entered.

✦ `Validation Rule`: A rule that data must pass before it is entered. This property works with the validation text rule. A validation rule property that applies to a whole record is in the Properties sheet. You find more on validation rules later in this chapter.

✦ `Required`: Specifies that the field must have a value in order for you to save the record. When no value is entered, Access doesn't create a new record when Tab or Enter is pressed, and the New Record button is grayed out.

✦ `Allow Zero Length`: Specifies whether or not a zero length entry "" (quotes without a space between them) is allowed (only for Text, Memo, and Hyperlink fields). A zero length field allows you to differentiate between information that doesn't exist, and a null value (blank) that is unknown or hasn't been entered. When this option is set, it allows a zero length string in a required field. You may want to use an input mask to make a zero length field look different than a null value when both are allowed.

✦ `Indexed`: When you choose to index a field, you can specify that no duplicate values are allowed in the field.

The rules that keep your data honest and help keep bad data out are sometimes called data integrity rules. You can change a field property that controls data integrity (filters out garbage data) in a field that already has data — Access tells you (when you ask to view the datasheet) that the data integrity rules have changed and gives you the option of checking existing data against the new rules. However, Access only tells you whether or not existing data violates the new rules — it doesn't flag the offending records in any way.

The rest of this chapter covers input masks, validation rules, and the Lookup Wizard, which allows you to create drop-down lists and pick from existing data, eliminating the possibility of misspelling a new entry.

When you use both the Format field property and an input mask, the field property is used and the input mask ignored.

Using Input Masks to Validate and Format Data

An *input mask* is sometimes called a *field template* — it both formats the data and defines a mold for the data — how the data looks. Input masks have two intertwined functions:

✦ **They format data by adding punctuation or changing the look of certain values (for example, displaying the text in passwords as asterisks).**

✦ **They block any data that doesn't fit the mold from being entered.** For instance, you can't enter twelve characters if the input mask specifies four, and you can't enter a digit followed by three letters if the input mask specifies two letters followed by two digits.

Use input masks when you know the form the data should take — for instance, a ten digit phone number, a nine digit zip code, or an item number that must be two letters followed by three or more digits. Using the input mask, you can add formatting characters — for instance, you can add parentheses and a hyphen to phone numbers, and you can change the way a value appears. The input mask for the field is in effect when you enter data into the field in a datasheet or a form.

If the data in a field varies or is not easily described, the field is probably not a good candidate for an input mask. For example, street addresses come in too many formats to describe easily, so making an input mask for an Address field is difficult. You can create input masks for Text, Number, and Currency field types; other data types don't have the Input Mask field property.

You can use an input mask with a validation rule to protect a field from data that is incorrect or that just doesn't belong there. Validation rules give you more flexibility in limiting the data you can enter. Validation rules are covered later in this chapter.

Input masks are commonly defined in Design view, where they become part of the field definition, and apply in forms also. However, you can also add input masks to queries and forms where data may be entered, and the input mask is defined only for that object. In all cases, you have to add an input mask from the Design view.

Using the Input Mask Wizard

The easiest way to create an input mask is to use the Input Mask Wizard. The wizard can help you create the input mask for your data — especially if the data in the field is a common type of data, such as a phone number or a zip code.

If your data is similar to one of the data types in the Input Mask Wizard, you may want to use the wizard and then edit the input mask in Design view.

To create an input mask with the Input Mask Wizard, follow these steps:

1. **Display the table in Design view.**

Press F11 to display the Database window, click the Tables button, select the table in the list, and click the Design button on the toolbar.

2. **Select the field you want to apply an input mask to by clicking the record selector, or put the cursor somewhere in the row for that field so that you see its field properties.**

3. **Click the** Input Mask **field property on the General tab of the field properties.**

Access displays the Build button to the right of the Input Mask line.

4. **Click the Build button.**

Access displays the Input Mask Wizard, shown in Figure 5-1.

5. **Select the input mask that looks the most like the data that you want to allow in the field.**

You may see an exact match for your field, or you may see something close that you can edit to fit your data.

You can add an input mask to the list displayed in the wizard by clicking the Edit List button in the first window of the Input Mask Wizard and filling in the details of the new input mask.

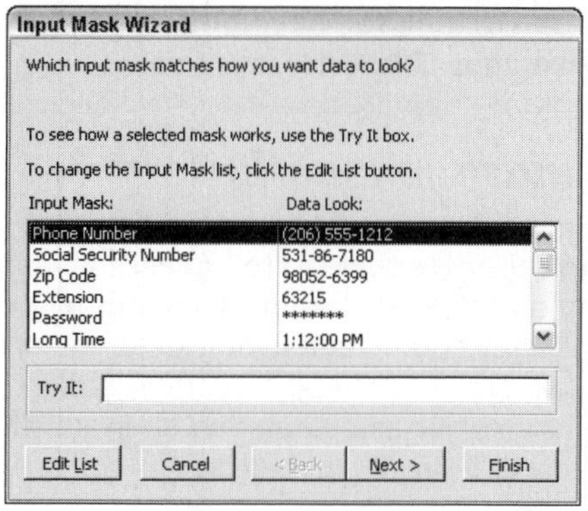

Input Mask Wizard

Which input mask matches how you want data to look?

To see how a selected mask works, use the Try It box.

To change the Input Mask list, click the Edit List button.

Input Mask:	Data Look:
Phone Number	(206) 555-1212
Social Security Number	531-86-7180
Zip Code	98052-6399
Extension	63215
Password	********
Long Time	1:12:00 PM

Try It: [   ]

[Edit List] [Cancel] [< Back] [Next >] [Finish]

Figure 5-1:
The Input
Mask
Wizard.

6. **Click in the Try It box and type some text to see how the field appears with data in it.**

Access displays a Try It box on each window so that you can see the effect of any changes you make — click in the Try It box to see what the input mask looks like when you enter data in the field.

7. **Click Next to see more questions about the input mask.**

The questions you see depend on the type of data you chose in the first window, so you may not see all the options in the next three steps.

8. **Edit the input mask, if you want to, using the characters listed in Table 5-1 (later in this chapter).**

Access displays the input mask it has created, and you have the opportunity to edit it.

9. **Choose a placeholder character and then click Next to see the next window of the wizard.**

A *placeholder* is a character that holds a place for every character that the user needs to enter. Choose one from the drop-down list.

10. **Choose how to store the data and then click Next to display the final window of the wizard.**

If you include punctuation or other additional characters in your input mask, you can choose how to save the data as it's entered — either save the characters entered plus the extra characters or just the characters entered. Generally you don't need to save the extra characters.

11. **Click Finish to tell the wizard to put the input mask it created into the** `Input Mask` **property for the field.**

Access displays the Design view with the new input mask.

12. **Save the table design by clicking the Save button on the toolbar —
otherwise, you may lose your nifty new input mask!**

Creating an input mask manually

To create an input mask manually, enter a series of characters in the Input
Mask property of the Field Properties pane to tell Access what kind of data
to expect. Data that doesn't match the input mask cannot be entered. To
block data from a field, first figure out exactly what data you want to allow
in a field; then use the characters in Table 5-1 to code the data in the Input
Mask field property. If you have trouble formulating an input mask, you may
find that a validation rule meets your needs better.

Table 5-1	Creating Input Masks
Input Mask Character	*What It Allows/Requires*
0	Requires a number
9	Allows a number
#	Allows a space, converts a blank to a space, allows + and -
L	Requires a letter
?	Allows a letter
A	Requires a letter or number
a	Allows a letter or number
&	Requires any character or a space
C	Allows any character or a space
<	Converts the following characters to lowercase
>	Converts the following characters to uppercase
!	Fills field from right to left, allowing characters on the left side to be optional
\	Displays the character following in the field (\Z appears as Z)
. ,	Displays the decimal placeholder or thousands separator
; : - /	Displays the date separator (the symbol used depends on the setting in the Regional Settings section of the Windows Control Panel)
Password	Creates a password entry text box; any character typed is stored as the character but displays as an asterisk (*)

Use input masks in these situations:

+ **AA00999:** Requires two letters followed by two digits and then allows
  an additional three digits.

✦ **00000-9999:** Zip codes — requires five digits, displays a hyphen, and provides space for an optional 4 digits.

✦ **L0L 0L0:** British postal codes — requires a letter, a number, a letter, displays a space, requires a number, a letter, and a number.

✦ **99:00:00 >LL:** Long time format — allows two digits, displays a colon, requires two digits, displays a colon, requires two digits, displays a space, requires two letters, which are displayed in upper case.

Creating a Lookup Field

**Book II
Chapter 5**

Avoiding "Garbage In, Garbage Out"

You want your database to be as easy to use as possible, right? But you also want data entered consistently. As orders are entered, for example, you want the name of each product entered so that Access can find it in the Products table. But what's the chance that the product name, entered as part of an order, actually matches the exact product name listed in the Products table? Pretty minimal . . . unless you create a lookup field.

A lookup field provides the user with a list of choices, rather than requiring users to type a value into the datasheet. You can create a drop-down list of products that you carry for users to choose from as orders are entered. Lookup fields enable you to keep your database small and the data entered accurate and consistent.

The items on the drop-down list can come from a list you type, or they can be from a field in another table. Storing values for your drop-down list in a table gives you much more flexibility to modify the list and the ability to store additional information about the values. (For instance, if your list contains state abbreviations, you may also decide to include full state names and even state tax rates.) Storing the drop-down list data in a table enables you to display one field (for instance, the customer's full name) and store another (such as the customer number). Working with the logical relationship you set up between tables, you can store less data — thus keeping the database compact — and entering and manipulating your data is easy. Lookup fields are very useful and not as complicated as they sound.

When you have two tables with a one-to-many relationship, the values of the connecting field may be perfect for a lookup field. When you enter records in the detail table (the *many* table in the relationship), the foreign key (related field) needs to match the primary key of the master (*one*) table. Consider making the foreign key in the detail table a lookup field, with the primary field in the master table providing the list of possible values. For example, if you have a Products table (the master table) and an Order Detail table (the detail table), make the Product Code field (or whatever field identifies the product the customer is ordering) in the Order Detail table a lookup field, using the Product Code field from the Products table as the list of values. You can find more information on relationships in Book I, Chapter 3 and Chapter 6 of this book.

Using the Lookup Wizard

An easy way to create a lookup field is with the Lookup Wizard. In this example, we show you how to use the Lookup Wizard to enter the Customer ID number (stored in the Address Book table) in the ContactID field in the Orders table. The Orders table lists information about each order, one record per order. Fields include the order date, the contact ID, payment, and shipping information.

Display the table you want set up to contain the lookup table in Design view and follow these steps:

1. **Find the field that you want to contain the drop-down list in the top half of Design view. Click the down arrow to display the Data Type drop-down list. Select the Lookup Wizard option.**

   Press F11 to display the Database window, click the Tables button, select the table and click the Design button on the Database window toolbar to display Design view.

   Access launches the Lookup Wizard.

2. **Tell the wizard whether the values you want to appear on the field's drop-down list come from a field in another table or from a list that you type. Click Next.**

   Storing the values in a table is easier, even if you have to cancel the wizard and create a new table!

   If you don't want the drop-down list to display every value in the field in another table, you can base the drop-down list on a field in a query. Find out all about queries in Book III.

3. **Choose the name of the table (or query) that contains the data that you want to appear in the drop-down list. Click Next.**

   If you want to see queries, click the Queries button. Click the Both button to show tables and queries.

   If you tell Access that you want to type in the values, a table appears in which you can type the lookup list. Click in the table in the wizard window (which currently has only one cell), and type the first entry in the list. Press Tab — not Enter — to create new cells for additional entries. Skip to Step 7.

4. **Tell Access which field(s) you want to display in the drop-down list by moving field names from the Available Fields list box to the Selected Fields list box.**

   Double-click a field to move it from one column to the other. Select multiple fields to display multiple fields on the drop-down list. For instance, you may display the First Name and Last Name fields in the drop-down list.

   Access always adds the primary key of the table that contains the data for the drop-down list to the list of selected fields, and it always saves the value of the primary key field. While you may see and select from another field — for instance, the First and Last Name fields — the primary key of the Address Book table (which is called ContactID in this example) is the value that is stored. Generally, this is exactly what you want (even if you don't know it). If you're sure that you don't want the primary key stored, you can customize the lookup field after the wizard finishes.

5. **If you select more than one field (or only one field that isn't the primary key), select a field to sort by, as shown in Figure 5-2. Then click Next.**

   You can sort by up to four fields. Click the Ascending button to sort in descending order (the button toggles between ascending and descending). In this example, we sort first by last name and then by first name.

Book II
Chapter 5

Avoiding "Garbage
In, Garbage Out"

Lookup Wizard

What sort order do you want for your list?

You can sort records by up to four fields, in either ascending or descending order.

1	Last Name	∨	Ascending
2	First Name	∨	Ascending
3		∨	Ascending
4		∨	Ascending

Cancel   < Back   Next >   Finish

Figure 5-2:
Choose fields to sort by and the sort order for each.

6. **Format your drop-down list — change the width of columns to fit your data, change the order of columns and choose whether to hide or display the primary key field. Then click Next.**

This window (shown in Figure 5-3) shows you a table with the values in the lookup list. You can change the width of the columns by clicking and dragging the border between field names; to automatically fit the widest entry, double-click the right edge of the field name that appears at the top of the column. You can change the order of columns by clicking the field name to select a column and then dragging the column to a new position.

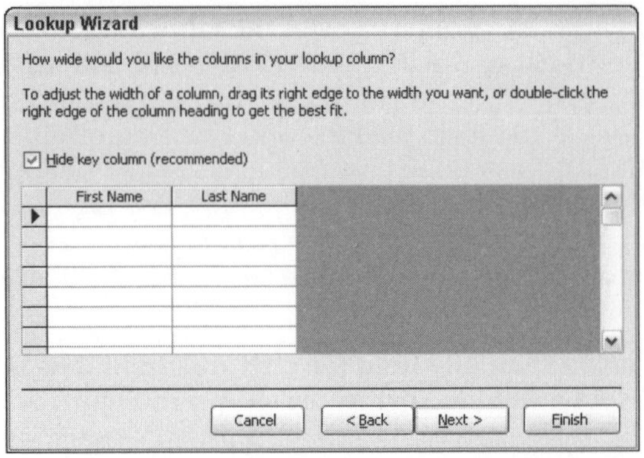

Figure 5-3:
Change the way your lookup list looks.

The window also contains a check box which, when selected, hides the key field. Depending on your application, you may want to display the key field by unselecting the Hide Key Column check box.

7. **In the final window, change the label (the field name) for the lookup column if you want to, and choose whether you want to display help on customizing the lookup column. Then click Finish.**

   Access may tell you that you need to save the table before relationships are created — go ahead and save the table. A relationship is created automatically when you use the Lookup Wizard — more about that in a minute.

View your table in Datasheet view to see your new lookup field. When you click within the field, you see an arrow to display a drop-down list. Go ahead and display the list. (Ours is shown in Figure 5-4.)

The default setting allows users to choose from the drop-down list or type in a value. To force users to choose from the drop-down list (or enter a value that's on the drop-down list), click the Lookup tab in the field properties and change the `Limit to List` property from the `No` setting to the `Yes` setting. Figure 5-5 shows Lookup properties. You may also want to enforce referential integrity, as covered in Chapter 6 of this book.

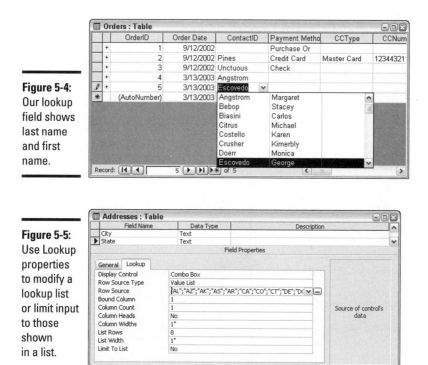

Figure 5-4:
Our lookup field shows last name and first name.

Figure 5-5:
Use Lookup properties to modify a lookup list or limit input to those shown in a list.

Using the Lookup Wizard creates a relationship between the table containing the lookup field and the table containing the data shown in the drop-down list for the lookup field — in our example, the relationship is between the ContactID field in the Orders table and the ContactID field in the Address Book table. If you display the Relationships window (click the Relationships button on the toolbar), you see the relationship the Lookup Wizard created. Find out more about relationships in Chapter 6 of this book.

Modifying the lookup list

Adding values to an existing lookup list is pretty easy. If the lookup list gets its values from a table, just add records to the table to see additional choices in the lookup list. If you typed values for the lookup list yourself, switch to Design view, click the field with the lookup, and click the Lookup tab in the field properties (refer to Figure 5-5). You can add options to the `Row Source` property — just be sure to separate the values with a semicolon.

You can use the Lookup tab in the field properties to edit the lookup field.

Validating Data As It's Entered

Often, you can state a rule that data must pass before being entered in a certain field. For instance, you may know that the date is not before 1999, that the price is zero or greater, and that the entry must be five characters and begin with P. The Validation Rule field property (in the field properties) enables you to specify a rule that data in a single field must pass in order to be entered in a particular field. Field validation rules are entered in the Validation Rule property for the field. Figure 5-6 shows a validation rule for the Order Date field.

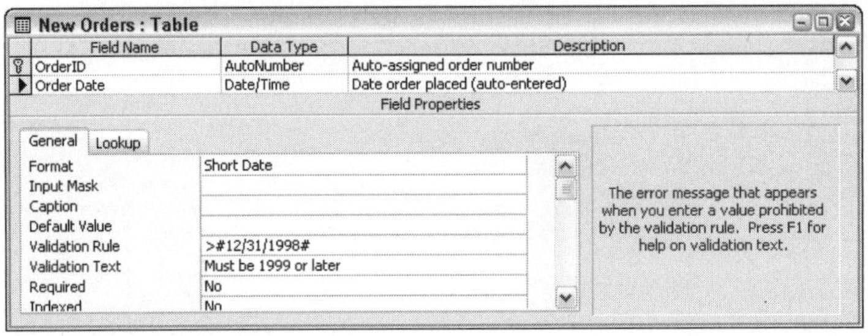

Figure 5-6:
The Order Date field must be after December 31, 1998.

New Orders : Table		
Field Name	Data Type	Description
OrderID	AutoNumber	Auto-assigned order number
Order Date	Date/Time	Date order placed (auto-entered)

Field Properties

General	Lookup
Format	Short Date
Input Mask	
Caption	
Default Value	
Validation Rule	>#12/31/1998#
Validation Text	Must be 1999 or later
Required	No
Indexed	No

The error message that appears when you enter a value prohibited by the validation rule. Press F1 for help on validation text.

If you just want to require that a value be entered, set the Required field property to the Yes setting.

You can also specify a validation rule for a record. Record validation allows you to create a rule to prevent internal inconsistency in a record — for instance, you may want to check that the ship date is not before the order date. You can enter record validation rules in the Validation Rule property of the field properties. Figure 5-7 shows a record validation rule.

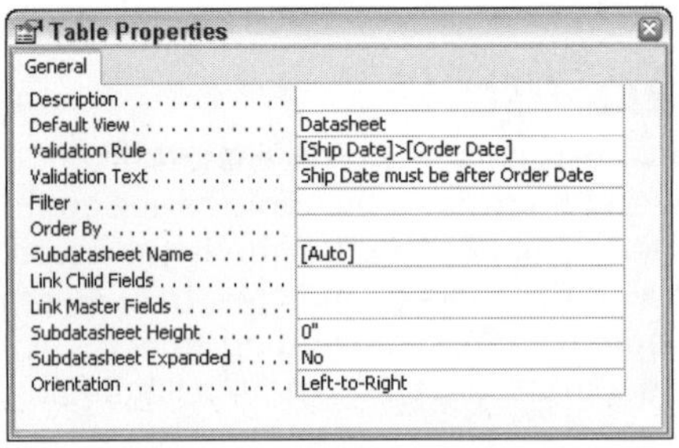

Figure 5-7:
The Ship Date field must be after the Order Date field.

Table Properties	
General	
Description	
Default View	Datasheet
Validation Rule	[Ship Date]>[Order Date]
Validation Text	Ship Date must be after Order Date
Filter	
Order By	
Subdatasheet Name	[Auto]
Link Child Fields	
Link Master Fields	
Subdatasheet Height	0"
Subdatasheet Expanded	No
Orientation	Left-to-Right

Table 5-2 shows a few examples of validation rules. If you have a complicated validation rule, read up on creating expressions. Use expressions the same way in validation rules as you do in query criteria. If the expression is true, then the data can be entered; if the expression is false, the validation text displays and the data cannot be entered. Criteria are covered in Book III, Chapter 1. Expressions are covered in detail in Book III, Chapter 2. The Build button that appears next to the Validation Rule box when you are entering a rule displays the Expression Builder, which is also covered in Book III, Chapter 2.

Table 5-2	Validation Rule Examples
Rule for the Field	*Validation Rule*
Date not before 1999	>#12/31/98#
Price zero or greater	>=0
Five characters beginning with P	Like P????
Ship date later than order date	[Ship Date]>[Order Date]

If a user attempts to enter data that does not pass a validation rule, the contents of the Validation Text field property pop up to guide the user, using the text you enter. Generally, the validation text guides the user to enter the right data. An exception may be if you don't want to give away too much information — maybe PO numbers are always two letters followed by three or more numbers, but you don't want users to guess at a PO number. Your validation text can simply say "Enter a valid PO number."

The validation text cannot be longer than 255 characters.

Use operators to tell Access how to validate your data. *Operators* are symbols, such as < and >, and words, such as AND and NOT, that tell Access how to limit your data. (+, —, *, and / are also operators, but you aren't as likely to use them in validation rules.) You can also use expressions that include functions to create validation rules.

The validation rule cannot be longer than 2,048 characters.

To create a validation rule, follow these steps:

1. **Display the table in Design view.**

Press F11 to display the Database window, click the Tables button, select the table, and click the Design button on the toolbar.

2. **Select the field to which you want to add a validation rule.**

   Place the cursor anywhere in the row that displays the field and data type, or click the record selector to select the field. When the field is selected, or when the cursor is anywhere in its row, you see the field properties for that field.

   If you want to create a record validation rule, click the Properties button on the toolbar.

3. **Click in the** `Validation Rule` **property.**

4. **Type your validation rule.**

   Table 5-3 tells you how to create your validation rule.

5. **Enter an explanatory message in the** `Validation Text` **property.**

   Validation text appears when data entered into the field does not meet the validation rule. In most cases, you want this script to be helpful for the user to understand why the input was not accepted. (In some cases, you may not want someone to make up data that passes the validation rule, so your validation text may be more cryptic.)

You can test data entered prior to the validation rule by right-clicking the title bar of the table and choosing the Test Validation Rules option from the shortcut menu or by displaying the datasheet by clicking the View button and clicking the Yes button when Access asks if you want to test existing data.

Table 5-3	Creating Validation Rules
Validation Rule Example	*How It Works*
"Boston" OR "New York"	Limits input in the field to just those two cities.
Is Null	Allows the user to leave the field blank.
<10	Allows values less than 10.
>10	Allows values greater than 10.
<=10	Allows values less than or equal to 10.
>=10	Allows values greater than or equal to 10.
=10	Allows values equal to 10.
<>0	Allows values not equal to 0.
In("Boston", "Concord")	Allows text that is *Boston* or *Concord*.
Between 10 And 20	Allows values between 10 and 20.

The Like operator deserves its own explanation. Use the Like operator to test whether an input matches a certain pattern — use wildcard characters, such as the ones shown in Table 5-4, to help define the pattern.

Table 5-4	Using the Like Operator
Wildcard	*What It Signifies*
?	Any single character
#	Any single number
*	Zero or more characters

For example, you may define a zip code field to only allow five digits, as follows:

```
Like "#####"
```

You can also define a field to contain only names that start with the letter S, as follows:

```
Like "S*"
```

According to the preceding rule, a person can choose not to type any characters after the S, because the * wildcard allows zero or more characters. If you always want a certain number of characters to follow the S, use the ? wildcard instead. If you want users to type exactly three characters after the letter S, use this validation rule:

```
LIKE "S???"
```

You can use more than one expression in a validation rule by separating the expressions with AND, OR, or NOT. AND and NOT limit the entries that pass the rule. In the case of AND, an entry must pass both rules; in the case of NOT, an entry must pass one rule and fail the other. Using OR increases the likelihood that an entry passes the rule, because the entry only needs to pass one of the two rules separated by OR.

Chapter 6: Protecting Your Data with Referential Integrity

In This Chapter

✓ **Protecting your relationships with referential integrity**

✓ **Using cascading updates and deletes to protect data integrity**

✓ **Printing the relationships between tables**

*R*elational database management systems, such as Microsoft Access, exist because the real world often requires that we store large amounts of data. And often one-to-many or many-to-many relationships exist between pieces of data. For example, any one customer may place many orders (a one-to-many relationship). Any one order may be an order for many different products. In a school, any one student may enroll in many courses. Any one course has many students enrolled in it.

When information is spread across multiple tables, the data must always "link up" correctly. For example, if customer Hortense Higglebottom places an order for 5 lawn flamingoes, the records from the various tables that record that information must jibe perfectly, so that she doesn't end up getting 37 Golden Whistles instead. The technical term for making absolutely sure that all the pieces line up correctly, at all times, is *referential integrity*. But before we get to the specifics of how you enforce referential integrity in your database, we provide you with a brief review of all the buzzwords and concepts surrounding the whole idea of storing chunks of data in separate tables.

Book I, Chapter 3 describes relationships among tables from a design perspective.

When two tables are related in a one-to-many relationship, the table on the "one-side" of the relationship must have a primary key field that uniquely identifies each record. For this reason, the table on the "one-side" is often referred to as the *master table*.

The table on the "many-side" of the relationship needs to contain a field that has (preferably) the same name, and (definitely) the same data type and field length as the primary key. In the table on the "many-side" of the relationship, that field is referred to as the *foreign key*. Because that table contains the foreign key, it's often referred to as the *detail table*.

Taken together, the primary key and foreign key are often referred to as the *matching keys*. (There's a load of technical jargon for ya.) Figure 6-1 shows an example of a one-to-many relationship between tables. The Address Book table is on the "one-side" (master table) of the relationship and the ContactID field is the primary key. The Orders table is on the "many-side" (detail table) of the relationship and the ContactID field is the foreign key.

You can see how the one-to-many relationship plays out when the two tables contain data. In Figure 6-2, looking up which orders are placed by Hortense Higglebottom is easy; the ContactID happens to be 10.

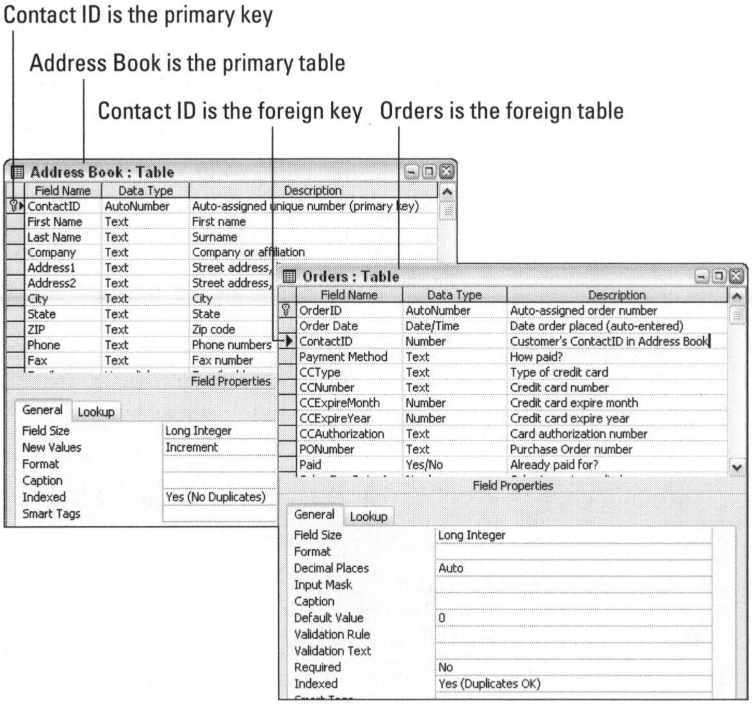

Contact ID is the primary key

Address Book is the primary table

Contact ID is the foreign key   Orders is the foreign table

Figure 6-1:
ContactID is the primary key on the "one-side," the foreign key on the "many-side."

Figure 6-2:
Sample data
in the
Address
Book and
Orders
tables show
the one-to-
many
relationship
between the
tables.

	ContactID	First Name	Last Name	Company	Address1
	6			Grandview Middle School	7724 Prospect St.
	7	Margaret	Angstrom		P.O. Box 1295
	8	Simpson	Sarah		1370 Washington L
	9	Nancy	O'Hara	ABC Productions	Haverston Square
▶	10	Hortense	Higglebottom		P.O. Box 1014
	11	Penny	Lopez		P.O. Box 10
	12				
	13	Hank & Matilda			

Record: 10

Orders : Table

	OrderID	Order Date	ContactID	Payment Method	CCType
▶	1	9/12/2004	12	Purchase Order	
	2	9/12/2004	11	Credit Card	Master Car
	3	9/12/2004	10	Check	
	4	9/13/2004	33	Check	
	5	9/13/2004	10	Credit Card	Visa
	6	9/14/2004	33	Purchase Order	
	7	9/14/2004	10	Check	

Record: 1 of 7

In any given database, one-to-many relationships likely occur between several tables. A *many-to-many* relationship is just two one-to-many relationships among three tables, as we show in the Students and Courses example in Book 1, Chapter 3. But you don't have to do anything special to define a many-to-many relationship. When you link two tables to a common third table, you create a many-to-many relationship.

Figure 6-3 shows how multiple tables in a database may relate to one another. In the Relationships window, field names in boldface are primary keys. The connecting lines show how the tables relate. In that example, the number 1 on a connection line represents the master table — the table on the "one-side" of the relationship. The many symbol (an infinity sign, or sideways 8) represents the detail table — the table on the "many-side."

Figure 6-3:
Multiple
one-to-
many
relationships
among
tables.

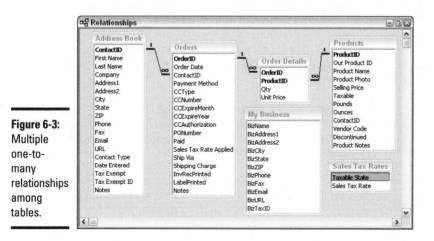

Protecting Your Relationships with Referential Integrity

We're not referring to your personal relationships. Well, maybe we are in an abstract sort of way. Before you join two tables in the Relationships window, think about whether or not you want Access to enforce referential integrity between those tables. *Referential integrity,* as the name implies, is all about making sure that the relationship between two tables doesn't turn to total garbage.

To see how you convert a one-to-many relationship to garbage, consider the following scenario. Suppose a table named Products contains a primary key field named ProductID that uniquely identifies each record. Say a hammer in that Products table has a ProductID value of 232.

The Order Details table in that same database also has a field named ProductID, which is the foreign key. Say 100 hammers are ordered to date, and 100 records in the Order Details table have the number 232 in their ProductID field.

So now someone comes along and decides to change the hammer's ProductID code to 98765. Or instead of changing the hammer's ProductID, that person just deletes that product from the Products table altogether. Either way, a record in the Products table no longer has a ProductID value of 232.

So what becomes of the 100 records in the Order Details table that still have 232 in their ProductID fields? Do we leave them referring to the now non-existent record 232? If we do that, we destroy the referential integrity of the relationship between the tables. How, you may ask, did we manage to do that? Well, a bunch of records in the Order Details table now point to absolutely nothing — there's no way to tell what product the customer bought. The referential relationship between the Products and Order Details tables has lost its integrity.

Enforcing referential integrity prevents these bad things from happening. When you enforce referential integrity, you prevent yourself from accidentally messing up your relationships. (That definitely doesn't apply to your personal relationships, even abstractly.)

Some rules exist to determine whether or not you can even choose to enforce referential integrity. You can only enforce referential integrity when all the following are true of the tables in the relationship:

+ In the master table, the matching field must be a primary key, or a field with its `Indexed` property set to the `Yes` (No Duplicates) setting.

+ In the detail table, the foreign key is of the same data type as the primary key. Or, if the primary key is an AutoNumber field, the foreign key is a Number field with its `Field Size` property set to the `Long` width.

+ Both tables are stored in the same Access database.

In Access projects (.adp files), Database Diagrams replace the Relationships window. See Book IX, Chapter 1 for more information on Database Diagrams.

Deciding on the best path to take

Assuming all the rules for enforcing referential integrity are met — see the previous section — you're ready to get started. Just keep in mind that you have a choice between two distinct types of referential integrity you can enforce:

+ **Cascade Update Related Fields:** This option ensures that if the value of the primary key field changes in the master table, the same change "cascades" to all records in the detail table. (This option doesn't apply if the primary key is an AutoNumber field. ***Remember:*** After an AutoNumber field receives a value, that value never changes.)

+ **Cascade Delete Related Records:** This option ensures that if a record is deleted in the master table, all corresponding records in the detail table are also deleted.

You can choose to enable referential integrity as soon as you join two tables in the Relationships window — more about said window later. You can change or disable referential integrity options at any time, so you're not making a lifelong commitment or anything.

Opening the Relationships window

The place where you actually join tables and enforce referential integrity between them is called the Relationships window, the same window you see back in Figure 6-3. Clearly then, if you want to be able to set up referential integrity between two tables, you're going to need some hints on how to open the Relationships window. What the heck? How about some explicit instructions, such as the following:

1. **If any tables are open, close them.**

The Relationships window can't handle open tables.

2. **Make sure the Database window is visible.**

   Press F11 if it's not.

 3. **Click the Relationships button on the Access toolbar.**

   Or choose Tools⇨Relationships from the main menu.

The Relationships window may be empty when you first open it, but if we know you, it won't be that way for long; you can (and probably will) add tables to the window at any time, as the next section makes clear.

Adding tables to the Relationships window

After the Relationships window is open, you can add tables to it by performing the following steps:

1. **Click the Show Table button on the toolbar.**

   Or choose Relationships⇨Show Table from the main menu.
   The Show Table dialog box appears.

2. **Click the name of any table you wish to add to the Relationships window, and then click the Add button.**

   Repeat Step 2 as many times as you wish to add multiple tables to the Relationships window.

3. **Click the Close button in the Show Table dialog box.**

The Show Table dialog box closes and — voilà — the tables you chose are visible in the Relationships window. Not the entire table, of course. That would be too big. Only a *Field list* that shows the names of all the fields in the table displays for each table you select. You can move those field lists around by dragging their title bars. You can size them by dragging any corner or edge.

Setting referential integrity between two tables

When you have two or more tables in the Relationships window, you can define their relationship and referential integrity. Here's how:

1. **Click the matching key in either table to select that field name.**

   For example, if you're joining the Address Book and Orders tables shown in Figure 6-3, you click the ContactID field in either table.

2. **Drag that selected field name to the corresponding field name in the other table, and drop it there.**

   The Edit Relationships dialog box, shown in Figure 6-4, opens.

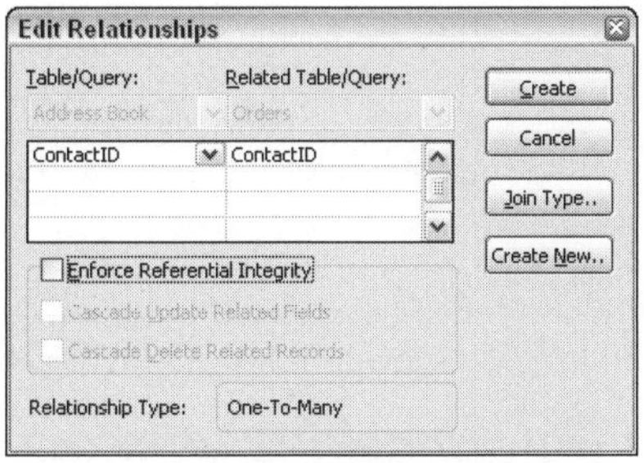

Figure 6-4:
The Edit
Relation-
ships dialog
box.

**Book II
Chapter 6**

**Protecting Your
Data**

3. **If you want to turn on referential integrity, select the Enforce Referential Integrity check box.**

   The Cascading options beneath the Enforce Referential Integrity check box are now enabled.

4. **If you want matching records in the detail table to update automatically when the value of a primary key field changes, select the Cascade Update Related Fields check box.**

5. **If you want matching records from the detail table to delete automatically after deleting a record in the master table, select the Cascade Delete Related Records check box.**

6. **Click the Create or OK button to save your changes and close the Edit Relationships dialog box.**

   (The OK button replaces the Create button when you edit an existing relationship as opposed to creating a new one.)

If you join two tables without enforcing referential integrity, the connecting line (or the *join* line) in the Relationships window is just a thin black line, as shown in the top two tables in Figure 6-5. If you enforce referential integrity, the connecting line shows a 1 near the master table, and a "many" symbol (an infinity sign, or sideways 8) near the detail table, as shown in the bottom two tables in Figure 6-5.

The relationship you define is not etched in stone. You can change the relationship between two tables at any time.

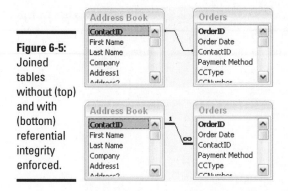

Figure 6-5:
Joined
tables
without (top)
and with
(bottom)
referential
integrity
enforced.

Editing and deleting Relationships window joins

To change or delete the relationship between two tables in the
Relationships window, you first need to select the relationship you want to
change. Selecting a relationship is trickier than you think. Follow these steps
to select the join line that represents the relationship you want to change:

1. **In the Relationships window, right-click the join line that you want to
change or delete.**

You see the options shown in Figure 6-6. If you see different options, you
right-clicked too close to a table. Clicking right on the line can be tricky:
Try right-clicking nearer to the center of the join line you want to change.

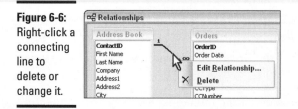

Figure 6-6:
Right-click a
connecting
line to
delete or
change it.

2. **Choose from the following:**

- If you want to delete the line (and therefore turn off referential
integrity), choose the Delete option.

- If you want to change something about the relationship, choose the
Edit Relationship option.

If you choose the Edit Relationship option, the Edit Relationships dialog box opens, where you can change or disable referential integrity. Make your changes and then choose OK.

The Join Type button in the Edit Relationships window allows you to set a default join type to be used in queries. Join types have no bearing on referential integrity.

Referential Integrity with Many-to-Many Relationships

As we discuss in Book I, Chapter 3, a many-to-many relationship often exists among chunks of data. For example, a school has many students, enrolled in many different courses. To design a database that contains information about students, courses, and enrollment, you need three tables. One table, perhaps named Students, contains a record for each student with a primary key field named StudentID that uniquely identifies each student.

A second table, perhaps named Courses, contains one record for each course with a primary key named CourseID that uniquely identifies each course. To keep track of which students are enrolled in which courses, you need a third table (called a *junction table*) that contains a record that pairs a StudentID with a CourseID. For the sake of the example, say the junction table is named Enrollments, as in Figure 6-7. When looking at data in the tables, you see how each record in the Enrollments table links a student to his or her courses.

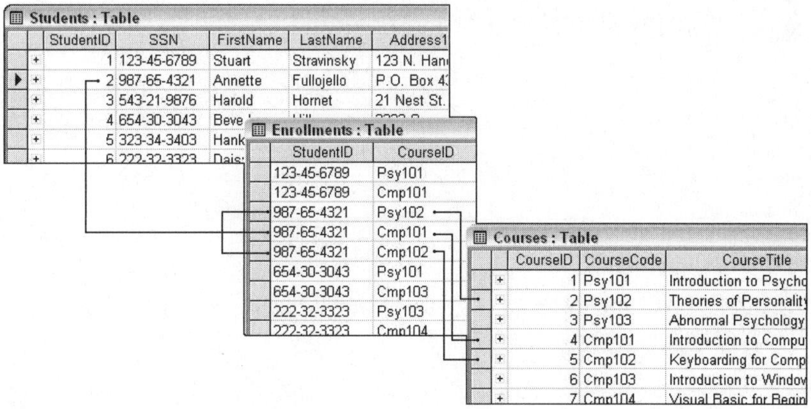

Figure 6-7:
Any one student can be enrolled in many courses.

The same tables, and same relationship, link any given course to the students that are enrolled in it, as shown in Figure 6-8.

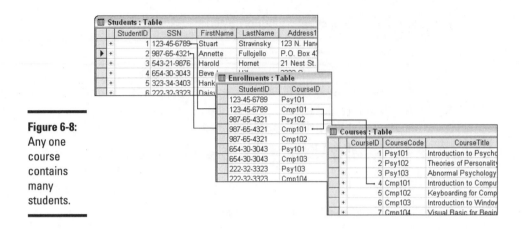

Figure 6-8:
Any one
course
contains
many
students.

While a many-to-many relationship is conceptually its own beast, Access only recognizes two one-to-many relationships. To set up referential integrity among the tables, you don't create a "special" many-to-many join. Rather, you just connect the fields and enforce referential integrity on each join line, as shown in Figure 6-9.

Figure 6-9:
The rela-
tionships
among the
Students,
Courses,
and
Enrollments
tables are
set to
enforce
referential
integrity, as
indicated by
the 1 and
infinity
symbol.

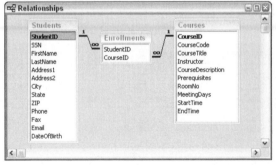

Printing the Relationships Window

You can print a copy of your Relationships window at any time. Doing so is not necessary. But if you'd like to have a printed copy to refer to in the future, you can just follow these steps:

1. **First make sure the Relationships window is open, and looks just the way you want the printed copy to look.**

2. **Choose File⇨Print Relationships from the main menu.**

   The printer won't start churning right away. Instead, a preview of what the printer will print appears in a new window.

3. **Click the Print button on the toolbar.**

   Now the printer actually prints the relationships.

4. **Click the Close button on the Print Preview toolbar.**

   A report design screen suddenly opens, but don't be alarmed. It appears in case you want to save a copy of the Relationships window as an Access Report. If you haven't gotten into reports yet, and don't know what that means, don't worry about it. You can just continue with the next step.

5. **Click the Close (X) button in the upper-right corner of the Report Design window, and then click the No button when asked if you want to save the changes to the Report.**

   You return to your Relationships window. To close the Relationships window, click the Close (red X) button in its upper-right corner.

Like we said, you don't need to concern yourself with this business of reports right now, so don't worry about the weird stuff that happens when you print your Relationships window. But just so you know, Access Reports are covered in Book V.

Book III

Queries

The 5th Wave   By Rich Tennant

"DO YOU WANT ME TO CALL THE COMPANY AND HAVE ANOTHER REVIEW COPY OF ITS DATABASE SOFTWARE SYSTEM SENT, OR DO YOU KNOW WHAT YOU'RE GOING TO WRITE?"

Contents at a Glance

Chapter 1: Creating Select Queries

In This Chapter

✔ **What do queries do and what kind of queries can you make?**

✔ **Creating a select query with a wizard**

✔ **Creating and editing a select query in Design view**

✔ **Getting the data you want out of your queries with criteria and sorting**

✔ **Using query datasheets to enter and edit data**

✔ **Saving your queries**

*Q*ueries are a way to ask questions of your data. Do you want to know who ordered a lawn flamingo? Which customers live in California? Which orders contain items that have been discontinued? What your top ten bestselling items are? Queries can tell you all that and more.

Like the tables covered in Book II, queries have two views: Design view and Datasheet view. In Design view, you define your query — you tell Access which fields you want to see, which tables they come from, and the criteria that any record has to meet in order to appear on the resulting datasheet. In Datasheet view, you see the fields and records Access finds that meet your criteria.

You can use queries to do the following:

✦ Look at data from related tables

✦ Look at subsets of your data — a selective slice that meets certain criteria that you specify

✦ Sort and alphabetize data

✦ Create new calculated fields

You can make as many queries as you want to — usually some are made on the fly and not saved, and some are saved, and even used as the basis for forms and reports.

To create a query, you need to know what data — more specifically, which fields — you want to see and which tables those fields are in. As you define the query, you may have criteria that limit the data. After you define the query, you can view the data in a datasheet. The datasheet created by a query is dynamic — that is, you see the data that meets the query definition each time you view the datasheet. If data has been added, edited, or deleted, the query datasheet may display different data.

To create a query, you use either a wizard or Design view (or both) to tell Access which data you want to see. The easiest way for a beginner to create a query is to use the Simple Query Wizard, but after you understand queries, you may prefer to go right to Design view.

We start this chapter by telling you about the different types of queries that Access offers, and then introduce you to Design view. This chapter concentrates on select queries, which are the most common type of query, and the skills you use to create select queries. Then we guide you through creating a query using the Simple Query Wizard. But because the Simple Query Wizard doesn't allow you to define criteria (such as limiting records to those ordered this month, or only viewing products that cost more than $20), you probably want to move quickly to the next sections on using Design view and criteria. At the end of the chapter, you find all the details on working with your query data in a datasheet.

Types of Queries

You use all types of queries to select and view specific data in your database. You choose the fields you want to see, and you define criteria to limit the data shown as necessary.

The following list includes the types of queries available in Access:

✦ **Advanced Filter/Sort:** The simplest kind of query, Advanced Filter/Sort allows you to find and sort information from a single table in the database. This option is available from any datasheet by choosing Records⇨ Filter⇨Advanced Filter/Sort.

✦ **Select Query:** A select query selects the data you want from one or more tables and displays the data in the order in which you want it displayed. A select query can include criteria that tell Access to filter records and display only some of them. Select queries that display individual records are called detail queries; those that summarize records are called Summary or Totals queries.

✦ **Totals or Summary Query:** These queries are a subset of select queries, but they allow you to calculate a sum or some other aggregate (such as an average) rather than displaying each individual record. Totals queries are covered in Chapter 2 of this book.

✦ **Parameter Query:** A query that asks you for one or more pieces of information before displaying the datasheet.

✦ **AutoLookup Query:** A query that fills in information for you. AutoLookup queries are covered later in this chapter.

✦ **Action Query:** Action queries change your data based on some set of criteria. Action queries can delete records, update data, append data from one or more tables to another table, and make a new table. We describe action queries in Chapter 3 of this book.

✦ **Crosstab Query:** Most tables in Access, including ones generated by queries, have records down the side and field names across the top. Crosstab queries produce tables with the values from one field down the side and values from another field across the top of the table. A crosstab query performs a calculation — it sums, averages, or counts data that is categorized in two ways as defined by the row and column labels. Crosstab queries are covered in Chapter 4 of this book.

Select queries are the most common type of queries used in Access. In fact, select queries are the simplest type of query, and all the other query types add features to select queries. When you define a select query, you select which fields and records to display in the new datasheet by using the design grid. The skills you use to define select queries are also used to define the other types of queries.

Creating a Query in Design View

If you're completely new to queries, this section is for you. Here we create a simple select query so that you can see what, exactly, a query does.

Just follow these steps to create a simple query:

1. **Click the Queries button in the Objects list on the left side of the Database window.**

Press F11 to display the Database window.

2. **Double-click the Create Query in Design View icon.**

Access displays Design view and the Show Table dialog box, shown in Figure 1-1.

3. **In the Show Table dialog box, select the table that contains the fields you want to display in the query datasheet and then click the dialog box's Add button.**

4. **Click the Close button in the Show Table dialog box.**

Now Design view displays the table you selected in its top pane and the empty design grid in its bottom pane.

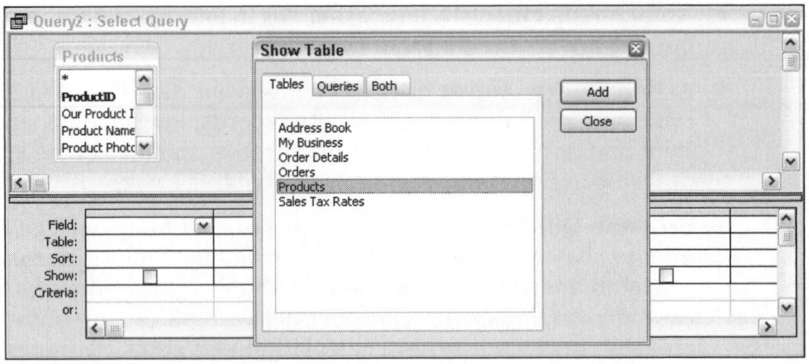

5. **Double-click a field name in the top pane to display that field name in the bottom pane — the design grid. Repeat to include any additional fields.**

You can drag a field name to the design grid or double-click a field name to move it to the grid. You can also use the drop-down Field and Table lists in the design grid to select the fields that you want to use. To select multiple field names in the Field list, use the standard Ctrl+Click or Shift+Click selection techniques, and then drag all selected field names to the design grid.

Figure 1-2 shows the query we created. Here we are asking to view three fields from the Products table — the ProductID, Product Name, and Selling Price fields.

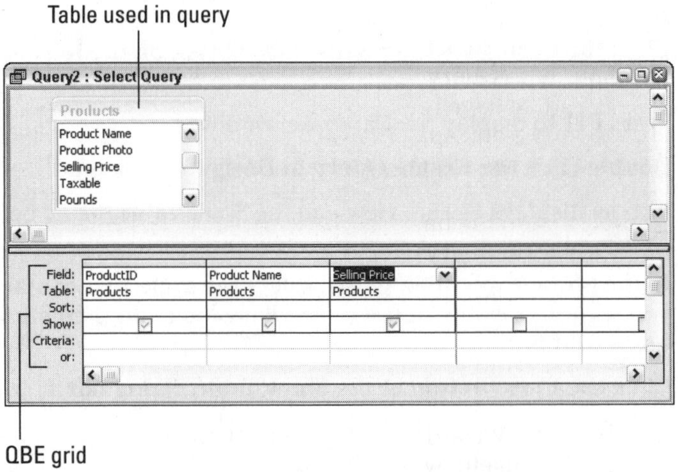

Table used in query

Figure 1-2:
This simple
query asks
to see
three fields
from the
Products
table.

QBE grid

6. Click the View button to see the datasheet with the data selected by your query.

Our datasheet, shown in Figure 1-3, shows the three fields we put in the design grid.

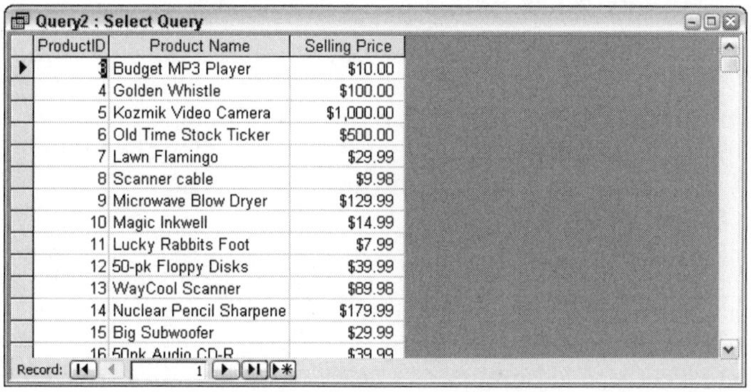

ProductID	Product Name	Selling Price
3	Budget MP3 Player	$10.00
4	Golden Whistle	$100.00
5	Kozmik Video Camera	$1,000.00
6	Old Time Stock Ticker	$500.00
7	Lawn Flamingo	$29.99
8	Scanner cable	$9.98
9	Microwave Blow Dryer	$129.99
10	Magic Inkwell	$14.99
11	Lucky Rabbits Foot	$7.99
12	50-pk Floppy Disks	$39.99
13	WayCool Scanner	$89.98
14	Nuclear Pencil Sharpene	$179.99
15	Big Subwoofer	$29.99
16	50pk Audio CD-R	$39.99

Figure 1-3:
The datasheet shows the data we asked for.

If you want to save the query, click the Save button in the query's Design or Datasheet view. Give the query a name that indicates the data it selects. Remember that the next time you open the query in Datasheet view, you see updated data — if any records have been added, deleted, or modified, the query reflects that. You may choose not to save the query, if you won't need it again. Just close it and click the No button when Access asks if you want to save it.

If you want to query just one table, the easiest way to create the query is to select the table in the Database window (click the Tables button for a list of tables) and then click the New Object: Query button on the Database window's toolbar. (Query is not always what the New Object button is set to create — you may have to use the New Object button's drop-down list.) The New Query dialog box appears. Select the Design View option and Access displays Design view with the table that you selected displayed.

Now that you have the hang of what a query is, you're probably ready for more — getting summary data out of a query, sorting the results, limiting results with criteria, and so on. Read on!

Creating a Query with the Simple Query Wizard

The Simple Query Wizard does a great deal of the work of creating a query for you. It's most useful when you want to use fields from different tables and when you want a query that summarizes your data.

**Book III
Chapter 1**

**Creating Select
Queries**

The Simple Query Wizard gives you the option of creating either a summary (totals) query or a detail query. A *detail query* lists every record that meets your criteria. A *summary query* (also called a totals query) performs calculations on your data to summarize it. You can create a summary query if the fields you choose for the query include both of the following:

✦ A field with values

✦ A field with repetitions or a field with dates, used to group the values

A summary query gives you the option of totaling (summing), averaging, counting the number of values in a field, or finding the minimum or maximum value in a field. A summary query creates new calculated fields that you can use in other queries or in reports.

Need an example? Here's one. If you have a field that lists the amount spent and a field that lists the dates on which the money was spent, the Simple Query Wizard creates a summary query for you that sums the amount spent by date. Pretty neat, huh?

Ready to give the Simple Query Wizard a spin? Just follow these steps to use the wizard to create a query:

1. **Click the Queries button in the Database window's Objects list, and then double-click the Create Query by Using Wizard icon.**

Access displays the first window of the Simple Query Wizard, as shown in Figure 1-4.

2. **Use the Tables/Queries list box to choose the first table or query that you want to use fields from.**

Figure 1-4:
Choose your fields with this window — they can come from more than one table.

Many queries are based on tables, but you also have the option of basing a query on another query. For instance, maybe you already created a query to select sales data from only the year 2003. Now, without modifying the original query, you want to create a query that lists 2003 sales by state, or limits the analysis to just a few salespeople.

When you select a table or query, fields from that object appear in the Available Fields list box.

3. **Move the fields you want to use in the query from the Available Fields list to the Selected Fields list by double-clicking a field name or by selecting the field name and then clicking the > button.**

4. **If you're using fields from more than one table or query, repeat Steps 2 and 3 to add fields from the additional tables or queries to the Selected Fields list and then click Next.**

From this point on, the windows you see depend upon the type of fields and the type of query (detail or summary) you choose.

5. **Choose the type of query you want: Detail or Summary. Depending on your selection, do one of the following:**

If you choose a summary query, click the Summary Options button.

If you choose a detail query, click Next and jump to Step 8.

The Summary Options window displays, shown in Figure 1-5, where you tell the wizard how to summarize each field.

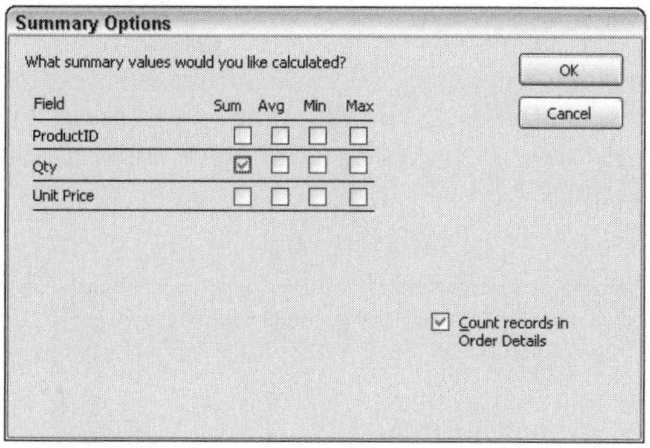

**Book III
Chapter 1**

**Creating Select
Queries**

Summary Options

What summary values would you like calculated?

Field	Sum	Avg	Min	Max
ProductID	☐	☐	☐	☐
Qty	☑	☐	☐	☐
Unit Price	☐	☐	☐	☐

[OK]
[Cancel]

☑ Count records in Order Details

Figure 1-5:
Choose how to summarize your data using these options.

6. **Choose how to summarize your data and click OK to close the Summary Options dialog box. Then click Next to see the next window of the wizard.**

Use the check boxes to indicate the new fields for Access to create with this query. For example, if you want to add all the values in the Qty field (to calculate how many of each item have been sold), click the Sum check box in the row for the Qty field.

Don't overlook the Count check box(es) that may appear in this window — selecting a Count check box tells the wizard to create a field that counts the records within each grouping.

7. **If the fields being summarized can be grouped by a Time/Date field, choose the time interval the records should be grouped by and click Next. (You will not see this window if your data does not contain a time/date field.)**

For example, if you choose to include the Order Date field in the query and to sum the Qty field, you can group by month to see how many of each item you sold in each month. You can choose to display total check amounts by the following options: Day, Month, Quarter, or Year. The Unique Day/Time option groups records by each unique date and time; if your data includes times, each record with the same date and time is grouped together. If your data only includes a date without the time, each record from the same day is grouped together (which is the same as the Day option).

8. **Type a name for the query in the box at the top of the window.**

Choose from the Open the Query to View Information option, which shows you the query in Datasheet view, and the Modify the Query Design option, which shows you the query in Design view. If you want to see the help screen on working with a query, click the Display Help on Working With the Query check box.

9. **Click Finish to view the query.**

If you chose the Open the Query to View Information option, you see the query in Datasheet view. If you chose the Modify the Query Design option, you see your resulting query datasheet, looking something like what you see in Figure 1-6.

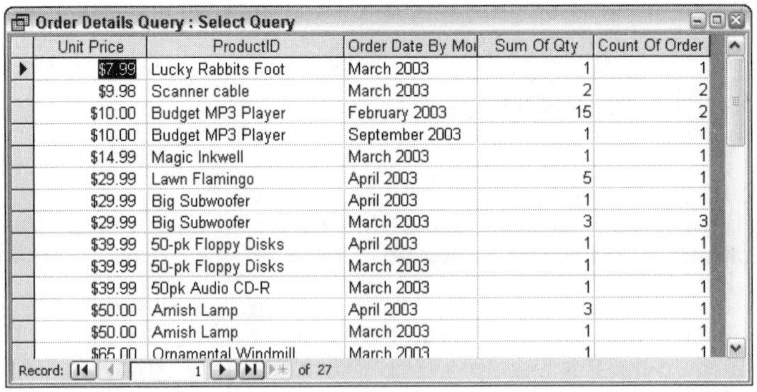

Figure 1-6:
The datasheet shows data summarized by date.

	Unit Price	ProductID	Order Date By Mo	Sum Of Qty	Count Of Order	
►	$7.99	Lucky Rabbits Foot	March 2003	1	1	
	$9.98	Scanner cable	March 2003	2	2	
	$10.00	Budget MP3 Player	February 2003	15	2	
	$10.00	Budget MP3 Player	September 2003	1	1	
	$14.99	Magic Inkwell	March 2003	1	1	
	$29.99	Lawn Flamingo	April 2003	5	1	
	$29.99	Big Subwoofer	April 2003	1	1	
	$29.99	Big Subwoofer	March 2003	3	3	
	$39.99	50-pk Floppy Disks	April 2003	1	1	
	$39.99	50-pk Floppy Disks	March 2003	1	1	
	$39.99	50pk Audio CD-R	March 2003	1	1	
	$50.00	Amish Lamp	April 2003	3	1	
	$50.00	Amish Lamp	March 2003	1	1	
	$65.00	Ornamental Windmill	March 2003	1	1	

Order Details Query : Select Query

Record: ◄◄ ◄ 1 ► ►► ►* of 27

You can edit the query created by the Simple Query Wizard using Design view, covered in most of the rest of this chapter.

The Simple Query Wizard doesn't allow you to include criteria to choose which records you want to include in the query datasheet. If you want to include criteria in your query, open the query created by the wizard in Design view and add the criteria. Design view is covered in detail in this chapter.

Viewing Your Query

After you create a query, you can open it in any of these views:

+ **Design view** displays the Design view where you can select tables, fields, create criteria, expressions, define sort order, and all the other things you need to do to define a query.

+ **Datasheet view** displays the fields from the query in a datasheet, just as if you were looking at a table datasheet.

+ **SQL View** displays the query definition in the form of a SQL (*Structured Query Language*) statement.

+ **PivotTable** and **PivotChart views** summarize and chart the data from the query. See Chapter 4 of this book for how to create PivotTables, and Book V, Chapter 3 for how to create PivotCharts.

When you open a query, you can open it in Datasheet or Design view by selecting the query name in the Database window and clicking the Open button (for Datasheet view) or the Design button (for Design view).

When a query is already open, you can switch between Design and Datasheet views by clicking the View button (the left-most button on the toolbar). To display SQL PivotTable, or PivotChart view, click the downward-pointing triangle at the right side of the View button. Choose the view you want.

Understanding Design View

If you're reading the chapter from the beginning, you created a simple, one-table query, and you used the Simple Query Wizard to create another query. Queries can do so much more, though, so dive into Design view and figure out what's what.

Design view

Design view is where you tell Access about the data you're looking for. In Design view you specify the tables (or other queries) where Access finds the data you want, the fields from those tables that you want to see, and any criteria that the data must pass in order to display. You also use Design view to choose the type of query, specify calculations, and define the sort order of the resulting data.

The following list describes our favorite ways to display a query in Design view (shown in Figure 1-7):

✦ Click the Queries button in the Objects list in the Database window, select the query name, and click the Design button on the toolbar.

✦ Click the Queries button in the Database window and Ctrl+double-click the query name.

✦ Click the View button when the query is displayed in Datasheet view.

Table 1-1 explains what the most useful buttons on the query's Design view toolbar do.

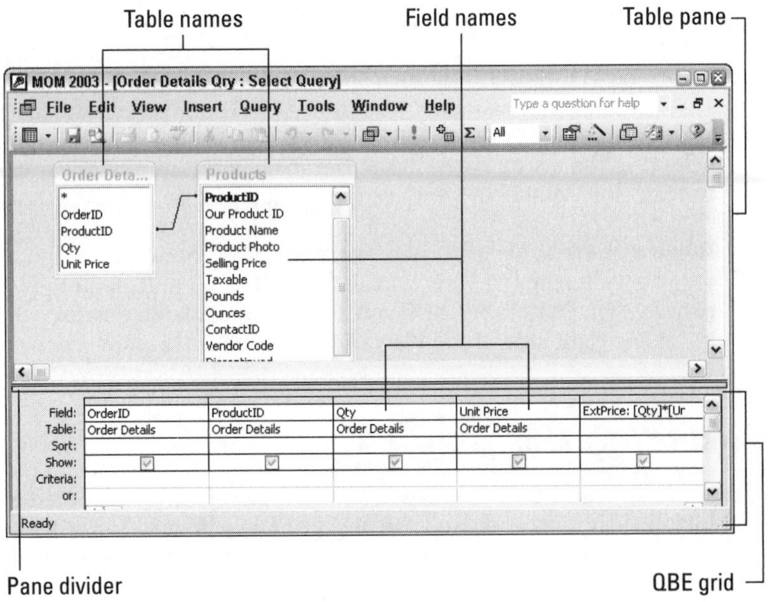

Figure 1-7: A query displayed in Design view.

Table 1-1   **Buttons in Design View**

Toolbar Button	*Button Name*	*What It Does*
	View	Displays Datasheet view — the data set defined by the query.
	Save	Saves the query design.
	Select Query Type	Displays a drop-down list from which you can choose a query type: Select Query, Crosstab Query, Make-Table Query, Update Query, Append Query, or Delete Query.
	Run	Runs the query. (For a select query, clicking the Run button does the same thing as clicking the View button. When the query is an action query, the Run button performs the action. Use this button carefully.)
	Show Table	Displays the Show Table dialog box so that you can add tables to the query.
	Totals	Displays the Total row in the design grid. (Use the Total row to create calculations that summarize your data.)
	Top Values	Limits the result of the query displayed in the datasheet to the number of records or the percentage of records displayed in this option (for example, All, 5, 25%, and so on). You can choose from the drop-down list or type values into this option.
	Properties	Displays properties for the selected field or Field list.
	Build	Displays the Expression Builder dialog box. (This button can only be clicked when the cursor is in the Field or Criteria row.) See more about building expressions in Chapter 3 of this book.
	Database Window	Displays the Database window.
	New Object	Create a new object (such as a form or report) based on the data produced by this query definition.

You can change the size of the panes in Design view by dragging the pane divider. Just move the mouse pointer to the divider, where it changes shape; then drag the mouse to move the divider.

Working with tables in Design view

The tables in the Table pane (the top pane of the Design View window) are really just little Field lists that you can move and size in the same way that you move and size windows. Change the size of a table window by moving the mouse pointer to the border of the window where it turns into a double-headed arrow; then drag the border to change the size of the window. To move a table in the Table pane, drag its title bar. This may be useful when you work with related tables and want to clearly see the relationships between them.

If your query contains tables that have relationships you previously defined (either with lookup fields or relationships you created in the Relationships window), you see the relationships as lines between the related tables. See more about relationships in Book II, Chapter 6.

Introducing the query design grid

The bottom pane of Design view is technically called the Query by Example (QBE) grid, but is often simply called the design grid. It is your handy visual aid for defining the data you want to select with your query. Each row in the design grid has a specific purpose. Table 1-2 lists how to use each of them.

Table 1-2	Rows in the Query Design Grid
Query Grid Row	*What It Does*
Field	Provides the name of a field that you want to include in a query.
Table	Provides the name of the table that the field comes from. (This row is not always visible.)
Total	Performs calculations in your query. (This row is not always visible — use the Totals button on the Design View toolbar to display or hide it.)
Sort	Determines the sort order of the datasheet produced by the query.
Show	Shows a field. (If you want to use a field to determine which records to display on the datasheet, but not actually display the field, remove the check mark from the Show column for the field.)
Criteria	Tells Access the criteria — such as records with values less than 10 or records with dates after 12/3/2002 — for the field in the same column.
Or	Use for additional criteria.

Each of these query features is covered in more detail later in this chapter.

Navigating Design view

You can work in Design view by using the mouse (to click the pane that you want) as well as the scroll bars (to see parts of the view that don't fit on-screen). Or if you prefer, you can use the keyboard to move around.

The keys in Table 1-3 move you around Design view.

Table 1-3	Shortcut Keys in Design View	
Key	*What It Does in the Table Pane*	*What It Does in the Design Grid*
F6	Switches to the other pane	Switches to the other pane
Tab	Moves to the next table	Moves to the next row to the right
Shift+Tab	Moves to the previous table	Moves to the next row to the left
Alt+↓ or F4	Nothing	Displays the drop-down list (if the row has one)
Page Down	Displays more field names in the active table	Displays more OR criteria
Home	Moves to the top of field names	Moves to the first column in the grid

Displaying or hiding table names

You can view table names for each field in the query design in the Table row, or you can choose not to see the Table row.

To make the Table row appear or disappear, do either of the following things:

✦ Right-click the design grid and choose the Table Names option from the shortcut menu.

✦ Choose View➪Table Names (to turn off the check mark).

Tips for Creating a Query

The "Creating a Query in Design View" section, earlier in this chapter, includes the basics for creating a query in Design view, but you can do so much more. This section delves into a few more aspects of the Creating Queries story.

Adding tables to the query

In order to use a table's fields in a query, you have to display the table name in the top pane of the Design view.

To do that, you need to view all table names by opening the Show Table dialog box. Open the Show Table dialog box using whichever of the following methods seems most convenient at the moment:

✦ Right-click the Table pane of Design view and choose the Show Table option from the shortcut menu.

✦ Click the Show Table button in Design view.

✦ Choose Query⇨Show Table from the Design View window's main menu.

After the Show Table dialog box opens, add a table to the query using whichever of the following methods is most convenient:

✦ Double-click the table name in the Show Table dialog box.

✦ Select the table and then click the Add button.

When you add all the tables that you need, click the Close button in the Show Table dialog box to get back to work in Design view.

To remove a table from a query, all you need do is press the Delete key on your keyboard when the table in the Table pane is selected (when a field in the table is highlighted). When a table is deleted from Design view, all the fields in the design grid from that table are deleted too. Because deleting a table from a query is so absurdly easy — and can have damaging consequences for your query — take care when your fingers get close to the Delete key.

If you want to include a field generated by another query, you can add queries to a query by clicking either the Queries or the Both tab of the Show Table dialog box and then double-clicking the query name.

Inserting fields in a design grid

You can move a single field from the Table pane to the design grid in three easy ways:

✦ **Double-click the field name.** Access moves the field to the first open column in the grid.

✦ **Drag the field name from the Table pane to the field row of an unused column in the design grid.** This option is for the dragging fans.

✦ **Use the drop-down list in the Field row of the design grid to choose the field you want.** If you use this method with a multiple-table query, you may find choosing the table name from the drop-down Table list before selecting the field name easier. If you don't have the Table row in your design grid, see the "Displaying or hiding table names" section, earlier in this chapter.

You can place all the field names from one table into the design grid in two ways:

✦ **Put one field name in each column of the grid:** If you have criteria for all the fields, you can put one field name in each column of the design grid in just two steps. Double-click the table name in the Table pane of Design view to select all the fields in the table. Then drag the selected names to the design grid. When you release the mouse button, Access puts one name in each column.

✦ **Put all the field names in one column:** This method is useful if you want to find something that could be in any field or if you have one criterion for all the fields in the table. Drag the asterisk (above the first field name in each table window) to the grid to tell Access to include all field names in one column. The asterisk is also available as the first choice in the drop-down Field list in the design grid — it appears as `TableName.*`.

Editing a Query

If you want, you can do some major reconstruction to your query in the design grid — you can move the columns around, delete a column, or delete all the entries in the grid.

To do any of those things, though, you first have to select the column in the grid by clicking the column selector — the gray block at the top of each column in the grid.

Table 1-4 lists some of the things you can do to make changes in the design grid.

Table 1-4	Editing Your Query
When You Want To . . .	*Here's What to Do*
Move a column	Click the column selector to select the column, click a second time, and then drag the column to its new position.
Delete a column	Click the column selector to select the column; then press the Delete key on your keyboard to delete the column.
Delete all columns	Choose Edit⇨Clear Grid from Design View menu.
Insert a column	Drag a field from the Table pane in Design view to the column in the design grid where you want to insert it. Access inserts an extra column for the new field, moving all other columns to the right to make space for the new column.
Change the displayed name	Use a colon between the display name and the actual name of the field in the Field row *(display name: field name)*.

Sorting a query

You can sort or alphabetize the results of a query in several ways. The first way is to use the Sort row in the design grid. Use the Sort row to tell Access which field to use to sort the datasheet. The second way is to use the Sort Ascending and Sort Descending buttons on the datasheet toolbar. For more on sorting in a datasheet, see Book II, Chapter 3.

If you sort a query by date, Access alphabetizes the months, which is usually not what you want. Reports know how to put months in chronological order. If you have monthly data that you want to sort, a report is a better object to use than a query.

To sort by a field, display your query in Design view and follow these steps:

1. **Move the cursor to the Sort row in the column that contains the field which you want to sort the records selected by the query.**

2. **Display the drop-down list for the Sort row.**

   Access displays the options for sorting: Ascending, Descending, and (not sorted).

3. **Choose to sort in ascending order or descending order.**

You can use the Sort row in the design grid to sort by more than one field. You may want to sort the records in the datasheet by last name, for example, but more than one person may have the same last name. You can specify another field (perhaps first name) as the second sort key.

When you sort using more than one field, Access always works from left to right, first sorting the records by the first field (the primary sort key) that has Ascending order or Descending order in the Sort row, and then sorting any records with the same primary sort key value by the second sort key.

You cannot sort by a Memo or OLE Data Type field.

Viewing top values

If all you care about are the top values produced by a query, you can tell Access to find and display only those records. Use the Top Values box in the Design View toolbar to see the top records produced by the query. A value in the Top Values box specifies exactly how many records in the datasheet you want shown; a percentage shows you that percentage of the records that the query finds.

Note that using a percentage does not show values that fall in the top *x*%, it shows you the top *x*% of values. Say you are looking at test scores of twenty students. The test scores fall between 0 and 100, but are mostly in the 80s and 90s. If you ask to see the top 20%, Access shows you the top 4 scores (20% of 20 records), not the scores that are 80 or above. To see the scores that are 80 or above, type the criteria >=**80** in the Test Score column in the design grid.

To display the top values found by a query, follow these steps:

1. **Create your query with all the fields and criteria that you need.**

2. **Choose the field you want to sort by and then set the Sort row to either Ascending order or Descending order.**

Access uses this to figure out which top values you're looking for. For instance, if we sort products using the Selling Price field, and sort in Ascending order, the cheapest products are at the top of the datasheet. When we ask for the top five prices, we get the five cheapest products. To get the most expensive products, we sort in Descending order so that the most expensive products appear at the top of the datasheet.

3. **Change the Top Values option by typing in a value or a value followed by a percent sign.**

You can also choose a value from the drop-down list. To see the top three values, type in **10**. To see the top 3% of values, type in **3%**.

4. **Click the View button to see only the top values in the datasheet.**

Hiding fields

You can use fields to sort data, or use criteria for the fields to filter data, but not display the field in the query datasheet. Deselect the Show check box (in the design grid) when you don't want to display the column in the datasheet. (The next time you open the query in Design view, you find that Access has moved the hidden field(s) to the right side of the grid. If the field is hidden and not used for sort order or criteria, Access removes it from the grid.)

Changing the format of a query field

The format of fields displayed in a query is determined by the field's properties in its native table. If the field is defined as having a currency format in its table, then that's what you see in the query. However, you can change the format of a field for the query.

To display a query in Design view, display the Database window by pressing F11, click the Queries button, select the query you want to display, and click the Design button.

To change the format of a field, follow these steps:

1. **In Design view, right-click anywhere in the column that contains the field you want to format.**

   A shortcut menu appears.

2. **Choose the Properties option.**

   Access displays the Properties sheet.

3. **Click in the** Format **property, and then click the arrow to display the format options.**

   The list of available formats drops down.

4. **Choose the format option that you want from the drop-down list.**

The format options in the Properties sheet are exactly the same as the options for the Format property in the field properties for a table, and you can use them in exactly the same way. However, when you format a field in a query, you affect how that field appears only in the query datasheet. Formatting fields is covered in detail in Book II, Chapter 1.

Limiting Records with Criteria Expressions

In addition to using queries to select only a few fields to show, you may also (even often) use queries to display a limited selection of records. Criteria enable you to limit the records that the query displays. You use the Criteria and Or rows in the design grid to tell Access exactly which records you want to see.

Querying by example

Querying by example — QBE, for short — makes defining criteria easy. If you tell Access what you're looking for, Access goes out and finds it. For example, if you want to find values equal to 10, the criteria is simply 10. Access then finds records that match that are equal to 10.

The most common type of criterion is a logical expression. A *logical expression* gives a Yes or No answer. Access shows you the record if the answer is yes, but does not show the record if the answer is no. The operators commonly used in logical expressions include <, >, AND, OR, and NOT.

Although we use uppercase to distinguish operators and functions, case does not matter in the design grid.

If you want to find all the addresses in California, the criterion for the state field is simply the following:

```
CA
```

You may want to add another criterion in the next line (OR) to take care of different spellings, as follows:

```
California
```

Access puts the text in quotes for you. The result of the query is all records that have either *CA* or *California* in the state field.

You can find records with null values by using the Is Null criterion. If you want all records except those with null values, use the Is Not Null criterion.

Using dates, times, text, and values in criteria

Access does its best to recognize the types of data that you use in criteria and relies on its best guess when using characters to enclose the elements of the criteria expression you came up with. You are less likely to create criteria that Access doesn't understand, however, if you use those characters yourself.

Table 1-5 lists the types of elements that you may include in a criteria expression and the character to use to make sure that Access knows that the element is text, a date, a time, a number, or a field name.

Table 1-5	Dates, Time, and Text in Criteria
Use This Type of Data . . .	*In an Expression Like This . . .*
Text	"text"
Date	#1-Feb-97#
Time	#12:00am#
Number	10
Field name	[field name]

You can refer to dates or times by using any allowed format. December 25, 1999, 12/25/99, and 25-Dec-99 are all formats that Access recognizes. You can use AM/PM or 24-hour time.

Using operators in criteria expressions

Often, your criteria are more complicated than "all records with California in the state field." You use operators in your criteria expressions to tell Access about more complex criteria.

Table 1-6 lists the operators that you're likely to use in a criteria expression.

Table 1-6	Using Operators in Criteria
Relational Operator	*What It Does*
=	Finds values equal to text, a number, or date/time ("equal to" is understood when you type a criteria without an operator — you don't need to type it)
<>	Finds values not equal to text, a number, or date/time
<	Finds values less than a given value
<=	Finds values less than or equal to a given value
>	Finds values greater than a given value
>=	Finds values greater than or equal to a given value
BETWEEN	Finds values between or equal to two values
IN	Finds values or text included in a list
LIKE	Finds matches to a pattern

When you type your criterion, you don't have to tell Access the field name. Just put your criterion in the same column as the field, and Access applies the criterion to the field that appears in the same column.

Table 1-7 explains how different criteria affect the records that display in the query datasheet.

Table 1-7	Examples of Criteria with Operators
When Field1 Has This Criteria	*These Are the Records You See*
<15	Displays records where Field1 is less than 15
<#9/1/03#	Finds records where Field1 contains dates before September 1, 2003
>15	Finds records where Field1 is greater than 15
>#12:00am#	Finds records where Field1 is after 12:00 a.m.
>[Max Price]	Finds records where Field1 is more than the value in the field Max Price
<>15	Finds records where Field1 is not equal to 15
>10 AND <20	Finds records where Field1 is between 11 and 19
>=10 AND <=20	Finds records where Field1 is between 10 and 20, including 10 and 20
BETWEEN 10 AND 20	The same as >=10 AND <=20
IN ("Virginia", "VA")	Finds records where Field1 contains either Virginia or VA
LIKE "A*"	Finds records where Field1 begins with the letter *A*. You can use LIKE with wildcards such as * to tell Access in general terms what you're looking for. For more information on the wildcards that Access recognizes, see Book II, Chapter 5

Using multiple criteria

Often one criterion is not enough. You may want to prune down the records displayed by using multiple criteria for a single field or multiple criteria for different fields. However, you do need to know how Access combines your criteria, so that you get the data you want.

When you have criteria for only one field, decide whether you want to see records that meet all the criteria (that is, join the criteria with AND) or whether you want records that meet only one criteria (that is, join the criteria with OR). Of course, you may have three or more criteria, and you can join them with both AND and OR.

To join criteria for a single field with AND, type them into the Criteria line of the grid with AND between them:

`>3 And <10`

shows you records with values less than three as well as those greater than ten.

To join multiple criteria for one field with OR, use one of these methods:

✦ Type your expressions into the Criteria row separated by OR.

✦ Type the first expression in the Criteria row, and type subsequent expressions using the Or rows in the design grid.

Whichever approach you take, the result is the same — Access displays records in the datasheet that satisfy one or more of the criteria expressions.

When you have criteria for different fields, you join them with either the OR or AND operator. The operator is implied in the way you put the criteria into the design grid:

✦ **Criteria on the same row are implicitly joined by AND.** Access assumes that you want to find records that meet all the criteria. If you type criteria on the same row for two fields, a record has to meet both criteria to display in the datasheet.

✦ **Criteria on different rows are joined by OR.** Access assumes that you want to find records that meet at least one criteria. If you type criteria on different rows for two fields, a record has to meet only one criteria to display in the datasheet.

✦ **When you use multiple rows for criteria, the expressions on each row are treated as though they are joined by AND, but each row's worth of criteria are treated as though they are joined by OR.** Access first looks at one row of criteria and finds all the records that meet all the criteria on that row. Then Access starts over with the next row of criteria, the Or row, and finds all the records that meet all the criteria on that row. The datasheet displays all the records that are found. A record has to meet all the criteria on only one row to display in the datasheet.

Using lookup fields in criteria

When you define a criteria for a query you tell Access what you are looking for either by entering a value or by using a logical expression. However, if you use a lookup field to limit records, you have to figure out exactly what value you want to find — it may not be the value you see in the table. See Book II for how to create a lookup field.

How about an example? You want to find orders for the Budget MP3 Player. The Order Details table stores this data, shown in Figure 1-8. Notice that the ProductID field is a lookup field — it displays values from the Product Name field of the Products table, but stores the values from the Products table primary key field, which is ProductID. The Product table is shown in Figure 1-9.

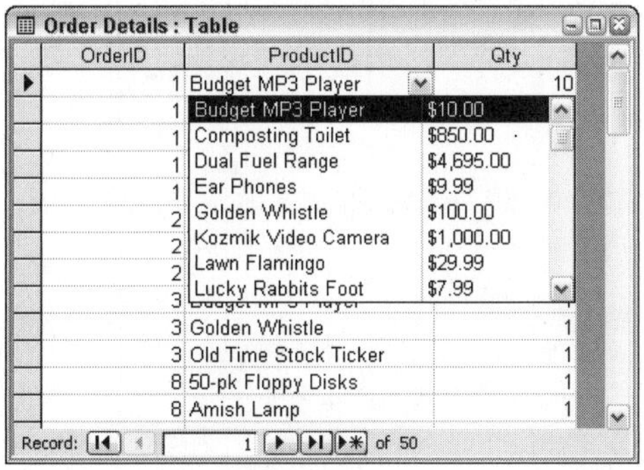

Figure 1-8: The ProductID field in the Order Details table is a lookup field.

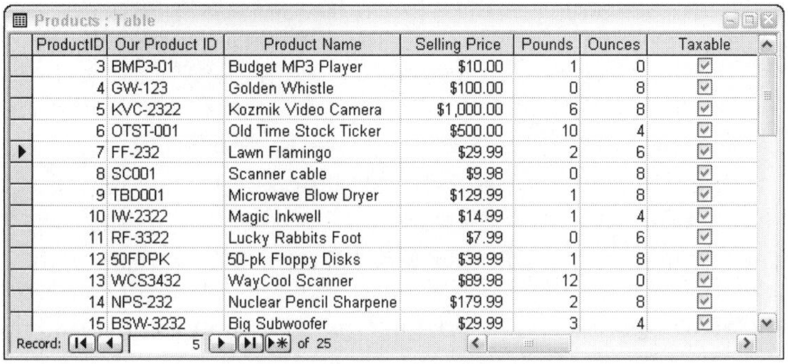

ProductID	Our Product ID	Product Name	Selling Price	Pounds	Ounces	Taxable
3	BMP3-01	Budget MP3 Player	$10.00	1	0	☑
4	GW-123	Golden Whistle	$100.00	0	8	☑
5	KVC-2322	Kozmik Video Camera	$1,000.00	6	8	☑
6	OTST-001	Old Time Stock Ticker	$500.00	10	4	☑
7	FF-232	Lawn Flamingo	$29.99	2	6	☑
8	SC001	Scanner cable	$9.98	0	8	☑
9	TBD001	Microwave Blow Dryer	$129.99	1	8	☑
10	IW-2322	Magic Inkwell	$14.99	1	4	☑
11	RF-3322	Lucky Rabbits Foot	$7.99	0	6	☑
12	50FDPK	50-pk Floppy Disks	$39.99	1	8	☑
13	WCS3432	WayCool Scanner	$89.98	12	0	☑
14	NPS-232	Nuclear Pencil Sharpene	$179.99	2	8	☑
15	BSW-3232	Big Subwoofer	$29.99	3	4	☑

Figure 1-9: The Products table holds the data shown in the Order Details table drop-down list.

When you create a query to look for Budget MP3 Player orders, you may have a query like the one shown in Figure 1-10 before you type any criteria. The datasheet for the query is shown in Figure 1-11.

Because the ProductID field in the Order Detail table is a lookup field, the criteria needs to refer to the value that is stored in the field, not the value that displays. The value that is stored is the primary key field from the Products table. The value that displays is the product name. If we enter Budget MP3 Player for the ProductID criteria and try to view the datasheet, we see a `Data type Mismatch in Criteria Expression` error message. We need to go back to the Products table and find the ProductID number for the Budget MP3 Player. (***Remember:*** A lookup field always stores the primary key field.)

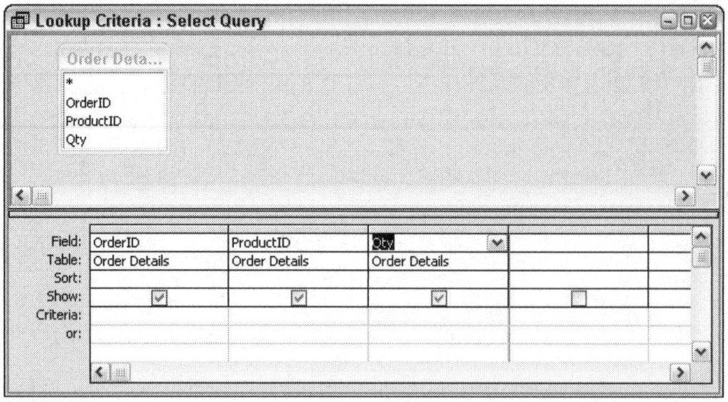

Figure 1-10:
This query
produces
the
datasheet in
Figure 1-11.

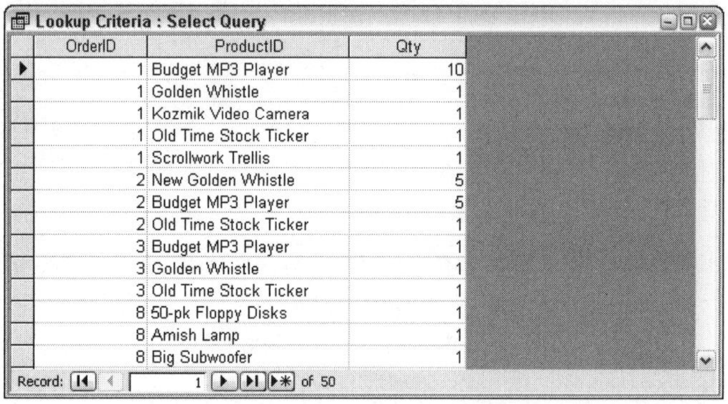

Figure 1-11:
The
datasheet
produced by
the query in
Figure 1-10.

The ProductID for the Budget MP3 Player is 3 (see the first line of Figure 1-9).
With that information we can create the query criteria — it is 3. The query is
shown in Figure 1-12, and the query datasheet in Figure 1-13.

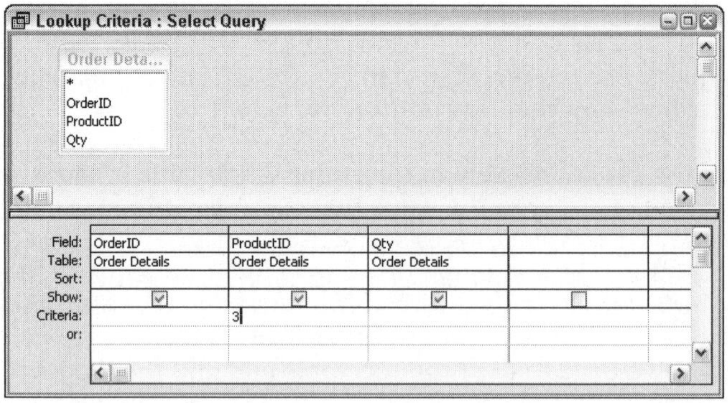

Figure 1-12:
The query
produces
the
datasheet in
Figure 1-13.

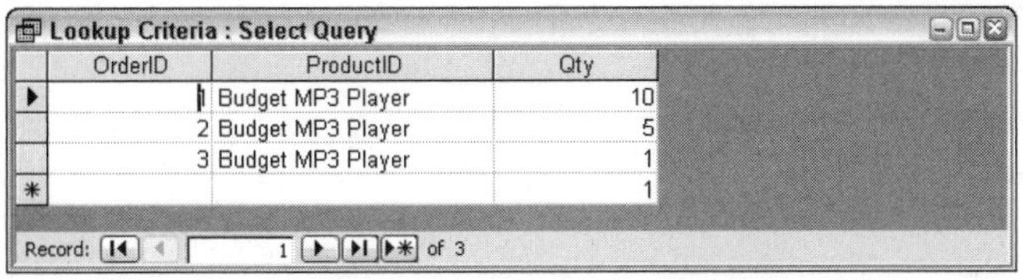

Figure 1-13:
The
datasheet
produced by
the query in
Figure 1-12.

	OrderID	ProductID	Qty
▶	1	Budget MP3 Player	10
	2	Budget MP3 Player	5
	3	Budget MP3 Player	1
*			1

Working with Multiple Related Tables

One powerful feature of queries is the ability to view related fields from different tables together in a query datasheet. For instance, using our database, we can create a query to list customer name and contact information with order dates and numbers, even though two different tables store the data. The relationship between the two tables is the ContactID field, which is the primary key of the Address Book table. The same field, ContactID, is in the Orders table — it identifies the customers who placed each order. For more information about relating tables, see Book I, Chapter 3 and Book II, Chapter 6.

In order for Access to display data from different tables, a relationship must be defined between the tables. The relationship between tables is created in one of these ways:

✦ A lookup field exists creating a relationship between two tables. For more on lookup fields, see Book II, Chapter 5.

✦ A relationship was defined in the Relationships window, as described in Book II, Chapter 6. (Creating a lookup field automatically creates a corresponding relationship in the Relationships window.)

✦ Access automatically creates a relationship when it finds related fields in two tables — that is, if the two fields have the same name and data type, and one of the matching fields is the primary key of its table.

✦ You create a relationship in Design view when defining a query.

When a relationship exists between two tables displayed in Design view, the tables appear joined by a line, as in Figure 1-14.

If you use data from two tables that are not directly related, you need to display any other tables that relate the fields you want to display in the query datasheet.

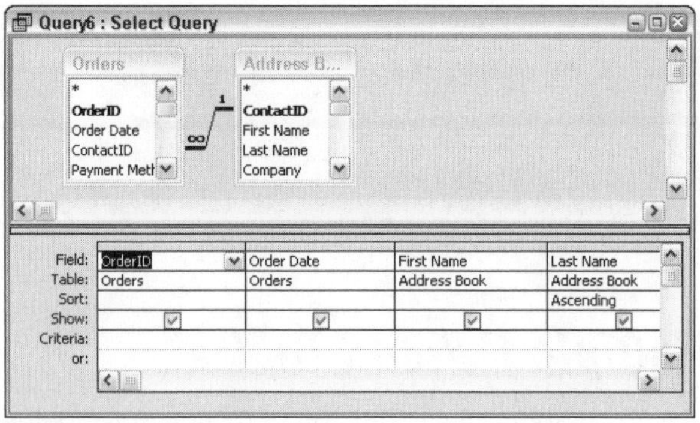

Figure 1-14:
A query combining data from two related tables and sorts the results alphabetically by last name.

If referential integrity is enforced, the 1 and ∞ symbols appear on the relationship line to denote the one and many sides of the relationship. If referential integrity is not enforced, those symbols do not appear on the line (see Book II, Chapter 6 for more on referential integrity).

Figure 1-15 shows the result of the query shown in Figure 1-14 — each order is listed once, with the name of the customer. Many customers have multiple orders, so they appear more than once in the datasheet.

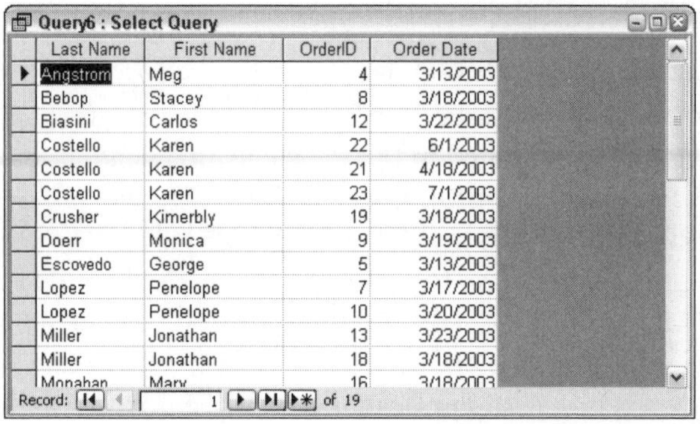

Figure 1-15:
The datasheet results of the query shown in Figure 1-14.

Last Name	First Name	OrderID	Order Date
Angstrom	Meg	4	3/13/2003
Bebop	Stacey	8	3/18/2003
Biasini	Carlos	12	3/22/2003
Costello	Karen	22	6/1/2003
Costello	Karen	21	4/18/2003
Costello	Karen	23	7/1/2003
Crusher	Kimerbly	19	3/18/2003
Doerr	Monica	9	3/19/2003
Escovedo	George	5	3/13/2003
Lopez	Penelope	7	3/17/2003
Lopez	Penelope	10	3/20/2003
Miller	Jonathan	13	3/23/2003
Miller	Jonathan	18	3/18/2003
Monahan	Mary	16	3/18/2003

Record: 1 of 19

Joining tables in Design view

You can create or edit a relationship between two tables in Design view. The relationship defined in Design view is used only for the query; it's not used in any other part of the database. You can use a type of join that you may not want to use in the database as a whole, but that you may find useful for a single query (which you may then use as the source data for a form or report). You can also delete a relationship in Design view without deleting the same relationship in the Relationships window. (To delete the join, click the line, and then press the Delete key on your keyboard.)

To create a join, you use the Table pane of Design view and follow the same procedure you use when creating a relationship in the Relationship window — you first identify the two related fields (each in a different table) you want to join and then you drag the field from one table to the related field in the other table. Voilà, a join!

Choosing the type of join and setting join properties

You can edit the join properties of a relationship for the query (remember, the new properties apply only in the current query, and not in any other objects in the database except those based on this query) in Design view. Double-click the relationship line to see the Join Properties dialog box, as shown in Figure 1-16. If you have trouble double-clicking the relationship line, keep trying! The tip of the pointer needs to be right on the line.

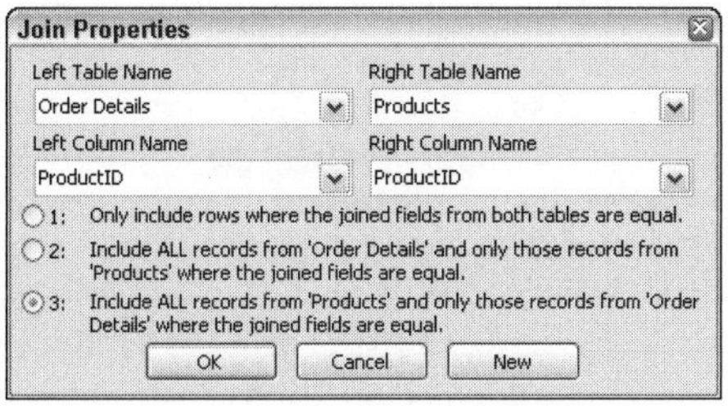

Figure 1-16: The Join Properties dialog box.

The Join Properties dialog box options are largely self-explanatory, but using the dialog box effectively requires certain foreknowledge of a few buzzwords used to describe particular types of relationships — buzzwords which don't appear in the dialog box. The buzzwords, *inner join*, *left outer join*, *right outer join* are included in the descriptions of the following three options:

✦ **Option # 1** (Inner join): A query displaying records from both tables displays only those records that have counterparts in the related table. Records that don't have matching partners in the opposite table are hidden, as though they didn't even exist. This is the default, meaning that if you don't set a join type, this is what you get.

✦ **Option # 2** (Left outer join): A query displaying records from both tables displays all records from the table on the left. From the table on the right, only records that have matching partners from the table on the left display.

✦ **Option # 3** (Right outer join): A query displaying records from both tables displays all records from the table on the right. From the table on the left, only records that have matching partners from the table on the right display.

The line that connects two tables in the Relationships view (and in Design view as well) reflects information about how the tables are joined, as shown in Figure 1-17. The arrow points to the table that contributes matching records — all records from the other table display in the query datasheet.

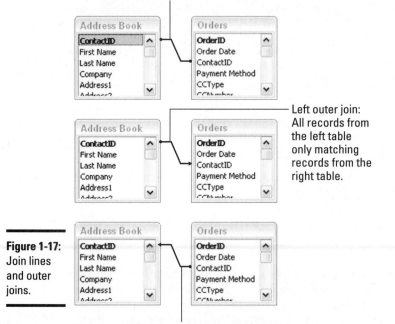

Inner join: Only matching records from both tables

Left outer join: All records from the left table only matching records from the right table.

Figure 1-17: Join lines and outer joins.

Right outer join: All records from the right table only matching records from the left table.

When would you use an outer join? If you create a sales report and want to see products that have not sold at all, you want an outer join that showed all the products from the Products table, regardless of whether or not they appeared in the Order Details table.

If you create a query with fields from two tables that don't have a relationship defined, Access doesn't know how to relate records, so every combination of records between the two tables displays. Generally these queries are not meaningful.

Working with Query Datasheets

A query datasheet (shown in Figure 1-18) looks a great deal like a table datasheet — you can sort, filter, navigate, and in some circumstances, enter data in the query datasheet. The data displayed in the query datasheet is sometimes referred to as a *dynaset*. Dynaset is used because the data that you see in the datasheet is a dynamic subset of your data.

The query result reflects changes in the data in your tables. The actual records displayed in a dynaset aren't stored in the database; only the design of the query is stored, and each time you open the query in Datasheet view, the query definition determines which records displays.

Because working with queries in Datasheet view is similar to working with tables in Datasheet view, turn to Book II for specific instructions on working in the Datasheet view.

To toggle between Datasheet and Design view, click the View button, the first button on the toolbar.

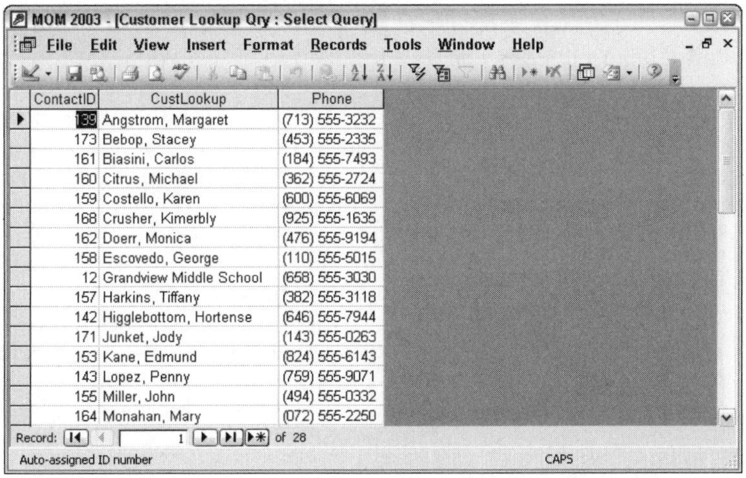

**Book III
Chapter 1**

**Creating Select
Queries**

ContactID	CustLookup	Phone
139	Angstrom, Margaret	(713) 555-3232
173	Bebop, Stacey	(453) 555-2335
161	Biasini, Carlos	(184) 555-7493
160	Citrus, Michael	(362) 555-2724
159	Costello, Karen	(600) 555-6069
168	Crusher, Kimberly	(925) 555-1635
162	Doerr, Monica	(476) 555-9194
158	Escovedo, George	(110) 555-5015
12	Grandview Middle School	(658) 555-3030
157	Harkins, Tiffany	(382) 555-3118
142	Higglebottom, Hortense	(646) 555-7944
171	Junket, Jody	(143) 555-0263
153	Kane, Edmund	(824) 555-6143
143	Lopez, Penny	(759) 555-9071
155	Miller, John	(494) 555-0332
164	Monahan, Mary	(072) 555-2250

MOM 2003 - [Customer Lookup Qry : Select Query]
File Edit View Insert Format Records Tools Window Help

Record: 1 of 28

Auto-assigned ID number   CAPS

Figure 1-18:
A query
datasheet.

Using the query datasheet to edit data

In many cases, you can edit the data in the query datasheet and use the datasheet to add new records. Any changes you make are reflected in the table that holds the data you changed — edits are permanent and apply to the underlying tables and not just to the query.

When your query includes fields from multiple tables you may see some funky things when you edit data — they are all features!

✦ You may see other data in the datasheet change when you make an edit. If your query includes related tables, you may see repeated data, such as the repeated names in Figure 1-15. If you make edits, you see all the repetitions of the name change when you change one instance. Because you are changing a single record repeated in the datasheet, the other instances change to reflect the change in the underlying table. When this happens, you create an AutoLookup query. The next section covers AutoLookup queries.

✦ Access may fill in fields after you enter a single value if your query meets the qualifications of an AutoLookup query.

If you work with a query datasheet that shows data from multiple related tables, you may not be able to modify data. The rules get complicated, but generally all data on the many side of a one-to-many relationship can be updated. Data on the one side usually can be updated if you are not editing the primary key field.

AutoLookup queries to fill in data automagically

AutoLookup queries can be a terrific tool when you want to enter one value (such as a customer number) and see other data from the same table (such as the customer's name, address, and phone number). You may want to use this feature as you enter a new order — you can enter a customer number and see the contact information, and then enter the particulars of the order, such as the date and payment method. AutoLookup queries sound like they're complicated, but in fact they are pretty simple.

The AutoLookup feature also works in forms.

The key to creating an AutoLookup query is that you must include the Join field from the many side of the one-to-many relationship (also known as the foreign key). Then when you enter a value for that field, Access fills in other fields from the one side of the relationship automatically.

For instance, the query in Figure 1-19 displays fields from the Orders and Address Book tables. The ContactID field comes from the Orders table (the key field on the one side, but displayed from the many table).

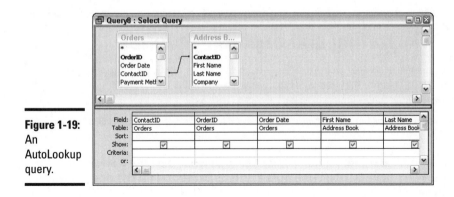

Figure 1-19:
An
AutoLookup
query.

When new orders are entered into the query datasheet, only the customer number needs to be entered — Access automatically fills in the first name, the last name, and other contact information from the Address Book table. The rest of the Order information can then be added.

Saving Queries

A query doesn't store data — it just pulls data out of tables for you to look at. A query is *dynamic* — as you add to or change your data, the result of the query also changes. When you save your query, you're not saving the table that the query produces — you're just saving the query design so that you can ask the same question again.

You don't have to save a query. Often, you create queries on the fly to answer a question. You don't need to clutter your database with queries that you're unlikely to need again.

That said, you can certainly save a query design when you need to. Use any of the following methods:

✦ **In Design or Datasheet view, click the Save button or choose File➪Save.** If you haven't saved the query yet, Access asks you for a name for the query. Type the name in the Save As dialog box and then click OK.

✦ **Close the query (clicking the Close button is a popular method).** If you've never saved the query, or if you've changed the query design since you last saved it, Access asks whether you want to save the query. Click the Yes button to save the query. If you've never saved the query, give it a name in the Save As dialog box and click OK.

Importing and exporting queries

If the query you need is in another Access database or if you create a query that you want to use in another database, simply import or export it. Information on importing and exporting objects is in Book II, Chapter 4.

Give your new query a name that tells you what the query does. That way, you won't have to open one query after another to find the one you're looking for.

If you want to create a query similar to one you already have in your database, select or open the query and choose File⇨Save As to save the query with a new name. You keep the original query and make changes to the new copy.

If you want to save the query dynaset, create a snapshot query with the data (covered in Book V, Chapter 2) or export the data to its own file using File⇨Export — either an Access table, an Excel spreadsheet, a Word document, or some other file. For more about exporting data, see Book II, Chapter 4.

Chapter 2: Letting Queries Do the Math

In This Chapter

- ✔ Doing calculations in queries
- ✔ Writing expressions for math
- ✔ Beyond basic arithmetic
- ✔ Calculating dates and times
- ✔ Manipulating text with expressions
- ✔ Writing decision-making expressions
- ✔ Creating flexible parameter queries
- ✔ Totals, subtotals, averages, and such
- ✔ Finding duplicate records

If you ever find yourself doing math to figure out what to put into a field, you made a mistake when designing your table. A table needs only the raw data — the factual information that cannot be calculated from known data. For example, a table may contain Qty and Unit Price fields to indicate how may items — and at what price — some product was ordered. But having an Extended Price or Subtotal field in the table is pointless, because Access is smart enough to determine that on its own by multiplying the Qty field by the Unit Price field for you.

Letting Access do the math for you has advantages beyond just saving you the time of doing the calculation yourself. For one thing, Access can do any mathematical calculation, no matter how complex, in less time than you take to blink your eye. Furthermore, the calculations are always correct. No need to worry about typing a wrong value into an Extended Price field, or forgetting to change the field after you change the Qty or Unit Price fields. Just let Access do all the math.

Doing Math in Queries

Access can do the math for you in queries, forms, reports, and macros. In many cases, doing the math in a query is easier than in a form, report, or macro, because that way any forms, reports, or macros that use the query automatically have access to the calculated value. To do the math in a query, you create a *calculated field* within the query. Unlike a regular field in a query, a calculated field's name does not match any of the field names in the tables. In fact, its value doesn't come directly from any field in any table. The calculated field exists only in the query.

A calculated field starts out with a field name followed by a colon and then an expression that defines the field's contents, in this order:

```
fieldname:expression
```

where *fieldname* is any name you want (provided it doesn't match the name of a field in a table) and *expression* is a formula that tells the query how to do the math.

Take a look at Figure 2-1, which shows a query in Design view. The first four field names at the top of the Query by Example grid — Order ID, Product Name, Qty, and Unit Price, are regular fields that get their values from either the Order Details or Products table in the top pane of the Design View window. The last field:

```
ExtPrice: [Qty] * [Unit Price]
```

is a calculated field. The field name is ExtPrice (short for "extended price"). The expression is [Qty] * [Unit Price], which means "The Qty (quantity field) times the Unit Price field."

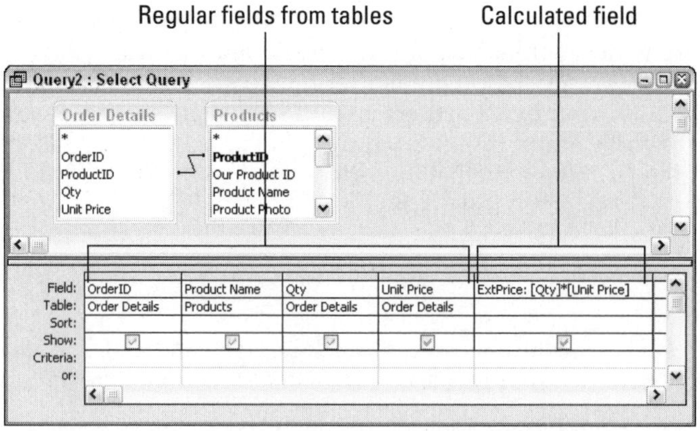

Regular fields from tables   Calculated field

Figure 2-1: The ExtPrice column is an example of a calculated field in a query.

Figure 2-2 shows the same query as Figure 2-1, but in Datasheet view. Notice two things about the Datasheet view:

✦ The ExtPrice field looks just like any other field.

✦ The value shown in the ExtPrice column is equal to the value of the Qty field times the Unit Price field in each column.

Figure 2-2:
The query from Figure 2-1 in Datasheet view.

OrderID	Product Name	Qty	Unit Price	ExtPrice
1	Golden Whistle	1	$100.00	$100.00
2	Golden Whistle	5	$100.00	$500.00
4	Golden Whistle	2	$100.00	$200.00
1	Kozmik Video Camera	3	$1,000.00	$3,000.00
3	Lawn Flamingo	1	$29.99	$29.99
3	Lucky Rabbits Foot	21	$7.99	$167.79

Record: 7 of 7

Even though the ExtPrice column in Datasheet view looks like a regular field, it doesn't behave exactly like a regular field. If you try to change the contents of the ExtPrice field, Access won't let you. The contents of the ExtPrice field in this query *always* show the quantity times the unit price, and cannot possibly show anything else, because it's a calculated field.

However, if you change the Qty or Unit Price field in any record, the ExtPrice field instantly — and automatically — changes to show the correct result based on the change you make. If you change the Qty field in the first record in Figure 2-1 from 1 to 2, the ExtPrice field for that record then shows $200.00.

Follow these steps to create calculated fields in queries:

1. **Create a normal select query, like any of those shown in Chapter 1 of this book.**

2. **Add any fields you want the query to display to the Field row of the QBE grid.**

3. **To add a calculated field, pick any empty column, type a unique field name into the Field row, followed by a colon (:) and an expression that performs the calculation — just like the ExtPrice calculated field shown in Figure 2-1.**

Your query can contain any number of calculated fields — you're not limited to having just one or two. The big trick, of course, is knowing how to write the expression. When writing expressions, the possibilities are almost endless. But some basic tools and rules exist to help you create any expression, as we discuss next.

**Book III
Chapter 2**

**Letting Queries
Do the Math**

Writing Expressions in Access

An *expression* tells Access how to perform some calculation. An expression can contain operators, field names, literal text, and may also use any of the Access built-in functions. Built-in functions can be mind-boggling, but if you take them one step at a time, you'll soon create them like a pro.

Literal text, in Access jargon, means text that isn't the name of some field or other object. Whereas LastName may be the name of a field in a table, "Smith," "Jones," and "123 Oak Tree Lane" are all examples of literal text.

Using operators in expressions

An *operator* is a character that operates on data. Some of the more commonly used operators are listed in Table 2-1. The operators are listed in *order of precedence,* meaning the order in which calculations are carried out when an expression contains two or more operators.

Table 2-1	Operators in Order of Precedence	
Operator	*Purpose*	*Example*
( )	Grouping	(2+2)*5 returns 20
^	Exponentiation	5^2 returns 25
* /	Multiplication, Division	5*6/3 returns 10
+ −	Addition, Subtraction	6+6-2 returns 10
&	String concatenation (connect chunks of text together)	"Hello" & "There" returns HelloThere

The order or precedence that operators follow can be a real "gotcha" if you're not careful. Take a look at the following simple expression that includes an addition operator (+) and a multiplication operator (*):

```
5+3*2
```

When you do the math, do you get 16, or do you get 11? If you do the addition first (5+3 equals 8) and then the multiplication (2 times 8), you end up with 16. But if you do the multiplication first (3*2 equals 6) and then the addition (6 plus 5), you end up with 11. So which is the correct answer, 11 or 16?

Give up? 11 is the correct answer (and the one Access comes up with) because the order of precedence rules state that multiplication and division are always performed before addition or subtraction.

Multiplication and division are at the same order or precedence. If an expression involves both of those operations, they're executed in left-to-right order. In the following expression, the division takes place first, because it's to the left of the multiplication:

```
10/5*3
```

The result of the expression is 6, because 10 divided by 5 is 2, and 2 times 3 equals 6.

Addition and subtraction work the same way. If an expression includes both addition and subtraction, the calculations take place in left-to-right order.

You can control the order of precedence using the parentheses. Access always works from the innermost parentheses to the outermost. The following expression is an example:

```
5^2+((5-1)*3)
```

When faced with this expression, Access goes inside the innermost parentheses first (5-1) and does that calculation. So the expression (for a brief instant in time) becomes:

```
5^2+(4*3)
```

Access next calculates the remaining pair or parentheses in the expression (4*3). For a brief moment the expression becomes:

```
5^2+12
```

Because no more parentheses are left, Access uses the regular order of precedence to do the rest of the calculation. Exponentiation has a higher order of precedence than addition, so for a brief instant the expression becomes:

```
25+12
```

Access then does the final math and returns the result, 37.

For the real math heads out there, two more operators have the same order of precedence as multiplication and division. One is the \ operator, which returns only the integer portion of a quotient, and the other is MOD, which returns only the remainder after division. For example, while 16/3 (normal division) returns 5.3333, 16\3 returns 5 and 16 MOD 3 returns 1.

Field names in expressions

If you're thinking "Big deal, I could have done those preceding calculations on my $2.00 calculator," that's certainly true. But Access expressions aren't limited to numbers and operators. You can use field names in expressions to perform math on data stored in fields. The sample query shown at the start of this chapter uses the field names [Qty] * [Unit Price] to multiply the value in the Unit Price field by the value in the Qty field.

Technically, you only need to enclose field names in square brackets when the field name contains a blank space, as in [Unit Price]. But you can put square brackets around any field name just in case. For the sake of consistency, and to make field names in expressions stand out, we always put them in square brackets throughout this book.

The sample expression shown in the first query at the start of this chapter, [Qty]*[Unit Price], is a prime example of using field names in expressions. The expression, in English, simply means "the contents of the Qty field in this record times the contents of the Unit Price field in this same record."

Using functions in expressions

Wait, there's more. An Access expression can also contain any number of functions. A *function* is sort of like an operator in that it performs some calculation and then *returns* some value. But the way you use a function is different. Every function includes a name followed by a pair of parentheses. For example, the Date() function always returns the current date.

Many functions accept *arguments,* which are enclosed within the parentheses. To calculate the square root of a number, you use a Sqr() function. The Sqr() function accepts one parameter — a number, the name of a field, or an expression that contains a number. The Sqr() function returns the square root of whatever value passes to it as an argument.

As an example, the following expression returns 9, because the square root of 81 is 9 (because 9 times 9 is 81). In this example, we use a number as the argument to the Sqr() function:

```
Sqr(81)
```

Note that in the example, we use 81 as the argument to the Sqr() function. Another way to state that is to say we *pass* the number 81 to the argument. In other words, the term *pass* in this context means to use as an argument in a function.

The following Sqr() function uses an expression, 5*20, as its argument:

```
Sqr(5*20)
```

Because the expression, 5*20, is inside the parentheses, the multiplication happens first. For a brief instant, the function contains Sqr(100). Then Sqr(100) returns 10, because 10 is the square root of 100.

You can use field names in functions as well. Suppose you have a table that contains a number field named bigNumber. The following Sqr() function returns the square root of whatever value is stored in the bigNumber field:

```
Sqr([bigNumber])
```

Dozens of functions are built into Access. In fact, memorizing all of the functions is nearly impossible. We recommend looking up functions as you need them, using the Expression Builder as your guide. What's the Expression Builder? Read on and find out.

Using the Expression Builder

The *Expression Builder* is a tool to help you write meaningful expressions using any combination of operators, field names, and functions. To use the Expression Builder while creating a calculated field in a query, do the following:

1. **If you haven't saved the current query yet, do so now to name it (choose File⇨Save from the main menu, type in a name for your query in the Save As dialog box, and click OK).**

2. **Type a new field name, followed by a colon (:) in the Field row of an empty column in the QBE grid.**

   The Query by Example grid, also known as the QBE grid, is in the bottom pane of the Design View window. For more on the QBE grid (and its lovely home, the Design View window), see Chapter 1 of this book.

3. **Right-click the empty space to the right of the colon you just typed and choose the Build option from the shortcut menu or click the Build button on the toolbar.**

   The Expression Builder opens, looking like Figure 2-3. Any text you already typed into the QBE grid is already in the Expression Builder.

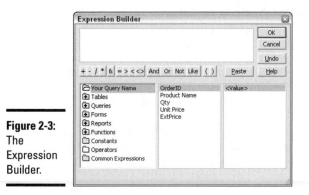

Figure 2-3:
The
Expression
Builder.

Within the Expression Builder, the large white area at the top is where you compose your expression, as shown in Figure 2-4. You can type and edit in that large area using the keyboard and all the standard Windows editing techniques. Or use the buttons and folders below the white area to build an expression without typing.

Not everything in the Expression Builder is geared toward creating expressions for queries. Some features of the Expression Builder are better suited to creating expressions in forms and reports. When you're working with a query, the main things you want to focus on are the following:

✦ **Operator buttons:** Click any of these buttons to insert an operator into your expression.

✦ **Query name:** Shows the name of the query that's currently open (not "Your Query Name"). When you click your query name, fields from that query appear in the center column. Clicking a field name in that center column adds the name to the expression.

> If you don't save the query before opening the Expression Builder, clicking the Query Name folder in the Expression Builder won't display anything!

✦ **Built-In Functions folder:** If you double-click the + sign next to the Functions folder, a couple of options appear. Click the Built-In Functions folder to see categories and names of available functions in the center column. Click a category name in the middle column to see in the right column names of functions within that category.

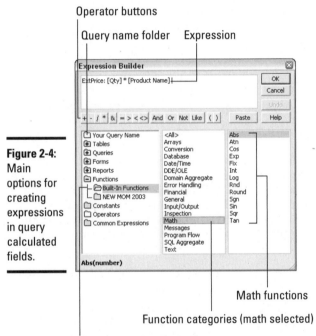

Operator buttons

Query name folder   Expression

Figure 2-4: Main options for creating expressions in query calculated fields.

Math functions

Function categories (math selected)

Built-In functions (selected)

Whatever you insert into your expression is inserted at the blinking cursor's position or at the end of whatever text is currently in the expression if no blinking cursor is visible. If you need to move the cursor before inserting something into an expression, just click at the spot where you want to position the cursor. You can also use the ←, →, Home, or End keys to position the cursor. Use the Backspace and Delete (Del) keys to delete text in the expression. To undo your most recent change to an expression, click the Undo button in the Expression Builder or press Ctrl+Z.

Getting help with functions

Just seeing the name of a built-in function in the third column of the expression builder doesn't tell you much. You don't know what the function does or how you use it. But you can get instant information by using the Help button. Follow these steps to access a Help window:

1. **In the left column of the Expression Builder, if the Functions folder has a + sign next to it, first click that + sign to expand the list.**

2. **Click the Built-In Functions folder in the first column.**

The category names appear in the center column.

3. **Click a category name in the middle column to see functions within that category listed in the third column. Or click on <All> in the middle column to see all functions in the third column.**

The functions for that category appear in the third column.

4. **In the third column, click the name of the function you want to find out more about.**

5. **Click the Help button on the top-right side of the Expression Builder.**

The Help window for that function opens.

In Figure 2-5, we selected the Financial category of functions in the center column, clicked the PV function in the third column, and then clicked the Help button. The Help page that opens not only describes what the PV function does, it also describes the syntax required for using the function. The *syntax* of a function describes what information you need to pass (provide) to the function in order for the function to do its calculation and return a result.

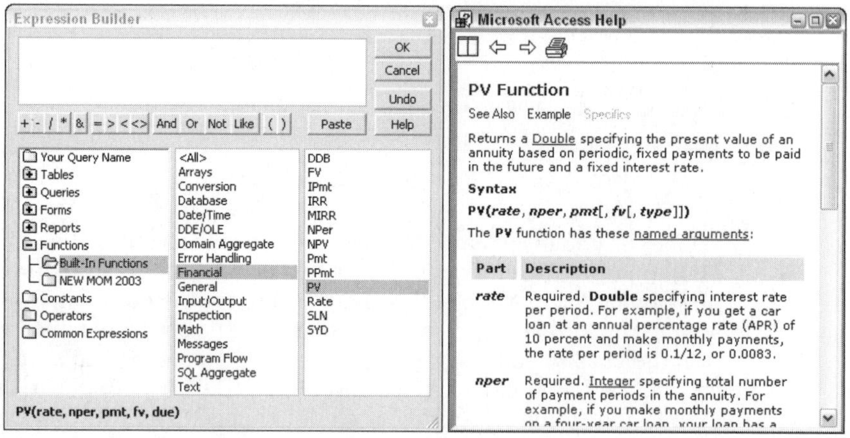

Figure 2-5:
Expression Builder and Help for the PV financial function.

The syntax for a function usually looks something like the following:

```
functionName(arg1, arg2, [arg3])
```

where *functionName* is the name of the function, and *arg1*, *arg2*, and *arg3* represent arguments the function accepts. The number of arguments a function accepts varies. Some functions take no arguments, some take many. If a function accepts two or more arguments, they must be separated by a comma.

Any argument name in square brackets is optional, meaning you can omit the entire argument if you wish. Whether you use an optional argument or not, you never type the square brackets into the function.

A function name is always followed by parentheses — even if the function accepts no arguments. `Now()`, `Sqr(81)`, and `PV(apr, TotPmts, Income)` are all examples of valid function syntax. Note as well that when typing an argument, you can use a literal value (like the name "Smith" or the number 10), a field name, or an expression as an argument. The following three expressions all pass literal values to their functions:

```
Sqr(100)
PV(.035,120,250)
UCase("howdy")
```

The next three expressions all pass data from fields to the function (provided that Hypot, Apr, Months, Amount, and Company are the names of fields in the current query):

```
Sqr([Hypot])
PV([Apr],[Months],[Amount])
UCase([Company])
```

In the next examples, we use expressions as arguments:

```
Sqr(227 * [Hypot])
PV([Apr]/12,[Months]*12,-1*[Amount])
UCase([First Name] & " " & [Last Name])
```

We know these examples look weird, but we do have a reason for the madness. The ability to pass literal data, field names, and/or expressions to functions gives you a lot of flexibility.

About text in < and > brackets

When you use the buttons in the lower half of the Expression Builder to insert text into your expression, that text often includes *placeholders* — text in angle brackets (< >). You may see placeholders, such as *<expr>*, *<interval>*, *<npers>*, or something equally bizarre in the Expression Builder. Each of these brackety things is a placeholder for an argument that you need to type in.

If a placeholder represents an optional argument and you don't plan to use that argument, then you can just delete the placeholder. But if the placeholder represents a required argument, then you need to replace the placeholder with valid data. Using the Help feature often when working with functions is very important. We doubt that anybody has ever managed to memorize all the functions because of the sheer number, all supporting so many different arguments.

Nesting functions

You can nest functions, meaning you can put a function inside another function. Because Access always works from the innermost parentheses outward, the inside function is always calculated first. For example, the `Date()` function always returns the current date. (It requires no arguments.) The `WeekDay()` function accepts any date as an argument, meaning its syntax looks like the following:

```
WeekDay(date)
```

Because the `Date()` function always returns a date, you can use it as the argument to the `WeekDay()` function. The expression turns out to be

```
WeekDay(Date())
```

A number between 1 and 7 returns, indicating which day of the week today is. If the current date is the 23rd, for example, and that day is a Tuesday, the `WeekDay()` function returns the number 3. (Day 1 is Sunday, 2 is Monday, and so forth).

Going Beyond Basic Arithmetic

Near the start of this chapter, we talked about how you can use the +, −, *, and / operators in expressions to perform simple arithmetic. As some of you know, not all math is quite that simple. Some calculations require more than addition, subtraction, multiplication, and division.

Access offers many mathematical and financial functions to help with more complex math. These functions all operate on numbers. For example, the math functions include Cos() (cosine), Tan() (tangent), and Atn() (arctangent), in case you need to do a little trigonometry in your queries. The financial functions include things such as IRR() (internal rate of return), Fv() (future value), Ddb() (double-declining balance depreciation). You're unlikely to need financial functions unless your work specifically requires those sorts of calculations. Rather than list all of the functions that allow you to do complex math, Table 2-2 lists a few examples to give you a sense of how they work.

Table 2-2	Examples of Built-In Math and Financial Functions	
Function and Syntax	*Returns*	*Example*
Abs(*number*)	Absolute value (negative numbers convert to positive numbers)	Abs(-1) returns **1**
Int(*number*)	Integer portion of a number	Int(99.9) returns **99**
Round(*number* [,*decimals*])	*Number* rounded to specified *decimals*	Round(1.56789,2) returns **1.57**
Pmt(*rate*, *nper*, *pv*[, *fv*[, *type*]])	Payment on a loan or annuity	Pmt(.058/12, 30*12, -50000) returns **293.3765** (payment on a $50,000 30-year loan at 5.8%)

If you need help with any function in the Expression Builder, just click the function name in the third column and then click the Help button. The Help window provides you with all the gory details you need to make the function work for you.

Formatting numbers in queries

When you create a table and define a field as the Number data type, you can choose a format, such as Currency, for displaying that number. In a query, you don't predefine a field's data type. The number that appears as the result of a calculation is often just displayed as a *General number* — no dollar sign, no fixed number of decimal places.

Figure 2-6 shows a query based on a hypothetical table named Loan Scenarios. Within the Loan Scenarios table, the APR (annual percentage rate) is a Number field with its Format property set to Percent. The LoanAmount field is a Number field with its Format property set to Currency. Those formats carry over in the results of the query (the query's Datasheet view). But the calculated MonthlyPayment field's result displays as a General number with no currency sign, no commas, and a lot of numbers to the right of the decimal point, as you see in the lower half of Figure 2-6.

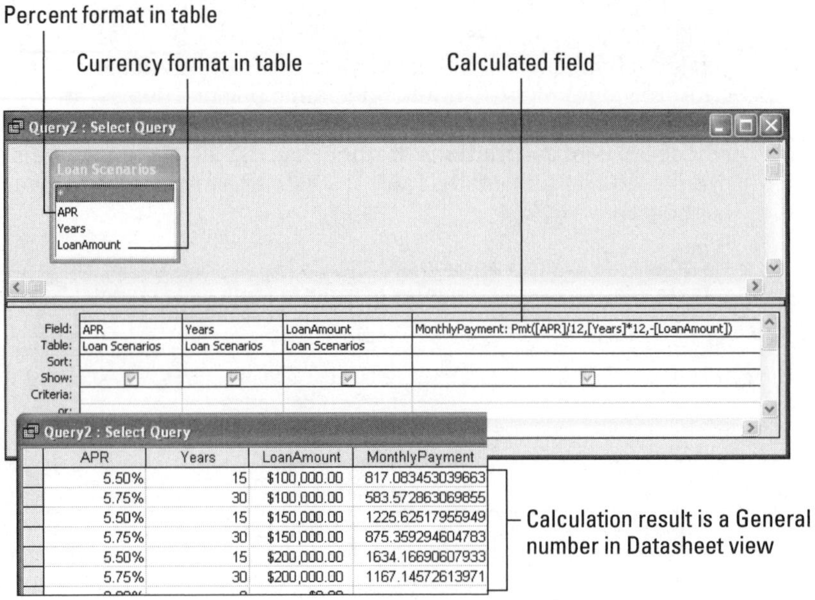
Percent format in table
Currency format in table
Calculated field
Query2 : Select Query
Loan Scenarios
APR
Years
LoanAmount
Field: APR | Years | LoanAmount | MonthlyPayment: Pmt([APR]/12,[Years]*12,-[LoanAmount])
Table: Loan Scenarios | Loan Scenarios | Loan Scenarios
Sort:
Show:
Criteria:
Query2 : Select Query
APR | Years | LoanAmount | MonthlyPayment
5.50% | 15 | $100,000.00 | 817.083453039663
5.75% | 30 | $100,000.00 | 583.572863069855
5.50% | 15 | $150,000.00 | 1225.62517955949
5.75% | 30 | $150,000.00 | 875.359294604783
5.50% | 15 | $200,000.00 | 1634.16690607933
5.75% | 30 | $200,000.00 | 1167.14572613971
Calculation result is a General number in Datasheet view

Figure 2-6: Calculated fields often display as General numbers.

You can format a calculated field so the result appears in `Currency` format in a couple ways. If you intend to build any forms or reports based on this query, you can just save the query and forget about formatting the field. Later, when designing a form or report based on the query, you just create a control for the calculated field as you do any other field in the query. Then set that control's `Format` property to the `Currency` format in the form or report. The data looks the way you want in the form or report, and you don't have to mess around with the query at all.

See Book IV, Chapter 1 for the goods on creating forms and reports. See the section on setting control properties in Book IV, Chapter 2 for the specifics on formatting controls.

Optionally, if you have no intention of creating any forms or reports based on the query, then you can use one of the conversion functions to format the data. The conversion functions are listed in Table 2-3. They're all accessible via the Conversion category of the Built-In Functions folder in the Expression Builder. As usual, you can click a conversion function name in the third column of the Expression Builder, and then click the Help button for more information on the function.

Table 2-3	Main Built-In Conversion Functions	
Function	*Acceptable Expression Type*	*Return Type*
CBool(*expression*)	String or number	Boolean
CByte(*expression*)	Number from 0 to 255	Byte
CCur(*expression*)	Number	Currency
CDate(*expression*)	Date/Time	Date
CDbl(*expression*)	Number	Double
CDec(*expression*)	Number	Decimal
CInt(*expression*)	Whole number from -32,768 to 32,767	Integer
CLng(*expression*)	Whole Number	Long
CSng(*expression*)	Number	Single
CStr(*expression*)	Any	String
CVar(expression)	Any	Variant

Think of the starting letter C in each conversion function's name as standing for "Convert to." For example, CCur means "Convert to Currency."

Be careful when you use a conversion function because you're defining the data type, as well as the appearance, of the calculated field. Setting the format of a calculated field in a form or report, rather than directly in the query, is often easier.

The big trick is to enclose the entire expression (everything to the right of the field name and colon) within the conversion function's paren-theses in the QBE grid. For example, to display the MonthlyPayment field from the sample Loan Scenarios query as Currency data, the entire expression must be contained within the CCur() parentheses as the following expression:

```
MonthlyPayment: CCur( Pmt([APR]/12,[Years]*12,-[LoanAmount]) )
```

Figure 2-7 shows the results of using CCur() in the MonthlyPayment calculated control to display the results of the expression in Currency format.

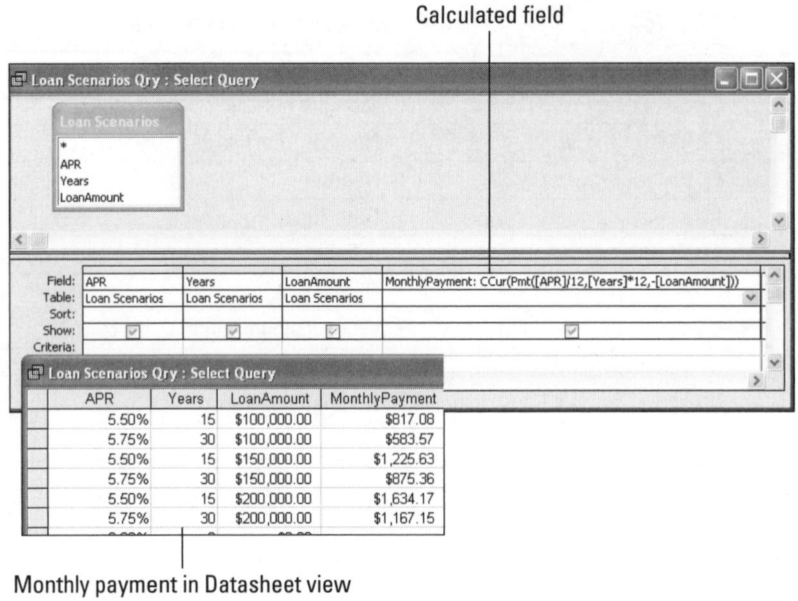

Calculated field

Figure 2-7:
Monthly
Payment
calculations
shown in
Currency
format.

Monthly payment in Datasheet view

Avoiding problems with null values

Sometimes a field in a record may be empty because nobody ever typed any
information into that field. The official name used to describe the value of an
empty field is *null*. If a field contains nothing, we say it contains a null value.

What's with the 12s in the expression?

In case you're wondering why the sample expression contains things like /12, *12 and such, it all has to do with the way the Pmt() function works. The APR value is the *annual* percentage rate, and the term of the loan is expressed in *years*. When you want the Pmt() function to return a *monthly* payment, you need to divide the annual percentage rate by 12 ([APR]/12). You also need to multiply the number of years by 12 to get the number of monthly payments ([Years]*12).

Normally, Pmt() returns a negative number as the result, because each payment is a debit (expense). By placing a minus sign in front of the LoanAmount field name (that is, -[LoanAmount]), we convert that to a negative number (a debit), which in turn makes the calculated monthly payment into a credit (a positive number).

Mathematical calculations don't automatically treat a null value as being the same thing as 0 (zero). If any field that's used in a calculated field contains a null, then the expression itself also returns null. In Figure 2-8, the SubTotal calculated field multiplies the contents of the HowMany field by the Price field. In the query results, shown at the bottom of Figure 2-8, any field that has a null in the HowMany or Price field ends up with a null value in the SubTotal field as well.

Calculated field

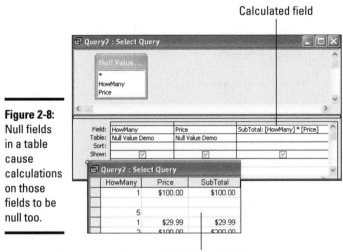

Figure 2-8:
Null fields
in a table
cause
calculations
on those
fields to be
null too.

Null calculated result

Use the Nz() function to convert a null to a zero. What Nz() really means is "if this field contains a null, then make that into a zero, and do the math using that zero." To use the Nz() function, put the entire field name within the function's parentheses. In Figure 2-9, the modified calculated field uses the following expression:

```
SubTotal: Nz( [HowMany] ) * Nz( [Price] )
```

In the Datasheet view of that same query, shown at the bottom of Figure 2-9, records that contain a null HowMany or Price field yield a zero result, rather than null, in the SubTotal field. That's because the modified calculated control tells Access to use a zero, rather than nothing (a null) to do the math when a field is null.

If you want the third column in Figure 2-9 to show results in Currency format ($100.00, $0.00, $0.00, and so forth), enclose the entire expression in a CCur() function, such as SubTotal: CCur(Nz([HowMany]) * Nz([Price])).

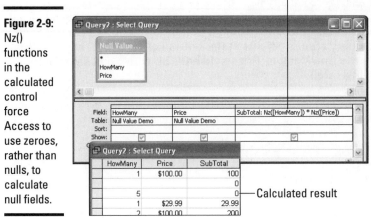

Figure 2-9:
Nz()
functions
in the
calculated
control
force
Access to
use zeroes,
rather than
nulls, to
calculate
null fields.

Modified calculated field

Calculated result

You can also use the IsNull() function to test for a null field. See the section "Testing for empty fields," later in this chapter, for more information.

Date and Time Calculations

The built-in Date and Time functions operate on data stored in Date/Time fields. You can perform some basic calculations, called date arithmetic calculations, on dates using simple + (addition) and – (subtraction) operators. Date arithmetic calculations follow a couple of simple rules:

✦ **If you subtract two dates, you get a number indicating the number of days between those dates.** For example, 1/15/2004 - 1/1/2004 returns 14, because there are 14 days between January 15 and January 1.

✦ **If you add a number to, or subtract a number from, a date, you get a new date, rather than a number.** That new date is the date that's *n* number of days away from the original date (where *n* stands for the number of days you add or subtract). For example, 1/1/2004 + 30 returns 1/31/2004 because January 31 is 30 days after January 1. The result of 12/31/2000-999 is 4/7/1998, because April 7, 1998 is 999 days before 12/31/2000.

Figure 2-10 shows a sample query that uses some basic arithmetic in query calculated fields. In the underlying table, the StartDate and EndDate fields are each defined as the Date/Time data type (with the Short Date format). The first calculated field is the following expression:

```
DaysBetween: [EndDate] - [StartDate]
```

and calculates and displays the number of days between the StartDate value and the EndDate value in each record. The ExtendedDate calculated field

```
ExtendedDate: [EndDate] + 15
```

adds 15 days to whatever date is stored in the EndDate field. The lower half of Figure 2-10 shows the query results in Datasheet view. The DaysBetween column shows the number of days between the StartDate value and the EndDate value. The ExtendedDate column shows the date 15 days after the EndDate value, as specified by the expression in the calculated fields.

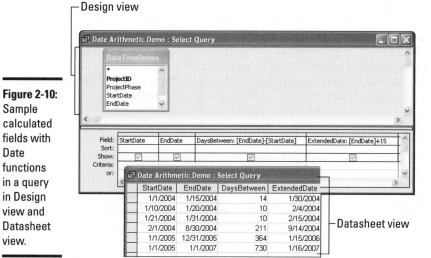

Figure 2-10:
Sample calculated fields with Date functions in a query in Design view and Datasheet view.

Using literal dates and times in expressions

When writing expressions that include dates, you can use a literal date, as opposed to the name of a field that contains a Date/Time value. A literal date is one that isn't stored in some field — it's just a specific date you want to use in the expression. But you can't just type in the date using an everyday format like 12/31/2005, because Access interprets that as "twelve divided by 31, divided by 2005." And you can't use quotation marks, because those are used to define literal text. Instead, you have to use the awkward # character to *delimit* (surround) a literal date.

For example, #01/01/2005# is literally the date January 1, 2005. The expression #01/01/2005# + 14 returns 1/15/2005, the date that's 14 days after January 1, 2005. The expression #3/31/2005# - #1/1/2005# returns 89, because March 31, 2005 is 89 days after January 1, 2005.

To express a literal time, use colons (:) to separate the hours, minutes, and seconds between the # delimiters. You can also tack on a blank space followed by AM or PM. For example, #7:30:00# is literally 7:30 AM, as is #7:30:00 AM#. The literal time #7:30:00 PM# refers to 7:30 at night. You can use military time as well: The literal time #19:30:00# is also 7:30 PM.

Using the Date/Time functions

You're not limited to basic date arithmetic in Access. Quite a few built-in Date/Time functions exist in Access that you can use to manipulate dates and times in other ways. Like all built-in functions, you can find the Date/Time functions in the Expression Builder. Again, if the Functions folder in the left column has a + sign next to it, click that + sign to expand the list. Then click on the Built-In Functions subfolder in the left column, and the Date/Time category in the center column. Then click any function's name from the right column and click the Help button for details on the function.

We spare you the details of every available Date/Time function. Chances are, you may never need to use the more obscure functions. Table 2-4 lists some of the more commonly used Date/Time functions and provides examples of their use.

Table 2-4	Examples of Access Date/Time Functions	
Function and Syntax	*Returns*	*Example*
Date()	The current date	Returns the current date, according to your computer's clock
Time()	The current time	Returns the current time, according to your computer's clock
Now()	The current date and time	Returns the current date and time, according to your computer's clock
CDate(*expression*)	Converts *expression*, which can be any string that looks like a date, to an actual Date/Time value	CDate("Mar 31, 2004) returns 3/31/2004
DateAdd(*interval, number, date*)	The date that is *number* of days, weeks, months (*interval*) from *date*	DateAdd("m",14, #1/1/2004#) returns 3/1/2005, the date that's 14 months after January 1, 2004

Function and Syntax	Returns	Example
`DateDiff(interval, date1, date2[, firstdayofweek[, firstweekofyear]])`	The number of hours, days, weeks, (*interval*) between two dates	`DateDiff("w", #1/1/2004#, #1/1/2005#)` returns 52 because there are 52 weeks between the two dates
`Day(date)`	The day of the month expressed as a number between 1 and 31	`Day(#1/15/2004#)` returns 15 because 1/15/2004 falls on the 15th day of the month
`Hour(time)`	The hour of a time	`Hour(Now())` returns a number representing the current hour of the day
`MonthName (monthNumber[, abbreviate])`	The month of a date, spelled out (if *abbreviate* is false) or abbreviated (if *abbreviate* is true)	`MonthName(12,False)` returns December, `MonthName(12,True)` returns Dec (because December is the 12th month of the year)

As you can see in Table 2-4, the `DateAdd()` and `DateDiff()` functions allow you to specify an *interval* argument. That argument defines the time interval used for the calculation.

For example, if you just use plain date arithmetic to subtract two dates, the difference between the dates automatically displays as the number of *days* between those dates. Using the `DateAdd()` or `DateDiff()` function, you can change that so that the difference between the dates is expressed in seconds, minutes, hours, weeks, months, or years, depending on which provides the accuracy you need.

To specify a time interval argument in a `DateAdd()` or `DateDiff()` function, you use one of the settings (enclosed in quotation marks) listed in the left column of Table 2-5.

Table 2-5	Settings for the *Interval* Argument in Date/Time Functions that Require an Interval
Setting	**Description**
"d"	Day
"h"	Hour
"m"	Month
"n"	Minute
"q"	Quarter

(continued)

Table 2-5 (continued)

Setting	Description
"s"	Second
"w"	Weekday
"ww"	Week
"y"	Day of year
"yyyy"	Year

Take a look at an example using an interval in a `DateDiff()` function. Without using the `DateDiff()` function at all, the expression #####2# returns 1, because there is one day between those dates, and "day" is the default interval when subtracting dates. On the other hand, the expression `DateDiff("h",#12/24/2005#,#12/25/2005#)` returns 24, because the "h" interval specifies hours, and there are 24 hours between those two dates.

Manipulating Text with Expressions

You can use the contents of Text fields (also called *strings,* short for "a string of characters") in expressions as well. Only adding, subtracting, multiplying, or dividing with strings doesn't make sense. After all "Smith times Jones" or "Smith divided by Jones" makes no sense at all. However, you can use the ampersand (&) operator to concatenate (join together) strings.

For example, the expression `[First Name] & [Last Name]` joins together the contents of the Last Name and First Name fields. If the Last Name field contains Pines, and the First Name field contains Tori, then the expression `[First Name] & [Last Name]` returns ToriPines.

Adding spaces to text expressions

"But wait," you say, "shouldn't that be Tori Pines with a space in between?" To you and me it should be. But that's not what the expression says. The expression says "stick the First Name value and Last Name value together." The expression doesn't say "and put a space between them." You can easily fix the problem using literal text.

Literal text is any text that doesn't refer to a field name or function or anything else that has special meaning to Access. To use literal text in a calculated field expression, enclose the text in quotation marks. A blank space is a character — a chunk of literal text. So if we re-write the previous example expression like this:

```
[First Name] & " " & [Last Name]
```

The result is Tori Pines with a space in between. The expression says "the contents of the first name field, followed by a blank space, followed by the contents of the Last Name field."

Two quotation marks right next to each other, with no blank space in between, is a zero-length string, which is basically nothing at all. So while [First Name] & " " & [Last Name] returns something like "Tori Pines", the expression [First Name] & "" & [Last Name] returns something like "ToriPines" (the first and last names with nothing in between).

Suppose a table contains City, State, and ZIP fields. The following expression displays the city name followed by a comma and a blank space, followed by the state name followed by two blank spaces, followed by the zip code:

```
[City] & ", " & [State] & "  " & [ZIP]
```

An example of the preceding expression may look something like this:

```
Los Angeles, CA  91234
```

Using the Access Text functions

Access provides several functions for working with text. You find them in the Text category in the middle column of the Expression Builder. We focus on some of the more commonly used functions and show examples of their usage. For information on more Text functions and additional details, use the Help button in the Expression Builder. Table 2-6 lists the more common Text functions.

Book III
Chapter 2

Letting Queries
Do the Math

Table 2-6	Examples of Built-in Text Functions	
Function and Syntax	*Returns*	*Example*
LCase(*string*)	*String* converted to lowercase	LCase("AbCdEfG") returns abcdefg
UCase(*string*)	*String* converted to uppercase	UCase("AbCdEfG") returns ABCDEFG
Left(*string*,*n*)	Leftmost *n* characters of *string*	Left("abcdefg",3) returns abc
Right(*string*,*n*)	Rightmost *n* characters of *string*	Right("abcdefg",2) returns fg
Mid(*string*, *start*[, *length*])	Middle *length* characters of string starting at *start*	Mid("abcmnyz",4,2) returns mn
Len(*string*)	Length of *string*	Len("Howdy") returns 5

(continued)

Table 2-6 *(continued)*

Function and Syntax	Returns	Example
`Trim(string)`	*String* with any leading and trailing spaces trimmed off	`Trim(" abc ")` returns abc
`InStr([start,] string1, string2)`	Position of *string2* in *string1* staring at *start*	`Instr("abcxdef", "x")` returns 4 (because x is the fourth character in *string1*)

Writing Decision-Making Expressions

One of the most useful functions in Access is the immediate if function, `iif()`, which accepts three arguments, as the following shows:

`iif(conditionalExpression, doThis, elseDoThis)`

where:

✦ *conditionalExpression* is an expression that results in a `True` or `False` value.

✦ *doThis* is what the function returns if the *conditionalExpression* proves `True`.

✦ *elseDoThis* is what the function returns if the *conditionalExpression* proves `False`.

The value of the `iif()` function lies in its ability to make a decision about what to return based on the current situation. For example, suppose your business requires charging 7.25% sales tax to New York residents and no sales tax to everyone else. The State field in the underlying table contains the state to which the order is shipped. The following expression says, "If the State field contains NY then return 0.7.25%, otherwise return 0 (zero)":

`iif([State]="NY", 0.0725, 0)`

Note in the preceding expression that 0.0725 is just a way of expressing 7.25% as a regular decimal number (remove the % sign and shift the decimal point two places to the left).

Another example of an `iif()` function is where a Paid field in a table is a Yes/No field. A Yes/No field can only contain either a `True` or `False` value.

The field name alone is a sufficient conditional expression for an `iif()` function, as in the following sample expression:

```
iif([Paid], "Receipt", "Invoice")
```

In English, the expression says, "If the Paid field contains True (or Yes), return the word Receipt. Otherwise (if the Paid field contains False), then return the word Invoice."

Making comparisons in iif()

Access offers several *comparison operators* that you can use to define expressions that result in the True or False values. Buttons for these operators appear alongside the arithmetic operators in the Expression Builder. Table 2-7 describes the Access comparison operators.

Table 2-7	Built-in Comparison Operators	
Comparison Operator	*Name*	*Meaning*
=	Equals	is equal to
>	Greater than	is greater than
>=	Greater or equal	is greater than or equal to
<	Less than	is less than
<=	Less or equal	is less than or equal to
<>	Not equal	is not equal to
Between	Between	is within the range of

An example of an `iif()` function that uses the `>=` comparison operator to make a decision based on the contents of a field named Qty is the following:

```
iif([Qty]>=10, "Discount", "No discount")
```

In English, the expression says, "If the Qty field contains a value greater than or equal to 10, then return Discount. Otherwise, return No Discount."

Combining comparisons

You can use the Access built-in *logical operators* to combine several comparisons into a single expression that results in a True or False value. The logical operators are listed in Table 2-8.

Table 2-8	Built-in Logical Operators
Logical Operator	*Meaning*
And	Both conditions are true
Or	One, or both, conditions are true
Xor	Exclusive "or," one condition, but not both conditions, are true
Not	Not true

As an example, take a look at the following iif() function which uses the And operator:

```
iif([Last Name]="Pines" And [First Name]="Tori","No Charge","Charge")
```

The conditional expression, [Last Name]="Pines" And [First Name]="Tori" says, "If the Last Name field contains Pines AND the First Name field contains Tori." So one condition is that the Last Name field contain Pines. The other condition is that the First Name field contain Tori. If both those conditions are true, the expression returns No Charge. If either one, or both, of those conditions is False, then the expression returns Charge.

Another example using the Or operator is the following expression:

```
iif([State]="NY" Or [State]="NJ", "Tax", "No Tax")
```

In the preceding example, the first condition is that the State field contain NY. The second condition is that the State field contain NJ. The Or operator says that either one (or both) of the conditions must be met for the whole conditional expression to return True. If the State field contains NY or NJ, the expression returns Tax. If the State field contains anything other than NY or NJ, then the expression returns No Tax.

To tax or not to tax?

A practical example of using an iif() function in calculated field expressions is whether to tax. Suppose you have a query like the one in Figure 2-11. Your business requires that you charge 7.25% to all orders shipped within the state of New York. You charge no sales tax on orders shipped outside of New York. The StateProv field in the query contains the state to which the order is shipped.

Obviously, you can't see all the expressions in the query — the QBE grid isn't wide enough to show all that. The following is a quick summary of what each field in the query represents:

✦ **StateProv:** A regular Text field from the underlying Address Book table representing the state to which the order is being shipped.

✦ **Qty:** A regular Number field from the Order Details table representing the quantity of items ordered.

✦ **Unit Price:** A regular Currency field from the Order Details table, representing the unit price of the item ordered.

✦ **ExtPrice:** A calculated field, `ExtPrice:[Qty]*[Unit Price]`, that multiplies the contents of the Qty field by the contents of the Unit Price field.

✦ **Sales Tax Rate:** A calculated field, `SalesTaxRate:iif([StateProv]= "NY",0.0725,0)`, meaning "If the StateProv field contains NY, then put 0.0725 into this field. Otherwise, put zero into this field."

✦ **SalesTaxAmt:** A calculated field, `SalesTaxAmt:CCur ([SalesTaxRate]*[ExtPrice])`, that multiplies the extended price by the sales tax rate. The `CCur()` function makes the result appear in Currency format, rather than as a General number.

✦ **TotalWithTax:** A calculated field, `TotalWithTax: [ExtPrice] + [SalesTaxAmt]`, that adds the extended price to the sales tax amount.

Figure 2-12 shows the results of the query. Records that have NY in the StateProv field show a sales tax rate of 7.25% (0.0725). Records that don't have NY in the StateProv field show 0 (zero) as the sales tax rate. The SalesTaxAmt and TotalWithTax fields show the results of adding sales tax. (Because the SalesTaxRate value is zero outside of NY, those records end up getting no sales tax added to them.)

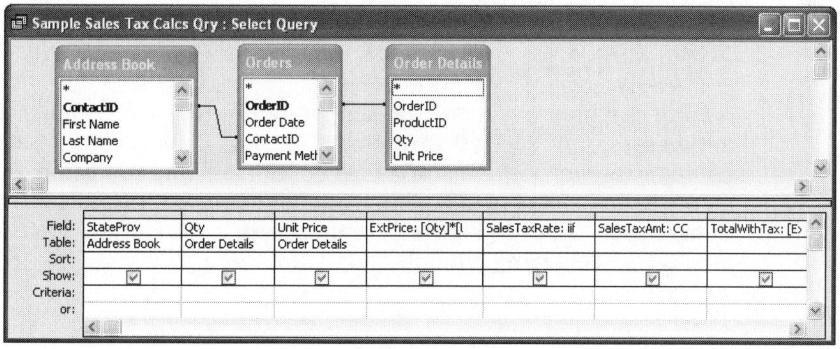

Figure 2-11: Query containing regular and calculated fields (calculated fields are partially hidden).

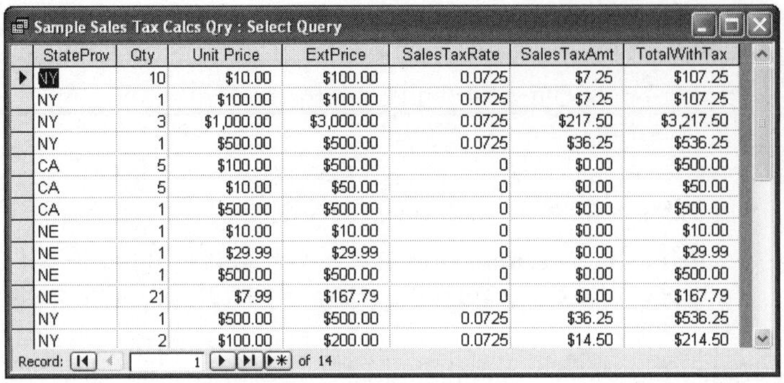

StateProv	Qty	Unit Price	ExtPrice	SalesTaxRate	SalesTaxAmt	TotalWithTax
NY	10	$10.00	$100.00	0.0725	$7.25	$107.25
NY	1	$100.00	$100.00	0.0725	$7.25	$107.25
NY	3	$1,000.00	$3,000.00	0.0725	$217.50	$3,217.50
NY	1	$500.00	$500.00	0.0725	$36.25	$536.25
CA	5	$100.00	$500.00	0	$0.00	$500.00
CA	5	$10.00	$50.00	0	$0.00	$50.00
CA	1	$500.00	$500.00	0	$0.00	$500.00
NE	1	$10.00	$10.00	0	$0.00	$10.00
NE	1	$29.99	$29.99	0	$0.00	$29.99
NE	1	$500.00	$500.00	0	$0.00	$500.00
NE	21	$7.99	$167.79	0	$0.00	$167.79
NY	1	$500.00	$500.00	0.0725	$36.25	$536.25
NY	2	$100.00	$200.00	0.0725	$14.50	$214.50

Figure 2-12: Results (Datasheet view) of the query shown in Figure 2-11.

Testing for empty fields

Sometimes having an expression know if a field is empty, or null, is useful. Access includes an `IsNull()` function that you can use to test if a field is empty. The syntax of the function is pretty straightforward:

```
IsNull[fieldname])
```

where *fieldname* is the name of the field you want to test.

If the specified field is empty, `IsNull()` returns a `True` value. If the specified field isn't empty, then `IsNull()` returns a `False` value. The next section provides an example of using `IsNull()` in an expression.

To treat a null field as a zero in mathematical expressions, use the `Nz()` function described in the section, "Avoiding problems with null values," earlier in this chapter.

Sort by name or company

A fairly common problem comes up in tables that store names and addresses. Some records in such a table may list a person's name, but no company name. Some records may contain a company name, but no person name. If you sort records in such a table by the Last Name, First Name, and Company fields, as in Figure 2-13, the records with empty Last Name and First Name fields are listed first.

Suppose you would prefer to see names listed in alphabetical order by person name or by Company name if there is no person name. In that case, create a calculated field in Design view. You can name this field anything you want, but in Figure 2-14, we named the field "CustLookup". The expression for that field reads:

```
CustLookup: iif(IsNull([Last Name]),[Company],[Last Name] & ", " & [First Name])
```

Sort by Last Name, First Name, Company fields

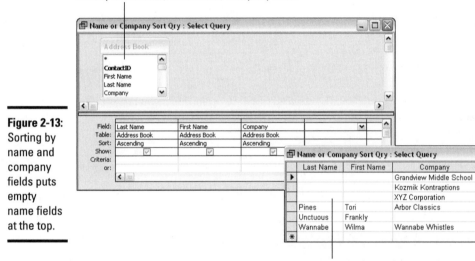

Figure 2-13:
Sorting by name and company fields puts empty name fields at the top.

In query results (Datasheet view), records with null Last Name field are listed first.

The iif() expression says, "If the Last Name field is null, put the Company name in this field. Otherwise, put the person's last name followed by a comma, space, and the person's first name (for example, Pines, Tori) into this field." Setting the Sort row for that calculated field to Ascending order puts records into alphabetical order by last name or company (if there is no last name), as shown in Figure 2-14.

Calculated field

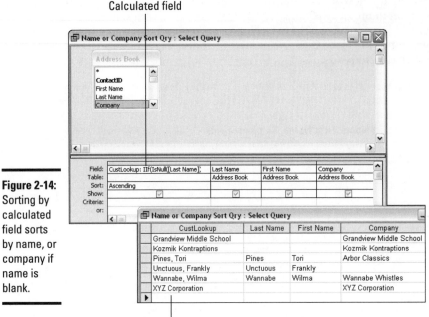

Figure 2-14:
Sorting by
calculated
field sorts
by name, or
company if
name is
blank.

Alphabetized by name or company

Creating Flexible Parameter Queries

A *parameter query* is a query intentionally missing a piece of needed information, so that you can enter the information on the fly when you open the query in Datasheet view. For example, suppose you create a query that shows orders from all records in a table (or tables) from all records in your database. You also like to have queries that show orders from each month.

Rather than create 12 different queries (one for each month), you can create a parameter query that asks for the month number. Then, as soon as you enter a month number, the query shows orders for just the month you specified. In other words, the month number that you're interested in becomes a parameter that you define and pass (provide) to the query just before the query opens.

To create a parameter query, start by creating just a normal select query. You can add tables and field names just as you would any other query. Then, follow these steps to make the query into a parameter query:

1. **In the Design View window, choose Query⇨Parameters from the window's menu.**

   The Query Parameters dialog box appears.

2. **Enter a parameter name and its Data Type in the appropriate columns.**

   The parameter name can be any name you like, so long as it doesn't match the name of a regular field or calculated field already included in the table. The data type matches the type of data that the parameter will ask for, such as Text for text, Currency for a dollar value, or Date/Time for a date or time. You can repeat this step to create as many parameters as you wish.

3. **Click OK to close the Query Parameters dialog box.**

In the QBE grid, you can then treat the parameter name as you do a value from a field. In fact, you enclose the parameter's name in square brackets just like a field name.

In Figure 2-15, we created a Month Number parameter that contains an integer. In the Criteria row for the Order Date field in the QBE grid, we used the parameter name in the following expression, as shown in Figure 2-15. The Criterion tells the query to show only those records where the month of the order date is equal to whatever we type in as the Month Number parameter.

```
Month([Order Date]) = [Month Number]
```

Month Number parameter defined

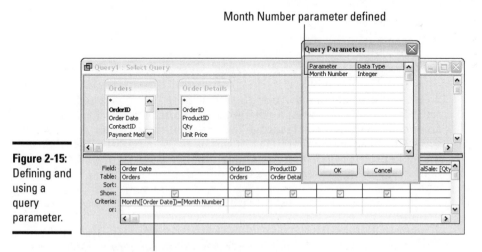

Figure 2-15:
Defining and
using a
query
parameter.

Month Number used in Criterion

After defining your parameter and using it in the QBE grid, you can save the query as you do any other query. The parameter doesn't really come into play until you open the query in Datasheet view. When you do, an Enter Parameter Value dialog box, like the one shown near the top of Figure 2-16, opens on-screen. You type in a value for the parameter and click OK. For the sake of our example, say you type 9 to view September orders only.

When you click the OK button in the Enter Parameter Value dialog box, the query opens in Datasheet view, using the parameter value you specified. In this example, the query shows only records that have 9 as the month number in the Order Date field, as shown in the bottom half of Figure 2-16.

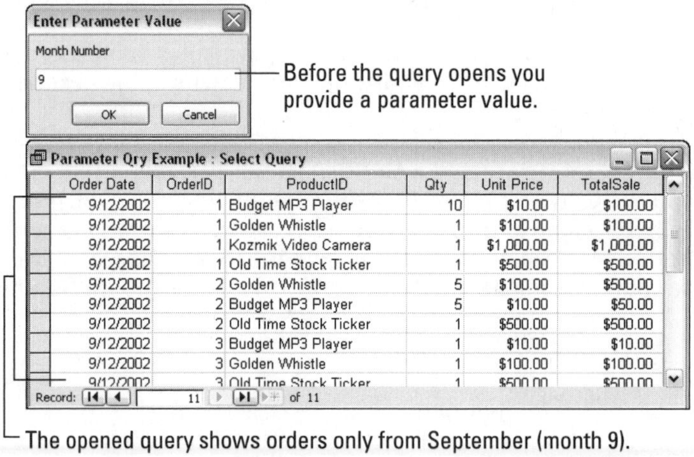

Enter Parameter Value

Month Number

9

OK   Cancel

————— Before the query opens you provide a parameter value.

Figure 2-16:
The result of opening a parameter query and specifying 9 as the Month Number.

Parameter Qry Example : Select Query

Order Date	OrderID	ProductID	Qty	Unit Price	TotalSale
9/12/2002	1	Budget MP3 Player	10	$10.00	$100.00
9/12/2002	1	Golden Whistle	1	$100.00	$100.00
9/12/2002	1	Kozmik Video Camera	1	$1,000.00	$1,000.00
9/12/2002	1	Old Time Stock Ticker	1	$500.00	$500.00
9/12/2002	2	Golden Whistle	5	$100.00	$500.00
9/12/2002	2	Budget MP3 Player	5	$10.00	$50.00
9/12/2002	2	Old Time Stock Ticker	1	$500.00	$500.00
9/12/2002	3	Budget MP3 Player	1	$10.00	$10.00
9/12/2002	3	Golden Whistle	1	$100.00	$100.00
9/12/2002	3	Old Time Stock Ticker	1	$500.00	$500.00

Record: |◄| ◄| 11 |►| |►I| |►*| of 11

————— The opened query shows orders only from September (month 9).

Totals, Subtotals, Averages, and Such

So far, all the calculations in our queries operate on individual fields within records. Suppose you want a different sort of total, such as the total dollar amount of all sales, in all records? You can perform such calculations in two ways. The best, and perhaps easiest way, is to use a report rather than a query. Reports provide more flexibility, and allow you to display the information in more meaningful ways than queries do.

For the goods on creating reports with totals and subtotals, see Book V, Chapter 1.

The other approach is to use a *totals query*. A totals query doesn't give you the flexibility or pretty output that a report does. But a totals query is useful when you just want to perform some quick calculations on the fly without formatting a fancy report.

If you just want to do some quick subtotals, totals, or other multi-record calculations — and don't really care how the data looks on-screen or in print — you can use a query to do the math. As to the other multi-record calculations we just mentioned, Table 2-9 lists all the calculations you can do in a totals query.

Table 2-9	**Operations Available in a Totals Query**
Choice	*Returns*
Avg	Average of records in field
Count	How many records
First	Value stored in first record
Group by	Nothing, used only for grouping
Last	Value stored in last record
Max	Highest value in all records
Min	Lowest value in all records
StDev	Standard deviation
Sum	Sum of records in field
Var	Variance

To create a query that performs calculations on multiple records, start with a normal select query that contains the table (or tables) on which you want to perform calculations. Then, do one or the other of the following:

Σ

✚ **Click the Totals button on the toolbar.**

✚ **Choose View⇨Totals from the main menu.**

The only change you see is a new row, titled Total, in the QBE grid. The next step is to drag any field name on which you want to perform math down to the Field row of the grid. Optionally, you can create a calculated field, and perform a calculation on that value.

After the field is in place, click the Total row, and then choose an option from the drop-down list, as shown in Figure 2-17. Repeat this process for each field on which you want to perform a calculation.

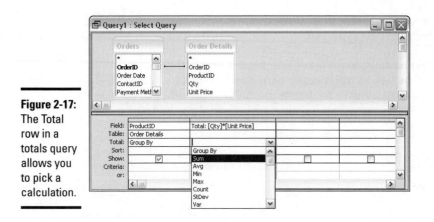

Figure 2-17:
The Total row in a totals query allows you to pick a calculation.

When you switch to Datasheet view to see the results of the query, don't be shocked if your large table, which consists of many records, is suddenly reduced to a single record. No, you didn't make an error — totals queries work this way.

The top half of Figure 2-18 shows a totals query containing one ExtPrice field, which is a calculated field showing the Qty field times the Unit Price field. Notice how the Total row for that field is set to the Sum value, so the query sums up that field for all records. The lower half of that same figure shows the query results.

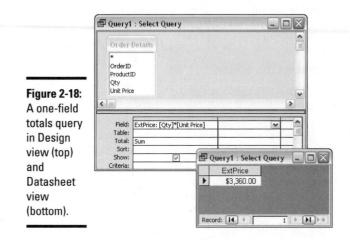

Figure 2-18:
A one-field totals query in Design view (top) and Datasheet view (bottom).

So what, exactly, is that $3,360.00 value shown in the results of the query in Figure 2-18? The result of the query, which goes in to each record in the Order Details table, multiplying the contents of the Qty field by the Unit Price field to come up with an Extended Price for each record, and then taking all those extended prices and adding them up. In other words, the $3,360.00 represents the total income from sales to date.

Calculating subtotals in a query

To calculate subtotals, add another field to the query that identifies the field the subtotals should be based on. Set the Total row for that field to a Group By value. In the top half of Figure 2-19, we added the ProductID field from the Order Details table to the QBE grid and set its Total row to a Group By value.

The bottom half of Figure 2-19 shows the results of that query in Datasheet view. Now, instead of getting just one huge grand total, we get the total extended price of orders for each individual product. The totals group by product. So we sold $160.00 worth of Budget MP3 Players, $700.00 worth of Golden Whistles, and so forth. If you add up the numbers in the ExtPrice field, you get $3,360.00 — the same grand total that the query in Figure 2-18 calculated and displayed.

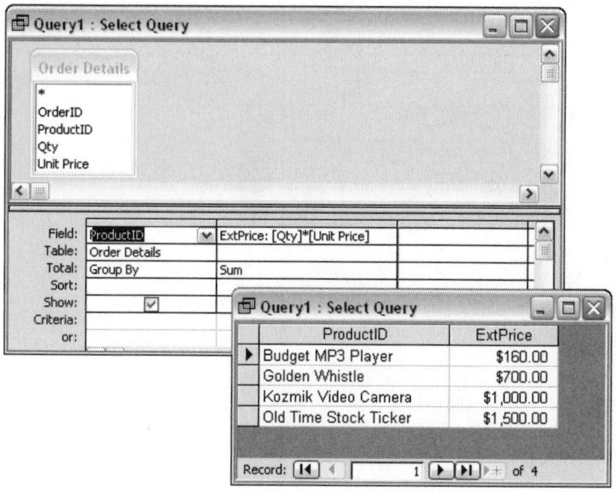

Figure 2-19:
A totals query with a Group By field in Design view (top) and Datasheet view (bottom).

As you can see from the previous two examples, the results of a totals query aren't always easy to interpret. Absolutely no detail in the query results does not make seeing what the calculated values are based upon easy. The lack of detail in queries is the real reason why reports are so much better than queries for totals and subtotals. In a report, you can include all the details you want and arrange things in such a way that you can easily grasp the meaning of every calculated total just by looking at the report.

Filtering records based on calculated fields

You can filter records based on the results of a calculated field. Suppose you want to do a query like the one in Figure 2-19, but you only want to see records where the total extended price is greater than or equal to $1,000. In that case, just set the Criterion row for the calculated field to >=1000 as in Figure 2-20. In the Datasheet view, only those products with sales totals results greater than or equal to $1,000 display, as in the lower half of Figure 2-20.

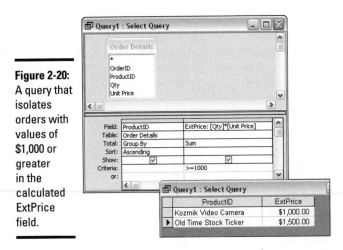

Figure 2-20: A query that isolates orders with values of $1,000 or greater in the calculated ExtPrice field.

Chapter 3: Doing Neat Things with Action Queries and Query Wizards

In This Chapter

✔ Using update queries to change data into tables

✔ Using make-table queries to create new tables

✔ Adding data from one table to another table with append queries

✔ Using the Find Duplicates Wizard

✔ Using the Find Unmatched Wizard

C hapter 1 of this book concentrates on creating select queries, which are the most common type of query created by Access users. You may not realize, though, that Access has other types of queries. Use action queries to make changes to your data — for example, you can set up a query to make a change to all the records that match a criterion. And two query wizards — the Find Duplicates Query Wizard and the Find Unmatched Query Wizard can help you clean up the data in your database.

Creating Action Queries

Action queries are a way to make global corrections to your database. They are very powerful, which means they can be tremendously useful and save you a lot of time, or they can make an enormous mess of your database if used incorrectly.

Action queries differ significantly from select queries. A select query shows you data that meet your criteria; an action query looks for the data that meets your criteria, and then does something with it, such as making changes to the data or moving records to a new table.

Four kinds of action queries, corresponding to four very specific tasks, exist. You may find that creating an action query saves you tons of time if you want to do any of the following things:

✦ Delete some records *(delete query)*

✦ Copy data from one table to another table *(append query)*

✦ Update (change) information in some records *(update query)*

✦ Create a new table from data stored in other tables *(make-table query)*

Make a backup before you run an action query. Action queries can make huge changes to your database, and even if you're careful, you may make a mistake. Making a backup doesn't take much time, especially compared to the time spent fixing what an action query did. You may want to back up the whole database or just the tables affected by the query. (To find out about making copies of a database object, see Book I, Chapter 2; to find out about backing up a database, see Book VII, Chapter 1.)

The usual way to create a query is to display the Database window (by pressing F11), click the Queries button, and double-click either the Create Query in Design View icon or the Create Query by Using Wizard icon. When you create a query using either of these methods, Access automatically creates a select query. You can change the query type of any query, whether it's brand new or well used. To change the query type, do either of the following things:

✦ Click the arrow next to the Query Type button on the Design View toolbar and choose the query type that you want, as shown in Figure 3-1.

✦ Choose the type of query you want from the Query menu in Design view. (You can choose Query⇨Make-Table Query, Query⇨Update Query, Query⇨Append Query, or Query⇨Delete Query to create an action query.)

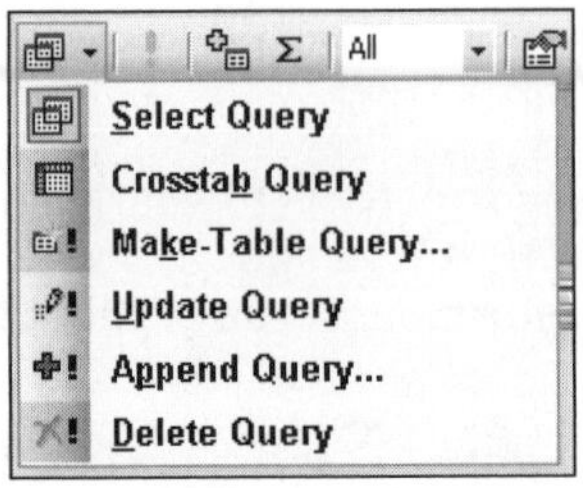

Figure 3-1:
The Query
Type button
shows six
types of
queries.

▣	**S**elect Query
▦	**C**rosstab Query
▣!	**M**ake-Table Query...
✎!	**U**pdate Query
✚!	**A**ppend Query...
✕!	**D**elete Query

The dangers of the Run button

As you may realize by now, action queries make changes; they don't just display data. You need to know how to safely create an action query without running it before you finish defining exactly how you want the query to work. The key is in when you use the View and Run buttons, and how you open the query. When you work with a select query, the View and Run buttons do the same thing. When you work with an action query, the View and Run buttons do completely different jobs:

+ The View button displays Datasheet view with all the records that match your selection criteria, which is a good way to preview what records will change when you run the action query. The View button is a safe way to look at the datasheet of an action query to see if the query will work the way you want it to.

+ The Run button executes the action — deletes or changes data in your database. You cannot undo the action after you click the Run button in an action query, so be very sure you set up the query correctly before you run it — and be sure to have backups of the affected tables just in case disaster strikes. (To find out about making copies of a database object, see Book I, Chapter 2.)

You also need to be careful how you open an action query. When you open an action query from the Database window by double-clicking the query name, selecting it, and clicking the Open button, you tell Access to run the query (not just to show it). Access warns you that you are about to run an action query that changes the database by updating records, deleting records, or whatever and gives you a chance to change your mind. If all you want to do is work on the design, make sure you select the query and click the Design button in the Database window toolbar.

Recognizing action queries in the Database window is easy because their icons are a little different from the icons select queries have — all action query icons have an exclamation point.

Creating action queries safely

You need to perfect an action query before you run it so that you don't wreck your data. (Of course, if you make a mistake you have a backup, right?) You make it, look at it, maybe test it on a few records in a test table, and then finally run it.

The process for creating an action query is as follows:

1. **Back up your database, or make copies of the tables that the action query will change.**

   Because action queries can do so much work (good or bad), make a backup before you run the query.

2. **Create the query as a select query.**

   In the Database window, click the Queries button and click one of the wizard icons. Add tables (or queries) and fields to the design grid. Define criteria and sort order as needed.

   The point is to create a query that displays the records that the action query acts on.

3. **View the records that the query will act on by clicking the View button.**

   You see the records that the query will act on. Make sure that you see the data you need.

4. **Use the Query Type button drop-down list or the Query menu to choose the type of action query you need — Make-Table, Update, Append, or Delete.**

5. **Add the information about what you want the query to do — update data, append data, make a table, or delete data.**

   The details are covered in the following sections on each type of query.

   You may want to use the View button again to see the records the query will act on.

6. **Click the Run button to run the query.**

   Access warns you that you are about to make changes that you can't undo.

7. **Click the Yes button to run the query.**

   Access runs the query.

8. **Check your results.**

   Checking the results in the underlying tables is a good idea. If the action query acts on a field that you use in a criteria, you may not see the records that change after the query has run — you may have to look at the table, or create a new query to view the results. The append and make-table queries create new tables. View those results in the affected tables, and not in the query datasheet.

9. **If you won't be using the action query again, delete it.**

   They are dangerous things to have laying around!

After you add an action query, each time you open your database you see a security warning telling you that the database contains macros, which may contain viruses. Unless you suspect a virus may actually exist, you can click the Enable Macros button and open the database. Book I, Chapter 2 covers the security error message in detail.

Changing Data with Update Queries

You can use an *update query* to change a pile of data at the same time — to raise prices by 10 percent, for example, or to replace a product number with a new product number.

For instance, you may create a query to find orders that haven't yet been shipped that include a Golden Whistle, an item that is discontinued but has a substitute. You could then use the update query to change the item number in records that meet those criteria to the New Golden Whistle, the replacement item.

Using the update query when you work on lots and lots of data or when you want to update multiple fields makes sense. But before you delve into the complexities of an action query, consider whether you can use the much simpler Find and Replace dialog box to find and replace data instead. See Book II, Chapter 2 for more information on the Find and Replace dialog box. You can use the Find and Replace dialog box in a datasheet created by a query, and if you change the data in the query, the table holding the underlying data reflects the change.

To create an update query, follow these steps:

1. **Back up the database and/or make copies of the tables that will be affected by the update.**

   Update queries can be hard to get right, so play it safe in case you need to get your data back the way it was before you ran the update query.

2. **Create a new select query in Design view.**

   See Chapter 1 of this book for more information on creating a query.

   Include tables that you plan to update or that you need to use fields to establish the update criteria.

3. **Put fields in the design grid.**

   Add fields that you want to see in the datasheet, fields that you want to use with criteria to tell Access exactly what to update, and the fields that you want to make changes to using the update query.

   See Chapter 1 of this book for more on using the design grid.

4. **Add the criteria to tell Access how to choose the records you want to update.**

   Figure 3-2 shows the select query that finds all unshipped orders for the Golden Whistle. You see two fields included in the query — the Shipped field, because we are looking for orders that haven't been shipped (this is a Yes/No field, and we are looking for No values), and the Product ID field, because we are looking for orders that contain Golden Whistle product.

**Book III
Chapter 3**

**Action Queries and
Query Wizards**

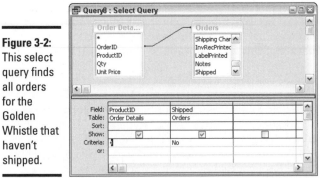

Figure 3-2:
This select query finds all orders for the Golden Whistle that haven't shipped.

5. **Click the View button to view the datasheet to check if all the records you want to update, and none that you don't, are included.**

   Edit the query as needed until you see only the records you want to update in the datasheet. Figure 3-3 shows the datasheet for the query shown in Figure 3-2.

   If you use an expression to define how a record is updated, you may want to create a test field now to write your expression and make sure it works the way you want. For instance, if you want to increase prices by 10 percent, you can create a new field: [New Price]: [Selling Price]*1.10. The test field appears in the datasheet when you view it, and you can check it for accuracy. For more information about writing expressions, see Chapter 2 of this book.

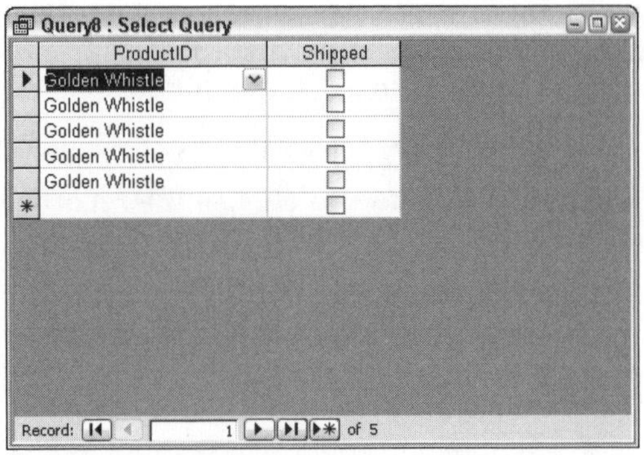

Figure 3-3:
The datasheet for the query in Figure 3-2, showing the Golden Whistle orders that haven't shipped.

6. **Click the arrow next to the Query Type button and choose the Update Query option from the drop-down list to change the query to an update query.**

Alternatively, choose Query⇨Update Query from the Design View menu.

Access adds an Update To row in the design grid.

7. Use the Update To row to tell Access how to update the field.

The easiest update is to change one value to another by simply typing the new value in the Update To box for the appropriate field. More complex updates include expressions that tell Access exactly how to update the field. For example, to increase the Selling Price field in a table by 10 percent, you use the expression [Selling Price]*1.10. You can use the Expression Builder to help you build an expression for the Update To row; just click in the box and then the Build button. (See Chapter 2 of this book for more information on using the Expression Builder to create expressions.)

If you created a test field in Step 5, move the expression to the Update To line for the field that will be updated, and delete the field you created to test the expression. Note that you move the part of the expression after the colon.

Figure 3-4 shows the update query that finds all orders for the Golden Whistle and changes them to orders for the New Golden Whistle.

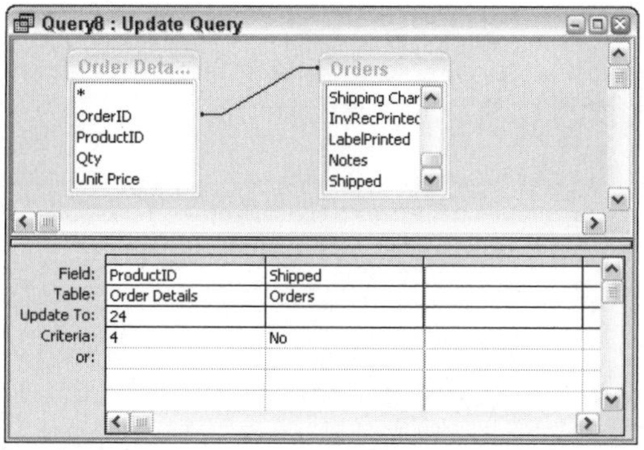

Figure 3-4:
This query finds all orders for Golden Whistle that haven't shipped, and changes them to New Golden Whistle.

8. Click the View button.

Access displays the datasheet with the records the query changes when you run it. If the data is not correct, return to Design view to correct the fields and criteria. This is the same data that you displayed in Step 5. You display it again to be sure you're making the changes you want to make. Check Design view over carefully to be sure that the Update To line is correct.

You can display only those fields in the datasheet that the update query is updating. If you want to get a fuller picture of the records you're updating (see the data for all the fields, for example), you can change the query back to a select query, add additional fields, and view the datasheet that your criteria produces. When you change the query back to an update query, the Update To options you added are still there. You need to remove any additional fields from the query grid before you run the update. Only fields that are updated or used for criteria are allowed in update queries.

Be aware that the datasheet shows the data that will be changed. You can't see what is changed until you run the query. If you use an expression in the Update To row, testing that your expression produces the desired result by using a calculated field in a select query is important (see Step 5).

9. **Click the Run button to run the update.**

   Access warns you that after the records update, you can't undo the changes, as shown in Figure 3-5.

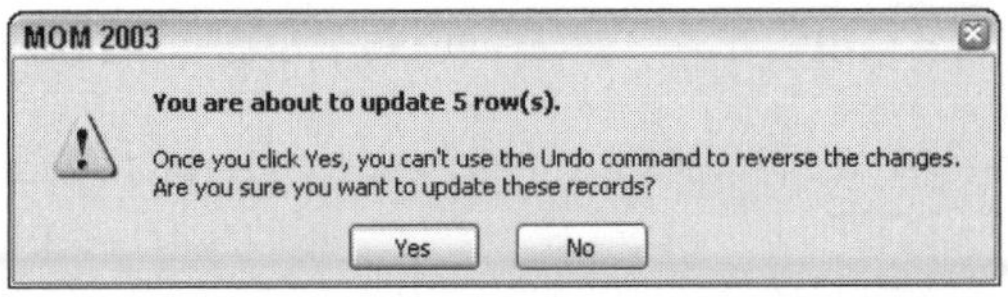

Figure 3-5:
When you click the Run button to run an update query, you see a warning like this one.

> **MOM 2003**
>
> ⚠ **You are about to update 5 row(s).**
>
> Once you click Yes, you can't use the Undo command to reverse the changes. Are you sure you want to update these records?
>
> [Yes] [No]

10. **Click the Yes button to update the data.**

11. **Check the tables with affected fields to see whether the update query worked correctly.**

    Figure 3-6 shows the Orders table with the Order Details subtable. Golden Whistles in unshipped orders are replaced by New Golden Whistles.

12. **Delete the query if you won't be using it again; press Ctrl+S to save it if you will need it again.**

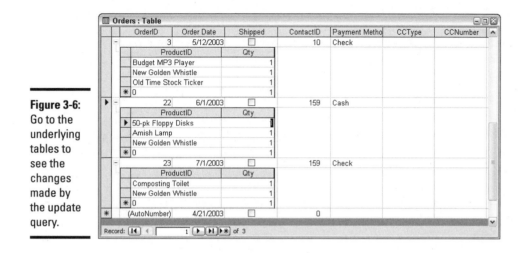

Figure 3-6:
Go to the
underlying
tables to
see the
changes
made by
the update
query.

Creating New Tables with Make-Table Queries

A *make-table query* is useful if you need to make a new table to export or to
serve as a backup. You can use a make-table query to make a new table that
contains a copy of the data in a table or query. The new table can contain
some or all of the fields and records from an existing table, or combine the
fields from two or more tables — similar to the results of a select query.

For instance, you can use a make-table query to create a table of customers
who bought Golden Whistles — you decided to share their addresses with a
school that offers whistle lessons.

To create a table with a make-table query, follow these steps:

1. **Create a select query that produces the records you want in a
   new table.**

   See Chapter 1 of this book for more information on creating a
   select query.

   Figure 3-7 shows a select query that finds the contact info for all customers who ever ordered Golden Whistles. Notice that although we only
   need fields from the Address Book and Order Details tables, the Orders
   table is also included in the query to define the relationship between
   the Order Details and the Address Book tables.

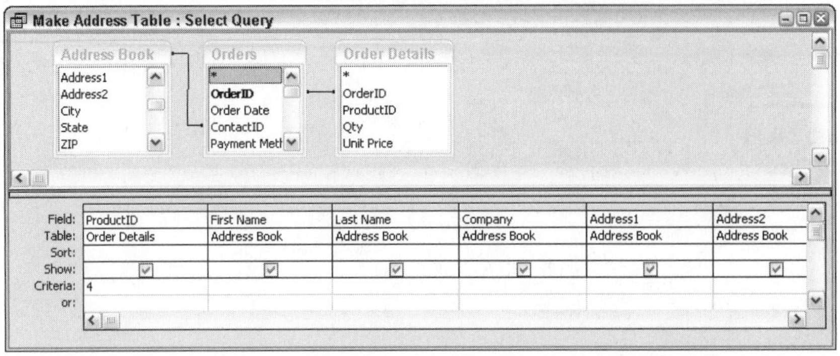

Figure 3-7:
The select
query finds
customers
who
ordered
Golden
Whistles
(item
number 4)
and lists
their names
and
addresses.

2. Click the View button on the toolbar to view the results.

Figure 3-8 shows the datasheet for our query.

We don't want to include the ProductID field in the table that the make-table query creates, so we return to Design view and de-select the check mark in the Show row for the ProductID field.

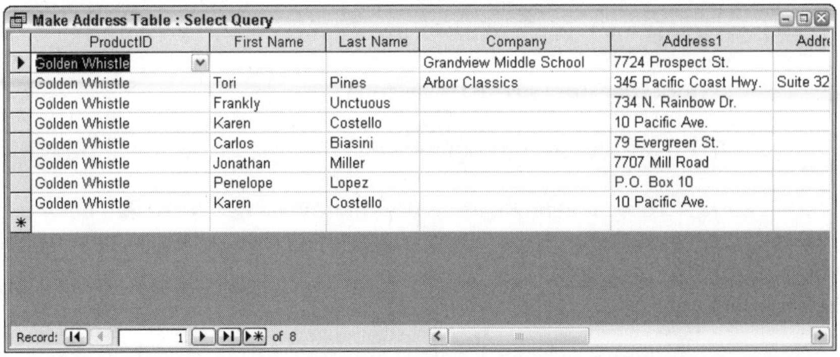

Figure 3-8:
The
datasheet
shows the
customers
and contact
info.

3. Click the View button on the toolbar to display Design view.

4. Change the query type to a make-table query by clicking the Query Type button.

Click the arrow next to the Query Type button and choose the Make-Table Query option from the drop-down list or choose Query⇨ Make-Table Query to change the query type.

Access immediately displays the Make Table dialog box shown in Figure 3-9.

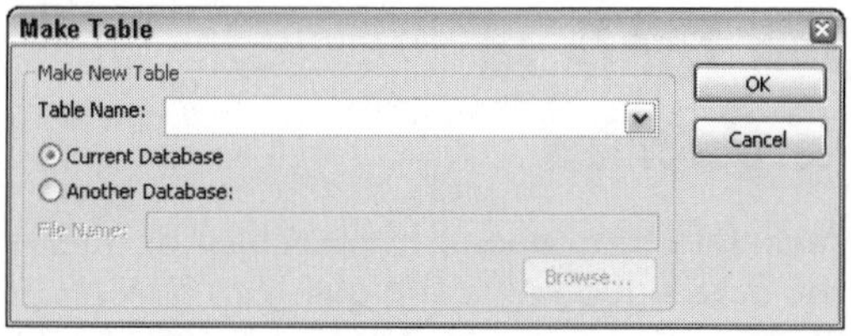

Figure 3-9:
The Make
Table dialog
box.

5. **Type the name of the table that you're creating in the Table Name box.**

   Although you're offered a drop-down list, you probably want to create a brand new table by typing a name for the table that is not the name of a table currently in your database.

6. **Choose whether to create the new table in the current database or in another database.**

   If you choose the Another Database option you can browse for an existing database. You cannot create a new database using a make-table query.

7. **Click OK to close the dialog box.**

   If you need to change the settings in the Make Table dialog box, display the drop-down list of query types from the Query Type button, and select the Make-Table Query option again.

8. **Click the View button to see the records that will be in the new table.**

   You may need to return to Design view to edit the query until all the records you want in the new table appear in the datasheet when you click the View button.

9. **Click the Run button to create the new table.**

   Access asks whether you're sure because you won't be able to undo your changes.

10. **Click the Yes button to create the new table.**

    Access quietly creates the new table.

11. **Check the new and old tables to make sure that you get what you need in the new table.**

You may want to edit the table design — the new table does not inherit the field properties or the primary key setting from the original table. See Book II, Chapter 1 for more information on table design.

Moving Data from One Table to Another with Append Queries

An *append query* copies data from one or more tables or queries in your database and adds the data selected by the query as new records to an existing table. As with other queries, you can use criteria to tell Access exactly which data to append.

Append queries are used to archive information, to move data between databases, as well as other useful housecleaning chores.

Cutting and pasting may be an easier way to append records from one table to another if you are only appending a few records. See Book II, Chapter 4, for more information.

Access gets a little picky about data that you append using an append query, especially with primary key fields. You must follow these rules when appending records to another table:

✦ Data that you want to append must have unique values in the primary key field. Each value in the primary key field must be unique in the table to which the data is being added, because by definition, no value can repeat in a primary key field. If the field is blank, or if the same value already exists in the table, Access does not append the records.

✦ If an AutoNumber field is in the table to which the data is being appended, do not append data in that field — Access automatically generates new numbers in the AutoNumber field for the new records and old values cannot be appended.

✦ The data type of each field that you're appending must match the data type of fields in the table to which they're being added.

To create an append query, follow these steps:

1. **Create a select query that produces the records that you want to add to another table. Display the query in Design view.**

See Chapter 1 of this book for details on creating a select query.

You can check the criteria by viewing the datasheet to see if the query is selecting the data you want to append. Click the View button on the toolbar to display the datasheet, and click the View button again to return to Design view.

2. **Change the query type to an append query by clicking the Query Type button.**

   Click the arrow next to the Query Type button and choose the Append Query option from the drop-down list or choose Query⇨Append Query from the menu.

   Access immediately displays the Append dialog box shown in Figure 3-10.

Figure 3-10:
The Append dialog box tells Access where you want to append data.

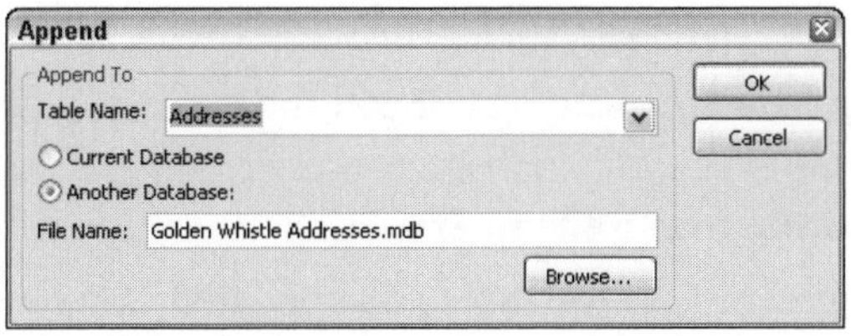

3. **Choose the table which you want to append the records to in the Table Name box.**

   You can display the names of all the tables in the open database by displaying the Table Name drop-down list.

   You can add the records to a table in another database — find the database by clicking the Browse button.

4. **Click OK.**

   Access adds an extra row to the design grid: the Append To row. If the field names match the names of the fields you're appending, Access automatically fills in the Append To row with the names of the fields in the table you're appending records to.

5. **Carefully check the Append To row of the query grid and make any necessary changes.**

   The Field and Table rows show where the field comes from, and the Append To row shows where the data will be appended.

Book III
Chapter 3

Action Queries and
Query Wizards

If some of the fields don't have field names in the Append To row, display the drop-down list in the Append row and select the name of the field you want to append to. When you're finished, check each column to ensure that

- The Field row contains the name of the field that contains data that you want to append to another table.

- The Table row contains the name of the table that contains the data.

- The Append To row contains the name of the field that the data will be appended to.

- No field appears more than once in the Append To row.

6. **Click the Run button to run the append query.**

   Access tells you that you're about to append rows and that you won't be able to undo the changes.

   Be careful about running this query. If you run it twice, you append the records twice!

7. **Click the Yes button to run the query.**

   Access adds the records to the table you specified. You now have the same information in two tables.

8. **Save the query by pressing Ctrl+S if you think that you'll use it again; otherwise, close it without saving.**

9. **Check your results.**

   Check the table you appended to as well as the table you appended from to make sure that Access copied all the records you wanted copied.

Deleting Lots of Records with Delete Queries

A delete query deletes whole records from tables, usually based on criteria you provide (although you can also use delete queries to delete all records in a table while keeping the field and table properties intact). Obviously, delete queries are a powerful feature, and should be treated with respect! Delete queries are dangerous — they actually delete data from the tables in your database.

Always make sure that you have a backup before you run a delete query. You may want to back up the whole database or just the tables affected by the delete query.

Because delete queries can wreak such havoc with your database, you may want to consider whether manually deleting records meets your needs. You can delete a record by selecting it (click the record selector, the gray box to the left of the record) and pressing the Delete key on your keyboard or clicking the Delete Record button on the toolbar. You can select a group of records by double-clicking the first record selector and dragging to the last in the group, or by selecting the first record and then Shift+clicking the last in the group.

Before you run a delete query you need to be aware of how the table you're deleting data from is related to other tables in the database. In some cases, running a delete query can delete records in related tables. If the table you're deleting data from is on the one side of a one-to-many relationship, and cascading deletes are enabled for the relationship, Access looks for related data to delete. For instance, the Products table (which holds information for all the sold products) is related to the Order Details table (where ordered items are listed). The relationship is one-to-many, with Products on the one side. If referential integrity is enforced and cascade related records are deleted between the two tables, then deleting records from the Products table results in Access deleting records from the Order Details table. Customers may not get the products they ordered, and no record of them ordering that item exists in the database. In this case, adding a Discontinued field to the Products table may be a better solution than deleting the records! For more information on one-to-many relationships, see Book I, Chapter 3. For more information on referential integrity, see Book II, Chapter 6.

When you tell Access to create a delete query, the Sort and Show rows in the design grid — the grid in the bottom pane of Design view — are removed and the Delete row is added. The Delete row has a drop-down list with two options that you only see with delete queries: the Where option and the From option. Use these two options to define the fields you want to see and the fields that you are using to define criteria to select the fields that will be deleted by the query:

✦ **Where:** Tells Access to use the criteria for the field to determine which records to delete.

✦ **From:** Displays the field when you view the datasheet for the query. You can choose the From option only when you use the * choice in the Field row to include all fields from a table. The asterisk appears as the first field for each table shown in the top half of Design view — when dragged to the design grid, Access displays all fields from the table. Viewing all fields from a table in the datasheet gives you a more complete picture of the data you're deleting; otherwise, all you see in the datasheet are the values from the fields that you include in the design grid with criteria rather than the entire record that the delete query will delete when you run it.

Follow these steps to create a delete query:

1. **In Design view, create a select query that produces the records you want to delete.**

   See Chapter 1 of this book for details on how to create a select query.

   Add to the query all tables that contain records that you want to delete.

2. **Drag the * option from each field list in the top half of Design view to the design grid to display all fields from the table or tables that contain records that you want to delete.**

   Using the * option allows you to view all fields in the table. When you change the query to a delete query, only the * allows you to display fields not being used for criteria.

3. **Add fields to the design grid that you have criteria for and define the criteria.**

4. **Click the View button on the toolbar to view the datasheet.**

   The records you see are the records that you want the delete query to delete.

5. **Click the View button again to return to Design view.**

   Make any changes needed so the query selects only those records that you want to delete.

6. **Change the query type to a delete query by clicking the Query Type button on the Design View toolbar.**

   Click the down arrow next to the Query Type button and choose the Delete Query option from the drop-down list or choose Query⇨Delete Query to change the query type.

   When you change the query type from select to delete, Access changes the rows in the design grid. The Sort and Show rows are removed, and the Delete row is added.

7. **Choose a value for the Delete row (if it's not set automatically) from the drop-down list in the following way: Set the fields that you want to view to the From option; set the fields to define criteria to the Where option.**

   Figure 3-11 shows an example of a delete query that will delete records with the ProductID value of 35 from the Order Details and Products tables. Note that when you view the datasheet you are seeing data from two different tables. All that data will be deleted, so data will be deleted from both tables.

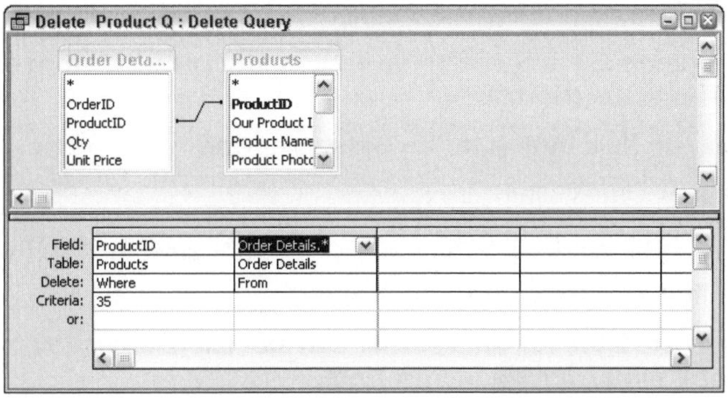

Figure 3-11:
This delete
query
deletes
records
with the
ProductID
value of 35
from the
Order
Details and
Products
tables.

8. **Click the View button to view the datasheet again. Check that you see only the records that the delete query should delete.**

   If you see data in the datasheet that shouldn't be deleted or if data that you want to delete is missing, correct the design of the query before you run it. *Remember:* A delete query deletes entire records.

9. **Return to Design view by clicking the View button.**

10. **Click the Run button to run the query.**

   Access deletes the data that you saw in Datasheet view — it's gone for good!

Finding Unmatched Records with a Wizard

Access has two categories of Neat Things You Can Do with Queries — action queries and the two query wizards covered here. The Find Unmatched Query Wizard finds records in one table that have no matching records in another, related table. For example, you may store orders in one table and details about customers in another table. If the tables are linked by, say, a Customer Number field, the Unmatched Query Wizard can tell you whether you have any customers listed in the Orders table who aren't listed in the Customers table.

Use the Find Unmatched Query Wizard to find unmatched records in the following way:

1. **Display queries in the Database window.**

Press F11 to display the Database window. Click the Queries button in the Objects list at the left side of the Database window to display all queries in the database.

2. **Click the New button in the Database window's toolbar.**

The New Query dialog box opens.

3. **Select the Find Unmatched Query Wizard option, and then click OK.**

The first window of the wizard appears.

4. **Select the table (or query) that may have unmatched records in a second table, and then click Next.**

For instance, if you are looking for customers with no orders, select the table that holds the names of customers in this window. If you are looking for orders for which you don't have the customer address, select the Orders table in this step. The final result of the query lists records from the table that you select in this step that don't have matching records in the table you select in the next step.

If you want to choose a query, click the Queries or Both radio button.

5. **Select the table (or query) that should contain the matching records for the data in the table you selected in the previous step, and then click Next.**

For instance, if you are looking for customers with no orders, select the table that holds the order information. If you are looking for orders which don't have the customer address, select the table that holds customer addresses in this step.

6. **Check that Access correctly guessed the related fields in the two tables you selected in the third window of the wizard (shown in Figure 3-12), and then click Next.**

The window shows field names in the two tables you selected. The names of the related fields are probably highlighted. Click the related field in each table if Access has not selected the correct related fields. The two fields that you select should contain the same information and be of the same data type.

7. **Select the fields you want to see in the query results in the next window of the wizard and click Next.**

To select all fields, click the double arrow pointing to the right.

8. **Accept the name Access gives the query or name the query yourself in the final window of the Find Unmatched Query Wizard.**

9. **Choose whether you want to view the results or modify the design (you can modify the design later, too) and click Finish.**

Access displays the query in Design or Datasheet view as you requested.

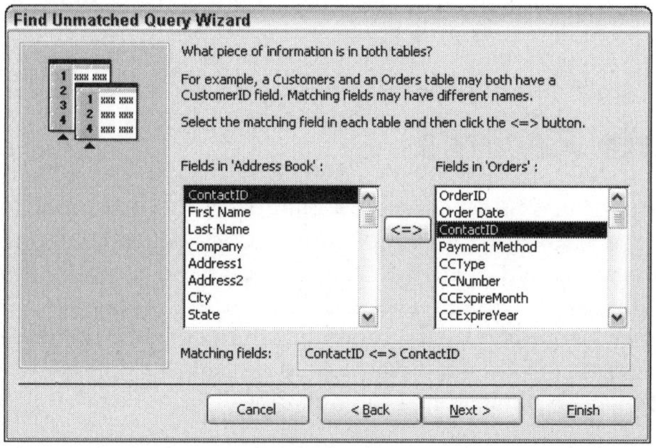

Figure 3-12:
Select related fields to find unmatched records.

Note that you don't have to use a wizard to create this kind of query. The query shown in Figure 3-13 finds unmatched records in the Address Book table by using an inner join between the tables and the Is Null criteria for the related field in the table where matching records are stored. For more about inner joins, see Chapter 1 of this book.

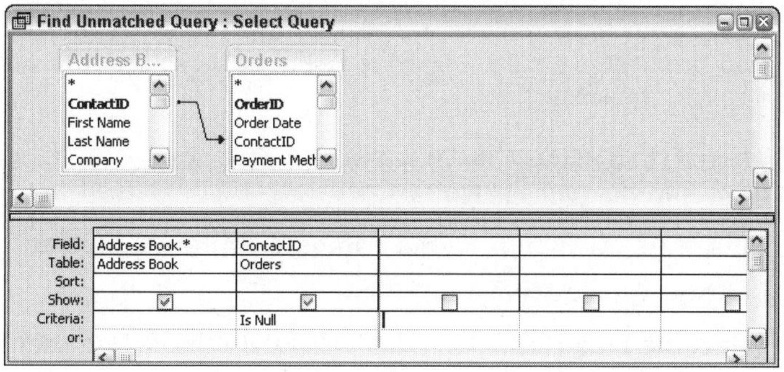

Figure 3-13:
Find unmatched records by using an inner join and the Is Null criteria.

In order to avoid unmatched records, define the relationship between the tables to enforce referential integrity. Define referential integrity in order to avoid creating orders for customers in the Orders table when you don't have contact information for them in the Address Book table. You may still find using the Find Unmatched Query Wizard useful though — for instance, you may want to find customers who have not placed any orders, or products that have not been ordered. For more information on referential integrity, see Book II, Chapter 6.

Finding Duplicate Records

When a table contains hundreds or thousands of records, spotting duplicates is not always easy. But the Find Duplicates Query Wizard can find them in an instant. Before you use the wizard, though, you need to really think about which combination of fields in a record constitute a duplicate. For example, in a table of names and addresses, you wouldn't necessary consider two records with the name Jones in the Last Name field duplicates, because two different people may have the name Jones in your table.

Not even the First Name and Last Name fields combined necessarily pinpoint duplicate records, because more than one Joe Jones or Chuma Jones can be in your table. On the other hand, if two or more records in your table contain the same information in the Last Name, First Name, Address1, and Zip Code fields, then there's a good chance that those records are duplicates. If you do mass mailings, you may be sending two or more of every item to the customers whose records are duplicated.

Before you go looking for duplicate records, think about which combination of fields in your table indicate records that are likely duplicates. Then, use the Find Duplicates Query Wizard to seek out those records. Follow these steps to run the wizard:

1. **Press F11 to display the Database window and click the Queries button in the Objects list.**

2. **Click the New button on the Database window's toolbar.**

   The New Query dialog box opens.

3. **Select the Find Duplicate Query Wizard option, and then click OK.**

   The Find Duplicates Query Wizard starts.

4. **Click the name of the table you want to search in the first window of the wizard and click Next.**

Optionally, you can click the Queries option and choose a query to use as the basis for the search.

5. **Use the > button to copy fields from the Available Fields list to the Duplicate-Value Fields list in the second window of the wizard and click Next.**

   Be sure to include all of the fields that contain the data needed to define duplicate records. For example, in Figure 3-14 we're about to find records that have identical information in the First Name, Last Name, Address 1, and ZIP fields.

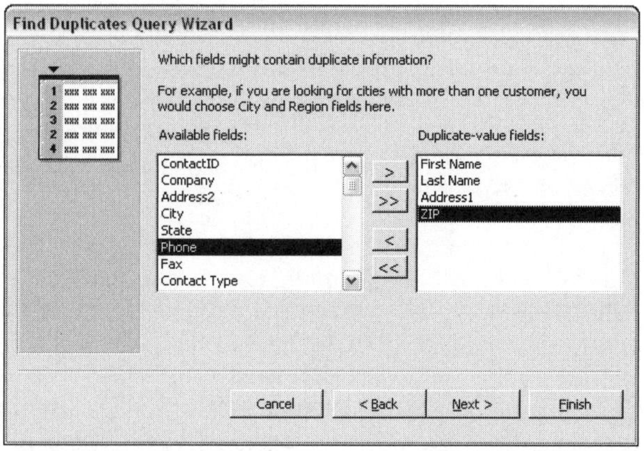

Figure 3-14: Specify fields to compare in the second window of the Find Duplicates Query Wizard.

Book III Chapter 3

Action Queries and Query Wizards

6. **Choose the fields to be shown for additional information in the third window of the wizard and click Next.**

   The fields you specify aren't used for comparing records. But they will display in the query results to help you better identify any duplicate records. If your table has a primary key and/or date entered field, both are good candidates for this third field.

7. **Change the suggested name for the query, if you wish, or use the suggested name in the last window of the wizard.**

8. **Choose the View the Results option, and then click the Finish button.**

The results of the query appear on-screen in Datasheet view. If no records display, that means no records have identical values in the fields you specified in the wizard. You have nothing to worry about.

The handy Unique Values and Unique Records properties

Sometimes, rather than finding duplicates and deleting them, you just want to hide them. For instance, you may only need to see a list of states that your customers come from — you don't need to see Massachusetts fifty-six times (if you have fifty-six customers in Massachusetts).

The Properties sheet has two properties that allow you to hide duplicate values:

✔ Unique Values: Set the Unique Values property to the Yes value when you want to see only unique values for the fields displayed in the query. The Unique Values property omits duplicate data for the fields selected in the query. Every row displayed in the query datasheet is different.

✔ Unique Records: Set the Unique Records property to the Yes value when you want to see only unique records based on all fields in the underlying tables. The Unique Records property only affects fields from more than one table. A record is considered unique if a value in at least one field is different from a value in the same field in another record. Note that the primary key fields are included when records are compared.

To display the Properties sheet, right-click an empty part of the Table pane (the top half of the design grid) and choose the Properties option from the shortcut menu or click the Properties button on the toolbar.

The Unique Values and Unique Records properties apply only to select, append, and make-table queries. Note that when both are set to the No value (which is the default), the query returns all records.

On the other hand, if records do appear, then you know you have duplicates. For example, in Figure 3-15, two records for Frankly Unctuous appear. Note the identical name, address, and zip fields. The ContactID and Date Entered fields allow us to see that two records for this customer are, indeed, in the table.

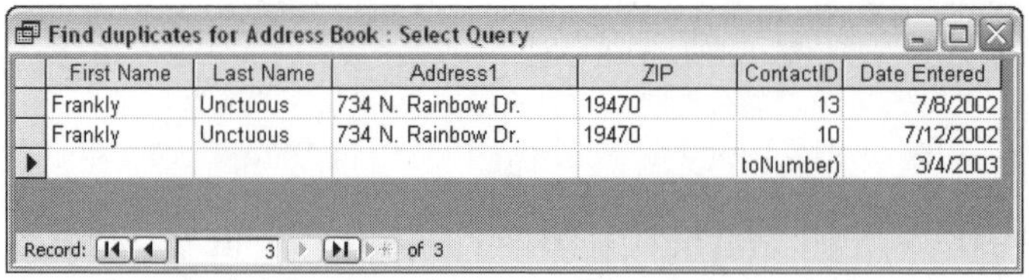

Figure 3-15:
Frankly
Unctuous
has two
records in
the table.

First Name	Last Name	Address1	ZIP	ContactID	Date Entered
Frankly	Unctuous	734 N. Rainbow Dr.	19470	13	7/8/2002
Frankly	Unctuous	734 N. Rainbow Dr.	19470	10	7/12/2002
				toNumber)	3/4/2003

Find duplicates for Address Book : Select Query

Record: 3 of 3

Chapter 4: Viewing Your Data from All Angles Using Crosstabs and PivotTables

In This Chapter

✔ Understanding crosstab queries

✔ Running the Crosstab Query Wizard

✔ Creating crosstab queries in Design view

✔ Understanding PivotTables

✔ Using PivotTable view

✔ Selecting filter, data, and category fields for your PivotTable

Sometimes, instead of viewing your data in records, you want to see it organized and categorized. You may want to see sales of each product by month and you may want to see that information in a compact table, with months as the column titles, product names as the row titles, and the sum of sales in the body of the table. Access creates that kind of table in two ways — with a crosstab query or a PivotTable. Both crosstabs and PivotTables organize data and create totals using the aggregate function of your choice — sum, average, and count being the most popular. You create crosstab queries in Design view, while the PivotTable view is all mouse driven — you drag and drop fields where you want them, use check boxes to create filters, and do nearly everything else with buttons and menu commands.

If you want to look at your data in lots of different ways in a short period of time, you'll prefer PivotTables — you can look first at product sales by month and then quickly shift the view to see which salespeople are selling the most of which product, and then shift again to see which states your customers come from for each product. But if you know exactly what you want with no need to look at the data in another way, or if you want to use the results of the query as the record source for a report, you may prefer crosstab queries. Take your choice — they're both covered in this chapter.

Aggregating Data in a Crosstab Query

A *crosstab query* is a specialized query for summarizing data. Instead of creating a table with rows showing record data and columns showing fields, you can choose a field and group it using two other fields as row and column labels. Access groups the data the way you tell it to and aggregates the grouped field in the body of the table — you can choose between the usual aggregate functions such as sum, average, minimum, maximum, count, and all other available functions. For instance, if you chose the Product field for the column labels, the Sales Month field for the row labels, and the field that contains the sales subtotal for the product (price × quantity) as the information to put in the body of the table, and you tell Access to sum the result, the crosstab query appears, shown in Figure 4-1, where sales of each product are shown by month. The result is a compact, spreadsheet-like presentation of your data.

If you want to aggregate data without using a crosstab query, see Chapter 2 of this book.

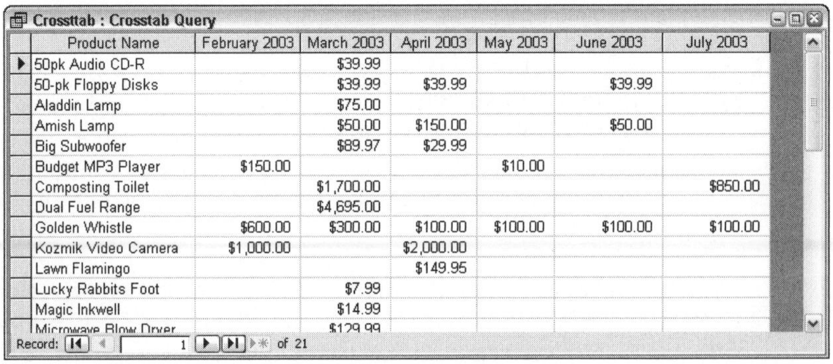

Figure 4-1: This crosstab query shows sales by product and month.

Product Name	February 2003	March 2003	April 2003	May 2003	June 2003	July 2003
50pk Audio CD-R		$39.99				
50-pk Floppy Disks		$39.99	$39.99		$39.99	
Aladdin Lamp		$75.00				
Amish Lamp		$50.00	$150.00		$50.00	
Big Subwoofer		$89.97	$29.99			
Budget MP3 Player	$150.00			$10.00		
Composting Toilet		$1,700.00				$850.00
Dual Fuel Range		$4,695.00				
Golden Whistle	$600.00	$300.00	$100.00	$100.00	$100.00	$100.00
Kozmik Video Camera	$1,000.00		$2,000.00			
Lawn Flamingo			$149.95			
Lucky Rabbits Foot		$7.99				
Magic Inkwell		$14.99				
Microwave Blow Dryer		$129.99				

Crossttab : Crosstab Query

Record: 1 of 21

Using the Crosstab Query Wizard

The Crosstab Query Wizard provides an automated way to create a crosstab query. The wizard works only with one table or query. If the fields you want to use in the crosstab query are not in one table, you have to create a query that combines those fields before you use the Crosstab Query Wizard. However, because the wizard does give you the option of aggregating date data (taking a Date/Time field and combining the data into months), you don't have to write an expression to aggregate data yourself. For instance, the Orders table saves the time and day an order is submitted. The Crosstab Query Wizard takes that date field and converts it to just the month (or the year, quarter, or day). In order to have the option to aggregate data, you must use the date field as a column heading.

Start the Crosstab Query Wizard by following these steps:

1. **Click the Queries button from the Objects list in the Database window.**

   Press F11 if the Database window isn't visible.

   In the right pane of the Database window, Access displays the names of any queries you have in your database.

2. **Click the New button on the Database Window toolbar.**

   Access displays the New Query dialog box.

3. **Select the Crosstab Query Wizard option and click OK.**

   Access starts the Crosstab Query Wizard, shown in Figure 4-2.

4. **Select the table or query that contains all the fields you need for your crosstab query, and then click Next.**

   If you create a query to hold the fields you need, click the Queries or Both button to see the query name.

5. **In the new window that appears, shown in Figure 4-3, select the field(s) whose values you want to use as row headings and click Next.**

   You can select up to three fields to fine-tune the breakdown of your data. As you select fields, the sample at the bottom changes to reflect how your finished query will look.

View box lets you choose Tables, Queries, or Both

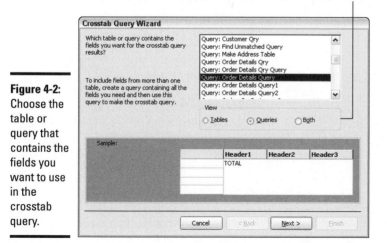

Figure 4-2:
Choose the table or query that contains the fields you want to use in the crosstab query.

Generally the fields you select as row and column headings contain repeated data that is grouped in the crosstab query. For instance, the ProductID field comes from the Order Details table and identifies products in each order. The crosstab query can show you how many times a product is ordered, or how many units of each product is sold.

TIP

If you want the option of grouping date values, don't pick the Date/Time field here — use it for column headings instead.

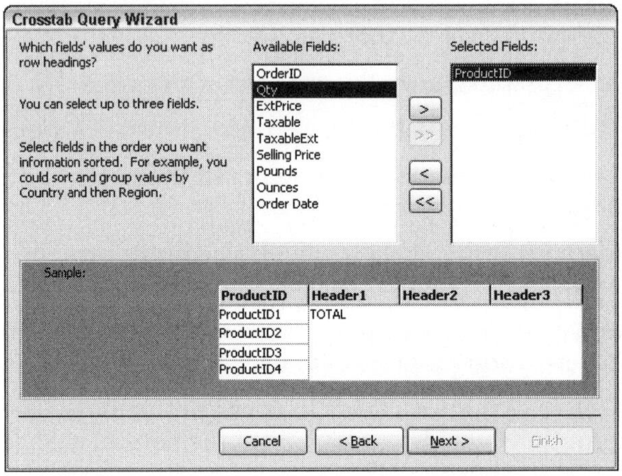

Figure 4-3:
Choose the field(s) that contains the data used as the row headings for the crosstab query.

6. **In the new window that appears, shown in Figure 4-4, select the field(s) whose values you want to use as column headings and click Next.**

You can only select one field to use as the column headings. You may want to use a field containing dates and tell Access to group date values.

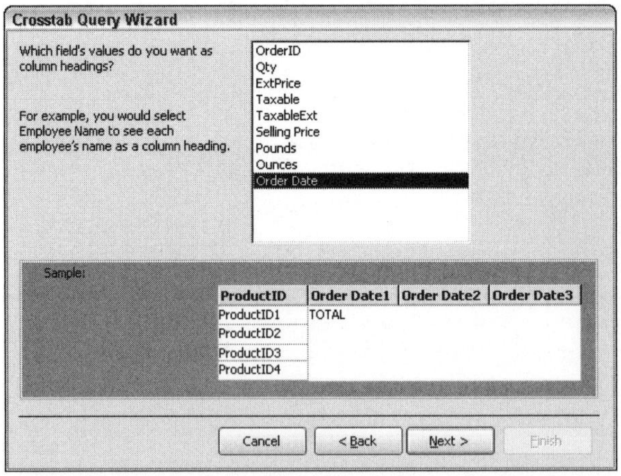

Figure 4-4:
Choose the field you want to use as column headings.

7. If you select a date field as the column headings, you see the window shown in Figure 4-5. Choose how to group dates from the list and click Next.

Choose one of the options listed. The Date/Time option shows data by unique Date and Time — data isn't grouped at all unless you have data with exactly the same time and date.

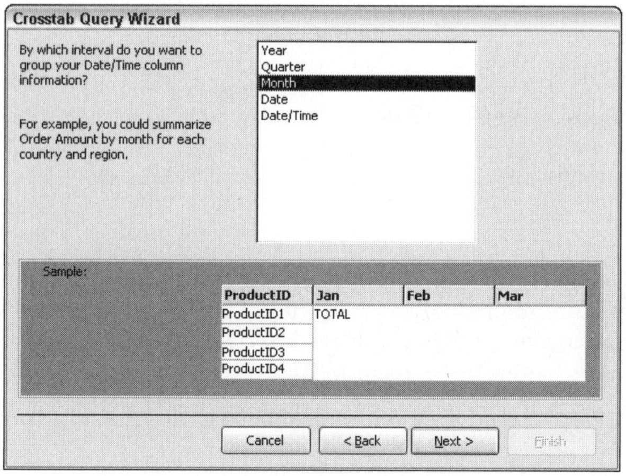

Figure 4-5:
Choose how to group date and time data.

8. In the new window that appears, shown in Figure 4-6, choose the field grouped by the row and column headings that you selected.

The field you select usually contains numerical data that can be aggregated in some way (added together, averaged, and so on). The exception is if you want to count instances — then the field doesn't need to contain numbers.

Figure 4-6 uses the extended price field, which is price × quantity — the dollar amount of sales for each product.

9. Select a grouping method from the Functions list.

You can find out more about these functions in Chapter 2 of this book. You can easily change this function in Design view if you change your mind after you view the crosstab query.

10. Choose whether to include row sums, and then click Next.

If you choose to include row sums, Access creates an extra column that contains the sum of the row — in this example, the total sales for the product.

**Book III
Chapter 4**

Using Crosstabs and PivotTables

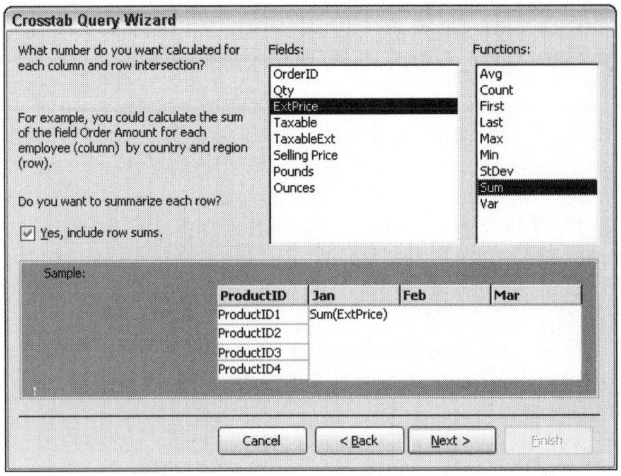

Figure 4-6:
Choose the
field that
contains
values for
the crosstab
query, and
how you
want to
aggregate
them.

Crosstab Query Wizard

What number do you want calculated for
each column and row intersection?

For example, you could calculate the sum
of the field Order Amount for each
employee (column) by country and region
(row).

Do you want to summarize each row?

☑ Yes, include row sums.

Fields:

OrderID
Qty
ExtPrice
Taxable
TaxableExt
Selling Price
Pounds
Ounces

Functions:

Avg
Count
First
Last
Max
Min
StDev
Sum
Var

Sample:

ProductID	Jan	Feb	Mar
ProductID1	Sum(ExtPrice)		
ProductID2			
ProductID3			
ProductID4			

Cancel   < Back   Next >   Finish

11. **Name the query (or use the name that Access suggests), choose how
you want to view the query — you have a choice between viewing the
query datasheet or viewing the query in Design view — and then
click Finish to see the crosstab query.**

See Figure 4-7 to see how our sample crosstab query turned out!

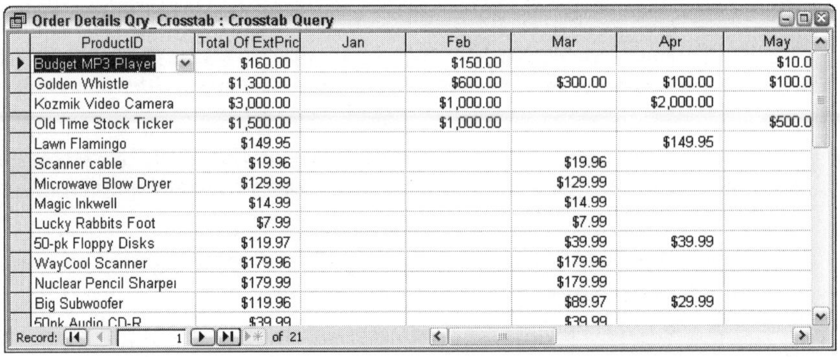

Figure 4-7:
This
crosstab
query
shows sales
of a product
by month.

Order Details Qry_Crosstab : Crosstab Query

ProductID	Total Of ExtPric	Jan	Feb	Mar	Apr	May
Budget MP3 Player	$160.00		$150.00			$10.0
Golden Whistle	$1,300.00		$600.00	$300.00	$100.00	$100.0
Kozmik Video Camera	$3,000.00		$1,000.00		$2,000.00	
Old Time Stock Ticker	$1,500.00		$1,000.00			$500.0
Lawn Flamingo	$149.95				$149.95	
Scanner cable	$19.96			$19.96		
Microwave Blow Dryer	$129.99			$129.99		
Magic Inkwell	$14.99			$14.99		
Lucky Rabbits Foot	$7.99			$7.99		
50-pk Floppy Disks	$119.97			$39.99	$39.99	
WayCool Scanner	$179.96			$179.96		
Nuclear Pencil Sharpei	$179.99			$179.99		
Big Subwoofer	$119.96			$89.97	$29.99	
50pk Audio CD-R	$39.99			$39.99		

Record: ◄ ◄ 1 ► ►► ►* of 21

Look at the results of the Crosstab Query Wizard in Design view to get ideas
about how to create a crosstab query from scratch. You can get your crosstab
query started with the Crosstab Query Wizard, and then put the finishing
touches on the query in Design view, which is covered in the next section.

Creating a crosstab query in Design view

A simple crosstab query has three fields:

✦ One used for row headings (Date, for example)

✦ One used for column headings (Product, for example)

✦ The Value field, which contains the data that you want to appear in the cells of the table (such as an item subtotal). Tell Access how to summarize your data in the crosstab query by choosing from these choices: Sum, Avg, Min, Max, Count, StDev, Var, First, or Last.

Follow these steps to create a simple crosstab query:

1. **Create a new select query in Design view with the tables that contain the fields you want to use in the crosstab query.**

   Chapter 1 of this book covers creating select queries.

2. **Change the query to a crosstab query by using the Query Type button drop-down list.**

   Click the arrow next to the Query Type button and choose the Crosstab Query option from the drop-down list. You can also choose Query⇨ Crosstab Query from the main menu.

   Access displays a Crosstab row in the design grid — the grid in the bottom half of the Design window. You use the Crosstab row to tell Access how to build the crosstab query. Access also displays the Total row in the design grid, which allows you to choose from the aggregate functions or choose the Group By option.

   In the next steps you double-click fields in the Table pane of Design view to move them to the design grid, and then choose from the Crosstab row drop-down list the way each field is used to create the crosstab.

3. **Double-click the field you want to use for row labels in the Table pane in the top half of Design view.**

   When you double-click the field name, Access moves it to the design grid.

   If you need to create the field with an expression, do that now.

4. **Click in the Crosstab row and then click the down arrow. Choose the Row Heading option from the drop-down list.**

   Set the Total row to the Group By option for this column in the grid.

5. **Double-click the field you want to use for column labels in the Table pane.**

   Access places the field in the design grid.

   If you need to create the field with an expression, do that now.

6. **Click in the Crosstab row for the new field and then click the down arrow. Choose the Column Heading option from the drop-down list.**

   Set the Total row to the Group By option for this column in the grid — chances are you won't have to make this change. (Click in the Total row to display the arrow for the drop-down list.)

7. **Double-click the field containing the values you want aggregated in your crosstab query in the Table pane to put it in the grid.**

   This field — the Value field — provides the values that fill up the crosstab query.

8. **Click in the Crosstab row for the new field in the grid and then click the down arrow in the Crosstab row. Choose the Value option from the drop-down list.**

9. **Choose the option to summarize the data from the drop-down list in the Total row for the Value field column.**

   Sum and average are common, but one of the other options may be the one you need. See Chapter 2 of this book for more on these aggregate options.

   Figure 4-8 shows the Design view for a crosstab query that creates a query similar to the one created by the Crosstab Query Wizard in the previous section.

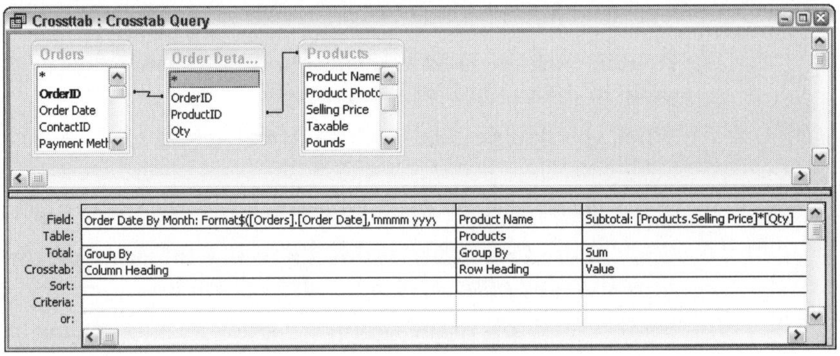

Figure 4-8:
This crosstab query shows sales by product and month.

10. **Click the View button to view your new crosstab query.**

You may want to edit your query design, or make some of the modifications described in the next section.

Modifying your crosstab query

After you figure out the basics of creating a crosstab query — choosing fields for the row headings, column headings, and the value field and how the data is aggregated — you may want to do any of the following to add more to the query design.

Using criteria

You can include criteria to narrow the data aggregated in a crosstab query. You add criteria in the design grid to the fields used for row headings and column headings, but not to the field used for values. If you want to specify a criteria for the value field, you can put the field in the query a second time, set its Total row to the Group By option, leave the Crosstab row option blank, and define the criteria. Using the same method, you can add any field to the design grid and define criteria — just leave the Crosstab row blank.

Multiple fields for row headings

You can use more than one field for row headings. The resulting crosstab query groups rows using both fields. Figure 4-9 shows hours grouped by company and project.

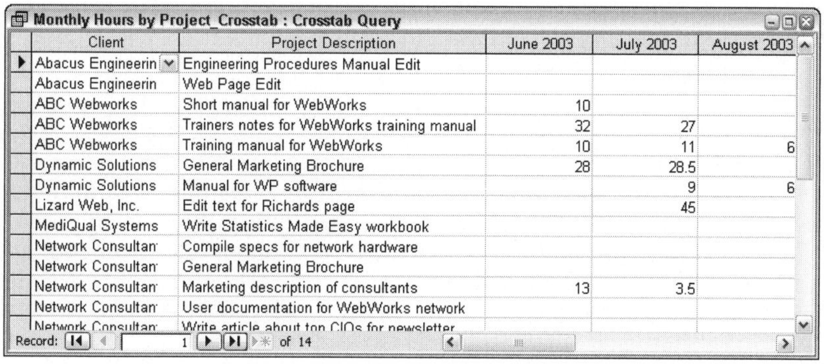

Figure 4-9:
This crosstab query uses two fields as row labels to group hours worked — the company field and the project field.

Client	Project Description	June 2003	July 2003	August 2003
Abacus Engineerin	Engineering Procedures Manual Edit			
Abacus Engineerin	Web Page Edit			
ABC Webworks	Short manual for WebWorks	10		
ABC Webworks	Trainers notes for WebWorks training manual	32	27	
ABC Webworks	Training manual for WebWorks	10	11	6
Dynamic Solutions	General Marketing Brochure	28	28.5	
Dynamic Solutions	Manual for WP software		9	6
Lizard Web, Inc.	Edit text for Richards page		45	
MediQual Systems	Write Statistics Made Easy workbook			
Network Consultan	Compile specs for network hardware			
Network Consultan	General Marketing Brochure			
Network Consultan	Marketing description of consultants	13	3.5	
Network Consultan	User documentation for WebWorks network			
Network Consultan	Write article about top CIOs for newsletter			

Monthly Hours by Project_Crosstab : Crosstab Query

Record: 1 of 14

To use multiple fields to group data by row, specify more than one field as a row heading in the design grid. Access figures out in which order to use the fields — the field on the one side of a one-to-many relationship displays first. Figure 4-10 shows the design grid for the same query.

Adding aggregate columns

A calculated column is an additional column in the query that totals rows displayed in the query. For instance, you may add a column that calculated the total number of the product sold to a query that displays sales by month and product.

You can add calculated columns to a crosstab query — they are added as row headings, and appear by default as the first column after the actual row headings. If you include row sums in a crosstab query, a calculated column is automatically created as a row heading that uses the Sum option in the Total row. You may want to calculate other values using other aggregate functions.

Getting months in order

By default, Access sorts column and row headings in alphabetical or numeric order. But usually, calculated dates (specifically months) need to appear in chronological order, rather than alphabetical and numerical order. PivotTables (described in the next section) are better at sorting data grouped in this way, but you can fix your crosstab query to appear in chronological order in one of two ways:

✦ Move columns manually in Datasheet view — click the column heading to select the column, and then drag the column heading to its new position.

✦ Specify the sort order in the Properties sheet for the query. First display the Properties sheet from within Design view by clicking the Properties button, and then type out the column headings in order in the `Column Headings` property, using quotes around the date and separating dates with commas as shown in Figure 4-11. Be sure to use the dates as they appear on the datasheet.

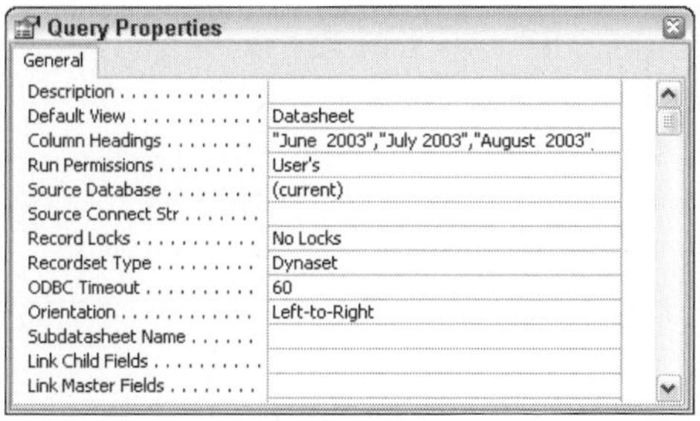

Figure 4-11:
Use the
Column
Headings
property to
list column
headings in
order.

Query Properties	☒
General	
Description	
Default View	Datasheet
Column Headings	"June 2003","July 2003","August 2003"
Run Permissions	User's
Source Database	(current)
Source Connect Str	
Record Locks	No Locks
Recordset Type	Dynaset
ODBC Timeout	60
Orientation	Left-to-Right
Subdatasheet Name	
Link Child Fields	
Link Master Fields	

Analyzing Data with PivotTables

A PivotTable is an interactive tool to help you analyze your data. When you work with a PivotTable, you can quickly drag fields and create new totals to present an entirely new view of your data, or drill down to see the individual pieces of data that make up a total. PivotTables are closely related to crosstab queries in the way they present your data — they group data into rows and columns, with the row and column headings defined by fields. Using a PivotTable, you can select how to categorize data into rows and columns, choose fields to be summarized in the body of the table, and filter the data. And rather than using Design view to define the table, you create and make changes to a PivotTable just by clicking the table and dragging field names or choosing from automatically created drop-down menus that reflect your data.

Creating a blank PivotTable

For many objects we recommend that you start with the wizard and then use Design view to make refinements that the wizard can't manage. However, the PivotTable Wizard doesn't do much for you except allow you to use fields from multiple tables or queries. You may choose to use the wizard for this reason, or you may want to gather all the fields you need into a single query, and go from there.

To create a blank PivotTable, shown in Figure 4-12, use one of the following options:

✦ Choose the Forms button from the Objects list in the Database window and then click the New button. Select the AutoForm: PivotTable option to create a new object — a blank PivotTable that allows you to use all the fields in one table or query.

✦ Choose the Forms button from the Objects list in the Database window and then click the New button. Select the PivotTable Wizard option to create a new object — a PivotTable that uses fields from more than one table or query. Unlike most other wizards, the PivotTable Wizard doesn't give you a lot of options. After you pick the fields you want to use, click Finish to create the blank PivotTable.

✦ Choose View⇨PivotTable View to view any table, query, or form in PivotTable view, or select the PivotTable View option in the View button drop-down list.

 After you create a PivotTable using one of the methods, you see a blank PivotTable with a PivotTable Field list. If you don't see the Field list, click the Field List button on the PivotTable toolbar.

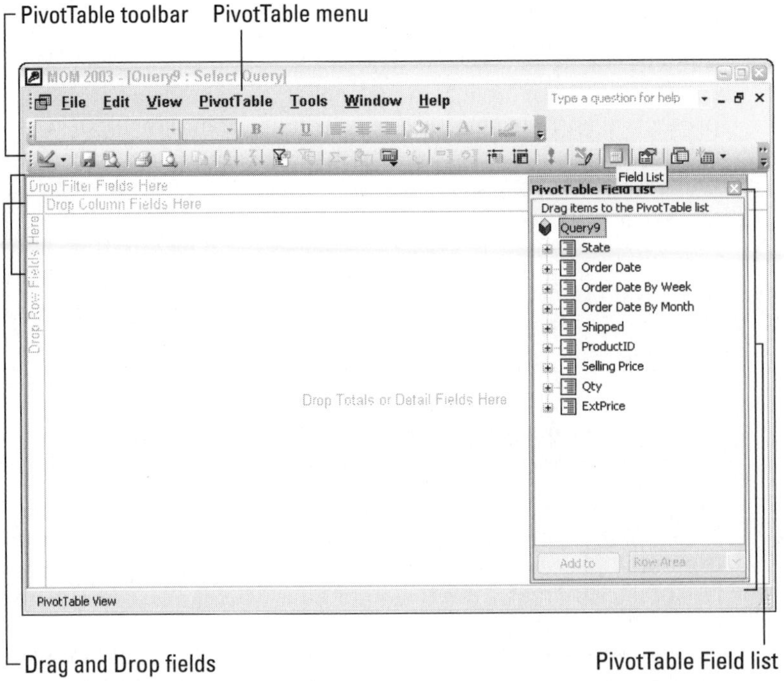

PivotTable toolbar   PivotTable menu

Figure 4-12:
At first your
PivotTable
is blank.

Drag and Drop fields

PivotTable Field list

Displaying data in your PivotTable

To see data after you create a blank PivotTable, you need to drag and drop fields into the drop areas. Each field name in the PivotTable Field list has a plus sign *(expand indicators)* or a minus sign *(collapse indicators)* next to it. Click an expand indicator in the PivotTable Field list to see more options for fields to drag and drop. In particular, Access adds fields to categorize date data by week, month, quarter, and so on.

The four drop areas are:

✦ **Totals or Detail Fields:** Drag the name of the field that contains the values you want displayed in the body of the PivotTable to this drop area. The values in this field are organized by the values in the column and row fields. After you drag a field to the Totals or Detail Fields drop area, you see data in your PivotTable.

✦ **Column Field:** Drag the name of the field you want to show as column headings to this area.

✦ **Row Field:** Drag the name(s) of the field(s) you want to show as row headings to this area.

✦ **Filter Fields:** Drag the names of any fields you want to use for filtering purposes to this area.

You can start dragging fields in any order. After you drop a detail field onto the PivotTable, you see data in the table. Figure 4-13 shows a PivotTable with the Product Name field in the rows drop area, the Order Date by Month field in the columns drop area, and the ExtPrice field in the body of the table. (The ExtPrice field is equal to price × quantity, and is the amount spent on the item — it accounts for records where a single person bought more than one of the item.) Fields used in the PivotTable appear in bold in the Field list.

Use these steps to see data in your PivotTable:

1. **Drag and drop a field from the PivotTable Field list into the main part of the PivotTable — the part labeled Drop Totals or Detail Fields Here.**

Choose the field that you want to see organized using other fields.

If the drop areas aren't visible in your PivotTable, choose View⇨Drop Areas.

A cell for each record of data appears. Now, by adding row and column labels, you can categorize that data. Later, you summarize it using the AutoCalc button.

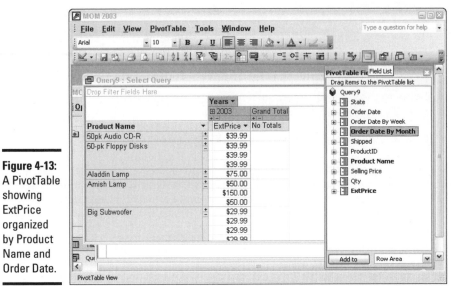

Figure 4-13:
A PivotTable
showing
ExtPrice
organized
by Product
Name and
Order Date.

If you prefer not to drag and drop, select the field in the Field list, use the drop-down list at the bottom of the Field list to tell Access where you want to use the field, and click the Add To button.

Fields used in the PivotTable appear in bold in the PivotTable Field list, as shown in Figure 4-14.

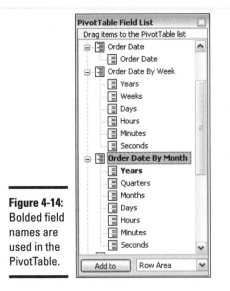

Figure 4-14:
Bolded field
names are
used in the
PivotTable.

2. **Drag and drop a field into the Drop Row Fields Here section of the PivotTable — the section on the left — to create row labels.**

   You may want to click an expand indicator in the PivotTable Field list to see more options for fields to drag and drop. In particular, Access adds fields to categorize date data by week, month, quarter, and so on.

3. **Drag and drop a field into the Drop Column Fields Here section of the PivotTable to create column labels.**

   Your table may look something like Figure 4-15.

   The resulting table may be confusing because you see each record rather than data totals. However, changing that isn't difficult.

Figure 4-15:
This PivotTable shows detail data — every record gets a value in the table.

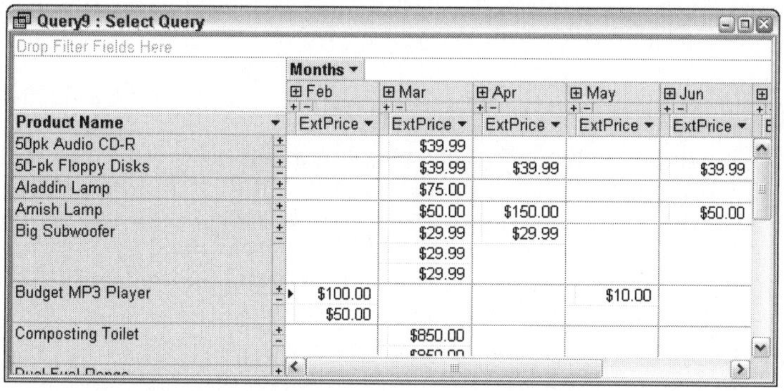

Query9 : Select Query						
Drop Filter Fields Here						
		Months ▼				
		⊞ Feb	⊞ Mar	⊞ Apr	⊞ May	⊞ Jun
Product Name ▼		ExtPrice ▼	ExtPrice ▼	ExtPrice ▼	ExtPrice ▼	ExtPrice ▼
50pk Audio CD-R			$39.99			
50-pk Floppy Disks			$39.99	$39.99		$39.99
Aladdin Lamp			$75.00			
Amish Lamp			$50.00	$150.00		$50.00
Big Subwoofer			$29.99	$29.99		
			$29.99			
			$29.99			
Budget MP3 Player		$100.00			$10.00	
		$50.00				
Composting Toilet			$850.00			
Dual Fuel Range			$950.00			

4. **Click a column label that names the field displayed in the body of the table to see the totaled data. (In Figure 4-15, that's the ExtPrice column.)**

   All like-named column headings are selected automatically.

5. **Click the AutoCalc button and choose the type of total you want to use.**

   See Chapter 2 of this book for more information about the aggregation choices. For Text fields, your only option is the Count total.

   You now see a Total column at the far right of the table and a Total row at the bottom of the table. Each cell in the table also gains an extra piece of information at the bottom of the cell: the sum, count, or other aggregation of the data in the cell. Also, the new field is added to the Pivot Table Field list.

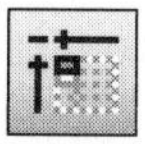

6. **Click the Hide Details button or choose PivotTable⇨Hide Details from the main menu.**

The table now displays aggregates, shown in Figure 4-16. You can show or hide the details for each row or column by clicking the expand (+) or collapse (-) indicator in the row or column heading.

You can now add or remove categories to see your aggregated data in different ways.

When you use a lookup field in a PivotTable, you see the data that Access stores in the field, not the data usually displayed. (*Remember:* A lookup field displays a drop-down list of data to choose from that is stored in a table or a list.) In general, you use the descriptive field in the PivotTable rather than the lookup field to see the appropriate data. We use the Product Name field rather than the Product ID field in this chapter even though in most views, those two fields display the same data. For more on lookup fields see Book II, Chapter 5. For information on using lookup fields in queries, see Chapter 1 of this book.

Modifying your PivotTable

After you have a basic PivotTable, you can modify it to look exactly how you want. You can add fields, move fields around to different drop areas, format your data, create new fields, expand and collapse details, and more.

For much of the work involved in modifying a PivotTable, your best friend is the PivotTable toolbar. Table 4-1 lists the buttons in the PivotTable toolbar and what they do.

If the data in your database changes while your PivotTable is open, be sure that the table reflects the most current data by clicking the Refresh (or Run) button on the PivotTable toolbar.

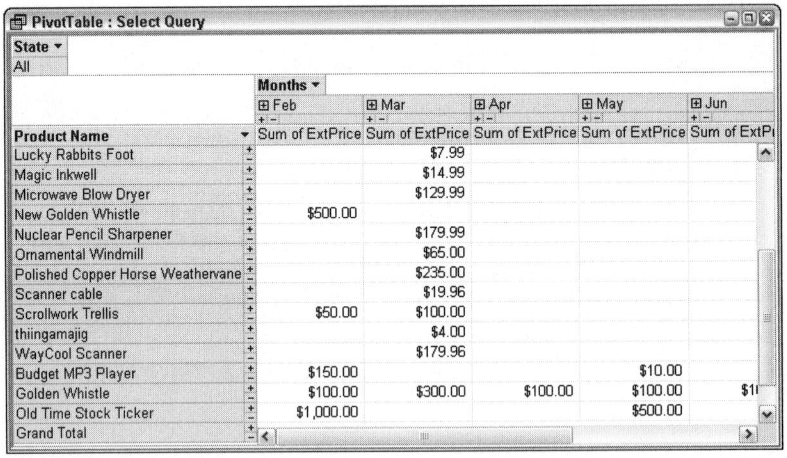

Figure 4-16:
This PivotTable shows aggregate data — total sales for each product for each month.

Product Name	Feb Sum of ExtPrice	Mar Sum of ExtPrice	Apr Sum of ExtPrice	May Sum of ExtPrice	Jun Sum of ExtP
Lucky Rabbits Foot		$7.99			
Magic Inkwell		$14.99			
Microwave Blow Dryer		$129.99			
New Golden Whistle	$500.00				
Nuclear Pencil Sharpener		$179.99			
Ornamental Windmill		$65.00			
Polished Copper Horse Weathervane		$235.00			
Scanner cable		$19.96			
Scrollwork Trellis	$50.00	$100.00			
thiingamajig		$4.00			
WayCool Scanner		$179.96			
Budget MP3 Player	$150.00			$10.00	
Golden Whistle	$100.00	$300.00	$100.00	$100.00	$1(
Old Time Stock Ticker	$1,000.00			$500.00	
Grand Total					

TIP

Working with dates

You may have noticed that the PivotTable Field list has a + next to each field name. Click the expand indicator (+) to see an indented list of fields, which is most useful when working with Date/Time fields.

Access does some neat things with Date/Time fields in the PivotTable Field list — it automatically creates fields to aggregate date data by year, quarter, month, week, day, hour, minute, and second. (Refer to Figure 4-14 to see date fields in the Field list.)

The two different date headings, Order Date By Week and Order Date By Month, allow you to use a date as a column field and a date as a row

field — but you must select the dates from different indented lists. For instance, you may want to see years in columns and months in rows to compare monthly sales from year to year.

To view data by month, find the Months field in one of the date fields and drop it in the PivotTable.

After you have a date field in the columns or rows heading, you can expand the heading using the expand indicator (+) next to the field in the PivotTable (not in the Field list) to display date data in more detail.

Table 4-1		PivotTable Buttons
Button	*Name*	*What It Does*
	View	View the PivotTable in another view. PivotChart is always available. The other options depend on which kind of object you use to create the PivotTable — table, query, or form.
	Save	Saves the format of the object, which includes the format of the PivotTable.
	Sort Ascending	Sorts the selected part of the PivotTable in ascending order.
	Sort Descending	Sorts the selected part of the PivotTable in descending order.
	AutoFilter	Applies (or removes) a filter already defined (such as a Show Top/Bottom Items filter).

(continued)

Table 4-1 *(continued)*

Button	Name	What It Does
	Show Top/Bottom Items	Choose to see top or bottom values. Choose from % of values or number of data points that you want to see. Click again to cancel the filter.
	AutoCalc	Calculates an aggregate field by selecting the field to aggregate by clicking a field name in the table and then choosing from the AutoCalc drop-down list.
	Subtotal	Calculates subtotals when the PivotTable has at least one total field and at least two fields as either row or column headings.
	Calculated Totals and Fields	Creates a new, calculated, total, or detail field.
	Show As	Displays the values or percentage of a total.
	Collapse	Collapses the selected cell, column, or row.
	Expand	Expands the selected cell, column, or row.
	Hide Details	Hides detail values (one value for each record of data) and displays only totals (if any are defined).
	Show Details	Shows detail values (one value for each record of data).
	Refresh	Displays new and updated data.
	Export to Microsoft Excel	Exports the PivotTable to Microsoft Excel (usually to make use of PivotTable functionality in Excel).
	Field List	Displays or hides the Field list available for this PivotTable.
	Properties	Displays PivotTable properties.

Working with PivotTable data

Changing the way your PivotTable displays data is the fun part! Drag fields around, in, and out of the table to your heart's content — or until you have a table that shows the data you need in an easy-to-analyze format.

To change the data in your PivotTable:

✦ **Add additional row and column categories:** Drag fields from the PivotTable Field list or from one part of the PivotTable to another. A blue line appears to show you where the field will drop. Watch the blue line — particularly the ends of the line — that tells you where you are dropping a field.

✦ **Remove categories:** Drag a field name off the table (until you see an x next to the pointer) to remove it from the table.

 If you want to save the PivotTable data, export it to Excel using the Export to Microsoft Excel button.

Showing/Hiding Details

By default, Access shows detail data, which means you see a heck of a lot of data. But you may be interested only in summary data, such as totals.

You may have noticed that every row and column label on the PivotTable has expand (+) and collapse (-) indicators. When a category expands, you see details; when it collapses, you see only the total. Use these buttons to see more or less data. You can change an individual row or column, or you can expand or collapse an entire category by clicking a heading and then clicking the Collapse or Expand buttons on the toolbar.

Adding totals and grand totals

 Use the AutoCalc button to create totals. Select the field you want to total; then click the AutoCalc button and choose how to total the values. (See the section, "Displaying data in your PivotTable," earlier in this chapter.)

To add grand totals to the PivotTable, scroll to the far right column of the PivotTable until you get to the Grand Total column. Drag the name of the field you want totaled from the Field list, or from somewhere else in the PivotTable to the Grand Total column, and drop it there. The empty Grand Total column fills with totals.

Adding a calculated field

You can also create a new, calculated field while in PivotTable view. Calculated fields are new fields that you create with an equation, know in Access-speak as an *expression*. When you create a calculated field in PivotTable view, you have the choice of creating a total or a detail field. A detail field has a value for every record, while a total field has only a value for every category shown on the PivotTable. For more about creating calculated fields, see Chapter 2 of this book.

Follow these steps:

1. **Click the Calculated Totals and Fields button.**

   Access displays a drop-down list.

2. **Choose the Create Calculated Total option or the Create Calculated Detail Field option.**

   Access displays the Calculation tab of the Properties sheet, shown in Figure 4-17.

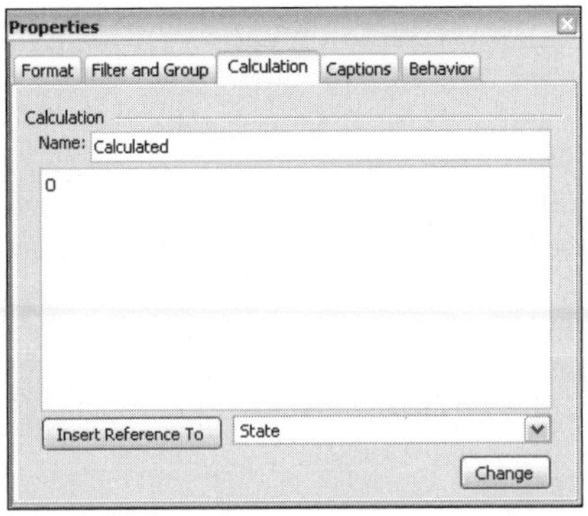

Figure 4-17: Create a new field using the Calculation tab of the Properties sheet.

3. **Name the new field.**

   Type a descriptive name for the new field in the Name box.

4. **Write the expression to calculate the new field.**

   You write the expression in the usual way (see Chapter 2 of this book). You can also use the Insert Reference To button to put a field name into the expression. You can use functions, but you must know the exact syntax. (You may prefer to create the new field in Design view — see the tip after these steps.)

5. **Click the Change button to create the new field.**

6. **Close the Properties sheet.**

The new field appears in the PivotTable Field list. If the new field is a total field, it appears indented under the Totals category, at the top of the Field list.

After you create a new field, you can drag it into the table.

You can also create a new field in Design view. If you work in the PivotTable view of a query or form, switch to Design view (click the View button) and create a new detail field. When you switch back to PivotTable view, the new field is available in the PivotTable Field list. You can use the Expression Builder when you create a new field using Design view — useful if you create an expression that uses functions.

Charting your PivotTable

You may find you want to view your PivotTable graphically. You can — with PivotChart view. Click the View button and choose the PivotChart option from the drop-down menu, or choose View➪PivotChart View from the main menu. PivotChart view reflects the layout of the PivotTable. See Book V, Chapter 3 for more on how to use PivotCharts.

If you change the layout of your PivotChart, the changes reflect in your PivotTable, and vice versa. If you want both a PivotChart and a PivotTable to work with, create two identical objects (queries or forms), one for the chart, and one for the table.

Formatting PivotTables

PivotTables do have some formatting options. You find some of the normal text formatting options through the Properties sheet. Click the Properties button. The Properties sheet appears, as shown in Figure 4-18. Click the Format tab.

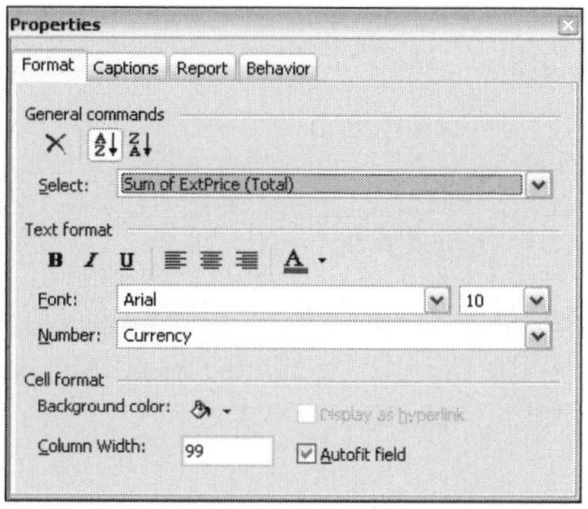

**Book III
Chapter 4**

Using Crosstabs and PivotTables

Figure 4-18:
The Format tab of the Properties sheet changes text formatting.

Properties	
Format	Captions	Report	Behavior

General commands

✕ ↑ ↓

Select: Sum of ExtPrice (Total)

Text format

B *I* U ≡ ≡ ≡ A ·

Font: Arial   10

Number: Currency

Cell format

Background color: 🎨 ·   ☐ Display as hyperlink

Column Width: 99   ☑ Autofit field

Before you select format options, click the Select drop-down list to tell Access what part of the PivotTable you are formatting. To make changes to the whole table, select the Microsoft Office PivotTable option. If you prefer, rather than choosing a field from the drop-down list, click a part of the PivotTable while the Properties sheet is open. The Select option changes to reflect the part of the PivotTable that you clicked.

Use the Delete (looks like an x) button to remove the field that appears in the Select box from the PivotTable, and the Sort buttons to sort the field. The other formatting options allow you to change the text format, alignment (where in the cell the data appears — left, center, or right), font, font color, font size, number format, background color, and column width. (Select the Autofit check box to select the best size for the column.)

You can also change column width without the Properties sheet, by using the drag method that you use in a datasheet.

Another formatting option that you may want to use is the `Caption` property on the Captions tab of the Properties sheet. Using the `Caption` property, you can change the label used for the field. First select the label you want to change by using the Select Caption drop-down list, or by clicking the caption in the table — the Properties sheet remains open. Then type the new caption in the `Caption` property. You can change the format of the caption too, using the formatting options.

Filtering the PivotTable data

You can filter data in a PivotTable in several ways. PivotTables can filter data, but they are set up for very simple criteria, such as excluding a single value at a time. To filter within a PivotTable, you select from a list of values. If you have a lot of data — as well as criteria that include a range of values — you may want to create criteria in a query, and then use the query data to create the PivotTable.

When you filter within the PivotTable, you can use a field in any drop area. If you don't want to use a field for the structure of the PivotTable (row, column, or data), then drop it in the Filter drop area, and use it just to filter the data in the PivotTable.

Every field used in the PivotTable has an arrow for a drop-down list. Use the drop-down arrow to display a check list of displayed data — click to remove check marks for data you don't want displayed.

Filter settings are retained when you remove a field. If you remove a field and later add the field back to the layout, the same items are again hidden.

Book IV

Forms

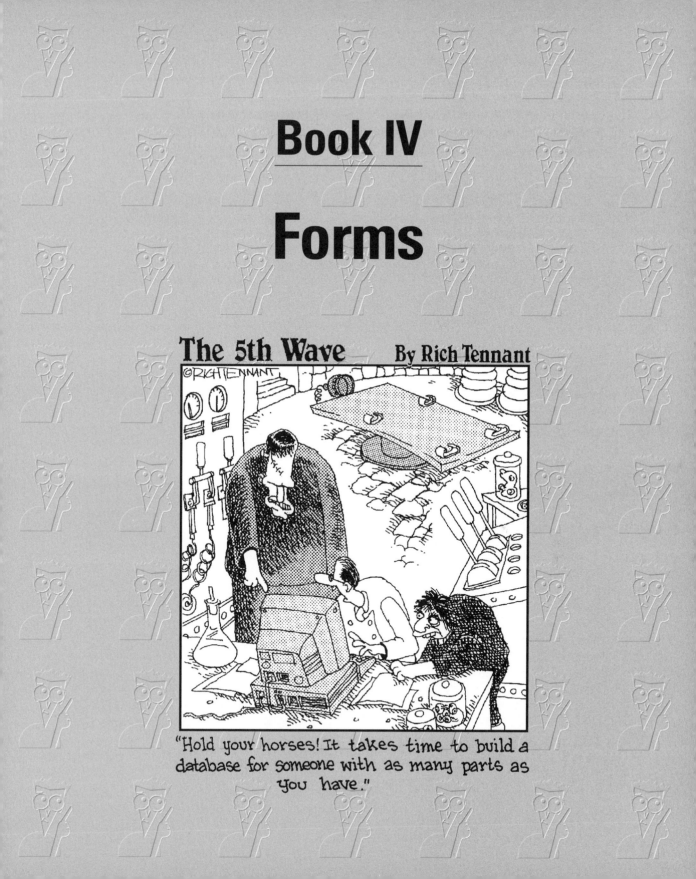

The 5th Wave   By Rich Tennant

"Hold your horses! It takes time to build a database for someone with as many parts as you have."

Contents at a Glance

Chapter 1: Designing and Using Forms (And Reports)

In This Chapter

✓ Understanding and using forms

✓ Understanding the difference between forms and reports

✓ Creating a form using a wizard (the easy way)

✓ Creating a form using Design view (the way with more options)

✓ Controlling what records appear, and in what order

✓ Using your new form to enter and edit records

✓ Saving, copying, printing, importing, and renaming your forms

*A*lthough datasheets are convenient for looking at, entering, and editing the information in tables and queries, there's a lot to dislike about them, as well. Datasheets show records one per row, and if your table or query has a lot of fields, you need to scroll left and right to see all the fields. Datasheets rarely look anything like the paper forms that your information may be coming from. And datasheets display information from only one table or query at a time, even though when you enter or edit data, you may need to make changes in related tables at the same time.

Forms to the rescue! When you design your own forms to display information on-screen, you choose where fields appear, what explanatory text appears, and what lines and boxes to add. Your forms can include calculations (such as the total number of items that a customer is ordering). You can also include *subforms,* which are small forms that display information (usually more than one record's worth) from a related table or query.

After you design a form (a first draft, anyway), you can save the form design as part of your database, and you can use it any time to view the table or query with which the form is associated. You can always change the design of a form later — no one makes a perfect form the first time. This chapter describes how to make simple forms (either using a wizard or from scratch). Chapter 2 of this book explains how to modify the design of a form after you create it. Chapters 3 and 4 of this book cover fancier forms, including forms with calculations, totals, and subforms.

Forms and Reports Are Secretly Related

This chapter describes how to make and edit forms, but it secretly also describes how to make and edit reports. Forms and reports are very similar. You *create* them with the same commands, tools, and properties to make stuff look good on-screen and on paper. But how you *use* forms and reports is different. Forms are for interacting with data on-screen, while reports are for printing data on paper.

If you need to know how to make reports, take a look at Book V, which is all about reports. But come back to this book, too, for the details of report layout and formatting.

Creating Forms with AutoForms and Wizards

Access provides several ways to create forms. The method you use depends on whether you want Access to do the work, whether you want complete control over what you see, or whether you want some combination of laziness and control.

You go a long way in your form design by using a wizard — we encourage starting that way. Save the form the wizard creates, even if it's not exactly right, and then use all your know-how to gussy up the form in Design view.

Your form creation options

As with most objects, you create forms from the Database window. Open your database and follow these steps to create a form from scratch:

1. **Display the Database window (press F11 or click the Database Window button on the toolbar).**

   Book I, Chapter 2 describes the Database window, if this is your first time looking at it.

2. **Click the Forms button on the Objects list.**

   Access displays a list of the forms in this database. If you haven't made any forms yet, you don't see much — just two options for creating forms.

3. **Click the New button on the Database window's toolbar.**

   Access displays the New Form dialog box, listing all the available methods of creating a form, as shown in Figure 1-1.

4. **Choose the method you want to use to create the form from the list.**

   See Table 1-1 for a summary of your options.

Figure 1-1:
Access
includes a
bunch of
automated
form
builders
in the
New Form
dialog box.

5. **Select the table or query on which you want to base the form from the drop-down list.**

Choose the table or query that contains most of the information on the form — the one for which the form usually displays one record at a time.

6. **Click OK.**

The appropriate wizard or AutoForm runs, or you see a blank form in a Design View window — a Form Design View window, to be precise.

Another way to create a form is by clicking the New Object button on the Access toolbar. (If you click the downward-pointing arrow on the button, you see the list of new objects you can create: Choose the AutoForm or Form options.) In fact, the default setting for the New Object button is to create a Columnar AutoForm form for the table or query selected in the Database window.

Table 1-1	Methods of Creating Forms	
Options	*What It Does*	*Where to Find More Info*
Design View	Allows you to design your own form from scratch, with little help from Access. (Design view is great for customizing a form, but getting it started with a wizard really helps.)	"Creating a form (or report) from scratch" later in this chapter.
Form Wizard	Walks you through the creation of a form, helping you to choose fields from multiple tables and queries and to add summary calculations. The results are bland and standard, but you can use Design view later to make changes.	"Wizard, make me a form!" later in this chapter.

**Book IV
Chapter 1**

Designing and Using
Forms (And Reports)

(continued)

Table 1-1 *(continued)*

Options	What It Does	Where to Find More Info
AutoForm: Columnar	Creates a quick and easy form for the table or query you specify, with field names in the left column and values in the right column.	"Running AutoForms for double-quick forms," coming up next.
AutoForm: Tabular	Creates a quick and easy form for the table or query you specify, putting data in rows, like a datasheet, but with more room for each row.	"Running AutoForms for double-quick forms," coming up next.
AutoForm: Datasheet	Creates a datasheet form for the table or query you specify, similar to Tabular AutoForm, but a little less spiffy.	"Running AutoForms for double-quick forms," coming up next.
AutoForm: PivotTable	Creates a PivotTable from a single table or query (this option was new in Access 2002). A PivotTable is an interactive table that summarizes data by multiple fields.	Book III, Chapter 4 for more on PivotTables.
AutoForm: PivotChart	Creates a PivotChart from a single table or query (this option was new in Access 2002). A PivotChart graphically analyzes data as a bar or line chart.	Book V, Chapter 3 for more on PivotCharts.
Chart Wizard	Creates a form consisting of a chart.	Book V, Chapter 3 for more on charts.
PivotTable Wizard	Creates a PivotTable from multiple tables or queries.	Book III, Chapter 4 for more on PivotTables.

Running AutoForms for double-quick forms

The easiest way to create a form is to use one of the five AutoForm choices. You don't have a lot of options — none, actually — but you get a usable form with no waiting. Display the Database window, click the Forms button from the Objects list, and click the New button on the toolbar to display the New Form dialog box. Choose one of the AutoForm options, choose the table or query for which you want a form, and click OK. Voilà — a form!

If you like the form, save it by clicking the Save button on the toolbar and typing a name for the form. (We usually name the form after the table or query whose data it displays.) If you don't like it, just close it and decline to save it when Access asks. See the section "Storing Your Forms and Reports" at the end of this chapter.

The first three types of AutoForms are the following:

✦ **Columnar:** You get a form with the fields arranged in a column, with the field names to the left, as shown in Figure 1-2. If Access runs out of space on-screen for your fields, it starts a second column of fields.

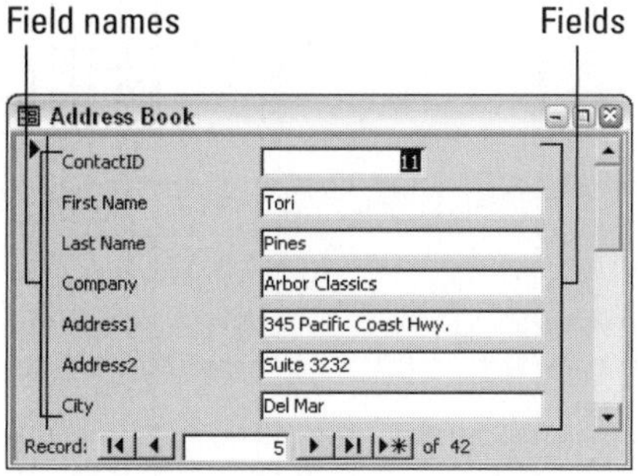

Field names   Fields

Figure 1-2:
A Columnar
AutoForm
lists the
fields in
your table
or query,
one per line,
in columns.

Address Book		
ContactID	11	
First Name	Tori	
Last Name	Pines	
Company	Arbor Classics	
Address1	345 Pacific Coast Hwy.	
Address2	Suite 3232	
City	Del Mar	

Record: 14 ◄ | 5 | ► ►I ►* of 42

✦ **Tabular:** Access creates a form arranged like a datasheet, with records in rows and fields in columns, as shown in Figure 1-3.

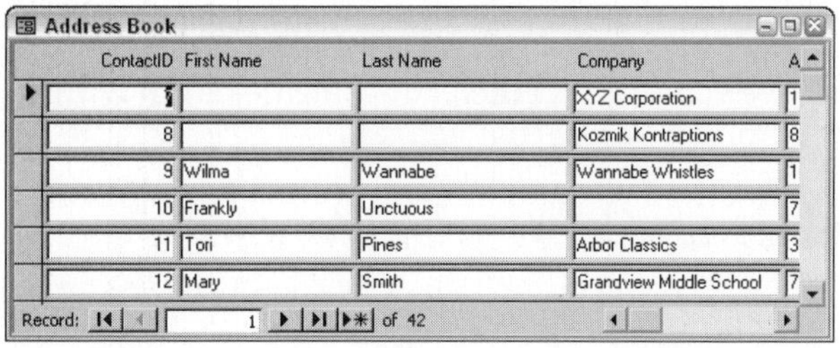

Figure 1-3:
A Tabular
AutoForm
looks a lot
like a
datasheet,
but you can
customize
the field
sizes later.

Address Book				
	ContactID	First Name	Last Name	Company	A
►	7			XYZ Corporation	1
	8			Kozmik Kontraptions	8
	9	Wilma	Wannabe	Wannabe Whistles	1
	10	Frankly	Unctuous		7
	11	Tori	Pines	Arbor Classics	3
	12	Mary	Smith	Grandview Middle School	7

Record: 14 ◄ | 1 | ► ►I ►* of 42

✦ **Datasheet:** Access creates exactly the same form as for the Columnar AutoForm, but displays it in Datasheet view, so it looks like a spreadsheet with one row per record. (See "Viewing a Form" later in this chapter for how to view a form in Datasheet view.)

PivotTable and PivotChart AutoForms are described in Book III, Chapter 4 and Book V, Chapter 3. We don't cover them here because these two views are for summarizing and graphing your data, not for entering and editing data.

**Book IV
Chapter 1**

**Designing and Using
Forms (And Reports)**

The PivotTable and PivotChart AutoForms don't exist in Access 2000.

After you create a form using an AutoForm, you can view it, close it, or use Design view to spiff it up.

Wizard, make me a form!

The Form Wizard is a step up from AutoForms — you choose which fields to include and in what order to place the fields. This wizard is especially useful if you want to create a form that includes data from more than one table or query. The wizard can create subforms for you, and even apply formatting to make the form look a little less vanilla. The Form Wizard can be a great way to get started with a complex form — you may not like the exact look of the finished form, but it works and it has all the fields you want. After the wizard finishes, you can make all the changes you want in Design view.

Follow these steps to create a form with the Form Wizard:

1. **Press F11 or click the Database Window button on the toolbar to display the Database window, and then click the Forms button in the Objects list.**

Access displays a list of the forms in this database. If you haven't made any forms yet, you don't see much — just two options for creating forms.

2. **Double-click the Create Form by Using Wizard icon to start the Form Wizard.**

Another way to get this wizard started is by clicking the New button in the Database window, and then choosing the Form Wizard option from the New Form dialog box that appears.

Whichever method you choose, you see the Form Wizard window, which looks like Figure 1-4.

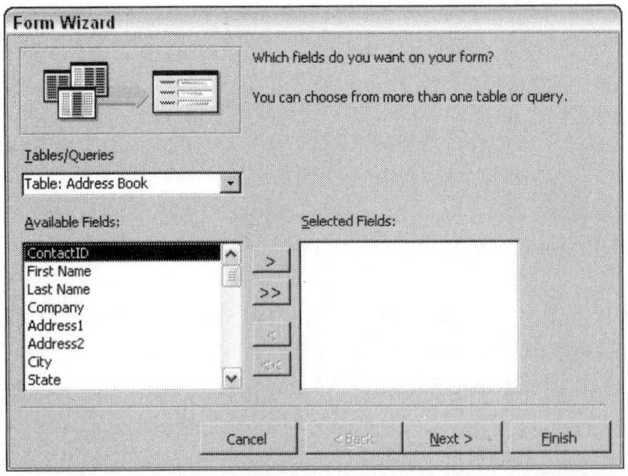

Figure 1-4:
The Form Wizard steps you through the process of creating a new form.

Form Wizard

Which fields do you want on your form?

You can choose from more than one table or query.

Tables/Queries

Table: Address Book

Available Fields:

ContactID
First Name
Last Name
Company
Address1
Address2
City
State

Selected Fields:

Cancel   < Back   Next >   Finish

3. **Use the Tables/Queries drop-down list to choose the first table or query for which you want to include fields.**

   Choose the table or query from which the form gets the data to display.

4. **In the Available Fields list, select the fields that you want to appear on the form. Move them to the Selected Fields list by double-clicking them or by selecting them and clicking the right arrow (>) button.**

   The order doesn't matter. If you decide you don't want a field after all, double-click it in the Selected Fields list — or select the field and click the left arrow button (<) button — to move it back to the Available Fields list.

5. **Repeat Steps 3 and 4 to choose fields from other tables or queries.**

   The additional tables or queries have to be related to the first table or queries. Otherwise, Access asks you to use the Relationships window to create relationships, and you have to start the wizard over. See Book II, Chapter 6 for how to create relationships between tables.

6. **When all the fields that you want to display in the form appear in the Selected Fields list, click the Next button.**

   The Form Wizard displays the next window. If you select fields from only one table or query, skip right to Step 11. Otherwise, the window asks how you want to view your data, as shown in Figure 1-5.

7. **Choose the organization you want for your form by clicking the table or query by which you want to group records.**

   In Figure 1-5, the form includes fields from the Address Book table (which contains a record for each customer) and the Orders table (with one record for each order). Do you want the form to display one customer, with all the orders for that customer? Or do you want to display one order, with all its customers? (The second option makes no sense, because each order is placed by only one customer.) You decide, by clicking an option from the list on the left side of the wizard's window.

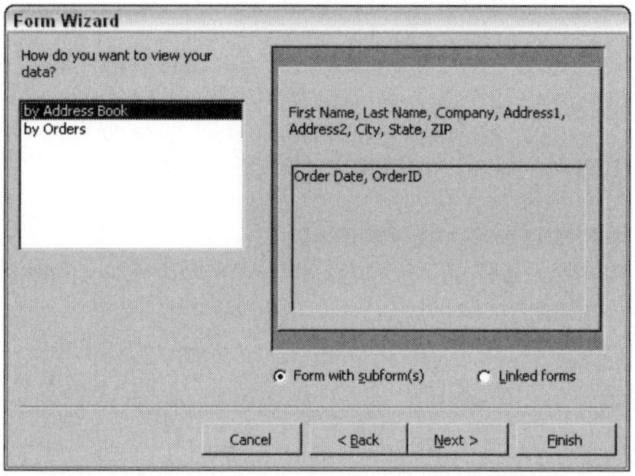

Figure 1-5:
The Form Wizard can create a form with a subform for information from a related table or query.

8. **Choose whether to include the second table or query as a subform or as a second form.**

   If you choose the Form with Subforms option, you end up with one form, with the records from the second table or query in a box (subform) on the form. If you choose the Linked Forms option, you get two separate forms, each in its own window, with a button on the first form to display the second form. When in doubt, try subforms (see Chapter 3 of this book for how subforms work).

9. **Click Next.**

   Access displays a window that asks you to choose the layout for the subform, if you are creating one. Otherwise, skip to Step 11.

10. **Choose the layout and click Next.**

    You can click a layout option to see what it looks like. If you're not sure which option to use, stick with the Tabular layout — using and editing the layout is easy.

11. **Choose the style for the form and click Next.**

    Click a style to see a sample of a form formatted with that style. None of the styles are gorgeous (in our humble opinions), so pick one and plan to fix it up later in Design view.

12. **Give the form a name in the last window. If you created a subform or second form, give it a name, too. Choose whether to open the form now (in Form view) or to make changes to the form design (in Design view). Then click Finish to create the form.**

    Why not open it first, to see how it looks? You can always edit the design later.

    Figure 1-6 shows a form with a subform as created by the Form Wizard.

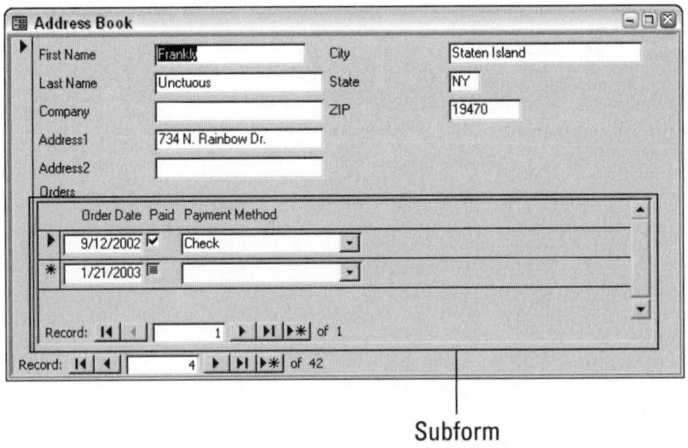

Figure 1-6:
A sample form created by the Form Wizard.

Subform

When you are done admiring your new form, close it with the Close button. To change its design, see Chapter 2 of this book.

Viewing a Form

After you create a form, you can open it in any of five views. When the form is open, you can switch views by clicking the View button, which is the left-most button on the toolbar. The View button changes depending on which view you are in. The five views (and their icons on the View button) are:

✦ **Form view** displays the form as you (or the Form Wizard or AutoForm) designed it, as shown in Figure 1-6.

✦ **Datasheet view** displays the fields from the form as a datasheet, just as if you were looking at a table or query. The datasheet includes only the fields included on the form, in the same order as on the form, even if your table includes additional fields.

✦ **Design view** displays the Design View window in which you can move form elements around, change them, add them, and delete them, as described in the next section.

✦ **PivotTable** and **PivotChart views** summarize and chart the information in the fields shown on the form. See Book III, Chapter 4 for how to analyze your data using PivotTables and Book V, Chapter 3 for how to make PivotCharts (and other kinds of charts).

The PivotTable and PivotChart views aren't available in Access 2000.

When you open a form, you can open it in Form or Design view by clicking the form name in the Database window (press F11 if it's not visible) and clicking the Open button (for Form view) or the Design button (for Design view).

When a form is already open in any view, you can switch among the views by clicking the downward-pointing triangle at the right side of the View button (the left-most button on the Access toolbar). Choose the view you want.

The View button provides different possible views depending on what type of object you are working on. The views available for tables and queries are different from those for forms.

When you are in Design view, the default for the View button is Form view, and when you're in Form view, the default is Design view. If you want to switch back and forth between Form and Design views (to make changes to your form and then see the results), just click the View button.

Creating Forms (And Reports) in Design View

As you work with forms, you'll find yourself using Design view in two situations: to create a form from scratch, and to change the layout of an existing form. Either way, you see controls — the objects on the form that tell Access what to display.

The information in this section (and most of the rest of the sections in this chapter) works for creating and editing reports, too. Just substitute the word "report" for "form" and give it a try!

Creating a form (or report) from scratch

To create a new form using Design view, follow these steps:

1. **Press F11 if the Database window isn't visible, and then click the Forms button on the Objects list in the Database window.**

   To make a report, click the Reports button.

2. **Click the New button on the Database window toolbar.**

   You see the New Form dialog box (refer to Figure 1-1). If you are making a report, it's the New Report dialog box, but it works the same way.

3. **Choose the Design View option from the list.**

   Chances are, it's already selected.

4. **From the drop-down list, choose the table or query that contains the fields you want to display on this form.**

5. **Click OK.**

   You see a blank form (or report) in Design view, as shown in Figure 1-7. (The Toolbox and Field list may not appear — yet.) After you create the form, you're ready to add controls to it, as explained in the section "Elements of Design view" section, later in this chapter.

You'd think that another easy way to start a form in Design view would be to click the Create Form in Design View icon in the list of forms in the Database window. However, this method doesn't allow you to select the table or query on which you want to base the form. If you create a form this way, you need to select the table or query that has the data, as described in the section "Where records come from," later in this chapter.

Ruler   Grid   Toolbox   Field list

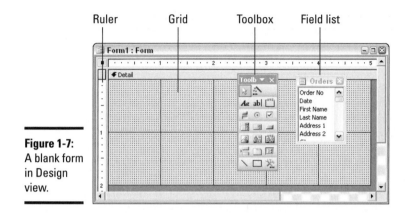

Figure 1-7:
A blank form
in Design
view.

Changing the layout of an existing form or report

To see an existing form or report in Design view, click its name in the
Database window and click the Design button on the Database window toolbar. Figure 1-8 shows a form in Design view.

Click here to select the entire form.

Label   Combo box   Command button

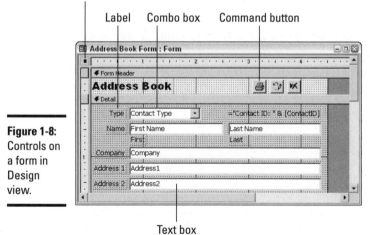

Figure 1-8:
Controls on
a form in
Design
view.

Text box

Elements of Design view

Design view shows the controls that make up your form or report, and
enables you to create, move, and delete the controls. You can also set the
properties of your controls to change how they look and act.

We can hear you asking, what's a control? A *control* is an object on a form or report that displays some information. Some controls display text, while others display check boxes, command buttons, drop-down menus, or pictures. You choose what information appears on your form or report by making controls to display that information. Figure 1-8 shows some of the all-time most popular controls: a text box (to show text, usually from a field in your table), a label (to show explanatory text), a combo box (to show a drop-down menu), and a command button (to run a little program, either a macro or a VBA module). Chapter 2 of this book includes a list of other types of controls.

Other things you may see in Design view are the following:

✦ **Grid:** Access displays a grid of lines and dots in the background of the Design View window to help you align objects neatly, as well as rulers at the top and left of the window. Figure 1-7 shows the grid.

 ✦ **Toolbox:** This little window contains a button for each type of control you may want to create (refer to Figure 1-7 for what it looks like). Display it by clicking the Toolbox button on the Access toolbar, choosing View⇨Toolbox from the menu, or right-clicking in the form and choosing the Toolbox option from the shortcut menu that appears. You can drag the Toolbox window to the edge of the Access window (called *docking*), where it turns into a toolbar. See Chapter 2 of this book for what each Toolbox button does.

 ✦ **Field list:** This floating window shows a list of the fields in the table or query that this form or report is based on (refer to Figure 1-7). You use it when creating a new control to display a field from your table or query. Display the Field list by clicking the Field List button on the Access toolbar or choosing View⇨Field List.

✦ **Toolbar:** The Access toolbar changes to include buttons for use in Design view, as shown in Figure 1-9.

Figure 1-9: Buttons on the toolbar in Design view.

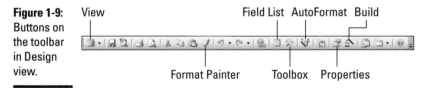

View · Field List · AutoFormat · Build · Format Painter · Toolbox · Properties

✦ **Formatting toolbar:** This toolbar appears beneath the regular Access toolbar and contains useful options depending on what part of the form or report is selected. We describe the buttons in Chapter 2 of this book where we explain how to format controls after you create them. If the Formatting toolbar isn't visible, choose View⇨Toolbars⇨Formatting (Form/Report).

✦ **Properties sheet:** This window (shown in Figure 1-10) displays the properties of the selected object, which can be the whole form or report, a section of the form or report, or an individual control. Tabs display the different types of properties. The properties listed depend on the type of object that you select. Click the All tab to see all the properties of the selected item in one long list.

Display the Properties sheet by clicking the Properties button, choosing View⇨Properties, right-clicking in the Design View window and choosing the Properties option from the shortcut menu, or double-clicking a control. To change which control's properties display, you can choose another control name from the drop-down list at the top of the Properties menu. You can also move and size the Properties sheet.

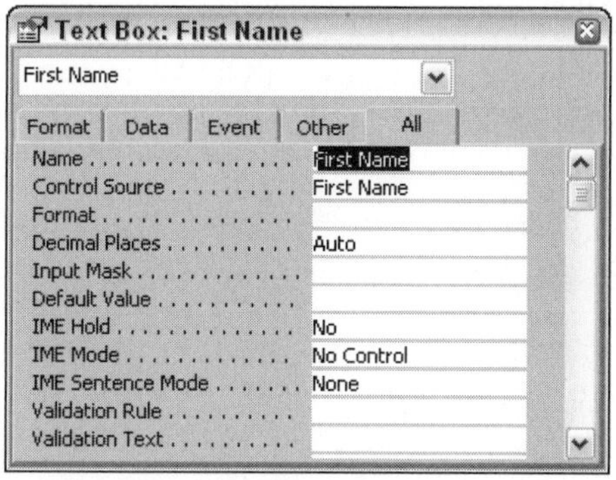

Figure 1-10:
The properties of a form control.

```
Text Box: First Name                           ✕
First Name                              ⌄
Format | Data | Event | Other | All
Name . . . . . . . . . . . . . .   First Name
Control Source . . . . . . . . .   First Name
Format . . . . . . . . . . . . .
Decimal Places . . . . . . . . .   Auto
Input Mask . . . . . . . . . . .
Default Value . . . . . . . . . .
IME Hold . . . . . . . . . . . .   No
IME Mode . . . . . . . . . . . .   No Control
IME Sentence Mode . . . . . . .    None
Validation Rule . . . . . . . . .
Validation Text . . . . . . . . .
```

If you use the Toolbox a lot, you can customize it. In addition to dragging it around your screen to a better position, you can change its shape by dragging its edges or by docking it at the edge of the Access window.

Configuring the Whole Form or Report

Some properties apply to an entire form, such as what records appear in the form or report, how many records appear at the same time, and what scroll bars and buttons appear around the edges. This section explains how to set these form and report properties, and why you'd want to.

Reports have additional properties and sections, which are described in Book V, Chapter 1.

**Book IV
Chapter 1**

**Designing and Using
Forms (And Reports)**

Follow these steps to display the properties that apply to the whole form or report:

1. **To select the entire form or report, click in the upper-left corner of the Design View window, in the little box where the two rulers intersect.**

Refer to Figure 1-8 for where this box is.

2. **If the Properties sheet isn't already open, click the Properties button on the toolbar to display it.**

The Properties sheet is shown in Figure 1-11.

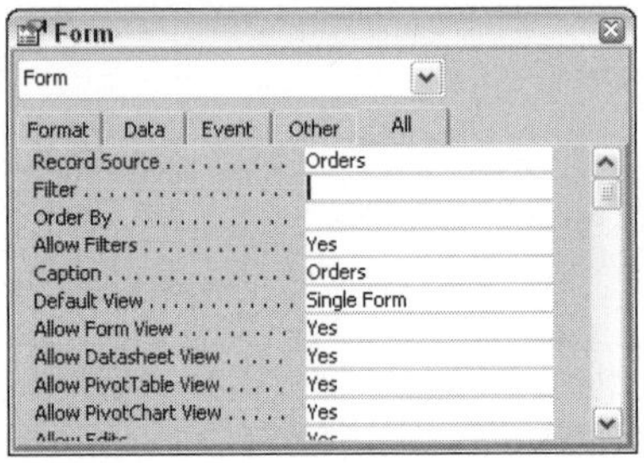

Figure 1-11: The properties of an entire form.

Here are two other ways to see the properties of the whole form or report:

✦ Double-click the gray area behind the grid.

✦ If the Properties sheet is already open, choose Form or Report from its drop-down list. (This list doesn't appear in Access 2002.)

The next few sections describe the most useful form and report properties.

Where records come from

When you created your form or report, you probably chose the *record source* — the table or query that provides the records to display. You rarely want to change the record source — if you want to use different data, you may as well start with a new form or report. An exception would be if you decide to use a query to sort or filter the data, but you are still displaying the same fields. To see or change the record source, open the form or report in Design view, display its properties, and follow these steps:

1. **Click the Data or All tab in the Properties sheet.**

Either way, the first property listed is the Record Source property. It shows the name of the table or query from which the form or report displays records (refer to Figure 1-11).

2. **If you want to change the record source to a different table or query, click the down-pointing triangle button at the right end of the** Record Source **property and choose a different table or query from the list that appears.**

   If the form or report is based on a query and you want to modify the query, click the Expression Builder button (the ... button to the right of the Record Source property). See Book III for how queries work.

If you are going to change the record source, do it before you spend a lot of time working on the design of the form. Having the correct record source makes creating and editing your form or report much easier, because Access already knows what fields may appear on it (the fields from the record source you choose appear in the floating Field list, making them easy to drag to the Design View window).

Deciding the order of the records

You can also control the order in which records appear. You may want to browse through your address book by last name or by city. Normally, Access displays the records in the same order as the record source. If the record source is a table, records appear in primary key order from that table. If the record source is a query, records are in the sort order specified in the query.

However, you can change the order of the records by changing the Order By property of the form or report, which appears on the Data tab of the Properties sheet. Type the field name into the Order By property (refer to Figure 1-11). If you want the records to appear in reverse order, type a space and **DESC** after the field name (for descending order).

One record or many?

You usually want your form to show only one record at a time, like a paper form. Most forms display one record at a time. For example, the Address Book forms shown in Figures 1-2, 1-3, and 1-6 each display one record from an Address Book table. But sometimes you want to see more than one record at a time, as in the form in Figure 1-12. (Reports use a different system to determine whether one or many records appear on the report, as described in Book V, Chapter 1.)

A form's Default View property determines whether the form displays one or several records. Display the form properties, click the Format tab of the Properties sheet, and look at the second property, Default View. The first three options are:

**Book IV
Chapter 1**

**Designing and Using
Forms (And Reports)**

✦ **Single Form:** Displays one record at a time. This setting is the default.

✦ **Continuous Forms:** Repeats the form for as many records as fit in the window, as shown in Figure 1-12.

✦ **Datasheet:** Displays a datasheet with the same fields that are included on the form. This option is used primarily for subforms, which are described in Chapter 3 of this book.

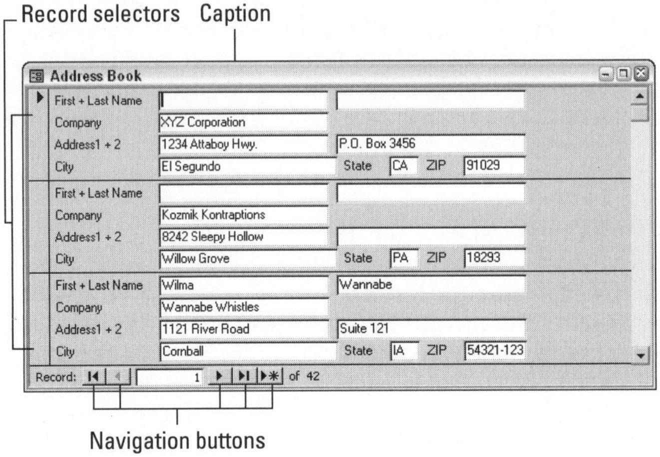

Record selectors ── Caption

Figure 1-12:
A form can display several records at the same time.

Navigation buttons

The last two options, PivotTable and PivotChart, are described in Book III, Chapter 4 and Book V, Chapter 3.

Some other cool form properties

A few other useful form properties appear on the Properties sheet for the form. Here's what they do:

✦ **Title bar text:** The Caption property, which appears on the Format tab, controls the text that appears in the title bar of the form. Normally, the title bar shows the same name as the form, but you can change this.

✦ **Scroll bars and navigation buttons:** Normally forms include horizontal and vertical scroll bars if the form is too large to fit in the window. You also see navigation buttons to move to the first, previous, next, and last records. You can turn the scroll bars and navigation buttons on and off using the Scroll Bars and Navigation Buttons properties, both of which appear on the Format tab.

✦ **Record selectors:** A gray box — the *record selector* — appears to the right of the information for one record, as shown in Figure 1-12. When you are editing records using your form, you can delete or copy a record by clicking its record selector and pressing the Delete key or Ctrl+C. You can control whether the record selectors appear on the form by setting the form's `Record Selectors` property, which appears on the Format tab.

✦ **Read-only forms:** You can make the information in a form *read-only* — that is, not editable (look, but don't touch!) — by setting the `Allow Edits` property, which appears on the Data tab. This property is normally set to the `Yes` value, but you can change it to the `No` value. You can prevent adding new records by setting the `Allow Additions` property to the `No` value, and you can prevent deletions by setting the `Allow Deletions` property to the `No` value.

Sizing Forms

How big will your form look on-screen? You can control two sizes: the height and width of the form itself, and the height and width of the window in which it appears.

To adjust the size of the form itself, drag the right and bottom edges of the form up, down, left, or right in the Design View window. You can't make the form smaller than the area that the controls occupy. We usually start with a large form, leaving lots of room to move things around, and then snug the controls closer together near the end of the design process, shrinking the edges of the form to match.

You adjust the size of the window in Form view. (You can adjust it in Design view, but it's easier in Form view.) Switch to Form view and drag the window borders. Easier yet, choose Windows⇨Size to Fit Form to shrink the window to the size of the form. When you save the design of the form, you save the size of the window, too.

If a form is too large to fit in its window, consider creating tabs, as described in Chapter 3 of this book.

The size of the window doesn't matter for reports, because it doesn't affect how the report looks when it's printed. The size of the report itself *does* matter, because the report needs to fit on your paper. See Book V, Chapter 2 for how to fit a report to the paper on which it can print.

Storing Your Forms and Reports

You spend oodles of time and energy getting your form or report looking just right. You don't want to lose all that hard work, do you? Save your form or report by clicking the Save button on the toolbar or pressing Ctrl+S. When Access displays the Save As dialog box, type a name. This name usually appears in the title bar of the form, although you can change this. (See the section "Some other cool form properties," earlier in this chapter for how.)

When you are done designing your form or report (or you're done for now, anyway), close it by clicking its Close button (the X in the upper-right corner). If you haven't saved it, Access asks whether you want to do so.

You can display the form or report any time from the Database window — click the Forms or Reports button in the Objects list and then double-click the name. If you want to change the design some more, select the name and click the Design button.

Form and report management

You can rename, delete, and copy forms and reports from the Database window, too. To rename one, click its name, press F2, edit the name in the little box that appears, and press Enter. To delete it, select the name and press the Delete key. And to copy it, select its name, press Ctrl+C, press Ctrl+V, and type a name for the new copy.

Importing forms and reports from other databases

What if you create a terrific form or report in one database and you want to use the same one in another database? You can import a form or report from another Access database:

1. **Choose File⇨Get External Data⇨Import to display the Import dialog box.**

2. **Choose the name of the database file and click Import.**

   You see the Import Objects dialog box (shown in Figure 1-13).

3. **Click either the Forms tab or the Reports tab.**

4. **Choose the form (or forms) or report (or reports) you want to import.**

   You can select a group of items by clicking the first one and Shift+click-ing the last. You can add a form or report to the ones you already selected by Ctrl+clicking it.

5. **Click OK.**

   If you already have an object of the same type with the same name, Access adds a *1* to the end of the name.

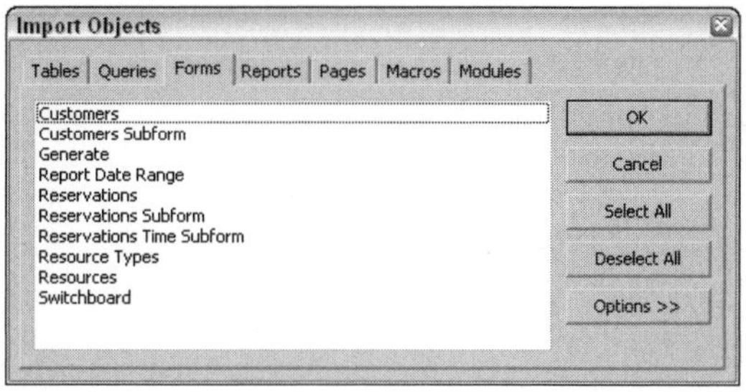

Figure 1-13:
You can import objects from one Access database to another.

Import Objects

Tables | Queries | **Forms** | Reports | Pages | Macros | Modules

Customers
Customers Subform
Generate
Report Date Range
Reservations
Reservations Subform
Reservations Time Subform
Resource Types
Resources
Switchboard

OK
Cancel
Select All
Deselect All
Options >>

Read Chapter 2 of this book if you want to add controls to your forms. Chapter 3 of this book describes advanced controls such as drop-down menus, sets of radio buttons, and subforms. If you're creating reports, jump to Book V.

Editing Data Using Forms

After you design and create your form, you can enter, edit, and display records. To open a form in Form view, double-click its name in the Database window. The data that a form displays comes directly from tables in the database, and any changes you make are stored in the tables. When you add a record via a form, Access stores the record in the table(s). If your form has subforms, as described in Chapter 3 of this book, you can edit records from several tables at the same time.

In general, you use all the same keystrokes you use when editing records in Datasheet view, as described in Book II, Chapter 2. You can also use the navigation buttons at the bottom of the form to move to different records, and you press Tab or Enter to move from one field to another.

If you prefer to use the keyboard to move around a form, the keys to use and where they move the cursor are listed in the following table.

To Move Here in a Form. . .	Press This Key
Following field	Tab, Enter, or →
Previous field	Shift+Tab or ←
First field of current record	Home
Last field of current record	End
Subform	Ctrl+Tab
Main form	Ctrl+Shift+Tab
New record	Ctrl+Plus Sign (+) (Plus sign)

**Book IV
Chapter 1**

Designing and Using Forms (And Reports)

You can cut and paste, search, and filter your records just as if you were working in Datasheet view, as described in Book II, Chapter 3. To select an entire record, click the record selector (the gray box at the left edge of the window). You can cut and paste a record from another table into your form as long as the field names match: For all the fields with matching names, Access pastes the data into the correct field on the form.

Saving your data

Access saves the record when you move to another record. You can also save what you typed so far by pressing Ctrl+S, choosing File⇨Save, or clicking the Save button on the toolbar.

Printing forms

Forms aren't designed to be printed — reports are the Access objects that give you the most printing and formatting options — but you can print them anyway. However, don't just click the Print button on the toolbar when you are using a form in Form view. Instead of printing just the record you are looking at, Access prints the form for every single record in the table or query, not just the record you're viewing!

One method of printing the form for just the current record is to apply a filter to select only the current record, and *then* click the Print button. Be sure to remove the filter before trying to move to any other records.

Book II, Chapter 3 explains how to create, apply, and remove a filter. Book VI, Chapter 2 describes how to create a command button on your form that prints just the current record.

Chapter 2: Jazzing Up Your Forms (And Reports)

In This Chapter

✔ Creating new controls on your form (or report)

✔ Adding controls to display text, numbers, dates, and Yes/No fields

✔ Spiffing up your form with lines and boxes

✔ Arranging and formatting the controls on your form

✔ Controlling how the cursor moves from field to field when you use the form

*C*hapter 1 of this book explains how to make a form or report by using either a wizard or your bare hands. In this chapter, you find out how to create *controls* — the objects on the form (or report) that actually display information. You use controls to add lines, boxes, and pictures to forms, too. You use Design view to fool around with your form (or report) and make it as clear and easy to use as possible.

The basic system is as follows:

1. **Switch to the Database window and click the Forms or Reports button in the Objects list on the left.**

   If the Database window isn't visible, click the Database Window button on the toolbar or press F11.

2. **Open the form or report in Design view by selecting its name from the list on the right and clicking the Design button on the Database Window toolbar.**

   See Chapter 1 of this book for an explanation of the toolbars, windows, and other items that you see in Design view.

3. **Make a change — add a control, change an existing control, turn the background purple, or whatever.**

   Read on to find out how to make all kinds of specific changes.

4. **To see how your form looks with the change, switch to Form view by clicking the View button on the toolbar.**

When you are in Design view, the View button on the toolbar shows a tiny form — it defaults to Form view. Clicking the View button when it's in tiny-form-mode tells Access to display your form in Form view — including a record from the table or query that the form is based on — so you can see whether you made the form better or worse. (See Chapter 1 of this book for the views available for forms.)

For reports, click the Print Preview button on the toolbar to see how the report will look on paper.

5. Switch back to Design view by clicking the View button again.

When you are in Form view (or Print Preview of a report), the View button shows a triangle, ruler, and pencil (which you maybe use if you create a paper form by hand!), which is the Access icon for Design view.

6. Repeat Steps 3 through 5 until your form or report is gorgeous and works perfectly.

Be smart: Click the Save button on the toolbar every few minutes to save your work, even before you are completely finished.

7. Close the form's or report's window (it doesn't matter whether you are in Design view, Form view, or Print Preview). If you haven't saved the form or report recently, Access asks whether you want to do so now — click the Yes button.

Taking Control of Your Form or Report

The heart of form design is the *controls* — the objects that appear on forms and reports. Controls on forms include boxes that display text and numeric data from fields, check boxes for Yes/No fields, drop-down menus for lookup fields, buttons you click to run a macro or VBA procedure, and other stuff you are used to seeing on computer screens. (On reports, all controls just sit there on the paper.)

To display or edit a field, you have to create a *bound control* — a control that is connected to a field in your table or query — so Access knows what information to display in the control. You can also display *unbound controls* that contain information that's not stored in your table or query, such as the form's title or explanatory text.

Designing a form or report (or changing the design of an existing one) consists mainly of adding controls where you want them to appear, getting rid of controls you don't like, and moving or configuring the controls that you've got.

Form and report design tips

When designing your form, keep the following design tips in mind for perfect, or at least tasteful, forms:

✔ **Make sure that the Snap to Grid feature is turned on.** This feature tells Access to make all the edges of your controls line up with the grid that appears in Design view, which makes your form or report look neater. To turn this feature on, click the Format menu on the toolbar and see whether a check mark appears to the left of the Snap To Grid command (you may need to click the downward-pointing arrow at the bottom of the Format menu to display this command). If the check mark doesn't appear, the feature is turned off: Choose Format⇨Snap To Grid

to turn it on. See the section "Neatening up your controls" for how to align existing controls with the grid.

✔ **Before you make any big changes to your form or report, be sure to save it (by clicking the Save button on the toolbar or by pressing Ctrl+S).** If you want to be double-sure, save it with a different name (like "Address Book Test") and fool around with the big change you are planning to make on the copy. Either way, if you don't like the results, close the modified version without saving it.

✔ **If you make a change and you're instantly sorry, press Ctrl+Z or choose Edit⇨Undo to reverse your change.** Whew!

Form control types

Table 2-1 lists the types of controls that can appear on forms and reports, along with the Toolbox button that creates each type of control. (The last button on the Toolbox displays a huge list of other types of controls, but few people use them.) As with any button, hover the mouse pointer over a Toolbox button to see the button's name.

To display the Toolbox window if it's not already on-screen, click the Toolbox button on the Access toolbar or choose View⇨Toolbox. See Chapter 1 of this book for other ways to display the Toolbox. Figure 2-1 shows the Toolbox.

The first two buttons on the Toolbox don't create controls, which are

 ✦ **Select Objects:** Click this button when you *don't* want to create another control. This buttons remains selected (with an orange background) while you do other kinds of editing in your form or report.

 ✦ **Control Wizards:** For some types of controls, Access includes a wizard that can step you through the process of creating it. If the background of the Control Wizards button on the Toolbox isn't orange (indicating that it's selected), click it to select it. Selecting this button tells Access

Book IV Chapter 2

Jazzing Up Your Forms (And Reports)

that when a wizard is available to help create a control, you'd like to run the wizard. This button remains selected (with an orange background) until you click it again.

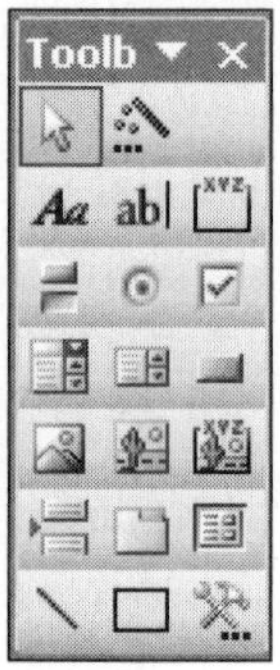

Figure 2-1:
The Toolbox helps you create controls on your form or report.

We usually keep the Control Wizards button selected — why not get help from a wizard when it's available?

Table 2-1	Types of Controls on Forms	
Toolbox Button	*Control Type*	*Description*
	Label	Text, not editable — hyperlinks are special types of labels (see the sidebar "It's a link!")
	Text Box	Contents of a field
	Option Group	Group of option (radio) buttons, check boxes, or toggle buttons
	Toggle	Button that is either on (pressed) or off (not pressed)
	Option Button	Option (radio) button that is part of an option group
	Check Box	Box that contains or doesn't contain a check mark
	Combo Box	Drop-down menu from which you can choose an option or type in a new one

Toolbox Button	*Control Type*	*Description*
	List Box	Drop-down menu from which you can choose an option, but you can't type new values
	Command Button	Button that performs an action when clicked
	Image	Bitmap picture
	Unbound Object Frame	OLE or embedded object (graph, picture, sound file, or video) that is not stored in a field in a table
	Bound Object Frame	OLE or embedded object (graph, picture, sound file, or video) that *is* stored in a field in a table
	Page Break	Division between one form page and the next
	Tab Control	A tab for displaying different controls (like those at the top of many dialog boxes)
	Subform/Subreport	Adds a subform or subreport to the form
	Line	A line, for visual effect
	Rectangle	A rectangle, for visual effect

Making a new control

Making most forms and reports consists mainly of setting up the bound controls to display the fields from the record source (table or query). Access makes this easy, with a quick drag-and-drop procedure. With your form open in Design view, follow these steps to create a bound control:

1. **If the Field list isn't already displayed, display it by clicking the Field List button on the toolbar.**

The Field list is shown in Figure 2-2. You see a list of the fields in your table or query. If your form or report doesn't have a record source, or the fields look like the wrong ones, see Chapter 1 of this book.

2. **Drag the field from the Field list to the Design View window, dropping it where you want a control for that field.**

   Access creates a control (usually a text box) and a label control. The label control contains the name of the field, followed by a colon. The text box (or other control) is where the contents of the field will appear.

Text boxes   Field list   Toolbox

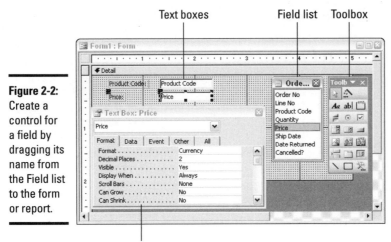

Figure 2-2:
Create a
control for
a field by
dragging its
name from
the Field list
to the form
or report.

Properties sheet

The Field list helps you create a control for your field, but you don't get to decide what kind of control to make. If you don't like what the Field list provides, or if you want to create an unbound control (one that doesn't display a field from the Field list), there is another way to create controls. To make any kind of control using the Toolbox, follow these steps:

1. **Click the Toolbox button for the type of control you want.**

   The Toolbox button turns a different color and has a box around it, so you know it's selected.

2. **Click the place in the Design View window where you want the control to appear.**

   Access creates a new control, and for some control types, runs a wizard to help you configure it.

Whether you use the Field list or the Toolbox to create a control, you usually need to configure it by setting its properties on the Properties sheet, as shown in Figure 2-2. You can change the text of a table control, change the field that a text box control displays, make text bold, huge, or a different color, and other changes. The rest of this chapter describes how to configure your controls.

This chapter tells you everything you need to know about making and configuring text boxes, labels, and check boxes, along with drawing lines and boxes on your form. The next chapter of this book describes how to create and configure more advanced controls, including combo boxes, list boxes, toggle buttons, option groups (of radio buttons), and command buttons.

Setting control properties

After you create a control on a form or report, you can change what information the control displays, how the control looks, and how the control acts by changing its properties. To see or change a control's properties, display the Properties sheet (by clicking the Properties button on the toolbar) and then click the control in Design view or choose the control's name from the drop-down list at the top of the Properties sheet. (In Figure 2-2, the Properties sheet displays the properties of the Price text box.)

Advanced form designers can make macros run when users move the cursor in or out of the controls on the form. (See Book VI for how to create macros and connect them to form events.)

The most important property of most controls is the `Control Source` property, which tells Access what information to display in the control. The `Control Source` property is usually a field in a table or query that is the record source for the form. For example, if a form's record source is the Products table in an order entry database, one text box may have the Product Code field as its control source — the text box displays the contents of the Product Code field in the current record of the Products table.

A control's name is usually the same as its control source, but not always. You can have a text box named TextBox123 for which the control source is the List Price field in the Products table. Naming your controls with the same names as the fields that they display is good practice, though, and cuts down on the confusion. When you drag a field from the Field list to the Design View window, Access usually names the new control after the field that it displays. In Figure 2-2, the Price text box has the Price field as its control source.

Making Controls That Display Text

Face it: The most important information on most forms and reports is text. Pictures are interesting, but text is usually where the heart of the matter is. Access has several types of controls that display text on forms and reports:

**Book IV
Chapter 2**

**Jazzing Up Your
Forms (And Reports)**

✦ **Label controls** display fixed text — text that isn't based on the record that you are displaying on the form.

✦ **Text box controls** display information from fields in the record source of the form, or calculated information.

✦ **List box and combo box controls** display drop-down menus of values, usually for a field in the record source.

This section describes how to create and format labels and text boxes. For combo and list boxes, see Chapter 3 of this book.

Making and editing labels

Every form has a title in the title bar of its window, which you can set by editing the `Caption` property of the form (as described in Chapter 1 of this book). But you may want some other titles on the form, including explanations of how to use the forms, headings for different sections of the form, or labels that apply to the controls for specific fields. Labels are unbound fields (they don't take their information from a table).

For reports, you use labels wherever you want to display text that doesn't come from the record source — such as the report title, the date, instructions, or any other text that's not stored in a table. For more formatting options that are available on reports, see Book V, Chapter 1.

To make a label, follow these steps:

1. **Click the Label button on the Toolbox.**

If you don't see the Toolbox, display it by clicking the Toolbox button on the toolbar.

2. **Click and drag in the Design View window to create a box the right size and position for your label.**

Don't worry — you can always move and resize it later.

3. **Type the text that you want to appear in the label and press Enter.**

If you want more than one line of text to appear in the label box, press Ctrl+Enter to start a new line.

Figure 2-3 shows a label that says "Order Details". When you create a label control, you may see a little error warning — an exclamation mark in a yellow diamond. Access thinks that you may have made a mistake: Are you *sure* that you don't want this label to be associated with another control? Most labels are associated with text boxes or other controls, to provide a visible name or prompt for that control.

TIP

It's a link!

You can make a special kind of label that consists of a Web address (hyperlink) that you click to display a Web page. This kind of label may be nice if you want to provide helpful information about using the form on a Web site, or if you are using data access pages for data entry.

Instead of clicking the Label button on the toolbar, choose Insert⇨Hyperlink, type the text that you want to appear on your form in the Text to Display box, type the Web address into the

Address box, and click OK. You get a clickable label control that displays the text you specified. In Form view, clicking the label switches to your browser (or runs it, if it's not already running) and displays the Web page you specified.

You can turn an existing label into a hyperlink label by changing its `Hyperlink Address` property. In the Properties sheet for the label control, click the Format tab and type a Web address into the Hyperlink Address box.

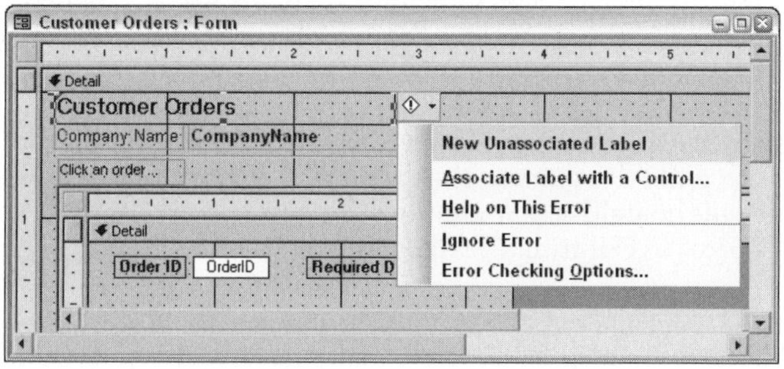

Figure 2-3:
When you create a text box, Access wants to know whether you want to associate it with another control.

If you see the error warning icon, click it to see your options. The first item on the shortcut menu that appears is the name of the error (in this case, New Unassociated Label). If the label isn't associated with another control — for example, it's a title for the whole form, or part of the form — choose the Ignore Error option. If the label applies to a nearby control, choose the Associate Label with a Control option and choose a control from the list that appears. The convenient thing about associating a label with the control to which it applies is that when you move the other control around, the label moves too.

To edit any text you entered, click the label box once to select it; then press F2 to edit the text. Press Enter when your edits are complete, or the Esc key to cancel editing. To change the font, size, or color of the label, see the section "Formatting Your Text," later in this chapter.

Putting Text and Memo fields in text boxes

Text, Memo, Hyperlink, and calculated fields usually appear in text boxes. You can adjust the size, shape, font size, and other features of each text box. You may want to make the most important fields appear in larger type, or in boldface.

To make a text box for a Text or Memo field, drag the field name from the Field List onto the form or report where you want the text box to appear. Or choose the Text Box button on the Toolbox and draw an outline where you want the text box to appear. Access makes a text box the size you indicated, along with a label control with the name of the field (see Figure 2-3 for three text boxes).

After you have the text box in place, you can make the text large, bold, or purple (or all three!) as described in the section, "Formatting Your Text," later in this chapter. The next chapter explains ways to make your text boxes smarter, starting with preset default values and validating the information that people type in.

How long should your text box be to fit the information that it may contain? Access has a nifty command that adjusts the width of a text box to match the width of the field that it contains. Select the text box and choose Format⇨Size⇨To Fit from the main menu.

You can format the contents of Text, Memo, and Hyperlink fields a bit, mainly controlling capitalization. See Book II, Chapter 1 for how to display text in upper- or lowercase, limit what you type to a certain number of characters, or add preset characters to a field (such as dashes or parentheses to phone numbers) — you find out what magic characters to type in the Format property of your text box. For other types of formatting, such as fonts and colors, see the section, "Formatting Your Text," later in this chapter.

Displaying Number, Currency, and Date Fields

Number, Currency, and Date fields appear in text boxes, too, just like Text and Memo fields. You create text box controls to display Number, Currency, and Date fields the same way you create them for Text fields, using the Field list or Toolbox.

You can set the format of numbers in a text box to display a currency sign (such as a dollar sign,) to control the number of decimal places that appear, and to display thousands separators (in the U.S. and Canada, we use commas for this). On the Format tab of the Properties sheet for the text box, click in the `Format` property and then click the downward-pointing triangle at the right end of the setting. You see a big, long list of formats to choose from, starting with date formats and continuing with numeric formats. To control the number of decimal places that appear, set the `Decimal Places` property (the `Auto` setting means that Access decides how many places to display).

For dates in a text box, you can control the order of the month, day, and year; whether to omit the day or year; how many digits to show for the year; and whether to display the name or number of the month. Make your choice from the `Format` property on the Format tab of the Properties sheet.

If you want to make fancier numeric or date formats, see Book II, Chapter 1. Forms and reports can include calculated numbers and dates, too. For example, an order form can display the sales tax based on the total amount of the order. See Chapter 4 of this book for how to get Access to do your arithmetic for you.

Moving, Renaming, Resizing, Deleting, and Copying Controls

The first step in doing all the stuff listed in the nice heading above is to select the control, so go ahead and click the control to select it. You can tell when the control is selected, because little black boxes, called *handles,* appear around it, as shown in Figure 2-4. If the control has a label associated with it, handles appear around the label control, too.

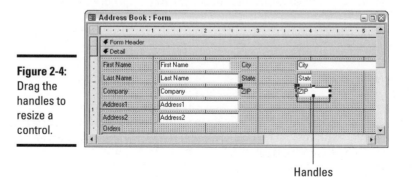

Figure 2-4:
Drag the
handles to
resize a
control.

Handles

After you tell Access which control you want to work on (by selecting the control), here are some things you can do:

✦ **Moving a control:** Drag the control to a new location with your mouse.

✦ **Renaming a control:** Change the Name property of the control, which appears on the Other tab of the control's Properties sheet.

✦ **Resizing a control:** Drag one of the handles to move that edge of the control. Exactly what happens depends on the control: Some controls can't be resized (such as a radio button). For labels, text boxes, and many other controls, the control stretches or shrinks as you drag its edge around the form or report.

✦ **Deleting controls:** Press the Del key. (Oops! If you didn't mean to delete it, then press Ctrl+Z or choose Edit⇨Undo.)

✦ **Copying controls:** Press Ctrl+C to copy the control to the Windows Clipboard. Then press Ctrl+V to paste a copy from the Clipboard back into the Design View window. Then drag the copy where you want it to be. Cleverly, if you press Ctrl+V *again* to paste another copy of the control, Access tries to figure out where you want the new one based on where you dragged the last copy (a nice feature, we thought). After you copy and paste the control, you can modify it as you like.

You can select the label associated with a control separately from the control itself. To select only the control and not the label, click the handle in the upper-left corner of the control (the mouse pointer turns into a little hand when you point to this handle). To select only the label, click the handle in the label's upper-left corner. This method enables you to move the label closer or farther away from its control.

You can also change the type of a control. For example, if you make a text box and wish later that it were a combo box (described in the next chapter), you don't have to delete the control and start over. Instead, right-click the control and choose the Change To command from the shortcut menu that appears. Access shows a submenu listing the types of controls to which you can change this control.

Formatting Your Text

You can format the label and text box controls in lots of ways, almost as if you were using a word processor. In fact, when you select a control with text in it, a Formatting toolbar appears above the regular Access toolbar. Figure 2-5 shows the Formatting toolbar.

Figure 2-5:
The
Formatting
toolbar
helps you
format your
labels and
text boxes.

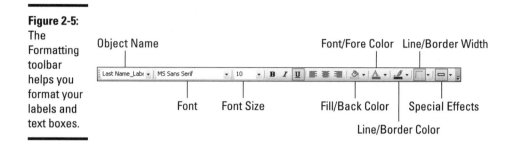

Object Name   Font/Fore Color   Line/Border Width

Font   Font Size   Fill/Back Color   Special Effects

Line/Border Color

Here are some of the properties of labels (and some other controls) that you may want to set:

✦ **Color:** Text doesn't have to be boring black on ho-hum gray. With the control selected, click the downward-pointing triangle on the right side of the Fill/Back Color button on the Formatting toolbar and choose the color you want as the background color. Click the triangle on the Font/Fore Color button and choose the text color.

If you want more colors, you can set them using the Format tab of the Properties sheet for the control. Set the `Back Color` property to the background color you want and the `Fore Color` property to the color for the text itself. These properties start as horrendous-looking 10-digit numbers, but they are easy to change. Click in the property and a Build button (it shows an ellipses) appears to its right. Click this button to display the Color dialog box, shown in Figure 2-6 (unfortunately, black-and-white printing really doesn't do this dialog box justice). Click a color and click OK. If you want an even fancier color that doesn't appear in this dialog box, click the Define Custom Colors button and go to town.

Figure 2-6:
You can
set the
foreground
and
background
colors of
labels and
text boxes.

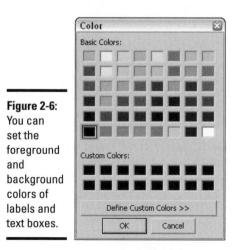

✦ **Box:** You can put a box around the control by clicking the downward-pointing triangle on the Line/Border Color button on the Formatting toolbar and choosing a color, or by setting the `Border Color` property on the Format tab of the Properties sheet. To change the thickness of the box, you can set the `Border Width` property by clicking the triangle on the Line/Border Width button on the Formatting toolbar and choosing a line width.

✦ **Special Effects:** You can make all selected labels and controls look sunken, raised (like a button), or shadowed. Click the downward-pointing triangle to the right of the Special Effect button on the Formatting toolbar and choose from the palette of options. (Or right-click the control and choose the Special Effect command from the shortcut menu.) If you wonder what a special effect does, hover your mouse on it until a description pops up.

✦ **Font:** You can control the typeface of the label text by editing the Font box on the Formatting toolbar (or the `Font Name` property on the Format tab of the Properties sheet). It's usually set to `MS Sans Serif`; don't try anything really fancy, or your text will be unreadable. Adjust the size of the text by setting the Font Size box on the Formatting toolbar, which also has buttons for boldface, italics, and underlining.

✦ **Alignment:** To left-align, right-align, or center the text within the edges of the control, click the Align Left, Center, or Align Right buttons on the toolbar, or set the `Text Align` property on the Format tab of the Properties sheet. If you really want to get weird, you can even display the text sideways within the box, by setting the `Vertical` setting on the Other tab of the Properties sheet to the `Yes` setting.

Copying your formatting

 After you go to the effort of prettifying one control, why reinvent the wheel to make another control to match it? You can simply copy the formatting from one control to another by using the Format Painter. The Format Painter copies all formatting — colors, fonts, font sizes, border sizes, alignment, and anything else that you can think of. Select the beautifully formatted control and click the Format Painter button on the toolbar. Your mouse-pointer now has a paintbrush attached to it, so you know you are doing format painting. Click the control that you want formatted like the original control.

Make it red if it's bad news

Access has a cool feature called *conditional formatting* that lets you make a control look one way normally and a different way — maybe boldface and red — under special circumstances. For example, the total amount of an order for an online store ought to be a positive, unless the customer is due a refund. Wouldn't it be great if the form reaches out and grabs you if the total order amount turns out to be negative? Well, Access can't reach out of the screen, but it can make the control appear in bright red, boldface, or both.

To set up conditional formatting, follow these steps:

1. **Right-click the control in Design view and choose the Conditional Formatting option from the shortcut menu that appears. Or choose Format⇨Conditional Formatting.**

You see the Conditional Formatting dialog box, shown in Figure 2-7. The Default Formatting section of the dialog box shows you how the control looks normally. The Condition 1 section shows how it will look under circumstances that you are about to specify.

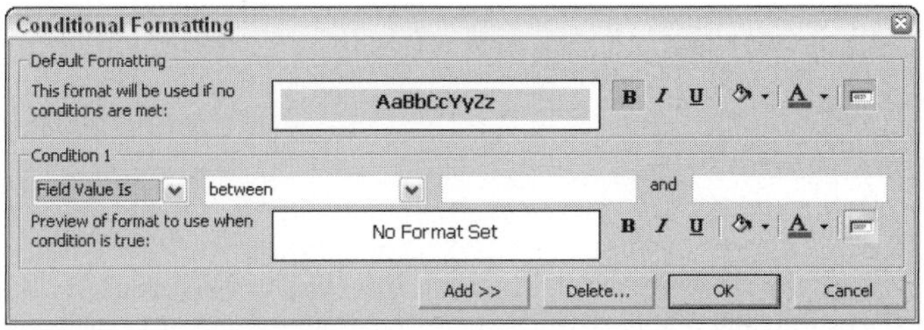

Figure 2-7:
You can tell Access to format a control based on the value displayed in the control.

2. **Set Condition 1 by choosing an option from the drop-down list and filling in the rest of the boxes.**

The drop-down list displays these options:

- **Field Value Is:** The formatting depends on the value of the field displayed in this control. You set the rest of the boxes to the right of the drop-down list to tell Access the value(s) for which you want the conditional formatting to take effect.

- **Expression Is:** The formatting depends on a calculation that you type into the box to the right of the drop-down list.

- **Field Has Focus:** The formatting takes effect when the control is active (when the user clicks in it or moves to it with the keyboard). This option is useful if you want to make it screamingly obvious when the user is editing this particular field.

3. **Set the format by clicking the formatting buttons in the Condition 1 box.**

If you want more than one condition, you can click the Add button to add a Condition 2 section to the dialog box and create a second set of conditions and formatting for the control.

4. **Click OK.**

Creating Check Boxes for Yes/No Fields

When you drag a Yes/No field from the Field list to the Design View window of your form or report, Access assumes that you want to display the field as a check box — a Yes value appears as a checked box, and a No value appears as a blank box. You can't change the size of a check box — dragging its edges expands the box around it, but the check box just sits there.

 Another way to create a check box is by clicking the Check Box button on the Toolbox and then clicking in the Design View window where you want a check box to appear. If you use this method, you need to set the check box's Control Source property on the Data tab of its Properties sheet to be the name of the field.

 Alternatively, you can display different information depending on whether the Yes/No field is Yes or No. For example, for tax-exempt companies, your order form can display a Tax Exempt ID box that only appears if the Tax Exempt field is set to the Yes value. See Chapter 3 of this book for how to display information that depends on other fields in this way.

Neatening Up Your Controls

You can spend hours fooling with the formatting of your forms and reports, moving controls around, getting all the labels to match, and choosing fonts and colors. (We certainly have!) One important aspect of design is neatness — forms are easier to use and reports are easier to read if they look neat and organized. People can find the information they are looking for — or the entries that they need to make — more easily if everything lines up nicely.

Luckily, Access has features that make it easy to line up your controls, so you don't have to squint at the screen and drag each control left or right by microscopic amounts. Instead, you can select a bunch of controls and deal with them all at the same time. To select more than one control, click one control and Shift-click the rest of the controls. Or drag around the group of controls with your mouse: Access selects all the controls that are within that area (even if only part of the control is in the area). In Figure 2-8, the City, State, and ZIP text boxes (and their labels) are selected.

Figure 2-8:
You can
select a
group of
controls and
move or
format them
together.

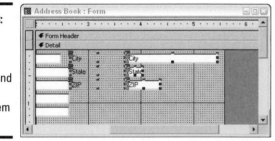

After you select a bunch of controls, you can do the following things with them:

✦ **Moving groups of controls:** If you want to move a bunch of controls together, select them all and then drag them to a new location. Access leaves the space between the controls unchanged.

✦ **Making controls the same size:** You can tell Access to make all the selected controls the same height or width. To make the widths all the same, choose Format⇨Size⇨To Widest from the menu to make all the controls as wide as the widest control you selected. Or choose Format⇨Size⇨To Narrowest to match the narrowest (left to right). To make the heights of the controls the same, choose Format⇨Size⇨To Tallest or Format⇨Size⇨To Shortest. For example, in Figure 2-9, choosing the To Widest option makes all the text boxes as wide as the City text box.

✦ **Lining up your controls:** You can adjust the edges of your controls to line up with the grid lines that appear in Design view. With the controls selected, choose Format⇨Align⇨To Grid. Access moves the edge of each control to the nearest gridline.

You can also get Access to move all the selected controls so that they are left-aligned (that is, the left edges line up) or right-aligned. Choose Format⇨Align⇨Left or Format⇨Align⇨Right. We like to see labels right-aligned next to text boxes that are left-aligned, but it's a matter of taste!

✦ **Spacing controls evenly:** Controls look better if there is a consistent amount of vertical space between one control and the next — for example, one gridline or two gridlines. Rather than moving controls up and down by hand, Access can do this task for you. Select the controls you want to space and choose Format⇨Vertical Spacing⇨Make Equal. You can also move all the controls together or apart by choosing Format⇨ Vertical Spacing⇨Decrease or Format⇨Vertical Spacing⇨Increase.

✦ **Setting the properties of all the controls:** After you select a group of controls, the Properties sheet changes to the Multiple Selections sheet. If you change the settings of any properties, Access makes the change to all the controls. Similarly, you can make changes on the Formatting toolbar to format all the controls at the same time.

✦ **Letting Access set the format:** Access has some preset formats that don't look half-bad. To change the formats of all the selected controls to one of the Access AutoFormats, choose Format⇨AutoFormat, select an AutoFormat (you have choices like Industrial and International), and click OK. If you don't like the results, choose the command again and choose the Standard AutoFormat, which looks like the Access default controls.

Figure 2-9 shows the steps you might follow to make your controls look neat: making the sizes match and aligning the labels to the right, nearer their controls.

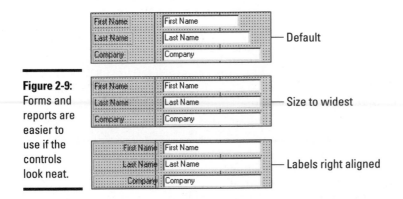

Figure 2-9:
Forms and reports are easier to use if the controls look neat.

Default

Size to widest

Labels right aligned

Adding Lines, Boxes, and Backgrounds

Some forms and reports have several sections, and they are easier to use if you separate the sections by lines or boxes. For example, an order form may have one section with information about the customer, another section showing what items were ordered, and a third section with payment information.

To draw a line, display the Toolbox (click the Toolbox button on the toolbar), click the Line button on the Toolbox, and draw the line in the Design View window using your mouse.

 Drawing a box works the same way. Click the Rectangle button on the Toolbox and draw the box, starting at one corner and dragging the mouse to the opposite corner.

You can set the colors and thickness of a line or box by using the Line/Border Color and Line/Border Width buttons on the Formatting toolbar.

You can specify a picture to display in the background of the form or report. Picture backgrounds seem like a demented idea to us — we hate forms and reports with clouds or sunsets in the background, because they make forms look busier and more confusing. But if you want to jazz up your form or report, set the `Picture` property, which is on the Format tab of the Properties sheet, to the file name of a picture — click the Build button (it shows an ellipses) to its right to navigate to the file.

Controlling How the Cursor Moves Around Your Form

You made a bunch of controls and formatted them nicely, and your form looks pretty spiffy. But here's a question you may not have thought about: When you (or other people) are using the form to enter or edit data, how does the cursor move from control to control? That is, when you press Enter or Tab to leave a text box or other control that allows you to edit information, which control does your cursor move to? Access calls this the *tab order* of the form.

Access stores the tab order for each form, which is a list of the editable controls on the form (that is, controls that allow data entry or editing in Form view). When you press Enter or Tab in Form view, your cursor moves from control to control in the same order as the Access list. Here's the problem: When you create a new control, Access adds it to the bottom of the list, even if the control is at the top of the form. As a result, your cursor skips around when you try to use the form.

The solution is to adjust the tab order of the form. To see the tab order list, follow these steps:

1. **With the form in Design view, choose View⇨Tab Order.**

You see the aptly named Tab Order dialog box shown in Figure 2-10.

2. **Change the order of the controls by dragging them up or down the list with your mouse.**

   Alternatively, click the Auto Order button to tell Access to put the controls into order based on their positions — from top to bottom and left to right — on the form.

   Access re-orders the controls, and you can look at the new order to see if Access got it right.

3. **Click OK when the controls are in the right order.**

Figure 2-10:
The tab order is the order in which the cursor moves from control to control in Form view.

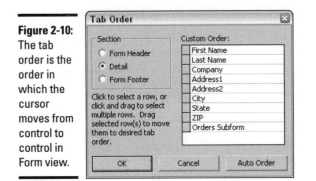

 You probably already guessed this, but this whole tab-order discussion doesn't apply to reports.

Chapter 3: Creating Smarter Forms

In This Chapter

- ✓ Making drop-down menus (combo boxes) and lists of values (list boxes) you can choose from
- ✓ Displaying Yes/No fields as option or toggle buttons
- ✓ Making groups of radio buttons
- ✓ Making a Find box so you can search for records
- ✓ Adding commands buttons that display forms, print reports, and other cool commands
- ✓ Adding headers and footers to your forms
- ✓ Making forms with tabs
- ✓ Validating what people type
- ✓ Creating a switchboard for your database

*I*n Chapters 1 and 2 of this book we explain how to make forms (and reports) and add labels, text boxes, check boxes, lines, and rectangles to them. You can go a long way with just those controls, but you'll miss a lot of the power of Access. If your database includes related tables, combo boxes and list boxes enable you (or your users) to choose values from lists instead of typing values in. If a field contains a small number of possible values, you may want to present them as radio buttons. And best of all, forms display records from more than one table through subforms. This chapter explains all this — and more.

This chapter doesn't apply to reports. Because you can't use reports for entering and editing data, the interactive features discussed in this chapter just don't work for reports (at least, not unless you have much fancier paper than we do!).

Creating and Configuring Combo and List Boxes

Combo boxes and *list boxes* are two controls that work like the drop-down lists that you see in Windows programs. Each box displays a list of values from which you can choose one value. The difference between the controls is how many values they display. A combo box shows only the currently selected value; you click the downward-pointing triangle on its right side to get the list to drop down so you can select a different value. A list box shows all the possible values (or as many that fit in the control, with a scroll bar to see the rest of the values), of which one is selected. Figure 3-1 shows a combo box and a list box.

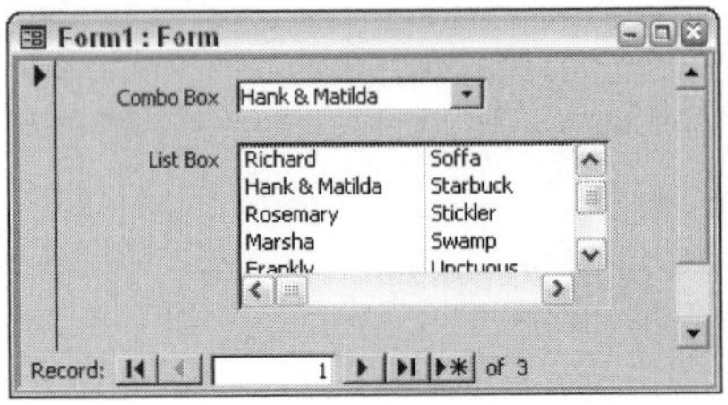

Figure 3-1:
You can use a combo box or list box to enable people to choose from a list of values.

List boxes take up more room on forms than combo boxes, so they are used far less often. On the other hand, they allow you to see more values at the same time. We explain how to create both list and combo boxes (the process is almost the same), but our examples concentrate on combo boxes.

Before you create a combo or list box, consider the following questions:

✦ **Where will the values come from?** The combo or list box displays a list of values. Are the values stored in a table, or will you type them in when creating the control? If you use this list of values in any other control on another form anywhere in your entire database, put the values in a table — just a plain old table, with one field for the value, and additional fields if you store other facts about each value. Make sure that the table has a primary key to uniquely identify each record. For example, if your bookstore has three types of products, these product codes need to be in a table, because you are sure to use them in lots of different forms and reports. Don't type them in as the values of a combo or list box.

✦ **If the values are stored in a table, which field (or fields) of the table do you want to appear in the control?** You can choose one or more fields, but don't choose too many or the list gets enormous. For example, a combo or list box for a StateAndProvince field can display the two-letter state or province abbreviation, the full state or province name, or both.

✦ **When the user of the form makes a choice from this control, what happens to the selected information?** Most forms are used for editing the records in a table or query (the record source for the form). If the purpose of the combo box or list box is to help the user enter a value in a field, then make a note of the field name. On the other hand, you may want to use the combo or list box for another purpose, such as allowing the user to find a record (as described in the section, "Making a Find box," later in this chapter).

For example, for an order entry database, you may want a combo box that lists the states and provinces in the United States and Canada. You have the two-letter abbreviations and full names stored in a table called StateAndProvince. You can have your combo box or list box display only the state or province name on the form, but have the control store only the abbreviation for the selected state or province in the order entry table that you are editing.

Making combo boxes the really easy way

If you set up a field as a lookup field — a field that must match the primary key field in a table of codes — Access creates a combo box when you drag it from the Field list to the Design View window of the form. Easy enough! By configuring the field as a lookup field, you've already told Access what table and field to use for the list of values.

To find out how to make a lookup field, see Book II, Chapter 5.

Running the Combo or List Box Wizard

To make a combo box or list box when you didn't designate the field as a lookup field, a wizard steps you through the process. Before you start, determine where the list of values comes from, as described in the previous section. The Combo Box and List Box Wizards ask the same questions that we pose, so you'd better have the answers. We describe the Combo Box Wizard, because combo boxes outnumber list boxes 10 zillion to one in actual usage, but the List Box Wizard is similar.

To create a combo box with the Combo Box Wizard, follow these steps:

1. **Open the form in Design view.**

Select the form in the Forms section of the Database window and click the Design button.

If Design view is new to you, jump back to Chapter 1 of this book for an overview of Design view.

2. **Display the Toolbox, if it's not already on-screen, by clicking the Toolbox button on the toolbar.**

Flip to Chapter 1 of this book if you're unfamiliar with the Toolbox.

3. **Click the Combo Box button on the Toolbox.**

4. **Click where you'd like the upper-left corner of the combo box to appear.**

Don't worry if the combo box isn't in exactly the right spot — you can always move the edges later. Access displays the Combo Box Wizard shown in Figure 3-2.

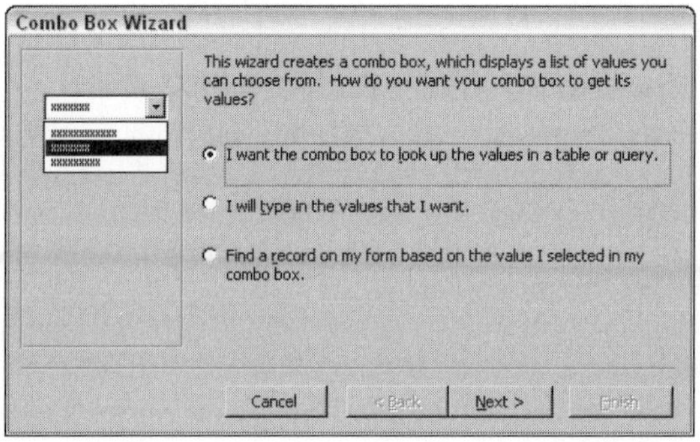

Figure 3-2:
The Combo
Box Wizard
steps you
through
creating a
combo box
(drop-down
list) on your
form.

5. **Choose where the list of values comes from and click Next.**

If the list comes from an existing table or query, choose the first option and go to Step 6. If the list of options doesn't exist in a table, choose the second option and go to Step 10. The third option is for creating a combo box that lets you jump to a specific record in your table (see the section, "Making a Find box," later in this chapter).

6. **If the list of values is already stored in your database, choose the table or query (as shown in Figure 3-3) and click Next.**

The wizard displays all the tables, all the queries, or both, so you can choose the table or query that you want. If the table doesn't have a primary key field, you can't choose it.

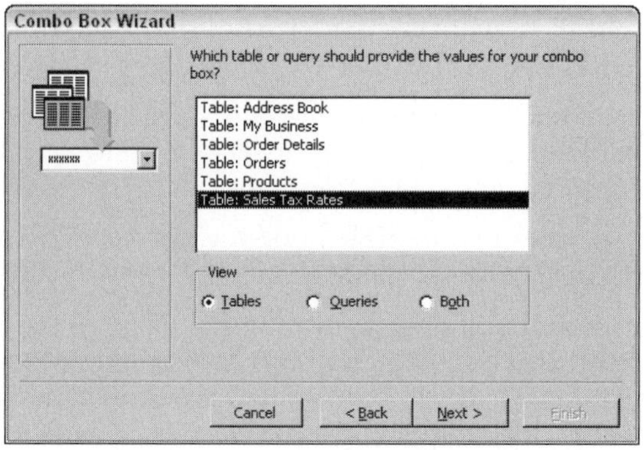

Figure 3-3:
Usually,
your combo
box displays
a list from a
table or
query in a
database,
so that you
can use the
same list
in other
combo
boxes or
lookups.

7. **When the wizard shows you a list of the fields in the table or query, choose the fields to display in the combo box and click Next.**

    You can choose more than one field if you want more than one to appear in the combo box.

8. **Choose the order in which you want the records to appear in the combo box, and click Next.**

    The wizard allows you to choose Ascending or Descending order for up to four fields. Be sure that the field on which you are sorting also appears in the combo box, or the order can be confusing. For example, if you sort states and provinces by their two-letter codes, the names don't appear in order, which looks weird if the codes don't also appear.

9. **Adjust the widths of the columns by dragging the column divider left or right, and then click Next. Skip to Step 11 unless you're typing in values instead of using a table.**

    If you want the primary key field to appear in the combo box (for example, the two-letter code in a list of states), uncheck the Hide Key Column check box.

10. **If you choose to type in the list of values, type them into the datasheet, one per row, and click Next.**

The wizard displays a datasheet into which you can type the list. When typing in a list of values, you can create more than one column (for example, a code and its meaning), of which one will be stored in the record source of the form.

11. **Choose the field that identifies each row of the combo box and click Next.**

The wizard asks which field uniquely identifies each row in the combo box — the equivalent of the primary key field in a stored table. (Aren't you beginning to wish you'd just stored the list in the table? Hint, hint!)

12. **Choose whether to remember the value for later use or store it in a field, as shown in Figure 3-4. Click Next.**

The wizard asks what you want to do with the value of the field when the form user chooses from the combo box: Remember the value for later use (for example, refer to it in a query parameter, macro, or VBA module); or store it in a field of the table or query that is the record source for the form. Most of the time, you want to store the value in a field; choose the field name from the list.

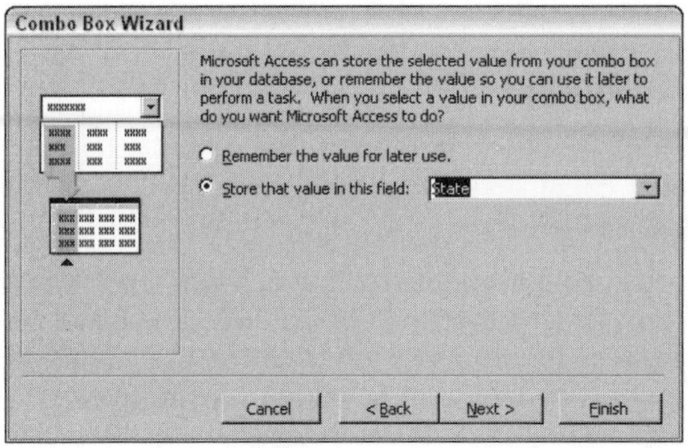

Figure 3-4:
If you are
using the
combo box
to choose
values for
a field
displayed on
the form,
choose to
store the
value in
the field.

13. **Type a label for the combo box and click Finish.**

The wizard creates your combo box.

14. **Adjust the edges of the control to resize the combo box. Drag its label to the right place.**

We never get the size and position of a combo or list box right the first time, and Access never puts its label in the right place. Good thing Access gives us a chance to touch things up a bit!

When the wizard finishes, you end up with a combo or list box that looks like Figure 3-5, which shows one of each in Design view.

The next section describes the properties you may want to change if you don't like the way your combo or list box turns out.

Figure 3-5:
A combo box or a list box provides values from which the user can choose, but combo boxes take up less space.

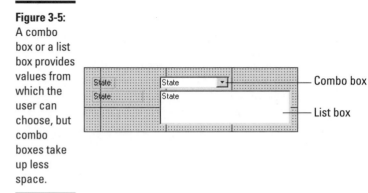

Combo box

List box

Changing the properties of a combo or list box

You can change the way a combo or list box works by editing its properties — you are never stuck with what a wizard creates. You can display its properties and change them on the Properties sheet (click the Properties button on the toolbar to display the Properties sheet). The properties you are most likely to change are shown in the following table.

Property	Description
Control Source	Field in the record source in which Access stores the value that you chose from the combo or list box.
Row Source Type	Where the items on the list come from: Table/Query, Value List, or Field List (that last option displays list of the fields in a table or query).

(continued)

(continued)

Property	Description
Row Source	If you choose the Table/Query or Field List options for the Row Source Type property, enter the name of a table or query (or a SQL statement). If you choose the Value List setting, type a list of values separated by semicolons (;).
Column Count	Number of columns to display in the combo or list box.
Column Heads	Whether or not to display headings for the columns of values.
Column Widths	Widths of the column(s). If you've got more than one column, separate the widths with semicolons.
Bound Column	Column number in the combo or list box of the column that gets stored in the control source.
List Rows	Number of rows that appear in the drop-down list of a combo box. (Not used for list boxes, because the size of the list box control on the form determines how many rows appear.)
Limit to List	Whether entries in the combo box are limited to values on the drop-down menu. Choose the No setting if you want to be able to type other values into the control. (Not used for list boxes, which are always limited to the values listed.)

Cool Looks for Yes/No Fields

Chapter 1 of this book describes how to create a check box for a Yes/No field, which looks pretty spiffy. But you have other options for Yes/No fields: option buttons (little round radio buttons) and toggle buttons (rectangular buttons that appear pressed in when selected). You can display a Yes/No field in a text box, too, but the Yes value appears as -1 and the No value appears as 0, which may not be what you want. Figure 3-6 shows a check box, option button, and toggle button.

Figure 3-6:
Display a Yes/No field as a check box, option button, or toggle button.

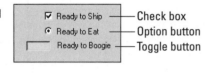

The easiest way to make a toggle or option button for a Yes/No field is to create a check box for it, and then change it into a toggle or option button. Drag the Yes/No field from the Field list to your form and drop it where you want the control. (Click the Field List button on the toolbar to display the Field list.) Access makes a check box for the field. Right-click the field and choose Change To⇨Option Button or Change To⇨Toggle Button from the shortcut menu that appears. Adjust the size and position of the control and its label, and you're done!

Creating Option Groups

If a field is set to one of a small number of numeric, integer values — such as 1 to 10 — you can display the values in a box, with an option button by each value. When editing records using the form, you click the option for the value to which you want to set the field. Only one option can be selected at a time; clicking one option deselects the other options.

Making a group of option buttons for a field requires creating an *option group* — a rectangle within which you put an option button for each possible value of the field. Figure 3-7 shows option buttons in an option group. Luckily, Access comes with the Option Group Wizard that creates the option group and all the option buttons.

Figure 3-7:
An option group contains an option button for each value that the field can take.

Categories
- ⦿ Audio   ○ Computers
- ○ Books   ○ Kitchen
- ○ Cameras ○ Other

TIP Before you run the Option Group Wizard, make a note of the values that the field takes. After the wizard is running, you can't open another table to see the values to which the field is limited. You may want to keep the table that lists the possible values open and visible in the corner of the Access window while you run the wizard.

Note that option groups work only with integer, numeric values. You can show any label you want next to each option button, but the value that Access stores for the option group has to be a whole number. In the option group shown in Figure 3-7, the actual category codes may be the numbers from 1 to 6.

An option group can contain option (radio) buttons, check boxes, or toggle buttons. However, most people expect check boxes and toggle buttons to stand by themselves, not to be in a group of mutually exclusive options. We recommend sticking with option buttons in option groups.

To make an option group and option buttons for a field, display your form in Design view and follow these steps:

1. **Click the Option Group button on the Toolbox and drag the mouse from one corner to the opposite corner of the area you want the option group to occupy.**

   Access draws a box for the option group and then runs the Option Group Wizard. (It may not be installed on your computer; if it isn't, Access asks if you want to install it now. Get your Microsoft Office CD and follow the prompts.)

2. **The wizard prompts you for a list of the labels for the individual option buttons. Type them in, one per line, and click Next.**

   Don't press Enter after typing in a value; the wizard thinks you're clicking Next. Instead, press Tab or the down arrow to move to the next row in the datasheet. (If you accidentally press Enter, click the Back button to get back to this screen.)

3. **In the next window, choose whether one of the choices that you just typed should be selected by default when you create a new record in the table. Choose the default value for the field, or choose the No I Don't Want a Default option. Click Next.**

4. **You see a list of the labels that you typed in Step 2. In the right-hand column, type the number to store for each value, as shown in Figure 3-8. Click Next.**

   Each label must have a different value, and all the values have to be whole numbers.

5. **Choose to save the value for later use or to store it in a field (and specify the field). Click Next.**

If you are creating a form for editing a table, choose the Store the Value in This Field option. If the form is unbound (not connected to a record source) and the options are for use as an input to a query, macro, or VBA module, choose the Save the Value for Later Use option. (See Book VI, Chapter 1 for how to run macros from a form, possibly using inputs from the form.)

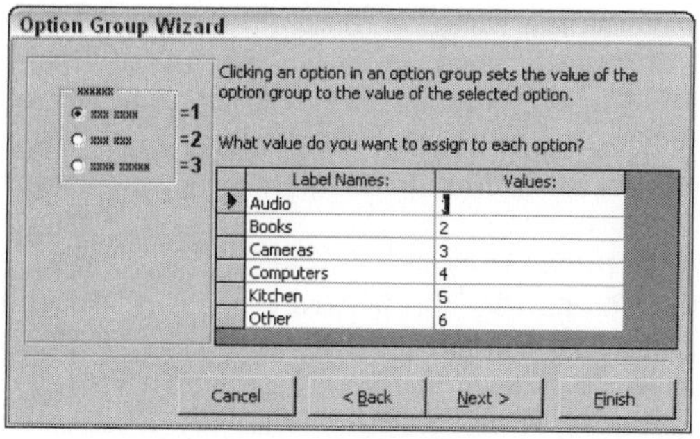

Figure 3-8:
When you create an option group, you specify a label and a value for each option button in the group.

Option Group Wizard

Clicking an option in an option group sets the value of the option group to the value of the selected option.

What value do you want to assign to each option?

Label Names:	Values:
Audio	1
Books	2
Cameras	3
Computers	4
Kitchen	5
Other	6

Cancel   < Back   Next >   Finish

6. Choose whether the options appear as option buttons, check boxes, or toggle buttons and choose the style for the option group box. Click Next.

We strongly recommend choosing option buttons (the default), because most people expect option buttons to be in groups of mutually exclusive options and check boxes and toggle buttons to work independently of each other.

7. Type a caption (label) for the option group and click Finish.

The caption appears at the top of the option group. When you click Finish, the wizard creates your option group and an option button (or check box or toggle button, if you callously disregarded our advice) for each value you specified.

After the wizard finishes, you can resize the option group box and move the option buttons around inside it.

If you change the list of possible values later, the option buttons on your form don't change automatically. For example, if a set of option buttons shows all the categories of products that your store sells and you add a new product category, you need to remember to edit the form and add a new option button to the option group. For this reason, combo boxes are used more frequently to provide lists of possible values, because when you update a table from which the combo box gets its list of values, the combo box updates automatically the next time you open the form.

Creating Command Buttons

Dialog boxes contain command buttons, such as Save and Cancel, and your forms can, too. When you create a command button, you tell Access what program the button should run. Programs can take two forms: macros (described in Book VI) and VBA modules (described in Book VIII). Luckily, wizards can do a lot of the work for you. You don't need to know how to create either macros or VBA modules to make nifty command buttons on your forms.

This section covers how to run the Command Button Wizard to make command buttons that do useful stuff. The wizard creates a VBA module for the form to contain the programs for the buttons on the form. The wizard makes buttons with actions that it divides into these categories:

✦ **Record Navigation:** These commands are for moving from record to record. Most of them duplicate the navigation controls that appear at the bottom of most forms (Go to First Record, Go to Previous Record, Go to Next Record, and Go to Last Record), but you can also make a Find Record button that displays the Find and Replace dialog box or a Find Next button to repeat the previous search. If you want to make a box right on the form into which you can type a value and a Find button that searches for that value, see the section, "Making a Find box," later in this chapter.

✦ **Record Operations:** This category includes buttons for adding, deleting, duplicating, printing, saving, and undoing the edits to a record (the current record, in most cases). The Duplicate Record button adds a new record that is a duplicate of the current record. The Print Record button prints the form with the data for the current record.

✦ **Form Operations:** These commands apply or edit filters (which are described in Book II, Chapter 3), close this form, open another form, or print another form. (*Warning:* If you print another form, you get *all* the records in that form, so you may want to come up with another method.) You can also make a button that reloads the data on the form, in case it has changed since you loaded the form.

✦ **Report Operations:** You can make command buttons to preview, print, or mail a report or save a report to a file. However, there's no way to restrict the report to a specific record without editing the code behind the form.

✦ **Application:** These commands run other Microsoft Office programs (like Word or Excel) or other applications.

✦ **Miscellaneous:** This last group of commands includes commands to dial a phone number (assuming that your computer is connected to a dial-up modem and a phone), print a table in Datasheet view, run a macro, or run a query and display the resulting datasheet.

Making a Close button

Who needs a Close button when forms already have a big X button in the upper-right corner? Some people like to have a Close button anyway, and it's easy enough to make. Here's how:

1. **With your form open in Design view, click the Command Button button on the Toolbox.**

2. **Click in the form where you want the button to appear.**

   Don't worry about the exact location; you can always move it later. Access starts the Command Button Wizard shown in Figure 3-9.

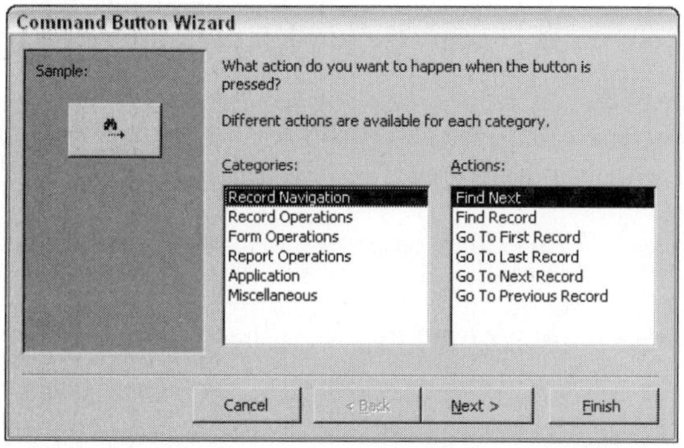

Figure 3-9:
The Command Button Wizard includes lots of pre-programmed commands for your button to run.

> **Command Button Wizard**
>
> Sample:
>
> What action do you want to happen when the button is pressed?
>
> Different actions are available for each category.
>
> Categories:
> - Record Navigation
> - Record Operations
> - Form Operations
> - Report Operations
> - Application
> - Miscellaneous
>
> Actions:
> - Find Next
> - Find Record
> - Go To First Record
> - Go To Last Record
> - Go To Next Record
> - Go To Previous Record
>
> Cancel   < Back   Next >   Finish

3. **Choose the Form Operations category and the Close Form action. Click Next.**

4. **Choose whether you'd like to have text or a picture on the button and click Next.**

   If you choose the Text option, you can edit the text in the box. If you choose the Picture option, you can choose from the list of suggested icons, or click the Browse button to look at the full set of icons Access provides. You can use any bitmap (.bmp) file as an icon.

5. **Type a name for your new control and click Finish.**

   The wizard creates a command button control where you originally clicked the form. Now you can drag the edges of the button to resize it, or drag the whole button to another location.

After creating a command button using the wizard, you edit its properties, as described in the "Customizing your command button" section, later in this chapter.

Making a button to display a related form

You can make a command button to display another form. You can display any old form in the database, but this kind of command button is most powerful when you use it to display a form that shows the records of a table that relates to the records in your original form. For example, you may be working on an Order form that displays information about each order of your online store. You can add a command button that opens the Address Book form showing the record for the customer that placed the current order, including the customer's address, phone number, and other information.

Here's how to add a button to display another form:

1. **With the form open in Design view, click the Command Button button on the Toolbox.**

2. **Click in the form where you want the button to appear.**

   The Command Button Wizard fires up to create your button.

3. **Choose the Form Operations category and the Open Form action. Click Next.**

4. **Choose the form name you want the button to open from the list and click Next.**

5. **In the next window, choose whether to display the form with all records available, or display a specific record on the form. Choose the Open the Form and Find Specific Data to Display option, and click Next.**

   This option tells the wizard that you want to display a specific record — in the next step, you tell the wizard which record you want to see.

6. **Choose the fields from the two forms that match. Click Next.**

   You see two list of fields, as shown in Figure 3-10: The left-hand list shows the field in the record source of the current form, and the right-hand list shows the fields in the record source of the form you want the button to open.

7. **Choose the text or picture to appear on the form, click Next, type a name for the control, and click Finish.**

   The wizard makes the command button. Switch to Form view by clicking the View button on the toolbar. Try out your new button!

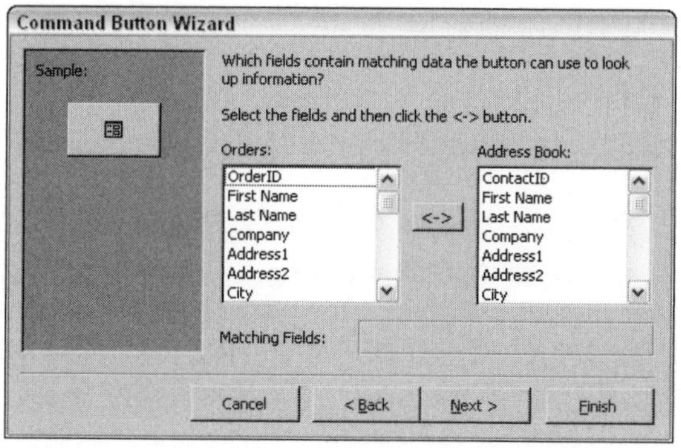

Figure 3-10: You can display a form with the record that matches the current record of the current form.

Making a button to print the current record

The Command Button Wizard offers a number of print actions, but most of them don't work the way you might wish. The Print a Form action prints a form once for every single record in the form, so you need to come up with a way to restrict the records to the one(s) you want. If you want to print the current record in the current form, run the Command Button Wizard and choose the Record Operations category and the Print Record action.

If you want to print a report for just the record in the current form, you need to do some extra work. Specifically, you need to make a macro that the button runs, and you need to set up the macro to print the report with the records limited to those records that match the record currently displayed on the form.

Luckily, this macro is short and easy to make — see Book VI, Chapter 1 for specific directions.

Making other cool buttons

You can run the Command Button Wizard to make lots of other useful buttons. Command buttons do some of our favorite things. The following list shows how the wizard creates them:

✦ **Add a new record that's a duplicate of the current record:** Choose the Record Operations category and the Duplicate Record action.

✦ **Save the current record:** Choose the Record Operations category and the Save Record action.

✦ **Display the results of a query in Datasheet view:** Choose the Miscellaneous category and the Run Query action.

✦ **Run a macro:** Choose the Miscellaneous category and the Run Macro action. Book VI describes how to make macros that do all kinds of things.

Customizing your command button

You can edit the properties of a command button after you create it. To display the button's Properties sheet, double-click the command button in Design view, or click the Properties button on the toolbar and select the command button.

Some of the most useful properties and what they do are in the following table.

Property	Description
Caption	Text that appears on the button unless it displays a picture. (If the Picture property specifies a picture, the button shows the picture, not the caption.)
Picture	Picture (icon) that appears on the button. (bitmap) indicates that you selected a picture. Click the Build button to the right of the property to select a different picture. If the picture is blank, Access displays the Caption text.
On Click	What program (macro or VBA module) Access runs when you click the button.

You can tell Access to run programs when you click, double-click, move into, or move away from the button (and other times, too). See Book VI, Chapter 1 for instructions.

Making a Find box

When you are using a form, choose Edit⇨Find or press Ctrl+F to display the Find and Replace dialog box that you can use to jump directly to a record that matches the criteria you specify. But wouldn't it be nice to have a combo box right on the form with the Find button next to it, so you can locate a record without bringing up a separate dialog box? Access makes this surprisingly easy.

For example, on an Address Book form, you could create a combo box that would list all the customers in your Address Book. When you choose a customer, the macro takes you right to that customer's record.

Follow these steps to create a Find box:

1. **With your form open in Design view, click the Combo Box button on the Toolbox.**

2. **Click in your form where you want the Find box to appear.**

   The Combo Box Wizard runs, as described in the section, "Running the Combo or List Box Wizard," earlier in this chapter.

3. **Choose the Find a Record on My Form Based on the Value I Selected in My Combo Box option and click Next.**

   Access displays a list of the fields in the record source of the form.

4. **Choose the table or query that contains the list of values from which the user can choose when finding a record. Click Next.**

   If you choose a field that is unique for each record (for example, the OrderID for a form that displays orders), the combo box provides you with a list of the values for the field, and choosing a value takes you right to the order. If you choose a field that's not unique, the combo box displays a list with duplicate values and finds records unpredictably.

5. **Adjust the width of the column to set the width of the drop-down list by dragging the column divider. Then click Next.**

6. **Type a name for the combo box control and click Finish.**

   The wizard creates the combo box. Switch to Form view by clicking the View button on the toolbar, and then test it out.

Adding and Linking Subforms

You use subforms to display related data from different tables. For example, for an online store, if you have a form that shows information about one order from your Orders table, it would be nice if you could also see a list of the items that were included in the order, which may be stored in the related Order Detail table. Figure 3-11 shows an example. The main form displays records from the "one" side of a one-to-many relationship and the subform displays records from the "many" side. As a result, the subform displays many records that relate to the one record on the main form.

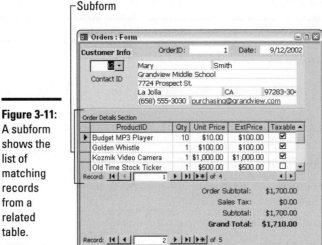

Subform

Figure 3-11:
A subform
shows the
list of
matching
records
from a
related
table.

Before you create a subform, make sure that the tables displayed by the form and proposed subform have a one-to-many relationship. Book I, Chapter 3 describes one-to-many relationships, master and detail records, and primary and foreign keys. Book II, Chapter 6 shows you how to tell Access about the relationships between tables by using the Relationships window.

A subform can have its own form layout and navigation buttons for moving around the records within the subform. One form can have more than one subform, if there's more than one table with a one-to-many relationship to the table shown in the main form.

Each subform is stored as a separate form in Access — you see the subform's name in the Database window. To display it as part of another form, you create a *subform control* on the main form, showing Access how and where you want the subform to appear on the main form.

If you want the main form to contain totals or counts of the records in the subform, see Chapter 4 of this book. For example, if a subform of an Orders form lists the items on the order, displaying the total cost of the items ordered on the Orders form is nice.

Creating a subform

The easiest way to create a form is by using a wizard (surprise, surprise!). You can always edit and improve the subform later. (If you are creating a report, see the section on subreports in Book V, Chapter 1.)

To add a subform to a form, follow these steps:

1. **Display the main form in Design view.**

2. **Display the Toolbox by clicking the Toolbox button on the toolbar.**

3. **Click the Subform/Subreport button on the Toolbox to tell Access that you want to add a subform to the form.**

4. **On the form, drag the mouse to create a box in which the subform will appear.**

   Access runs the SubForm Wizard to lead you through the process of creating the subform. (If the wizard isn't installed on your system, Access offers to install it; get out your Microsoft Office CD and follow the instructions on-screen.)

5. **Unless you already have a form that works as a subform, choose the Use Existing Tables and Queries option. If you already created a form, choose the Use an Existing Form option. Click Next.**

   If you choose the Use Existing Tables and Queries option, then the wizard needs to know the name of the related table, and which fields in that table you want to display. You can choose to display records from a query, if the query contains a unique field that can act as the primary field in a one-to-many relationship with the records on the main form.

   If you choose the Use an Existing Form option, then skip to Step 7.

6. **In the Tables/Queries box, choose the table or query from which you want to display records. Then choose the fields you want to display by selecting fields and clicking the > button. Click Next when you are finished.**

   Alternatively, you can double-click a field name to move it from one list to the other. If you want to display all the fields, click the >> button. As you select fields, they move from the Available Fields list to the Selected Fields list. Don't choose too many fields — they need to fit in the subform!

Don't choose to include the primary key, which relates to the record in the main form. For example, if you are adding an order detail subform to an orders form, the main form displays one order at a time, including its order number. The subform displays all the order detail records that have the same order number. If you include the order number on the subform, you just see the same order number over and over, once for each record in the subform. What a waste of screen space!

7. **Choose a relationship from the list, or select the Define My Own option and choose the matching fields on the form and subform. Click Next.**

   The wizard needs to know how the records in the subform relate to the records in the main form, as shown in Figure 3-12. It displays a list of the relationships known, and this list usually contains the right relationship. For example, in Figure 3-12, the wizard suggests Show Order Details for each record in Orders Main Qry using OrderID — it uses the OrderID field in the Order Details table to match the OrderID field in the Orders Main Qry query (the record source of the main form).

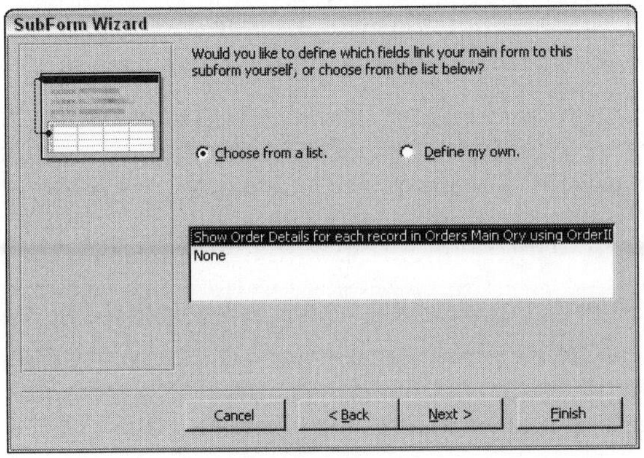

Figure 3-12: Tell the SubForm Wizard how the records in the subform relate to the records in the main form: What fields match?

If you choose the Define My Own option, the wizard's window changes to allow you to choose the matching fields on the form (the "one" side of the relationship) and the subform (the "many" side).

8. **Type a name for the subform or accept the wizard's suggestion. Click Finish.**

The wizard creates the subform as a separate form in your database. It also creates a subform control on the main form, as shown in Figure 3-13. You can adjust the edges of the subform control by dragging them.

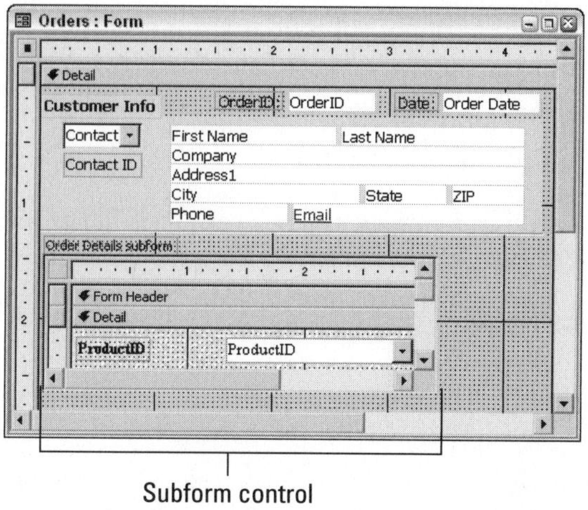

Figure 3-13: A subform control displays the subform in Design view.

Subform control

The subform may look totally wrong in Design view but fine in Form view. The subform appears in Datasheet view when the main form is in Form view, so the exact placement of the controls, background color, and other features doesn't matter.

To adjust the column widths of the subform, which is usually in Datasheet view, just drag the column dividers left or right in Form view. After you have nice-looking columns, switch the main form back to Design view and adjust the width of the subform control until it's the right size to fit your columns.

The properties of subform controls

After you create the subform, you edit it from the main form or in its own Design View window. In the Database window, you can click the Forms button to see your list of forms, select the form you want to edit, click the Design button, and make your changes. When you save the changes and reopen the main form, you see the changes in your subform, too. However, updating a subform's design is easier: Open the main form in Design view and double-click the subform control. Now you can edit the subform right within the main form. When you save your main form, Access saves changes to your subform, too.

While you're fooling with the fields on the subform, you may want to change the properties of the subform control that displays the subform on the main form. To see the properties of the subform control, display the main form in Design view, display the Properties sheet by clicking the Properties button on the toolbar, and then click in the subform. (*Note:* Don't click in the gray box in the upper-left corner of the subform, or you end up seeing the properties of the form you are using as a subform, rather than the properties of the subform control.) The box at the top of the Properties sheet should show the name of the subform control; if it doesn't, click the drop-down list and choose the subform control name.

Some useful entries you can change on the Properties sheet for the subform control are the following:

✦ **Source Object:** The name of the form you are displaying in this subform control.

✦ **Link Child Fields:** The field name in the record source of the subform. This field must match the Link Master Fields field.

✦ **Link Master Fields:** The field name in the record source of the main form. This field must match the Link Child Fields field.

Other properties have to be changed in the subform itself. Open the subform in Design view and click the Properties button to display the properties of the form. Or, with the main form open in Design view, click the subform control to select it, and then click the gray box in the upper-left corner of the subform to select the form properties. Some properties you may want to change are

✦ **Default View:** The default setting is Datasheet view, so that the subform appears as a small datasheet of records. You can change the `Default View` property to the `Continuous Forms` setting if you prefer: You need to adjust the layout of the subform to make it look right.

✦ **Navigation Buttons:** If a subform doesn't show many records, you may not want to waste space on navigation buttons. Having two sets of navigation buttons — one for the subform and one for the main form — can be confusing, too. However, without navigation buttons, you need to click or use the keyboard to move from record to record in the subform.

If you are editing the properties of a subform in Design view of the main form, click elsewhere on the main form to tell Access to update the subform properties. Otherwise, your changes don't appear to have taken effect when you switch to Form view.

Adding Form Headers and Footers

Normally, a form contains one section: the Detail section. You can see the Detail header at the top of the Design View window (take a look at Figure 3-13, for example). You can usually ignore this section header (and the idea that forms have sections at all).

However, you may want to display information at the top and bottom of your form. Yes, you can just put controls at the top and bottom of the Detail section of your form, and most people do just that. However, if the window displaying the form is too small for the whole form to fit, the information may not always be visible.

You can add a Form Header and Form Footer section to your form by opening the form in Design view and choosing View⇨Form Header/Footer. (You can get rid of the sections by giving the same command again.) Access creates a new, blank Form Footer section at the top of the Design View window and a matching new, blank Form Footer at the bottom. Next you can add controls to these sections, using the Toolbox or Field list.

When you switch to Form view by clicking the View button, the controls in the header and footer sections are always visible, no matter what the size of your Form window.

Creating Tabbed Forms

Sometimes you need to fit tons of information on a form, and you can see that the form is getting to be the size of Nebraska. In addition to not fitting on the screen, large forms are confusing: Where is the right box to type this information?

One way to fit lots of information on a form while keeping the window size down and making the form less confusing is to divide the form up into tabs. We're talking about the kind of tabs that stick up from the tops of folders. Lots of dialog boxes have them: Take a look at the Properties sheet for a nice example. Your forms can have tabs, too, with different controls on each one. The entire form can be on the tabs, or the tabs can occupy part of the form, with controls that remain visible regardless of which tab you are looking at. (We recommend the latter approach.)

To create tabs, you create a *tab control* on the form, and then you create controls on the tab. Before you start, decide how many tabs you want, and what controls go on each tab. Then follow these steps:

1. **With your form open in Design view, make some space on your form where you want the tabs to go.**

If your form is already crowded, just expand the form outrageously by dragging its bottom edge downward, and drag groups of controls out of the way of your new tabs.

2. **Click the Tab Control button on the Toolbox.**

3. **Click in the form where you want the upper-left corner of the tabs to appear.**

Access creates a tab control and two tabs (also called *pages*), usually named Page1 and Page2, as shown in Figure 3-14.

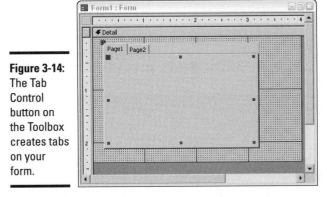

Figure 3-14:
The Tab Control button on the Toolbox creates tabs on your form.

4. **Drag the edges of the tab control to fix the size of the control.**

If you want to move the whole tab control, click the first page (usually Page1) so it's selected, and drag the black handle that appears in its upper-left corner.

After you have a tab control, the things you can do with it are as follows:

✦ **Rename the pages:** Page1 and Page2 are probably not what you want to call your tabs. Click the tab to select the page, display the Properties sheet by clicking the Properties button on the toolbar, and change the Name property on the Properties sheet.

✦ **Add, delete, or reorder the pages:** If you want more than two pages, right-click the tab control (or any of its pages) and choose the Insert Page option from the shortcut menu that appears. To delete a page, select it, right-click it, and choose the Delete Page option from the shortcut menu. To switch the order of the pages, right-click any of the pages and choose the Page Order option; on the Page Order dialog box that appears, use the Move Up and Move Down buttons to reorganize the list of pages.

✦ **Put controls on the pages:** This is the good part — you can drag existing controls from the rest of the form, or you can create new controls on the form in the same way you create controls for the rest of the form. Click the page on which you want to put the controls, so that page appears "on top." Then move or create the controls you want.

Figure 3-15 shows a form with three tabs in Design view.

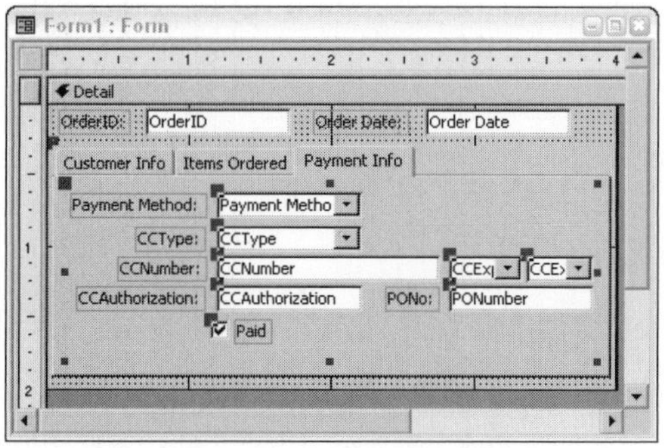

Figure 3-15:
This tab
control
contains
three pages,
and each
page
contains
controls.

You Can't Type That Here!

The main purpose of forms is to provide easy-to-use on-screen display and editing for your records. Most people use forms rather than datasheets for entering and editing data. Book II, Chapter 5 describes how to create defaults and validation rules for your tables, to prevent the dreaded "garbage in, garbage out" syndrome that so many databases suffer from. You can add validation to your form controls, too.

Use validation in your tables when you want data to follow rules all the time, no matter how it is entered. Use validation in form controls when you want to validate one field against another. For example, you may want to make sure the Ship Date can't be earlier than the Order Date, which you can't enforce using field validation in the table design.

Form controls that display data have properties with which you can validate and format that data. In fact, they are the very same properties that you can set as part of your table design:

✦ **Default Value:** The starting value for this field when you add a new record.

✦ **Input Mask:** A pattern for field data to follow, including where letters, numbers, and punctuation appear, and how letters are capitalized.

✦ **Validation Rule:** A rule Access applies to values entered in this field.

✦ **Validation Text:** An error message you see if you try to enter data that breaks the validation rule.

These settings appear on the Data tab of the Properties sheet for controls. For help with creating input masks and validation rules (which can be a little complicated, frankly), click in the setting on the Properties sheet and then click the Build button (to the right of the setting). For input masks, you see the Input Mask Wizard, and for validation rules, you see the Expression Builder. For details about using these settings, see Book II, Chapter 5.

Making Switchboards — A Friendly Face for Your Database

If you use an Access template to create your database, the database probably includes a special kind of form called a switchboard. *Switchboards* are forms that contain buttons for different database maintenance tasks, usually including adding records, printing reports, and closing the database. For example, if you use the Contact Management template to create a database, you see the switchboard shown in Figure 3-16 when you open the database. Choosing Enter/View Other Information displays another switchboard with other options, and choosing Preview Reports displays a switchboard listing the reports that the template created. Very nice!

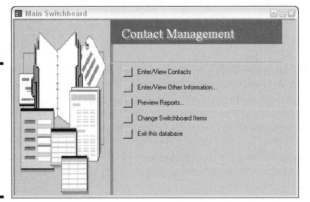

Figure 3-16:
A switch-
board
serves as
mission
control
for your
database.

The secret life of switchboards

A switchboard is a special kind of Access form. One form, called Switchboard (good choice of names, we thought), appears in the list of forms in the Database window. To open the main switchboard, double-click the Switchboard file name on the forms list in the Database window. You can't open the other switchboards directly from the Database window — you must open them from the main switchboard.

You may want to make changes to the switchboards in your databases. For example, if you create a few really useful reports, adding them to the Preview Reports switchboard is a good idea. You can open a switchboard in Design view to make changes. However, the list of buttons and what they do is stored in an unusual (and clever) way — your database includes a Switchboard table with one record for each switchboard button. There's one table for the buttons on all your switchboards. When Access displays a switchboard, it uses the information in the Switchboard table to create the buttons and the labels next to them.

You can edit switchboards by using Design view or by editing the values in the Switchboard table, but we don't recommend it. Instead, you can use the Switchboard Manager to create and edit switchboards.

Switchboard Manager, boss of the switchboards

To start the Switchboard Manager (shown in Figure 3-17), choose Tools⇨ Database Utilities⇨Switchboard Manager. You see a list of the switchboard pages. (*Switchboard pages* are the different switchboards that appear in this database; Access thinks of them as different pages of the same switchboard. Whatever!)

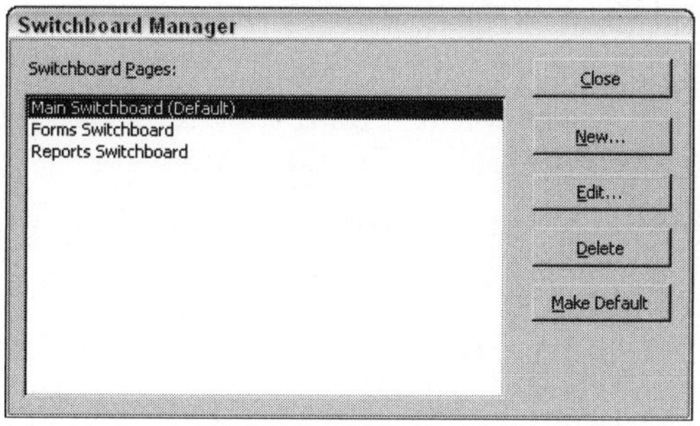

Figure 3-17: Use the Switchboard Manager to change your switchboards or to create new ones.

The Switchboard Manager lists all the switchboard pages. One of the pages is shown as the default; this page is the starting page — the page that appears first, and from which you can display all the other pages. The default page usually has a name like Main Switchboard.

If you want to change the entries on a switchboard, follow these steps:

1. **Display the Switchboard Manager by choosing Tools⇨Database Utilities⇨Switchboard Manager.**

2. **Select the switchboard page you want to change, and click the Edit button.**

    You see the Edit Switchboard Page window, with a list of the items (buttons) on the switchboard.

3. **To edit what a switchboard button does or what its label says, click the entry on the Items on This Switchboard list and click the Edit button.**

    The Edit Switchboard Item dialog box appears, as shown in Figure 3-18.

4. **Change the entries for the item and click OK.**

    You can edit the contents of the Text box to change the label that appears next to the button. To change what the button actually does, choose a different Command entry. For most commands, you see a third entry in which you can specify more information about the command (for example, which switchboard page to open or which report to print).

5. **To get rid of a switchboard button, select it, click the Delete button, and click the Yes button to confirm the deletion.**

6. **To create a new switchboard button, click the New button.**

    The Edit Switchboard Item dialog box appears.

7. **Specify the text (label for the button), command (what the button does), and other information. Then click OK.**

    The new button appears on the Items on This Switchboard list.

8. **To change the order of the buttons on the switchboard, select a button and click the Move Up or Move Down button.**

9. **Click the Close button to return to the Switchboard Manager window.**

    You see the list of switchboard pages again.

10. **If you want a different page to be the default (starting) page, select it and click the Make Default button.**

    The default page should have buttons that display each of the other pages. Otherwise, you have no way to display the other switchboard pages. Most default pages also have an Exit This Database button.

11. **When you finish making changes, click the Close button.**

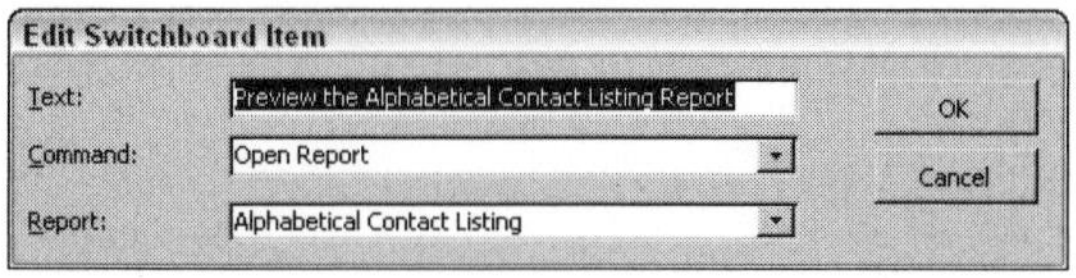

Figure 3-18:
Change what switchboard buttons do and what their labels say.

The alternative to switchboards

You don't have to use switchboards to make a main menu form for your database. You can use a regular old form with command buttons on it instead.

To make a main menu form, create an unbound form (a form for which the `Record Source` property for the form is blank). (See Chapter 1 of this book for how to set the record source of a form.) Use labels to give the form a title (such as "Main Menu") and create a command button for each command you want available on the form.

Many people use a one-record table to contain constants about their business or project (see Book I, Chapter 3). If you use this trick, you may want to set this table as the record source of your main menu form. The form shown in Figure 3-19 contains two controls at the bottom of the form, showing data from a Constants table. These controls make seeing and editing these values easy for a database user.

Figure 3-19:
You can use a regular form with lots of command buttons as a main menu, too.

Chapter 4: Doing Calculations in Forms (And Reports)

In This Chapter

✔ Including calculated results on your forms (and reports)

✔ Using numbers in calculations

✔ Using dates in calculations

✔ Using strings, that is, text in calculations

✔ Totaling and counting information from subforms (and subreports)

The first three chapters in Book IV explain how to make forms with all kinds of controls, showing information in all kinds of ways. In the process, you find out how to create reports, because creating and editing reports is so similar to working with forms. However, up to this point all the information we deal with is sitting there waiting for us, nicely contained in tables and queries. How about calculating data that *isn't* stored anywhere? Your forms and reports can calculate and display information, which you can also store in the record source for the form (that is, store the results so that you can use them in other objects). For example, you may want the Order form for an online store to calculate the total price of all items ordered, the sales tax, and the grand total for the order.

In addition to calculating numbers, you can also do text, date, and logical calculations. For example, you can give Access instructions like "If Tax Exempt is True, then Sales Tax is 0; otherwise it's Tax Rate times Product Total." Text calculations include things such as keeping only the first five digits of a zip code, or capitalizing a text entry.

Doing Elementary Calculations

Sounds like algebra class, doesn't it? Don't worry; creating calculated values for your forms won't cause you to scream in terror like your high school algebra teacher did. You'll recognize some arithmetic signs (especially the equal sign), but the calculations are all easy.

A *calculated value* is a value that Access creates by doing a calculation based on other information, usually using fields from your tables. For example, Access can add the product total to the shipping cost for an order, to come up with the total cost.

To include a calculated value on a form or report, create a text box and then enter an expression in the `Control Source` property of the text box. An *expression* is a formula that tells Access how to calculate an answer from field values and other values. Expressions start with an equal sign (=). If field names include spaces, enclose them in square brackets. (Actually, we enclose *all* field names in square brackets, just so we don't forget.) For example, this is an expression:

```
= [Product Total] + [Shipping Cost]
```

And another one:

```
= "Your total will be " & [GrandTotal] & "."
```

The expressions you use on forms and reports are the same as the expressions you use to create calculated fields in queries. Turn to Book III, Chapter 3 for how expressions work in queries, including the operators and functions that they can include.

Making a calculated control

A *calculated control* is a control that uses an expression, rather than the field name, as its `Control Source` property (as explained in Chapter 2 of this book). Usually it's a text box control. To create a calculated control, follow these steps:

1. **With the form or report open in Design view, display the Toolbox by clicking the Toolbox button on the toolbar.**

For an introduction to the Toolbox, see Chapter 1 of this book. You have to use the Toolbox, rather than the Field list, to create a control with a blank control source. (A control with no control source is called an *unbound control.*)

2. **Click the Text Box button on the Toolbox. Click the form where you want the text box, or drag from one corner to the other in the space where you want the text box to appear.**

A text box appears, with *Unbound* showing in it. The control has no Control Source — Access doesn't know what to display in the text box.

3. **Display the Properties sheet for the control by clicking the Properties button on the toolbar. Click the Data tab on the Properties sheet that appears.**

The `Control Source` property is the first property on the Data tab — and lo! It's blank.

4. **Type an expression in the** `Control Source` **property of the text box.**

You can click in the text box on the form and type the expression, as shown in Figure 4-1. Or click in the `Control Source` property on the Properties sheet. Your choice.

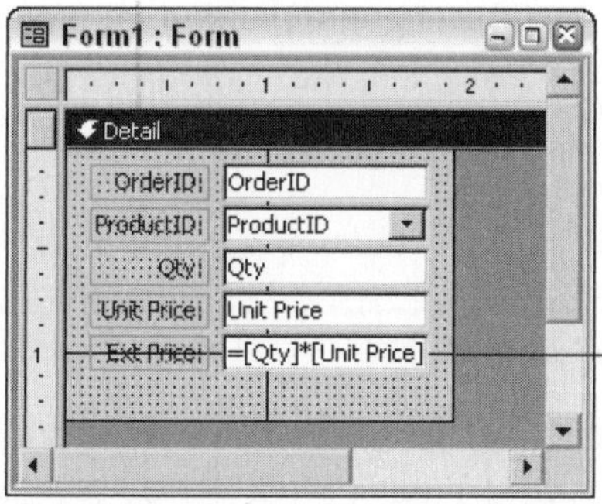

Figure 4-1:
When you type an expression as the value of a text box, be sure to start it with an equal sign.

Form1 : Form

Detail	
OrderID	OrderID
ProductID	ProductID
Qty	Qty
Unit Price	Unit Price
Ext Price	=[Qty]*[Unit Price]

———— Expression

If you want to edit the expression later, you can change your entry on the Properties sheet.

Another way to enter or edit an expression is to click the Build button — the button to the right of the Control Source box — or press Ctrl+F2 to run the Expression Builder, which steps you through writing an expression. See Book III, Chapter 3 for how the Expression Builder works.

Expressions can get long, and it can be hard to see them. When editing an expression, press Shift+F2 to display it in a Zoom box, as shown in Figure 4-2.

Zoom

=[Qty]*[Unit Price]

OK

Cancel

Font...

Figure 4-2:
A Zoom box displays an expression.

Should you put your calculations in queries or on forms and reports?

When you want to include a calculated value in a form or report, you can do it in one of two ways:

✔ In a query, which you use as the record source for the form or report

✔ In a text box control on the form or report

Both methods work fine. If you plan to use the calculated value to select which records to include in the form or report, you need to calculate the value in a query, and then set the Sort row for that field to ascending or descending. We usually calculate values in a query if we plan to sort or select by the calculation, or display the calculation in more than one form or report.

Don't name the text box control with the same name as a field in the record source for the form or report! For example, if the table or query that provides the records has a field called Full Name, don't create a calculated text box with that name. Two items with the same name confuse Access if you refer to that name — Access doesn't know whether you want the field or the control.

Checking your expression

After you type an expression into the `Control Source` property of a text box (or use the Expression Builder to create it), you see the expression itself in the text box. What about the answer?

To check whether the expression works, switch to Form view by clicking the View button on the toolbar or choosing View⇨Form View. (For reports, switch to Print Preview.) Check the answer in several records to see whether the expression works as you expect.

Troubleshooting expressions

If you make a mistake in your expression, you may see one of three things in Form view or Print Preview: a wrong answer, #Name?, or another error message that starts with a #. If you find an error, check out these ideas for fixing your calculated text box and its expression:

+ *#Name?* indicates that Access can't understand a field name in your expression. The most likely reason is that you forgot the equal sign (=) at the beginning of the expression. Or you may have spelled a field name wrong, or you may have forgotten to enclose it in square brackets. If your text box control has the same name as a field, Access can't tell which one you are referring to, so check the name of the text box, too. (It's the Name property on the All tab of the Properties sheet.)

+ *#Div/0!* means you are dividing something by zero, which is impossible in standard arithmetic. Check the fields in your expression to see if one might be zero for some records.

+ *#Error* indicates some other problem — check the expression carefully.

Calculating and Formatting Numbers

To display a numeric calculation on a form or report, you can use the arithmetic operators that we describe in Book III, Chapter 3. Access also has numeric functions, described in the same section.

Some sample numeric expressions (you can guess what the fields contain from their names) are included in the following table.

Numeric Expression	Purpose
=[TaxableTotal]*[SalesTaxRate]	Sales tax on an order
=3.50 + ([ItemCount] * 2)	Shipping is $3.50 plus $2 per item
=[OrderSubtotal] + [SalesTax] + [Shipping]	Grand total for an order

After you type an expression in the Control Source property of a text box and switch to Form view or Print Preview to check that it works, you usually want to format the number — you may not like the number of decimal places, use of commas, or lack of a currency symbol in your calculated text box.

To format a number, display the properties of the text box and click its Format tab, as shown in Figure 4-3. For a text box with numeric values, you can click in the Format property and click the down arrow at the right end of the property to see a list of numeric formats. Details about numeric formats are in Book II, Chapter 1 — they are the same formats you can use to format the fields in your tables.

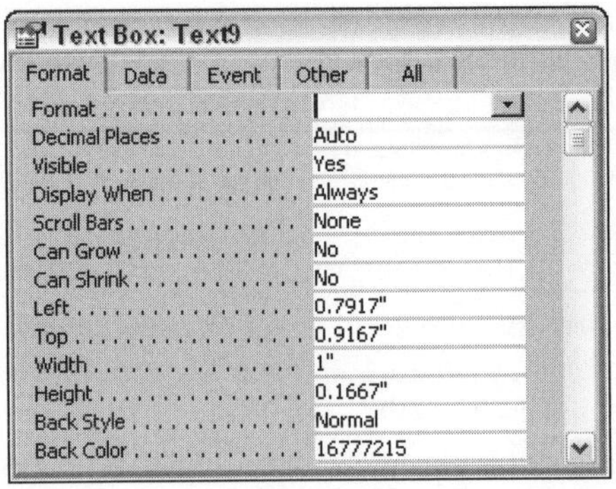

Figure 4-3:
Formatting a
calculated
value in a
text box.

Calculating and Formatting Dates

Access includes operators and functions that work on dates, including finding the number of days between two dates, separating a date into its component parts (day, month, year, hour, minute, and second), and adding days to a date. Book III, Chapter 3 describes the operators and functions you can use. A few examples are in the following table.

Date Expression	Purpose
=DateDiff("w", [OrderDate], [ShipDate])	Number of weeks between ordering and shipping
=[InvoiceDate] + 30	30 days after the invoice date
=Date() + 10	10 days after today
=DatePart("q", [OrderDate])	Quarter in which order was placed

Access gives you lots of date formats to choose from, as listed in Book II, Chapter 1.

Calculating and Formatting Text

For forms and reports, you want things to look just right, and text expressions allow you to do all kinds of things to slice and dice the text that appears in your text boxes. Book III, Chapter 3 describes the operators and functions you can use with text values. A few examples are in the following table.

Text Expression	Purpose
=[FirstName] & " " & [LastName]	First and last names, with a space in between
=[LastName] & ", " & {FirstName]	Last name first, with a comma in between
=UCase([LastName])	Last name, in all capital letters
=Left([ProductCode], 2)	First two characters of the product code

You can create a so-called *input mask* that determines the formatting of a calculated text box, as we describe in Book II, Chapter 1. For example, an input mask can add parentheses and dashes to a phone number, or dashes to a Social Security Number. A nifty way to explore input masks is to click in the Input Mask property on the Data tab of the Properties sheet for your text box, and then click the Build button to its right. The Input Mask Wizard runs and shows you a list of input masks you can use, as shown in Figure 4-4. (See Book II, Chapter 5 for more information on input masks.)

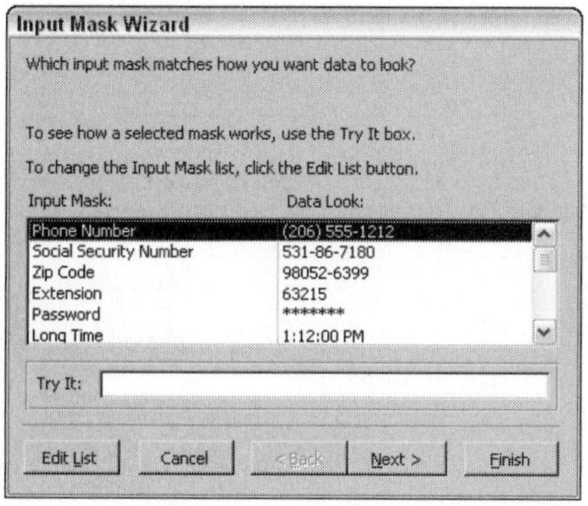

Figure 4-4:
The Input
Mask
Wizard
helps format
text in a
form or
report.

Input Mask Wizard

Which input mask matches how you want data to look?

To see how a selected mask works, use the Try It box.

To change the Input Mask list, click the Edit List button.

Input Mask:	Data Look:
Phone Number	(206) 555-1212
Social Security Number	531-86-7180
Zip Code	98052-6399
Extension	63215
Password	*******
Long Time	1:12:00 PM

Try It: |

Edit List   Cancel   < Back   Next >   Finish

Displaying Values That Depend on Conditions

Some calculations have an *if-then* component — basically, *if* this is true, *then* we do this. For example, if the order is from your home state, then charge sales tax; otherwise, don't. Or if the order is above $100, then shipping is free. Access handles these types of if-then calculations using its iif() (*immediate-if*) function, which we describe in Book III, Chapter 3.

For example, if you charge sales tax only for Vermont orders, you use this expression:

```
= iif([State]="VT", [TaxableTotal]*.05, 0)
```

The condition ([State]="VT") is either true or false; if it's true, the expression is [TaxableTotal]*.05 (5 percent of the taxable total); if it's false, the expression is 0.

The condition can be a Yes/No field: if the field is yes (true), the function returns the first value, and if it's no (false) you get the second value. For example, the following expression looks at the Yes/No field, TaxExempt, to determine whether this customer is exempt from sales taxes. For taxable customers, the function returns the value of the TaxableTotal field. For tax-exempt customers, it returns zero:

```
= iif([TaxExempt], 0, [TaxableTotal])
```

Here's the mind-boggling part: You can *nest* functions, including the iif() function — you can use a function inside another function. This expression combines the last two examples to calculate sales tax based on both the customer's tax-exempt status and the customer's state:

```
= iif([State]="VT", iif([TaxExempt], 0, [TaxableTotal]*.05), 0)
```

Adding Subtotals and Totals from Subforms

If your form includes a subform (or your report includes a subreport), and the information shown in the subform includes quantities, you may want to display a total on the main form. For example, on an Orders form that contains an Order Detail subform, the main form can include the total cost of all the items in the subform, and maybe a count of the records in the subform. Figure 4-5 shows an Orders form with a subform listing the items that the customer is buying.

Unfortunately, you can't make a control on the main form that calculates a total for the records on the subform. You can, however, make a control on the subform that calculates the total, and then make a control on the main form that displays the value of this control. Seems like an extra step to us, but it works. The following sections cover what you need to know to create totals and counts of subform records.

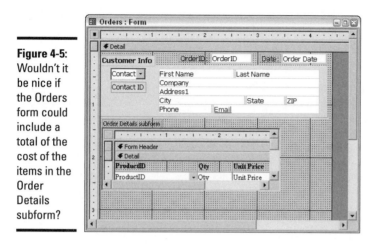

Figure 4-5:
Wouldn't it
be nice if
the Orders
form could
include a
total of the
cost of the
items in the
Order
Details
subform?

Using aggregate functions

An *aggregate function* is a function that combines a bunch of values together.
For example, the Sum( ) function adds a bunch of numbers together. (Simple
enough!) When doing calculations based on a bunch of records, you can use
the aggregate functions outlined in the following table.

Function	Description
Sum( )	Totals the values
Count( )	Counts the values
Avg( )	Averages the values (sum divided by count)
Min( )	Calculates the smallest value (for numeric values), the earliest date (for date values), or the first value in alphabetical order (for text values)
Max( )	Calculates the largest value (for numeric values), the latest date (for date values), or the last value in alphabetical order (for text values)
First( )	Uses the value from the first record
Last( )	Uses the value from the last record

Aggregate functions work only where Access knows what set of records you
want to work with. On forms, they work in the form footer of a subform. (See
Chapter 3 of this book for a description of a form footer, unless you already
guessed that a form footer is a section that appears at the bottom of a form.)

Summarizing lots of records

In addition to the functions that work with the field values in the current record, Access has *domain aggregate functions* — functions that work with field values in some or all of the records in a table or query. (A *domain* is a fancy name for a table or query.) For example, you may want a form to display the grand total of all the orders so far this year, or the amount of the largest order placed. To total the value of a field for a bunch of records, you use the DSum function, which has this syntax:

```
DSum(expression, domain,
   criteria)
```

Replace *expression* with the field name that you want to total (or an expression such as [Price] * [Qty]), in quotes. Replace *domain* with the table or query name, in quotes. Optionally, you can include a *criteria* that limits which records to include.

For example, the following expression totals the extended price (price times quantity) for all the records in the Order Detail table:

```
DSum("[Price] * [Qty]", "Order
   Details")
```

Some of the other domain aggregate functions you can use (they have the same syntax as DSum) are

- ✓ DAvg: Averages the values
- ✓ DCount: Counts the values
- ✓ DFirst: Value for the first record
- ✓ DLast: Value for the last record
- ✓ DMin: Minimum value (for numbers it's the smallest; for text it's the first in alphabetical order; and for dates it's the earliest)
- ✓ DMax: Maximum value (for numbers it's the largest; for text it's the last in alphabetical order; and for dates it's the latest)

One other useful domain aggregate function is DLookup, which returns the value of a specific field for a specific record in a table or query. For example, the following expression returns the date of OrderID 5000 from the Orders table:

```
DLookup("[Order Date]",
   "Orders", "[OrderID] =
   5000")
```

In this DLookup function, the expression is "[Order Date]", the date of the order. The domain is the Orders table. The criteria is "[OrderID] = 5000", which limits the records to include only the record with that specific ID.

For example, in Figure 4-5, the total of the Qty field in the Order Detail subform tells the shipping clerk how many items need to be shipped for this order. The expression is

```
= Sum([Qty])
```

If a field name contains spaces, you have to enclose it in square brackets. We enclose all field names in square brackets, just to be safe.

You can also total a calculation. To come up with the total cost of the items ordered, you use this expression:

```
= Sum([Unit Price] * [Qty])
```

If you want to total, average, or count all the records in an entire table or query, or selected records in a table or query, use the functions described in the sidebar, "Summarizing lots of records."

Referring to a control on a subform

To create a control on the main form that shows information from the sub-form, you need to know how to refer to a control on the subform. The format of an expression that displays a value from a subform is the following:

```
= [subform control name].Form![control name]
```

(This looks hideous, but hold on!) Replace *subform control name* with the name of the subform control on the main form that displays the subform. Replace *control name* with the name of the text box on the subform that displays the value that you want to see.

For example, if your main form is the Orders form shown in Figure 4-5, its subform control is called "Order Details subform." If you want to display the information from that subform's Order Subtotal text box, the expression would look like this:

```
= [Order Details subform].Form![Order Subtotal]
```

Creating the controls to total a subform

To calculate a total (or a count) of the values of a control on the subform and to display it on the main form, you create two controls: one in the form footer of the subform and one on the main form, wherever you want the total to appear.

Be careful when entering the expressions for calculating and displaying the total: In some cases, you type the name of the field while in other cases you type the name of the control that displays the field. It can get confusing!

Follow these steps to display the subform total on the main form:

1. **Open the subform in Design view and display its Properties sheet by clicking the Properties button.**

If you already have the main form open in Design view, you can click in the subform control and choose View⇨Subform in New Window.

**Book IV
Chapter 4**

Doing Calculations
in Forms (And
Reports)

2. **Add a Form Footer section (assuming that it doesn't already have one) by choosing View⇨Form Header/Footer.**

   Figure 4-6 shows a form in Design view with header and footer sections. (See Chapter 3 of this book for more about form headers and footers.)

3. **Note the name of the field (not the control on the form) that contains the values you want to count or total.**

   Frequently, the control that displays a field has the same name as the field itself, but not always. Be sure to use the field name, not the name of any control on the form that displays the field.

4. **In the Form Footer, make a text box by clicking the Text Box button on the Toolbox and clicking in the form footer.**

5. **Open the Properties sheet for the text box, and enter the expression that you want to calculate in the** Control Source **property.**

   For example, type = **Sum([Unit Price] * [Qty])** into the Control Source property, as shown in Figure 4-6.

6. **Enter a descriptive name for the control in the** Name **property.**

   Make a note of the control name, because you need it to display the value on the main form. For example, you may name the control *OrderSubTotal*.

7. **Switch to Form view by clicking the View button, to make sure that the new text box works.**

   Because you're looking at the subform as an independent form, the subform shows all the records in its record source, and the calculation totals all the records, not just those for one order. But when this form is used as a subform, the linkage between the subform and the main form restricts the records in the subform to one order at a time, and the control totals the records for only the current order.

8. **If you plan to display the subform in Form view, not just in Datasheet view, hide the Form Footer section by setting its** Visible **property to a** No **setting.**

   Otherwise, you display the subtotal once on the subform and once on the main form, which looks odd. Most subforms appear in Datasheet view, which don't display form headers and footers.

9. **Save and close the subform.**

   Press Ctrl+S to save your changes, and go ahead and close its Design View window — you're done with it.

10. **Open the main form in Design view. Click the Properties button to display the Properties sheet and the Toolbox button to display the Toolbox, if they aren't already on-screen.**

11. **Create a text box to control the total, by clicking the Text Box button on the Toolbox and clicking in the Design View window where you want the calculated control.**

You get a new unbound control, ready to display your calculated total.

12. **Set the text box's** Control Source **property to an expression that refers to the calculated control on the subform.**

For example, the expression referring to the calculated control shown in Figure 4-6 is this:

```
= [Order Details subform].Form![Order Subtotal]
```

13. **Format the new control with the numeric format you want and switch to Form view to test it out.**

If you don't format the text box, Access usually displays way too many decimal places for calculated values. On the Format tab of the Properties sheet, set the Format property to the Currency setting, or whatever format you prefer.

If you see #Name or #Error instead of the subtotal, check the expression for the control on the main form carefully, and make sure that you entered the expression, the name of the control on the subform, and the name of the subform control — the control you put on the main form — correctly. (What a zoo!)

Figure 4-6:
Create a
calculated
control in
the form
footer to
calculate
totals of
records on
the form.

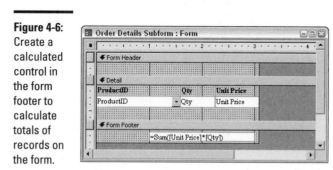

Formatting Calculated Controls

When you display calculated values on a form, the value isn't editable in Form view — that is, you can't type a different value in its place, or delete it. The expression controls what appears in the text box.

To make it clear which text boxes are editable, we like to make calculated text boxes look different from text boxes we type in. We recommend that you display the Format tab on the Properties sheet for each calculated control and make the following changes:

✦ **Set the** Back Style **property to the** Transparent **setting, so the background of the calculated value matches the background of the form itself.**

✦ **Set the** Special Effect **property to the** Flat **setting, so the value doesn't appear in a box at all.**

Figure 4-7 shows the Orders form with three calculated controls at the bottom.

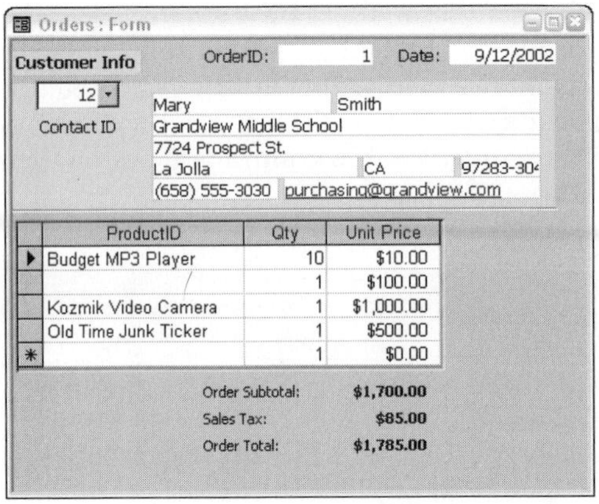

Figure 4-7:
Order
Subtotal,
Sales Tax,
and Order
Total are
calculated
controls.

Book V

Reports

The 5th Wave   By Rich Tennant

"Oh, Scarecrow! Without the database in your laptop, how will we find anything in Oz?"

Contents at a Glance

Chapter 1: Creating and Spiffing Up Reports

In This Chapter

- How reports are like forms
- Creating reports by running wizards and AutoReports
- Editing reports in Design view
- Adding page headers and footers
- Creating groupings and subtotals
- Including subreports on your report to print information from related tables
- Making reports that print mailing labels

*R*eports are the best way to put information from your database onto paper. In a report, you can choose how to display your data, including which information to include (which tables and fields); where to print each field on the page; text fonts, font sizes, and spacing; and printing lines, boxes, and pictures.

Reports can include information from different tables — for instance, you can display the customer information, followed by all the items that the customer has bought from all orders. The Report Wizard simplifies creating reports that list, summarize, and total your data. You can also use calculations in reports to create totals, subtotals, and other results. You can create invoices, packing slips, student rosters, and all kinds of other reports. Thanks to the trusty Label Wizard, reports are also the best way to create mailing labels from addresses in your database.

This chapter explains how to create and modify reports, so they are ready to print. The next chapter talks about previewing and printing them. Chapter 3 of this book describes graphical reports — graphs and charts.

If You Know Forms, You Already Know Reports

Reports and forms are used very differently, but you create them in similar ways. You can create both forms and reports by running wizards. You can create or modify both forms and reports in Design view, where you can create, move, and customize controls and their properties.

To see a list of the reports in your database — and, eventually, to open or modify a report — press F11 to display the Database window and then click the Reports button in the Objects list at the left. A nice list of reports in your database appears in the Database window, as shown in Figure 1-1. The first two entries help you create new reports, and the rest of the entries are your report names.

Figure 1-1:
The Database window lists all your reports.

You can look at a report in two views: Design view (where you can look behind the scenes at what fields the report displays where) and Print Preview, which shows how the report will look when you print it. To see a report in Design view, click its name in the Database window and click the Design button on the Database window toolbar. To see the report in Print Preview, double-click its name in the Database window. If you already opened the report in Design view, switch to Print Preview by clicking the Print Preview button on the toolbar or by choosing File⇔Print Preview. From Print Preview, you can switch to Design view by clicking the View button on the toolbar (the left-most button).

This chapter describes how to make reports by running wizards, as well as how to customize reports in ways that don't work for forms. For information about how to create and customize reports in Design view, including adding controls and setting properties, see Book IV, Chapter 1.

However, reports can't include features that don't appear on forms, including these:

✦ **Grouping and sections:** When you design a report, you frequently want to have information grouped together. For example, a monthly sales report may list sales by product, with subtotals for each product. A mailing label report may start a new page for each new zip code, and print the total number of labels that are in each zip code. You can have up to four grouping levels. You can add grouping levels by adding section headers to your report in Design view (see the section, "Adding sections that group your records," later in this chapter).

✦ **Page headers, footers, and numbers:** Most reports have page numbers and many need other information printed at the top or bottom of every page. See the section, "Adding page headers, footers, and numbers," later in this chapter.

✦ **Margins, paper size, and paper orientation:** Reports usually end up on paper, and you can configure your report to fit. See the section, "Creating Mailing Labels," later in this chapter, along with most of the sections in Chapter 2 of this book.

But first, we cover how to create some reports the easy way — by using wizards.

Creating Reports Automagically

You create a report the same way that you create other objects in your database. Follow these steps:

1. **Display the Database window (press F11 or click the Database Window button on the toolbar).**

Book I, Chapter 2 describes the Database window, if this is your first time looking at it.

2. **Click the Reports button in the Objects list in the Database window.**

A list of existing reports appears in the Database window, but you can ignore these for now. You're here to create a new report.

3. **Click the New button on the Database Window toolbar.**

Access displays the New Report dialog box, giving you lots of choices for creating a new report, as shown in Figure 1-2.

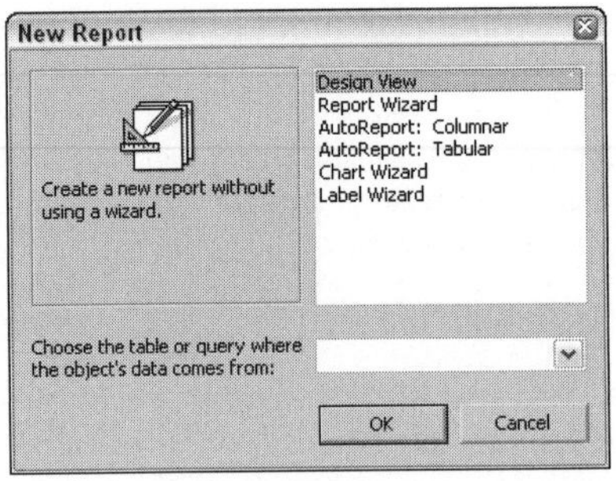

Figure 1-2:
Access
comes with
several
built-in
Report
Wizards.

New Report

Create a new report without using a wizard.

Design View
Report Wizard
AutoReport: Columnar
AutoReport: Tabular
Chart Wizard
Label Wizard

Choose the table or query where the object's data comes from:

OK   Cancel

Don't click the New button on the Access toolbar, which makes a new
database!

4. **Choose the method you want to use to create the report.**

Table 1-1 lists the choices in the New Report dialog box and tells you
when to use each of them.

5. **Select the table or query on which you want to base the report.**

Click the drop-down list and choose from the list of tables and queries
in the database. Choose the one that contains most of the information
you want to include on the report.

6. **Click OK.**

The appropriate wizard or AutoReport runs, or, if you decide to go it
alone by choosing Design view, you see the Design View window.

When you view a table or query in Datasheet view, you can create a new
report by clicking the downward-pointing triangle button next to the New
Object button on the toolbar and choosing the Report option.

Table 1-1	Options in the New Report Dialog Box	
Option	*When To Use It*	*Where to Find More Info*
Design View	When you want to design your report from scratch in Design view.	See Book IV, Chapter 1.
Report Wizard	When you want Access to create a report, using the fields, grouping, and sorting that you provide.	See the next section in this chapter.

Option	*When To Use It*	*Where to Find More Info*
AutoReport: Columnar	When you want to create a report from one table or query and arrange the fields from each record on a separate page, with field names in a column down the left and the data for the fields down a column on the right.	See "Running AutoReports" later in this chapter.
AutoReport: Tabular	When you want to create a report from one table or query and arrange the fields in a table, with field names at the tops of the columns and data from each record displayed as a row in the table (as in a datasheet).	See "Running AutoReports" later in this chapter.
Chart Wizard	When you want to create a chart from data stored in one table or query.	See Chapter 3 of this book.
Label Wizard	When you want to print data from one table or query on labels.	See "Creating Mailing Labels" later in this chapter.

You can also run the Report Wizard by double-clicking the Create Report by Using Wizard option in the Database window, and you can create a report in Design view by double-clicking the Create Report in Design View option in the Database window.

Running the Report Wizard

The first step in creating almost any report is to run the Report Wizard — especially if you want to create a report that groups data using one or more fields, with headings or subtotals for each group. When the wizard finishes, you can switch to Design view and add your own formatting touches in Design view.

One big advantage of using the Report Wizard is that you can choose fields for the report from more than one table or query — you don't have to gather all the data you want into one query. For example, using the MOM sample database (which stores order and customer information for a mail-order store), you may want to create a report that lists all the orders for each customer. The information for this report comes from several tables: Address Book (which stores one record for each customer, including name and address), Orders (with one record for each order, including the order date), and Order Details (with one record for each item in an order, including the quantity ordered and the price each).

If you want your report to include a calculated field, you need to create a query that calculates the field. For example, for our customer order listing, we need the extended price (price × quantity) for each item in each order, so we can calculate the total amount of each order. See Book III, Chapter 2 for how to create calculated fields in queries. Alternatively, you can add a calculated control to your report in Design view: See the section, "Formatting Tips and Tricks," later in this chapter for how this works.

The Report Wizard asks different questions depending on the data in the record source and on options you select, so don't be surprised if you don't see every window each time you run it. Follow these steps to create a report:

1. **Click the Reports button in the Database window to see your list of reports. Then double-click the Create Report by Using Wizard option.**

Access displays the first Report Wizard window, as shown in Figure 1-3. You can also start the wizard by displaying the New Report dialog box as described in the previous section.

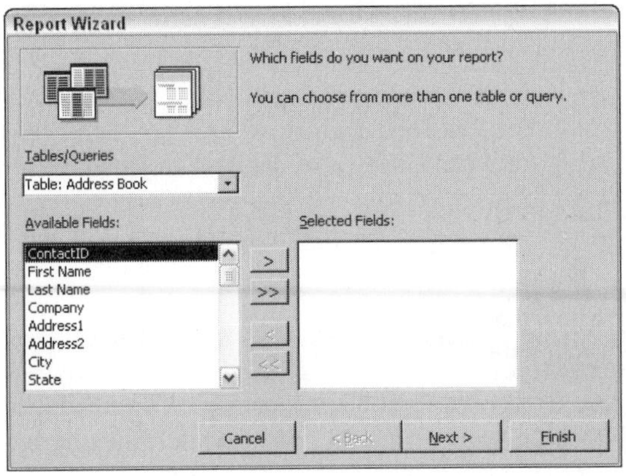

Figure 1-3:
The Report
Wizard can
build a
report from
one or more
tables and
queries.

> Report Wizard
>
> Which fields do you want on your report?
>
> You can choose from more than one table or query.
>
> Tables/Queries
> Table: Address Book
>
> Available Fields: Selected Fields:
> ContactID
> First Name
> Last Name
> Company
> Address1
> Address2
> City
> State
>
> Cancel   < Back   Next >   Finish

2. **Set the Tables/Queries drop-down list to the table or query that stores the records you want to include in the report.**

If you plan to use information from several tables or queries, choose one of them. The Available Fields box lists the fields in the selected table or query.

3. **Select the fields you want to display in the report in the Available Fields box and add them to the Selected Fields list by clicking the > button.**

Double-clicking a field name also adds it to the Selected Fields list. Click the >> button to add all the fields.

4. Repeat Steps 2 and 3 for fields in other tables or queries until all the fields you want to include in the report appear in the Selected Fields list.

You can use some fields from tables and other fields from queries. For our customer order listing, we select fields from the Address Book table, the Orders table, and the Order Details Qry query (which includes the Ext Price field, a calculated field that equals Price × Qty).

5. Click Next to see the wizard's next window.

Access gives you a chance to choose how you want to group the data. For example, in our customer order report, grouping by customer is a good idea in order for all the information about one customer to be together. Within the section for each customer, the secondary grouping is by order, so that all the items in each order are listed together.

If your report includes fields from more than one table or query, Access makes an educated guess about how you want to group your data, based on the relationships among the source tables. In Figure 1-4, the report includes records from the Address Book table (the customer list), the Orders table, and the Order Details Qry query, and Access has automatically created three ways of grouping your data: one by customer (Address Book table), one by order (Orders table), and one by Order Details Qry. Click an option in the How Do You Want to View Your Data list and look at the example on the right side of the window. For the selected way of grouping your data, Access shows how it plans to arrange your data in the report.

Click an option to see how the
wizard plans to group your data.

Figure 1-4:
The Report
Wizard
guesses
how you
want to
group the
information
in the report,
based on
the relation-
ships
between the
underlying
tables.

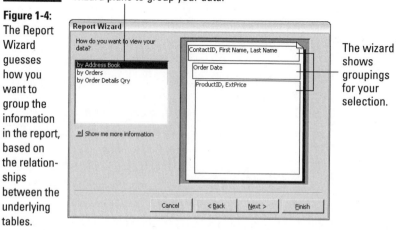

The wizard
shows
groupings
for your
selection.

In this example, if you choose the By Address Book option, the report prints information about a customer, followed by all of the customer's orders, each with its order detail information. Then the next customer, with that customer's orders, prints.

6. Click the option that's the closest to the way you want to organize your report and click Next.

The guesses Access makes about how to group data are not always on the mark, so the wizard gives you a chance to make your own changes, as shown in Figure 1-5.

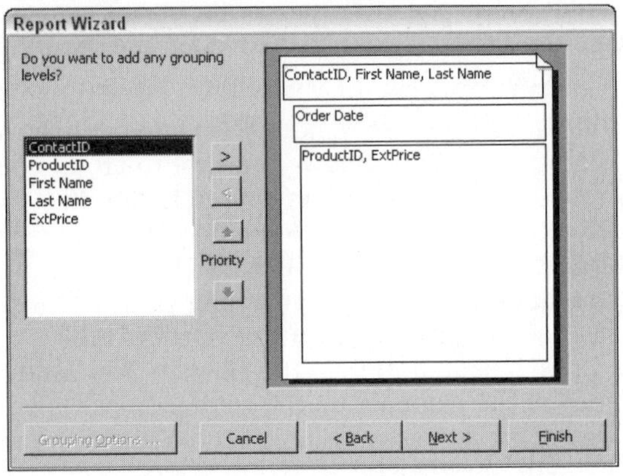

Figure 1-5:
You can adjust how the Report Wizard plans to group the records in your report.

7. Add or change the grouping fields if you want, and then click Next.

The wizard displays the grouping levels that you chose in the previous step on the right side of the window. To add an additional level of grouping, select a field from the list and click the > button. You can remove it by selecting it and clicking the < button.

However, you can't change the groupings that the wizard created in Steps 5 and 6. Instead, you have to click the Back button and choose a different way to group your records.

After you add a field, you can change the importance (grouping level) of a field by selecting the field and clicking the up-arrow and down-arrow Priority buttons (refer to Figure 1-5).

In the customer order report, the wizard's suggested groups are right, so you wouldn't have to make any changes.

Clicking the Grouping Options button (which is not always available, depending on your groupings) displays the Grouping Intervals dialog box, where you can specify exactly how to group records using the fields you choose. For data fields, you can group by day, month, or year. For number fields, you can group by 10s, 50s, 100s, 500s, 1,000s, 5,000s, and 10,000s so that you can categorize values by magnitude. For text fields, you can group on the first 1, 2, 3, 4, or 5 characters. Click OK to exit the Grouping Intervals dialog box and return to the main wizard window.

8. **Choose how you want to sort the records within the lowest-level grouping and click Next.**

   Access automatically sorts by the fields on which you are grouping records. For example, if you are grouping records by customer and then by order, the customers appear in alphabetical order by name or in order of customer number. Within the lowest level of grouping, you can choose what order the records appear in, specifying up to four fields on which to sort. If you aren't grouping your records at all, you can also sort them here.

   Click in the 1 box (shown in Figure 1-6), choose a field, and click the Ascending button if you want to switch to a descending sort. Additional sort fields are used only when the "1" sort field is identical in two or more records — then the "2" field is used. If the "1" and "2" fields are identical in two records, Access sorts by the "3" and then the "4" field.

   In the customer order report, you don't need to sort your records — the groupings take care of all the sorting you need.

Figure 1-6:
You can sort the records in your report within the lowest-level grouping.

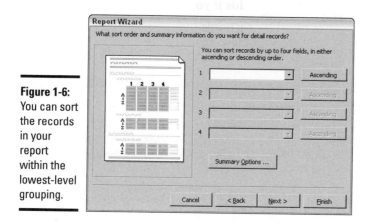

9. **Click the Summary Options button if you want to print counts, averages, or totals; specify which numeric fields to summarize; choose between the Detail and Summary and the Summary Only options; click OK; and click Next.**

Access displays a list of the numeric fields in your report, with a check box for Sum (total), Avg (average), Min (minimum or smallest value), and Max (maximum or largest value), as shown in Figure 1-7. If you want only the summary values, without information for individual records, click the Summary Only radio button. If you want Access to calculate the percent of the total that each grouping represents (for example, the percentage of orders that each customer represents), click the Calculate Percent of Total for Sums check box.

In the customer order report we are making, you click the Sum check box for the Ext Price field, to get a total of the items in each order and for each customer.

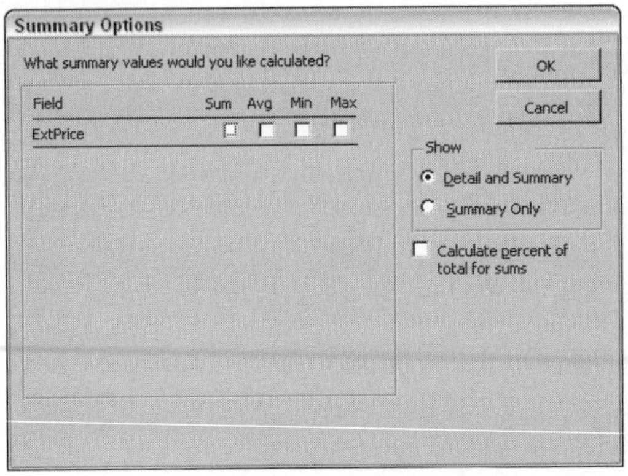

Figure 1-7:
The Report
Wizard can
add totals,
subtotals,
averages,
percent-
ages, and
other
summary
statistics to
your report.

10. **Choose the layout for your report from among the Access canned layouts and click Next.**

You can preview the layout options by clicking one of the Layout radio buttons. The sample box on the left changes to show what your chosen layout looks like. If you want to print your report sideways on the paper, click the Landscape radio button.

11. **Choose the style — typefaces, colors, lines, and boxes — for your report and click Next.**

Access has six preset styles to choose from. Click a style to see a sample.

12. **Type a title for the report. Choose whether to display the report in Print Preview or in Design view and click Finish.**

The title appears at the top of report. The Report Wizard takes a moment to create the report, and then displays it in the view you chose.

The report may look close to perfect, or it may look like a complete wreck. For example, the customer order report as created by the Report Wizard contains the right information, but it looks lousy (take a look at Figure 1-8). Luckily, you can switch to Design view to fix it up. Click the View button on the toolbar or choose View➪Design View. Then see Book IV, Chapter 1 for how to make changes in Design view.

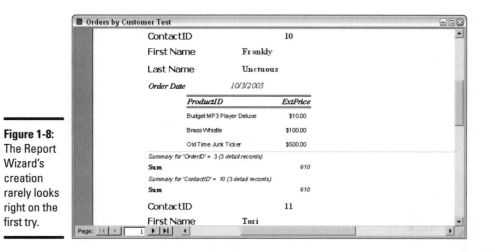

Figure 1-8:
The Report Wizard's creation rarely looks right on the first try.

Running AutoReports

AutoReports are simple wizards that you can use to create a report using the data from a single table or query. AutoReports don't have the flexibility that the Report Wizard provides — you can't group data from related tables, for example — but they are an excellent way to get your data into a report quickly. After you create a report using an AutoReport, you can customize it just like any other report — just open the report in Design view and have at it.

Access has two AutoReports: columnar and tabular. The columnar AutoReport prints the field names in a column on the left and the data for the record in a column on the right, as in Figure 1-9. (Hmm, the Product Photo is *under* the field name instead of to its right. We don't know why.) The tabular AutoReport looks similar to a datasheet, with data in columns and field names as the column headers, as in Figure 1-10.

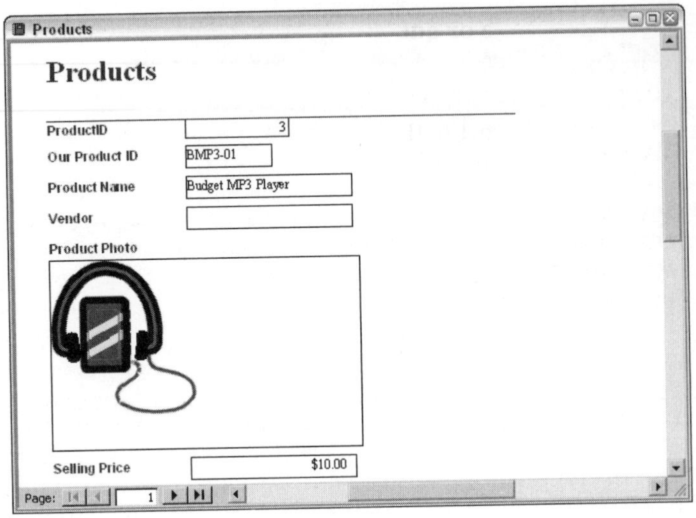

Products

Products

ProductID	3
Our Product ID	BMP3-01
Product Name	Budget MP3 Player
Vendor	

Product Photo

Selling Price | $10.00

Page: |◄ ◄ | 1 | ► ►| | ◄

Figure 1-9:
The columnar AutoReport lists field names and values.

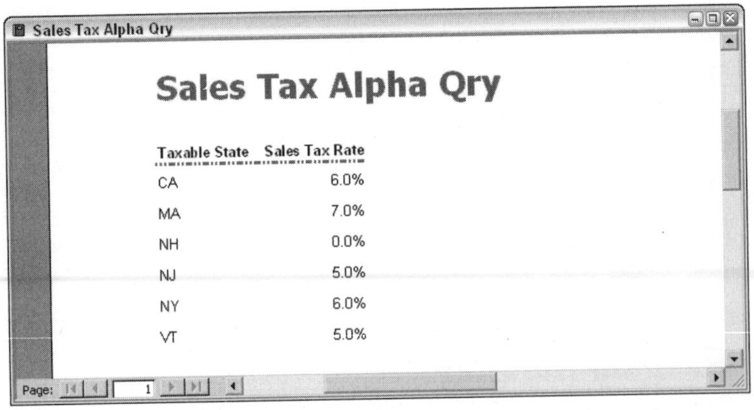

Sales Tax Alpha Qry

Sales Tax Alpha Qry

Taxable State	Sales Tax Rate
CA	6.0%
MA	7.0%
NH	0.0%
NJ	5.0%
NY	6.0%
VT	5.0%

Page: |◄ ◄ | 1 | ► ►| | ◄

Figure 1-10:
The tabular AutoReport looks like a datasheet.

To run an AutoReport, follow these steps:

1. **Click the Reports button in the Objects list of the Database window and then click the New button on the Database window toolbar.**

   (Press F11 if the Database window isn't visible.) The New Report dialog box appears. (Refer to Figure 1-2.)

2. **Click the AutoReport Columnar or AutoReport Tabular option from the list of wizards.**

3. **Choose the table or query from which you want the data to come.**

4. **Click OK.**

Access creates a report in the format you choose, showing all the fields and records in the table or query.

Another way to create a columnar AutoReport is to open the table or query, click the downward-pointing triangle button next to the New Object button on the toolbar, and choose the AutoReport option. (No option appears to make a tabular report.)

If your table or query has more than four or five fields, the tabular report usually looks lousy. Because the report tries to fit all the fields across the page, field names and data may be truncated, producing an unreadable report. You can use Design view to get rid of the unwanted fields, widen the controls for the fields and field names you want to keep, or switch to landscape printing (or all three).

Editing Reports in Design View

Book IV, Chapter 1 describes how to edit forms in Design view, and most of the same information holds true for editing reports. Figure 1-11 shows a report in Design view (specifically, a report created by the tabular AutoReport).

Toolbox

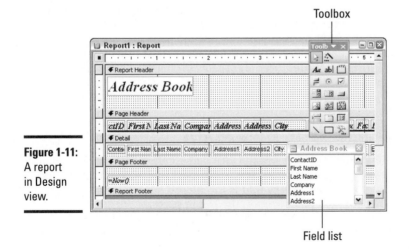

Figure 1-11:
A report in Design view.

Field list

You can modify your report in many ways, some of which work just as they do when modifying a form. Check out the following list for some of the ways, with the section in Book IV that describes each one:

✦ **Creating, editing, moving, and deleting controls:** Controls are the boxes on the Design grid that display labels, data from fields, and other information. See the sections, "Taking Control of Your Form or Report" and "Setting control properties," in Book IV, Chapter 2.

✦ **Drawing lines and boxes:** See the section, "Adding Lines, Boxes, and Backgrounds," in Book IV, Chapter 2.

✦ **Setting report properties:** See the section, "Configuring the Whole Form or Report," in Book IV, Chapter 1.

✦ **Saving, importing, copying, and renaming reports:** See the section, "Storing Your Forms and Reports," in Book IV, Chapter 1.

When you are in Design view, the Access toolbar looks like Figure 1-12, with most of the same buttons that are used when designing a form.

Figure 1-12:
The Access
toolbar in
Design view.

Print Preview   AutoFormat

View   Sorting and Grouping

However, some things work differently for forms and reports. Reports don't have command buttons and drop-down lists (they wouldn't work on paper!). Reports also have to fit correctly on the printed page and need page headers, footers, and headings for subsections. The rest of this chapter describes report-specific features and the next chapter describes controlling how reports print.

Report Sections and How They Work

In Design view, your report is broken into parts, called *sections*. The main part of the report is the *Detail section* — the part that shows information from fields in the table or query that is the record source for the report. The other sections come in pairs around the Detail section.

Sections provide headers and footers for your pages and allow you to group data using a particular field. If you have a number of reports with the same value in a field, you can display those records together in the report. For example, if your record source has a Date/Time field, you can create a section for that field and group records that have the same date, with subtotals by date. Table 1-2 lists the different sections that a report can include, with tips for how to use the section.

Table 1-2	Sections of Reports
Report Section	*Where It Appears and How to Use It*
Report Header and Footer	Appears at the beginning and end of the report. These sections are for summary information about the entire report. The Report Header can include a title page. The Report Footer can include totals for all the records in the report.
Page Header and Footer	Appears at the top and bottom of each page, and usually includes the report name, the date, and the page number.
Section Header and Footer	Appears at the top and bottom of each grouping before the first record and after the last record in a group that has the same value for a field. Your report may have more than one Section Header and Footer: You get one pair for each grouping. The Section Footer may include subtotals. Format Section Headers and Footers to make the hierarchy of the report obvious (for instance, larger fonts for first-level groups and smaller fonts for second-level groups).
Detail	Appears after each Section Header or after the Report Header if your report has no additional sections. Displays values for each record and can contain calculated fields.

In Design view, each section has a specific place. The gray bar names the section, and the controls appearing underneath the bar appear each time that section of the report prints. In the report shown in Figure 1-13, the Report Header prints only once, at the very beginning of the report. The Page Header section is blank, so nothing prints at the top of each page. Records are grouped by company name, with the company name and address printing at the beginning of the section for each company (in the Company Header). The Detail section prints information about each product, with the products for each company appearing under its Company Header. The Company Footer section is blank (a little space is left before the next company). The Page Footer section includes the current date and time, the page number, and the total number of pages in the report. The Report Footer section is blank. Figure 1-14 shows the report when printed.

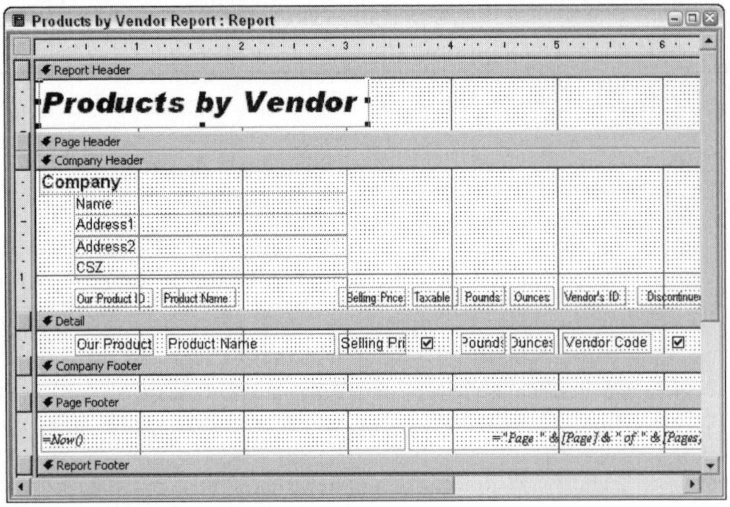

Figure 1-13:
Report
sections
determine
what prints
at the
beginning
and end of
the entire
report and
each
section of
the report,
as well as at
the top and
bottom of
each page.

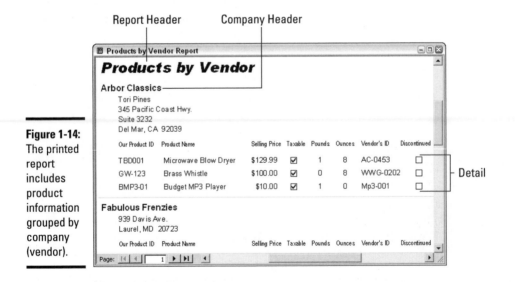

Figure 1-14:
The printed
report
includes
product
information
grouped by
company
(vendor).

Most sections are repeated many times in the report when you print it. For example, the Company Header in Figure 1-13 prints once for each company that has products. The Detail section prints once for each product. The Page Header and Page Footer sections print once (each) per page.

When you create a report using a Report Wizard, you get sections for each field on which you grouped the records. When you create a report from scratch in Design view, Access gives you just the Page Header, Detail, and Page Footer sections. You can add or delete sections in Design view, as described in the next two sections of this chapter. You can also adjust the size of each section by dragging the section dividers upward and downward.

You can't delete the Detail section. You can leave it blank, though, if you want a summary report with subtotals and totals but no data for individual records. Drag its lower edge (the top of the next section divider) upward to shrink the section to nothing. (In Figure 1-13, the Page Header section is shrunk to nothing.)

Setting report and section properties

As with most Access objects, each section and control in your report — as well as the entire report itself — has properties. You can display and change the properties on the Properties sheet (see Figure 1-15). To display the Properties sheet for the whole report, double-click the report selector (the gray box in the top-left corner of the Design View window) or right-click the title bar of the Design View window and choose the Properties option. Click the tabs to see the different categories of properties (or click the All tab to see all of them). Click in a property to change it.

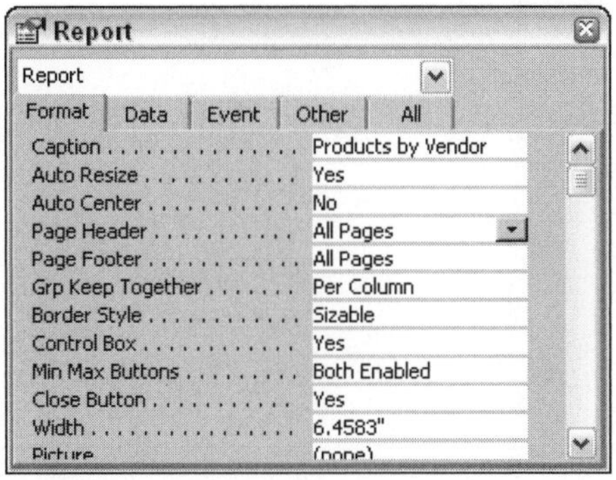

Figure 1-15:
You can
set the
properties
of the entire
report or of
individual
sections or
controls.

Report	
Report	⌄

| Format | Data | Event | Other | All |

Caption	Products by Vendor
Auto Resize	Yes
Auto Center	No
Page Header	All Pages
Page Footer	All Pages
Grp Keep Together	Per Column
Border Style	Sizable
Control Box	Yes
Min Max Buttons	Both Enabled
Close Button	Yes
Width	6.4583"
Picture	(none)

To see or change the properties of a particular section, double-click the section header or select the section header and click the Properties button on the toolbar. After the Properties sheet is visible, you can click a section header or control to see its properties.

Adding page headers, footers, and numbers

To add Report or Page Header or Footer sections, choose View⇨Page Header/Footer or View⇨Report Header/Footer. Access adds these in pairs: If you have a Page Header, you have a Page Footer. You can leave one or the other blank, though. To delete the Page or Report Header or Footer sections, choose the same command again: Access deletes the Header/Footer pair and all the controls in the sections.

If you want just a header or just a footer, change the height of the section you don't want to delete by dragging the bottom border of the section up to the top border.

Adding page numbers

After you have a Page Header or Footer to put controls in, you can create controls in the sections, or drag them there from other sections. The easiest way to add page numbers — probably one of the most common controls you find in a report — is to choose Insert⇨Page Numbers from the menu. When you see the Page Numbers dialog box (shown in Figure 1-16), choose the format of the numbering, the position, and the alignment (Left, Center, Right, Inside, or Outside). Inside and Outside page numbering refers to alternating left and right positions on odd and even pages. You can also omit the page number on the first page by deselecting the Show Number on First Page check box.

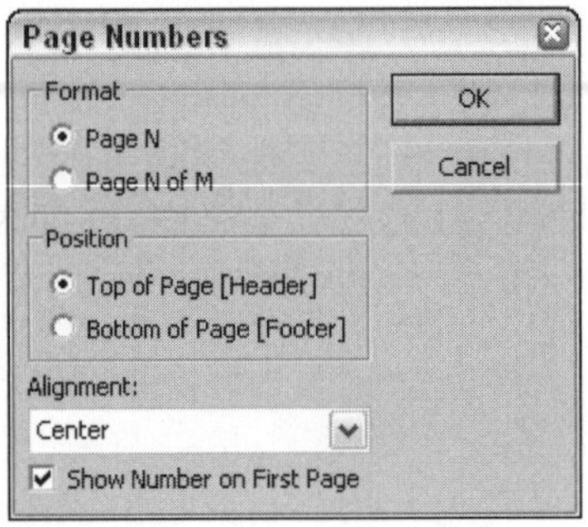

Figure 1-16:
Adding
page
numbers to
your report.

If you'd rather make your own page-numbering controls, you can create your own text box control by following these steps:

1. **With the report open in Design view, display the Toolbox (if it's not already on-screen) by clicking the Toolbox button on the toolbar.**

You can read about the Toolbox in Book IV, Chapter 1.

2. **Create a text box control in the Page Header or Footer section by clicking the Text Box button on the Toolbox and clicking in the header or footer section.**

   Don't worry if the text box doesn't appear in exactly the right place — you can drag it around later.

3. **If Access created a label to go with the text box, delete the label by clicking in the label and pressing the Delete key.**

   Your page number doesn't need a label.

4. **Display the Properties sheet if it's not already on-screen by clicking the Properties button on the toolbar.**

   You see the Properties sheet with the properties of the text box you just created.

5. **Click the Data tab on the Properties sheet, click in the** Control Source **property, and type the following expression:**

   ```
   = Page
   ```

   To display the word *Page* as well as the number, type

   ```
   = "Page " & Page
   ```

Adding the date and time

If you want to include the current date or time on your report, follow the same steps as in the preceding section, but type the following expression into the Control Source property of another text box:

```
= Now()
```

The Now() function returns both the date and time (for example, *6/25/04 1:55:48 PM*). If you want to print only the current date, format the box as a date using the Format property. (In the Properties sheet for the text box, click the Format tab and set the Format property to one of the date formats, which omit the time.)

Controlling which pages get page headers and footers

You can also choose whether the Page Header and Footer sections print on all pages, all but the Report Header page (so your cover page isn't numbered), all but the Report Footer page, or all but the Report Header and Footer pages. The following steps explain how to change the Page Header and Footer sections properties:

1. **With the report open in Design view, double-click the report selector (the gray box in the top-left corner of the Design window, where the rulers intersect) or right-click the title bar of the Design View window and choose the Properties option.**

You see the Properties sheet for the report (refer to Figure 1-16).

2. **Click the Format tab.**

3. **Set the** `Page Header` **and** `Page Footer` **properties.**

Your options are `All Pages`, `Not With Rpt Hdr`, `Not With Rpt Ftr`, and `Not With Rpt Hdr/Ftr`.

Displaying the first value of a field in the Page Header section to make a telephone-book-style header is easy. Just create a text box in the Page Header section that displays the field. When you print the report, the text box shows the value for the first record on the page. You can also print the value of the last record on the page in the Page Footer section.

Adding sections that group your records

To create *grouping sections* (also known as *group sections*), you tell Access to group the records in your report by the value of one or more fields. For each field, you get a header and footer section for that field. For example, on a report that lists products, you may want to group the records by category, and within category by vendor. If you choose to add both a header and footer section for the group, you end up with Category Header, Vendor Header, Vendor Footer, and Category Footer sections (in that order).

To create new grouping sections, display the report in Design view and follow these steps:

1. **With the report open in Design view, click the Sorting and Grouping button on the toolbar.**

Access displays the Sorting and Grouping dialog box, shown in Figure 1-17. You see any fields that are currently used for sorting or grouping the records on your report. If more than one field appears, the top-most field is the major grouping and other fields are subgroups.

2. **Move your cursor to a blank row and select a field from the Field/Expression drop-down list to add a section (grouping).**

You see a list of the fields in the record source for your report. After you select a field, Access automatically uses an ascending sort for the new field.

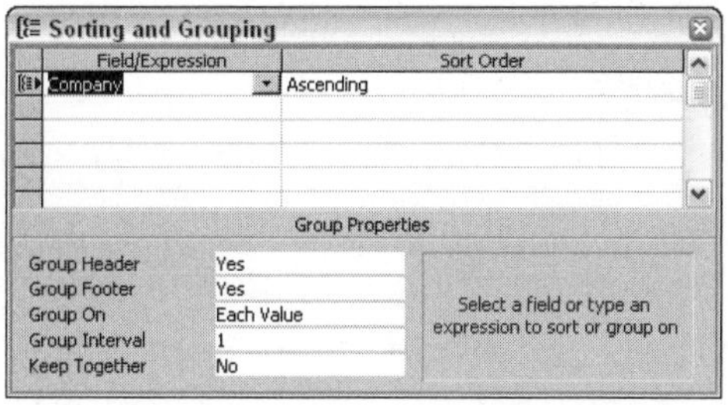

Figure 1-17:
The Sorting
and
Grouping
dialog box
defines how
the records
in your
report are
grouped for
subtotals.

3. **Choose the Descending order in the Sort Order column if you want to sort this field in descending order. Click in the column, click the down-arrow at the right end of the box, and choose the value.**

   The lower pane of the dialog box shows the properties for the selected grouping. The default settings for a new grouping have neither a header nor a footer section, group by individual values of the field, and don't keep all records in each group together on a page.

4. **Change the Group Header or Group Footer property to the Yes setting if you want a header or footer section for the group.**

   Use the Group Header or Group Footer property if you want to print something before the first record or after the last record in the group.

   If the group includes either a header or footer (if the Group Footer or Group Header setting for the group is Yes), then Access adds the grouping symbol to the field in the top part of the box.

5. **Close the Sorting and Grouping dialog box by clicking its X button.**

   Access adds the new section(s) to the report design.

Access makes a new grouping with a header and/or footer, as shown in Figure 1-18. You can also use the Sorting and Grouping dialog box to delete groupings, or the dialog box can add or delete header or footer sections for groupings. You can also set the group properties shown in Table 1-3 by changing the properties in the lower half of the Sorting and Grouping dialog box.

Prints before each group of records

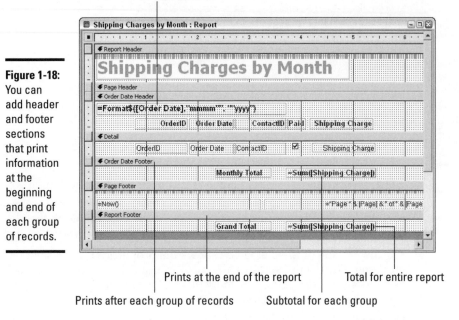

Figure 1-18:
You can
add header
and footer
sections
that print
information
at the
beginning
and end of
each group
of records.

Prints at the end of the report   Total for entire report

Prints after each group of records   Subtotal for each group

Table 1-3	Properties of Report Groups
Group Property	*What It Does*
Group Header	Specifies whether the report contains a header section for the group.
Group Footer	Specifies whether the report contains a footer section for this group.
Group On	Specifies the size of the group. Usually, you group on the Each Value setting (each different value of the field defines a new group when the report is printed). For numbers, choose an Interval setting to specify an interval (for example, 1-10, 11-20, 21-30, and so on) For dates, you can group on year, quarter, month, week, day, hour, or minute. For text fields, choose a Prefix Characters setting to group on values that start with the name first character(s).
Group Interval	If you choose a setting other than the Each Value setting for the Group On property, specifies the size of the interval on which groups occur.
Keep Together	Specifies whether all the records for a group appear on one page or whether the group can be split and printed on more than one page. If all the records can't fit, Access begins a new page before starting the group. Select the No setting to allow splitting, the Whole Group setting to print each group together on a page, or the With First Detail setting if you want the group header to always appear on the same page with at least one record.

You have some control over whether your groups start on a new page, or can be broken over several pages. If you want to start a new page each time a new group starts, change the Force New Page property to the Before setting on the Format tab of the Properties sheet for the group header section. You can also set the Keep Together property for the group header: The Yes setting keeps the entire group together on one page and the No setting allows Access to break a group over multiple pages.

Sorting the records in your report

You can sort a report by sorting the record source — the table or query that provides the records for the report. But a more foolproof method is to use the Sorting and Grouping dialog box to make a group for the field(s) by which you want to sort, even if you don't want to print anything extra when the field value changes. When you tell Access to group by a field, you get sorting thrown in for free. Set the Group Header and Group Footer properties to the No setting, which tells Access to sort by the field, but not print any grouping sections.

To sort the records in a report by two fields, decide which field is the primary sort field and which is the secondary one. The secondary sort field, like a tiebreaker, is used only when two or more records have the same value for the primary sort field. For example, to sort order records by customer name, you usually sort by last name (primary sort field) and the first name (secondary sort field).

In the Sorting and Grouping dialog box, type the primary sort field in the Field/Expression column on the first row and the secondary sort field on the second row. If you have a large number of records, you may want additional sort fields (for example, you could sort a mailing list by zip code, then last name, and then first name).

You can sort by a calculated value that is not one of the fields in the record source of the report. Just enter an expression in the Field/Expression column of the Sorting and Grouping dialog box. See Book III, Chapter 3 for an introduction to expressions. For example, if you print a listing of products, you may want to sort them by profit margin — by [Selling Price]-[Purchase Price]. You can type that expression into the Field/Expression column (hence the name of the column!).

Calculating group subtotals and report totals

If you use the Report Wizard to create a report, and you use the Summary Options button to request sums, averages, minimum values, or maximum values for each group, you already have subtotals and totals on your report. But you can make them yourself in Design view, too.

After you group your report on one or more fields, you can add subtotals. In the group footer section, create a text box control for each sum, count, or other summary information that you want to print. To print totals and counts for the entire report, make a text box in the Report Header or Report Footer section. Type an expression in the Control Source property for the text box using aggregate functions, such as Sum( ), Avg( ), and Count( ). (See Book IV, Chapter 4.)

When you use aggregate functions in a group header or footer section, Access automatically restricts the records to those in the current group. For example, the Sum( ) function totals the values of a field for all the records in the group. To subtotal the amount paid for each product in the current group, you use the following expression in a text box control:

```
= Sum([Price])
```

To print the number of records in the report, type the following expression in the Control Source property for a text box in the Report Header or Report Footer section:

```
= Count(*)
```

Don't use aggregate functions in the Page Header or Page Footer sections of a report; you see an #Error message.

Figure 1-18 (earlier in this chapter) shows a report in Design view with Sum( ) functions in both the Order Date Footer and Report Footer sections. The Sum( ) function in the Order Date Footer section prints a subtotal of the shipping charges for each month's orders, and the Sum( ) function in the Report Footer section prints the total shipping charges for the whole report.

Formatting Tips and Tricks

The following list details a few tricks for making nicely formatted controls for your reports. Most of them involve setting report, section, or control properties on the Properties sheet:

✦ **Printing calculations:** Print a *calculated field* — a field decided by an expression — the same way you display one on a form: Create a text box and enter an expression in the Control Source property. Be sure to set the control's Format property, too. Book IV, Chapter 4 contains excruciating detail about displaying calculations on forms, and the same methods work for reports.

✦ **Prompting for information to print:** Just as Access can prompt for information when running a query (as described in Book III, Chapter 2), you can use parameters when printing a report. Parameters allow you to specify information — usually in the Report or Page Header or Footer sections — that you want to print. Create a text box control where you want the information to print. For the `Control Source` property of the text box, enter the parameter prompt in square brackets, such as the following:

```
[Enter title line]
```

✦ **Avoiding space between fields:** When you display several fields in a row, you may not want to leave gaps between them. For example, in a mailing label or form letter, you may want to print fields containing first names and last names with only one space between them. To eliminate extra space between fields, regardless of the length of the values in the fields, concatenate them (glue them together) using the & operator. (We describe calculated fields and the & operator in Book III, Chapter 3.) Create a text box control and type an expression in its `Control Source` property, such as the following expression:

```
= [First Name] & " " & [Last Name]
```

This expression glues the first name, a space, and the last name together. If the first name were *Elvis* and the last name were *Presley*, you end up with *Elvis Presley*.

✦ **Use conditional calculations:** You can print one thing in some circumstances and another thing in others by using the `iif()` function. (For more on the `iif()` function, see Book IV, Chapter 4.) For example, you may make a report that can print either an invoice or a receipt, depending on whether the customer has paid. At the top, you include a text box with an expression in the `Control Source` property that spells out that Access should print either an invoice or a receipt depending on the value of the Paid field. That expression looks something like the following:

```
= iif([Paid], "Receipt", "Invoice")
```

✦ **Calculating a running sum:** You can tell Access to sum the values of a numeric field, showing the total of the current record (a *running sum*). Set the `Running Sum` property of the text box control displaying that field to the `Yes` setting. You may want to include two text box controls for the numeric field: one to show the value for the current record (with the `Running Sum` property set to the `No` setting), and the running sum (with the `Running Sum` property set to the `Yes` setting).

✦ **Hiding duplicate values:** If a group of records have the same value for a control, and you want the value to print only the first time it appears, you can set the `Hide Duplicates` property of the field to the `Yes` setting. This setting is especially useful in tabular reports, in which each field appears in a separate column.

Don't use a field name as the control name for a calculated control. When you create controls, Access names them automatically, although you can change the names later. If you rename a calculated control, make sure that the name you assign isn't the same as any field mentioned in the expression (or any field in the record source of the report). Access gets confused about whether references to that name are to the field or to the control and the report displays an #Error message.

Copying Forms to Reports

If you have a form that you want to print, you can certainly go ahead and print it as is, but you have a lot more control over the format if you turn the form into a report first. You can then change the design for the report to print nicely without changing the format of the original form.

To save a form as a report, open the form and choose File➪Save As from the menu. (Alternatively, display the Database window, click the Forms button, click the form name, and choose File➪Save As.) When you see the Save As dialog box, type a name for the new report and set the As drop-down list to the Report option. Access creates a new report based on the design of the form.

Most forms have gray backgrounds. After saving a form as a report, be sure to change the background of your new report to white before printing the report, or you waste a lot of ink (or toner). Right-click the background of each section, choose the Fill/Back Color option from the shortcut menu that appears, and choose the white box in the palette of colors.

Adding and Formatting Subreports

A *subreport* provides detail information from other tables. For example, if you have a report about customers, a subreport can list the orders for each customer. Figure 1-19 shows a report with two subreports in Design view and Figure 1-20 shows the same report in Print Preview.

You can create a *subreport control* to print another report as part of your report. An *unbound subreport* is not connected to the records in the main report: No relationship exists between the record source of the main report and the subreport. The unbound subreport in Figure 1-19 displays information from the My Business table, which contains one record, with the business's name, address, and other information. (We like to create a My Business table to store this information in one place, for use in all the forms and reports in the database. If your phone number changes, for example, you change it in the My Business table, and all your forms and reports are updated automatically.)

Unbound subreport

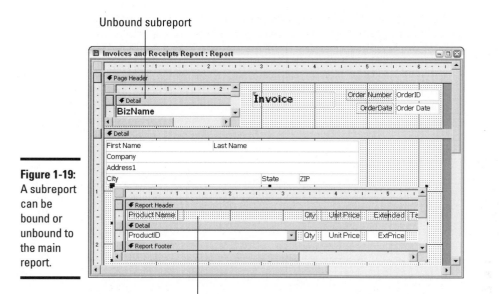

Figure 1-19:
A subreport can be bound or unbound to the main report.

Bound subreport

Unbound subreport prints the same data for every record.

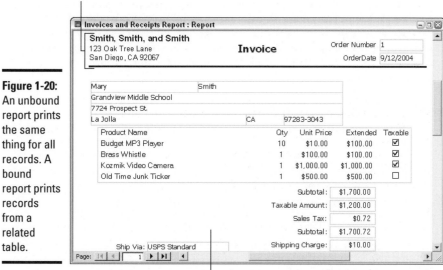

Figure 1-20:
An unbound report prints the same thing for all records. A bound report prints records from a related table.

Bound subreport prints data that relates to the current record.

With an unbound subreport, Access prints the same information for each record in the main report. In Figures 1-19 and 1-20, the business information from the My Business table is printed at the top of each invoice.

A *bound subreport* provides detail from other tables. In Figures 1-19 and 1-20, the bound subreport lists the items in the current order, pulling the information from the Order Details table. Bound subreports help you print information from a one-to-many relationship: The main report displays records from the master (*one*) table and the subreport displays records from the detail (*many*) table.

If you always print two or more reports at the same time, include them as unbound subreports in a new, unbound report. When you print the new report, Access prints each of the subreports. Just make sure that all the reports require the same kind of paper!

Making a subreport

To create a subreport, whether bound or unbound, follow these steps:

1. **Create the report you plan to use as a subreport and save it.**

For example, to make the report in Figures 1-19 and 1-20, you make one report appear as the unbound subreport, with the My Business table as its record source. You create another report as the bound subreport, with the Order Details table as its record source. When you preview the report by itself, Access displays all the records in the record source, but as a subreport, Access restricts the records each time the subreport prints to the records that match the current record in the main report.

When you create this report, nothing about it says "subreport." Any report can be used as a subreport. We like to use the word "subreport" in the name of reports that never print on their own, only as subreports of other reports.

2. **Open the main report in Design view.**

3. **Make space for the subreport control (also called a Subreport/ Subform control) in the Detail section of the report.**

Drag your other controls out of the way.

4. **Display the Database window (press F11 if it's not visible) so that the Design View window for the main report and the Database window are both at least partially visible. Click the Reports button in the Objects list of the Database window to display the list of your reports.**

You're going to drag the subreport from the Database window to the Design View window.

5. **Select the subreport-to-be from the Reports list in the Database window and drag it into the Design View window, dropping it where you want the subreport to appear.**

   Access creates a subreport control on the main report, containing the report you selected. The `Source Object` property for the subreport control contains the name of the report that you dragged.

6. **Delete the label that Access created for the subreport if you don't like it.**

   Access creates a label for the subreport with the name of the report, but you can select it and delete it if you want.

7. **Move and size the subreport control.**

   Drag the control to the location you want and drag its edges to adjust its size.

8. **Click in the subreport control and then click the Properties button on the toolbar to display the Properties sheet for the subreport control.**

   If you double-click in the subreport, Access displays the properties for the report that appears in the subreport control, rather than for the control itself. (Confusing? Yes! You've got a report within a report.) Figure 1-21 shows the Properties sheet for a subreport control with the Data tab selected. (While you've got the Properties sheet displayed, you can fool with the format properties, too.)

Figure 1-21:
The properties of a subreport control include the link between records in the subreport and those in the main report.

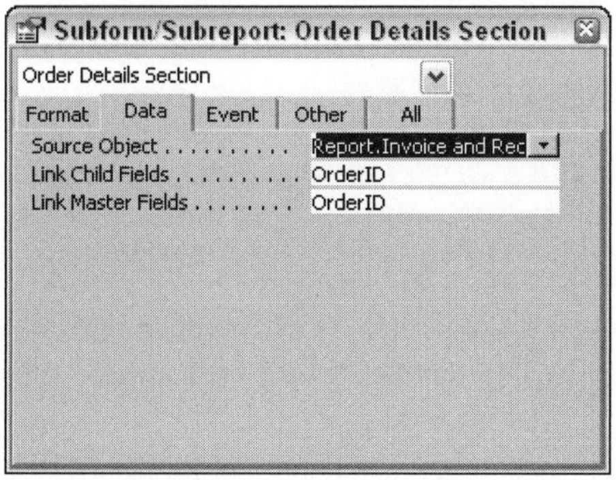

9. **Check the** `Link Child Fields` **and** `Link Master Fields` **properties on the Data tab of the Properties sheet.**

   These properties contain the names of the fields that relate the main and subreports. The `Link Master Fields` property should contain the name of the field in the record source of the main report that relates to a field in the subreport. The `Link Child Fields` property contains the name of the matching field in the record source of the subreport.

Printing information from a subreport on the main report

Just as you can display totals from a subform on a main form, you can print totals from a subreport on the main report. See Book IV, Chapter 3 for how to create a control on the main report to display a total from a subreport.

When entering the expression in the text box control on the main report, use this format:

```
= [subreport control name].Report![total control]
```

Replace *subreport control name* with the name of the subreport control. Replace *total control* with the name of the text box control in the subreport that displays the total. For example, the following expression may display the total extended price (price times quantity) for the records in the report that displays in the `Order Detail Subreport` subreport control:

```
= [Order Detail Subreport].Report![Total Ext Price]
```

Displaying Empty or Long Fields

Text and Memo fields can pose problems on reports, because they can contain one or hundreds of characters. Anticipating how much space to leave for them is hard. Luckily, Access has some features to help deal with long fields.

Displaying long text

If a Text or Memo field in your report contains more than a few words, you may want the field to wrap onto additional lines. For example, the Description field in a Products table may contain a whole paragraph about the product. You could display the field in a very large text box control that can fit the largest description in the table, but Access would leave a large empty space in the report after short descriptions. Instead, each text box can expand or shrink vertically to fit the amount of text in the field for each record.

To make a text box grow, start off by making it big enough to fit just one line of text. (See Book IV, Chapter 1 for how to make a text box control.) Display its Properties sheet by clicking the Properties button on the toolbar. Then set its Can Grow property (which is on the Format tab) to the Yes setting. When Access prints each record, the text box control expands until the entire value of the field fits. The remaining controls move down the page.

When you set a control's Can Grow property to the Yes setting, Access sets the Can Grow property for the section that contains the property, too. When Access prints the report, the section expands as well as the control, so that nothing gets cut off. If you don't want the section to expand, you can change its Can Grow property back to the No setting, and information is omitted that doesn't fit in the section. Set the Can Grow property to the No setting when printing on forms of a predetermined size, such as mailing labels. (Later in this chapter, we show you how to set up a report that prints mailing labels.)

Displaying fields that may be empty

To avoid leaving blank lines when a field is blank, set the Can Shrink property for the text box to the Yes setting. (This setting is on the Format tab of the Properties sheet.) For example, many address lists are stored in tables that have two lines for the street address. If the second line is empty, the mailing label looks better if the city/state/zip line prints right below the first address line with no gap.

To make a text box control that shrinks when the value is blank, make the text box big enough to fit the longest value in the table. Then set its Can Shrink property to the Yes setting. When printing the report, Access omits the control if the field value is blank.

When you set the Can Shrink property of a control to the Yes setting, Access does not automatically change the Can Shrink property of the section that contains the control. Leave the Can Shrink properties of the Detail section set to the No setting if the Detail section must always be the same size — for example, mailing labels or other pre-printed forms. Otherwise, set these properties to the Yes setting.

Creating Mailing Labels

A perennial database task is printing mailing labels from lists of names and addresses. The easiest way to create a report that prints on labels is to use the Label Wizard, which contains a long list of preset formats for all standard Avery brand and compatible labels. (Most boxes of label sheets include an Avery number that specifies the size of your labels.) After you create a report with the wizard, you can make further changes in Design view.

Running the Label Wizard

To run the Label Wizard, follow these steps:

1. **In the Database window, click the Reports button in the Objects list to see a list of reports and then click the New button.**

   You see the New Report dialog box (refer to Figure 1-2).

2. **Choose the Label Wizard option from the list of methods of making a report.**

3. **Choose the table or query that contains the names and addresses you want to print. Then click OK.**

   You see the Label Wizard, as shown in Figure 1-22.

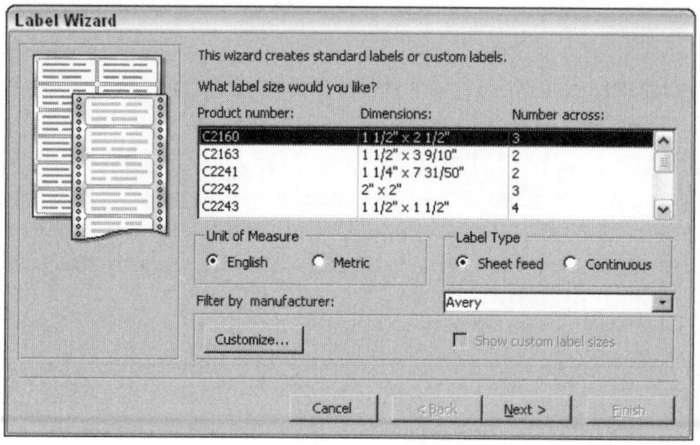

Figure 1-22:
The Label
Wizard
knows the
sizes and
shapes of
most sheets
of labels.

4. **Choose the type of label from the Product Number list, checking that the label size and number across match what Access displays. Click Next.**

   Access normally shows the labels according to the numbers assigned by Avery, a major manufacturer of labels. But you can see other types of labels by changing the Filter by Manufacturer box. If you plan to print continuous-feed labels (where the sheets are connected together) rather than sheets of labels, change the Label Type setting. If you are printing on custom-printed labels, click the Customize button, click the New button in the New Label Size dialog box that appears, and tell Access about your labels.

5. **Choose the font, font size, weight (light, normal, or bold, among others), and color. Click Next.**

   Access uses these settings for the text boxes in the report.

6. **Choose the fields that you want to include on the label, as shown in Figure 1-23. Click Next.**

The Prototype Label box shows the layout of fields on the label, including spaces, punctuation, and text that prints on every label (for example, "First Class" or your return address). You arrange the fields and other information in the Prototype Label box. One line in the Prototype Label box is selected (it's gray), showing that new fields are added to this line. You can press the ↑ and ↓ keys to move to a different line.

To print a field on your mailing labels, click the field in the Available Fields box and then click the > button to add it to the current line of the Prototype Label box. (Double-clicking a field does the same thing.) To add text, such as a space, comma, other punctuation, or words, just move your cursor to the location in the Prototype Label box where you want the text to appear, and type it.

For example, the first line of a mailing label usually consists of the first name, a space, and the last name. With the first line of the Prototype Label box selected, you double-click the First Name field (whatever it's called in your table), type a space, and double-click the Last Name field. To move to the next type, press Enter or ↓.

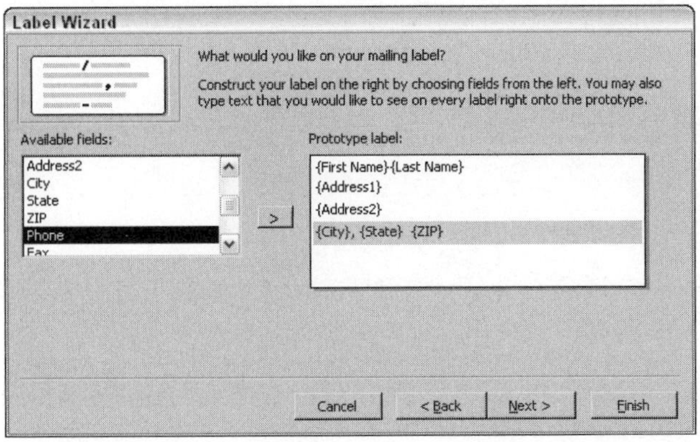

Figure 1-23:
You tell the
Label
Wizard
what fields
you want on
your label
and the
wizard
creates the
text box
controls.

If you put a field in the wrong place, click it in the Prototype Label box and press the Delete key to remove it.

Be sure to type a comma and a space between city and state/province fields in the Prototype Label box, and a space between state/province and zip/postcode fields, too.

7. **Choose the field(s) by which to sort the records. Click Next.**

   For example, to sort by last name within zip code, choose the ZIP field and then the Last Name field.

8. **Type a name for the report and click Finish.**

If the label report looks good in Print Preview, print it on a blank piece of paper before wasting sheets of labels. Hold the printed sheet up to a blank sheet of labels and see whether the names and addresses line up with the labels. This method avoids wasting sheets of expensive labels while you refine your label report.

Behind the scenes in a mailing label report

The Label Wizard makes a report that looks like Figure 1-24 in Design view. You see the fields and text that you told the wizard to include, followed by enough blank space to reach down to where the text should start on the next label. Where more than one field (or text) appears on a line, the Label Wizard has cleverly written expressions (starting with =) that use the & operator to concatenate (glue together) the information. In expressions, the wizard encloses each field name in square brackets (for field names that contain spaces, these brackets prevent the spaces from confusing Access). The wizard also uses the Trim() function to eliminate any extra spaces at the ends of fields.

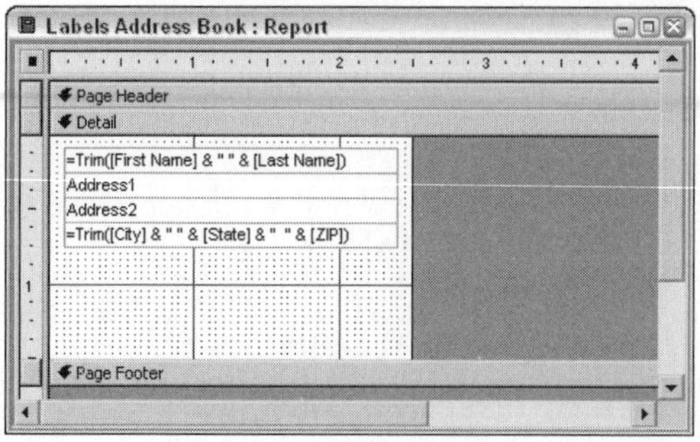

Figure 1-24:
The Label
Wizard
creates a
report the
size of a
single label.

▣ Labels Address Book : Report
· · · · · 1 · · · 1 · · · 2 · · · 1 · · · 3 · · · 1 · · · 4 ·
✦ Page Header
✦ Detail
=Trim([First Name] & " " & [Last Name])
Address1
Address2
=Trim([City] & " " & [State] & " " & [ZIP])
✦ Page Footer

For example, the first line of the label in Figure 1-24 contains a text box with this expression as its Control Source property:

```
=Trim([First Name] & "" & [Last Name])
```

This scary-looking expression glues the first name, a space, and the last name together, and then discards any spaces at the right end.

If you don't like the way information appears on your mailing labels, you can delete the text boxes, add new ones, alter the expressions in the existing text boxes, and change the formatting of the text boxes — the same kind of changes you can make to the controls in any report.

Changing the page setup for labels

Unexpectedly, the report is only the size of a single label. You don't see a whole page full of labels. How does Access know how many labels to print across a row? The Page Setup dialog box for the report contains this information. If you specified the wrong Avery number in the Label Wizard, or if you have labels that don't have an Avery number, you can change these settings.

With the report open in Design view or Print Preview, choose File⇨Page Setup and click the Columns tab in the Page Setup dialog box that appears (as shown in Figure 1-25). You see the following settings:

✦ **Number of Columns:** How many columns of labels per page.

✦ **Row Spacing:** How much blank space to leave between one row of labels and the next (usually zero, because Access includes this space in the report design).

✦ **Column Spacing:** How much blank space to leave between one column and the next (that is, between one label and the next across each row).

✦ **Column Size Width and Height:** The size of the labels. If you leave the Same as Detail check box selected, Access sets these settings to be the same size as the Detail section of the report.

✦ **Column Layout:** The order in which the labels print on each page.

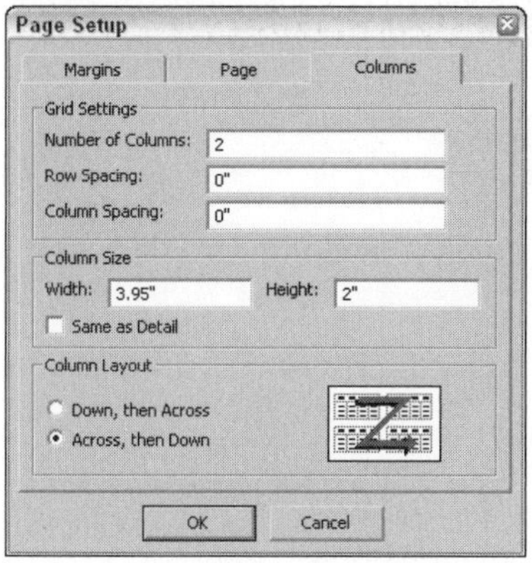

Figure 1-25:
The Columns tab of the Page Setup dialog box defines how your report prints on sheets of labels.

See the next chapter for how to print labels and other reports.

You can use the settings on the Columns tab of the Page Setup dialog box to create newspaper-style "snaking" columns for any report, not just mailing labels. Make the Detail section of the report narrower than half the width of the paper, specify two columns, and set the `Column Layout` property to the `Down Then Across` setting.

Chapter 2: Printing Beautiful Reports

In This Chapter

✓ Previewing your report on-screen

✓ Controlling report margins and page orientation

✓ Choosing which printer to print on

✓ Creating snapshot reports that others can view on-screen without Access

✓ Including Access reports in other Office documents

*A*fter you create a good-looking report on-screen, the next step is to see whether it looks good on paper. To make it perfect, you need to be able to control how the printer prints the report. This chapter describes page formats, margins, and other printer settings.

Viewing Your Report

You can see how the printed report will look *before* you spend the time, paper, and ink or toner to print it. Using Print Preview, you can see on-screen whether your controls are positioned as you want them, whether the right information appears in each control, and whether your headers and footers appear correctly. To see how your report looks in Print Preview, try the following:

✦ With the report open in Design view, click the Print Preview button on the toolbar.

✦ In the Database window, click the Reports button in the Objects list to display a list of your reports, and double-click the report. (Or click the report and click the Preview button on either the Database window toolbar or the main Access toolbar.)

The Print Preview window appears, showing you the top of the first page of your report, looking a lot like Figure 2-1. (Of course, your own report looks different.)

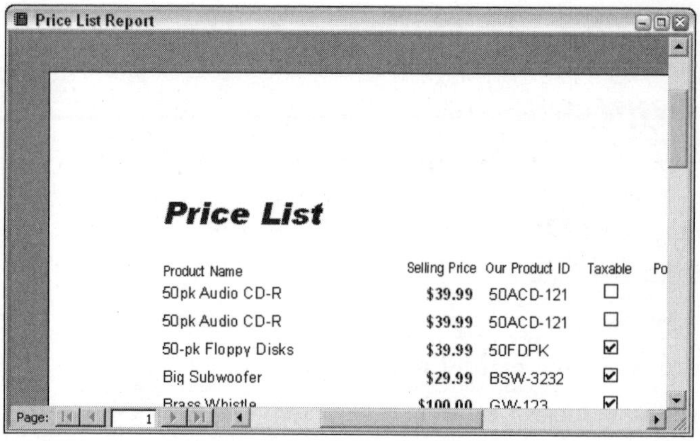

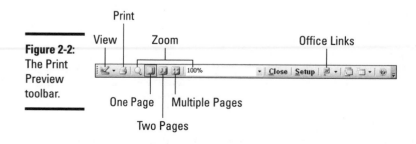

Figure 2-1:
A report
in Print
preview.

 You can display almost any Access object in Print Preview and then print it. When you are looking at a table in Datasheet view or a form in Form view, the Print Preview button is available on the toolbar. Reports have more formatting options than any other type of object in Access, but sometimes datasheets and forms are worth printing, too.

When the Print Preview window is active, the Access toolbar looks like Figure 2-2.

Print

View   Zoom   Office Links

Figure 2-2:
The Print
Preview
toolbar.

One Page   Multiple Pages

Two Pages

Adjusting the view

 If your report is shrunk to fit in the window, click the Zoom button on the toolbar — the mouse pointer turns into a magnifying glass. Click the report to zoom in, and click it again to zoom out (the Zoom button provides just two zooms — in and out). Alternatively, click in the Zoom box on the toolbar (the one that says something like "Fit" or "100%") and choose a magnification level.

When the report is large enough to read, you can rarely see much of it. Drag the edges of the Print Preview window outward to expand the window, or click the Maximize button near the upper-right corner of the window to maximize its size to take up the whole Access window. Use the vertical scroll bar or press the Down Arrow, Up Arrow, Page Down, and Page Up keys on your keyboard to scroll the report up and down within the Print Preview window. Use the horizontal scroll bar or press the Left Arrow and Right Arrow keys on your keyboard to pan sideways. To see other pages of the report, use the navigation buttons in the lower-left corner of the Print Preview window.

Looking at lots of pages

You can zoom *way* out by displaying two or more pages at the same time. Click the Two Pages button on the toolbar to display two pages at a time, side by side. Though useless for close proofreading, with this view you can tell where section breaks come and how full the pages are, as shown in Figure 2-3. To see more than two pages, click the Multiple Pages button on the toolbar and choose an arrangement of pages: Your options are 1 x 1, 1 x 2, 1 x 3, 2 x 1, 2 x 2, and 2 x 3. Use the Zoom button to zoom in and out on Two Pages view and Multiples Page view.

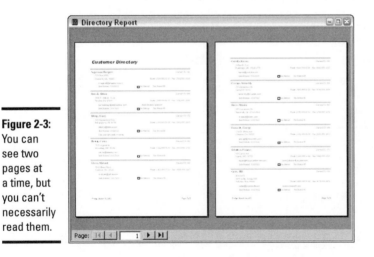

Figure 2-3:
You can see two pages at a time, but you can't necessarily read them.

Previewing reports with parameters

Some reports use parameters — the record source for the report or one or more report controls that contain prompts for information. (See Chapter 1 of this book for how to make a control that prompts for a parameter; see Book

III, Chapter 2 for how to make a parameter query.) If your report has parameters, Access prompts you to type values for the parameters each time you preview the report. After you look at the report, you may want to try different values for the parameter(s). To enter new parameters, close the report and reopen it or switch to Design view and back to Print Preview.

Formatting the Page

Access stores print setup information with each report, so you can design different reports to be used with different printers or with different paper.

Selecting a printer

When formatting your report in Print Preview, Access takes into account what printer you plan to use, as well as the size and shape of the paper. (Okay, most paper is rectangular, but you know what we mean.) Before you're ready to print, specifying what printer you plan to use is important.

Setup

Choose File⇨Page Setup, or click the Setup button on the Print Preview toolbar, to display the Page Setup dialog box, shown in Figure 2-4. Click the Page tab. If you plan to use your system's default printer (the printer that Windows uses unless you tell it otherwise), click the Default Printer option. To use another printer, click the Use Specific Printer option, click the Printer button, and specify the printer in the dialog box that appears.

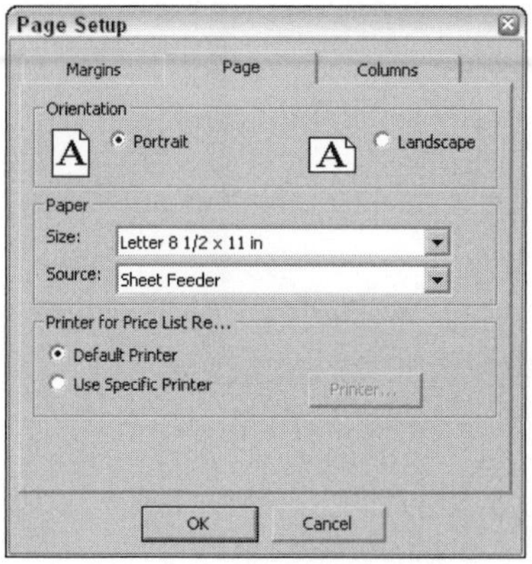

Figure 2-4:
Configuring
the report to
fit on the
page.

While you're on the Page tab, tell Access which paper bin to use — if your printer has more than one bin — by clicking in the Source box and choosing from the bins listed for your printer.

To see what printers your computer is configured to use, including the default, choose Start⇨Printers and Faxes (or Start⇨Control Panel⇨Printers and Other Hardware⇨Printers and Faxes, depending on how Windows is configured). The Printers and Faxes window appears, listing all the printers that your computer is configured for. The printer with an icon that includes a little check mark is the default printer. Right-click a printer and choose the Properties option from the shortcut menu to see how the printer is configured. To make a printer the default printer, right-click it and choose the Set as Default Printer option from the shortcut menu that appears.

Setting margins, paper size, and paper orientation

Other print settings you can configure in the Page Setup dialog box are the following:

✦ **Margins:** On the Margins tab (shown in Figure 2-5) you can change the Margins settings, typing new numbers (in inches or your default unit of measurement).

✦ **Paper orientation:** On the Page tab, click the Portrait option to print normally on the page, or click the Landscape option to print sideways.

✦ **Paper size:** On the Page tab, click in the Size box and choose the size of the paper (or envelope or sheet of labels) on which you plan to print the report.

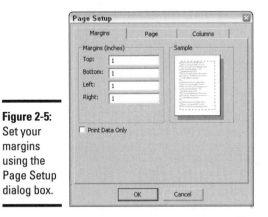

Figure 2-5:
Set your
margins
using the
Page Setup
dialog box.

If you find that you end up changing the margins for almost every report you create, you can change the default margins for all new reports. Choose Tools⇨Options to display the Options dialog box. Click the General tab and change the default Print Margins settings.

Controlling page breaks

Normally, Access fills each page from top to bottom, starting a new page only when the previous one is full. However, you can insert a page break (start a new page) at other times. You can add page breaks to a report in several ways:

+ **After each record (print one page per record):** Set the Force New Page property of the Detail section to either the Before Section or After Section setting. If you choose the Before & After setting for this property, Access prints a blank page both before and after the page(s) for each record. With the report only in Design view, double-click the gray bar at the top of the Detail section to display the Properties sheet for the section, and then click the Format tab to see the Force New Page property.

+ **After each group of records:** See Chapter 1 of this book for how to group records. Set the Force New Page property for the Group Footer to the After Section setting. Access prints the Group Header section, the Detail section for each record in the group, the Group Footer section, and then starts a new page for the next group of records.

+ **Within a section of your report:** Use a page break control. For example, the Detail section of the report may print a packing slip and an invoice for each order on separate pages. To add a page break control to the Detail section of the report, click the Page Break button on the Toolbox, and then click where you want the page break to occur. Access puts the page break control at the left margin of the report.

Don't place page break controls in the Page Header or Page Footer sections. Doing so starts a new page at the top or bottom of every page, which just creates confusion (and an error).

Avoiding blank pages

Almost every Access user winds up with blank pages between each printed page of a report. The blank pages appear in Print Preview, but what causes them?

Access knows the width of your paper and how much space to leave for the left and right margins because these sizes are specified in the Print Setup dialog box. Access adds the width of your report to the left and right margins to come up with the total width of the printed report. If the total is wider than your paper, Access splits the report into vertical bands, and prints the left and right halves of the report onto separate pieces of paper, so you can tape them together to create a very wide report.

If the report is just a *little* bit too wide to fit across one piece of paper, the text of the report is all in the left half, leaving the right half blank. These blank right halves are the blank pages that Access prints. To get rid of them, follow these steps:

1. **Choose File➪Page Setup from the menu.**

   You see the Page Setup dialog box with the Margin tab displayed (refer to Figure 2-5).

2. **Subtract the left and right margin settings from the width of your paper to get the maximum width of the report.**

   Standard U.S. paper is 8-1/2 inches wide. If the left and right margins are too wide, make them smaller in this dialog box, and use the new values in your calculation. For example, if your paper is 8-1/2 inches wide and you have half-inch left and right margins, your report can't be more than 7-1/2 inches wide.

3. **Click OK to exit the Page Setup dialog box.**

4. **In Design view of the report, note the report's width — the location along the ruler of the right edge of the grid area.**

   Alternatively, look at the `Width` property of the report in the Properties sheet. (Double-click the gray box in the upper-left corner of the Design View window where the rulers meet to display the Properties sheet.)

5. **If the report is too wide to fit on the page, drag the right edge of the report leftward.**

   If the edge won't move, a control extends to the right of where you want the page to end. Move or shrink any control that extends too far to the right and move the right edge of the report to the left. Alternatively, change the `Width` property of the report.

Another possible reason for blank pages is an incorrect setting for the `Force New Page` property of one of the sections of the report. See the preceding section for how to control page breaks before or after groups.

Printing only the data

If you are printing on a form, rather than on blank sheets of paper, you can design a report that looks like the form, including labels and lines that match the form. When you print the report, you can skip printing the labels and lines and print only the data. In Print Preview, click the Setup button to display the Page Setup dialog box, click the Margins tab if it's not already selected, and select the Print Data Only check box.

Printing the Report

After you have your page and margin options set, you are ready to risk wasting paper to print your report. You can print your report when it's open in Print Preview, in Design view, or not open at all. Choose the report you want to print, either by selecting the report in the Database window or by opening the report in Design view or Print Preview. Then click the Print button on the toolbar, choose File⇨Print, or press Ctrl+P.

If you choose File⇨Print or press Ctrl+P, you see the Print dialog box shown in Figure 2-6 (the same Print dialog box that most Microsoft programs display). Click the Setup button if you want to take a look at the Page Setup dialog box. Otherwise, click OK to send your report to the printer.

Clicking the Print button on the toolbar sends your report directly to the printer without displaying the Print dialog box. Make sure you are really ready to print before you click!

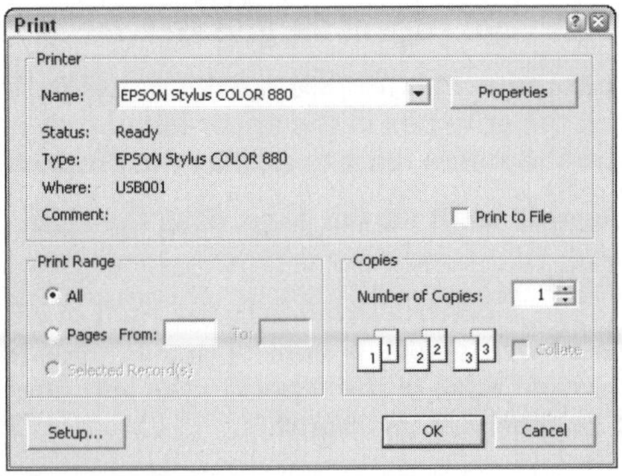

Figure 2-6:
Printing
your report.

You may want to print only part of a report. For example, you may want to print just the first page to see how the margins look, or you may need to reprint a specific page. On the Print dialog box (shown in Figure 2-6), in the Print Range section, click the Pages radio button and enter the starting and ending page numbers in the From and To boxes.

Printing, But Not on Paper

In the old days, "printing" meant printing with ink on paper. Nowadays, the term expands to include other ways of creating a final version of a report suitable for showing to others.

Creating snapshot reports for distribution

Access can save a report as a *snapshot report* in a file with the extension .snp. After you create a snapshot report file, you can e-mail it to other people as an attachment and the recipients can view the report without needing either Access or your database — the snapshot report contains all the information for the report.

To create a snapshot report after you create the report of which you want a snapshot, follow these steps:

1. **In the Database window, click the Reports button in the Objects list to see the list of your reports and then click the name of the report.**

   Or double-click the report to open it. The report can be open or closed — either way works.

2. **Choose File⇨Export from the menu.**

   The Export Report dialog box opens, which looks just like all the Open and Save As dialog boxes you've ever seen.

3. **Click in the Save As Type box and set it to Snapshot Format (*.snp).**

4. **Type a name for the snapshot report file.**

   This name doesn't appear on the report — it's just the filename. Leave off the extension, because Access adds .snp to the end of the name you type. You can navigate to another folder to store the file there.

5. **Click the Export button.**

   Access creates the file with the name you specified.

The snapshot report file contains all the pages of the report, with both the data and the formatting. You can attach it to an e-mail, store it in a shared folder on your local area network, or pass it out via diskette or CD.

To display and print a snapshot report, double-click the file in Windows Explorer (My Computer). The first time you open a snapshot report, Windows prompts you to install the Snapshot Viewer — if you have Microsoft Office 2000, XP, or 2003 installed. Follow the instructions on-screen to install the viewer; you need to insert your Microsoft Office program CD.

Reports viewed through the Snapshot Viewer look like Figure 2-7. You can use the navigation buttons in the lower-left corner to either move around the page itself or move from page to page.

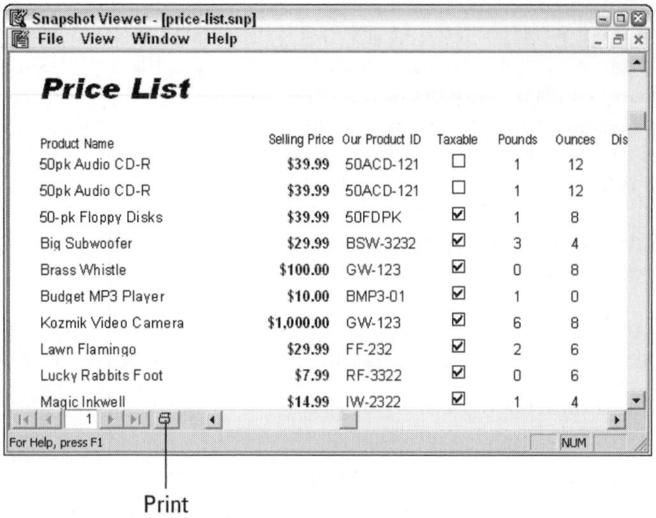

Figure 2-7:
The
Snapshot
Viewer
displays a
snapshot
even if
Access isn't
loaded.

Product Name	Selling Price	Our Product ID	Taxable	Pounds	Ounces	Dis
50pk Audio CD-R	$39.99	50ACD-121	☐	1	12	
50pk Audio CD-R	$39.99	50ACD-121	☐	1	12	
50-pk Floppy Disks	$39.99	50FDPK	☑	1	8	
Big Subwoofer	$29.99	BSW-3232	☑	3	4	
Brass Whistle	$100.00	GW-123	☑	0	8	
Budget MP3 Player	$10.00	BMP3-01	☑	1	0	
Kozmik Video Camera	$1,000.00	GW-123	☑	6	8	
Lawn Flamingo	$29.99	FF-232	☑	2	6	
Lucky Rabbits Foot	$7.99	RF-3322	☑	0	6	
Magic Inkwell	$14.99	IW-2322	☑	1	4	

Snapshot Viewer - [price-list.snp]

File   View   Window   Help

Price List

For Help, press F1

NUM

Print

If a coworker has an older version of Microsoft Office or uses Corel Office,
Star Office, or other software, he or she can install and run the Snapshot
Viewer separately from Office. Tell your coworker to go to `www.microsoft.`
`com/accessdev/prodinfo/snapshot.htm` for a description and a download
link for the Snapshot Viewer.

Sending a report to another application with OfficeLinks

The nice thing about Microsoft Office is that all the programs are designed
to work together. Sometimes they even *do* work together.

For example, what if you want to include a report from your Access database in a Word document or an Excel spreadsheet? Office has a cool feature
called OfficeLinks that makes this incredibly easy. Follow these steps:

1. **Open the report that you want to include in a Word document or
    Excel spreadsheet.**

    Open the report in Print Preview.

2. **Click the downward-pointing arrow to the right of the OfficeLinks
    button on the toolbar and choose either Publish It with Microsoft
    Word or Analyze It with Microsoft Excel.**

Your choice! Access outputs the report, fires up either Word or Excel, and displays the report in that program. When exporting a report to Word, Access stores it as a Rich Text Format (RTF) file. When exporting to a spreadsheet, Access creates an Excel spreadsheet file (with the extension .xls, as shown in Figure 2-8).

3. **In Word or Excel, make any desired changes to your new document or spreadsheet, save it, and print.**

   The exported file is a normal document or spreadsheet: You can use it like any other file.

That's all there is to it!

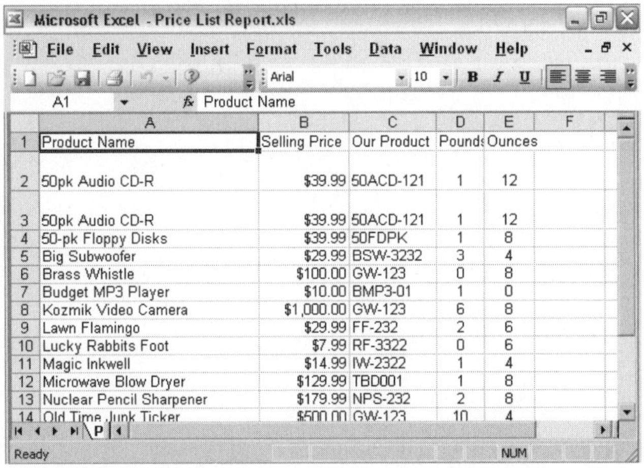

	A	B	C	D	E	F
1	Product Name	Selling Price	Our Product	Pounds	Ounces	
2	50pk Audio CD-R	$39.99	50ACD-121	1	12	
3	50pk Audio CD-R	$39.99	50ACD-121	1	12	
4	50-pk Floppy Disks	$39.99	50FDPK	1	8	
5	Big Subwoofer	$29.99	BSW-3232	3	4	
6	Brass Whistle	$100.00	GW-123	0	8	
7	Budget MP3 Player	$10.00	BMP3-01	1	0	
8	Kozmik Video Camera	$1,000.00	GW-123	6	8	
9	Lawn Flamingo	$29.99	FF-232	2	6	
10	Lucky Rabbits Foot	$7.99	RF-3322	0	6	
11	Magic Inkwell	$14.99	IW-2322	1	4	
12	Microwave Blow Dryer	$129.99	TBD001	1	8	
13	Nuclear Pencil Sharpener	$179.99	NPS-232	2	8	
14	Old Time Junk Ticker	$500.00	GW-123	10	4	

Figure 2-8:
A price list report exported to an Excel spreadsheet.

If you want to use a table or query with the Microsoft Word merge feature, you can. Select the table or query in the Database window, choose Tools⇨ Office Links⇨Merge It with Microsoft Word, and follow the prompts of the Microsoft Word Mail Merge Wizard. When you open the document in Word into which you want to merge your data, click Insert Word Field to include a field from your table or query in the document.

Chapter 3: Creating Charts and Graphs from Your Data

In This Chapter

✓ Making charts and graphs using the Chart Wizard

✓ Drawing bar charts

✓ Crafting line and area charts

✓ Displaying pie and doughnut charts

✓ Doing XP scatter and bubble charts

✓ Changing the format of your chart

✓ Making PivotCharts from PivotTables, tables, and queries

✓ Tweaking your PivotChart

Charts and graphs often communicate the meaning of your data better than columns of names and numbers. (What's the difference between a chart and a graph? Actually, they are two words for the same thing.) Microsoft Office 2003 comes with a charting component called Microsoft Graph (also called Microsoft Chart) that you can use from within Access to create a wide variety of graphs. You can run a Chart Wizard to create charts using Microsoft Graph.

PivotCharts are another Microsoft Office component that you can use with Access. A PivotChart is dynamic, which means that you can easily adjust it while you're looking at it. As you drag field names around the PivotChart, or make choices from drop-down lists, the chart changes immediately on-screen.

Which should you use, charts, or PivotCharts? PivotCharts are designed for the screen, where you can fool around with their settings and explore your data graphically. Regular charts (the kind that Microsoft Graph draws) are designed to print out, and include many more formatting options.

PivotTables are like PivotCharts — they also let you analyze your data on-screen. PivotTables display your data as text, while PivotCharts graph your data. For more information about PivotTables, see Book III, Chapter 4.

Displaying Information with Charts and Graphs

Access databases contain different types of objects: tables, queries, forms, reports, and the rest. But what about charts? Where are they stored?

Strangely, Access stores charts as controls on forms or reports. Before you make a chart, you create a new form or report — or open an existing one — and then add a chart control. In this chapter, we describe storing your chart controls in reports, but you can include them in forms if you prefer — depending on whether you want to view the charts on-screen or print them out.

Actually, storing charts as controls on forms or report makes sense if you know what's going on behind the scenes. Access itself doesn't include any graph-drawing features at all. Instead, chart controls are *object frame* controls that can contain a wide variety of things, including pictures, Word documents, Excel spreadsheets, sound files, video clips — you name it. What we call a *chart control* is actually an object frame control that contains a Microsoft Graph chart object. Luckily, you don't need to worry about object frames — you can just create your new chart control using a wizard. If you insist on making a chart control manually, see the sidebar, "Making charts the old-fashioned way," later in this chapter, but don't say we didn't warn you.

We recommend starting with the Chart Wizard and then customizing the chart afterward. Heck, why not make the wizard do most of the work?

The Access Chart Wizard is very limited — Microsoft Graph can draw more types of charts. If you want to create a stacked bar chart, radar chart, or multi-ring doughnut chart, the wizard can't help you. You can make a similar chart with the wizard, and then modify the chart afterwards using Design view. Another method of making better charts is to export your data to Microsoft Excel 2003 — yet another component of Microsoft Office 2003 — and use its more powerful Chart Wizard. See Book II, Chapter 4 for how to export records from Access to Excel.

Creating charts with the Chart Wizard

If you want to create charts in Access, the Chart Wizard is the only good way to start. You may want to add a chart to an existing report, or create a chart that stands alone (no other controls are on the report). The Chart Wizard allows you to do either.

Whether you create a new report for your chart or add a chart to an existing report, you start at the Reports list in the Database window. If the Database window isn't visible, press F11 or click the Database Window button on the toolbar. Then click the Reports button in the Object list to see the list of your existing reports.

Starting the Chart Wizard to add a chart to an existing report

You can add a chart to a report that you already created by adding a chart control to your report. Follow these steps:

1. **Open the report in Design view (by selecting the report and clicking the Design button on the Database window toolbar) and choose Insert⇨Chart.**

Access gives you no clue that you in fact have issued this (or any other) command, except that when you move your mouse pointer back to the Design View window, it appears as a teeny little graph.

2. **Click the section of the report where you want the chart to appear.**

The Chart Wizard starts.

3. **Click the Tables, Queries, or Both tab to display the list from which to make your choice. Make your selection and click Next.**

The wizard is now up, running, and ready to ask lots more questions about what you want your chart to look like. Skip forward to the section, "Answering the Chart Wizard's questions."

Starting the Chart Wizard to create a chart in a new report

Perhaps you'd like to make a standalone chart — one that is all by itself in a report. You can create a new report with a new chart object in it by following these steps:

1. **Click the New button in the Database window.**

The New Report dialog box makes an appearance.

2. **Select the Chart Wizard option, choose the table or query containing the data you want to chart, and click OK.**

Read on in order to find out how to tell the wizard how you want your chart to look.

Answering the Chart Wizard's questions

After you start the Chart Wizard and choose the table or query that provides the data, follow these steps to create a chart:

1. **Choose the fields you want to chart by moving them from the Available Fields list to the Fields for Chart list, and then click Next.**

To move a field from one list to the other, select the field and click the arrow button between the two lists, as shown in Figure 3-1.

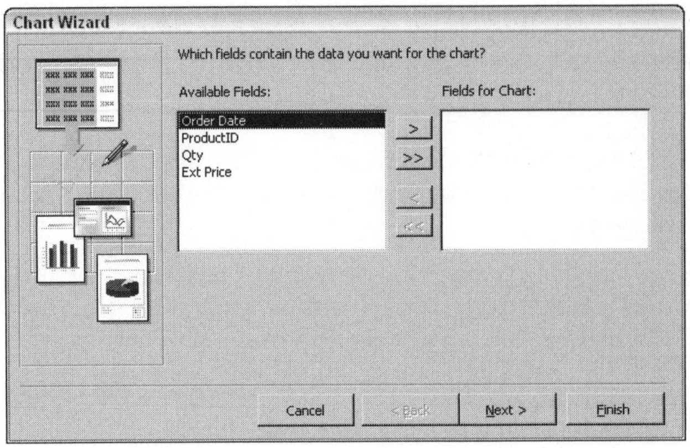

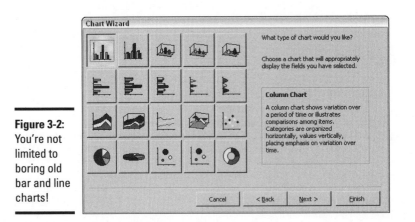

Figure 3-1:
Choose which fields to include in the chart.

If you are charting values by date, make sure that you include the field that contains the date value. For example, if you want to chart sales per week for each week of the year, you need to choose both the field that contains the sales numbers and the field that contains the dates of the sales. The fields don't have to be weekly totals: The Chart Wizard can total your fields for you.

In Step 3, you tell the wizard how to represent each field, and you don't have to represent all the fields you choose here. Go ahead and include any field that you *may* want to include on the chart.

2. **In the next window of the Chart Wizard (see Figure 3-2), select the type of chart that you want to create, and then click Next.**

   When you select a chart type, the wizard displays the name of that type of chart as well as some information about that type of chart and the kind of data that it displays best.

Figure 3-2:
You're not limited to boring old bar and line charts!

3. **Drag fields onto the chart on the left side of the wizard window and tell the wizard how to use the fields you've selected, as shown in Figure 3-3.**

Data   Series

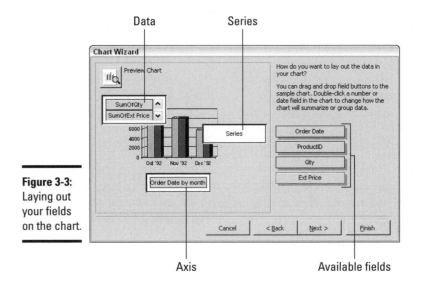

Figure 3-3:
Laying out
your fields
on the chart.

Axis   Available fields

The chart shows three labels: the Axis (the horizontal X-axis on most types of graphs), the Data (usually the vertical Y-axis), and the Series (usually fields displayed in the chart as bars, lines, or other shapes). The fields that you choose appear as buttons on the right side of the window. You specify how to use each field by dragging its field name to the sample chart. If Access guessed wrong about how to use the fields, you can drag the field name from the chart on the left side back to the field list at the right.

Double-click a field's box to see more detail. You see a dialog box that allows you to change the totaling or grouping for that field.

How the Axis, Data, and Series settings work depends on the type of chart you are creating. The next four sections describe how to specify fields for bar, line, pie, and other types of charts. Remember, you don't need to use all the fields.

4. **Click the Preview Chart button in the top-left of the window to see how your chart looks so far. Check out the results and click the Close button to return to the Chart Wizard window.**

The Sample Preview window (shown in Figure 3-4) helps you figure out whether you chose the right fields for the X-axis, Y-axis, and Series settings.

 5. **Repeat Steps 3 and 4 until the chart looks right. When it does, click Next.**

Figure 3-4:
Preview
your chart
to see
whether
you have
correctly
specified
which fields
go where.

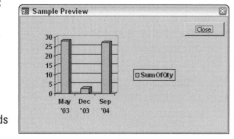

 6. **Specify a title, whether to display legends, and whether to open the report containing the new chart control in Design view or Print Preview. After making your selections, click Finish.**

   The title for your report appears at the top of the report. The wizard suggests the name of the table or query you chose as the record source Legends show what the colors of the bars, lines, or pie sections mean.

   The wizard creates a new chart control in your new or existing report.

After the Chart Wizard creates your chart control, you can move the control around your report by dragging it. You can also resize the chart by selecting the control and then dragging the black handles on the edges of the control. If you double-click the chart control, you find yourself in a strange new editing mode described in the section, "Formatting charts with colors, legends, and titles," later in this chapter.

In Design view, Access shows a sample chart, not the actual chart. The chart is of the type that you select, but with sample data. Don't worry, your real chart is on the report — switch to Print Preview to see the actual chart.

A report can contain more that one chart control. You may want to make a report that contains three chart controls that display three different charts. Just make the additional controls in Design view by choosing Insert⇨Chart and clicking where you want the new control to appear.

Now you know how to use the Chart Wizard to create a chart. The next few sections describe popular types of charts — bar, line, and pie charts.

Making bar charts

The Chart Wizard can make a bunch of different kinds of bar charts. The types of bar charts in which the bars run vertically appear on the first row of buttons on Figure 3-2:

+ **Column Chart:** Flat, vertical bars.

+ **3-D Column Chart:** Three-dimensional-looking vertical bars.

+ **Cylinder Column Chart:** Same thing as a column chart, but the bars are cylindrical.

+ **Cone Column Chart:** Another column chart, but with cones instead of bars.

+ **Pyramid Column Chart:** Ditto, but with pyramids.

You can also make the same charts run horizontally (these appear on the second row of buttons in Figure 3-2):

+ **Bar Chart:** Flat, horizontal bars.

+ **3-D Bar Chart:** Three-dimensional-looking horizontal bars.

+ **3-D Cylinder Bar Chart:** Same thing as a bar chart, but the bars are cylindrical.

+ **3-D Cone Bar Chart:** Ditto, with horizontal cones (they look rather odd, we think).

+ **3-D Pyramid Bar Chart:** Ditto, with horizontal pyramid (which look even odder).

To see little pictures of these, look at the top two rows of buttons in Figure 3-2, earlier in this chapter. Unfortunately, the Chart Wizard can't draw stacked bar charts — to make them, you need to choose another type of bar chart in the Chart Wizard, and then change the chart type later (see the section, "Changing your chart," later in this chapter).

The key to creating bar charts with the Chart Wizard is to specify the right fields for the Axis, Data, and Series — the field selections you made in Step 3 of the previous section. Keep reading to find out how the Axis, Data, and Series settings work.

The Axis setting

For graphs with vertical bars (or other vertical shapes), set the Axis to the field that determines the labels that run along the bottom of the graph. For horizontal bar graphs, the Axis runs up the left side of the graph. This setting also determines what bars sprout up from the axis. A bar graph has one bar (or group of bars) for each value (or range of values) of the Axis setting. Figure 3-5 shows two bar charts, one vertical (select Column Chart to get this particular chart type) and one horizontal (select Bar Chart for this one). The Axis setting in Figure 3-5 is the Order Date field.

Figure 3-5: Vertical and horizontal bar charts, with Order Date as the Axis setting.

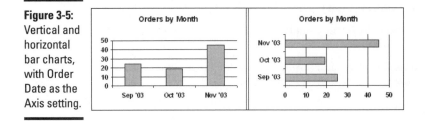

If you use a Date/Time field for the Axis setting, you can choose to group the dates into time periods such as a month or year. The Axis setting in the Chart Wizard window tells you how Access plans to group the information by date: An Order Date field may appear as "Order Date by month" — refer to Figure 3-3. To change the grouping, double-click the Axis field to display the Group dialog box, as shown in Figure 3-6. You can choose to group your data by year, quarter, month, and so on. The Group dialog box also allows you to choose to limit the values plotted on your graph to values within a specified date range. Just select the Use Data Between check box and enter the beginning and end dates you want for your chart. Access ignores records with dates outside that range.

Figure 3-6: How would you like to group values by date?

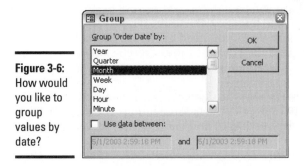

Strangely, you can't control how numeric or text values are grouped, or limit their ranges on the graph.

The Data setting

For vertical bar charts, drag the fields that determine the heights of the bars — along with the values that appear up the left side of the chart — to the Data setting. On horizontal bar charts, the Data fields control the lengths of the bars and the values that run along the bottom of the chart. In Figure 3-5, the Data field contains the number of items sold; it runs up the left side of the chart on the vertical bar chart and across the bottom of the chart on the horizontal bar chart.

If you group dates together along the X-axis, you can specify how the values are combined into the bars. If you want to graph sales by year and your record source has one record for each order, you may set the Data field to be the Grand Total field of each order. You can then specify how to combine the values of the orders into years — you may want the total value of all the orders for the year, or you may want the average value. The Data setting in the Chart Wizard window indicates how the values are combined: In Figure 3-3, the Data setting contains two variables, SumOfQty and SumOfExtPrice, so Access sums up the Qty and Ext Price fields for the orders in each year.

To change how Access combines the values of a Data field, double-click the Data field to display the Summarize dialog box, as shown in Figure 3-7. Then choose how you want the values for each time period combined: Sum, Avg (average), Min (minimum value), Max (maximum value), or Count (number of records).

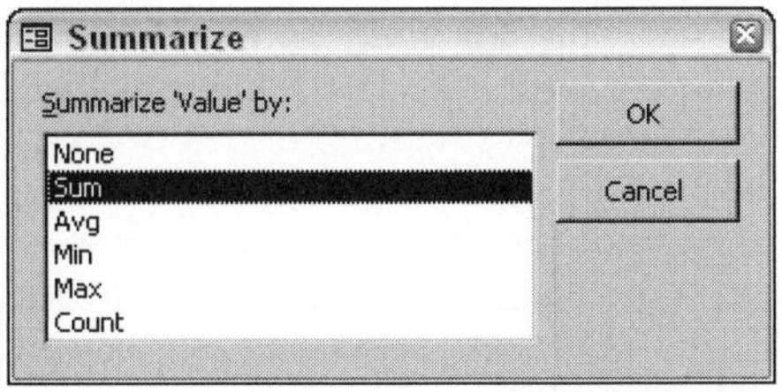

Figure 3-7:
How do
you want to
combine the
values for
each bar?

Summarize	
Summarize 'Value' by:	OK
None	Cancel
Sum	
Avg	
Min	
Max	
Count	

Unlike the Axis setting, the Data setting can be more than one field. If you drag more than one field to the Data setting, you see a listing of the Data fields, as shown in Figure 3-8. For each Data setting, you get a separate bar.

You can drag the same field to the Data setting twice — for example, you may want to see the count and the total of the same field.

Two fields for the Data setting

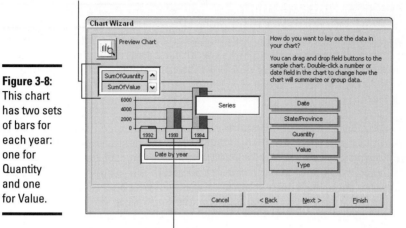

Figure 3-8:
This chart
has two sets
of bars for
each year:
one for
Quantity
and one
for Value.

Two bars appear in each chart entry

The Series setting

Unlike the Axis and Data settings, the Series setting in the Chart Wizard is
optional — most charts leave this setting blank. The field used for the Series
setting tells Access how to break down the bars (or columns, cones, or pyramids) into a group of smaller bars.

If you graph sales by month, each bar normally shows the total of the sales
records for that month. If you drag a field to the Series setting, Access
divides the bar for each month up into several bars according to the value
of the Series field. If you set the Series setting to a field that represents what
type of product was sold in each order, you get a group of bars for each
month, with one bar for each type of product. Figure 3-9 shows the Chart
Wizard settings for a graph that separates sales by Category, and Figure 3-10
shows the resulting chart (there are four categories).

If you choose three or more fields to use in your chart, the Chart Wizard
usually guesses that you want to use one of the fields as the Series setting.
But for most charts, you use only the Axis and Data settings — just leave the
Series setting blank. If the wizard puts a field there, drag it back over to the
list of fields on the right side of the wizard's window.

Making line and area charts

Line and area charts work similarly to bar charts. A bar chart draws a bar
(or other shape) for each value of the Axis series, with its height determined
by the Data series. A line chart works the same way, but instead of drawing

a bar, Access draws a dot where the top of the bar would be, and then connects the dots. An area chart is basically the same thing, but Access colors in the area under the line, as shown in Figure 3-11. Line and area charts appear on the third row of buttons in Figure 3-2 (they are all but the last button in that row.)

Figure 3-9: The Category field is used as the Series setting, which splits each month's sales into separate bars for each product category.

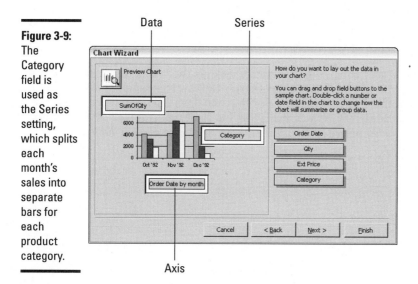

Figure 3-10: The Axis field contains sales dates grouped by month, the Data field contains the values of the products sold, and the Series field contains the product category (1, 2, 3, or 4).

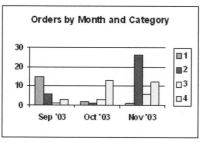

Figure 3-11:
Line and
area charts
work
the same
way bar
charts do.

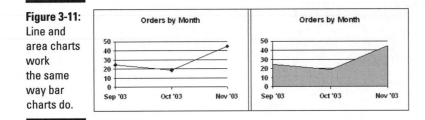

In a line or area chart, the Axis series defines the labels that run along the bottom of the graph and the Data series defines the distance from the bottom of the chart up to each dot that the lines connect. If you have two or more Data series, Access draws a line for each one and (for an area chart) colors the area between one line and the next (see the left-hand chart in Figure 3-12).

Figure 3-12:
An area
chart with
two Data
fields shows
one area in
front of the
other (left).
The Series
field splits
the quantity
of the Data
field into
several lines
or areas
(right).

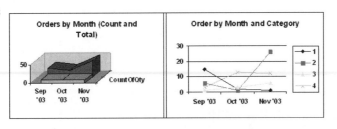

As with bar charts, Access uses the Series field to split the amounts for each line into several, lower lines. The right-hand chart in Figure 3-12 shows a line chart with Category as the Series field. (This is the same data that Figure 3-10 displays as a bar chart.)

Making pie and doughnut charts

A pie chart shows how a total amount is split up by percentages. Access needs to know what field contains the numbers you want summed to make the total amount as well as what field contains the information by which to split this total into pie slices. A doughnut chart is a line pie chart with a hole in the middle, except that you can specify more than one field, and you get a concentric ring for each field. Pie and doughnut charts appear on the fourth row of buttons in Figure 3-2.

When you run the Chart Wizard, choose just two fields to include in the chart:

✦ The Data field is the one that contains numbers for Access to sum up to create the total pie. For a doughnut chart, you should be able to specify more than one Data field, and get a concentric ring for each field. If you can't specify all the fields in the Chart Wizard, you can add them later; see "Changing which data is charted," later in this chapter.

✦ The Series field can be numeric, text, Yes/No fields, or Date/Time fields. Access makes a separate pie slice for each value of this field.

The left-hand chart in Figure 3-13 shows a pie chart in which the Data field is a numeric field with the total amount of each order and the Series field is a category field. The right-hand chart is the same thing as a doughnut chart.

Figure 3-13:
A pie chart (left) and a doughnut chart (right).

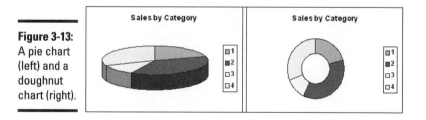

Making bubble and XY scatter plots

An XY scatter plot needs two numeric fields and plots one field against the other. For each record, you see a point with the horizontal and vertical position determined by the numbers in the fields. A bubble chart works the same way, except that Access draws a circle instead of a point, and the numeric value of a third field determines the size of the circle.

Making charts the old-fashioned way

By far the best way to create a chart is by using the Chart Wizard. However, if you want to create one without a wizard, be our guest — just don't say we didn't warn you. Follow these steps:

1. **With a report or form open in Design view, display the Toolbox by clicking the Toolbox button on the toolbar.**

2. **Click the Unbound Object Frame button on the Toolbox, and then click in the Design View window where you want your chart to appear.**

   You see a Microsoft Access dialog box (which really ought to be called something like the Insert Object dialog box).

3. **If you've created a graph in some other program (perhaps in Excel or Word), choose** the Create from File option, click the Browse button, and choose the file. If you are making a new chart, choose the Create New option and choose Microsoft Graph Chart from the Object Type list. Then click OK.

Yes, that's "Microsoft Graph Chart," which sounds redundant, but the point is that you are creating a chart by using the Microsoft Graph program. Makes sense!

Access creates a sample bar chart based on sample data that appears in a Datasheet window. To replace the data with your own data, type your own headings and numbers in the Datasheet window. To change the type of chart, see the section, "Changing your chart."

You can try making these graphs in the Chart Wizard, but we haven't had much luck. (Consider exporting the data to Microsoft Excel and charting it there.) If you want to try the Chart Wizard, drag the numeric field you want to graph along the horizontal (X) axis to the Series setting and drag the field you want to graph along the vertical (Y) axis to the Data setting. If the wizard decides to aggregate either of the fields (you see "Sum Of" the field name), double-click the field name and change the aggregation to the None setting.

Changing your chart

The Access Chart Wizard can't make all the types of charts the Microsoft Graph can draw. It can't even make all the charts that the Excel Chart Wizard can make — wouldn't you think that these two wizards would get together sometime and compare notes? Luckily, you can change the settings of a chart after the wizard creates it. You can fix charts that don't look quite right, as well as create charts that the Chart Wizard doesn't know about.

To modify a chart, you change the properties of the chart control on the report that contains the chart. This section gives you the general idea of how to modify a chart after you make it, while the next two sections provide more details.

To modify an existing chart, follow these steps:

1. **Open the report that contains the chart in Design view. (Click the Reports button in the Objects list of the Database window, select the report, and then click the Design button on the Database window toolbar.)**

   If the Database window isn't visible, press F11 to display it. If the report is already open in Print Preview, then click the View button to switch to Design view. You see the report in Design view, including the chart control that defines the chart.

   In Design view, the chart control displays sample data, not the actual data. Don't worry — Access hasn't forgotten the actual data you want to plot. Just switch to Print Preview to see the real chart.

2. **Click once in the chart control to select it.**

   Now you can drag it to a different location on the report, or resize it.

   You can tell when the chart control is selected because a selected control sprouts handles — little black squares at the corners and the middle of the sides — as shown in Figure 3-14. Drag anywhere in the middle of the chart control to move the chart. Drag a handle to resize the chart control.

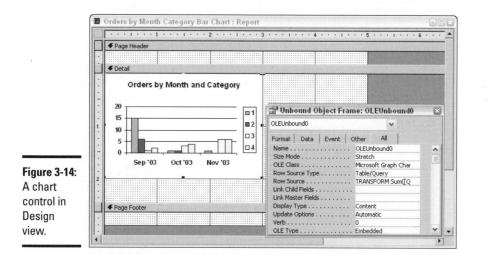

Figure 3-14: A chart control in Design view.

When the chart control is selected, click the Properties button on the toolbar to display the Properties sheet, which is also shown in Figure 3-14. In the Properties sheet, you can change configuration settings for the graph, as described in the next two sections.

The chart control appears as an Unbound Object Frame, because the chart frame contains information that comes from another program, Microsoft Graph. The chart control is unbound because it's not connected to the records in a table or query.

3. **Double-click the chart control to start the Microsoft Graph program.**

When Microsoft Graph is running, the chart control appears with a hatched line around it, as shown in Figure 3-15.

Three new toolbars appear: the Microsoft Graph Standard, Formatting, and Drawing toolbars. Your menu options change to include Microsoft Graph commands. The next two sections describe what some of the buttons do.

Inexplicably, Microsoft Graph also displays a datasheet containing the sample data it uses to make the graph that appears in Design view. Editing this sample data changes the chart in Design view; however — and this is important — editing the sample data has absolutely no effect on the real chart that appears in Print Preview (or on the data in the database).

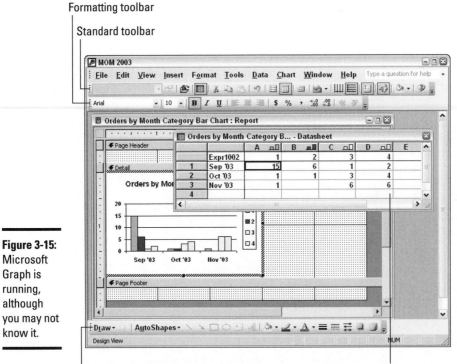

Figure 3-15: Microsoft Graph is running, although you may not know it.

Click the View button on the Standard toolbar to get rid of the datasheet, which just clutters up the screen.

4. **Make changes to your chart, as described in the next three sections.**

   The next three sections explain how to change colors, legends, titles, fields, and chart type.

5. **Exit Microsoft Graph by clicking in the Design View window, outside the chart control.**

   The extra toolbars disappear, the funny border around the control disappears, and you are back in Access.

6. **Click the View or Print Preview button to see how your graph looks now.**

Repeat these steps until you have the chart the way you want it. When you save the report that contains the chart control, you save the changes to the control, too.

The next three sections describe changes you can make to your chart. You make some of these changes in the Properties sheet for the chart control, some using buttons on the various Microsoft Graph toolbars, and some by giving commands while Microsoft Graph is running. (Don't worry — we tell you when to do what.)

Formatting charts with colors, legends, and titles

The Chart Options dialog box, shown in Figure 3-16, enables you to change the titles, axis labels, gridlines, legends, data labels (which appear on the graph itself), and data table placement. To display it, first double-click the chart control in the Design View window to get Microsoft Graph up and running, and then choose Chart➪Chart Options from the main menu.

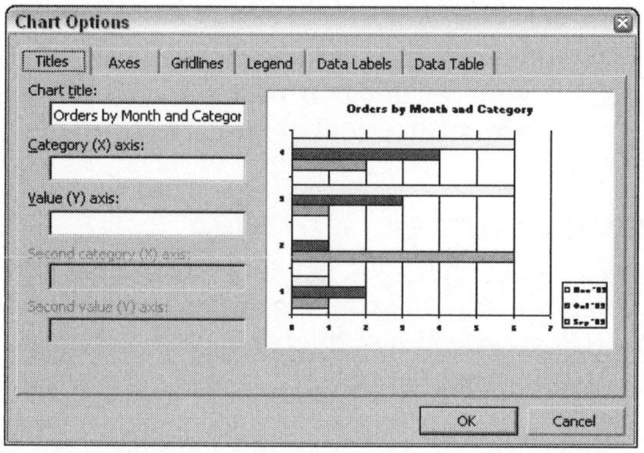

Figure 3-16:
The Chart Options dialog box contains lots of formatting settings for your graph.

Some other ways you can format your graph when Microsoft Graph is running (that is, when the chart control has a hatched border) are the following:

✦ **Background color:** Click a part of the graph and then click the down-arrow to the right of the Fill Color button on the Standard toolbar and choose a color. You can also right-click the plot area (the graph itself) or a blank part of the chart and choose the Format Chart/Plot Area option from the shortcut menu that appears.

✦ **Gridlines:** To add or remove gridlines within the chart, click the Category Axis Gridlines and Value Axis Gridlines buttons on the Standard toolbar.

✦ **Title:** To change the title that appears on the graph, just double-click the title and edit the text. Move the title by selecting it (with one click) and dragging. You can also change the font by right-clicking it and choosing the Format Chart Title option from the shortcut menu that appears.

✦ **Legends:** To display or remove the legend — the table that explains the meanings of the colors or symbols in the graph — click the Legend button on the Standard toolbar. Move the legend by dragging it to a new location within the chart control. Change the fonts by double-clicking the legend to display the Format Legend Entry dialog box.

✦ **Data table:** Click the Data Table button on the Standard toolbar to add a table to the chart showing the data used in the table.

You can choose how the border of the graph looks by setting the following options. These options are available only when you've selected the chart control but have not yet double-clicked the control to get Microsoft Graph up and running:

✦ **Border:** To set the color of the border, click the down-arrow to the right of the Line/Border Color button on the Formatting toolbar and choose a color. Then set the width of the border by clicking the down-arrow to the right of the Line/Border Width button.

✦ **3-D effect:** You can give the edge of the chart a raised, sunken, or 3-D shadow effect by clicking the down-arrow to the right of the Special Effect button on the Formatting toolbar and selecting the look you like.

Changing how the data is graphed

You can modify what type of chart you get and what data it shows, but you have to get Microsoft Graph up and running again before you start scrambling things around. (***Remember:*** Just double-click the chart control in Design view to call up Microsoft Graph.)

✦ **Type of chart:** If you want to switch from a bar chart to a line chart, from one kind of bar chart to another kind of bar chart, or if you want to make one of the types of charts that the Chart Wizard doesn't even know about, click the down-arrow to the right of the Chart Type button and choose a different type of chart. For more options, choose Chart⇨ Chart Type from the main menu, or right-click the chart control and choose the Chart Type option from the shortcut menu that appears.

✦ **Axes:** Because Microsoft Graph treats your data as if it were stored in a spreadsheet — graphing the data row by row or column by column — switching which field is represented along which axis of the chart is pretty easy. To see other ways of representing your data on the same type of graph, just click the By Row and By Column buttons on the Standard toolbar.

Save your chart first, in case you don't like the results. Switching your chart back to its original format is not always easy.

✦ **Trendline:** If your graph shows information over time (a Date/Time field is shown along one axis), you can add a *trendline* that shows the general direction of growth or decline in the numbers. Choose Chart⇨Add Trendline.

Changing which data is charted

If you want to change the fields included in the chart, you can change the Row Source setting of the chart control. Display the Properties sheet for the chart control by single-clicking (not double-clicking) the chart control in the Design View window and clicking the Properties button. (Microsoft Graph can't be running when you do this; to exit Microsoft Graph, click in the Design View window outside the chart control.)

The Row Source setting (on the Property sheet Data tab) contains an SQL statement that describes the fields to be graphed. (See Book VIII, Chapter 5 for information about SQL.) You can change the statement by clicking in the Row Source setting and then clicking the Build button to its right. You see the SQL Query Builder window, which looks just like the Design View window when creating queries. Each column in the QBE grid corresponds to a field in the graph, although the exact number and use of the columns depends on the type of the chart.

If you make changes to the QBE grid, Access asks whether you want to save your changes when you close the window. (Or press Ctrl+S or click the Save button on the toolbar before closing the window.) When you switch the report containing the chart control to Print Preview, you see the results of your changes.

Access 2000 doesn't provide a handy Build button for changing your data source. Instead, you set the Row Source Type property of the chart object to the Table/Query setting, and the Row Source property to a table or query in your database.

Analyzing Your Data Graphically with PivotCharts

A PivotChart, like a PivotTable, is an interactive tool that helps you analyze your data, selecting and summarizing your data by the fields that you designate. Both PivotTables and PivotCharts cross-tabulate records in a table or query, but a PivotTable presents the results as text while a PivotChart graphs the results. Unlike a regular chart, you can instantly make changes to a PivotChart by dragging field names to the chart or choosing from drop-down lists that reflect your data. Figure 13-17 shows a PivotTable that analyzes orders for audiotapes (A), CDs (C), DVDs (D), and videos (V) by year. Figure 3-18 shows the same information as a chart. The beauty of PivotCharts is that you don't have to create a whole bunch of different charts to show different types of data. Instead, create one flexible PivotChart that can be tweaked to show whatever you're interested in seeing at the moment. (PivotCharts were new in Access 2002.)

Order Detail Query : Select Query

Drop Filter Fields Here

	Type				
	A	C	D	V	Grand Total
Years	Sum of Quantity	Sum of Quantity	Sum of Quantity	Sum of Quantity	Sum of Quantity
(Blank)	421.00	43.00	3.00	1185.00	1652.00
1997	94.00	16.00		191.00	301.00
1998	214.00	21.00		934.00	1169.00
1999	321.00	9.00		1114.00	1444.00
2000	443.00	24.00		1347.00	1814.00
2001	420.00	49.00		1513.00	1982.00
2002	366.00	132.00	16.00	1537.00	2051.00
Grand Total	2279.00	294.00	19.00	7821.00	10413.00

Figure 3-17: A PivotTable analyzes your data and shows it as text.

Figure 3-18: When you view a PivotTable as a PivotChart, Access uses the same fields that you specified for the PivotTable.

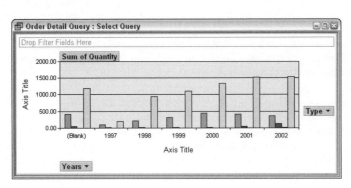

You can read all about PivotTables in Book III, Chapter 4.

Creating PivotCharts

You can display the information from any table, query, or PivotTable as a PivotChart. When you create a PivotChart, you actually create a special view of a form, and the PivotChart is stored in the form. The easiest way is by using the PivotChart AutoForm, which was new in Access 2002.

To create a PivotChart based on a PivotTable, open the PivotTable and choose View➪PivotChart View from the main menu. Access displays the same information contained in the PivotTable as a PivotChart. (Refer to Figure 3-18.)

To create a PivotChart from any table or query, follow these steps:

1. Click the Tables or Queries button in the Objects list of the Database window, and then select the table or query that contains the information you want to analyze.

   If the Database window isn't visible, press F11. You don't need to open the table or query — just select it.

2. Choose Insert➪Form from the main menu and, in the New Form dialog box that appears, select the AutoForm PivotChart option, and then click OK.

   Access creates a new, blank form and a control containing the PivotChart. The Chart Field list also appears, showing the fields from the table or query on which the PivotChart is based, as shown in Figure 3-19. A new toolbar also appears: the PivotChart toolbar.

3. Specify what's on your chart by dragging fields from the Chart Field list to the PivotChart drop areas.

   If the Chart Field list doesn't appear, click the Field List button on the PivotChart toolbar. The Chart Field list is like the Field list that appears when you edit a form: It lists the available fields to drag to the PivotChart.

   The PivotChart drop areas are

   • **Filter fields:** Fields you want to use to filter the data shown in the chart. To filter the data, click the drop-down list and click to remove check marks — only checked data is included in the chart. This drop area works like the Criteria row in an Access query.

- **Data fields:** Fields containing the data you want to chart (for example, the numbers that are represented by the heights of the bars of a bar chart). The values of these fields are measured by the numbers on the Y-axis.

- **Category fields:** Fields that contain values that you want to run along the bottom edge (X-axis) of the chart.

- **Series fields:** Different values in these fields are represented by different lines in a line chart, different bars in a bar chart, or different colored graph elements. To display legends for the series, click the Show Legend button the PivotChart toolbar or choose PivotChart⇨ Show Legend from the main menu. If you want a stacked or clustered bar chart, a line graph with more than one line, or a multi-ring doughnut chart, drag more than one field to the Series drop area.

4. **Make changes to the type of chart, which fields are graphed, and which values of each field are included.**

   See the section, "Sprucing up your PivotCharts," at the end of this chapter, for details.

5. **To see the chart better, close the Chart Field list by clicking its X button.**

   You can always open it again if you want to add more fields: Right-click in the PivotChart and choose the Field List option from the shortcut menu that appears.

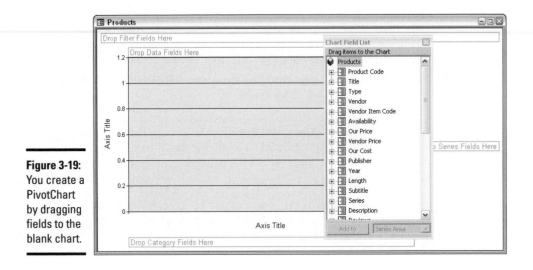

Figure 3-19:
You create a
PivotChart
by dragging
fields to the
blank chart.

Saving and viewing your PivotChart

Like PivotTables, a PivotChart is a special view of an Access object (tables and queries have pivot views available to them, too). When you close a PivotChart, Access asks you to name the form that contains the PivotChart, and then stores the form with your other forms. When you close a PivotChart view of a table or query, Access just saves the information as part of the table or query. You can save your changes while editing a PivotChart by choosing File⇨Save or pressing Ctrl+S.

To avoid confusion, we like to include the word "PivotChart," "Pivot," or "PC" in the names of forms that contain PivotCharts.

To open a PivotChart again, click the Forms button in the Objects list of the Database window and, from the list that appears in the right pane of the window, double-click the name of the form that contains the PivotChart. Access opens the form in PivotChart view. The title bar of the PivotChart View window shows the name of the table or query that provides the record source for the chart.

You can switch to other views by clicking the View button on the toolbar or choosing View⇨Datasheet View, View⇨Form View, View⇨PivotTable View, or View⇨Design View. Switching to PivotTable view shows the same information as rows and columns of text. Switching to Datasheet, Form, or Design views is usually pointless, though — you see only the datasheet or AutoForm of the underlying table or query.

Sprucing up your PivotCharts

After you create a PivotChart, you can change the type of chart, which fields appear where, and which values are included. As you make your changes, Access redraws the PivotChart immediately — unlike with charts made by Microsoft Graph, you don't need to switch views to see your results.

Another dynamic aspect of PivotCharts is that you can see what each part of the chart means by simply hovering the mouse pointer over it. Figure 3-20 shows a chart of the products that an online video and CD store sells, with a bar for each vendor from which the product is purchased. When you point to a section of the stacked bar chart shown in Figure 3-20, Access displays a pop-up box with the values that make up that bar ("V" for "video" and "ROU" for Rounder Kids, the name of the vendor that sells those videos), along with its numeric value (196, the number of videos that the store sells that come from that vendor).

Click to filter records

Data field

Series field

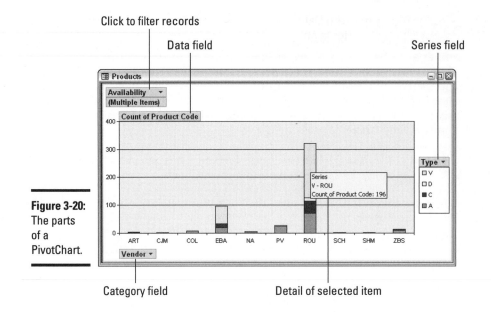

Figure 3-20:
The parts
of a
PivotChart.

Category field

Detail of selected item

The following list details some changes you can make to your PivotChart
with it open in PivotChart view:

✦ **Changing chart type:** If you don't want a bar chart (the default chart
type), change the chart type by clicking the Chart Type button on the
PivotChart toolbar. Or right-click a blank place on the chart and choose
the Chart Type option from the shortcut menu that appears. Either way,
you see the Properties sheet for the PivotChart with the Type tab
selected, as shown in Figure 3-21. Click a type from the list at the left,
and then a format from the examples shown.

✦ **Changing which fields are graphed:** For each field on the PivotChart,
you see a gray button with a downward-pointing triangle — a *field
button*. Figure 3-20 shows buttons for the Availability, Type, and Vendor
fields. You can change or add the fields to the graph. Display the Chart
Field list by clicking the Field List button on the toolbar. Then drag a
field from the Chart Field list to one of the drop areas. (Turn to the section, "Creating PivotCharts," earlier in this chapter, if you need a
refresher on drop areas.) You can have more than one field in each of
the drop areas. To remove a field from a drop area, drag it anywhere
outside the PivotChart window.

You can switch the Data and Series fields (the fields shown along the X-axis and the fields shown by colors or symbols) by clicking the By Row/By Column button on the toolbar. Click the button again to switch back.

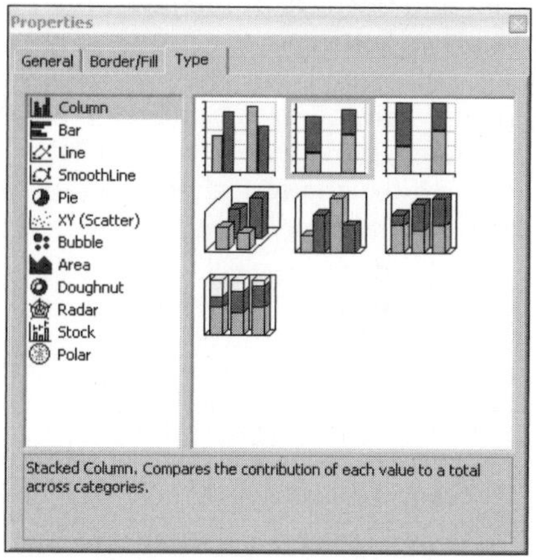

Figure 3-21:
Change the type of chart from the Properties sheet for a PivotChart.

✦ **Changing which values are included:** When you click a field button on the PivotChart (for example, the Vendor or Type button on Figure 3-21), the button expands into a list of the values for that field (as shown in Figure 3-22). The field button(s) at the top left corner of the chart are for fields that don't appear on the chart, but which are used to filter the records included. In the list of values, you can clear the check box for any value that you don't want included in the chart.

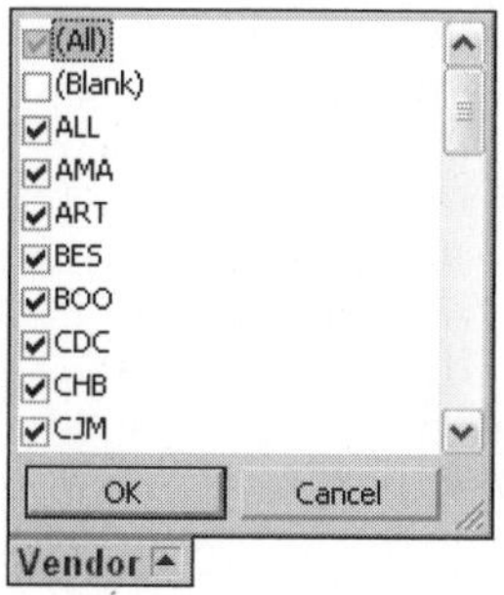

Figure 3-22:
Click a field's button on the PivotChart to see a list of values to include in the chart.

✦ **Displaying or hiding legends:** Click the Show Legend button on the PivotChart toolbar to display or hide the legend that shows the meanings of the colors and symbols on the chart.

✦ **Changing other properties:** Click an item in the PivotChart and click the Properties button on the toolbar to see the Properties sheet for that item. You can set the colors and borders of the bars, the background color, gridlines, fonts, and other settings.

Another way to change which fields are on the PivotChart, which values are included, and how they are arranged is to switch to PivotTable view (choose View⇨PivotTable View) and make your changes there. When you switch back to PivotChart view, the same data is included in the chart.

Book VI

Macros: Automating Stuff in Access

The 5th Wave   By Rich Tennant

"Our automated response policy to a large, company-wide data crash is to notify management, back up existing data and sell 90% of my shares in the company."

Contents at a Glance

Chapter 1: Making Macros Do the Work

In This Chapter

✔ What macros do

✔ Creating a macro

✔ Macro actions and arguments

✔ Running macros

✔ Making your forms smarter with macros

A ccess is a pretty smart program. Throughout the program are thousands of nice little features that make Access so intelligent, such as validation rules and formats that allow Access to help you keep your data neat and tidy. However, sometimes you want Access to be even smarter. You may want to format a field in a way Access doesn't allow. Or you may want your form to include a command button that the Command Button Wizard doesn't make. No problem — you can make Access even smarter by writing your own programs within Access.

Strangely, Access includes two (count 'em) ways of putting a program together: macros and VBA. The differences between the two are

✦ **Macros** are the original Access do-it-yourself program makers, dating back to the Dawn of Access (1991). However, Microsoft is phasing out macros, and suggests that you not use them for any major programming tasks.

✦ **Visual Basic for Applications (VBA)** is the newer create-a-program-in-Access programming language. VBA is a version of Visual Basic that works with all the programs in Microsoft Office. Microsoft recommends VBA for all significant programs. We describe VBA in detail in Book VIII.

So why use macros at all? Here's why: If you want to do something small and simple, making a little macro is a piece of cake (as you find out in this chapter). And you can always convert the macro to VBA later with the Access conversion command.

What Is a Macro?

A *macro* is a list of actions that happen when you run the macro. (That's a general definition that works for almost any programming language, actually.) For example, you may have a macro that performs these actions when you click a button on a form:

1. Saves the current record.

2. Prompts you to put a blank mailing label in the printer.

3. Prints a report, filtering the records to include only those that match the record currently displayed on the form.

Most macros are short and sweet, like this example. For more complex programs, you need VBA.

Creating and Editing Macros

Creating a macro is easy:

1. **Click the Macros button in the Objects list of the Database window (you may need to scroll down the list to find it).**

   Press F11 if the Database window isn't visible. Access shows you the macros that already exist in the database, as shown in Figure 1-1.

Figure 1-1:
The Database window shows you the macros in your database.

2. **Click the New button in the Database window.**

   Don't click the New button on the main Access toolbar, which creates an entirely new database!

   Access displays the Macro window, where you enter the actions that make up the macro. Figure 1-2 shows a macro with one action already entered.

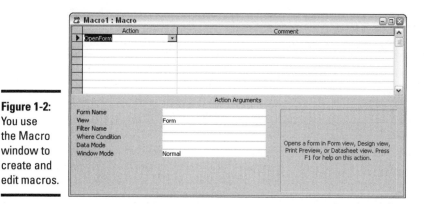

The upper part of the Macro window shows the list of actions, with space for a comment after each action. The Action Arguments part of the window shows the *arguments* — additional information that Access needs to perform the action — of the currently selected action.

3. **Enter the action that you want the macro to take in the first row of the Macro window.**

   When you click in the Action column and then click the downward-pointing button at the right side of the column, a drop-down menu appears listing all the Access macro actions. Choose the one you want. For example, choose the OpenForm action to display a form on-screen, or the SetValue action to set a field or control to a specific value. The next section lists many useful actions.

   After you choose an action, a description of the action appears in the lower-right part of the Macro window. Access also displays the arguments of that action in the lower half of the Macro window — the Action Arguments pane.

4. **For each action, specify the arguments for that action in the Action Arguments page.**

   Click in each box in turn and set the value of the argument. For some arguments you type a value, and for others you can choose from a list. If a downward-pointing triangle button appears at the right end of the box, click it to see a drop-down menu of your options.

5. **Repeat Steps 3 and 4 for each action you want the macro to take.**

   When you run the macro, Access executes the actions you specified, starting on the first row of the macro and proceeding until Access reaches a blank row.

Taking action!

To tell Access what to do when running the macro, you specify actions and arguments to actions. Access provides you with 56 actions that you can use in your macros. Table 1-1 lists the most commonly used actions.

Table 1-1	Macro Actions
Action	*Comments*
Apply Filter	Applies a filter to the records in a datasheet, form, or report. Set the Filter Name argument to the name of an existing query or type a SQL WHERE statement as the Where Condition argument.
Beep	Beeps. (You were perhaps expecting it to do something else?)
Close	Closes an Access object. Set the Object Type to Query, Form, Report, or other object. Set the Object Name to the specific object you want to close. Set Save to specify whether to save any changes.
FindNext	Repeats the last search you performed. (Perfect for a Find Next button on a form!)
FindRecord	Searches the current datasheet or form for the record you specify in the Find What and other arguments.
GoToControl	Moves the focus (cursor) to the control you specify in the Control Name argument. Useful on forms.
MsgBox	Displays a message box with the text you specify in the Message argument.
OpenDataAccessPage	Opens a page in Browse or Design view.
OpenForm	Opens a form in Form or Design view or in Print Preview. You specify the Form Name. The Filter Name and Where Condition arguments let you filter the records that appear in the form.
OpenQuery	Opens a query in Datasheet or Design view or Print Preview.
OpenReport	Opens a report in Design or Print Preview, or just prints the report, depending on what you specify for the View argument. The Filter Name and Where Condition arguments let you filter the records that appear in the report.
OpenTable	Opens a table in Datasheet or Design view or in Print Preview.
OutputTo	Exports the data from the specified object to an Excel spreadsheet file, Rich Text Document (RTF), text file, Web page (HTML), or Snapshot Report.
PrintOut	Prints the object that you specify. You can specify the page range and the number of copies to print.

Action	Comments
ReQuery	Recalculates the value of the current control, or reruns the record source query.
RunApp	Runs another program. The Command Line argument specifies the program name.
RunCode	Runs a VBA function. (See Book VIII.)
RunCommand	Runs an Access menu command. You specify the command by choosing from a long list.
RunMacro	Runs another macro. When the other macro finishes running, the first macro continues with the next action.
Save	Saves the object that you specify.
SelectObject	Selects the object that you specify.
SendKeys	Types the keystrokes that you specify in the Keystrokes argument, as if you were typing the keystrokes in the current application.
SetValue	Sets the value of a control, field, or property to the value you specify (which can be an expression).
ShowAllRecords	Removes any filter from the current table, query, or form.

Specifying arguments to actions

After you select an action, Access displays its arguments in the Action Arguments section of the Macro window (refer to Figure 1-2). Click in an argument's box to set it. Pressing F6 switches between the list of actions in the top part of the Macro window and the Action Arguments pane.

When you click in the box for an argument, Access displays information about that argument in a box on the right side of the Action Arguments pane.

Some arguments start out blank, while others start with a default value. For example, the OpenForm action has a View argument that specifies which view you want the form to appear in. The default value for the View argument is Form view (you usually want forms to open in Form view).

For example, Figure 1-3 shows a macro that prints three reports. The macro contains three OpenReport actions. Each OpenReport action has the Report Name argument set to a different report — three reports that print at the end of each month. For each action, the View argument is set to the Print mode, which prints the report rather than displaying it on-screen. Running the macro prints the three reports. Note, however, that only the action arguments for the currently selected action are visible in the window. You only see the Action Arguments for the third macro action in Figure 1-3.

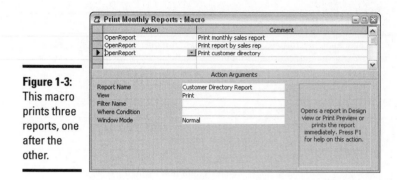

These arguments appear in many macro actions:

✦ `View:` What view Access opens the object in. For example, the `OpenForm` action includes the `View` argument, and you can choose the `Form`, `Design`, `Print Preview`, `Datasheet`, `PivotTable`, or `PivotChart` arguments from a drop-down menu — all the possible views for a form.

✦ `Object Type:` Type of object. Access provides a drop-down menu from which you choose the `Table`, `Query`, `Form`, `Report`, `Macro`, `Modules`, or `Data Access Page` objects.

✦ `Object Name:` Name of the object (table, query, form, report, macro, modules, or data access page) the action affects. Choose the `Object Type` argument first, and Access provides a drop-down menu of the objects of that type. For example, the `Close` action uses this argument to tell Access what to close.

✦ `Filter Name:` Name of a query (or filter saved as a query) that specifies which records to include in the action.

✦ `Where Condition:` Expression that specifies which records to include. Click the Build button to the right of the argument to display the Expression Builder.

Naming, saving, and editing macros

Before you run a macro, you need to save it with a name. Press Ctrl+S, click the Save button on the toolbar, choose File➪Save, or click the Close button and click the Yes button to save the macro. The Save As dialog box appears the first time you save a macro. Name the macro and click OK.

⬩ Design   You can edit your macro by clicking the Macros button in the Objects list of the Database window, selecting the macro's name in the list of stored macros that appears and then clicking the Design button. (Or right-click the macro name and choose the Design View option from the shortcut menu that appears.) You see the Macro window again, with the name of the macro appearing in the title bar of the Macro window. (In Figure 1-3, the macro is called `Print Monthly Reports`.)

In the Macro window, you can change actions and arguments as described in the preceding sections. You can also insert rows if you need to add macro actions in the middle of a macro: Choose Insert⇨Rows to add a row above the current row. You can delete a row by clicking the gray box at the left of the row to select the row, and then pressing the Delete key.

Adding comments

You can type anything you like in the Comment column in the Macro window. We usually explain what each action is supposed to do. You can also leave a blank row or two at the top of the macro, with no actions in the rows, and type the name and purpose of the macro in the Comment column.

Storing macros in related groups

Because most macros are short — frequently only one or two actions — storing them in groups is efficient. We like to store all the macros used for each form in one macro group. To create a macro group, follow these steps:

1. **Create a new macro by clicking the Macros button in the Objects list of the Database window and then clicking the window's New button.**

   You see the Macro window.

2. **Press Ctrl+S or click the Save button on the toolbar to save your new, blank macro group. Type a name for the group and click OK.**

   For example, if these macros run from the Purchase Order form, name the group something like *Purchase Order Form*. So far, this macro looks just like a single macro, not like a macro group, but stay tuned!

 3. **Choose View⇨Macro Names from the menu or click the Macro Names button on the toolbar.**

   Access adds a column to the Macro window: the Macro Name column. This new column provides a place to specify the names of the individual macros in the group.

4. **For the first macro you want to store in the group, type the name in the Macro Name column.**

   For example, if you're writing a macro to print the current purchase order, type **Print** in the Macro Name column. The full name of the macro is the group name followed by a dot and the macro name. Your macro may end up with the name *Purchase Order Form.Print*.

5. **Enter the macro's actions and arguments as usual, using as many rows as you need.**

6. **For the next macro you want to store in the group, type the name in the Macro Name column on the next row.**

   For readability, you can leave a blank row between one macro and the next, but you don't need to. Each macro starts on the line where its name appears and ends on the line just before the next macro's name appears.

7. **Enter the next macro's actions and arguments as usual.**

8. **Repeat Steps 6 and 7 for all the macros in the group.**

9. **Save and close the macro group the same way you save and close a single macro: Press Ctrl+S or click the Save button on the toolbar to save your changes, and click the X button to close the Macro window.**

Figure 1-4 shows a macro group that includes macros named `CopySellPrice`, `CopyTaxRate`, and `PaymentInfo`. The name of the group is `Purchase Order Form` (hmm, sounds like these macros must be used on the Purchase Order form). The full names of these macros are `Order Form Macros.CopySellPrice`, `Order Form Macros.CopyTaxRate`, and `Order Form Macros.PaymentInfo`.

Leave a row with no action above each macro name, to separate one macro from the next. Type the name and purpose of the macro in the Comment column.

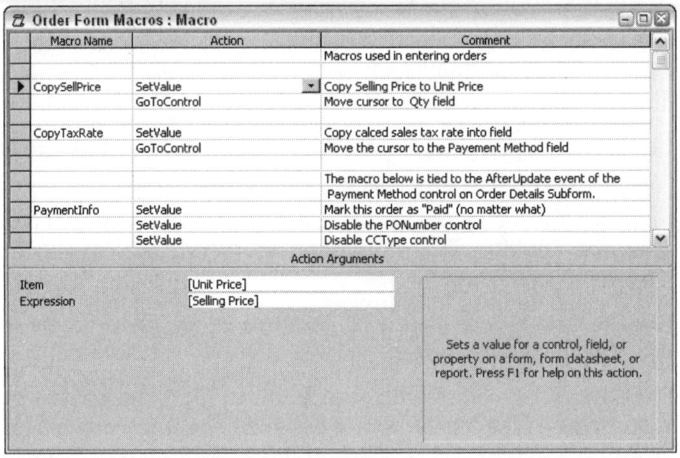

Figure 1-4:
You can store a group of macros together.

Macro Name	Action	Comment
		Macros used in entering orders
CopySellPrice	SetValue	Copy Selling Price to Unit Price
	GoToControl	Move cursor to Qty field
CopyTaxRate	SetValue	Copy calced sales tax rate into field
	GoToControl	Move the cursor to the Payement Method field
		The macro below is tied to the AfterUpdate event of the Payment Method control on Order Details Subform.
PaymentInfo	SetValue	Mark this order as "Paid" (no matter what)
	SetValue	Disable the PONumber control
	SetValue	Disable CCType control

Action Arguments

| Item | [Unit Price] |
| Expression | [Selling Price] |

Sets a value for a control, field, or property on a form, form datasheet, or report. Press F1 for help on this action.

Running Macros

You can run a macro directly by selecting the macro in the Database window and clicking the Run button. To run a macro without going to the Database window, choose Tools⇨Macro⇨Run Macro and choose the macro name from the Run Macro dialog box that appears. If you stored a bunch of macros in a macro group, Access runs just the first macro in the group. (You can't run the second or following macros in a group from the Run Macro dialog box.)

For example, to run the `Print Monthly Reports` macro (refer to Figure 1-3), click the Macros button in the Database window, select the Print Monthly Report macro from the list of macros, and click the Run button. Or just double-click the macro name.

The most common way to run a macro, however, is to assign it to an event on a form — for example, the `On Click` event of a command button. You specify the full name of the macro (macro group name, a dot, and the name of the individual macro) in one of the properties of a command button. But before we cover macros with forms (later in this chapter), you can run macros in two other cool ways: auto-execution when the database opens and execution when certain keystrokes are used.

Running a macro when the database opens

We like our databases to automatically display a Main Menu form, or some other commonly used form, as soon as the database opens. If the first thing you usually do after opening the database is to open the Order Entry form, why not tell Access to open it for you? You may have other actions you'd like Access to take when your database opens — you may want to prompt the user for his or her name, or display a list of reports.

In order to tell Access to do something automatically when the database opens, you can write a macro with the actions you want Access to take, and then tell Access to run the macro on startup.

Running a macro when the database opens is a snap: Just name the macro `AutoExec`. That's the whole thing. When you open a database, Access looks in the database for a macro named `AutoExec`, and if there is one, Access runs the macro. Enter the actions and arguments for the `AutoExec` macro in the usual way — in the Macro window.

If you *don't* want the `AutoExec` macro to run when you open the database, hold down the Shift key while the database is loading.

Assigning macros to keys

Your database can contain a *key-assignment macro* — a macro that assigns keys on the keyboard to run macros. If you create a macro group named AutoKeys, and it contains macros with the names of keys (or key combinations) on the keyboard, then Access runs the appropriate macro when you press the key. Figure 1-5 shows an AutoKeys macro with macros assigned to Ctrl+T, Ctrl+1, and Ctrl+P.

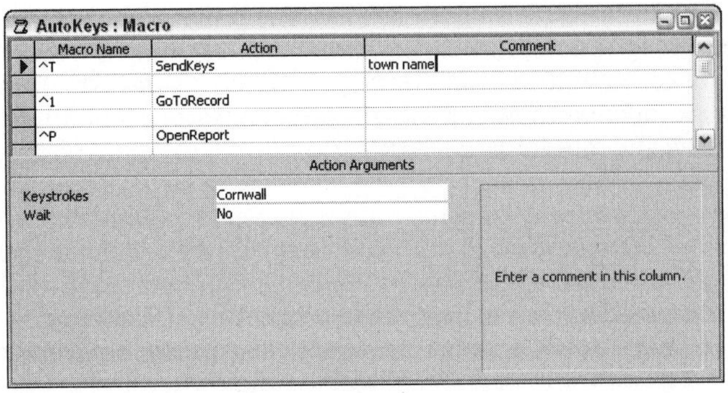

Figure 1-5:
An
AutoKeys
macro
group
assigns
macros to
keystrokes.

To name a key-assignment macro, use ^ to indicate the Ctrl key, + for the Shift key, and { } around key names that are more than one letter long. Table 1-2 shows the names of the keys you can use: You are restricted to letters, numbers, Insert, Delete, and the functions keys, used in conjunction with the Shift and Ctrl keys. A few examples of key-assignment macros are the following:

✦ ^G: means Ctrl+G

✦ +{F2}: means Shift+F2

✦ {INS}: means the Insert key

Table 1-2	Key Names in AutoKeys
Key Name	**Key**
A	A letter key (ditto for the rest of the letter and number keys)
{F1}	F1 function key (ditto for the rest of the function keys)
{INS}	Insert or Ins key
{DEL}	Delete or Del key

If you assign a macro to a key that normally does something else (such as Ctrl+F, which usually chooses Edit⇨Find from the menu), your macro overrides the Access command.

Opening Databases That Contain Macros

Access 2003 has a new feature to guard against databases that contain viruses in the form of macros. Unfortunately, this feature also guards against normal databases that contain macros, action queries, and VBA procedures. When you open a database that contains one of these types of objects, you may see a dialog box asking whether you really want to take a chance on running the macros in the database. You can choose whether to open the database with the macros enabled. (See Book I, Chapter 2 for details.)

Can a macro be a virus?

Writing a virus is no small feat, and requires pretty advanced programming skills. In order to qualify as a virus, the macro has to be intentionally written to do bad things to your computer, and to replicate itself. Writing code that does harmful things is not easy. If you're concerned that you may accidentally create a virus, you can stop worrying about that. Creating a virus by accident is about as likely as writing an entire book, or driving across country, by accident.

If the database is something you created yourself, then it's absolutely, positively, 100 percent safe to enable the macros. You have three options:

✦ Put up with the annoying security warning message every time you open the database, and choose the Enable Macros button each time.

✦ Set your Access security level to the Low setting, so that Access never notifies you when you open a database that may contain viruses. See the section, "Turning down your Access security setting," later in this chapter.

✦ *Digitally sign* your database by adding the security code that tells Access, "It's okay, this is my own database, and I can vouch for its safety." This digital signature works only when you open the database on your own computer. The next section describes how to sign your database.

We recommend this last option: you don't have to put up with annoying messages, and you don't want to open up your Access program to viruses from other people.

Signing your database

Signing a database for your own use is easy to do. First you create your own digital signature, and then you use it to sign your databases. This signature works only on your own computer: When other people open your database, they still see the security warning message. If you want to create a digital signature that works everywhere, then you need to contact a certification authority and buy one.

Follow these steps to create a digital signature for use on your own computer:

1. **Choose Start⇨Programs⇨Microsoft Office⇨Microsoft Office Tools⇨Digital Signature For VBA Projects.**

   Windows prompts you to install this program, unless you've used it before.

2. **Follow the prompts to install Digital Signature For VBA Projects.**

   You probably need your Microsoft Office CD. When the program is installed you see the window shown in Figure 1-6.

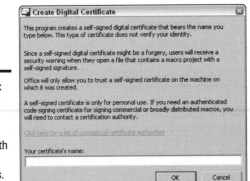

Figure 1-6:
Creating a digital signature for use with your own databases.

3. **Type a name for your certificate (such as your own name) and click OK.**

   The program reports that it created a certificate, or digital signature.

4. **Click OK.**

If you plan to distribute your database to other people and you need a certificate that works on computers other than yours, you need to buy a digital certificate. See the VeriSign Web site:

`www.verisign.com/products/signing`

After you have a digital certificate, sign your database with the following steps:

1. **With your database open, choose Tools⟳Macro⟳Visual Basic Editor (or press Alt+F11).**

You see the Microsoft Visual Basic window, which is described in Book VIII, Chapter 1.

2. **Choose Tools⟳Digital Signature.**

You see the Digital Signature dialog box shown in Figure 1-7.

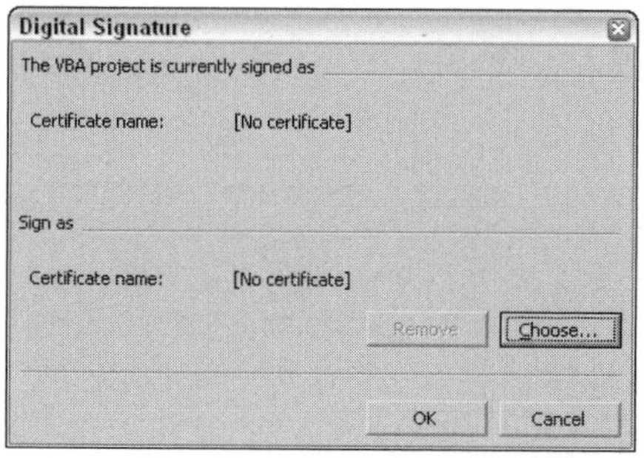

Figure 1-7:
You can add your own digital signature to your database.

3. **Click the Choose button and choose from a list of the digital signature certificates stored on your computer. Click OK twice.**

Now when you open your own database, Access doesn't complain. Whew!

Turning down your Access security setting

If you don't expect to open any database that you or your trusted associates didn't create, you can tell Access not to warn you about any databases. Follow these steps:

1. **Choose Tools⟳Macro⟳Security.**

You see the Security dialog box.

2. **Click the Security Level tab to see the options.**

The Medium option is usually selected as in Figure 1-8.

3. **Choose the Low option.**

4. **Click OK.**

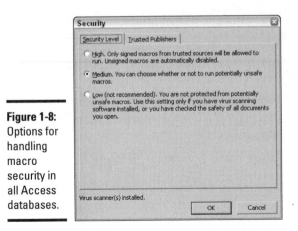

Figure 1-8:
Options for
handling
macro
security in
all Access
databases.

Access no longer displays warning messages when you open databases that contain macros.

Attaching Macros to Forms

Most macros are used with forms — to make form controls smarter or to power command buttons. Every control in a form has *events* connected to it — things that happen when the user clicks the control. You can tell Access to run a macro when an event happens.

Events are properties of the control. To tell Access to run a macro when the event happens (for example, any time the value of a field changes or a command button is clicked), you enter the macro name in the event property for the control or for the whole form. Follow these steps:

1. **Create and save the macro you want to run.**

You can store the macro by itself, or as part of a macro group. (We usually create one macro group for each form, and store all the macros for that form in the group.) Save the macro before continuing. (But you can keep the Macro window open if you plan to make further changes to your macro.)

2. **Open the form in Design view.**

Refer to Book IV, Chapter 2 for how to edit a form in Design view.

3. Display the Properties sheet by clicking the Properties button on the toolbar. Click the Event tab.

See Book IV, Chapter 1 for information about the Properties sheet. The Event tab displays all the events for the selected object.

4. If you are attaching a macro to a control (such as a command button), click that control. If you want to attach the macro to the form itself, click the box where the rulers intersect in the upper-left corner of the form.

Now the Properties sheet shows the available events for the form or control.

5. Click in the event property you want to use.

For example, if you are attaching a macro to a command button, click in the `On Click` property to run the macro when the user clicks the command button. If you want the macro to run whenever you insert a record using the form, click in the `Before Insert` property.

6. Click the downward-pointing arrow at the right end of the property and choose the name of the macro.

Access lists all the individual macros as well as macros in groups, in alphabetical order. For example, if the `Order Form Macros` macro group contains a macro named `AddRecord`, choose `Order Form Macros.AddRecord`.

Most controls have a number of different events to which you can assign a macro, including when your cursor enters and exits the control, when you click or double-click it, or when its value changes. Figure 1-9 shows the Event tab of the Properties sheet for a text box control, with a macro name in the `After Update` event property of a combo box.

Table 1-3 shows the most commonly used events that can happen to controls in a form.

Book VI Chapter 1

Making Macros Do the Work

Figure 1-9: The events properties of a combo box control on a form.

```
Combo Box: ContactID                              ⊗
ContactID                          ⌄
Format   Data   Event   Other   All
Before Update . . . . . . . . . |
After Update . . . . . . . . . . Order Form Macros.CopyTaxRate
On Dirty . . . . . . . . . . . .
On Undo . . . . . . . . . . . .
On Change . . . . . . . . . .
On Not in List . . . . . . . . .
On Enter . . . . . . . . . . . .
On Exit . . . . . . . . . . . . .
On Got Focus . . . . . . . . . .
```

Table 1-3	Some Form Control Events
Event	*Description*
Before Update	When the control or record is about to be updated
After Update	Immediately after the control or record is updated
On Not in List	When a user tries to enter a value in combo and list boxes that's not in the list of values
On Enter	When focus (cursor) moves to the control
On Exit	When focus (cursor) leaves the control
On Click	When you click the control
On Dbl Click	When you double-click the control

For example, you can make a macro for an order form that automatically moves you to the last record in the table. (You rarely want to edit the oldest order in the table, but you more likely want to continue editing the newest order.) The macro runs when you open the form. The macro, which we named LastRecord and stored in our Order Form Macros macro group, is

Action	*Arguments*
GoToRecord	Record: Last

To make the macro run each time you open the form, set the form's OnOpen event property to the name of the macro, Order Form Macros.LastRecord.

Creating command buttons on forms

Book IV, Chapter 3 describes how to make command buttons on a form. The Command Button Wizard can write VBA procedures for many tasks that you may want a button to do, such as going to the first or last record, applying a filter, or finding a record. However, you may want a command button to do something that the wizard doesn't know how to do. In that case, you have to write your own macro or VBA procedure and link it to an event property of the command button. (Book VIII explains how to write VBA.)

For example, if you want to make a button that prints three end-of-month reports, you use the Command Button button in the Toolbox to create a new command button control and then set its On Click event to the name of the macro you created for printing those three reports.

Referring to form controls in macros

When you write a macro that runs from a form, you frequently need to refer to the current value of a control on the form. In arguments to macro actions, you can just type the name of the control that displays either the field or the field name. For example, to set the shipping charge to three dollars per item, you use this macro:

Action	Arguments
SetValue	Item: [Shipping & Handling] Expression: [Total Qty] * 3

Book VI
Chapter 1

However, if you are referring to a control on a form other than the form from which the macro was called, you need to specify which form the control is on, such as

[Forms]![*formname*]![*controlname*]

**Making Macros
Do the Work**

Replace *formname* with the name of your form and *controlname* with the name of the control on the form.

For example, the OpenReport action displays or prints a report. You can use its Where Condition argument to restrict the records that appear in the report. If you want the report to include only records with the same Order No value as the order displayed on the Orders form, you type this value in the Where Condition argument of the OpenReport action:

[Order No] = [Forms]![Orders]![Order No]

In the Where Condition argument of many actions (an argument you use to filter records), you must always use this longer version of the name of the control you want to refer to.

Printing matching records from a form

Now you know everything to create a very useful command button: a button that prints a report for the record displayed in the form. For example, an order form may have an Internal Report button to print an internal report, a Mailing Label button to print the Mailing Label report, and an Invoice/Receipt button to print the Invoice or Receipt report — all filtered to include only the order that is currently displayed in the form. Put all these macros into a macro group for the form (for example, the Order Form macro group).

The `Internal Report` macro saves any changes made to the current record on the form, and then prints the `Internal Report` for the current record:

Action	Arguments
RunCommand	SaveRecord
OpenReport	Report Name: Internal Report View: Print Where Condition: [Order No] = [Forms]![Orders]![Order No]

For each macro, you create a button that calls the macro via the button's `On Click` property. Figure 1-10 shows the Properties sheet for the `InternalReport` command button.

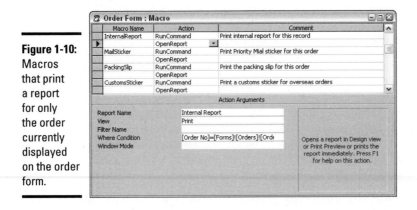

Figure 1-10: Macros that print a report for only the order currently displayed on the order form.

Chapter 2: Making Macros Smarter

In This Chapter

✔ **Making macros run conditionally**

✔ **Changing form control properties with a macro**

✔ **Creating your own switchboard or main menu form**

*W*hile macros are simple and powerful, they aren't the full-featured programming language that VBA is. (We want to repeat that for writing programs of any size, use VBA, not macros.) This chapter describes some nifty ways to use macros with your forms, including how to create a "Mission Control" or switchboard form for your database.

If you create a macro and decide later that you wish you'd written a VBA procedure to do the job, Access can convert the macro to VBA. See Book VIII, Chapter 1 for how to convert a macro to a VBA program. If you want to use the Access built-in switchboards rather than regular forms, see Book IV, Chapter 3.

Only Run This If I Say So

Every programming language worth its salt has an if-then feature, which ensures that a command is only carried out under specific circumstances. For instance, you may want Access to print a report for the current order only if the order number isn't blank: If the order number *is* blank, don't print the report and if the order number *isn't* blank, then do print the report. The technical term for such an if-then situation is *conditional execution.*

If-then macros

The way you add a condition to a macro action is by adding a Condition column to the Macro window and typing a condition into the column. Follow these steps:

1. **Display the Database window (by pressing F11), click the Macros button in the Object list, select your macro from the list of macro names, and click the Design button on the Database window's toolbar.**

You see the Macro window with your macro, ready to edit. (See Chapter 1 of this book for how the Macro window works.)

2. Choose View⇨Conditions from the menu or click the Conditions button on the toolbar to add a Condition column to the Macro window.

The Condition column appears to the left of the Action column, as shown in Figure 2-1.

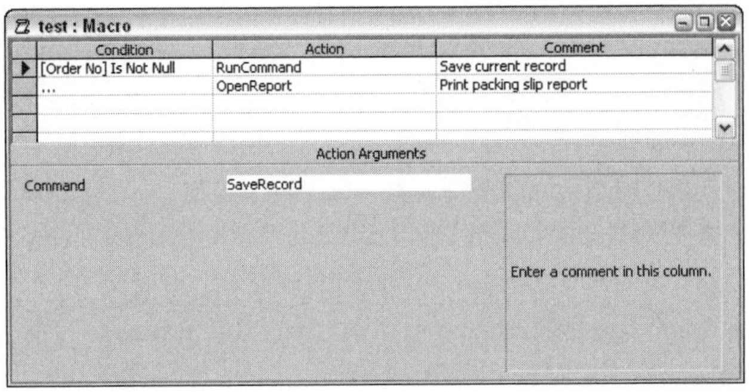

Figure 2-1:
The Condition column in the Macro window enables you to type a condition that controls whether Access performs an action.

3. Enter actions and arguments.

Click in the Action column, click the downward-pointing triangle button at the right side of the Action box, and choose the action from the drop-down list. Then enter the arguments for the action in the Action Arguments page in the lower half of the Macro window.

4. When you get to a conditional action, type the condition into the Condition column.

For example, you may want to print a report for the current order (using the OpenReport action), but you don't want to print a blank report if no order is displayed. You use the [Order No] Is Not Null condition to specify that Access performs the action only if an order number appears on the form.

For the condition, you can use any expression that comes out to be either True (Yes) or False (No). Conditions work just like the criteria that you use when creating queries, as described in Book III, Chapter 1. You can compare values using comparison operators such as =, <, and >, and you can use Is Null and Is Not Null to spot blank and non-blank values.

5. **If you want to perform several actions based on the same condition, type the condition in the Condition column on the row for the first action, and type . . . (three periods) in the Condition column for the other actions.**

The . . . condition means "use the condition from the preceding row."

For example, the following macro (the same one shown in Figure 2-1) saves the current record and prints a report with records that match the current record but *only* if the current record isn't blank:

Condition	Action	Arguments
[Order No] Is Not Null	RunCommand	Command: SaveRecord
. . .	OpenReport	Report Name: Packing Slip View: Print Where Condition: [Order No] = [Forms]![Orders]![Order No]

Book VI
Chapter 2

Making Macros
Smarter

On the first line, the RunCommand action only happens if the Order No control isn't blank (null). On the second line, the . . . condition means to use the same condition for this line, too — only print the report if the order number isn't blank. (Otherwise, you get a blank report!)

In the second row of the macro, the OpenReport action prints the Packing Slip report, printing only the records for the current order. The Where Condition argument makes the selection, comparing the Order No control in the record source for the report to [Forms]![Orders].[Order No], the Order No control on the Orders form. (This long and confusing way of referring to a control on a form is described near the end of Chapter 1 of this book.)

If-then-else macros

If you want an if-then-else condition — you want to run one set of actions if the condition is true and another set if the condition is false — you use the StopMacro action. Your macro looks like this:

Condition	Action	Arguments
condition	*action*	
. . .	action	
. . .	StopMacro	Ends the macro execution
	action	

On the first line, you enter the condition and the first command to run if that condition is True. On the following lines, enter . . . (three periods) as the condition and choose the additional actions that you want to happen when the condition is True. On the line after the final action that happens when the condition is True, enter . . . (three periods) for the condition and **StopMacro** for the action. This line tells the macro to stop executing, but Access only runs this action if the condition is true. On the following lines, leave the condition blank and enter the actions that happen if the condition is False.

When you run an if-then-else macro, Access checks whether the condition is true. If it is, Access runs the actions, line by line, until it reaches the StopMacro action, and then stops. If the condition is false, Access skips down to the first line that has a blank condition, and starts executing there.

For example, the macro shown in Figure 2-2 prints a report if the Order No condition isn't blank, and displays a message if it is:

Condition	Action	Arguments
[Order No] Is Not Null	RunCommand	Command: SaveRecord
. . .	OpenReport	Report Name: Packing Slip View: Print Where Condition: [Order No] = [Forms]![Orders]![Order No]
. . .	StopMacro	
	MsgBox	Message: Order No. is blank Beep: Yes

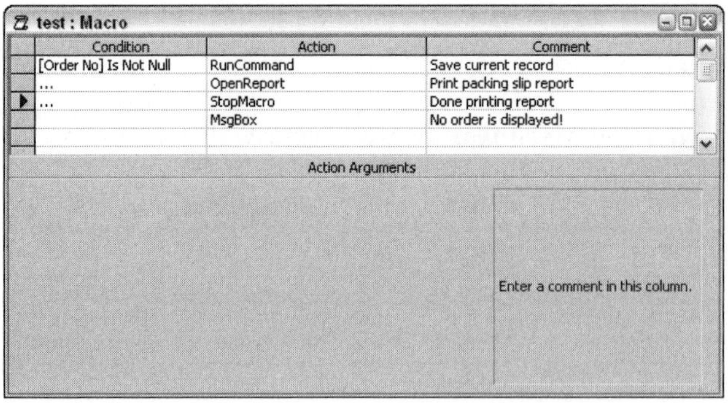

Figure 2-2: An if-then-else macro does one set of actions if a condition is true, and another set if the condition is false.

Changing the Way Your Form Looks Dynamically

A really smart form changes based on the information you type into it. Making smart forms is not hard: You only need to know how to make a macro display, hide, enable, and disable the controls on the form in response to what you enter.

Setting the properties of form controls

Macros have no problem changing the values of controls — a macro can copy a value from one control to another, for example, or store a calculation in a control. But that's not all. Macros can also change the *properties* of controls, in essence changing how controls look or act on-screen. The following properties, for example, are all eminently changeable once a macro gets its hands on them:

+ Fore Color: We're guessing Fore Color is short for "Foreground Color." In any event, Fore Color refers to the text color property of a label. Changing the Fore Color property makes the text appear in a different color. Why is this neat? A macro can change the color of a label to, say, bright red based on whether an order is paid for or not, which makes tracking down deadbeats much easier for you.

+ Visible: If the Visible property is set to a No setting, the control is hidden. You can have a macro make controls invisible based on the values of other controls. For example, if an order is paid by check, the credit card controls aren't needed and can be hidden.

+ Enabled: If the Enabled property is set to the No setting, the cursor won't move to it, and you can't change the control's value. You can make a macro that sets the value of some controls and then disables them so that the value can't be changed.

Follow these steps to add an action to a macro that changes the properties of a form control:

1. **Open your macro in the Macro window. (Select the macro in the Database window and click the Design button.)**

   If you want to create a new macro instead of adding to an existing macro, click the New button in the Database window.

2. **Display the Condition column if you want to make your action conditional by choosing View➪Conditions from the menu or clicking the Conditions button on the toolbar.**

   In Figure 2-3, the macro hides a label if a control is blank (null) and displays the label if the control isn't blank.

3. **In the Condition column, type the condition under which you want to change the property of the control.**

   In Figure 2-3, the condition for the first row of the macro is [Notes] Is Null. This condition means "perform this action if the Notes control on the current form is blank."

4. **Click in the Action column, click the downward-pointing arrow at the right end of the box, and choose the** SetValue **action from the menu.**

   The SetValue action works for setting properties, too.

5. **In the Item argument box, type the name of the control whose property you want to set, followed by a dot and the name of the property.**

   If the control name includes spaces, enclose it in square brackets. (If there are no spaces, the square brackets can't hurt.) Access adds brackets around the property name for you. In Figure 2-3, the Item argument is [SeeNotes].[Visible] — the Visible property of the SeeNotes label.

6. **In the Expression argument box, type the value to which you want to set the property.**

   To hide the SeeNotes label when the Notes field is empty, the macro in Figure 2-3 sets the Visible property to the No setting.

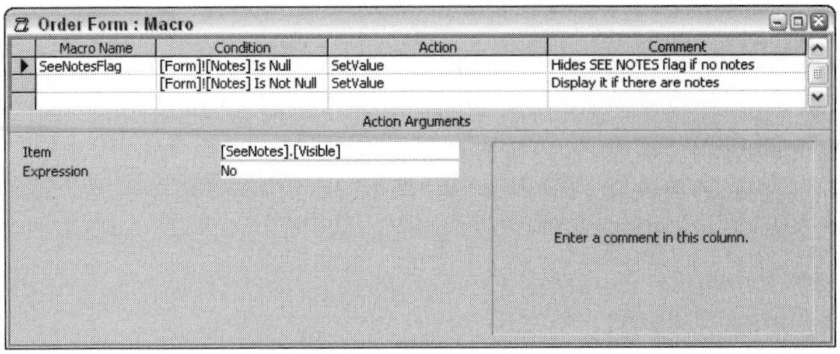

Figure 2-3:
The See
NotesFlag
macro
changes the
Visible
property of
the Notes
field.

Macro Name	Condition	Action	Comment	
SeeNotesFlag	[Form]![Notes] Is Null	SetValue	Hides SEE NOTES flag if no notes	
	[Form]![Notes] Is Not Null	SetValue	Display it if there are notes	

Action Arguments

Item	[SeeNotes].[Visible]
Expression	No

Enter a comment in this column.

When you set the Item argument of the SetValue action to the property you want to change, you can click the Build button to the right of the Item box to use the Expression Builder. In the Expression Builder window, delete anything in the box at the top of the window where the finished expression appears. Double-click the Forms option in the left-hand column, double-click the All Forms option (or Loaded Forms, if the form is currently open on-screen), and double-click the name of the form that contains the control. In the middle column of the Expression Builder window, click or double-click the name of the control. In the right-hand column, double-click the property. The complete expression appears in the box at the top of the window. Click

OK to return to the Macro window — your new expression appears in the Item box.

Running a macro during data entry

If you want to run a macro in response to a value entered in a control, set the control's `After Update` property to run the macro: Any change in the value of the control runs the macro. The `After Update` property is on the Event tab of the Properties sheet for the control.

For example, an order form may have a `PaymentMethod` combo box from which you choose Cash, Check, Purchase Order, or Credit Card. You can run a macro based on the value of the `PaymentMethod` combo box that enables the appropriate other controls: `PONo` (purchase order number), `CCNo` (credit card number), `CCMonth` (credit card expiration month), `CCYear` (credit card expiration year), and `CheckNo` (check number). The macro, which is run by the Payment Method's `After Update` property, looks like this:

Condition	Action	Arguments
	SetValue	Item: [PONo].[Enabled] Expression: False
	SetValue	Item: [CCNo].[Enabled] Expression: False
	SetValue	Item: [CCMonth].[Enabled] Expression: False
	SetValue	Item: [CCYear].[Enabled] Expression: False
	SetValue	Item: [CheckNo].[Enabled] Expression: False
[PaymentMethod]= "PO"	SetValue	Item: [PONo].[Enabled] Expression: True
. . .	GoToControl	Control Name: PONo
[PaymentMethod]= "CC"	SetValue	Item: [CCNo].[Enabled] Expression: True
. . .	SetValue	Item: [CCMonth].[Enabled] Expression: True

Condition	Action	Arguments
. . .	SetValue	Item: [CCYear].[Enabled] Expression: True
. . .	GoToControl	Control Name: CCNo
[PaymentMethod]= "CH"	SetValue	Item: [CheckNo].[Enabled] Expression: True
. . .	GoToControl	Control Name: CheckNo

First it disables all the controls specific to purchase orders, credit cards, and checks. The macro uses the SetValue action to set the Enabled property of each of these controls to False (disabled). Then the macro enables only the appropriate controls, based on the value of the PaymentMethod control. For each payment type, the macro also moves the cursor to one of the controls that are enabled, using the GoToControl action.

You can also make a macro run when you move your cursor to a control (using the On Entry property) or when you move your cursor out of the control (the On Exit property).

Displaying Forms and Datasheets

Making a macro that opens another form or a table or query in Datasheet view is easy. Just use the OpenForm, OpenTable, or OpenQuery action in your macro. For example, you may want a button on the Access database Orders form that displays the Products form, so you can see detailed information about the products that a customer is thinking of ordering. The macro looks like this:

Action	Argument
OpenForm	Form Name: Products View: Form
Simple enough!	

Setting Up Your Own Main Menu Form

If you create a database using an Access template (as we describe in Book I, Chapter 3), Access makes a *switchboard,* a form with bunches of buttons for opening forms and printing reports. You can make your own main menu form by creating an *unbound form* (a form with no record source) with command buttons that run macros. For some commands, you can use the Command Button Wizard to write VBA code instead of having to write a macro.

First (as the next few sections explain), create the main menu form. Second, create the AutoExec macro so Access displays the form automatically when you open the database. Third, create each command button that you want on the main menu form. For command buttons that do something that the Command Button Wizard doesn't offer, write a macro for the command button to run (and create a macro group to store these macros in).

Creating a form that displays when the database opens

To create an unbound form (a form with no record source) that displays when you open the database, follow these steps:

1. **Create a new form by clicking the Forms button in the Objects list of the Database window, clicking the New button in the window's toolbar, and then clicking OK in the New Form dialog box that appears.**

In the New Form dialog box, don't choose a table to base the form on — this is an unbound form that doesn't display table data. Leave the Design View setting selected, too. Access opens a form in Design view.

2. **Save the form by clicking the Save button on the toolbar or by pressing Ctrl+S. In the Save As dialog box, type a name for the form and click OK.**

Call the form something like Main Menu. Leave the form open — you make buttons for it in Step 11.

Now you are ready to make the AutoExec macro that opens the form automagically.

3. **Press F11 or click the Database Window button on the toolbar to return to the Database window.**

4. **Click the Macros button in the Objects list of the Database window and then click the New button in the window's toolbar to create a new macro.**

A blank macro appears in the Macro window.

5. **Choose the OpenForm action from the drop-down menu in the first row of the Action column of the Macro window.**

6. **In the Action Arguments section of the Macro window, set the Form Name argument for the OpenForm action to the name of the form you just created.**

You click in the Form Name argument, click the down-arrow button, and choose the form from the list that appears.

7. Close the macro, click the Yes button to save it, and name it AutoExec.

You have to name your macro AutoExec if you want the macro to run automatically each time you open the database.

8. Click the New button again in the Database window to make another macro.

Your main menu form needs a macro group for the macros.

A blank macro appears in the Macro window.

9. Choose View⇨Macro Names.

The Macro Names column appears in the Macro window, which enables you to give each macro in the group a name.

10. Click the Save button or press Ctrl+S to save the new macro group, type a name for the macro group, and click OK.

You don't *have* to name the macro group with the same name as the switchboard form, but you'll find yourself less confused if you do! If you took our advice in Step 2, name the macro group Main Menu or Main Menu Form.

Now you are ready to return to your main menu form (the one you created back in Step 1 — remember?) and add command buttons.

11. Click in the Design View window for the form, and display the Toolbox, if it's not already on-screen, by clicking the Toolbox button on the toolbar.

12. Click the Control Wizards button in the Toolbox.

The Control Wizards button remains selected, and makes Access run a wizard (where available) when you create a new control.

13. Click the Label button in the Toolbox and click in the upper-left corner of the form. Type a title for the form: We suggest the name of the database.

Main Menu is also an appropriate title for this form — use whatever text makes the function of the form clear. Format the title any way you want (how about large and centered?).

The form is ready and appears when you open the database — all it needs is buttons!

Creating command buttons for your main menu form

For each button you want on the main menu form, create a command button and (if necessary) a macro for it to run. When you create a command button, the Command Button Wizard writes VBA procedures to open forms, print reports, and run queries. The most useful Command Button Wizard choices for buttons on a main menu form are

✦ **Open Form** (in the Form Operations category): Opens any other form.

✦ **Preview Report** (in the Report Operations category): Opens a report in Print Preview.

✦ **Print Report** (in the Report Operations category): Prints a report without previewing it.

✦ **Run Query** (in the Miscellaneous category): Runs an action query or opens a select query in Datasheet view.

✦ **Run Macro** (in the Miscellaneous category): Runs a macro. The macro needs to exist before you create the command button.

If you want to do something else, you need to create a macro in your macro group and then tell the command button to run it. The next two sections describe both ways to make a command button — letting the Command Button Wizard write a VBA procedure for your button, or writing your own macro for your button.

Letting the wizard make your command button

If the Command Button Wizard knows how to write the VBA procedure for your button, use the wizard. Open your main menu form in Design view, make sure the Control Wizards button is selected in the Toolbox, and follow these steps:

1. **Click the Command Button button in the Toolbox and then click the form where you want the button to appear.**

Access starts the Command Button Wizard. (See Book IV, Chapter 2 for the details.)

2. **Look in the categories and actions that the wizard offers for the action that you want the button to do. Choose the category and the action and click Next.**

Depending on which action you choose, the wizard asks for specific information about what you want to do. For example, if you choose Open Form for the action, the wizard asks which form you want to open and whether you want it to display all or specific records.

3. **Answer the wizard's questions about what form you want to display, what report you want to preview or print, or what query you want to open or run. Click Next.**

4. **When the wizard asks what the button should look like, click Text or Picture and specify the text or icon to appear on the button. Click Next.**

5. **Type a short name for the command button. Choose a name that has something to do with what the button does and click Finish.**

   The wizard creates the command button and sets the button's On Click property to the VBA code it just wrote. This property causes Access to run the VBA procedure when someone clicks the command button.

6. **Move or resize the command button as you like and create a label to go next to it.**

   If the button displays text, it may not need a label.

The Command Button Wizard sets the On Click property of each command button to a VBA procedure that it writes. In the Properties sheet, you see Event Procedure in the property, which means that this event runs a VBA procedure rather than a macro; click the Build button to see the VBA code. (See Book VIII for what the code means and how to change it.)

If you want to change the button to run a macro, you can click in the On Click property on the Event tab of the Properties sheet, click the down-arrow button for the property, and choose your macro from the list that appears.

If you're not sure whether the Command Button Wizard can write a VBA procedure for the task you want the button to perform, run the wizard according to the preceding steps to find out. In Step 2, browse through the various programs that the wizard knows how to write. If you don't see the program you need, cancel the wizard and try the steps in the next section of this chapter.

Making command buttons that run your macros

You ran the Command Button Wizard, but couldn't find the VBA program you need — the wizard just doesn't do everything. Instead, you can create a button and then write a macro for the button to run.

If you followed the steps in the section, "Creating a form that displays when the database opens," earlier in this chapter, you already created a macro group for the macros run by command buttons on your main menu form. Follow these steps for each command button that runs a macro:

1. **Open the macro group in the Macro window by clicking the macro name in the Database window and clicking the Design button.**

The Macro window opens, showing the macro group in which you store the macro for your new command button. If you already created macros for this form, this macro group already contains macros. No problem! Just skip down to the first blank row in the Macro window. (Or skip down an extra row or two, to leave some blank space between one macro and the next.)

If the Macro Name column doesn't appear in the Macro window, choose View⟹Macro Names to display the column.

2. **Type a macro name in the Macro Name column — we suggest typing the name of the command button that will run this macro.**

For example, if the Print Packing Slip command button will run this macro, why not name it Print Packing Slip, too?

3. **Create the macro choosing the actions and entering the arguments.**

Chapter 1 of this book describes how to choose the actions and arguments for a macro.

4. **Save the macro group by pressing Ctrl+S or clicking Save.**

You can't assign the macro name to the command button's On Click property if the macro isn't saved.

5. **Switch to the form's Design View window.**

If your main menu form isn't open in Design view, open it now. (In the Database window, click the Forms button, click the form name, and click the Design button.)

6. **Click the Command Button button in the Toolbox and then click the form where you want the button to appear.**

Access starts the Command Button Wizard.

7. **Choose the Miscellaneous category and the RunMacro action. Click Next.**

8. **When the wizard asks which macro you want to run, choose the macro name from the list. Click Next.**

The macro name is macrogroup.macroname. For example, if the macro group is named Main Menu and the macro name is OrderForm, choose Main Menu.OrderForm.

9. **Click Text or Picture and specify the text or icon to appear on the button. Click Next.**

10. **Type a short name that has something to do with what the button does and click Finish.**

    The wizard creates the command button.

11. **Move or resize the command button as you like, and create a label to go next to it.**

    If the button displays text, it may not need a label.

The Command Button Wizard writes a VBA procedure that runs the macro you specified, and sets the command button's On Click property to run the procedure. We think running a VBA procedure to run a macro is a little odd, but that's the way the wizard works.

If you'd rather run the macro directly (so no VBA procedure is involved), or you want to change to running a different macro, double-click the command button you just created (to display its Properties sheet), click the Event tab, and set its On Click property to the macro you want to run.

Book VII

Database Administration

The 5th Wave By Rich Tennant

"We're here to clean the code."

Contents at a Glance

Chapter 1: Database Housekeeping

In This Chapter

✔ **Taking out the garbage (compacting your database)**

✔ **Backing up the whole, or part of the, database**

✔ **Analyzing how the objects in your database work together**

✔ **Loading Access add-ins**

✔ **Creating an MDE file**

An Access database can get big and complicated, with hundreds of different objects — tables, queries, forms, reports, macros, and other stuff you find about in other parts of the book. Given this fact, you need to keep your database neat and tidy, or the file size balloons and it becomes just plain confusing to use. This chapter describes how to compact, repair, back up, analyze, and configure your database.

Compacting and Repairing Your Database

As you make changes to your database, Access stores new information in the database file and marks the old information for deletion. However, the old information isn't actually removed from your database file right away. In fact, most database files have a tendency to get larger and larger, just because Access (like most other programs) isn't very good at taking out the garbage. To shrink your database back down, you *compact* the database file.

The process of compacting a database also repairs errors that crop up in the file. Occasional Access bugs, Windows bugs, or cosmic rays from the planet Jupiter can cause objects in the database to become *corrupted* — or broken, if you prefer a more straightforward term. Compacting the database repairs these corrupted objects.

To compact and repair your database when the database is open, follow these steps:

1. **Close all tables, queries, forms, reports, and other database objects, including the Visual Basic Editor.**

   Access can't compact the database if objects are open.

2. **Choose Tools➪Database Utilities➪Compact and Repair Database from the main menu.**

   Access compacts the database. When the status indicator at the bottom of the Access window hits 100 percent and the mouse pointer stops appearing as an hourglass, the compacting is done. If you don't see any error messages, the compacting worked perfectly, and no repairs were needed.

If your computer is on a network and you suspect other people may be using your database, make sure that no one else has your database open before compacting it.

You can also compact a database that's not open. Access leaves the original database unchanged and asks you for a new file name to use for the compacted version — the original database is left as a backup. With no database open, follow these steps:

1. **Choose Tools➪Database Utilities➪Compact and Repair Database.**

   Access displays the Database to Compact From dialog box that looks just like an Open dialog box.

2. **Choose the name of the database you want to compact and click the Compact button.**

   The Compact Database Into dialog box appears that looks just like a Save As dialog box.

3. **Type a new name for the compacted database and click the Save button.**

   Access compacts the database and saves it with the new name.

Making Backups

Backing up your database is vital. If you're not sure about this, think about the amount of effort required if the database vanishes from your hard disk. Think about your boss's fury. Think about the killing boredom of typing all that information in again. Okay, you get the idea — backups are a good thing.

Ideally, you should back up your entire hard disk, or at least the files that you create or edit. (Backing up program files is usually pointless: You should have all the CDs to reinstall your programs, if need be.) A good backup system creates backup copies of all your files — perhaps all the files in the My Documents folder of your computer — on a regular basis (nightly?) on tapes, ZIP disks, or writable CDs.

For a listing of Windows-compatible backup programs, go to the Microsoft Windows Catalog site at www.windowscatalog.com and click the Software tab. Then choose Utilities⇨Backup from the list on the left side. (If Microsoft redesigns this site, just look for the equivalent links or buttons.)

For more information about backups, see *Troubleshooting Your PC For Dummies*, by the amazing Dan Gookin (published by Wiley Publishing, Inc.).

Backing up your database

We can't force you to make backup copies of all the files on your hard drive, but we *can* suggest in the strongest terms possible that you at least create regular backup copies of your Access database. Follow these steps:

1. **Make sure that all the objects in your database are closed. Click the X (Close) button in the upper-right corner of all the windows in your Access window *except* the Database window. (Clicking that particular X closes the database itself.)**

   If the Microsoft Visual Basic window is open, close that, too.

2. **Choose File⇨Back Up Database.**

   You see the Save Backup As dialog box, which looks just like a Save As dialog box. In the File Name box, Access suggests a file name for the backup copy, consisting of the original file name with today's date stuck on the end — an excellent suggestion, in our opinion.

3. **Change the folder or file name if you want, and then click Save.**

   Access creates a duplicate copy of your database.

Backing up your database on the same hard disk that stores the original database is a good first step, but what if your hard disk dies? Consider backing up the database on a ZIP disk or CD-R disc. To make a backup copy on a ZIP disk or another hard disk, use the File⇨Back Up Database command from within Access, or use Windows Explorer (My Computer) to copy the file. To make a copy on a CD-R disc (recordable CD), use the software that came with your CD burner. (Windows XP users can also use its CD-burning facility, which is built into Windows Explorer.)

Backing up specific objects

You may also want to back up only part of your database — maybe only a few tables contain data that changes frequently. You can export objects to another Access database for backup. First you need to create a blank database to which you can export objects, and then you can export them.

Follow these steps to create a new, blank database:

1. **Choose File⇨Close or close the Database window to close the database you're working with (if any).**

   Don't close the Access window — you still need to use Access.

 2. **Choose File⇨New, press Ctrl+N, or click the New Database icon on the toolbar.**

   Access displays the New File task pane.

3. **Click the Blank Database link in the New section of the task pane.**

   You see the File New Database dialog box, which looks just like a Save As dialog box.

4. **Type a name for the database (how about "Backup" followed by the name of your main database?) and click the Create button.**

   Access makes the new database and opens its Database window.

5. **Close your new backup database.**

   It's ready to hold backup copies of your most important Access objects.

Now follow these steps each time you want to back up an object in your Access database.

1. **Open the database that contains the object that you want to export.**

   While you're at it, display its Database window (press F11).

2. **Select the object that you want to export in the Database window.**

   For example, click the Tables button in the Objects list of the Database window and, from the list that appears in the window's right pane, click the table whose data changes the most often.

3. **Choose File⇨Export.**

   You see the Export To dialog box. Actually, the dialog box title includes the type and name of the object you are exporting, such as Export Table Orders To.

4. **Select the name of the backup database that you created earlier and click the Export button.**

   The Export dialog box appears, as shown in Figure 1-1, listing which object is exporting and what its name is in the backup database.

5. **Edit the name that the object will have in the backup database.**

   For example, if it's Christmas Eve and you are exporting the Orders table, you may want to name it "Orders 12-24-03." We like to use file names that sort in chronological order, so we'd name it "Orders 03-12-24."

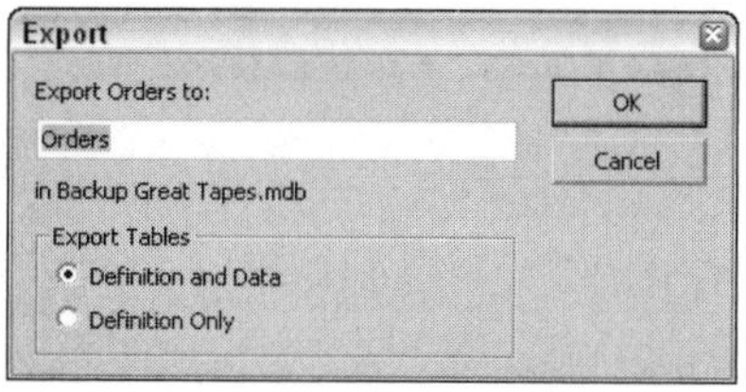

Figure 1-1:
Exporting a
table to a
backup
database.

Export

Export Orders to:

Orders

in Backup Great Tapes.mdb

Export Tables
- ⦿ Definition and Data
- ○ Definition Only

OK

Cancel

6. **Choose whether to export the structure only or the data, too, if you are exporting a table.**

   Select the Definition and Data radio button if you want all the records in the table, or the Definition Only radio button if you want a blank table with no records. For backup purposes, go with the Definition and Data option.

7. **Click OK.**

   Access creates a duplicate object in the backup database with the same information stored in the current database.

Converting Databases

Access 2003 uses the same file format as Access 2002 (Office XP) for storing its database. However, earlier versions of Access use slightly different file formats. Book I, Chapter 3 describes how to choose between Access 2002 and previous file formats. See Book I, Chapter 2 for what happens when you open older Access databases in Access 2003.

You can tell what version a database is by opening it in Access and looking at the title bar of the Database window. (Press F11 if the Database window isn't visible.) The title bar may say "(Access 2000 file format)" or "(Access 2002-2003 file format)." If the title bar says nothing at all about file formats, your file is in Access 2002 format.

To convert a database from an older file format to the Access 2002-2003 format, open the database, close all the windows except the Database window, and choose Tools➪Database Utilities➪Convert Database➪To Access 2002-2003 File Format. Type a new file name for the converted database and click the Save button. Access creates a new database with all the objects in the old database, but stored in the new format.

You can use almost the same command to convert an Access 2003 database into an older format. Choose Tools➪Database Utilities➪Convert Database and choose the older format — your choices are Access 2000 and Access 97. (Access 2003 can't convert database formats older than those.)

Analyzing and Documenting Your Database

Access includes a number of commands that help you analyze your database, especially in terms of how the objects in your database connect together. The following sections detail some of them.

Viewing relationships in the Relationships window

Keeping the relationships straight between tables can be a tricky business. For help, choose Tools⇨Relationships or click the Relationships button on the toolbar to display the Relationships window, which shows you how your tables connect together. For example, in an order entry database, your Customers table has a one-to-many relationship with your Orders table, because one customer may place zero, one, or many orders. (See Book II, Chapter 6 for how to use this window, including how to move stuff around.)

Looking at a list of the objects in your database

Need a handy list of all the objects in your database? Choose File⇨Database Properties to display the Properties sheet for your database. Click the Contents tab, shown in Figure 1-2, to see a list of all the objects in the database, listed by type. This list is cool, but printing is impossible.

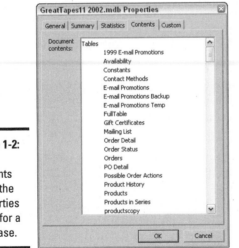

Figure 1-2:
The Contents tab in the Properties sheet for a database.

Viewing object dependencies

Access can show you a list of the tables, queries, forms, and reports that depend on an object. Say you have a query in your database that you never use, but you're not sure you can delete it because it may very well be the record source for a form or report. Access can ease your worried mind on this subject. To display the Object Dependencies task pane shown in Figure 1-3, right-click an object in the Database window and choose the Object Dependencies option from the shortcut menu that appears.

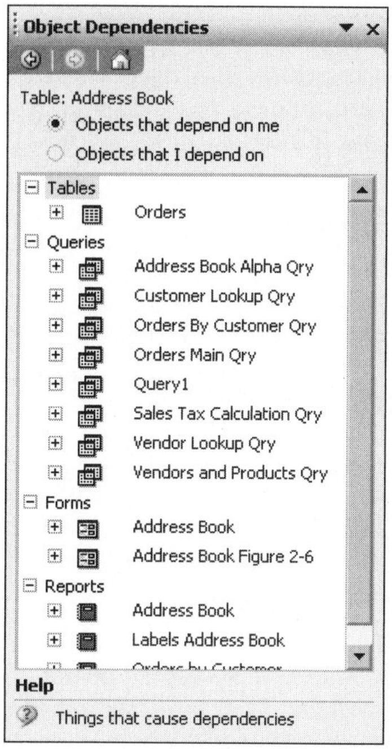

Figure 1-3:
What tables, queries, forms, and reports depend on this query?

Book VII
Chapter 1

Database
Housekeeping

⚠️ **WARNING!**

Before you can use this feature, you have to turn on the Name AutoCorrect feature (see the sidebar "Tracking name changes" in this chapter, to find out why). When you choose View➪Object Dependencies, if Name AutoCorrect is turned off, Access asks whether Name AutoCorrect can be turned on. The View➪Object Dependencies command is new in Access 2003, and it isn't available for databases stored in the Access 2000 or 97 format.

At the top of the Object Dependencies task pane is the name of the object that you are analyzing. (It has to be a table, query, form, or report: Access can't show the dependencies of data access pages, macros, or VBA modules.) After the object name are two options:

✦ **Objects That Depend On Me:** Choosing this option lists the tables, queries, forms, and reports that use this object as a data source. The objects that depend on a table include the queries based on the table and the forms and reports that use the table as a record source. The objects that depend on a form include forms of which this is a subform.

✦ **Objects That I Depend On:** Choosing this option lists the tables, queries, forms, and reports that directly provide input for this object. The objects that a report depends on include the query or table that makes up its record source, as well as any reports used as subreports on this report.

After the Object Dependencies task pane displays information about one object, you can't simply switch to another object. To see the dependencies for another object, right-click the object in the Database window and choose the Object Dependencies option from the shortcut menu. When you are done looking at object dependencies, click the X button in the upper-right corner of the Objects Dependencies task pane to make the task pane disappear.

Tracking name changes

In early versions of Access (before Access 2000), if you changed the name of a field in a table, the old name would remain in all the forms, queries, and reports that referred to that field. You needed to find all the field name references by hand and change them to the new field name. Ditto for changes to the names of objects on forms and reports. What a pain!

Access 2000 added a feature called Name AutoCorrect that notices if you change a field or object name and tries to correct it wherever the name appears in queries, forms, and reports. (Macros or VBA procedures are not updated.)

For Name AutoCorrect to work, you need to turn it on. Choose Tools➪Options to display the Tools dialog box, click the General tab, and select the Track Name AutoCorrect Info check box (if it's not already). When you turn on this feature, Access creates a *name map* for all the objects

in the database, which takes a few minutes. After the name map is created, Access updates the name map whenever you make changes to field or object names, and tries to update all the references to them.

You need to turn on Name AutoCorrect tracking if you want to display object dependencies. However, if you actually want Access to fix references to objects when you rename them, you need to select the Perform Name AutoCorrect check box on the General tab of the Options dialog box, too. This option tells Access to not only maintain the name maps, but also to use them for renaming.

Name AutoCorrect isn't perfect. It doesn't fix the names in objects that you create before you turned tracking on, because no name map exists for them. And it doesn't fix macros or VBA module names. But it's better than nothing!

Analyzing database performance

The Performance Analyzer looks at and improves the speed and efficiency of your database, and it also suggests changes, such as shrinking unnecessarily large fields and adding indexes. Creating indexes for fields in your tables speeds up sorts and searches. (See Book II, Chapter 1 for how to create an index for a field in a table.)

To improve your database's performance, follow these steps:

1. **Open the database and then close all the objects in it — except the Database window itself.**

2. **Choose Tools⇨Analyze⇨Performance.**

You see the Performance Analyzer dialog box, shown in Figure 1-4.

Figure 1-4:
The Performance Analyzer improves your database's performance.

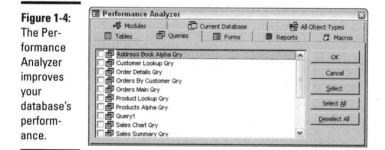

Book VII
Chapter 1

Database
Housekeeping

3. **Select the objects you want to analyze.**

To do so, click the Tables, Queries, Forms, Reports, Macros, or Modules tab and then click the check boxes next to the specific objects to include in the analysis. To select all the objects of a type, click the tab for the type and click the Select All button. On the Current Database tab, click the Relationships check box to ask Access to look at the relationships among your tables. If you want Access to analyze everything, click the All Object Types tab and the Select All button.

4. **Click OK to begin the analysis.**

This may take a few minutes. When the analysis is complete, a new Performance Analyzer dialog box appears, as shown in Figure 1-5. Each result on the list is classified as a Recommendation (a change that Access recommends and can fix for you), a Suggestion (a change that may have some drawbacks, but that Access can make for you), or Idea (a change that Access can't make, but that you can make yourself).

When you click a result, more information about the result appears in the lower part of the Performance Analyzer dialog box.

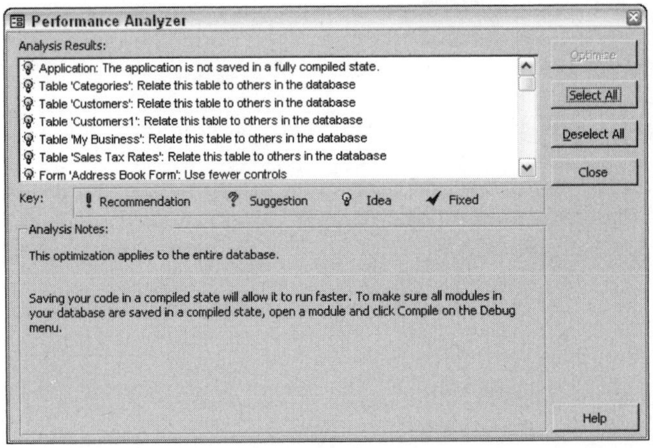

Figure 1-5:
The Per-
formance
Analyzer
lists its
results.

5. **For each recommendation or suggestion that you want Access to fix for you, select the result and click the Optimize button.**

   Access tries to make any recommended or suggested change, and displays a message about its success or lack thereof.

6. **Make a note of the ideas that you may want to try.**

   Write down any of the ideas that you want to look into, because you can't print out the ideas, and you can't give any commands until you close the Access windows.

7. **Click the Close button to close the Performance Analyzer dialog box.**

We haven't found the Performance Analyzer's suggestions to be particularly useful, but giving it a try is worth the effort — we expect Microsoft to improve this feature in future versions of Access. The Performance Analyzer does a good job of spotting fields that should be indexes to speed up searches and sorts.

Documenting your database

You can create reports that describe the design and properties of the objects in your database. With the database open and all objects other than the Database window closed, choose Tools⇨Analyze⇨Documenter to open the Documenter dialog box, shown in Figure 1-6.

Figure 1-6:
Access
prints doc-
umentation
about the
objects
in your
database
from the
Documenter
dialog box.

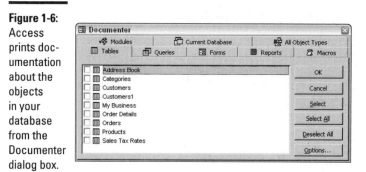

The Documenter dialog box works (and looks) just like the Performance Analyzer dialog box shown in Figure 1-4 — you click tabs and select check boxes to specify which objects in your database you want to document. When you click OK, Access creates a report showing details about the properties of the object. If you select a table, the report looks similar to Figure 1-7, with information about the table itself as well as about each field (column) in the table. The report about a form or report includes the properties of all the controls in the form or report design.

Choose just one object to document at a time — the report about each document can be many pages long!

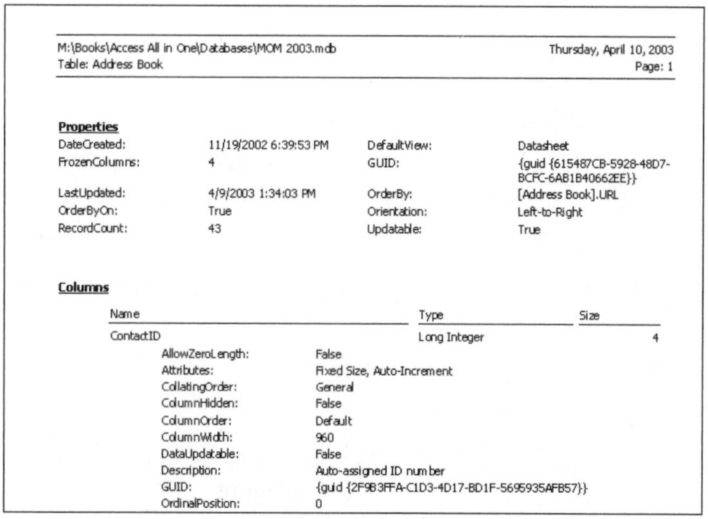

```
M:\Books\Access All in One\Databases\MOM 2003.mdb          Thursday, April 10, 2003
Table: Address Book                                                      Page: 1


Properties
DateCreated:         11/19/2002 6:39:53 PM    DefaultView:     Datasheet
FrozenColumns:       4                        GUID:            {guid {615487CB-5928-48D7-
                                                               BCFC-6AB1B40662EE}}
LastUpdated:         4/9/2003 1:34:03 PM      OrderBy:         [Address Book].URL
OrderByOn:           True                     Orientation:     Left-to-Right
RecordCount:         43                       Updatable:       True


Columns
        Name                                  Type              Size
        ContactID                             Long Integer         4
                AllowZeroLength:      False
                Attributes:           Fixed Size, Auto-Increment
                CollatingOrder:       General
                ColumnHidden:         False
                ColumnOrder:          Default
                ColumnWidth:          960
                DataUpdatable:        False
                Description:          Auto-assigned ID number
                GUID:                 {guid {2F9B3FFA-C1D3-4D17-BD1F-5695935AFB57}}
                OrdinalPosition:      0
```

Figure 1-7:
The Docu-
menter's
report
includes the
gory details
about a
table.

Loading and Managing Add-Ins

As with all of the programs in Microsoft Office, Access allows you to extend the functionality of Access through the use of add-ins. An *add-in* is a custom component, usually created by professional programmers. If you work in a large corporation that has an Information Technology (IT) department, programmers may create an add-in to make Access easier to use with your company's data.

Running the Add-in Manager

To use an add-in, you must first copy it to your computer's hard disk. To do that, you need the name and location of the add-in. If the add-in was created by your company's IT department, they can tell you the name and location of that add-in. After you copy the add-in to your hard drive, using the add-in is simple. Just follow these steps:

1. **Choose Tools⇨Add-Ins⇨Add-In Manager from the Access main menu.**

The Add-in Manager dialog box appears, as shown in Figure 1-8.

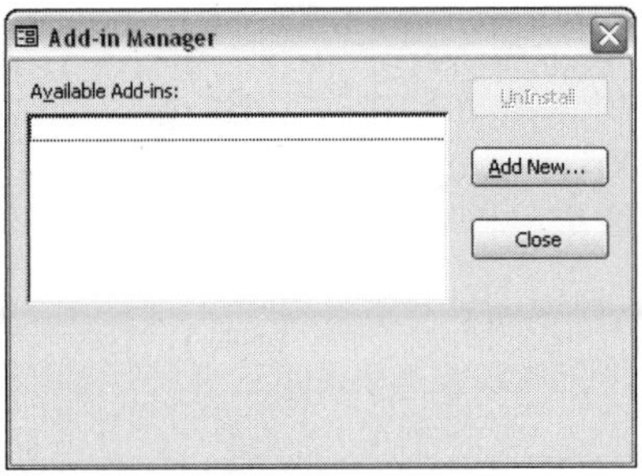

Figure 1-8: The Add-in Manager allows you to add, and remove, add-ins.

2. **To install an add-in, click the Add New button.**

An Open dialog box opens.

3. **Navigate to the folder in which the add-in is stored, and then click the Open button.**

4. **Repeat Steps 2 and 3 to add as many add-ins as you wish. Then click the Close button in the Add-in Manager dialog box.**

To remove an add-in, choose Tools⇨Add-Ins⇨Add-In Manager. In the Add-in Manager dialog box, select the name of the add-in you want to remove, and then click the Uninstall button.

Creating add-ins

Creating add-ins is the turf of serious programmers. Read this section if you are already a programmer — it's one big "Technical Stuff" section. This section points out the main things that you need to be aware of, such as creating wizards, custom menu items, or custom builders for Access. If you're not a programmer, skip to the next section of this chapter.

Office versus Access add-ins

Be aware that you can create two different types of add-ins. One is the *Component Object Model (COM) add-in.* A COM add-in works in multiple Office 2003 applications. You can write a single COM add-in to perform the same function in Access, Word, Excel, and PowerPoint. To create a COM add-in, you need to use Microsoft Visual C++, C#, J++, J#, or any of the languages available in the Microsoft Office 2003 Developer Edition. COM add-ins are dynamic link libraries (.dll files), and need to be registered with the operating system to allow them to be loaded by Microsoft Office 2003 applications.

The second of the two types of add-ins is the *application-specific add-in,* which works only in a single application, such as Microsoft Access. An *Access add-in* is designed only to work with Access. Access add-ins are easier to create than COM add-ins, and you don't need an entirely separate programming language. You can create Access add-ins using Visual Basic for Applications (VBA), which comes with Access. Access add-ins are stored in files that have an .mda or .mde extension.

To see what Visual Basic for Applications is all about, see Book VIII.

Types of add-ins

But even though Access add-ins are easier to create than COM add-ins, they're still far from simple to create. You really need to be fluent in VBA first in order to create any code at all. But you can create three main types of add-ins:

+ **Wizards:** Custom wizards are similar to the many wizards available throughout Access, to help less sophisticated users with complex tasks in a step-by-step manner.

+ **Builders:** Custom builders, similar to the Expression Builder, help users create complex expressions.

+ **Menu Add-In:** Make complex procedures available as options on the Access menu.

In order for your custom code to function as an add-in, you also need to create a USysRegInfo table that defines a subkey or value to be added to the Windows Registry. For details, go to the Microsoft Developer Network Web site at `msdn.microsoft.com` and search for the phrase *Access+Add-In*.

Locking Up Your Database as an MDE File

If you make an Access database for other people — especially people who may be a teeny bit clueless about Access — you may want to lock up your database to prevent other users from making changes that may break it. Chapter 3 of this book talks about adding security in the form of user names and passwords, but a simpler option is to turn your database from an MDB file to an MDE file.

What's an MDE file, we hear you asking. An *MDE file* is the same as a regular Access MDB database file, with the following changes:

✦ All VBA procedures are *compiled* — converted from human-readable code (more or less readable, anyway) to a format that only the computer understands. This change prevents a database user from reading or changing your VBA code. (See Book VIII for how to write VBA procedures.)

✦ No one can create forms or reports or modify the existing ones (you can't even open them in Design view). You can't import any, either.

Be sure to keep a copy of your original MDB file! If you need to make changes to your VBA code, forms, or reports (or create new ones), you need to use the MDB file, not the MDE file. MDE files are most commonly used for the front-end database when you split an application into two databases (front end and back end), as we describe in Chapter 2 of this book.

Creating an MDE file

Saving your MDB file as an MDE file is easy. Follow these steps:

1. **Make sure your database is in Access 2002/2003 file format by opening the database.**

Take a look at the title bar of the Database window. (Press F11 if it's not visible.) If the title bar says "(Access 2000 file format)" then you need to convert it to the latest file format. See the section, "Converting Databases," earlier in this chapter.

2. **Choose Tools⇨Database Utilities⇨Make MDE File.**

    Access closes the database to do the conversion. Then you see the Save
    MDE As dialog box.

3. **Specify the folder and file name for the file and click the Save button.**

    Access creates the new MDE file while leaving the original MDB file
    untouched. Then the new MDE file opens.

If Access runs into a problem while making the MDE file, a message appears
with a Show Help button. Click the button to find out what's wrong.

Making updates later

Sooner or later, you are going to want to make a new report or fix an annoying typo in a form. You have to go back to your MDB file to make these kinds
of changes, because you can't make changes in an MDE file.

If the MDE file is a front-end file, with no data stored in it, you can just make
your changes to the original MDB file and resave it as an MDE file. Because
all your data lives in the back-end database, you're all set. (If you don't know
what we are talking about, see Chapter 2 of this book.)

However, if your MDE file contains tables full of valuable information, you
can't just abandon it. If you use the MDE file to do data entry and editing,
that file contains your up-to-date tables. The original MDB file has editable
forms, reports, and VBA code, but doesn't have the latest version of the
data stored in your tables.

Not a problem. Follow these steps:

1. **Rename your MDE file as a backup file.**

    For example, add today's date to the end of the file name (right before
    the .mde part). You're about to create a new MDE file, but you don't
    want to lose the data in this file.

2. **Open the original MDB file and make any changes to contain the
    forms, reports, and VBA code that you want.**

    If you plan to make drastic changes, make a backup copy of the MDB
    first.

3. **Choose Tools⇨Database Utilities⇨Make MDE File and save it as an
    MDE file with the name that your MDE file originally had.**

    Now you have an updated MDE file with new, improved forms, reports,
    and VBA procedures, but with old data. You also have an updated MDB

file with your new, improved forms, reports, and VBA code (but out-of-date tables).

4. **Delete all the tables from this new MDE file.**

   In the Database window, click the Tables button in the Objects list, click each table in the list that appears in the right pane and then press the Delete key for each table. You need to confirm each deletion by clicking the Yes button. Deleting tables sounds dangerous, but remember you have all these tables stored safely in your old MDE file.

5. **Import the tables from the old MDE file to the new one.**

   Choose File⇨Get External Data⇨Import and choose the name you gave your old MDE file in Step 1.

   You see the Import Objects dialog box, with tabs for Tables, Queries, Forms, Reports, and other objects.

6. **Click the Select All button with the Tables tab selected and then click OK.**

   Access imports your tables from the original MDE to the new MDE files, replacing the older data in the tables.

7. **Import any queries or macros in the old MDE database that you created or changed.**

   Repeat Steps 5 and 6, but use the Queries and Macros tabs on the Import Objects dialog box to import whatever changed.

If you are going to do this often, consider splitting your table into a front end and a back end, as described in Chapter 2 of this book. With a split database, you don't have to re-import your updated tables: You can just leave them in the unchanged back-end database.

Chapter 2: Sharing the Fun — and the Database: Managing Multi-User Access

In This Chapter

✔ Sharing an Access database over a LAN

✔ Setting up groups of objects that people use frequently

✔ Splitting your database into a front end (for each user) and a back end (where the data lives)

✔ Editing data when someone else may be editing the same record

*Y*our database probably contains such terrific information that lots of people in your organization want to use it. If the database stores customer names and addresses, your colleagues may want to use this information — and wouldn't it be great if only one person had to enter an address correction in a shared address book, instead of everyone maintaining a separate one?

Access has been a *multi-user database* right from the beginning. More than one person can get at the information in your database in these ways:

✦ **Everyone uses Access to open the database.** If your computer is on a LAN (local area network), you can store your Access database on a shared network drive and other people can run Access and open your database — keep reading to find out more.

✦ **Some people see the database information via Web-based forms.** Book IX, Chapter 1 describes how you can create *data access pages* that allow anyone on your LAN (anyone with access to the database file, anyway) to see and/or edit database information by using a Web browser.

✦ **Store your data in a big, industrial-strength database server application. Everyone uses Access to see the database.** If your database gets really large, or you want a lot of people to be able to see and maintain it simultaneously (more than, say, 40 or 50 people), Access may not be able to handle the load. Not a big problem. Move the tables to a database server program such as Oracle or SQL Server, and continue to use your Access queries, forms, or reports to work with it. You link your Access database to the tables in the database server.

How you link an Access database to a database server depends on which server you use. Book II, Chapter 4 tells you how to link to tables in other database programs. Book IX, Chapter 2 explains how to scale an Access database up to an Access project, for use with a database server program.

✦ **Use database replication.** Access has a feature that allows you to make copies of a database and pass them out to people who can make changes to the database. When you get the updated copies of your database back, Access combines all the information together. However, this method is complicated and (in our experience) error-prone, so we recommend that you use database replication only if you can't use another method.

This chapter describes how to set up a database in order for more than one person to open it at the same time, using computers that connect to a LAN.

Putting Your Database Where They Can See It

For other people on a LAN to be able to open your Access database, you need to store it in a *shared folder* — a *share,* for short. Follow these steps to make a shared folder in Windows XP:

1. **Choose Start⇨My Computer to start Windows Explorer.**

You see the My Computer window, listing your folders and disks. (See *Windows XP For Dummies*, by Andy Rathbone, if you want to know more about it.)

2. **Move to your Shared Documents folder.**

In Windows XP, other LAN users have access to this folder.

3. **Choose File⇨New⇨Folder from the menu, type in a name for the folder, and press Enter.**

Shared Databases or *Databases* may be a good name for the folder.

If you store your database file in this new folder, other people on the LAN can open it. Check with your LAN administrator to find out how to see a shared folder from each computer on the LAN that may want to use your database.

You don't have to make this folder in the Shared Documents folder. If you create it somewhere else, though, you need to share the folder with other people. In Windows Explorer, right-click the new folder and choose the Sharing and Security option from the shortcut menu that appears. A Properties dialog box appears for the folder, with the Sharing tab selected.

Choose the Share This Folder on the Network option and type a name in the Share Name box for the folder by which other people will see it. Click OK. You can tell that a folder is shared because its icon includes a little hand.

If you store a shared database on your computer, everyone else depends on the stability and speed of your computer. If you restart Windows after installing the latest update to your favorite game of solitaire, everyone else loses the edits they make to the database. If you decide to run a big, hairy application that slows your computer down to a crawl, the other users of your database crawl, too. If your database is important, consider storing it on a network server, or at least on a little-used or lightly used PC.

Splitting Your Database into a Front End and a Back End

If you create a multi-user database, consider splitting your database into two pieces: the data (the tables and the relationships among them) and everything else. The database with the data is called the *back end* and the database with everything else — the queries, forms, reports, macros, and VBA procedures — is called the *front end*. You and other database users open the front-end database, which contains links to the tables in the back-end database. Figure 2-1 shows how the two databases connect.

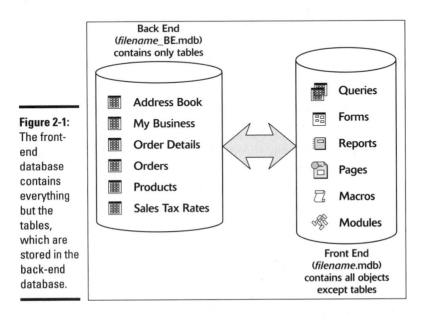

Figure 2-1: The front-end database contains everything but the tables, which are stored in the back-end database.

Back End
(*filename*_BE.mdb)
contains only tables

- Address Book
- My Business
- Order Details
- Orders
- Products
- Sales Tax Rates

- Queries
- Forms
- Reports
- Pages
- Macros
- Modules

Front End
(*filename*.mdb)
contains all objects
except tables

What if some people have Access 97?

Be aware of what Access version you use for your database files. Access 2000 (which comes with Office 2000), 2002 (Office XP), and 2003 all use the same file format. If anyone uses Access 97, you have two options: Upgrade this person to Access 2000 or later or make your database readable by Access 97. If people are using even earlier versions of Access, make them upgrade — too much has changed since Access 95!

If you have to support Access 97 users, then your back-end database must be stored in Access 97 format. In Access 2003, choose Tools⇨Database Utilities⇨Convert Database⇨ To Access 97 File Format to convert your back-end database to Access 97. Put this database — in place of your Access 2003 version — in the shared folder, which everyone now links to. Luckily, later versions of

Access can all link to tables in an Access 97 database.

You also need to create an Access 97 version of the front-end database for your Access 97 users. The best idea is usually to maintain two front ends: one version in Access 2000 (for your 2000, 2003, and 2003 users) and one in Access 97 (for your 97 users). Name them *filename_2000_fe.mdb* and *filename_97_fe.mdb*, store them in a shared folder, and tell your users to copy the appropriate version to their computer for their use.

When you convert the front-end database to Access 97, you may see error messages if your database uses features that don't exist in Access 97. You may need to recreate an Access 97 front end, starting with a blank database in Access 97 format and importing only the database objects that work.

Why split?

Splitting your database in two has some advantages. Two scenarios you could come across that have nothing to do with multi-user databases are

✦ **You don't need to back up the front end nearly as often as the back end, because the front end rarely changes.** By splitting your database into two files, you can back up just the back end, where the constantly updated data lives. (You do back up your data every day, right? See Chapter 1 of this book to find out how.)

✦ **If you create a database that you plan to hand out to other people and each person has his or her own data, storing data in a separate back-end database is important.** But all the users have the same front-end database. When you improve the front-end database, you replace everyone's old front-end database with your new one, without messing up each person's data, which is stored safely in the back end. For example, you may create a church management database program that tracks church members, committees, and donations, and then sell the database to zillions of congregations. By splitting the database, you can provide updates to the front end later (with improved forms, reports, and programming), without disturbing each congregation's data in the back-end database.

Splitting your database is even more important if you create a multi-user database in which everyone opens the same forms and edits the same data, possibly at the same time:

✦ **Each person has his or her own front-end database with user-specific forms and reports.** But all the front ends can connect to the same shared back-end database.

✦ **You can protect the front-end database by saving it as an MDE file.** (See Chapter 1 of this book.) People can't change the VBA code, macros, forms, or reports in an MDE file.

✦ **If the database grows into a huge project, the back-end part can migrate to a larger database system, such as MySQL or SQL Server, without changing the Access front end.** Your Access front end can link to large corporate databases as well as to an Access back-end database.

Of course, a few disadvantages exist:

✦ **You need to keep track of both files.** You can't get far with only one of the two databases. If you need to move your database to another computer, be sure to move both files. Back up both files regularly, too.

✦ **If you want to change the design of the tables in your database, you need to remember to make your changes in the back-end database.** Then make sure that the links still work from the front end.

Let's split!

Access comes with a Database Splitter Wizard that splits a database into front and back ends — and even creates the links between the two databases.

To split your database into front-end and back-end databases, follow these steps:

1. **Make a backup copy of your database.**

You never know what could go wrong, and you certainly don't want your entire database to be trashed. (See Chapter 1 of this book for info on backing up your database.)

2. **Open the database in Access and close all the windows except the Database window.**

   Close all tables and anything that may refer to a table because the wizard can't run if any are open.

3. **Choose Tools⇨Database Utilities⇨Database Splitter from the main menu.**

   The Database Splitter Wizard appears, as shown in Figure 2-2.

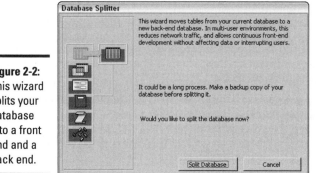

Figure 2-2: This wizard splits your database into a front end and a back end.

4. **Click the Split Database button.**

   You see the Create Back-End Database dialog box, which looks just like a Save As dialog box.

5. **Type a name for the back-end database and click the Split button.**

   The wizard suggests the same name as your original database, followed by "-be" (for *back end*). You may want to use the original name plus the word "Data".

   Access creates a new, empty database with the name you specify. Each table exports to this new database, including the relationships among the tables, and then attaches the tables in the new back-end database to the current database, which has become the front-end database.

   The wizard displays a message when finished, indicating whether the split was successful.

6. **Click OK.**

If you open the back-end database directly in Access, you find only tables — no queries, forms, reports, macros, or VBA modules. If you open the original database (which is now the front end), the tables are replaced by links to the tables in the back end.

Splitting by hand

Some people just don't trust wizards. If you'd rather split your database by hand rather than using the wizard, follow these steps:

1. **Create a blank database in your shared folder and name it** *filename*_be.mdb, **where** *filename* **is the original database name (or whatever name you want to use for the database).**

   This database is the back end. Make sure to store it in the shared folder where the back-end database lives and where other users can access it. Refer to Book I, Chapter 3 for how to make a new database.

2. **Choose File⇨Get External Data⇨Import with the new database open.**

   You see the Import dialog box.

3. **Choose the name of the database you want to split and click the Import button.**

   You see the Import Objects dialog box with a tab for each type of database object you can import.

4. **Click the Select All button with the Tables tab selected and then click OK.**

   Access imports all the tables from your original database — their names appear in the Database window. The back-end database is ready to roll!

5. **Close the back-end database.**

6. **In Windows Explorer (My Computer), make a copy of the database you want to split. Name the copy with the same name you used in Step 1, but ending with "_fe" instead of "_be".**

   This copy is the front end. You are making a copy so that you leave your original database untouched, just in case something goes wrong.

7. **Open the new front-end database.**

8. **Click the Tables button in the Objects list of the Database window to see all your tables — the ones you just imported into the back-end database — displayed in the right pane of the Database window.**

9. **Delete all the tables, one by one, by selecting each one, pressing the Delete key, and clicking the Yes button to confirm the deletion.**

   If Access reports that a relationship exists between the table you are deleting and other tables, click the Yes button to delete it.

   If you don't want to have to click the Yes button each time, choose Tools⇨Options, click the Edit/Find tab, and uncheck the Document Deletions check box.

10. Choose File⇨Get External Data⇨Link Tables.

You see the Link dialog box, which looks just like the Import dialog box.

11. Choose your back-end database and click the Link button.

You see the Link Tables dialog box with a list of the tables in the back-end database.

12. Click the Select All button and then OK to make links to all the tables in the back-end database.

Your table names reappear in the Database window, but with an arrow next to the icon for each one, to indicate that the table links from another database. Access even imports the relationships between the tables!

Handing out front ends

Each person who uses your shared database needs a copy of the front-end database on his or her own computer. (You can open a front-end database from a shared folder, but it loads and runs much more slowly.) You can copy the front end to each person's computer, or copy the front end to a shared folder and tell everyone to copy the file.

Before you pass out the front-end database, consider saving it as an MDE file, so that people can't accidentally mess up the forms, reports, or VBA code. (See Chapter 1 of this book for more on saving a database file as an MDE file.) If you do, save a copy of the MDB file, too, so that you have a way to make updates.

Relinking your tables

The links between the two databases work only as long as the files are in the same positions relative to each other. If you create the back-end database in the same folder as the original database, the two databases need to be in the same folder to work. If you need to move one of the files (you move the back-end database to a network drive where you can share it with other users on a LAN and give copies of the front-end to the computers of various people in your office), you need to re-link the tables. To do so, follow these steps:

1. Put the front and back ends in their new locations.

The two databases need to be in their new positions in order to be sure that everything works.

2. **Open the front-end database and click the Tables button in the Database window.**

   All your tables appear in the right pane of the Database window.

   Now you're ready to re-link tables.

3. **Right-click any table name and choose the Linked Table Manager option from the shortcut menu that appears, or choose Tools⇨ Database Utilities⇨Linked Table Manager from the Access menu.**

   The Linked Table Manager opens.

4. **Click the Select All button, and then click the OK button.**

   The Select New Location Of dialog box opens.

5. **Navigate to the folder in which you put the back-end database, and click the icon for that back-end database.**

6. **Click the Open button in the dialog box, and then click the Close button in the Linked Table Manager dialog box.**

   Now Access knows the correct locations of your linked tables.

See Book II, Chapter 4 for more on how to create a link in one database to a table in another database.

Putting Your Favorite Objects into Groups

The Objects list in the Database window has a button for each type of object that makes up an Access database, but having to click and scroll around the list for the forms and reports that you use the most can be annoying. If several people use a database, each person may have favorite objects that are used every day.

Access has a solution to this problem — groups. A *group* is like a folder in which you can put shortcuts to your favorite objects. Instead of having to search in the list for the forms and reports (or other objects) that you usually open, you can collect shortcuts to them in one place.

To see the groups in an Access database, click the Groups button at the bottom of the Database window's Objects list. When you click it, the existing groups appear. If you haven't created any groups, you see only one, named Favorites.

If you have a lot of groups, click the Groups button in the Database window twice. Access shrinks the Objects list down to a single button (Objects) and uses the left side of the Database window for a list of your groups, as shown in Figure 2-3. To see your tables, queries, and other objects again, click the Objects button.

Groups button

Objects button

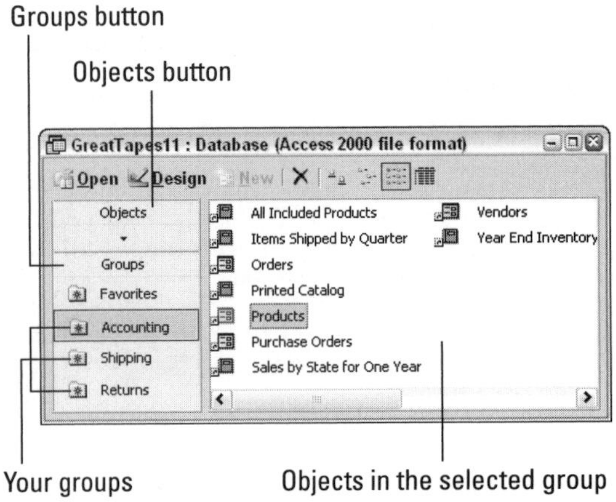

Figure 2-3:
A group contains shortcuts to your favorite objects.

Your groups

Objects in the selected group

Putting objects in a group

To put a shortcut to an object into a group, follow these steps:

1. **Click the Objects button in the Database window to see the usual Objects list, and then click the button for the type of object you want a shortcut for.**

If you want to add the Orders form to your Favorites group, click the Forms button.

2. **Right-click the object you want and choose the Add to Group option from the shortcut menu that appears. Then choose the name of the group to which you want to add it.**

If you haven't created any groups yet, your only option is the Favorites group.

Nothing appears to happen, but if you click the Groups button and the group name, a shortcut icon now appears in the Database window.

Making and unmaking new groups

If only one person (you) uses the database, you can simply use the Favorites group. But if several people use this database (whether it's a single-file database or a front-end database), you can make a group for each person — or group of people — who use the database. For example, you may make groups for Accounting, Shipping, and Returns because the people in these three departments tend to use different forms and reports.

To create a new group, follow the steps in the previous section to put an object in a group, but choose Add to Group⇨New Group when you right-click the object. Or click the Groups button to display the names of existing groups, right-click a group name, and choose the New Group option from the shortcut menu that appears. With an object selected in the Database window, choose Edit⇨Groups⇨New Group from the Access menu. Then type a name for the new group and click OK. The new group appears after the Groups button.

To rename a group, right-click it and choose the Rename Group option from the shortcut menu that appears. Type a new name and click OK. If you want to get rid of a group, right-click it and choose the Delete Groups option from the shortcut menu that appears. Click the Yes button to continue. Don't worry — the original objects aren't deleted, only the shortcuts.

Using groups

Why bother creating groups and putting shortcuts to objects in them? You'll like having shortcuts to all your favorite objects in one place. To open any object in a group, just double-click it. After you add all your favorite forms and reports to a group, you can use the group as a sort of main menu for the database.

Editing with Multiple Users

Actually, to set up Access for more than one person to open your database, you don't have to do a thing other than store the database file in a shared folder. Access has multi-user features built in! Just open the database once on your computer and again from a second computer. Poof! You're both using the database!

Everything works fine if multiple people use front-end and back-end data-bases, too. One back-end database lives in a shared folder and multiple people have copies of the front-end database running on their computers. When several people open the front end at the same time, they all link to tables in the back end. No problem!

Multi-user access works just great as long as everyone looks at the data without making any changes. Two people can look at the same table — even the same record — at the same time. People can open forms and print reports. Peachy.

Fixing exclusive access

Well, okay, you may have to do one thing. If the second person tries to open your database gets an error message saying that the database is already in use, you have Access in *exclusive mode,* in which the database opens for its own exclusive use. (How very exclusive!) If this happens, the person who has the database open needs to follow these steps:

1. **Choose Tools⇨Options from the Access menu.**

You see the Options dialog box, shown in Figure 2-4.

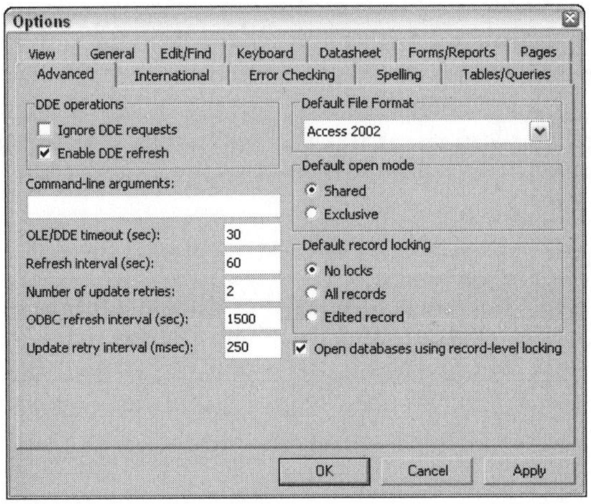

Figure 2-4:
You can set the default open mode and record-locking options for each database in the Options dialog box.

2. **Click the Advanced tab.**

The Default Open Mode section shows how Access opens each database.

3. **Click the Shared option in the Default Open Mode section and click OK.**

4. **Close the database and reopen it.**

Access now opens the database in *shared mode*.

Managing record-locking

Okay, everyone can look at the information in the database. But what happens when two people want to edit a table at the same time? Or worse, two people want to edit the same record at the same time? The Access *record-locking* feature handles this situation.

To turn on the record-locking feature, choose Tools⇨Options, click the Advanced tab in the Options dialog box, and look at the Default Record Locking section (refer to Figure 2-4). You have three options: No Locks, All

Records, and Edited Record. The following sections detail how these three options work.

No Locks (no record-locking)

Multi-user editing works as follows without record-locking, when you check the No Locks check box in the Options dialog box:

1. Person A opens a table or query (or a form based on a table or query) and begins editing a record.

2. Person B opens the same table or query, or a form or other query based on the same table that Person A is editing. Person B starts making changes to the exact same record that Person A is editing.

3. When Person A or Person B tries to save the record, Access displays the Write Conflict dialog box shown in Figure 2-5.

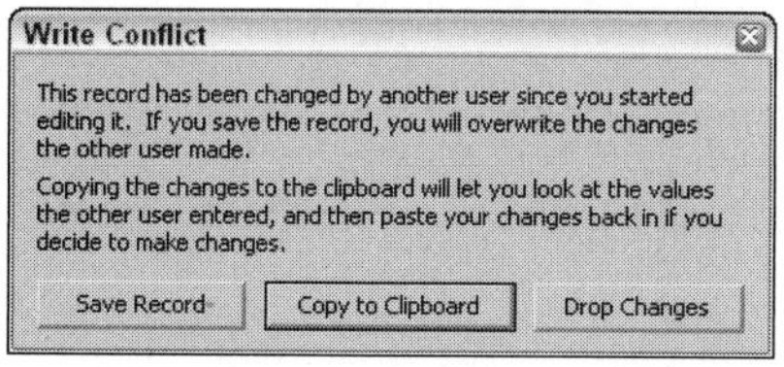

Figure 2-5:
Two people are trying to change this record at the same time.

Write Conflict	✕

This record has been changed by another user since you started editing it. If you save the record, you will overwrite the changes the other user made.

Copying the changes to the clipboard will let you look at the values the other user entered, and then paste your changes back in if you decide to make changes.

| Save Record | Copy to Clipboard | Drop Changes |

**Book VII
Chapter 2**

**Sharing the Fun —
and the Database**

4. If the person clicks the Save Record button, his or her changes write over whatever changes the other person made to the record. Not good. If the person clicks the Drop Changes button, he or she loses the changes in process. Also not good. Clicking the Copy to Clipboard button allows the person to compare the two people's changes and either choose between them or combine them. (This process is usually a pain — you need to check with the other person to compare changes and decide which to keep.)

Sometimes Access just beeps, or beeps and displays a message that says that the record is locked, even though you turned locking off.

The No Locks option is usually a bad choice, because people can end up losing changes to records. Why not let Access prevent this from happening?

The solution is for Access to lock the information that someone is editing. While the user is editing the information, no one else can make any changes. When the first person saves all changes, then the next person can start editing — each takes a turn; simple enough.

Records versus pages

Sometimes, Access locks more than just the record being edited. Access (and most other programs) stores information in chunks called *disk pages* or *pages* (these pages have nothing to do with the data access pages described in Book IX, Chapter 1). Access retrieves information from your hard disk a page at a time, and Access can lock an entire page worth of information much more easily than locking a single record, which is usually smaller than a page. (How many records fit in a page depends on how big each record is. If your table has large records with lots of fields, a record may even be larger than a single page of storage.)

Rather than locking individual records, this system is called *page-level locking* rather than real record-level locking. Page-locking is faster and easier for Access than real record-locking, but in some applications, page-locking just isn't good enough. If you have several people entering and editing orders in an order entry database at the same time, they may end up constantly locking each other out of records — very annoying.

You can control whether Access does true record-level locking or just page-level locking. On the Advanced tab of the Options dialog box (refer to Figure 2-4), check the Open Databases Using Record-Level Locking check box to use record-level locking.

All Records (lock the whole table)

If you choose the All Records option, when someone starts editing a record, Access locks the entire table that contains the record. When someone else tries to edit any record in the table, Access just beeps and refuses to allow changes. This option means that two people can't change different records at the same time. Some databases require this option — for example, if each record contains information based on the records before it. However, for most databases, each record stands on its own and you can allow simultaneous editing of separate records.

Edited Record (lock one record)

Our favorite record-locking setting is to just lock the record you are editing. Leave the rest of them available for other people to edit.

If you try to edit a record that someone else is editing, Access beeps and doesn't allow you to make changes. The international "don't even think about it" symbol also appears in the record selector when a record is locked, as shown in Figure 2-6. Within a few seconds after the other person saves the changes, Access displays the changes on-screen, too. Then you can make your changes.

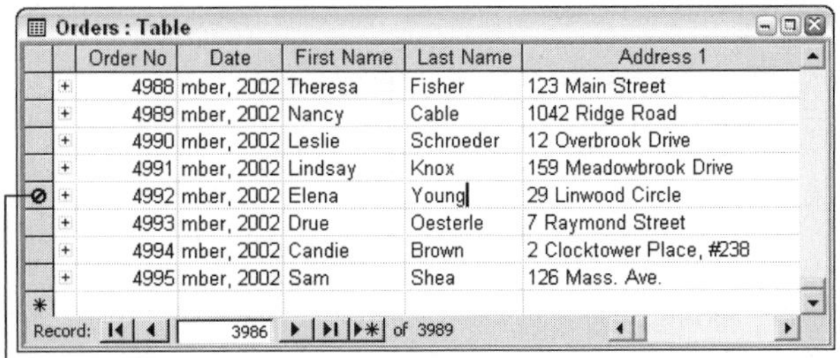

	Order No	Date	First Name	Last Name	Address 1
+	4988	mber, 2002	Theresa	Fisher	123 Main Street
+	4989	mber, 2002	Nancy	Cable	1042 Ridge Road
+	4990	mber, 2002	Leslie	Schroeder	12 Overbrook Drive
+	4991	mber, 2002	Lindsay	Knox	159 Meadowbrook Drive
Ø +	4992	mber, 2002	Elena	Young	29 Linwood Circle
+	4993	mber, 2002	Drue	Oesterle	7 Raymond Street
+	4994	mber, 2002	Candie	Brown	2 Clocktower Place, #238
+	4995	mber, 2002	Sam	Shea	126 Mass. Ave.

Record: ⏮ ◀ 3986 ▶ ⏭ ▶* of 3989

Figure 2-6:
The icon shows this record is locked.

Record is locked

Programming your locks

If you use forms to edit your tables (and most people do), you can control how each form locks records when someone uses the form to edit a record. Display the form in Design view by selecting it in the Database window and clicking the Design button. Display the Properties sheet for the form by clicking the Properties button on the toolbar. Click the Data tab on the Properties sheet and look at the Record Locks property of the form. You can set it to the No Locks, All Records, or Edited Records (the default) option.

You can also write VBA code to control the way that tables and records are locked. See Book VIII, Chapter 5 for how to write VBA code that edits records.

If you want different people to have permission to see or change different information, you need to find out about the Access security features, which we describe in Chapter 3 of this book.

**Book VII
Chapter 2**

**Sharing the Fun —
and the Database**

What's happening behind the scenes

Whenever anyone opens an Access database, Access creates a *Locking Information File* that contains information about who's doing what with the information in the database. Even if only one person opens the database, Access makes the file in the same folder and with the same file name as the database, but with the extension .ldb (people usually refer to this file as the *LDB file*). When you close the database, Access deletes the file: If more than one person has the database open, Access doesn't delete the folder until the last person closes the database.

Chapter 3: Securing Your Access Database

In This Chapter

✔ **Types of Access security**

✔ **Setting your startup options to secure the database**

✔ **Setting a database password**

✔ **How user-level security works**

✔ **Creating a workgroup information file**

✔ **Creating users and user groups in your database**

✔ **Assigning permissions to groups of users**

✔ **Password-protecting your VBA modules**

*A*fter you create a database, you may want to be able to control who can open it, look at the data, and change the data. If you're creating a database in which many people link to a shared back-end database, you should design security from the beginning — otherwise, your data is sure to deteriorate as different people use the database in different ways. Consistency may be the hobgoblin of little minds but it is vital for clean data. You owe the users of your database protection from them accidentally doing something dumb.

Be sure to use validation in your tables and forms, too — read all about it in Book II, Chapter 5.

Access has several mechanisms for adding security to your database:

+ **Startup options that you use to display your own forms, menus, and toolbars instead of the standard Access ones.** See the section, "Setting Startup Options," later in this chapter.

+ **Password-protecting your database.** See the section, "Setting a database password," later in this chapter.

+ **Converting your database to an MDE file to prevent anyone from editing forms, reports, and VBA modules.** Chapter 1 of this book describes this process.

✦ **User-level security, which allows you to create a system of users and permissions for what each user can do in your database.** See the section, "Granting Database Access to Specific Users," later in this chapter for the lowdown.

In addition, you can encrypt (encode) your database, regardless of what other security systems you use. (See the section, "Encrypting your database," later in this chapter.)

Windows Security

Your first line of defense for your Access database, no matter what Access security options you choose, is securing the computer where you store the database. Be sure you set a Windows password. If the database lives in a shared folder on a local area network, check with your LAN administrator to make sure that only the right people have access to the shared folder.

Part of security is making sure no one walks off with your database — such as copying it and taking it off-site — or deletes it! That's why Windows-level and LAN-level security is important.

For information about networking and Windows security, see *Networking For Dummies* (by Doug Lowe) or *Windows XP For Dummies* (by Andy Rathbone) — both are published by Wiley Publishing, Inc.

Setting Startup Options

If you don't want users entering data (except in the forms you create); modifying your tables, queries, forms, and other database objects; and generally screwing up your lovely Access system, you can prevent them from using (or even seeing) the normal toolbars and menus in Access. In both regular Access databases (.mdb files) and Access projects (.adp files, described in Book IX, Chapter 2), you can set the startup options to control what the database user can see and do.

Choose Tools⇨Startup from the main menu to display the Startup dialog box, shown in Figure 3-1, which is where most of the action takes place. The settings in the dialog box apply to the current database (or project). If you change them, many don't take effect until you exit and reopen the database. Table 3-1 lists the settings that control what users see and can do when they open your application.

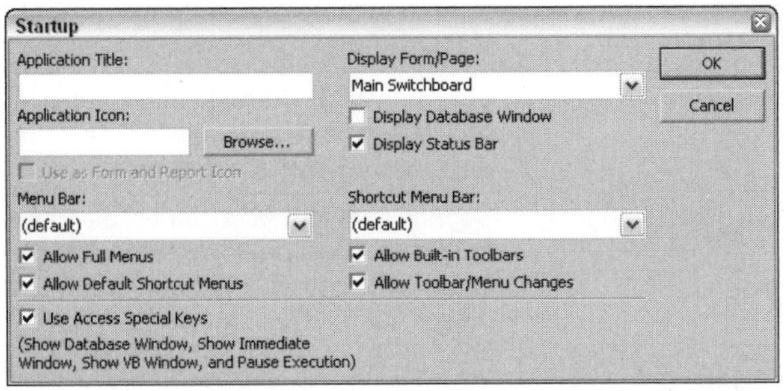

Figure 3-1:
The Startup
dialog box
shows
settings that
control what
appears
when
someone
opens your
database.

Table 3-1	The Startup Dialog Box Security Settings
Setting	*What It Does*
Application Title	Displays this title in the title bar of the Access window, instead of the usual Microsoft Office Access 2003.
Application Icon	Displays a different icon for this file, in place of the Access icon.
Display Form/Page	Specifies the form or data access page to open when the database opens. (Choose a switchboard or other main-menu-type form.)
Display Database Window	Controls whether the Database window is visible or hidden. You should hide it unless you want users able to open, rename, and delete all database objects!
Display Status Bar	Controls whether the status bar appears at the bottom of the Access window.
Menu Bar	Specifies what menu displays when the program starts. The default is the standard Access menu, but you can create your own. Other menus may appear as the user opens forms and reports that have their own menus. To associate your own menu bar with a form or report, see "Creating your own menus," later in this chapter.
Allow Full Menus	Controls which menus Access displays. If you deselect this check box, Access doesn't display any menu commands that allow the user to change the design of any database object.
Allow Default Shortcut Menus	Controls whether the usual Access shortcut menus appear when the user right-clicks something.

(continued)

Table 3-1 *(continued)*

Setting	What It Does
Shortcut Menu Bar	Specifies what shortcut menu appears when the user right-clicks in your database. See "Customizing shortcut menus," later in this chapter.
Allow Built-in Toolbars	Controls whether users can see and use the Access built-in toolbars. You can associate your own toolbars with forms and reports. See "Creating your own toolbars," later in this chapter.
Allow Toolbar/Menu Changes	Controls whether users can customize any toolbars or menu (the Access built-in ones or ones you provide).
Use Access Special Keys	Controls whether some key combinations work in Access (specifically, key combinations that display the Database, Immediate, and Microsoft Visual Basic Editor windows). Deselect this check box, if you don't want users displaying the Database window, by pressing F11.

After you customize a database using the Startup dialog box, when you (or anyone) open this database, Access performs the startup actions you specified. Then Access runs the AutoExec macro, if any, which performs additional actions. (See Book VI, Chapter 2 for how to create an AutoExec macro.)

Sometimes you need to bypass the settings in the Startup dialog box. No problem! Hold down the Shift key while the database opens. Of course, if other people use this shortcut, you have a huge security hole. You can set the AllowBypassKey property to the False setting for your database (using a macro or VBA procedure), but then *you* won't have a way in either. Be sure to save a version of your database *without* this command!

Creating your own toolbars

The built-in toolbars in Access contain all kinds of commands that allow the users of your database to make changes to objects in the database. For example, when you enter or edit data in a form, the toolbars include buttons that allow you to filter, add, and delete records — or even switch to Design view in order to change the form! What if you don't want to allow your users access to those commands? You need to get those buttons off your toolbars, or display your own toolbars.

You can create your own toolbars, and then associate them with forms and reports. You can make a toolbar that appears when your Order Entry form opens, with buttons that are useful for someone entering orders (but without dangerous buttons, such as the one that switches to Design view).

Making the toolbar

To get this toolbar-making show on the road, follow these steps:

1. Choose Tools⇨Customize from the main menu.

You see the Customize dialog box, shown in Figure 3-2, with the Toolbar tab selected.

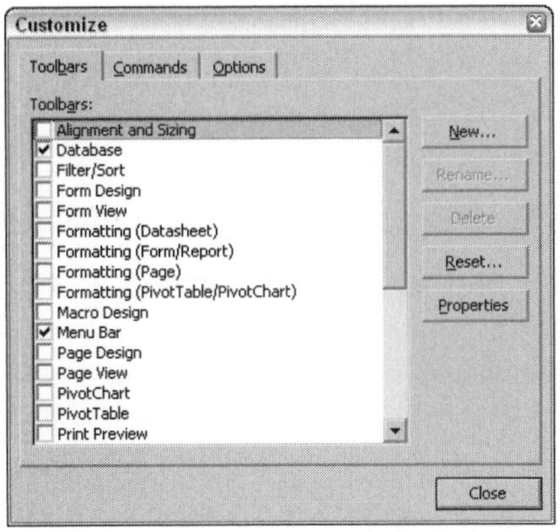

Figure 3-2: Creating a custom toolbar to display when a form or report is open.

2. Click the New button, type a name for your new toolbar, and click OK.

The toolbar now appears in the list of toolbars, and displays floating in the Access window. Because no buttons are on the toolbar yet, it's rather small.

3. Drag the toolbar to the top of the Access window with the other toolbars if you like all your toolbars together.

When your new toolbar gets near the other toolbars, it turns into a normal-looking toolbar (just smaller).

4. Select your new toolbar from the list on the Toolbars tab, click the Properties button to display the Toolbar Properties dialog box, and uncheck the Allow Customizing check box to prevent users from customizing the toolbar.

The check boxes by the toolbars in the Customize dialog box control whether the toolbars are currently displayed on-screen — they don't control which toolbar is selected for customization. You can tell which toolbar is selected because its entire name displays on a gray background.

The Toolbar Properties dialog box (shown in Figure 3-3) also allows you to control the size and shape of the toolbar, but why not let users follow their own preferences for these settings?

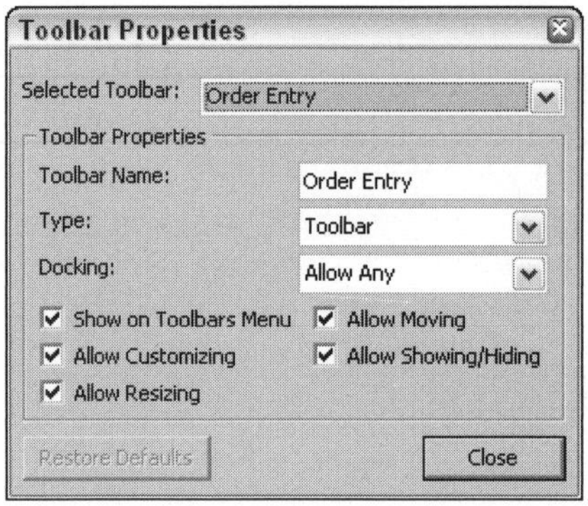

Figure 3-3:
You can prevent users from changing toolbars.

Toolbar Properties

Selected Toolbar: Order Entry

Toolbar Properties

Toolbar Name: Order Entry

Type: Toolbar

Docking: Allow Any

☑ Show on Toolbars Menu ☑ Allow Moving
☑ Allow Customizing   ☑ Allow Showing/Hiding
☑ Allow Resizing

Restore Defaults   Close

5. **Click the Close button to return to the Customize dialog box.**

6. **Click the Commands tab and drag buttons to your new toolbar, as described in Book I, Chapter 2.**

   Just poke around the categories of buttons until you find useful ones. Drag each button to the spot on the toolbar where you want the button to appear.

7. **Click the Close button in the Customize dialog box when your new toolbar is loaded with useful buttons.**

Now you have a toolbar — you just need to display it. You can display the toolbar any time by right-clicking any visible toolbar and choosing your toolbar name from the shortcut menu that appears. However, if you create an Access database for other people to use, displaying the toolbar automatically is nice.

Displaying a toolbar when a form or report is open

You can associate a toolbar with a form or report. Access displays the toolbar when the form is open in Form view or when the report is open in Print Preview. Follow these steps to assign a toolbar to a form or report:

1. **Open the form or report in Design view.**

   Press F11 to display the Database window, click the Forms or Reports button in the Objects list, select the one you want, and then click the Design button.

2. **Click the Properties button or choose View➪Properties to display the Properties sheet for the form or report.**

   If a control or section is selected, use the drop-down menu at the top of the Properties sheet and select the form or report to see the properties for the whole form or report.

3. **Click the Other tab.**

4. **Click in the** `Toolbar` **property, click its down-arrow button, and choose the name of a toolbar that you created.**

When you display the form in Form view or the report in Print Preview, Access displays your custom-made toolbar instead of the toolbar that Access normally shows.

Creating your own menus

Any Access menu contains lots of commands that you probably don't want Joe or Josephine Average User to give. You probably don't want your users to edit table relationships via the Relationships table, so you probably want to hide the Tools⇨Relationships command. For safety, you may want to remove commands from your menus, or better yet, display your own custom menus that include commands that are useful for the folks using your database.

Creating your own menu is less common than creating toolbars: Most database designers include the commands users need right on their forms, or on a toolbar. But if you want to create a custom menu, to replace the usual File Edit View menus and commands, you can do so.

Make sure you have some way to get back to the regular menus, or you may lock yourself out of your own application! Also, don't make changes to the main Access menu — if you do, the changes apply to other databases that you open.

Making a menu

Follow these steps to create a custom menu that displays in your Access database:

1. **Choose Tools⇨Customize and click the Toolbars tab if it's not already selected.**

   You see the Customize dialog box. (Refer to Figure 3-2.)

2. **Click the New button, type a name for your menu, and then click OK.**

   The Customize dialog box now shows your new menu in the Toolbars list.

   We know — it says Toolbars, but hold your horses.

   Include *Menu* or *Menu Bar* in the name, so you remember it's (or is about to be) a menu, not a toolbar.

3. **Select the new item in the Toolbars list and click the Properties button.**

   The Toolbar Properties dialog box displays. (Refer to Figure 3-3.)

4. **Change the Type setting from Toolbar to Menu Bar and then click the Close button.**

   You return to the Customize dialog box.

   See? We told you it turns out to be a menu — your new menu appears above the Access menu with only one command on it: the Type a Question for Help box that appears on the right end of the standard menu.

5. **Click the Commands tab in the Customize dialog box.**

   The Commands tab of the Customize dialog box appears, listing all the available commands.

   Most of the items on the Commands tab add icons to your menu rather than menus.

6. **If you want to create your own menu with its own commands, scroll all the way to the bottom of the Categories list on the Commands tab, click the New Menu category, and drag the New Menu item from the Commands list to your menu.**

   You get the new menu —it starts out with the name *New Menu*. When you click it, you see no commands, as shown in Figure 3-4.

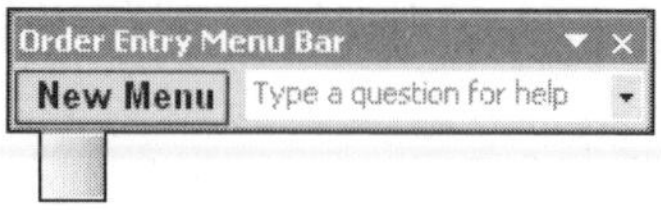

Figure 3-4:
A new menu is born — now you just have to add commands.

| Order Entry Menu Bar | ▼ × |
| New Menu | Type a question for help ▼ |

7. **Right-click your New Menu item and choose the Name option from the shortcut menu that appears. Name the menu (the text that appears in place of "New Menu") and press Enter.**

8. **Drag commands from the Commands tab of the Customize dialog box to the new menu.**

   Drag the command to the new menu, keep the mouse button down, wait a second until the menu expands to show the commands on it (initially, none) and drop the command on the expanded menu.

9. **Click the Close button in the Customize dialog box when the new menu contains the menus and commands you want.**

   You can always make more changes, or add additional commands, later.

If you want to add an entire menu (such as File or Edit) to your custom menu, select the Built-In Menus category in the Commands tab of the Customize dialog box and drag a menu from the Commands list to your menu. The entire built-in menu appears on your menu.

Displaying the menu bar with forms and reports

Follow the steps in the section, "Displaying a toolbar when a form or report is open," earlier in this chapter. Instead of setting the Toolbar setting in the Properties sheet for the form or report, change the Menu Bar setting.

Customizing shortcut menus

The last kind of menu that allows your users to access commands that you may not want them to use is the shortcut menu — the menu that appears when you right-click an object in the Access window. Access has zillions of built-in shortcut menus that vary depending on what window you are in and what kind of object you right-click.

To prevent users from making changes to your database objects, we recommend that you prevent shortcut menus from appearing. Choose Tools➪ Startup and uncheck the Allow Default Shortcut Menus check box. Now when you (or anyone else) right-clicks in the Access window, nothing happens.

You *can* modify your built-in shortcut menus, but these changes apply to your installation of Access, not just to the current database. If you do want to change the built-in shortcut menus, choose Tools➪Customize and select the Shortcut Menus option from the list on the Toolbars tab. The Shortcut Menus floating menu appears, as shown in Figure 3-5. You can drag commands on or off of the menus — but first, you need to poke around to figure out which one(s) you want to change.

Figure 3-5:
Customizing your built-in shortcut menus.

Shortcut Menus	▾ ×
Database ▾ Filter ▾ Form ▾ Index ▾ Macro ▾ Module ▾ Query ▾ Relationship ▾ Report ▾ Table ▾ View Design ▾ Other ▾	
Custom ▾	

Password-Protecting Your Database

Halt — who goes there? You can tell Access not to allow anyone to open your database until he or she types in the right password.

This system is all-or-nothing, which is a problem: After you allow someone to open the database, he or she can do anything to the database unless you take additional security measures. You also can't set a password on an Access project file (.adp file), only on a regular database file (.mdb file).

Setting a database password

Follow these steps to create a password for your database:

1. **Make a backup copy of the database and store it somewhere safe.**

This copy doesn't have a password. If you lose the password to the database, at least you have this backup. You may want to burn it to a CD and store the CD in something that's locked.

2. **Make sure no one else has the database open.**

You need sole access to the database to assign a password. In fact, you need exclusive access, in which everyone is temporarily locked out.

3. **Close the database. Then choose File⇨Open and select the name of the database.**

4. **Click the little arrow to the right of the Open button in the Open dialog box (instead of the Open button) and choose the Open Exclusive option from the menu that appears.**

Access opens the database with exclusive access.

5. **Choose Tools⇨Security⇨Set Database Password.**

You see the Set Database Password dialog box, shown in Figure 3-6.

Figure 3-6:
Setting a
password
for a
database.

6. **Type the database password once in each box and click OK.**

If you don't type the password the same way in both boxes, Access complains, and you have to type them again. Note that capitalization counts in passwords. A password can be up to 20 characters, and can include letters, numbers, and some punctuation.

Opening a password-protected database

After you set a password, whenever you (or anyone else) try to open the database, you see the Password Required dialog box shown in Figure 3-7.

Password Required

Enter database password:

OK   Cancel

WARNING!

If you forget your database password, you are hosed. No command, service, or secret incantation can get your password back.

But what happens if another database (one with no password) links to your password-protected database? Answer: When you create a link to a password-protected database, Access asks you for the password. If you don't know it, you can't create the link. However, after you create the link, Access saves the password so that you can see the linked table in the future without entering a password — you have an unguarded backdoor into your password-protected database (at least, to the linked tables in your database).

Encrypting your database

Setting a database password ensures that no one opens it in Access without the password. However, someone can still open the database in a programming editor (a text editor that can deal with the control characters that live in data files). To prevent this, you can *encrypt* the database. Encryption — writing the database file in a scrambled format that can be unscrambled only with the password — doesn't do any good if you haven't also protected the database from Access, either by setting a password or by creating user-level security, as described in the next section.

To encrypt a database, choose Tools➪Security➪Encrypt/Decrypt Database. When you see the Encrypt Database As dialog box (which looks just like a regular Windows Save As dialog box), type a file name for the database and click the Save button. The database doesn't appear to change at all, because Access decrypts the database automatically when you open and work with the database. The database may work a little more slowly, however, because Access has to encrypt and decrypt the information each time it reads or writes the database file.

Granting Database Access to Specific Users

For most databases (and computer systems in general), giving different people permission to do different things makes sense. A data entry clerk may have permission to enter information, but not to edit existing information or delete anything. The system manager may have permission to do almost anything. And other users fall somewhere in between.

Access has a system of *user-level security* in which you can create users and groups of users. You grant specific permissions to specific users or groups. When each user opens the database, he or she types a user name and password, so Access always knows who is using the database and allows or disallows commands accordingly. This system works with both Access databases (.mdb files) and Access projects (.adp files).

This section covers the basics of converting a regular database to a secured database using user-level security. For a detailed, if slightly out-of-date, write-up about Access user-level security, see the following Web page:

support.microsoft.com/support/access/content/secfaq.asp

How user-level security works

With user-level security, Access maintains a database of users and groups. *Users* can log in to Access and use your database. *Groups* are objects to which users can belong. For example, you can have users named *Zac*, *Neil*, and *Stuart*, and they can all belong to a group named *Users*. Zac may also belong to a group called *Administrators* and Neil and Stuart may also belong to a group named *Managers*.

This database of users and groups is stored in a *workgroup information file* or *workgroup file* or *system database* with the file name extension .mdw (Microsoft Database Workgroup). Each time Access opens a database, it looks for a workgroup file, checks whether users are required to log in with passwords, and asks for user names and passwords, if needed.

After you set up your users and your groups, you grant *permissions* to them. You give a user or group permission to use a database object in a specific way — you can give the Managers group permission to create reports, but not to change the design of tables. When you grant a permission to a group, you grant it to all the members of that group. When you use a database with user-level security, each time you open, print, or otherwise work with a database object, Access checks the permissions of your user account to make sure that the action is allowed.

Every object in an Access database has an *owner* — a user or group that owns the object. The owner of an object has full permission to do anything with that object. The person who creates the object is initially the owner of the object, but you can transfer ownership to someone else.

The default workgroup file

Actually, all Access databases have user-level security — you've been secretly using it since you started using Access. Access comes with a generic workgroup file that contains one user — Admin — and two groups — Users and Admins. The Admin user has no password and full permission to do anything to any database object. Whenever you run Access, Access logs you in as the Admin user. You never encounter the user-level security system until you secure your database.

The Admin user owns all the objects in an unsecured database, because you log in as the Admin user when you create all the objects. You normally have full permission to do anything with all database objects, because you are their owner.

If you want to create a secure database that only people who can open or change things are the people you designate, you need to create users and groups and grant permissions to those users and groups. But you also need to *remove* ownership and permissions from the Admin user, because every Access installation has the same Admin user: Whatever your Admin user has permission to do, someone using the generic workgroup file can do, too. Similarly, the Users group has full rights to all database objects. You need to revoke those rights, leaving only the specific permissions you want to give to specific users and groups.

The generic workgroup file is called System.mdw and is stored in this folder:

```
C:\Documents And Settings\username\Application Data\Microsoft\Access
```

(Replace *username* with your Windows user name.) To secure your database, you stop using this workgroup file and create a new one.

Windows also has a system of users and passwords, which you can control by choosing Start⇨Control Panel⇨User Accounts (in Windows XP). Access user-level security is unconnected to Windows security; no relationship exists between Windows users and Access users.

Your new workgroup file

When you secure your database, you make a new workgroup file. You have two options:

✦ Make the new workgroup file the default for all the databases you open in Access.

✦ Leave your default workgroup file alone and continue to use it with databases that don't need to be secure. Tell Access to use your new workgroup file only with specific databases.

Choosing your users and groups

The first step in setting up user-level security is to choose your users and groups. Choosing your users is easy — just make a list of all the people who may possibly use your database. Make each one a user.

Next, create a group for each department, committee, or other group of people who need the same access to database objects. A user can be in more than one group — the sales manager can be in both the Sales group and the Managers group. A user gets all the permissions from all the groups of which he or she is a member. If you are a member of the Accounting and Admins groups, you have the permissions from both groups.

The default groups

All workgroups include two groups:

✦ **Users:** Includes all the users. Every Access workgroup file has a Users group, and they are all identical internally. Any permissions that your Users group has can be exploited by someone with a copy of the default Access workgroup file.

✦ **Admins:** Includes all administrative users — users to whom you want to grant permission to administer the security system, create users and groups, change passwords, and grant permissions. The Admins group must have at least one member (like you), or no one is able to fix security problems.

User and group do's and don'ts

Some tips for choosing your users and groups include the following:

✦ **Don't assign permissions to users, only to groups.** Having a group with only one user is okay. When a receptionist is promoted to the Sales Department, you can move him or her from the Receptionists group to the Sales group, with all the rights and privileges thereunto appertaining. Moving someone from one group to another is easy: Changing the permissions for every object in the database to which this person does or should have access is a pain.

✦ **Don't plan for people to share a user name.** If three people work as the company receptionist over the course of the day, and spend their spare time doing data entry, don't create a user named Receptionist. Instead, create individual user accounts for each person, and a group named Receptionists or Data Entry Folks. This method allows you to grant extra permissions to someone who takes on an additional responsibility, without giving the same permissions to anyone else — you just add the person to an additional group.

✦ **Use plural words for the names of groups and singular words for the names of users.** This system clarifies what's a user and what's a group and avoids the situation where you try to give a user and a group the same name. Department or committee names for groups can be an exception to the rule (for example, Accounting or Marketing).

PIDs, GIDs, and SIDs

When you create a user or group, you type in three pieces of information:

✦ **User name:** Use a consistent naming convention to avoid confusion. Use first names followed a last initial, or full names, or last names only.

✦ **Company name:** If you're not part of an organization, then make something up. Use the same entry for all the users and groups.

✦ **Personal identifier (PID) or Group identifier (Group ID or GID):** A string of letters and numbers that you make up, from 4 to 20 characters long. Capitalization counts.

Access combines the user name, company name, and PID or GID to create a secret *security ID (SID)* for each user and group. Access uses this SID to keep track of what the user or group has permission to do to each object in the database.

If you lose the workgroup file that contains all the users and groups, you can recreate the file by entering the exact same user names, company names, and PIDs — with the same inputs, Access creates the exact same SID for each user and group, and your database is up and running. Keep a list of the PIDs that you use: You may lose the workgroup file and have to re-create it. Keep this list secret, so that no malefactor can create the workgroup file and use it to break into your database.

Securing a database

For your database to be safe, you need to create a new workgroup file with your new users and groups, remove ownership and permissions from the Admin user and Users group, encrypt the new database, and grant ownership and permissions to your new users and groups for each object in the Access database. Sounds like a lot of work! Luckily, Access comes with a wizard that can do a lot of it — the User-Level Security Wizard.

To get the User-Level Security Wizard working for you, follow these steps:

1. **Open the database for which you want user-level security.**

   Making a backup beforehand wouldn't be a dreadful idea, either.

2. **Choose Tools➪Security➪User-Level Security Wizard from the main menu.**

   The Security Wizard window opens, and asks whether you want to create a new workgroup file or edit an existing one. If you haven't already created a workgroup file, the second option isn't available.

3. **Make sure that the Create a New Workgroup Information File option is selected and click Next.**

   The Security Wizard window now looks like Figure 3-8.

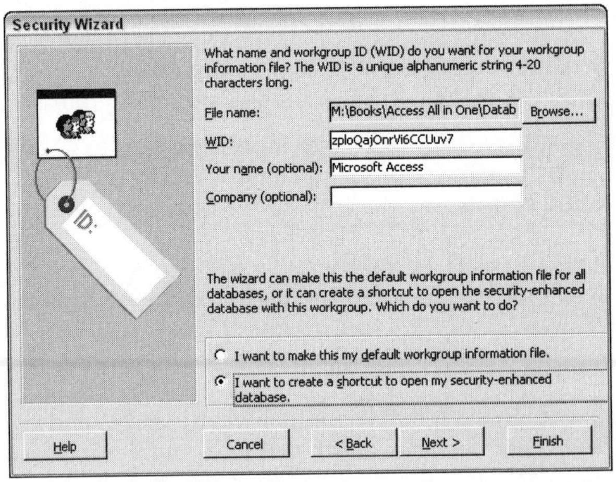

Figure 3-8: Creating a workgroup file with the User-Level Security Wizard.

4. **Enter the following information, which Access needs to create a new workgroup file:**

   - **File Name:** The name and location of the new workgroup file you are creating. The default is `Secured.mdw`, located in the same folder in which the database is stored, but you can click the Browse button to choose a different location.

   - **WID:** A string of numbers and letters, from 4 to 20 characters long, that Access uses to create an encrypted *Workgroup SID* (security ID). The Workgroup SID is what makes your new workgroup file different from the default workgroup file. Type a series of characters that no one is likely to guess.

- **Your Name:** Optional.

- **Company:** Optional.

You may want to write down all this information, because you need it to re-create the workgroup file. However, you don't have to, because in Step 12 you print an Access report that includes this information.

5. **Choose whether to use this workgroup file as the default whenever you run Access, or just for this database. Then click Next.**

   If you choose the I Want to Make This My Default Workgroup Information File option, the wizard configures Access (via your Windows Registry) to use this new workgroup file whenever you run Access, unless you override the default for a specific database.

   If you choose the I Want to Create a Shortcut to Open My Security-Enhanced Database option, your default workgroup file is unchanged. The wizard creates a shortcut on the Windows desktop that runs Access, opens the database, and tells Access to use this workgroup file. See the sidebar, "Starting Access with a specific workgroup," later in this chapter.

   If you decide to replace your default workgroup file (System.mdw), make a backup of the original version first. (See the section, "The default workgroup file," earlier in this chapter for its default location.)

6. **Leave all the objects selected, as shown in Figure 3-9, and then click Next.**

   A tab for each type of database object is in this window, except VBA modules, which are secured separately. (See the section, "Securing your VBA modules," later in this chapter.)

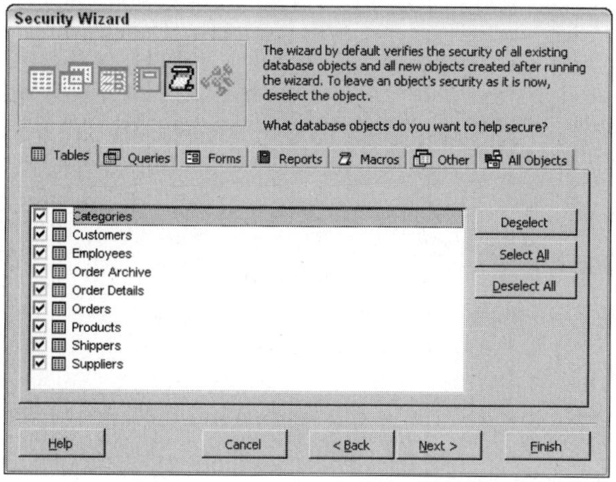

Figure 3-9:
Select all
the objects
for which
you want
user-level
security.

Security Wizard

The wizard by default verifies the security of all existing database objects and all new objects created after running the wizard. To leave an object's security as it is now, deselect the object.

What database objects do you want to help secure?

Tables | Queries | Forms | Reports | Macros | Other | All Objects

☑ Categories
☑ Customers
☑ Employees
☑ Order Archive
☑ Order Details
☑ Orders
☑ Products
☑ Shippers
☑ Suppliers

Deselect
Select All
Deselect All

Help | Cancel | < Back | Next > | Finish

7. **For each group that you want Access to create, click its check box and type a Group Identifier (GID), as shown in Figure 3-10. Then click Next.**

   You can make a note of the name of each group you choose to create, along with the exact GID that you type, at least until you print a report that includes this information (in Step 12).

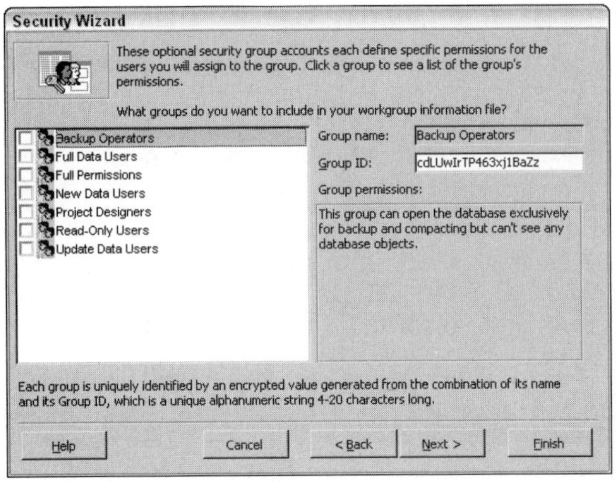

Figure 3-10: The User-Level Security Wizard can create some groups for you.

8. **Choose whether or not the Users group will have any permissions (choose No), and then click Next.**

   If you choose to grant permissions to the Users group, keep the following in mind: You're not just granting permission to the users you create in your workgroup file. Anyone with an Access installation can use his or her default workgroup file, with its default Users group, to open the database and use the permissions that you grant. We recommend that unless you don't mind *anyone* doing anything, leave this option set to the No setting. Why risk it? You can create your own groups and give them permissions.

   If you do decide to ignore our advice and grant the Users group permissions, see the section, "Setting permissions for groups," later in this chapter for what the various permissions mean.

9. **Enter the information in order for Access to create each user name and click Add This New User to the List, as shown in Figure 3-11. When you finish, click Next.**

   The pieces of information you need to enter include the following:

   - **User Name:** The name for the user account. Be consistent with your names. Use each person's first and last names (spaces are allowed).

- **Password:** The starting password for this user. The user can change it later.

- **PID:** A string of numbers and letters, from 4 to 20 characters long, that Access uses to create an encrypted *SID* (security ID). Access uses the SID when storing permissions in databases. Type a series of characters that no one is likely to guess.

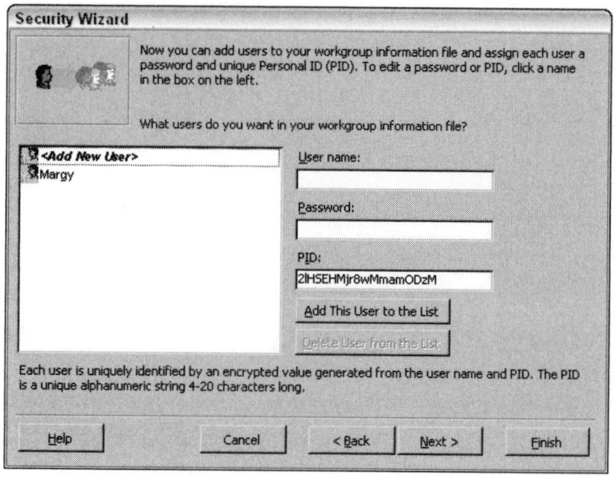

Figure 3-11:
Creating users in the User-Level Security Wizard.

Book VII Chapter 3

Securing Your Access Database

You can edit the password and PID for a user by clicking the user name on the list and editing the entries. Click the Add New User option on the list to continue adding users. (You may want to write down this information, but you'll print it all out in a report in Step 12.)

The wizard creates a user — you — using your Windows user name. You can't delete or change this name.

10. **Assign at least one user to the Admins group, as shown in Figure 3-12. If you create other groups, you can assign users to those groups, too. Then click Next.**

The wizard creates the Admins group no matter what, which is the group of users who have administrative permissions (permission to create and edit users, groups, and passwords). It puts you (the user name created for you) in the Admins group.

You can look at one user at a time or one group at a time, whichever you find easier. To switch, choose the Select a User and Assign the User to Groups options or the Select a Group and Assign Users to the Group option.

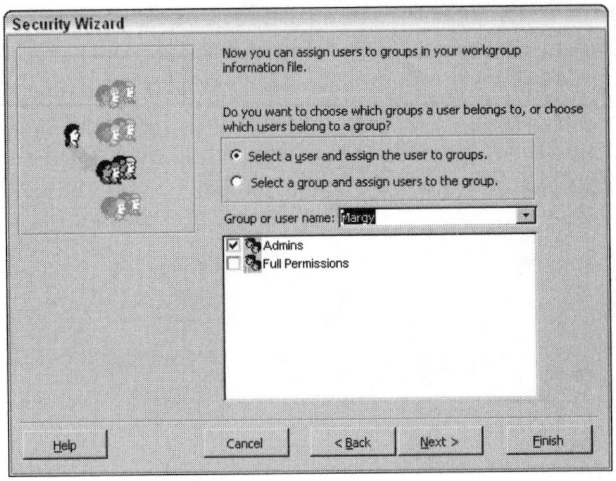

Security Wizard

Now you can assign users to groups in your workgroup information file.

Do you want to choose which groups a user belongs to, or choose which users belong to a group?

   ● Select a user and assign the user to groups.

   ○ Select a group and assign users to the group.

Group or user name: Margy

   ☑ Admins
   ☐ Full Permissions

| Help | Cancel | < Back | Next > | Finish |

Figure 3-12: Which users are in which groups?

11. **Change the name or path for the backup copy of the database if you don't like the one that the wizard suggests, and then click Finish.**

   Access proposes to use the same name and folder as the original database, with the extension .bak, for an unsecured backup version.

   The wizard creates a workgroup file, creates the user and groups that you specified, creates a copy of the database, transfers ownership of the database objects that you selected from Admin to your user name, encrypts the new database, and displays a report about its success.

12. **Print the report, which lists all the information you need if you ever need to re-create the workgroup file.**

13. **Select the security report and choose File⇨Export, set the Save as Type box to Rich Text Format, and click the Export button.**

   Access saves the report as an RTF file, which you can open with Word, WordPerfect, WordPad (which comes with Windows), or most other word processors.

14. **Close the security report, and click the Yes button when the wizard asks whether to save it as a snapshot report.**

   See Book V, Chapter 2 for how to view a snapshot report. The snapshot report file has the same name and folder as the database, but with the extension .snp.

15. **Click OK when the wizard displays a message confirming it created a new, encrypted version of your database. Then close Access.**

   You need to close and restart Access to open the new workgroup file.

16. **Copy the RTF file and the snapshot report to a diskette or burn them to a CD, stick it in a sealed envelope with the printout of the security report, and store it somewhere safe. Then delete the RTF file from your hard disk.**

This information enables anyone who finds it to create a workgroup information file and open your database, so keep it safe.

Okay, you have a new workgroup file, a partially secured database, and your workgroup information backed up.

Opening your secure database

After the User-Level Security Wizard secures your database, you may need to open the database in a different way. If you chose to make your new workgroup file the default for all databases, then you don't need to do anything differently: Whenever you open a database from now on, Access uses your new workgroup file.

However, if you chose to make a workgroup file for use with one (or more) specific database(s), then the wizard creates a shortcut that runs Access and opens the database with the workgroup file you just created. Look on your Windows desktop for a new icon with the name of your database. Double-click this shortcut to open your secured database. You can copy this shortcut to any folder, or drag it to the Start menu.

See the sidebar, "Starting Access with a specific workgroup," for how secure database shortcuts work.

To check whether your database is secure and to see the name of the workgroup file you are using, choose Tools➪Security➪Workgroup Administrator. You can use the Create button on the Workgroup Administrator dialog box to create a new workgroup, but we recommend using the User-Level Security Wizard instead, because creating a workgroup doesn't do much good unless you change the Admin and Users settings, encrypt the database, and do all the other good stuff that the wizard does for you. You can click the Join button to switch which workgroup file this database uses.

Setting passwords

The database isn't secure until you enter a password for your user account — you find the account in the Admins group — and the rest of the Admins users set their passwords. To set your password, choose Tools➪Security➪User and Group Accounts to display the User and Group Accounts dialog box and then click the Change Logon Password tab. Type your old password (if you typed one when you created the user) and then a new password two times.

Starting Access with a specific workgroup

You may not want to use the same workgroup file for all the databases you create. You may want most of your databases to remain wide open, with no user-level security, while securing one specific database.

You can tell Access which workgroup file to use with which database. Access uses only one workgroup file at a time, and you have to exit Access and restart to switch to another workgroup. If the same group of people use several secured databases, using the same workgroup file for all the databases makes sense — you make changes to users and groups in just one place.

When you start Access, you provide the name of the database, the name of the workgroup file, and even the user you want to log in as. You specify this information as part of a shortcut to the Access database. Make a shortcut to each secured Access database that includes the workgroup file required to open that database.

A *shortcut* is a Windows feature — you see them on your Windows desktop. Shortcuts can live in folders, too. You can tell a shortcut by examining its icon: If the icon includes a little bent arrow, it's a shortcut.

Luckily, you don't have to make a shortcut if you want a specific database opened with a specific workgroup file, because the User-Level Security Wizard creates one for you on the Windows desktop.

If you know how to create Windows shortcuts, you can make your own. The Target box needs to include:

- **Path to Access program:** Usually `"C:\ Program Files\Microsoft Office\ Office11\Msaccess.exe"` (with the quotes, because the pathname includes spaces).

- **Database pathname:** The full pathname of your database file.

- **Workgroup pathname:** `/WRKGRP` followed by the full pathname of your workgroup file.

Here is a shortcut target for the Northwind.mdb database using the Secured.mdw workgroup:

```
"C:\Program Files\Microsoft Office\
    office11\Msaccess.exe""
    D:\Databases\Northwind.
    mdb" /WRKGRP "D:\Databases\
    Secured.mdw"
```

If someone forgets a password, clear the password by clicking the Users tab on the User and Group Accounts dialog box, setting the Name box to the user, and clicking the Clear Password button. Then tell the person to log in to the database with a blank password and set a password (as described in the preceding paragraph) right away.

Never clear the password for the Admin user! Access only prompts for user names and password if the Admin user has a password. If you secure a database and you clear the Admin password, the next time you open the database you get a message that you don't have permissions for this database, and you have no chance to log in.

Creating the rest of your users and groups

You may create all your users in the User-Level Security Wizard, but creating all your groups with the wizard is unlikely, because the wizard doesn't provide many options for group names. You can create more users and groups any time: Choose Tools⇨Security⇨User and Group Accounts to display the User and Group Accounts dialog box shown in Figure 3-13.

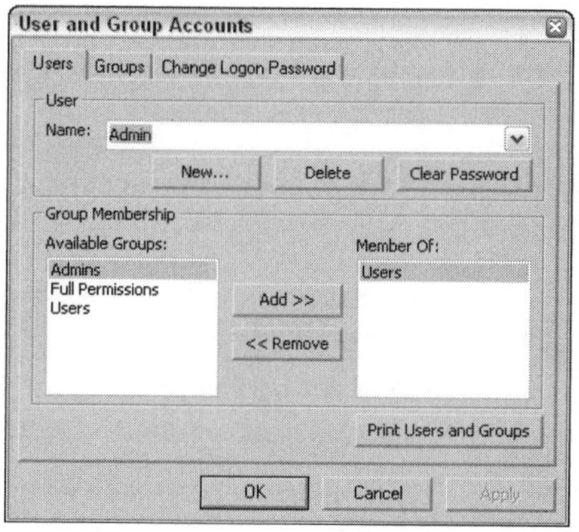

Figure 3-13:
Creating or deleting user and group accounts, and assigning users to groups.

On the Users tab, you can create new users, delete existing users, and assign users to groups. When you choose a user name in the User section of the dialog box, Access lists the groups of which the user is a member in the Member Of list. Click the Add and Remove buttons to move group names from the Available Groups list to the Member Of list.

The Groups tab allows you to create additional groups. Then switch back to the Users tab to add people to your new group. Access stores the changes to your users and groups in the workgroup file, not in the database.

When you create new users or groups, be sure to type something into the Personal ID box. This entry is the PID or GID that Access uses to create the SID for the user or group. Write down your entries, taking careful note of the exact text (including capitalization) of the user name and PID, or group name and GID, in case you ever need to re-create the workgroup file.

The Admin user can't be deleted, and it creates a security hole in your database if you give Admin *any* permissions. Remove the Admin user from all groups except the Users group. (***Remember:*** The Admin user is a different thing from the Admins group.)

Setting permissions for groups

The information about specific permissions is stored in your database, not in the workgroup file. When you log in, you tell Access who you are, and Access knows your SID (security ID). Each time you try to open a database object, Access checks whether your SID has permission to use that object in the way you are trying to use it — creating, editing, displaying, printing, and so on.

Types of permissions

For each type of database object (including the database as a whole), you can set the permissions listed in Table 3-2.

Don't grant these permissions to individual users: Grant them to groups, and then add users to those groups.

Table 3-2	Permissions for Database Objects	
Object	*Permission*	*What It Lets You Do*
Database	Open/Run	Open database
	Open Exclusive	Open database for exclusive access
	Administer	Set database password; change startup options
Table	Read Design	View table in Design view
	Modify Design	Edit table in Design view; delete table
	Administer	Anything, plus assign permissions
	Read Data	View records
	Update Data	View and edit records
	Insert Data	View and insert records
	Delete Data	View and delete records
Query	Read Design	View query in Design view
	Modify Design	Edit query in Design view; delete query
	Administer	Anything, plus assign permissions
	Read Data	View records
	Update Data	View and edit records
	Insert Data	View and insert records
	Delete Data	View and delete records
Form	Open/Run	Open form
	Read Design	View form in Design view
	Modify Design	Edit form in Design view; delete form
	Administer	Anything, plus assign permissions

Object	Permission	What It Lets You Do
Report	Open/Run	Open report in Print Preview
	Read Design	View report in Design view
	Modify Design	Edit report in Design view; delete report
	Administer	Anything, plus assign permissions
Macro	Open/Run	Run macro
	Read Design	View macro in Design view
	Modify Design	Edit macro in Design view; delete macro
	Administer	Anything, plus assign permissions

Granting permission for an object to a user or group

After you run the User-Level Security Wizard, the Users group has no permissions, and neither do any of the other groups, except for the Admins group, which has full permissions. The next step in securing your database is to grant permissions to the groups you created.

To assign permissions, choose Tools⇨Security⇨User and Group Permissions to display the User and Group Permissions dialog box. On the Permissions tab, shown in Figure 3-14, click the Groups radio button in the List options to assign permissions to groups.

Help! I can't get into my database!

Your workgroup file is destroyed, replaced with another file, or otherwise out of commission, and you can't log into your database. If you followed all the steps in the section "Securing a database," your database is locked up tight. You are out of luck unless you remembered to keep a list of the user names, company names, and PIDs (personal identifiers) that you entered when creating the workgroup file. If you saved this information, you can create a new workgroup file that is identical to the original one, and you should be able to log in to your database.

In an unsecured blank database, choose Tools⇨Security⇨Workgroup Administrator to display the Workgroup Administrator dialog box, and click the Create button. In the Workgroup

Owner Information dialog box that appears, type the Name, Organization, and Workgroup ID that you used when you created the original workgroup. Specify a file and pathname and click OK. Access creates the workgroup. Still in the blank database, click the Join button in the Workgroup Administrator dialog box and specify the new workgroup file name. Use the User and Group Accounts dialog box to create the same users and groups, with the same PIDs and GIDs, as the original workgroup file. (Aren't you glad you saved that User-Level Security Wizard report, with all this information?) Finally, rename this new workgroup file with the same name as the original workgroup file, and try opening your database again.

Converting a secured database from an older version of Access

Access has had user-level security since version 2.0. If you want to upgrade a secured database from an older Access version to the latest version, create a new workgroup file in Access 2003 that exactly matches your old workgroup file. You need the Workgroup ID and all the group IDs (GIDs) and personal IDs (PIDs) used to create the original workgroup file. Then upgrade the database by choosing Tools➪Database Utilities➪Convert Database, as described in Chapter 1 of this book.

If you don't have this information, you can't create a replacement workgroup file. In this case, removing the security, upgrading the database, and then re-creating the security is the best method. (You probably have some better ideas for the design of your users and groups, anyway!) To remove security, grant full permissions to the Users group, in order for everyone to do anything within the database. Add the Admin user to the Admins group (for a database to be secure, the default Admin user can never be in the Admins group), and remove the password for the Admin user.

Figure 3-14:
Assigning permissions to groups to access specific objects.

For each group, follow these steps:

1. **Select the group from the User/Group Name list.**

2. **Set the Object Type option to the Database type and, in the Permissions section of the dialog box, check the check boxes next to those permissions you want to assign for the entire database.**

   Normally, only the Admins group has Administer permission for the database.

3. **Set the Object Type option to the Table type.**

   The Object Name box lists all the tables in the database.

4. **With *<New Tables/Queries>* selected, use the Permissions check boxes to set the default permissions you want this group of users to have for any new objects of that type.**

   Setting default permissions saves having to set them for each new object that you create later. Refer to Table 3-2 for what the permissions mean for this type of object.

5. **Select each object in turn, and set the permissions that you want this group to have for this object.**

6. **Repeat Steps 3 through 5, setting the object type to the Query, Form, Report, and Macro types — one at a time.**

7. **Click OK to close the dialog box.**

The Admins group normally has all permissions for all objects, and you should probably leave it that way. Don't chance locking yourself out of your own database!

Displaying or changing an object's owner

The owner of an object has full permissions for that object, regardless of what other permissions you do or don't grant. You can see who owns any database object by looking at the Change Owner tab of the User and Group Permissions dialog box, shown in Figure 3-15.

To see an object's owner, set the Object Type option to the type of the object and find the object from the Object list — the owner's user name appears to its right. To change ownership, select the object, set the New Owner option to another user or group name, and click the Change Owner button.

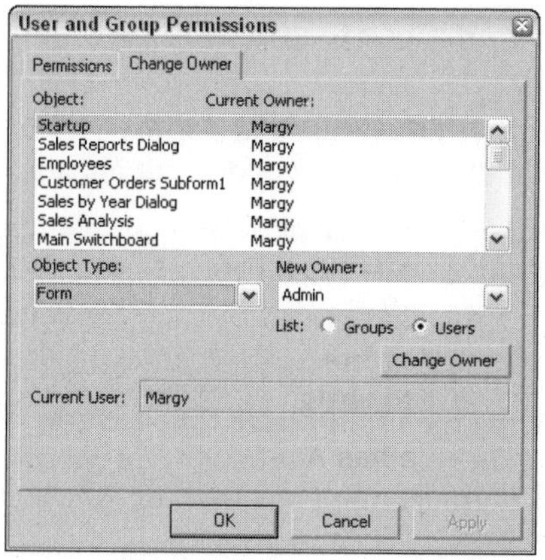

Figure 3-15:
You can change the owner of any object in the database.

Securing your VBA modules

Before Access 2000, you used the same user-level security system to protect VBA modules that you use for the rest of your database objects. However, starting with Access 2000, you use a separate password to secure your VBA procedures.

To set a password for viewing or editing your VBA procedures, follow these steps:

1. **Choose Tools⇨Macro⇨Visual Basic Editor (or press Alt+F11).**

   You see the Microsoft Visual Basic window, which we describe in Book VIII.

2. **Choose Tools⇨*databasename* Properties.**

   The actual name of the database appears in place of *databasename*. You see the Project Properties dialog box.

3. **Click the Protection tab, and type the same password in the Password and Confirm Password text boxes.**

4. **Click OK.**

   To remove the password, follow the same steps but delete the entries in the Password and Confirm Password text boxes.

Securing front-end and back-end databases

If you split your Access application into a front end and a back end, as described in Chapter 2 of this book, how do you secure it? You need to secure both databases. Follow these steps:

1. **Secure both the front-end and back-end databases, using the same workgroup.**

2. **Create users and groups.**

3. **In the back end, grant permissions to groups to view and/or edit the records.**

   Users access only the tables in the back-end database. What permissions they have for other database objects doesn't matter.

4. **In the front end, grant Open/Run permission to all groups for the Database object. Also grant groups permission to use the appropriate forms and reports.**

Not granting any permissions in the back-end database is another approach. Instead, create queries in the front-end database that include tables in the back-end database, and you set the RunPermissions property of each query to provide the needed permissions — search for *RunPermissions* in Access Help for more information.

Book VIII

Programming in VBA

The 5th Wave — By Rich Tennant

FIRED
YOU

"NIFTY CHART, FRANK, BUT NOT ENTIRELY NECESSARY."

Contents at a Glance

Chapter 1: What the Heck Is VBA?

In This Chapter

✔ Understanding Visual Basic for Applications (VBA)

✔ Using the Visual Basic Editor

✔ Discovering code as you go

*V*isual Basic for Applications, often abbreviated *VBA*, is a programming language that you can use to extend the functionality of Microsoft Access and other products in the Microsoft Office suite of programs. A *programming language* is a means of writing instructions for the computer to *execute* (perform). Programmers often refer to the written instructions as *code*, because the instructions aren't in plain English. Rather, they're in a code that the computer can interpret and execute.

You can create sophisticated Access databases without using VBA at all. In most cases, the other objects offered by Access — tables, queries, forms, reports, and macros — offer more than enough flexibility and power to create just about any database imaginable. But once in a while you come across a situation where you want to do something that none of those other objects can do. That's where VBA comes in. If you can find no other way to accomplish some goal in Access, writing code is usually the solution.

Finding VBA Code

So what the heck is VBA code, anyway? To the untrained eye, VBA code looks like gibberish — perhaps some secret code written by aliens from another planet. But to Access, the code represents very specific instructions on how to perform some task.

Within any given database, Access stores code in two places:

✦ **Class modules (Code Behind Forms):** Every form and report you create automatically contains a *class module* (also called *Code Behind Forms*), as illustrated in Figure 1-1. The class module for a given form or report is empty unless you place controls that require VBA code on that form or report.

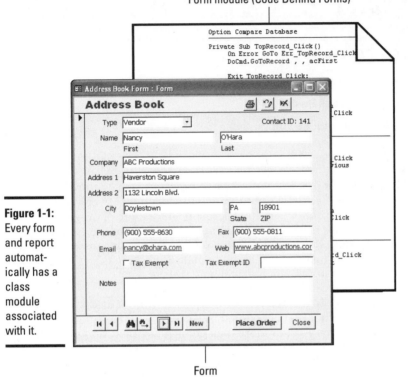

Figure 1-1:
Every form
and report
automat-
ically has a
class
module
associated
with it.

+ **Standard modules:** Code can also be stored in *standard modules*. When
you click the Modules button in the Objects list of the Database window,
the larger pane on the right lists standard modules (if any) contained
within the database, as shown in Figure 1-2. Code in standard modules is
accessible to all objects in your database, not just a given form or report.

Opening a class module

If you want to view or change the code for a form or report's class module,
or add code to that module, you first have to open the module. To open a
class module, you first need to open, in Design view, the form or report to
which the module is attached. After you're in the Design window, you can
click the Code button on the Design View window toolbar or choose View⇒
Code from the Access main menu to view the class module for the form or
report.

Modules   Standard
button   modules

Figure 1-2:
Standard
modules are
listed in the
Modules
section
of the
Database
window.

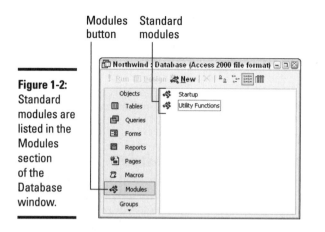

You can also get to a class module from the Event tab of the Properties
sheet in the Design View window. The Properties sheet allows you to zoom
right in on the VBA code that's associated with a given control. For example,
if you use a Control Wizard to create any controls on the form or report, you
see [Event Procedure] entered as the property name. *Event Procedure*
means that a VBA *procedure* (chunk of code) executes when the event is
triggered. You can click [Event Procedure], and then click the Build
button (as shown in Figure 1-3) to see the VBA procedure that the Control
Wizard created.

Event tab
on the
Properties   Selected   Code   Build
sheet   control   button   button

Figure 1-3:
Use the
Code button
or Build
button to
view VBA
code in a
class
module.

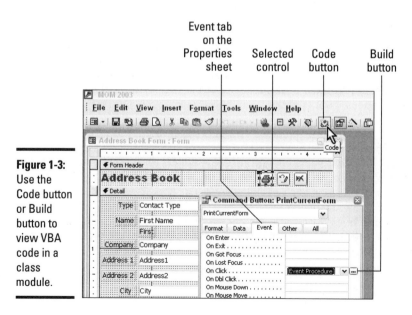

**Book VIII
Chapter 1**

**What the Heck
Is VBA?**

To write custom code for a control, select the control in Design view, open the Properties sheet, click the Event tab, click the event to which you want to attach some custom code, and then click the Build button and choose Code Builder.

After you open a module, you're taken to an entirely separate program window called the Visual Basic Editor, where you see the module in all its glory.

Creating or opening a standard module

Standard modules contain VBA code that isn't associated with a specific form or report. The code in a standard module is available to all tables, queries, forms, reports, macros, and other modules in your database. The techniques for creating and opening standard modules are the same as those for other objects in the Database window:

✦ To open a standard module, click the Modules button in the Objects list of the Database window, and then double-click the module name when it appears in the right pane of the window.

✦ To create a new module, click the Modules button in the Objects list of the Database window, and then click the New button in the window toolbar.

The module opens in the Visual Basic Editor.

How code is organized

All modules organize their code into a Declaration section at the top, followed by individual procedures, as shown in Figure 1-4. The Declaration section contains options, written in code format, that apply to all procedures in the module. Each procedure is also a chunk of VBA code that, when executed, performs a specific set of steps.

Procedures in a module fall into two major categories, *sub procedures* and *function procedures*. Both types of procedures use VBA code to perform some task. The next sections outline some subtle differences in how and where they're used.

Sub procedures

A *sub procedure* is one or more lines of code that make Access perform a particular task. Every sub procedure starts with the word Sub (or Private Sub) and ends with End Sub, using one of the following general structures:

```
Sub name()
    ...code...
End Sub

Private Sub name()
    ...code...
End Sub
```

Name is the name of the procedure, and *...code...* is any amount of VBA code.

Text that appears to be written in plain English within a module represents *programmer comments* — notes for other programmers. The computer ignores the comments. All comments start with an apostrophe (').

In a class module, sub procedures created by a Control Wizard are always named using a combination of the control name and the event that triggers the code to run and do its job.

Function procedure

Function procedure

Sub procedure

Declaration

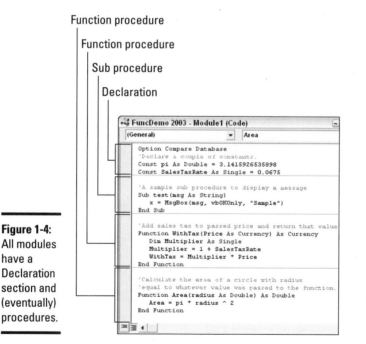

Figure 1-4:
All modules have a Declaration section and (eventually) procedures.

For example, in Figure 1-5, the selected button (named `PrintCurrentForm`) prints the current form when you click it. Viewing the Event tab of the Properties sheet for that control shows that an Event Procedure is associated with that control. Clicking the Build (...) button next to Event Procedure opens the class module, where you see the name of the procedure, `PrintCurrentForm_Click()`, is constructed from the name of the control to which the code is attached (`PrintCurrentForm`) and the event that triggers the code into action (On Click).

The keyword, Private, in front of the word Sub tells Access that the procedure is visible only to the form (or report) to which the code is attached. You can have different `PrintCurrentForm` buttons and `PrintCurrentForm_Click()` procedures in any number of forms with a `Private Sub`. The names won't conflict with one another because each is private (visible only to) the form or report to which the class module is attached.

Function procedures

A *function procedure* is enclosed in `Function...End Function` statements, as the following code shows:

```
Function name()
    <...code...>
End Function
```

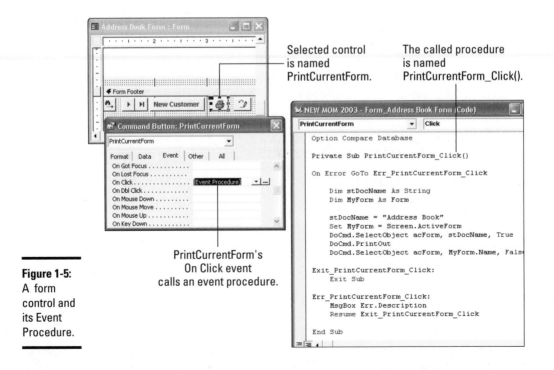

Selected control is named PrintCurrentForm.

The called procedure is named PrintCurrentForm_Click().

PrintCurrentForm's On Click event calls an event procedure.

Figure 1-5:
A form control and its Event Procedure.

Unlike a sub procedure, which simply performs some task, a function procedure performs a task and returns a value. In fact, an Access function procedure is no different from any of the built-in functions you use in Access expressions. And you can use a custom function procedure wherever you can use a built-in procedure.

If you open the sample Northwind database that comes with Access and click the Modules button in the Objects list of the Database window, you see that Northwind already contains a couple of standard modules. If you double-click on the Utility Functions module, that module opens in the Visual Basic Editor, revealing that it contains one function procedure named IsLoaded(), as shown in Figure 1-6.

The name of a function procedure isn't tied to any particular control or event, because a function procedure can be called upon from any Access object, control, or event. When you create a custom function procedure, you can name it anything you wish.

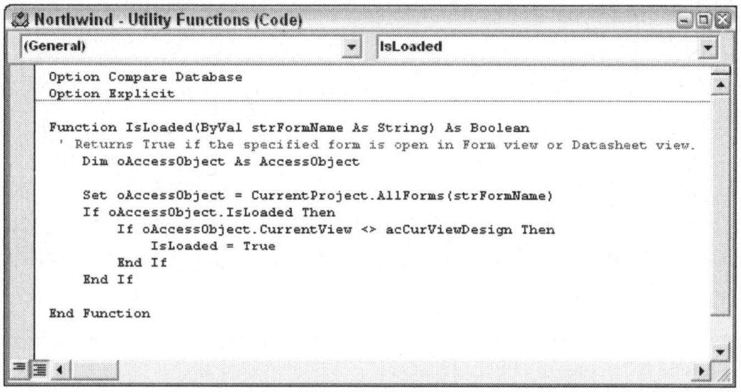

Figure 1-6:
A sample
function
procedure
from the
Northwind
database.

```
Northwind - Utility Functions (Code)
(General)                          IsLoaded

Option Compare Database
Option Explicit

Function IsLoaded(ByVal strFormName As String) As Boolean
' Returns True if the specified form is open in Form view or Datasheet view.
    Dim oAccessObject As AccessObject

    Set oAccessObject = CurrentProject.AllForms(strFormName)
    If oAccessObject.IsLoaded Then
        If oAccessObject.CurrentView <> acCurViewDesign Then
            IsLoaded = True
        End If
    End If

End Function
```

Using the Visual Basic Editor

Regardless of how you open a module, you end up in the Visual Basic Editor. The Visual Basic Editor is where you write, edit, and test your VBA code. The Visual Basic Editor is entirely separate from the Access program window. If you click outside the Visual Basic Editor window, the window may disappear as whatever window you clicked comes to the front.

Like all program windows, the Visual Basic Editor has its own Windows taskbar button, as in the top half of Figure 1-7. If the taskbar is particularly crowded with buttons, the editor and Access may share a taskbar button,

Book VIII
Chapter 1

What the Heck
Is VBA?

as in the bottom half of Figure 1-7. If you suddenly lose the VBA Editor window, click its taskbar button to bring the window back to the top of the stack of program windows on your desktop.

Microsoft Access   Visual Basic Editor

Figure 1-7:
The Visual
Basic Editor
has its own
program
window
and taskbar
button.

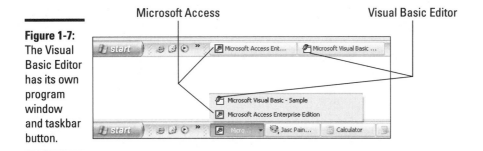

In most versions of Windows, you can right-click the Windows taskbar and choose the Tile Windows Vertically option from the shortcut menu to make all open program windows visible on-screen without overlap.

The Visual Basic Editor provides many tools designed to help you write code. Most of the tools are optional and can be turned on or off using the View menu in the Visual Basic Editor menu. The windows are shown in Figure 1-8. We provide more information on each of the optional windows when they become relevant to the type of code we're demonstrating. For now, knowing how to make them appear and disappear is sufficient.

Talkin' the talk

Programmers have their own slang terms to describe what they do. For example, the term *code*, which refers to the actual instructions written in a programming language, is always singular, like the terms *hardware* and *software*. You don't add *hardwares* and *softwares* to your computer system. You add *hardware* and *software*. Likewise, you never write, or cut and paste *codes*. You write, or cut and paste, *code*.

The term *gooey* refers to Graphical User Interface, abbreviated GUI. Anything you can accomplish using a mouse (that is, without writing code) is considered the GUI. You create tables, queries, forms, reports, data access pages, and macros using the GUI. You only need to write code in modules.

A database may be referred to as an *app*, which is short for *application*. If a programmer says "I created most of the app with the GUI; I hardly wrote any code at all," he means he spent most of his time creating tables, queries, forms, reports, data access pages, and macros using the mouse, and relatively little time typing code in VBA.

Project Explorer　　　Code Window　　　Immediate Window

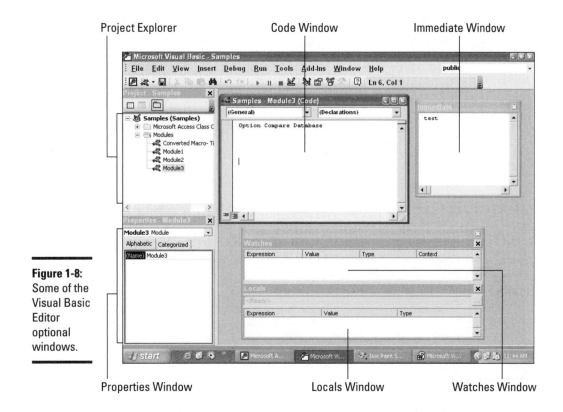

Figure 1-8:
Some of the
Visual Basic
Editor
optional
windows.

Properties Window　　　Locals Window　　　Watches Window

You can move and size most of the windows in the Visual Basic Editor using
standard methods. For instance, you can move most windows by dragging
their title bars. Size windows by dragging any corner or edge. Most of the
time, you won't need to have all those optional windows open to write code.
Feel free to close any optional window open in your editor by clicking its
Close (X) button. To open a window, choose View from the menu, and click
the name of the window you want to open.

If you have multiple monitors connected to your computer, you can put the
Access window on one monitor and the Visual Basic Editor window on the
other.

Using the Code window

The Code window is where you type your VBA code. The Code window, similar to a word processor or text editor, supports all the standard Windows
text-editing techniques. You can type text and use the Backspace and Delete

keys on your keyboard to delete text. You can use the Tab key to indent text. You can select text by dragging the mouse pointer through it. You can copy and paste text to, and from, the Code window. In short, the Code window is a text editor.

Like all windows in the Visual Basic Editor, the Code window can be docked (attached to the larger editing window) or free-floating. When the Code window is docked, you can click the Restore button to make it free-floating. When the Code window is free-floating, you can click its Maximize button to dock it again, as illustrated in Figure 1-9.

Restore
(undock Code window)

Maximize
(dock Code window)

Figure 1-9:
The Code
window
Maximize
and Restore
buttons.

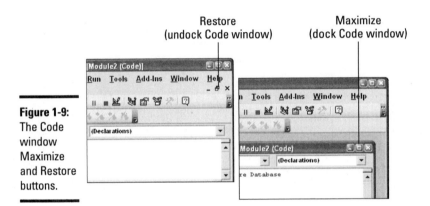

Other tools in the Code window are pointed out in Figure 1-10 and summarized in the following list.

✦ **Object box:** When viewing a class module, the Object box shows the name of the object associated with the current code and allows you to choose a different object. In a standard module, only the word General appears, as a standard module isn't associated with any specific form or report.

✦ **Procedure/Events box:** When viewing a class module, the Procedure/ Events box lists events supported by the object whose name appears in the Object box. When viewing a standard module, the Procedure/Events box lists the names of all procedures in that module. To quickly jump to a procedure or event, just choose its name from the drop-down list.

✦ **Split bar:** Drag the Split bar down to separate the Code window into two independently scrollable panes. Drag the Split bar back to the top of the scroll bar to unsplit the window.

✦ **Procedure View:** When clicked, declarations are hidden and only procedures are visible.

✦ **Full Module View:** When clicked, declarations and procedures are both visible.

✦ **Sizing handle:** Drag to size the window (you can drag any corner or edge as well).

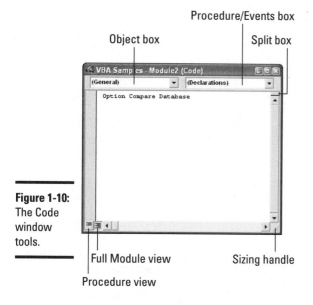

Procedure/Events box

Object box   Split box

Figure 1-10:
The Code
window
tools.

Full Module view   Sizing handle

Procedure view

Using the Immediate window

The *Immediate window,* or *debug window,* in the Visual Basic editor allows you to run code at any time, right on the spot. Use the Immediate window for testing and debugging (removing errors from) code. If the Immediate window isn't open in the Visual Basic Editor, you can bring it out of hiding at any time by choosing View⇔Immediate Window from the editor's menu.

When the Immediate window is open, you can anchor it to the bottom of the Visual Basic editor just by dragging its title bar to the bottom of the window. Optionally, you can make the Immediate window free-floating by dragging its title bar up and away from the bottom of the Visual Basic Editor program window. You can also dock and undock the Immediate window by right-clicking within the Immediate window and choosing the Dockable option from the shortcut menu that appears.

The Immediate window allows you to test expressions, run VBA procedures you create, and more. To test an expression, you can use the `debug.print` command, or the abbreviated ? version, followed by a blank space and the expression. Which command you use doesn't matter, though obviously typing the question mark is easier. You may think of the ? character in the Immediate window as standing for "What is?" Typing ? 1+1 into the Immediate window and pressing Enter is like asking "What is one plus one?" The Immediate window returns the answer to your question, 2, as shown in Figure 1-11.

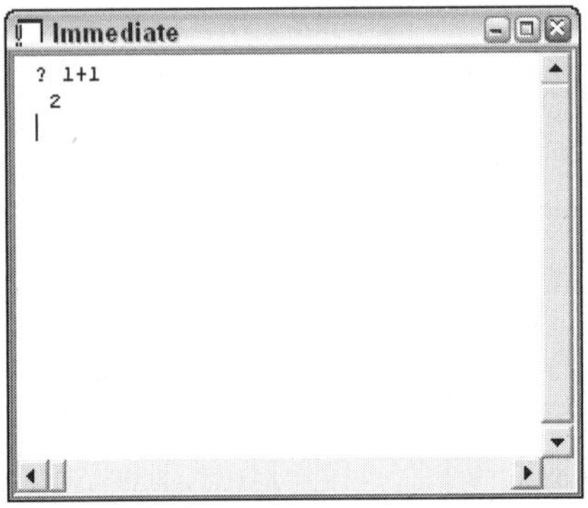

Figure 1-11: The free-floating Immediate window answers the grueling question "What is 1+1?"

```
? 1+1
 2
|
```

If you want to re-execute a line that you already typed into the Immediate window, you don't need to type that same line in again. Instead, just move the cursor to the end of the line that you want to re-execute and press Enter. To erase text from the Immediate window, drag the mouse pointer through whatever text you want to erase. Then press the Delete (Del) key or right-click the selected text and choose the Cut option from the shortcut menu.

You see many examples of using the Immediate window in the forthcoming chapters of this book. For the purposes of this chapter, knowing the Immediate window exists and basically how it works is enough. Do bear in mind that the Immediate window is just for testing and debugging. The Code window is where you type (or paste in) VBA code.

Using the Object Browser

VBA code can manipulate Access objects *programmatically*. **Remember:** Virtually everything in Access is an object — tables, forms, reports, and even a single control on a form or report are objects. Every Access object you see on-screen in Access is managed either *interactively* or *programmatically*. When you work with objects in the Access program window, using your mouse and keyboard, you use Access interactively. You do something with your mouse and keyboard and the object responds accordingly.

When you write code, you write instructions that tell Access to manipulate an object *programmatically*, without user intervention. You write instructions to automate some task that you may otherwise do interactively with mouse and keyboard. In order to manipulate an object programmatically, you write code that refers to the object by name, which is where the Access *object model* comes into play. The Access object model provides the names you use to refer to objects from within your VBA code.

The organization of the object model reflects the organization of the objects themselves. Take a look at the highest-level objects in the Access object model, shown in Figure 1-12. At the top of model is the Application object, which refers to the Microsoft Access program as a whole.

Beneath the Application object are several other objects and collections. For example, the Forms collection is contained within the Application object. Any given form can have any number of controls (Control Objects). Every single control has a set of properties (Properties). These relationships are represented by the arrangement and connections between the first four boxes in the upper-left corner of Figure 1-12.

The object model you work with is actually composed of one or more object libraries. An *object library* is an actual file on your hard disk that provides the names of objects that VBA refers to and manipulates. To view the objects that VBA can access, follow these steps to open the Object Browser:

1. **Make sure you're in the Visual Basic Editor.**

2. **Click the Object Browser button in the toolbar, or choose View⇨Object Browser from the menu, or press the F2 key.**

The Object Browser opens. Figure 1-13 shows the Object Browser and points out some of the major features of its window. The following list describes each component:

✦ **Project/Library list:** Allows you to choose a single library or project to work with, or <All Libraries>.

✦ **Classes list:** Shows the names of all classes in the currently selected library or project name (or all libraries).

✦ **Members list:** When you click a name in the Classes list, this pane shows the members (properties, methods, events, functions, objects) that belong to that class.

✦ **Details pane:** When you click a member name in the Members list, the Details pane shows the syntax for using the name, as well as the name of the library to which the member belongs. You can copy text from the Details pane to the Code window.

✦ **Split bar:** Drag the Split bar left or right to adjust the size of the panes. (Drag any edge or corner of the Object Browser window to size the window as a whole.)

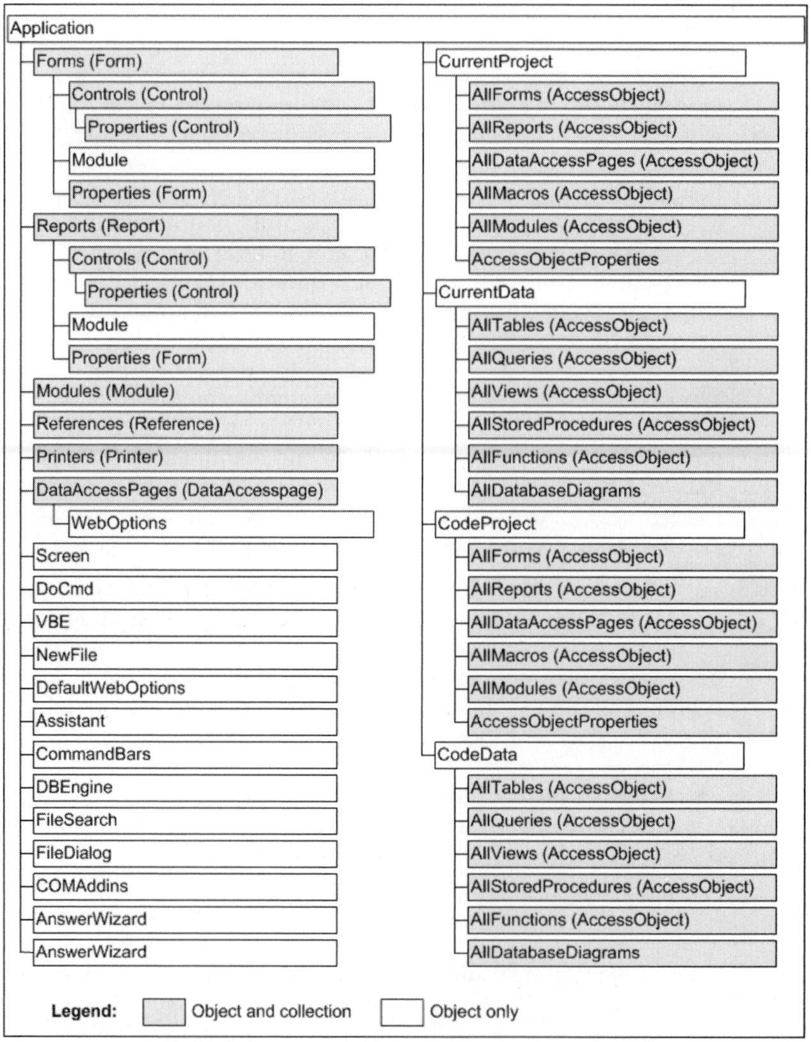

Figure 1-12:
The highest levels of the Access object model.

Project/Library list

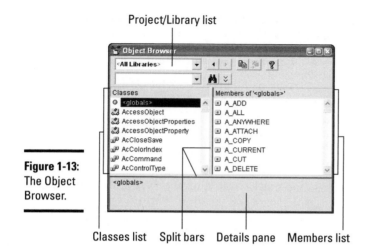

Figure 1-13:
The Object
Browser.

Classes list   Split bars   Details pane   Members list

Clicking the Project/Library drop-down list displays the names of all currently loaded object libraries. Many object libraries are available to you. By default, you likely see at least the four main libraries, which are summarized in the following list:

◆ **Access:** Contains classes that provide programmatic access to Access features, such as the commands that are available from the Access menu.

◆ **ADODB (ActiveX Data Objects):** Provides access to tables, queries, and the data within them; can also be used to access data from external SQL database servers.

◆ *Database/Project Name*: The name of the project or database in which you work is an object library. This object library provides access to the objects you created within your database.

◆ **VBA:** Contains all the functions that are built into Visual Basic.

When <All Libraries> is selected in the Project/Library drop-down list, the Classes list shows classes from all of the currently open object libraries. The currently open libraries are those that appear under <All Libraries> in the drop-down list.

Searching the Object Library

For a beginning programmer, the sheer quantity of items in the Object Browser is daunting. However, learning about the pre-written code you pick up elsewhere is useful. Suppose you find and use a procedure that has a DoCmd object in it. You're wondering what this DoCmd thingy is.

**Book VIII
Chapter 1**

**What the Heck
Is VBA?**

You can search the Object Library for information about any object, including DoCmd, by following these steps:

1. In the Object Browser, type the word you're searching for in the Search box.

In this example, type **DoCmd**, just like in Figure 1-14.

2. Click the Search button.

The search results appear in the Search Results pane.

3. Click the word you searched for.

4. Click the Help (Question mark) button on the Object Browser toolbar.

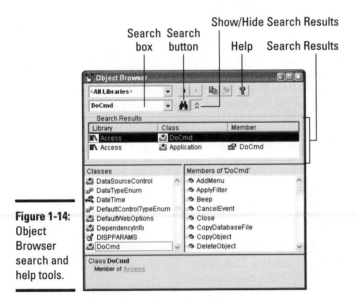

Figure 1-14:
Object
Browser
search and
help tools.

Figure 1-15 shows the Help window for the DoCmd object. For the absolute beginner, even the information in the Help text may be a bit advanced. However, as you gain experience and learn more about VBA, you'll find the Object Browser and Help windows useful for constructing references to objects, properties, and methods from within your code.

Referring to objects and collections

Objects in the object model all have a syntax, just as the statements in VBA have a syntax. The general syntax works this way: You start with the largest, most encompassing object, and work your way down to the most specific object, property, or method. Sort of like a path to a filename, as in C:\My Documents\MyFile.doc, where you start with the largest container (disk drive C:), down to the next container (the folder named My Documents), and then to the specific file (MyFile.doc).

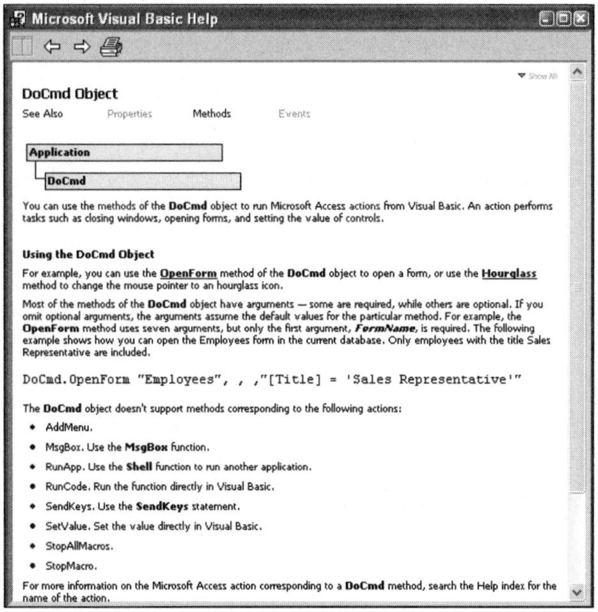

Figure 1-15:
The Help window for the DoCmd object.

For example, the Application object, shown back in Figure 1-12, includes a `CurrentProject` object. If you were to look up the `CurrentProject` object in the Object Browser and view its Help window, you see `CurrentProject` houses several collections, including one named `AllForms`. The `AllForms` collection contains the name of every form in the current database.

The `AllForms` collection, in turn, supports a `Count` property. That property returns the number of forms in the collection. Say that you have a database open and that database contains some forms. If you go to the Immediate window and type:

```
? Application.CurrentProject.AllForms.Count
```

and then press Enter, the Immediate window displays a number matching the total number of forms in the database.

Book VIII
Chapter 1

What the Heck
Is VBA?

At the risk of confusing matters, typing the following line in the Immediate window returns the same result:

```
? CurrentProject.AllForms.Count
```

The shortened version works because the `Application` option is the *default* parent object used if you don't specify a parent object before `CurrentProject`. (The `Application` object is the *parent* of `CurrentProject`, because `CurrentProject` is a member of the Application object library.)

The bottom line is that when you see a bunch of words separated by dots in code (such as `CurrentProject.AllForms.Count`), be aware that those words refer to some object. In a sense, the words are a path to the object, going from the largest object down to a single, specific object, property, method, or event. You can use the Object Browser as a means of looking up the meanings of the words to gain an understanding of how the pre-written code works.

As you gain experience, you can use the Object Browser to look up information about objects, collections, properties, methods, events, and constants within your code. For now, consider the Object Browser as yet another tool for discovering VBA as you go.

Choosing object libraries

Most likely, the object libraries that appear automatically in the Object Browser's Project/Library drop-down list (shown in Figure 1-16) are all you need. However, should a given project require you to add some other object library, follow these steps to add it:

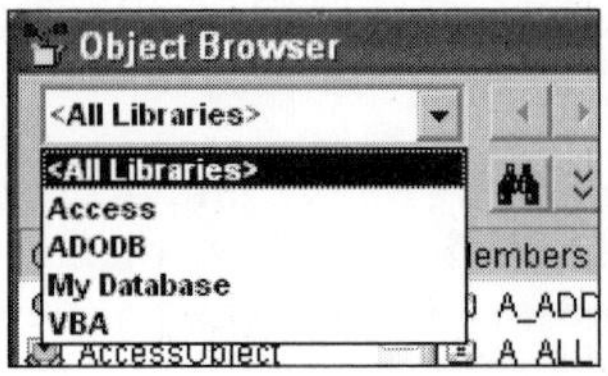

Figure 1-16:
The Project/
Library list
in the Object
Browser.

1. **Choose Tools⇨References from the Visual Basic Editor main menu.**

   The References dialog box opens.

2. **Choose any library name from the list.**

In the unlikely event that you need a library that isn't in the list, but you know you stored it on your hard disk, click the Browse button, navigate to the folder that contains the object library you need, click its name, and then click the Open button.

3. **Click OK when the object libraries you need have check marks.**

The Project/Library list in the Object Browser now includes all of the libraries you selected in the References dialog box.

Closing the Visual Basic Editor

When you're done working in the Visual Basic Editor, you can close it using whichever of the following techniques is most convenient for you:

✦ Choose File➪Close and Return to Microsoft Access from the Visual Basic Editor main menu.

✦ Click the Close button in the upper-right corner of the Visual Basic Editor program window.

✦ Right-click the Visual Basic Editor taskbar button and choose the Close option from the shortcut menu.

✦ Press Alt+Q.

Access continues to run even after you close the Visual Basic Editor window.

Discovering Code as You Go

Most beginning programmers start by working with code they pick up elsewhere, such as code generated by code wizards, or code copied from a Web site. You can also create VBA code, without writing it, by converting any macro to VBA code.

Converting macros to VBA code

Any macro you create in Access can be converted to VBA code. Converting macros to code is easier than writing code from scratch. For example, say you need to write some code because a macro can't do the job. But a macro can do 90 percent of the job. If you create the macro and convert it to VBA code, then 90 percent of your code is already written. You just have to add the other ten percent (especially helpful if you can't type worth beans).

See Book VI, Chapter 1 for how macros work and how to create them.

As an example, suppose you click the Macros button in the Objects list of the Database window, click the New button, and create a small simple macro, such as the example shown in Figure 1-17.

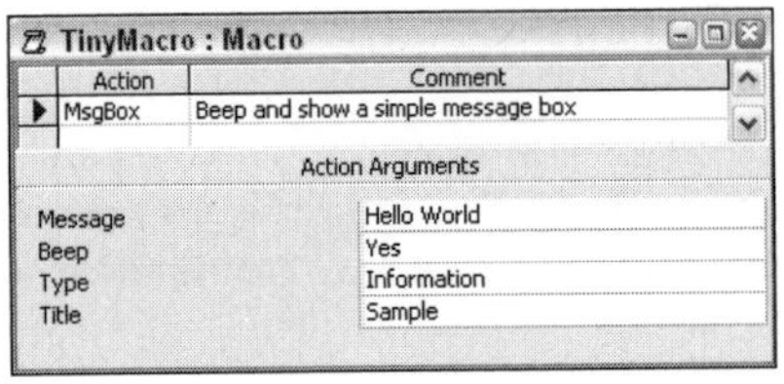

Figure 1-17:
A simple macro named TinyMacro.

When you convert a macro to VBA code, you actually convert all the macros in the macro group to code. Follow these steps for the basic procedure of converting macros to VBA:

1. **If the macro group that contains the macro is open, close that macro group and save any changes.**

2. **Click the Macros button in the Objects list of the Database window.**

   All stored macros appear in the right pane of the Database window.

3. **Click the name of the macro group you want to convert to VBA code to select (highlight) that name.**

4. **Choose Tools⇨Macro⇨Convert Macros to Visual Basic from the Access main menu, as shown in Figure 1-18.**

   The TinyMacro macro shown is just an example. You can convert any macro that's available in the database window.

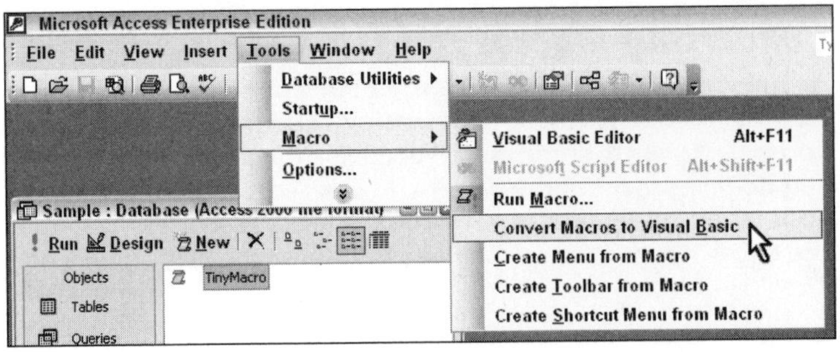

Figure 1-18:
About to convert TinyMacro to Visual Basic code.

A dialog box appears, asking if you want to include error-handling code or comments in the code. If you want to keep the code relatively simple, you can clear the first option and select only the second option.

5. Click the Convert button.

You see a message indicating when the conversion is complete.

6. Click OK.

The converted macro is in a standard module named Converted Macro - *macro name*, where *macro name* is the name of the macro you converted. For example, Figure 1-19 shows the Database window after converting a sample macro (named TinyMacro) to VBA code, and then clicking the Modules button in the Objects list of the Database window.

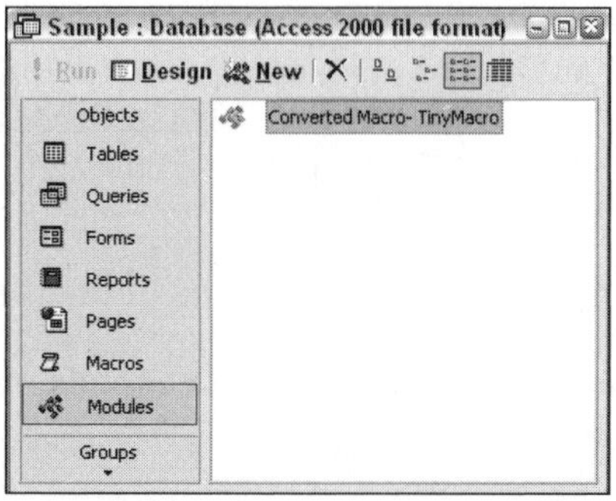

Figure 1-19: Macros converted to VBA are stored in modules.

7. Double-click the name of the converted macro in the Database window to view the VBA code.

Like all VBA code, the code from the converted macro opens in the Visual Basic Editor Code window, as shown in Figure 1-20.

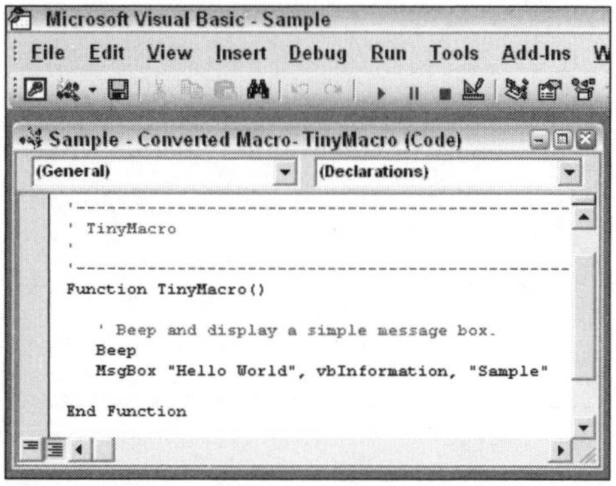

Figure 1-20: The converted macro in the Visual Basic Editor.

You don't need to do anything to the converted code — it works fine as it is. To get back to Access, just close the Visual Basic Editor window again.

Cutting and pasting code

Many VBA programmers post examples of code they've written on Web pages. When you come across some sample code you want to incorporate into your own database, re-typing it all into the Visual Basic Editor is not necessary. Instead, just use standard Windows cut-and-paste techniques to copy the code from the Web page into the Visual Basic Editor.

Say you come across some code in a Web page you want to use in your own database. In the Web page, you drag the mouse pointer through the code you want to copy to select that code. Then press Ctrl+C to copy that selected code to the Windows Clipboard.

Back in Access, create a new module or open an existing module in which you want to place the code. In the Code window, click at the position you want to put the copied code. Then paste the code to the cursor position by pressing Ctrl+V.

Bear in mind, however, that just pasting code into the Code window doesn't make the code do anything. Code, like a macro, doesn't do anything until called upon to do its job. Exactly how you call code depends on many factors, as we discuss in the next chapter of this book.

Chapter 2: Writing Code

Writing VBA code is different from writing in English or some other human language. When you write in English, you're presumably writing to another human being who speaks the same language. If your English isn't so great (bad spelling, poor grammar), your recipient can probably still figure out what your message means. Humans have flexible brains that can figure things out based on context.

Not so for computers. Computers don't have brains, and can't figure out anything based on context. When you write code, the computer does exactly what the code tells it to do. If the computer can't read and process a statement, the procedure stops running and an error message appears on-screen.

Before you start writing your own custom code, you need to know about syntax, and the resources available for finding the syntax for the tasks you want to program. And you need to know at least some basic techniques for testing your code to see if it's going to work before you try putting it to use.

How VBA Works

VBA code is organized into procedures. Each *procedure* contains any number of lines of code called statements. Each *statement* instructs VBA to perform some action. The procedure sits in its module, doing nothing, until some event calls the procedure.

When a procedure is called, each statement *executes* (runs) one at a time. VBA fully executes the first statement, then fully executes the second statement, and so forth, until the End Sub or End Function statement, which marks the end of the procedure. At that point, the code stops executing. Figure 2-1 summarizes how procedures work.

Actually, the pure top-to-bottom flow of execution can be altered using loops and decision-making code, as we describe in Chapter 3 of this book.

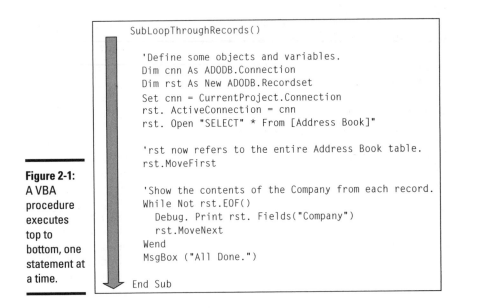

```
SubLoopThroughRecords()

    'Define some objects and variables.
    Dim cnn As ADODB.Connection
    Dim rst As New ADODB.Recordset
    Set cnn = CurrentProject.Connection
    rst. ActiveConnection = cnn
    rst. Open "SELECT" * From [Address Book]"

    'rst now refers to the entire Address Book table.
    rst.MoveFirst

    'Show the contents of the Company from each record.
    While Not rst.EOF()
        Debug. Print rst. Fields("Company")
        rst.MoveNext
    Wend
    MsgBox ("All Done.")

End Sub
```

Figure 2-1:
A VBA
procedure
executes
top to
bottom, one
statement at
a time.

Each statement within a procedure must follow strict rules of syntax. You can't just write text that looks like VBA code. All languages, including English and VBA, have rules of syntax. Rules of *syntax* define the order in which words must be placed so that a statement makes sense. For example, the following sentence — which is English, by the way, and not VBA — doesn't make sense because grammar rules are broken (similar to some of those e-mails we get):

> moon the yapped sullen dog at irritating the.

If we rearrange the letters and words of that sentence so that they follow the correct rules of syntax for the English language, the sentence makes sense:

> The irritating dog yapped at the sullen moon.

The rules of VBA syntax are more rigid than the rules of human language. Even the slightest misspelling or missing punctuation mark causes a statement to fail. Every VBA *keyword* (any word that VBA recognizes as its own) has a *syntax chart* that defines the rules of syntax for that keyword.

Finding a keyword's syntax

You can find the syntax for any keyword by searching the Help system in the VBA Editor program window (not the Access program window). The simplest thing to do, after you have a sense of what keywords are available to you, is to first make sure you're in the VBA Editor by opening any module. Then, in the Code window, type the keyword with which you need help.

Then select that word (by double-clicking the word), and press the Help key, F1. The keyword appears in a Help window.

Figure 2-2 shows what happens if you select the `MsgBox` keyword and press the F1 key. The Help window shows information about the `MsgBox` keyword. Blue text in the Help window, such as See Also and Example, are links to related Help pages. You can click any blue underlined text, such as the <u>String Expression</u> and <u>Numeric Expression</u> links, to see a definition of the underlined term. The syntax chart for the keyword is located under the Syntax heading. Most of the information below the syntax chart defines how you can use the various *arguments* (words such as *prompt*, *button*, and so forth in the syntax chart) to create exactly the action you're seeking.

A VBA keyword is any word that has meaning in the language. Some keywords are statements, some are functions. Some, such as `MsgBox`, can be used either as a function or a statement. The important point to remember is if a word or name has any meaning at all in VBA, then it's considered a VBA keyword.

Selected keyword MsgBox   Help for the MsgBox keyword

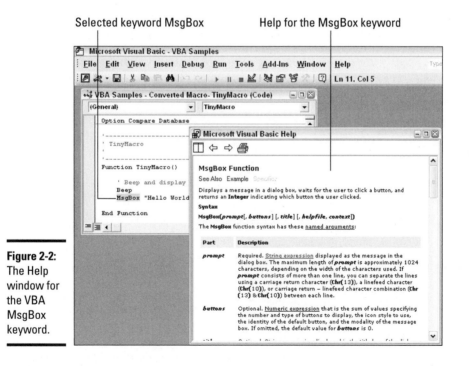

Figure 2-2:
The Help
window for
the VBA
MsgBox
keyword.

Reading the syntax charts

The syntax chart for most keywords resembles the example shown for the `MsgBox` keyword, which looks like the following:

`MsgBox(prompt[, buttons] [, title] [, helpfile, context])`

A lot of information is packed into the preceding syntax. A quick overview of the various elements of the syntax indicate the following:

✦ **Bold:** An actual keyword or character that must be typed exactly as shown.

✦ *Italic* or ***bold italic:*** Represents an *argument* — a placeholder — for a value you supply when writing code. ***Bold italic*** represents named arguments.

✦ [ ]: Anything in square brackets is an optional part of the statement and can be omitted. Do not type the square brackets into the statement.

Beneath the syntax line you find detailed information on each argument that `MsgBox` supports. Beneath the descriptions of the arguments are the various settings you can use for the arguments. In most cases, you can use either a *constant* (a word that has a specific meaning in VBA) or a *value* (a number) to specify the setting of an argument. For example, Figure 2-3 shows valid settings for the optional `buttons` argument offered by the `MsgBox` function.

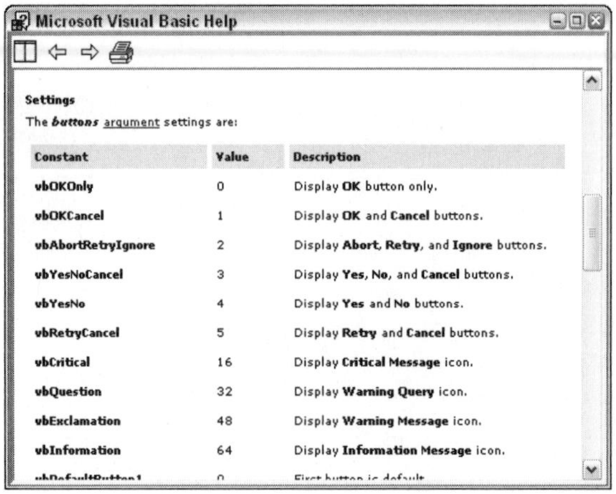

Figure 2-3: Settings for the MsgBox function's optional buttons argument.

Constant	Value	Description
vbOKOnly	0	Display **OK** button only.
vbOKCancel	1	Display **OK** and **Cancel** buttons.
vbAbortRetryIgnore	2	Display **Abort**, **Retry**, and **Ignore** buttons.
vbYesNoCancel	3	Display **Yes**, **No**, and **Cancel** buttons.
vbYesNo	4	Display **Yes** and **No** buttons.
vbRetryCancel	5	Display **Retry** and **Cancel** buttons.
vbCritical	16	Display **Critical Message** icon.
vbQuestion	32	Display **Warning Query** icon.
vbExclamation	48	Display **Warning Message** icon.
vbInformation	64	Display **Information Message** icon.
vbDefaultButton1	0	First button is default.

Most settings can be either a *string expression* or a *numeric expression*. The rules for these expressions are identical to the rules for expressions used throughout Access. A string expression can be a literal string enclosed in quotation marks (such as "Smith" or "Jones"), or the name of a field or variable (described in the next chapter of this book) that contains a string, such as [LastName] (refers to a field in a table). A numeric expression can be anything that results in a valid number. For example 10 is a valid numeric expression, as is 2*5 (two times five), as is the name of a field or variable that contains a number.

Given all this information, take a look at some MsgBox statements that follow the rules of syntax, and are considered valid:

```
MsgBox("Slow Children at Play")
```

The preceding statement is valid because the one-and-only required named argument is included — the placeholder text prompt duly replaced by the Slow Children at Play phrase. When executed, the MsgBox() statement displays the message shown in Figure 2-4.

Figure 2-4:
Message box display by MsgBox statement with one argument.

If you want the message box to display some button or buttons other than OK, then you have to specify a value for the buttons argument. You also have to precede the statement with a variable name (any name of your own choosing — we just use x because it's easy to type). You can also use the optional title argument to put a specific word into the title bar of the message box.

For example, the following statement is perfectly valid syntax for the MsgBox keyword, where vbYesNo is the setting that tells the box to display Yes and No buttons — and replaces the placeholder text buttons in the MsgBox syntax chart — and "Question" is literal text that appears in the title bar of the message box (and replaces the placeholder text title in the same chart).

```
x = MsgBox ("Are we having fun yet?",vbYesNo,"Question")
```

The following statement is identical to the preceding statement, but uses the value 4 (from the Value column of Figure 2-3) rather than the vbYesNo constant to specify that the message box display Yes and No buttons.

```
x = MsgBox ("Are we having fun yet?",4,"Question")
```

The preceding MsgBox statements are just two different ways of saying the same thing. They both tell Access to display a message box showing the message "Are we having fun yet?" with Yes and No buttons, and the word "Question" in the title bar. Each example, when executed, displays the message shown in Figure 2-5.

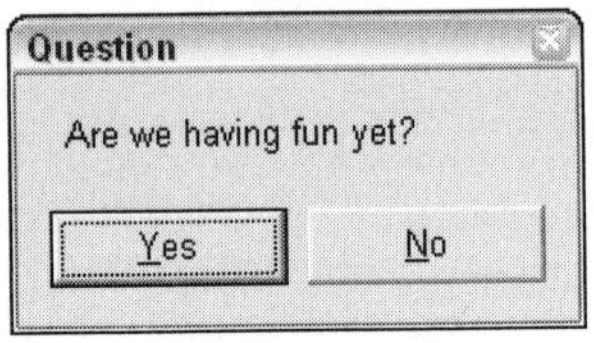

Figure 2-5:
The message box displayed by the MsgBox statement with three arguments.

Because the buttons argument is a numeric expression created using numeric values or the pre-defined constants (such as vbYesNo and vbQuestion), you can combine two or more to define both an icon and the buttons for the message box. For example, the preceding MsgBox statement uses the vbYesNo and vbQuestion constants to specify that the box show a Question icon as well as the Yes/No buttons:

```
x= MsgBox ("Are we having fun yet?",vbYesNo+vbQuestion,
    "Question")
```

You could accomplish the same goal using the numeric values for those settings, as the following statement shows:

```
x = MsgBox ("Are we having fun yet?",4+32,"Question")
```

Because 4 + 32 equals 36, you can also just use the sum of the two numbers to specify the setting for the buttons argument, as the following statement does:

```
x = MsgBox ("Are we having fun yet?",36,"Question")
```

Any one of the statements, when executed, shows a message box similar to Figure 2-5, but with a Question icon added in, as in Figure 2-6.

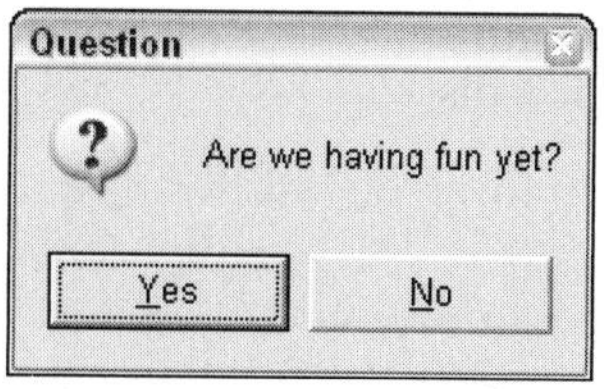

Figure 2-6:
Message
box with a
Question
icon and
Yes/No
buttons.

Using named arguments

While you have some flexibility in how you express values for arguments, you have almost no flexibility in terms of the order in which you place the arguments within a statement. For example, if you want to use just the first and third arguments in a syntax chart, such as the Prompt and Title arguments of the MsgBox function, you still need to include a comma for the second argument to make clear that the last argument is the title, as in the following example:

```
x = MsgBox("Howdy",,"I am the Title")
```

The first comma after the "Howdy" prompt shows the start of the second argument. No argument shows between the two commas because you're not using that argument. The second comma then shows that the next argument is actually the third one, Title, and hence the text, "I am the Title," displays in the title bar of the message box.

You can get around the strict order of arguments. If a statement supports *named arguments,* you can ignore the order of arguments if you precede each value by its name and a colon (:). When viewing the syntax chart for a keyword, named arguments are shown in italics. If you refer to Figure 2-2, you see the prompt and buttons arguments (and other arguments currently scrolled out of view) are all named arguments. Because the MsgBox function supports named arguments, you could also use this syntax rather than the two commas:

```
x = MsgBox(prompt:"Howdy",title:"I am the Title")
```

Module level versus procedure level

As you work with the VBA Help windows and syntax charts, you often come across the terms module level and procedure level. These terms refer to the location of code within the module. Simply stated, anything that's defined near the top of the module above the first Function or Sub procedure is a *module-level declaration.* Anything defined within a procedure is said to be defined at the *procedure level,* as illustrated in Figure 2-7.

Module-level stuff

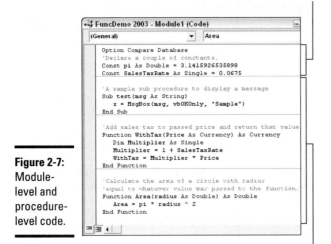

```
FuncDemo 2003 - Module1 (Code)
(General)                          Area

Option Compare Database
'Declare a couple of constants.
Const pi As Double = 3.1415926535898
Const SalesTaxRate As Single = 0.0675

'A sample sub procedure to display a message
Sub test(msg As String)
    x = MsgBox(msg, vbOKOnly, "Sample")
End Sub

'Add sales tax to passed price and return that value
Function WithTax(Price As Currency) As Currency
    Dim Multiplier As Single
    Multiplier = 1 + SalesTaxRate
    WithTax = Multiplier * Price
End Function

'Calculate the area of a circle with radius
'equal to whatever value was passed to the function.
Function Area(radius As Double) As Double
    Area = pi * radius ^ 2
End Function
```

Figure 2-7:
Module-
level and
procedure-
level code.

Procedure-level stuff

All procedures that you add to a module should be placed below the declarations section of the module. When you see one or more Option statements at the top of a module, make sure that any procedures you add to the module start below all the Option statements at the top of the module.

Declaring Module Options

Most modules, even one you just create that is otherwise blank, contains at least one declaration at the top. Typically it reads Option Compare Database, which doesn't even seem to make any sense. And frankly, changing or deleting that is extremely unlikely. But the declaration actually has meaning.

The word, Option, tells the VBA to set an option. The specific option to set is the Compare option. The Compare option tells VBA what rules to use when comparing values. The word, Database, means to use the same rules that the rest of the database uses when comparing values. Using the same rules is always a good idea because otherwise things could get very confusing. But the other two possible settings are the Binary and Text options, as the following summarizes:

✦ **Option Compare Binary:** When comparing strings, uppercase letters are considered to be smaller than lowercase letters. (With Option Compare Database, uppercase and lowercase letters are considered equal.)

✦ **Option Compare Text:** The sort order of your system's *locale* (the country and spoken language of your location) is used to compare strings. This option may be useful when creating a database that's used in non-English speaking countries.

Writing Your Own VBA Procedures

Just about all code you write is contained within procedures. A procedure is a single chunk of code that performs a series of actions when called. As mentioned in Chapter 1 of this book, a sub procedure always begins with a Sub statement, or Private Sub statement, and ends with an End Sub statement. A function procedure begins with a Function statement and ends with an End Function statement. You can add new procedures to class modules or standard modules. How you do so depends on where you want to place the procedure.

Creating a new standard procedure

A procedure in a standard module is available to all Access objects, and isn't tied to any particular control or event. To create a new procedure in a standard module:

1. **Create a new standard module by clicking the Modules button in the Objects list of the Database window, and then clicking the New button in the window's toolbar.**

   or

   Open an existing module by clicking the Modules button in the Objects list of the Database window, and then double-clicking the module name in the right pane of the window.

2. **Choose Insert⇨Procedure from the Visual Basic Editor menu.**

   The Add Procedure dialog box opens, as shown in Figure 2-8.

3. **Type a name for the procedure in the Name box.**

   The name can be anything you choose, but must start with a letter and cannot contain any blank spaces.

4. **Choose a type of function — Sub to create a sub procedure or Function to create a function.**

   The Property option in Type list has to do with creating custom objects, which isn't relevant to the topic at hand.

5. **Choose either the Public procedure type (to make the procedure available to all Access objects) or the Private procedure type (to make the procedure visible only to the current module) in the Scope section.**

If you're not sure whether to choose the `Public` procedure or the `Private` procedure, choose public. Private procedures are generally used only in class modules, not standard modules.

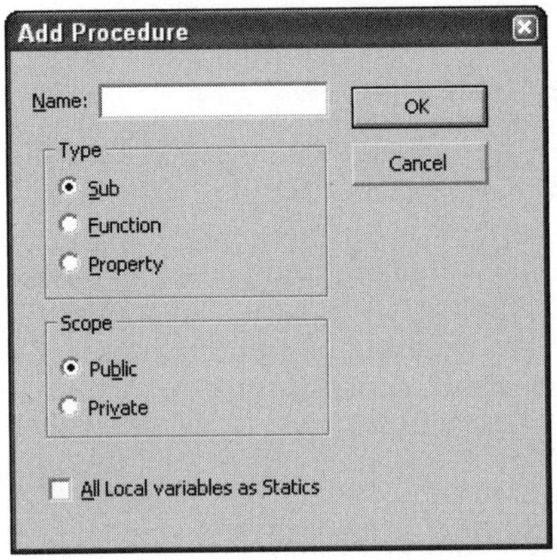

Figure 2-8:
The Add
Procedure
dialog box.

6. **Check the All Local Variables as Statics check box if you want to ensure that variables in the procedure retain their values between calls.**

   If you're not sure what to do with the All Local Variables as Statics option, your best bet is to leave it unselected.

7. **Click the OK button in the Add Procedure dialog box.**

   You see a new, empty procedure in the Code window.

If you chose the `Function` procedure type, the procedure looks something like this:

```
Public Function name()
End Function
```

If you chose the `Sub` procedure type, the code looks something like this:

```
Public Sub name()
End Sub
```

Where *name* is the name you typed into the Add Procedure dialog box.

Creating a procedure through the Add Procedure dialog box is not really necessary. You can just type the `Function` statement or `Sub` statement into the Code window, and VBA automatically adds a corresponding `End Function` or `End Sub` statement.

The statements that the Add Procedure dialog box adds to the module use only the bare minimum of optional arguments supported by the `Function` and `Sub` statements. Depending on what the procedure does, you may need to define some additional arguments, as discussed in the section, "Using arguments in procedures," later in this chapter.

Creating a new event procedure

Recall that an event procedure is already tied to some event, such as the clicking of a button on a form. If you want to create a new event procedure for a control on a report or form, follow these steps:

1. **In Design view, open the form or report that contains the control for which you want to create a new procedure.**

   In the Database window, select the name of the form or report you want to open, and choose the Design button.

2. **Select the control for which you want to create a procedure.**

3. **Click the Event tab in the Properties sheet.**

   If the Properties sheet isn't open, right-click the selected control and choose the Properties option from the shortcut menu to see its properties, and then click the Events tab.

4. **Click in the event that should trigger the procedure into action, and then click the Build (...) button that appears.**

   For example, if the selected control is a button, and you want a user to click that button to trigger the procedure into action, click in the On Click event, and then click its Build button.

   The Choose Builder dialog box opens.

5. **Click the Code Builder button, and then click the OK button.**

   The class module for the form or report opens in the Visual Basic Editor, with the cursor resting in a new procedure.

The name of the new procedure is a combination of the control's name and the event that triggers the procedure into action, as illustrated in the example shown in Figure 2-9.

Using arguments in procedures

All procedures are capable of accepting *arguments* (also called *parameters*). Arguments have nothing to do with verbal disagreements among people. Rather, an argument is data that's passed to the procedure from outside the

procedure. Forgetting about VBA for a moment, we can use any built-in function to illustrate what an argument is. The built-in UCase() function accepts
one argument — a string (text). You pass text to the UCase() function, as in
the following example:

```
=UCase("howdy world")
```

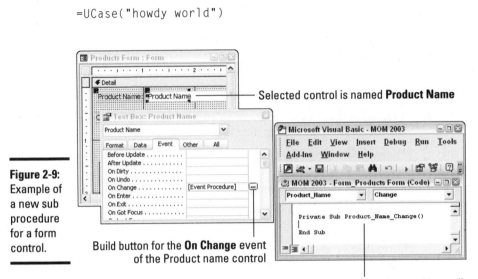

Figure 2-9:
Example of
a new sub
procedure
for a form
control.

Selected control is named **Product Name**

Build button for the **On Change** event
of the Product name control

New sub procedure is automatically named **Product_Name_Change()**

Or in the Immediate window of the Visual Basic Editor, you can type the following to test the built-in UCase() function:

```
? UCase("howdy world")
```

The UCase() function returns that same chunk of text, but with all the letters converted to uppercase. When you pass "howdy world" to the UCase()
function, it spits back (*returns*) HOWDY WORLD.

When you create your own procedures, you can define what arguments, if any,
the procedure is capable of accepting. If you create a function procedure, you
can also define what the procedure returns. (A sub procedure doesn't return a
value.)

If you were to look at the syntax chart for the Sub statement, and take away
some of the optional stuff from that chart, you see the syntax for the Sub
statement looks something like this:

```
Sub name [(arglist)]
End Sub
```

What's with the simplified syntax?

Many of the optional arguments available in VBA statements represent very advanced concepts that are difficult to describe out of context. This book often shows a simplified version of the syntax for a given statement, focusing just on those arguments you either need to use or are likely to want to use. When you compare the simplified syntax shown in this book with the actual syntax shown in the Visual Basic Editor Help windows, the two may not be the same. Don't be alarmed. It's not a mistake.

Using the simplified syntax in this book allows you to discover VBA programming in a manner that focuses on the most basic — and most important — stuff first. You can work your way to the more advanced — and mostly optional — stuff as needed. The simplified syntax may well be all you ever need to use when writing your own code.

The simplified syntax for the Function statement (with some of the optional stuff removed) looks similar, as the following:

```
Function name [(arglist)] As type
End Function
```

In both cases, the *arglist* is optional, as indicated by the square brackets. But even the optional *arglist* has a syntax, the simplified version of which is:

```
name [As type]
```

where *name* is a name you make up. You can list multiple arguments by separating their names with commas.

The *type* component specifies the data type of the data. Like Access tables, VBA supports multiple data types. These data types are similar (but not identical) to data types defined for fields in the structure of a table. For example, the String data type in VBA is similar to the Text data type in an Access table, in that both contain text.

Table 2-1 lists all the VBA data types. Admittedly, Table 2-1 shows more information than you probably need to know. The Storage Size column shows how many bytes each data type assumes. The Declaration character shows an optional character used at the end of a name to specify a data type. For example, the name, PersonName$, defines PersonName as containing a string. But in the real world, you really need not concern yourself too much with those columns. The first two columns in the table provide the information you really need to know.

**Book VIII
Chapter 2**

Writing Code

The Decimal data type can't be used in an arglist. Officially, the Decimal data type can only be used as a subtype of the Variant data type, using the cDec() function.

Table 2-1	VBA Data Types		
Data Type	*Acceptable Values*	*Storage Size*	*Declaration Character*
Boolean	True (-1) or False (0)	2 bytes	
Byte	0 to 255	1 bytes	
Currency	-922,337,203,685,477.5808 to 922,337,203,685,477.5807	8 bytes	@
Date	January 1, 100 to December 31, 9999	8 bytes	
Decimal	+/-79,228,162,514,264,337, 593,543,950,335 with no decimal point; +/-7.922816 2514264337593543950335 with 28 places to the right of the decimal; smallest non-zero number is +/-0.0000000000000000000 000000001	14 bytes	
Double	-1.79769313486231E308 to -4.94065645841247E-324 for negative values; 4.94065645841247E-324 to 1.79769313486232E308 for positive values	8 bytes	#
Integer	-32,768 to 32,767	2 bytes	%
Long	-2,147,483,648 to 2,147,483,647	4 bytes	&
Object	Name of any object	4 bytes	
Single	-3.402823E38 to -1.401298E-45 for negative values; 1.401298E-45 to 3.402823E38 for positive values	4 bytes	!
String (fixed length)	Any text from 1 to 65,400 characters in length	10 + string length	$
Variant (no text)	Any number up to the range of the Double data type	16 bytes	
Variant (with text)	Any text up to 2,000,000,000 characters in length	22 + string length	

You define the names and data types of arguments within the parentheses that follow the name of the procedure. Separate the name from the data type using the word "As." For example, the following Sub statement defines a sub procedure named SampleSub(). That sub procedure accepts two arguments: a single-precision number named Amount and a string named Payee:

```
Sub SampleSub(Amount As Single, Payee As String)
...code...
End Sub
```

Unlike a sub procedure, a function procedure can return a value. You define the data type of the returned value after the parentheses and the word "As." The returned data doesn't need a name, just a data type. For example, the following Function statement defines a function procedure named IsOpen(). That function accepts one argument — a string. The name FormName refers to that passed string within the function. The function returns either a True or False value (the Boolean data type).

```
Function IsOpen(FormName As String) As Boolean

        ...code...
End Function
```

Don't bother to type either of the preceding procedures because they don't actually do anything. They just demonstrate the syntax of the Sub and Function statements. Figure 2-10 further points out the purpose of the various components of the sample Function statement.

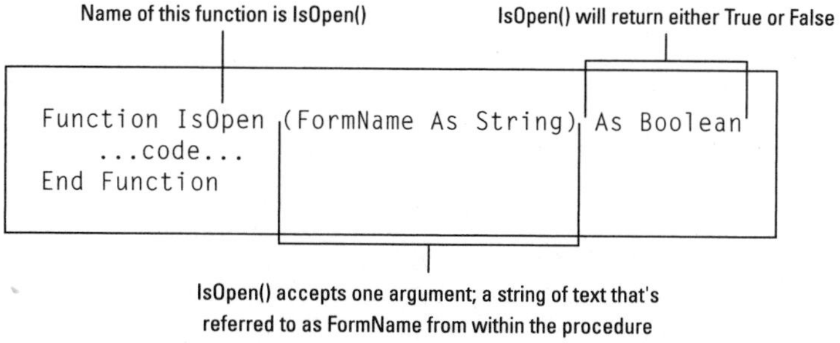

Figure 2-10: Components of the sample function statement.

Name of this function is IsOpen()

IsOpen() will return either True or False

```
Function IsOpen (FormName As String) As Boolean
        ...code...
End Function
```

IsOpen() accepts one argument; a string of text that's referred to as FormName from within the procedure

Returning a value from a function

Any function can return a value. To define the value that a function returns, you use the following syntax within the body of the function:

```
functionName = value
```

where *functionName* is the name of the function, but without the parentheses. And *value* is the value that the function returns. The following function is an example:

```
Function WithTax(AnyNumber As Currency) As Currency
    WithTax = AnyNumber * 1.065
End Function
```

Notice that the function is named WithTax() and accepts one argument, a value stored as the Currency data type under the name AnyNumber. The function also returns a Currency number because of the expression WithTax = AnyNumber * 1.065, as illustrated in Figure 2-11.

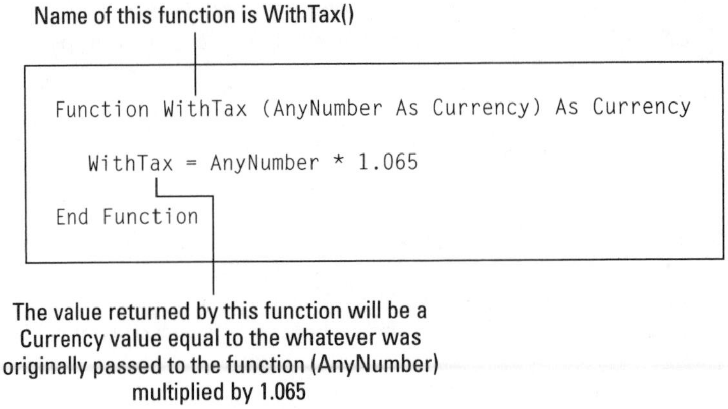

Name of this function is WithTax()

Figure 2-11:
The
WithTax()
function
returns the
passed
value
multiplied
by 1.065.

```
Function WithTax (AnyNumber As Currency) As Currency

    WithTax = AnyNumber * 1.065

End Function
```

The value returned by this function will be a
Currency value equal to the whatever was
originally passed to the function (AnyNumber)
multiplied by 1.065

Multiplying a number by 1.065 is equivalent to adding 6.5 percent sales tax to that number. Do this little trick with any sales tax rate. For example, to add 7.75 percent sales tax, you would multiply by 1.0775.

The WithTax() function is a complete VBA procedure that actually works. You can use the function like any built-in Access function anywhere within the current database. You could even test it out in the Immediate window. For example, type the function into the Code window, exactly as shown, and then type the following code into the Immediate window:

```
? WithTax(10)
```

The Immediate window displays 10.65, as shown in Figure 2-12, because 10 times 1.065 equals 10.65.

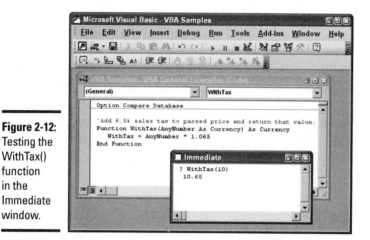

Figure 2-12: Testing the WithTax() function in the Immediate window.

Typing and Editing in the Code Window

In order for a procedure to actually do anything, it needs to contain some valid VBA code. As you type statements in the Code window, the VBA Editor offers a little help along the way, in the form of small syntax charts and drop-down lists of acceptable values for arguments.

For example, if you type MsgBox(or x = MsgBox(into the Code window, the syntax chart for MsgBox appears near where you're typing, as shown in Figure 2-13.

Within the syntax chart, boldface indicates which argument you're about to type. For example, the boldface Prompt in Figure 2-13 shows that you're expected to type the contents of the Prompt argument. If you were to type a prompt and a comma, or just a comma, the boldface would move to the second argument, buttons, to show that you're now expected to type a value for the second argument, and so forth. As in the Help windows, optional arguments are shown in square brackets ([ ]) and can be omitted.

Figure 2-13:
Syntax for
MsgBox
appears
after typing
the first part
of a
MsgBox
statement.

When you get to an argument where you can use a constant to specify a setting, a drop-down list of possible choices appears automatically, as in Figure 2-14. You can either type the constant name, or just double-click a constant name to have that name inserted into your code.

Figure 2-14:
A list offers
acceptable
constants
for the
second
argument.

Shortcut keys used in the Code window

While typing in the Code window, you can use the various shortcut keys listed in Table 2-2 to navigate around, make changes, and so forth. Most of the shortcut keys are identical to those found in other text-editing programs and word processors.

Table 2-2	Shortcut Keys You Can Use in the Code Window
Action	*Shortcut Key*
Move cursor right one character	→
Select character to right	Shift+→
Move cursor right one word	Ctrl+→
Select to end of word	Shift+ Ctrl+→
Move cursor left one character	←

Action	Shortcut Key
Select character to left of cursor	Shift+←
Move cursor left one word	Ctrl+←
Move cursor to start of line	Home
Select text to start of line	Shift+Home
Move cursor to end of line	End
Select text to end of line	Shift+End
Move cursor up a line	↑
Move cursor down a line	↓
Move cursor to next procedure	Ctrl+↓
Move cursor to previous procedure	Ctrl+↑
Scroll up one screen	PgUp
Scroll down one screen	PgDn
Go to top of module	Ctrl+Home
Select all text to top of module	Shift+Ctrl+Home
Go to bottom of module	Ctrl+End
Select all text to bottom of module	Shift+Ctrl+End
Cut selection	Ctrl+X
Copy selection	Ctrl+C
Paste	Ctrl+V
Cut current line to Clipboard	Ctrl+Y
Delete to end of word	Ctrl+Delete
Delete character or selected text	Delete (Del)
Delete character to left of cursor	Backspace
Delete to end of word	Ctrl+Delete
Delete to beginning of word	Ctrl+Backspace
Undo	Ctrl+Z
Indent line	Tab
Outdent line	Shift+Tab
Find	Ctrl+F
Replace	Ctrl+H
Find Next	F3
Find Previous	Shift+F3
View Object Browser	F2
View Immediate window	Ctrl+G

**Book VIII
Chapter 2**

Writing Code

(continued)

Table 2-2 *(continued)*

Action	Shortcut Key
View Code window	F7
View shortcut menu	Shift+F10 (or right-click)
Get help with currently selected word	F1
Run a Sub/UserForm	F5
Stop code execution	Ctrl+Break

Typing comments

When typing VBA code, you can mix in programmer comments (usually called comments for short). A *comment* is plain-English text for human consumption only. VBA ignores all comments and processes only the code. As such, comments are entirely optional. The purpose of a comment is simply to "jot down notes" within the code, either as a future reminder to yourself or to other programmers working on the same project.

The first character of a comment must be an apostrophe ('). In the Code window, comments appear as green text. Each comment is on its own line or follows a line of VBA code. Never put VBA code to the right of a comment on the same line because VBA assumes all text after the apostrophe (on the same line) is just a comment, and ignores everything to the right of the apostrophe.

Breaking lines of code

Unlike a word processor, where long lines of text are word-wrapped (broken between words as necessary), text in the Visual Basic Editor never wraps. You (and Access) really need to be able to see each line independently. If the Visual Basic Editor were to word-wrap, you wouldn't really know exactly where one line ends and the next one begins.

Sometimes you may end up typing a statement that extends beyond the right border of the window. For example, the line that begins with `AnyText =` in Figure 2-15 is actually much longer than it appears. Most of the line is invisible, cut off at the right margin. The statement works as is. But you may want to see the entire statement when writing, testing, or modifying your code.

If you want to break a single long statement into two or more lines, you must insert a *continuation character* (an underscore _) at the end of the line, just before you press Enter to break the line. Essentially, the continuation character tells Access "the line break that follows isn't the end of this statement. Rather, I want to break up this lengthy line." Figure 2-16 shows the lengthy line broken into three shorter lines using the continuation character.

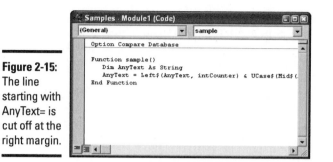

Figure 2-15:
The line starting with AnyText= is cut off at the right margin.

While you can break a statement into two or more lines using the continuation character, you cannot break a literal string in the same manner. A *literal string* is text enclosed in quotation marks, as in the following example:

```
SomeChunk = "A literal string is text in quotation marks"
```

If you try to break a literal string into two lines, by using a continuation character, as the following example does, you get an Expected end of statement **error message:**

```
SomeChunk = "A literal string is _
    text in quotation marks"
```

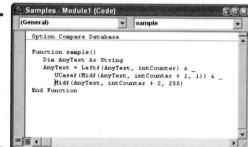

Figure 2-16:
The long line from Figure 2-15 broken into three shorter lines.

To break a literal string, you need to terminate the top line with a quotation mark ("), followed by an ampersand (&), and then the continuation character (_). On the next line, enclose the entire second half of the literal text in quotation marks, as the following example shows:

```
SomeChunk = "A literal string is " & _
    "text in quotation marks"
```

Because breaking up lines is entirely optional, you may never have to concern yourself with these nit-picky details of breaking lines within literal text. However, when you cut and paste code written by others, you may find that the programmer has broken up lengthy lines to make them more readable. Just be aware that an underscore (_) at the end of a line means, "The line below is actually a continuation of this line, not a new, separate statement."

Dealing with compile errors

Each statement in VBA code must be syntactically correct, complete, and must be either on its own line or correctly broken across several lines using the continuation character. (See the previous section for more on how to correctly break a line.) If you press Enter to end the line before you type a complete, syntactically correct statement, an error message appears on-screen. For example, Figure 2-17 shows what you see if you type `MsgBox("Hello World"` and press the Enter key. The `MsgBox()` statement requires a closing parenthesis, missing in this example. The editor displays an error message. (On-screen, the faulty line is shown in red.)

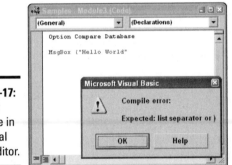

Figure 2-17: An error message in the Visual Basic Editor.

The Compile Error part of the message tells you that the line you typed cannot be compiled, which is a fancy way of saying that the code cannot be translated to instructions that Access can perform. Access can only compile and execute syntactically correct and complete statements. The part that says `Expected: list separator or )` tells you that Access expected to find either a comma (to separate the first argument from the second) or a closing parenthesis.

The box displaying the error message contains two buttons:

✦ **OK:** Closes the error message box so you can type in the correction.

✦ **Help:** Provides some general information about the type of error discovered and provides some suggestions for fixing the problem.

Regardless of which button you click, you need to correct the statement before it can work correctly. After you type the correct statement and press Enter, the error message no longer appears, and the line no longer displays in red.

Indenting the lines within the procedure is customary, just to make the starting and ending lines stand out more. But indentations are optional and have no effect on how the code will behave when executed.

Testing and Running Your Code

A completed procedure is generally called from some object, such as a button on a form. But as you write code, you may want to make sure it will work before you start attaching a procedure to objects in your database. You can use the Immediate window to run the procedure right on the spot. The syntax varies depending on whether you're testing a sub procedure or function, and whether or not the procedure accepts arguments.

Testing sub procedures

To test a sub procedure that accepts no parameters, you simple type the name of the sub procedure into the Immediate window, and then press Enter. The following procedure accepts no parameters and displays a message box when called:

```
Sub ShowThanks()
    MsgBox ("Thank you")
End Sub
```

To test the preceding procedure, simply type its name without the parentheses into the Immediate window, as the following:

```
ShowThanks
```

The procedure switches to the Access window and shows a message. Then close the message box and switch back to the Visual Basic Editor to continue writing code.

If a sub procedure accepts arguments, then you follow the procedure name by a blank space and the value to pass to the sub procedure. For example, the following sub procedure accepts one argument:

```
Sub WarnUser (msg as String)
    x=MsgBox(msg,vbCritical,"Warning")
End Sub
```

Access assumes that the passed parameter is a string. To test the procedure you need to pass some text to it. Type the following into the Immediate window to test this procedure:

```
WarnUser "Don't move!"
```

When you press Enter, the procedure executes, displaying a message box in the Access window. Close the message box and return to the Visual Basic Editor.

If a procedure accepts more than one argument, then separate the arguments by a comma. The following procedure accepts two string arguments:

```
Sub TakeTwo(msg as String, tBar As String)
    x = msgbox(msg,vbOKOnly,tBar)
End Sub
```

To test the procedure, you need to pass two parameters to it from the Immediate window, as in this example:

```
TakeTwo "Hello World", "Sample"
```

The result is a message box with "Hello World" on-screen, a single OK button, and "Sample" in the title bar. The result is the same if you execute this statement directly:

```
    x = msgbox("Hello World",vbOKOnly,"Sample")
```

Running sub procedures from Access

The real goal of a sub procedure, of course, is to run when appropriate from within Access. Sub procedures in a class module are usually tied to a control on the corresponding form or report. To actually run a procedure, open the corresponding form or report and trigger the event that causes the code to run. For example, if the code is attached to the On Click event of a button on a form, then you need to open the form in Form view and click the button that runs the code.

Calling a procedure from another procedure

Any VBA procedure can call another procedure, using exactly the same syntax used to test the procedure in the Immediate window. If the sub procedure accepts no arguments, then just call the procedure by name. If the sub procedure does contain arguments, include the passed values in the command.

You can use the `Call` keyword in front of the procedure name as a reminder that you're calling some other procedure. But the `Call` keyword is optional.

Figure 2-18 shows two sub procedures, one named `SampleSub()`; the other named `SecondSub()`. The `SampleSub()` procedure includes a `Call` statement that calls upon `SecondSub()` to do its job. What happens when you execute `SampleSub()` is

✦ *Statement1A* and *Statement2A* in `SampleSub()` are each executed.

✦ The `Call SecondSub "Howdy World"` statement is executed, causing *Statement1B* and *Statement 2B* in `SecondSub()` to be executed.

✦ The `End Sub` statement at the end of `SecondSub()` returns control to the next line in the calling procedure — *Statement3A*.

✦ Both *Statement3A* and *Statement4A* in `SampleSub()` are executed next.

✦ The `End Sub` statement at the end of the `SampleSub()` procedure is executed, and no more VBA code is executed.

Figure 2-18:
Example of
one sub
procedure
calling
another.

```
Sub SampleSub()
     Statement1A
     Statement2A
     Call SecondSub "Howdy World"
     Statement3A
     Statement4A
End Sub

Sub SecondSub (AnyText As String)
     Statement1B
     Statement2B
End Sub
```

Running sub procedures from macros

You can also call VBA sub procedures from macros, though technically, a macro only calls a function procedure, not a sub procedure. You have two choices if you still like to have a macro call a sub procedure:

✦ Either convert the sub procedure to a function procedure.

✦ Write a function procedure that calls the sub procedure, and then call the function procedure from the macro.

Converting a sub procedure to a function procedure is a simple matter of changing the `Sub` keyword at the top of the procedure to `Function`, and the `End Sub` statement at the bottom of the procedure to `End Function`.

If you want to leave the procedure as is and call it from a function, place the call to the sub procedure within a function procedure. When executed, the following DoMySub() function procedure calls the MySub() sub procedure.

```
'The sub procedure below is named MySub()
Sub MySub()
...Code
   Code...
End Sub

'Function procedure below calls MySub sub procedure.
Function DoMySub()
    Call MySub
End Function
```

To run MySub from a macro, you choose RunCode as the macro action. Then type the name of the function procedure — in this example, DoMySub() — as the Action Argument for the RunCode action, as shown in Figure 2-19.

For a reminder on defining macro actions, see Book VI, Chapter 1.

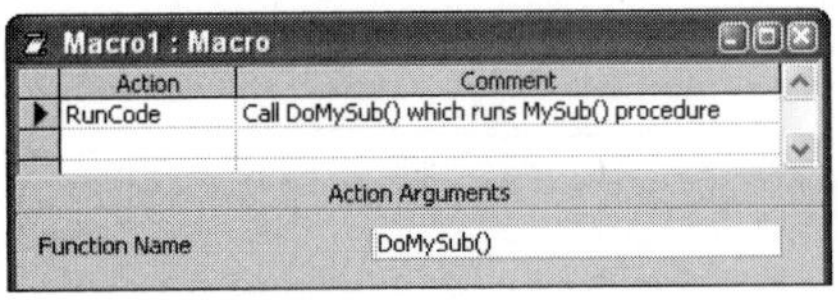

Figure 2-19:
A macro
action that
calls a
function
procedure.

Macro1 : Macro	
Action	Comment
RunCode	Call DoMySub() which runs MySub() procedure

Action Arguments	
Function Name	DoMySub()

Testing function procedures

Unlike sub procedures, which return no value, a function procedure always returns a value. To test a function from the Immediate window, use the ? ("What is?") symbol followed by the function name and, if necessary, values that pass to the function.

For example, the following custom function accepts no arguments. When called, the day of the week is returned:

```
Function Today() As String
    Today = WeekDayName(Weekday(Date))
End Function
```

To test the function, type the following into the Immediate window and press Enter:

```
? Today()
```

The Immediate window then displays the value returned by the function. If you ran the test on a Monday, the function would return

```
Monday
```

The following function procedure accepts a single number as an argument (and returns a number).

```
Function Area(radius As Double) As Double
   Area = 3.141592654 * (radius ^ 2)
End Function
```

To test the function, call it with the ? symbol and pass some number to it, as in this example:

```
? Area(10)
```

The Immediate window then displays the value returned by the function, as the following shows:

```
314.1592654
```

If the function accepts multiple arguments, you just separate the arguments with commas, as when using the Access built-in functions.

Using function procedures in Access

When you create a function procedure in VBA, you can use that function any place within the database where you use a built-in function. Wherever you use an expression in Access, that expression can contain built-in functions, custom function procedures, or both. Some examples include:

✦ In an expression used in the Control Source property of a calculated control on a form or a report.

✦ In an expression that defines a calculated field in a select query.

✦ In an expression in the Update To row of an update query.

✦ In an expression used in a macro.

✦ As a custom action called from a macro, such as the example shown back in Figure 2-19.

In Access, function procedures are generally easier to use than sub procedures. Calling a function procedure from within any expression is easy. Most pre-written custom VBA code you may find on the Web is organized into function procedures, rather than sub procedures.

**Book VIII
Chapter 2**

Writing Code

Chapter 3: Writing Smarter Code

In This Chapter

✔ **Using variables and constants to store temporary data**

✔ **Having your code make decisions**

✔ **Executing the same code repeatedly**

✔ **Examples of managing data with custom VBA functions**

*L*ike all programming languages, VBA offers certain concepts and statements designed to allow you to write the code necessary to make a computer do — well, *anything*. Those concepts and statements are the subject of this chapter.

We must point out, though, that the underlying VBA concepts described in this chapter aren't unique to VBA. Virtually all programming languages are built around these same concepts. If you ever have aspirations of learning to program in any language, be it Java, JavaScript, C++, C#, VBScript, or whatever, the concepts you discover in this chapter apply equally to most programming languages.

Creating Variables and Constants

Within a procedure, you define and use variables. A *variable* is a name — a placeholder — for any data that may change. You make up your own variable names — choose names that indicate what information the variable contains, so you don't have to wonder later. Variable names must begin with a letter, cannot contain spaces or punctuation, and not be the same as any built-in keyword.

Unlike data stored in a table, data stored in a variable is not permanent. Data stored in a variable is fleeting and exists only for as long as VBA needs the information contained within the variable.

Make me a variable

You can create variables in a couple of ways in VBA code. The quick-and-dirty way is to simply make up a variable name, assign a value by following the name with an equal sign (=) and the value to be stored in the variable. The following VBA statements define three variables named x, y, and ExtPrice. The variable x stores the number 10, the variable y stores the number 9.99, and the variable ExtPrice stores the result of multiplying the contents of x by the contents of y (or 99.9 by the time all three lines are executed):

```
x = 10
y = 9.99
ExtPrice = x * y
```

These statements are all examples of *implicit variable declarations*.

Explicit variable declaration, as the name implies, requires that you assign a data type to each variable *before* you assign the variable a value. Explicit variable declaration is a little more work, but your code runs more smoothly and efficiently because Access doesn't have to figure out the best data type to use when encountering the data in the variable. Two steps go into using a variable explicitly. First you *define* (or *declare*) the variable, which gives the variable a data type. After the variable exists, you assign a value using the same syntax as for implicit declarations: *variableName = value*.

The command for defining a variable explicitly is Dim, short for *dimension*. But thinking of Dim as standing for "Define In Memory" may be easier because variables exist only in the computer's random access memory (RAM). The simplified syntax for the Dim statement is:

```
Dim varname [As type] [,...]
```

where *varname* is a name of your own choosing. The *type* refers to one of the acceptable VBA data types or object types. The data types you assign to variables in a Dim statement are the same as those used in defining arguments in a Function or Sub statement.

See Chapter 2 of this book for a summary of VBA data types. When you create a variable implicitly (by just using it, with no Dim statement), VBA creates a variant type, a catch-all data type used to store any kind of information.

The comma and ellipsis in the syntax chart mean that you can define multiple variables, separated by commas, within a single statement. For example, the following statement declares one variable, named ReportName, as a string (textual data):

```
Dim ReportName as String
```

The following sample `Dim` statement declares two variables: a string named `ReportName` and a long integer named `Qty`. The lines after the `Dim` statement then assign a value to each variable using the standard *variableName = value* syntax:

```
Dim ReportName as String, Qty as Long
ReportName = "Sales Summary Report"
Qty = 50
```

Scope and lifetime of variables

All variables and constants have a scope and a lifetime. The *scope* of a variable defines to which procedures the variable is *visible*. You determine the scope of a variable when you declare the variable. Variables declared at the beginning of a module (before the first procedure in the module) can be either *private* (visible only to procedures within the same module) or *public* (visible to all procedures in all modules). These variables have *module-level scope.*

If you use the `Public` keyword (rather than `Dim`) to declare a variable at the module level, then the variable is visible to all procedures in all modules. On the other hand, if you use a `Dim` or `Private` statement to define a variable at the module level, then the variable is private to the module. All procedures defined within the same module can see the variable, but the variable is invisible to procedures defined in other modules.

When you define a variable within a procedure, that variable has *procedure-level scope,* meaning that the variable is *private* (visible only) to the procedure in which it is defined. Only the procedure in which the variable is defined can see, and use, the variable.

Figure 3-1 shows a module with several variables declared using `Dim`, `Private`, and `Public` keywords. Comments in the code describe the scope of the variables declared within the module as follows:

✦ `Public farReaching As String`: The variable named `farReaching` is visible to all procedures in all modules, because it's declared using the `Public` keyword.

✦ `Private notSoFarReaching As String` and `Dim alsoNotSoFarReaching As String`: These variables are visible to all procedures in the same module, but not visible to procedures defined in other modules. `Dim` and `Private` have the same meaning in this context.

✦ `Dim existsOnlyHere As String`: Because this variable is declared within a procedure, the variable is visible only to that procedure.

Book VIII Chapter 3

Writing Smarter Code

```
VBA Samples - Module2 (Code)                                    _ □ ✕
(General)                          ▼    doSomething                  ▼
  Option Compare Database
  Option Explicit

  'You can use Dim, Private, or Public to declare variables at the procedure level
  'as in the examples below. Public variables are visible to all procedures in
  'all modules. Dim and Private are identical in meaning in that both limit the
  'scope of the variable to procedures within the same module.

  Public farReaching As String        'Visible to all procedures in all modules.

  Private notSoFarReaching As String  'Visible to all procedures in this module.
  Dim alsoNotSoFarReaching As String  'Visible to all procedures in this module.

  Function doSomething()

      'The variable declared below has procedure-level scope.

      Dim existsOnlyHere As String   'Visible only to doSomething() procedure.

  End Function

  |
```

Figure 3-1:
Examples of defining a variable's scope.

The *lifetime* of a variable defines how long a variable retains a value. When you open a database, variables defined at the module level of standard modules are created and can be assigned a new value at any time. The lifetime of such variables is lengthy — these variables exist and can contain values for the entire session — from the time you open the database to the time you close it.

Variables declared with a Dim keyword at the procedure level have a much shorter lifetime. The variable retains its value only for as long as the procedure runs. A second call to the same procedure re-creates the variables and assigns new values to them.

Though rare, you may want one or more variables to retain their values between calls to the procedure in some instances. For example, you may have a variable that keeps track of how many times the procedure is called. In that case, you can use the Static keyword, rather than Dim, to declare the variable or variables. The following statement defines a static variable named howMany, which stores an integer (whole number).

```
Static howMany as Integer
```

You can make all variables declared within a procedure static by preceding the Sub or Function keyword with Static. All variables defined within the following procedure are static, because the Static keyword in front of the word Function makes all that procedure's variables static:

```
Static Function myFunction()
    'Both variables below are static
    Dim var1 As String
    Dim var2 As Byte
End Function
```

If you find this terribly confusing, you rarely need to be so picky about the scope and lifetimes of variables. In fact, if you never use the Public, Private, or Static keywords in any code you write, chances are the code will still work perfectly — the default scope and lifetime assigned to a variable through the Dim statement is usually exactly what you need. Exceptions are few and far between, and not likely to show up until you start developing huge and complex databases.

Defining constants

A *constant* is similar to a variable: It has a name, a data type, and a value. However, unlike a variable whose contents can change at any time, a constant's value never changes. Constants are often used to assign a short name to some value that must be used repeatedly throughout the code, but never changed.

To declare a constant, you use the Const keyword. The simplified syntax for the Const keyword is:

```
Const name [As type]=value [, name [As type]=value]...
```

You define the name, data type (type), and value of the constant on a single line. The rules for coming up with a name are the same as those for a variable — it must start with a letter, cannot contain blank spaces or punctuation, and cannot be the same as a VBA keyword.

As an example of creating a constant, the following statement defines a constant named pi as a double-precision number containing the value 3.141592654:

```
Const pi As Double = 3.141592654
```

You can declare multiple constants in a single Const statement by separating them with a comma. For example, the following statement declares two constants, a number named x of the Byte data type with a value of 10, and a string named myName containing the text "Alan":

```
Const x As Byte = 10, myName As String = "Alan"
```

Constants tend to be private to the module in which they're defined. If you want to ensure that a constant is available to all objects and all modules within the database, precede Const with the Public keyword, as the following shows:

```
Public Const pi As Double = 3.141592654
```

Organizing Variables into arrays

An *array* is a collection of variables organized into a list or table. Each item's name is the same, but each has one or more *subscripts* that uniquely identify each item in the array based on its position in the array. The subscript is one or more numbers, enclosed in parentheses, that follows the name. If `Colors` is the name of an array, `Colors(1)`, pronounced *colors sub 1,* is the first item in the list, `Colors(2)` is the second item in the list, and so forth.

In a sense, an array is like a database table, in that the data can be organized into rows and columns. And you can use VBA to manipulate data stored in tables. The only time you really want to use an array is when you work with a small amount of data that either never changes, or changes only while the code is running. The data in an array is defined in code, not in a table, so getting to the data stored in the array is not easy.

The syntax for declaring an array is almost identical to that of creating a variable. However, you need to define the number of *dimensions* in the array, and the number of *elements* in each dimension of the array. An array can have up to 60 dimensions, and virtually any number of elements within each dimension. The basic syntax for declaring an array using the `Dim` statement is:

```
Dim varname[([subscripts])] [As type]
    [,varname[([subscripts])] [As type]] . .
```

In this statement

+ *varname* is the name assigned each element in the array.

+ *subscripts* is the number of elements in each dimension, with each dimension separated by a comma. It can contain the optional keyword `To` to specify the starting and ending subscripts.

+ *type* is any valid VBA data type.

All arrays are zero-based, unless you specify otherwise, which means that the first item in the array has a subscript of zero, rather than one. The number of elements specified is actually one less than the total number of elements that the array contains.

For example, the following `Dim` statement declares a one-dimensional array named `Colors` that contains four string elements (numbered 0, 1, 2, and 3):

```
Dim Colors(3) as String
```

The following lines of code show how you can then assign a value to each element in the array. Because the first item always has a subscript of zero, you actually place four, rather than three, items into the array:

```
Colors(0)="black"
Colors(1)="red"
Colors(2)="blue"
Colors(3)="green"
```

Having the first element in an array start with a zero can be counterintuitive for we humans, who tend to think of the first item in a list as being number 1. You can force the first element to be 1 by specifying a range, rather than a number, of elements in the `Dim` statement. The following `Dim` statement declares an array of three elements, with subscripts ranging from 1 to 3. The lines after the `Dim` statement assign a value to each of those elements:

```
Dim Colors(1 To 3) as String
Colors(1)="red"
Colors(2)="blue"
Colors(3)="green"
```

Another alternative, if you want all of your arrays to start at 1 rather than 0, is to simply put the following statement up in the Declarations section of the module, before the first procedure in the module:

```
Option Base 1
```

After you add the `Option Base 1` statement to the top of a module, all arrays within that module start at 1 rather than zero. Thus the `Dim Colors(3)` statement creates an array of three elements, numbered 1, 2, 3, as you expect. There is no `Colors(0)` when the optional base for arrays is set to 1 via the `Option Base 1` module declaration.

Multidimensional arrays

A *multidimensional array* is one that offers more than one subscript per name. The simplest example is a two-dimensional array, which you can envision as a table. The first subscript in a two-dimensional array represents the element's row position in the array. The second subscript represents the elements column position in the array. For example, in the following array, `State(3,2)` refers to "row 3, column 2" in the `States` array, which contains "AZ".

State(1,1)="Alabama"	State(1,2)="AL"
State(2,1)="Alaska"	State(2,2)="AK"
State(3,1)="Arizona"	State(3,2)="AZ"
State(50,1)="Wyoming"	State(50,2)="WY"

The Dim statement that creates a two-dimensional array named States, with 50 row elements and 2 column elements, is shown with the following statement. If you use the Option Base 1 statement in the Declarations section, the starting number for each array is 1:

```
Dim States (50,2) as String
```

The code to *populate* (assign each variable a value) the array looks like this:

```
State(1,1)="Alabama"
State(1,2)="AL"
State(2,1)="Alaska"
State(2,2)="AK"
State(3,1)="Arizona"
State(3,2)="AZ"
...
State(50,1)="Wyoming"
State(50,2)="WY"
```

Though all programming languages support multidimensional arrays, you won't use them in Access very often. Instead, you can use a table to store lists and tables of data, and then use Access code to extract data, as needed, from that table.

Naming conventions for variables

Some programmers use *naming conventions* to identify the data type of a variable as part of the variable or constant's name. The naming conventions are entirely optional — you don't have to use them. But a lot of VBA programmers follow them, so you're likely to see them in any code you happen to come across.

The idea behind a naming convention is simple. When you define a new variable, make the first three letters of the name (referred to as the *tag*) stand for the type of variable or object. The following line creates an Integer variable named intMyVar, where "int" is short for "integer."

```
Dim intMyVar As Integer
```

The tag added to the front of the name doesn't affect how the variable is stored or how you can use it. The tag serves only as a reminder that MyVar is an Integer. Table 3-1 summarizes the tags you'll most likely encounter when reading other people's code. In the Sample Declaration column of the table, the italicized word *Name* means that you can put in any variable name of your own choosing.

Table 3-1	Naming Conventions Used Among VBA Programmers	
Tag	*Stands For*	*Sample Declaration*
byt	Byte data type	Dim byt*Name* As Byte
cur	Currency data type	Dim cur*Name* As Currency
dtm	Date/Time data type	Dim dtm*Name* As Date
dbl	Double data type	Dim dbl*Name* As Double
int	Integer data type	Dim int*Name* As Integer
lng	Long integer data type	Dim lng*Name* As Long
sng	Single data type	Dim sng*Name* As Single
bln	Boolean data type	Dim bln*Name* As Boolean
str	String data type	Dim str*Name* As String
var	Variant data type	Dim var*Name* As Variant

Making Decisions in VBA Code

Decision-making is a big part of programming — most programs need to be smart enough to figure out what to do depending on circumstances. Often, you want your code to do one thing if "such-and-such is true," and do something else if "such-and-such is false." You use conditional expressions to determine if something is true or false. A *conditional expression* is one that generally follows the syntax

```
Value ComparisonOperator Value
```

where *Value* is some chunk of information and the *ComparisonOperator* is one of those listed in Table 3-2.

Table 3-2	Comparison Operators
Operator	*Meaning*
=	Equal to
<	Less than
<=	Less than or equal to
>	Greater than
>=	Greater than or equal to
<>	Not equal to

For example, the expression

```
[Last Name] = "Smith"
```

compares the contents of the `Last Name` field to the string "Smith". If the `[Last Name]` field does, indeed, contain the name Smith, then the expression is (or *returns*) `True`. If the `[Last Name]` field contains anything other than Smith, then the expression returns `False`.

Another example is the following statement:

```
[Qty] >= 10
```

The content of the `Qty` field is compared to the number 10. If the number stored in the `Qty` field is 10 or greater, the expression returns `True`. If the number stored in the `Qty` field is less than 10, the expression returns `False`.

You can combine multiple conditional expressions into one using the logical operators summarized in Table 3-3.

Table 3-3	**Logical Operators**
Operator	*Meaning*
and	Both are true
or	One or both are true
not	Is not true
xor	Exclusive or: One — but not both — is true

The following conditional expression requires that the `[Last Name]` field contain "Smith" and the `[First Name]` field contain "Janet" in order for the entire expression to be `True`:

```
[Last Name]="Smith" and [First Name]="Janet"
```

An example of an expression that returns `True` if the `State` field contains either NJ or NY is the following:

```
[State]="NJ" or [State]="NY"
```

Using If...End If statements

You can have VBA code make decisions as the code is running in several ways. One method is to use the `If...End If` block of code. The syntax for `If...End If` looks like this:

```
If condition Then
    [statements]...
[Else
    [statements]...
End If
```

where *condition* is an expression that results in True or False, and *statements* refers to any number of valid VBA statements. If the condition proves True, the statements between Then and Else execute, and all other statements are ignored. If the condition proves False, then only the statements after the Else statement execute, as illustrated in Figure 3-2.

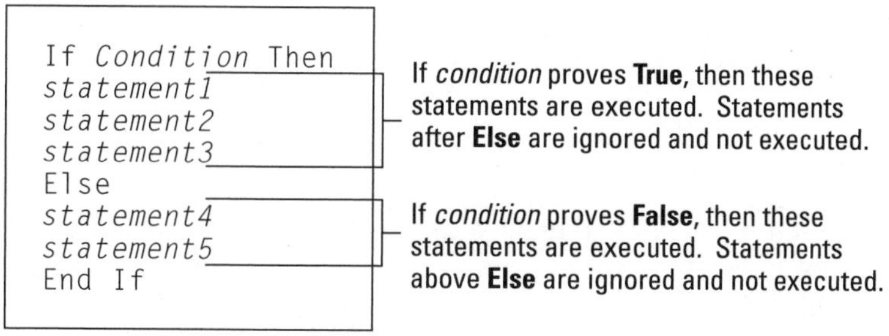

Figure 3-2:
The basic idea behind the If...End If statement.

```
If Condition Then
    statement1
    statement2
    statement3
Else
    statement4
    statement5
End If
```

If *condition* proves **True**, then these statements are executed. Statements after **Else** are ignored and not executed.

If *condition* proves **False**, then these statements are executed. Statements above **Else** are ignored and not executed.

As an example, imagine that a State variable contains some text. The following If...End If block checks to see if the State variable contains NY. If the State variable does contain NY, then the TaxRate variable receives a value of 0.075 (7.5%). If the State variable does not contain NY, then the TaxRate variable receives a value of 0.

```
If State="NY" Then
    TaxRate=0.075
Else
    TaxRate=0
End If
```

You have a little bit of flexibility when using If...End If. If only one line of code executes for a True result, and only one line executes for a False result, then you can put the whole statement on a single line and omit the End If statement, as the following shows:

```
If State="NY" Then TaxRate=0.075 Else TaxRate=0
```

Because you can use any built-in function in VBA, and Access supports the use of the iif() (immediate if) function, you can also write the preceding statement as an expression:

```
TaxRate = iif([State]="NY",0.075,0)
```

**Book VIII
Chapter 3**

Writing Smarter Code

For a review of the iif() function, see Book III, Chapter 3.

In the block format, you can also write code that tests for more than just two possible conditions, using the optional ElseIf statement. Suppose the Reply variable stores a string of text. If Reply contains the word "Yes", your code does one thing. If Reply contains "No", your code does something else. If Reply contains neither "Yes" or "No", then you want your code to do something else instead. You could set up an If...End If block to test for and respond to all three conditions, as the following:

```
If Reply = "Yes" Then
    statements for "Yes" reply
ElseIf Reply="No" Then
    statements for "No" reply
Else
    statements for any other reply
End If
```

When the code has to make a decision from many possibilities, you may find using a Select Case...End Select block is easier, described in the section, "Using a Select Case block," later in this chapter.

Nesting If...End If statements

What if you have more than two possible scenarios? No problem — you can *nest* If...End If blocks, meaning you can put one complete If...End If block inside another If...End If block. For example, in the code shown in Figure 3-3, the innermost statements execute only if *Condition1* and *Condition2* result in True.

The *'condition1* and *'condition2* text after the words "End If" in Figure 3-3 are both comments — text preceded by an apostrophe. You can only put comments, or nothing, to the right of an End If statement. Don't put an actual expression or any code to the right of an End If statement.

You can see why the nested If...End If statements work if you look at what happens when either test proves False. For example:

✦ If *condition1* proves False, all code down to the last End If statement is skipped over. The inner If...End If block isn't seen or executed.

✦ If *condition1* proves True, but *condition2* proves False, all the statements in the nested block are ignored. The innermost statements still don't execute.

✦ If both *condition1* and *condition2* prove True, then no code is skipped over and the innermost statements execute normally.

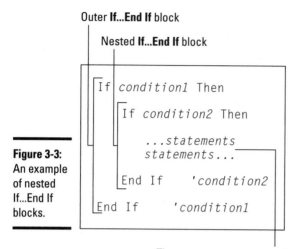

Outer **If...End If** block

Nested **If...End If** block

```
If  condition1 Then

    If condition2 Then

        ...statements
        statements...

    End If      'condition2

End If      'condition1
```

Figure 3-3:
An example
of nested
If...End If
blocks.

These statements executed
only if both *condition1* and
condition2 result in **True**

You can nest If...Else...End If blocks as deeply as you wish. However, you have to make sure each one has its own End If statement.

Using a Select Case block

But what if you have more than two or three cases to check for? For example, what if you need to perform different statements depending on which of 10 product types a person ordered? You could nest a lot of If...End If blocks, but it would be confusing. Luckily, Access provides a better way.

A Select Case block of code is one that performs a particular set of instructions depending on some value. Typically, the value is stored in a variable or field in a table, and is a number that represents some previously made selection. The basic syntax of a Select Case block of code looks like this:

```
Select Case value
    [Case possibleValue  [To possibleValue]
        [statements]]
    [Case possibleValue [To possibleValue]
        [statements]]...
    [Case Else
        [statements]]
End Select
```

where *value* is some value, like a number, and *possibleValue* is any value that could match the *value*. You can have any number of Case

Book VIII
Chapter 3

Writing Smarter
Code

possibleValue statements between the Select Case and End Select statements. Optionally, you can include a Case Else statement, which specifies statements that execute only if none of the preceding Case *possibleValue* statements prove True.

Each Case statement can have any number of statements beneath it. When the code executes, only those statements after the Case statement that matches the *value* at the top of the block execute. Figure 3-4 shows the idea.

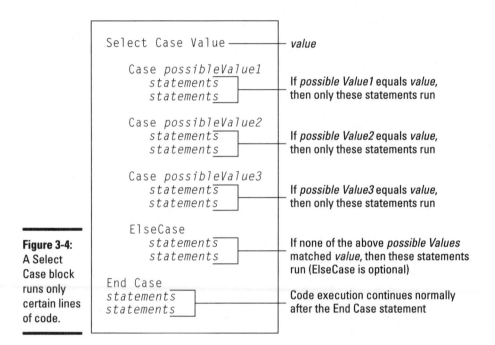

Figure 3-4:
A Select
Case block
runs only
certain lines
of code.

As an example, suppose you create a custom dialog box — a form, in other words — such as the one in Figure 3-5. On that form, the five options shown are in an Option Group control named WhereTo. The value of the WhereTo control is a number from 1 to 5, depending on which item is selected, or Null if no item is selected. The button on that form is named OKButton.

In the class module for that form, a sub procedure named OKButton_Click() executes whenever someone clicks the OK button. The sub procedure, shown in Figure 3-6, opens a form, exits Access, or does nothing, depending on what's selected in the WhereTo option group.

The OKButton_Click() procedure does its job this way: When called, the following statement executes first:

```
Select Case Me!WhereTo.Value
```

This statement uses the `Me!WhereTo.Value` expression to refer to the value of the WhereTo option group on the form. The word `Me!` is used mainly in class modules to refer to the form or report to which the class module is attached. `Me!WhereTo.Value` is a number between 1 and 5 when the code executes. If no option is selected, `Me!WhereTo.Value` equals `Null`. In that case, the code after the `Case Else` statement executes.

Option group named **WhereTo**

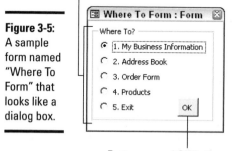

Figure 3-5:
A sample form named "Where To Form" that looks like a dialog box.

Button named **OKButton**

If you omit the `Case Else` statement from the sample code, no code within the `Select Case...End Case` block executes when `Me!WhereTo.Value` contains something other than a number from 1 to 5. Execution still continues normally, however, at the first line after the `End Case` statement.

```
VBA Samples - Form_Where To Form (Code)
OKButton                              Click

Option Compare Database

'Whenever someone clicks on the OK button on Where To Form,
'the Sub procedure below is called to perform whatever
'action the user requested.
Private Sub OKButton_Click()
    Select Case Me!WhereTo.Value

        Case 1
            DoCmd.OpenForm ("My Business Main Form")

        Case 2
            DoCmd.OpenForm ("Address Book Form")

        Case 3
            DoCmd.OpenForm ("Orders Main Form")

        Case 4
            DoCmd.OpenForm ("Products Form")

        Case 5
            DoCmd.Quit

        Case Else
            MsgBox ("You didn't pick an option!")

    End Select
End Sub
```

Figure 3-6:
A sub procedure attaches to the On Click event of OKButton in the Where To form.

The optional `To` keyword of the `Case` statement can be used to specify a range of values to compare against. In the following code, statements after `Case 1 To 9` execute only if `SomeNumber` contains a value from 1 to 9. Statements after `Case 10 To 99` execute only if `SomeNumber` contains a value from 100 to 999, and so forth.

```
Select Case SomeNumber
    Case 1 to 9
       Statements for when SomeNumber is between 1 and 9
    Case 10 to 99
       Statements for when SomeNumber is between 10 and 99
    Case 100 to 999
       Statements for when SomeNumber is between 100 and 999
End Select
```

Executing the Same Code Repeatedly

Occasionally a situation occurs where you want to execute one or more VBA statements multiple times. Say you write some VBA statements that need to operate on each record in a table, and there are 1,000 records in the table. You have two choices: Write each set of statements 1,000 times or create a loop that repeats the one set of statements 1,000 times. Needless to say, typing the statements once rather than 1,000 times saves *you* a lot of time. A *loop* is your best bet.

Using Do...Loop to create a loop

The `Do...Loop` block is one method of setting up a loop in code to execute statements repeatedly. Two syntaxes for using `Do...Loop` exist. The first syntax evaluates the condition of the loop, as the following shows:

```
Do [{While | Until} condition]
    [statements]
    [Exit Do]
    [statements]
Loop
```

The second syntax provides the option of defining the condition at the bottom of the loop, using this syntax:

```
Do
    [statements]
    [Exit Do]
    [statements]
Loop [{While | Until} condition]
```

As an example of the first syntax, the code in the following `Do Until` loop executes once for each record in a recordset named `rst`. (A recordset, discussed in Chapter 4 of this book, is the VBA equivalent of a table in Access.)

```
'Code to define a recordset named rst.
rst.MoveFirst
Do Until rst.EOF()
    Debug.Print rst.Fields("Product Name")
    rst.MoveNext
Loop
```

How the loop works is as follows: The `rst.MoveFirst` statement moves the cursor to the first record in the table. At that point, `EOF()` (which stands for "End Of File") is `False`, because `EOF()` means "past the last record in the table." Because the cursor is at the first record, `EOF()` is `False`.

Within the loop, the `rst.MoveNext` statement moves the cursor to the next record in the table. But `EOF()` remains `False` until `rst.MoveNext` executes a sufficient number of times to have visited every record in the table. After visiting the last record, `rst.MoveNext` moves the cursor to the end of the file — past the last record. When the cursor is past the last record, `EOF()` becomes `True`, and the loop doesn't repeat anymore. Instead, Access resumes executing your code normally at the first statement after the `Loop` statement.

Using the alternative syntax, where you define the condition at the bottom, rather than at the top of the loop, you can construct that same sort of loop as follows:

```
'Code to define a recordset named rst.
rst.MoveFirst
Do
    Debug.Print rst.Fields("Product Name")
    rst.MoveNext
Loop Until rst.EOF()
```

You'll notice one subtle difference between setting the loop condition at the top of the loop rather than at the bottom of the loop. Access checks the condition *before* the loop executes for the first time (and each time thereafter). When you set the condition at the top of the loop, none of the statements in the loop may execute. Forgetting about recordsets and tables for the moment, consider the following more generic example:

```
Counter = 101
Do While Counter < 100
    Counter = Counter +1
Loop
'Statements below the loop.
```

Because `Counter` already has a value of 101 when the `Do While Counter < 100` statement executes, the looping condition is `False` right off the bat. So everything between the `Do While` and `Loop` statements is skipped over completely, and code execution resumes at the statements after the loop.

In the following code, we move the looping condition, `While Counter < 100`, to the bottom of the loop:

```
Counter = 101
Do
    Counter = Counter +1
Loop While Counter < 100
'Statements below the loop.
```

In the preceding loop, `Counter` receives a value of 101. The `Do` statement doesn't specify a condition for starting the loop. So the `Counter = Counter + 1` statement within the loop executes. The `Loop While Counter < 100` condition then proves `False` (because Counter = 102 by then), so code execution continues at the statements after the `Loop` statement at the bottom of the loop.

In short, when you define the condition for the loop at the top of the loop, the code within the loop may not execute at all. But if you define the condition at the bottom of the loop, then the code within the loop executes at least once.

Using While...Wend to create a loop

The `While...Wend` loop is similar to `Do...Loop`, but it uses the simpler (and less flexible) syntax shown in the following code:

```
While condition
    [statements]
Wend
```

where *condition* is an expression that results in a `True` or `False` value, and *statements* are any number of VBA statements, all of which execute with each pass through the loop.

The condition is evaluated at the top of the loop. If the condition proves `True`, all lines within the loop execute (down to the `Wend` statement), and then the condition at the top of the loop is evaluated again. If the condition proves `False`, then all statements within the loop are ignored, and processing continues at the first line after the `Wend` statement.

Using For...Next to create a loop

When you want to create a loop that keeps track of how many times the loop repeats, you can use the `For...Next` block of statements. The syntax for a `For...Next` loop is as follows:

```
For counter = start To end [Step step]
    [statements]
    [Exit For]
    [statements]
Next [counter]
```

where

+ *counter* is any name you want to give to the variable that keeps track of passes through the loop.

+ *start* is a number that indicates where the loop should start counting.

+ *end* is a number that indicates when the loop should end.

+ *step* is optional and indicates how much to increment or decrement *counter* with each pass through the loop. If omitted, *counter* increments by 1 with each pass through the loop.

+ *statements* are any number of VBA statements that execute with each pass through the loop.

Figure 3-7 shows a simple example of a `For...Next` loop within a sub procedure. This loop starts at 1, and increments the `Counter` variable by 1 with each pass through the loop. The loop continues until `Counter` reaches a value of 10, at which point the loop is done and processing continues at the first line after the `Next` statement. Within the loop, the `Debug.Print` statement simply prints the current value of the `Counter` variable to the Immediate window.

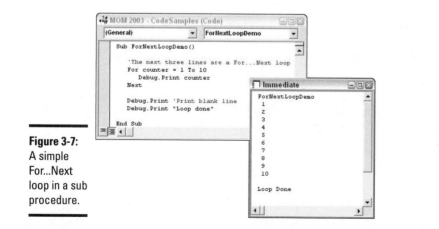

Figure 3-7: A simple For...Next loop in a sub procedure.

Book VIII
Chapter 3

Writing Smarter Code

The results of testing the procedure in the Immediate window are shown in the Figure 3-7. As you can see, the Counter value displays once with each pass through the loop. Then processing continues at the lines that use Debug.Print to display a blank line and the words "Loop done."

Note that if you change the loop so that it counts from 2 to 10, and adds 2 (rather than 1) to Counter with each pass through the loop, the code looks like the following:

```
For counter = 2 to 10 Step 2
    Debug.Print counter
Next
```

Running the preceding loop displays the following in the Immediate window:

```
2
4
6
8
10

Loop done
```

Looping through an array

You can use the Counter variable for a For...Next loop as the subscript for elements in an array. You can use the LBound() (lower boundary) and UBound() (upper boundary) functions to automatically return the lowest and highest subscripts in the array. You can use those values as the *start* and *end* values in the For... statement. The following code creates an array of four elements and assigns a value — a color name — to each element in the array. The For...Next loop that follows the array prints the contents of each array element by using the Counter value as the subscript for each pass through the loop:

```
'Declare and fill a sample array.
Dim Colors(3) As String
Colors(0)="black"
Colors(1)="red"
Colors(2)="blue"
Colors(3)="green"

'Create a loop that displays the contents
' of each array element.
For counter = LBound(Colors) to UBound(Colors)
    Debug.Print Colors(counter)
Next
```

On the first pass through the loop, the Debug.Print statement prints the contents of Colors(0). On the second pass through the loop, Debug.Print displays the contents of Colors(1), and so forth, until all array elements print.

Analyzing each character in a string

You can also use a For...Next loop to look at each character in a string. First, be aware that two built-in Access functions help with the loop:

✦ **Len(*string*):** Returns the length of a string in number of characters.

✦ **Mid(*string,start,length*):** Returns a portion of *string* starting at character *start* that's *length* characters long.

As an example, if *string* is "Hello World" then Len(*string*) returns 11, because there are eleven characters in "Hello World" (counting the blank space that separates the two words). The expression Mid(string,7,3) returns a substring of *string* starting at the seventh character that's three characters in length. Which, in this case, would be "Wor" (because "W" is the seventh character, and the returned substring is three characters in length).

Text-handling functions are described in more detail in Book III, Chapter 3.

To create a loop that looks at each character in a string, one at a time, start the loop at 1 and end it at Len(*string*). Within the loop, use Mid(*string,counter*,1) to isolate the single character at the position indicated by Counter. A simple loop that just prints each character from the string names strFull in the Immediate window looks like this:

```
Sub LookAtEachCharacter()

'Declare a couple of string variables.
Dim strFull As String, thisChar As String

'Give strFull a value.
strFull = "Hello World"

'Now isolate and display each character from strFull.
For Counter = 1 to Len(StrFull)
    thisChar = Mid(strFull,Counter,1)
    Debug.Print thisChar
Next

End Sub
```

Admittedly, just printing each character to the Immediate window isn't a very practical example. In real life, you use such a loop to analyze each character in a string to somehow change the string. The sample `PCase()` custom function presented in the section, "Converting text to proper case," later in this chapter, uses a similar type of loop to convert text to the proper case.

The `For Each...Next` loop is a slight variation on the `For...Next` loop, and is discussed in Chapter 4 of this book.

Making Your Own Functions

One of the most powerful reasons to use VBA is to create your own functions (sometimes called *user defined functions* or *UDFs*). In this section, we look at a couple of examples of VBA functions that act like built-in Access functions, but do things that no built-in function is capable of.

Converting text to proper case

Importing text into Access creates a problem that comes up more often than you may think. You beg, borrow, steal, or pay for some long list of names and addresses. But when you get them into your Access database, you realize that everything is in uppercase, as shown in Figure 3-8. Ugly!

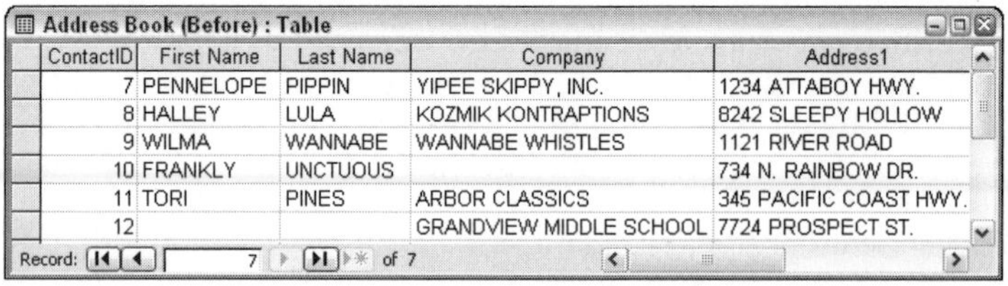

Figure 3-8: Names and addresses are all in uppercase.

	ContactID	First Name	Last Name	Company	Address1
	7	PENNELOPE	PIPPIN	YIPEE SKIPPY, INC.	1234 ATTABOY HWY.
	8	HALLEY	LULA	KOZMIK KONTRAPTIONS	8242 SLEEPY HOLLOW
	9	WILMA	WANNABE	WANNABE WHISTLES	1121 RIVER ROAD
	10	FRANKLY	UNCTUOUS		734 N. RAINBOW DR.
	11	TORI	PINES	ARBOR CLASSICS	345 PACIFIC COAST HWY.
	12			GRANDVIEW MIDDLE SCHOOL	7724 PROSPECT ST.

Address Book (Before) : Table

Record: [◄◄] [◄] 7 [►] [►►] [►*] of 7

Printing everything in all uppercase letters doesn't look too professional on your forms and reports. The question is, how are you going to fix this? You certainly don't want to go in and re-type all the information (especially if there are thousands of them). And Access doesn't include a built-in command or function that can instantly correct the problem.

Well, if you create a custom function that converts any string to proper case (take any string and spit it back with only the first letter of each word capitalized), then you solved the problem. The custom function you need to write, named `PCase()`, is shown in Figure 3-9.

The PCase() function, and all the other useful functions described in this chapter, is available on the Web site. If you don't want to re-type this function, cut and paste it from the Web page to your VBA procedure. Each posted procedure includes a <u>How It Works</u> link that shows you, step by step, exactly how each one works. See this book's Web page at www.dummies.com/go/access03_allinone to access this function.

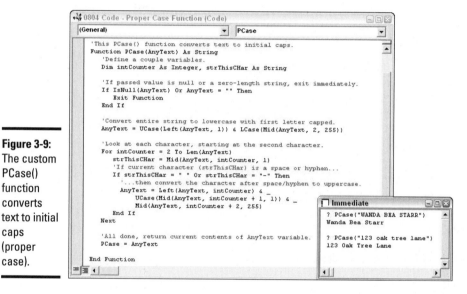

Figure 3-9:
The custom PCase() function converts text to initial caps (proper case).

Because you use PCase() as a general-purpose function — just like any built-in Access function — place the procedure in a standard module. It can be any standard module with any name. If you put PCase() in a class module, it is private to the form or report to which that module is attached, and you can't use it anywhere else in your Access project.

After the PCase() function is in a standard module, test it out in the VBA Editor Immediate window. For example, entering ? PCase("WANDA BEA STARR") returns "Wanda Bea Starr." Entering ? PCase("123 oak tree lane") returns "123 Oak Tree Lane." When you know the function works, you can put it to use on that table with all those nasty uppercase names in it.

The easiest way to apply the custom function to all the records in the table is to use an update query. For example, say the table with the data that needs to be converted is in an Address Book table. You create a query that includes the Address Book table, and then add the field names that need to be converted to the Query by Example.

**Book VIII
Chapter 3**

**Writing Smarter
Code**

WARNING!

Because update queries act on all records in a table, be sure to make a copy of the original table before creating and running the update query. If the update query does more harm than good, you can just delete the converted table and rename the original table back to its original name.

Next, choose Query➪Update Query from the Access menu. An Update To row is added to the QBE grid, where you can enter an expression that defines a new value for the field. In this case, you convert the contents of fields to the `PCase()` function's version of each field's contents. The expression to place in each field's Update To row is `PCase([`*`fieldname`*`])` where *fieldname* is the name of the field being displayed in the column. Figure 3-10 shows how the update query looks in this example.

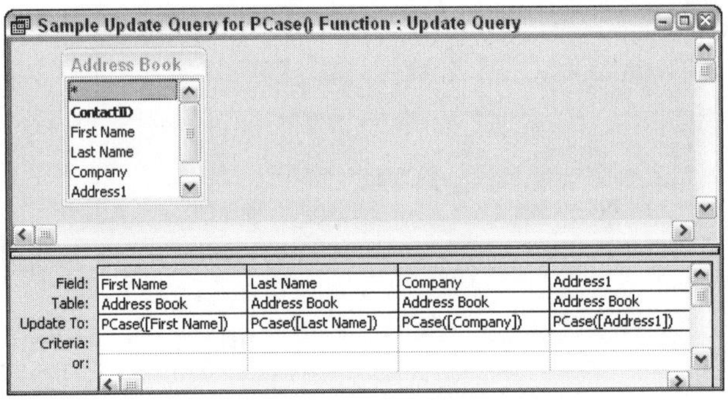
Sample Update Query for PCase() Function : Update Query
Address Book
*
ContactID
First Name
Last Name
Company
Address1
Field: First Name | Last Name | Company | Address1
Table: Address Book | Address Book | Address Book | Address Book
Update To: PCase([First Name]) | PCase([Last Name]) | PCase([Company]) | PCase([Address1])
Criteria:
or:

Figure 3-10: An update query converts text to proper case in several fields.

Because the query is an action query, you have to click the Run button in the Access toolbar (or choose Query➪Run from the menu) to run the query. Access responds with a message telling you how many records will be updated (and a healthy reminder that you won't be able to undo this action, which is why we mention making a backup earlier). Clicking OK runs the query and does all the updates. Opening the table after the update reveals all the text converted to proper case, as in Figure 3-11.

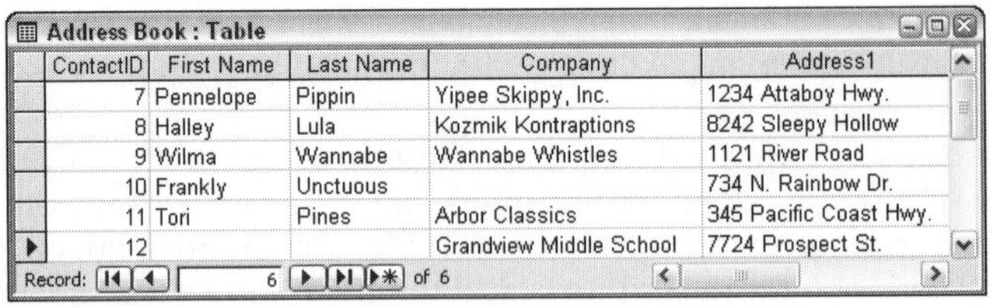
Address Book : Table
ContactID | First Name | Last Name | Company | Address1
7 | Pennelope | Pippin | Yipee Skippy, Inc. | 1234 Attaboy Hwy.
8 | Halley | Lula | Kozmik Kontraptions | 8242 Sleepy Hollow
9 | Wilma | Wannabe | Wannabe Whistles | 1121 River Road
10 | Frankly | Unctuous | | 734 N. Rainbow Dr.
11 | Tori | Pines | Arbor Classics | 345 Pacific Coast Hwy.
12 | | | Grandview Middle School | 7724 Prospect St.
Record: 6 of 6

Figure 3-11: A sample Address Book table after running the update query.

See Book III, Chapter 3 for the lowdown in creating and running update queries.

Spelling out numbers for printing checks

Suppose you have a table that contains information about checks to be written, as in Figure 3-12. You also have some checks that you can run through your printer. You want Access to print the checks. You can easily create a report to print the checks. But how do you fill out the part of the check where you write out the amount (for example, $1,234.56) in words, for example, One Thousand Two Hundred Thirty-Four and 56/100)?

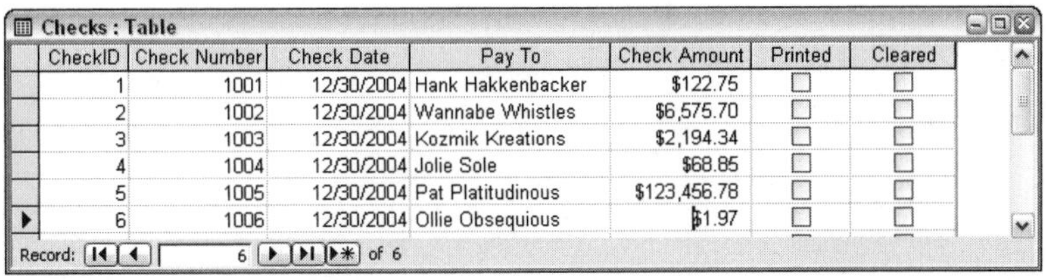

Figure 3-12:
A table containing data to be printed on checks.

CheckID	Check Number	Check Date	Pay To	Check Amount	Printed	Cleared
1	1001	12/30/2004	Hank Hakkenbacker	$122.75	☐	☐
2	1002	12/30/2004	Wannabe Whistles	$6,575.70	☐	☐
3	1003	12/30/2004	Kozmik Kreations	$2,194.34	☐	☐
4	1004	12/30/2004	Jolie Sole	$68.85	☐	☐
5	1005	12/30/2004	Pat Platitudinous	$123,456.78	☐	☐
6	1006	12/30/2004	Ollie Obsequious	$1.97	☐	☐

Checks : Table

Record: 6 of 6

Creating a function to convert numbers to words takes more than a few lines of code. If you actually need this function, you'd be wise to cut and paste the code from the Web site for this book (www.dummies.com/go/access03_allinone). But if you want to take a look, the code looks like the following:

```
'NumWord converts a number to its words,
'Useful for printing checks.
Function NumWord(AmountPassed As Currency) As String
    'Declare all variables and arrays.
    Dim English As String, strNum As String
    Dim Chunk As String, Pennies As String
    Dim Hundreds As Integer, Tens As Integer
    Dim Ones As Integer, LoopCount As Integer
    Dim StartVal As Integer, TensDone As Boolean
    Dim EngNum(90) As String
    EngNum(0) = ""
    EngNum(1) = "One"
    EngNum(2) = "Two"
    EngNum(3) = "Three"
    EngNum(4) = "Four"
    EngNum(5) = "Five"
    EngNum(6) = "Six"
    EngNum(7) = "Seven"
    EngNum(8) = "Eight"
    EngNum(9) = "Nine"
```

```
EngNum(10) = "Ten"
EngNum(11) = "Eleven"
EngNum(12) = "Twelve"
EngNum(13) = "Thirteen"
EngNum(14) = "Fourteen"
EngNum(15) = "Fifteen"
EngNum(16) = "Sixteen"
EngNum(17) = "Seventeen"
EngNum(18) = "Eighteen"
EngNum(19) = "Nineteen"
EngNum(20) = "Twenty"
EngNum(30) = "Thirty"
EngNum(40) = "Forty"
EngNum(50) = "Fifty"
EngNum(60) = "Sixty"
EngNum(70) = "Seventy"
EngNum(80) = "Eighty"
EngNum(90) = "Ninety"

'** Initialize some variables
strNum = Format(AmountPassed, "000000000.00")
'strNum is original number converted to string

Pennies = Mid(strNum, 11, 2)
'Pennies variable contains last two digits of strNum

English = ""
LoopCount = 1
StartVal = 1

'** If amount passed is 0 just return "VOID"
If AmountPassed = 0 Then
NumWord = "VOID"
Exit Function
End If

'** Now do each 3-digit section of number.
Do While LoopCount <= 3
    Chunk = Mid(strNum, StartVal, 3)        '3-digit chunk
    Hundreds = Val(Mid(Chunk, 1, 1))        'Hundreds portion
    Tens = Val(Mid(Chunk, 2, 2))            'Tens portion
    Ones = Val(Mid(Chunk, 3, 1))            'Ones portion

    '** Do the hundreds portion of 3-digit number
    If Val(Chunk) > 99 Then
        English = English & EngNum(Hundreds) & " Hundred "
    End If

    '** Do the tens & ones portion of 3-digit number
    TensDone = False
```

```
        '** Is it less than 10?
        If Tens < 10 Then
            English = English & " " & EngNum(Ones)
            TensDone = True
        End If

        '** Is it a teen?
        If (Tens >= 11 And Tens <= 19) Then
            English = English & EngNum(Tens)
            TensDone = True
        End If

        '** Is it evenly divisible by 10?
        If (Tens / 10) = Int(Tens / 10) Then
            English = English & EngNum(Tens)
            TensDone = True
        End If

        '** Or is it none of the above?
        If Not TensDone Then
            English = English & EngNum((Int(Tens / 10)) * 10)
            English = English & " " & EngNum(Ones)
        End If

        '** Add the word "Million" if necessary
        If AmountPassed > 999999.99 And LoopCount = 1 Then
            English = English + " Million "
        End If

        '** Add the word "Thousand" if necessary
        If AmountPassed > 999.99 And LoopCount = 2 Then
            English = English + " Thousand "
        End If

        '** Do pass through next three digits
        LoopCount = LoopCount + 1
        StartVal = StartVal + 3
    Loop

    '** Done: Return English with Pennies/100 tacked on
    NumWord = Trim(English) & " and " & Pennies & "/100"
End Function
```

The NumWord( ) function can handle any number in the range of zero to 999,999,999.99. Presuming you entered NumWord( ) into a standard module in your database, you can test it out in the Immediate window. Just don't type any commas, dollar signs, or spaces in the number you pass to it. For example, if you type ? NumWord(76543.21) into the Immediate window, the function spits back Seventy Six Thousand Five Hundred Forty Three and 21/100.

Say you have this big blob of VBA code sitting in a standard module. How do you go about actually printing checks? Well, you can use NumWord() any place that you use a built-in function, such as in the Control Source property of a calculated control on a report designed to print your checks. Figure 3-13 shows an example.

See Book V, Chapter 1 for the goods on putting calculated controls on reports.

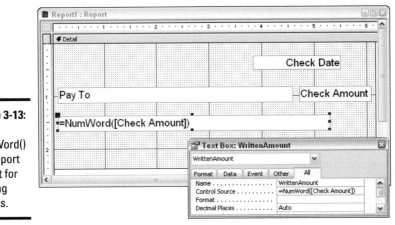

Figure 3-13:
Using
NumWord()
in a report
format for
printing
checks.

Chapter 4: Controlling Forms with VBA

In This Chapter

✔ **Displaying — and responding to — custom messages**

✔ **Opening a form with the DoCmd object**

✔ **Changing form controls with VBA**

✔ **Using objects and collections in code**

*W*hen you create a database for other people to use, making things as automatic as possible is to your advantage. The more automated your overall database, the less likely *users* — the people who actually use the database — will make mistakes (even if the user is you!). This chapter explores some techniques for using Visual Basic for Applications (VBA) to display custom messages to users, to automatically open and close forms, to change form controls, and more.

Displaying Custom Messages

In your day-to-day work with your computer, programs occasionally pop little messages on-screen to ask you questions, such as, "Are you sure you want to delete . . .?" You can then click the Yes or OK button to delete, or click the No or Cancel button to change your mind. You can add similar custom messages to your database.

Displaying a message box

As you may recall from Chapter 2 of this book, VBA can also display custom messages. By using a variable and the MsgBox() function, you can display a question and then have VBA perform some task based on the user's answer to that question. The syntax for creating such an interactive message box is

```
Dim myVar as Byte
myVar = MsgBox(prompt[, buttons] [, title])
```

where the Dim statement defines a variable as the Byte (Yes/No) data type, *myVar* is any variable name of your choosing, *prompt* is the text of the message, and *title* is the text to appear in the title bar of the message. The buttons argument is a constant, or sum of constants, that specify the buttons and icons to show in the box, as summarized in Table 4-1.

Table 4-1	Constants Used for the MsgBox Buttons Argument
Constant	*Description*
vbOKOnly	Display OK button only
vbOKCancel	Display OK and Cancel buttons
vbAbortRetryIgnore	Display Abort, Retry, and Ignore buttons
vbYesNoCancel	Display Yes, No, and Cancel buttons
vbYesNo	Display Yes and No buttons
vbRetryCancel	Display Retry and Cancel buttons
vbCritical	Display Critical icon
vbQuestion	Display Question icon
vbExclamation	Display Warning icon
vbInformation	Display Information icon

For example, the following statement shows a message box that contains a Question icon and Yes and No buttons. Figure 4-1 shows the message box that the code displays when executed.

```
Dim myVar as Byte
myVar = MsgBox("Are you sure?",vbYesNo+vbQuestion)
```

Figure 4-1: The message displayed by MsgBox.

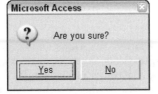

When someone clicks a button in the message box, the variable (myVar in this example) receives a value. That value tells you which button the person clicked, as summarized in Table 4-2.

Table 4-2	Values That MsgBox Passes to the Variable	
Button Clicked	*Variable Receives*	*Numeric Value*
OK	vbOK	1
Cancel	vbCancel	2
Abort	vbAbort	3
Retry	vbRetry	4

Button Clicked	Variable Receives	Numeric Value
Ignore	vbIgnore	5
Yes	vbYes	6
No	vbNo	7

Responding to what the user clicks

By using decision-making code, you can then have your VBA procedure do something when someone clicks a button on your message box, based on the contents of the myVar variable. For example, the sample message box displays a Yes button and a No button. If the user clicks the Yes button, myVar contains vbYes (or 6). If the user clicks the No button, myVar contains vbNo (or 7). The skeletal structure of the code that decides what to do based on the button clicked (where Do these statements... can be any number of VBA statements) is the following:

```
'Show a message box with Yes and No buttons.
Dim myVar as Byte
myVar = MsgBox("Are you sure?",vbYesNo+vbQuestion)

'Decide what to do next based on button clicked in box.
If myVar = vbYes Then
    'Do these statements if Yes
Else
    'Do these statements if No
End If
```

You can use either the constant or the numeric value to refer to the contents of the myVar variable. The following code works exactly the same as the preceding code:

```
'Show a message box with Yes and No buttons.
Dim myVar as Byte
myVar = MsgBox("Are you sure?",vbYesNo+vbQuestion)

'Decide what to do next based on button clicked in box.
If myVar = 6 Then
    'Do these statements if Yes
Else
    'Do these statements if No
End If
```

If you need three buttons, you can use a Select Case statement to choose what to do. For example, the following code displays a message box with Yes, No, and Cancel buttons. The Select Case block of code then decides what to do based on the button that was clicked. (Again, Do these statements... represents any number of VBA statements.)

```
'Show a message box with Yes, No, and Cancel buttons.
Dim myVar as Byte
myVar = MsgBox("Overwrite?",vbYesNoCancel+vbQuestion)

'Decide what to do next based on button clicked in box.

Select Case myVar

    Case vbYes
        'Do these statements if Yes clicked

    Case vbNo
        'Do these statements if No clicked

    Case vbCancel
        'Do these statements if Cancel clicked
End Select
```

Message boxes are handy for presenting short little messages on-screen. Often, though, you want your code to open an entire form.

Opening Forms with DoCmd

Although you can access (seemingly) countless objects in VBA, the DoCmd object (pronounced *do* com-*mand*) is one of the easiest and handiest for manipulating Access objects. The DoCmd object gives you access to all the commands — including options on all menus, toolbars, and shortcut menus — found in the Access program window. The basic syntax of a DoCmd statement is as follows:

```
DoCmd.methodName(arglist)
```

where *methodName* is any method that's supported by the DoCmd object, and *arglist* represents required and optional arguments that a given method accepts.

Like with any VBA keyword, as soon as you type **DoCmd.** into the Code window, a menu of acceptable words that you can type next appears, as shown in Figure 4-2. Use the scroll bar at the right side of the list to see all your options. Of course, you can also use the VBA Help system to find more information on the DoCmd object and its methods, also shown in Figure 4-2.

Umpteen ways to open a form

Although many methods are available to choose from in the DoCmd object, the OpenForm method provides a good example. The syntax of the OpenForm method is

```
DoCmd.OpenForm FormName, [View], [FilterName],
    [WhereCondition], [DataMode], [WindowMode], [OpenArgs]
```

where

- ✦ `FormName`: Represents the name of the form that you want to open.

- ✦ `View`: Represents the view in which you want to open the form using the built-in constants:

  - `acNormal`: Form view. This view is used if you omit the `View` argument in the statement.

  - `acDesign`: Design view.

  - `acFormDS`: Datasheet view.

  - `acFormPivotChart`: PivotChart view.

  - `acFormPivotTable`: PivotTable view.

  - `acPreview`: Print Preview.

- ✦ `FilterName`: The name of a query within the current database, which limits records displayed by the form. If omitted, no query filter is applied.

- ✦ `WhereCondition`: An expression, enclosed in quotation marks, that specifies records to include. If omitted, all records are available. For example, entering a `WhereCondition` such as `"[State] = 'CA' "` displays only records that have `CA` in the State field.

- ✦ `DataMode`: Specifies the data entry mode in which the form opens, using one of the following constants:

  - `acFormatPropertySettings`: Opens the form in its default view as specified in the form's `AllowEdits`, `AllowDeletions`, `AllowAdditions`, and `DataEntry` properties. If you don't specify a `DataMode` argument in the statement, this setting is used by default.

  - `acFormAdd`: Opens the form with the ability to add new records enabled and the cursor in a new, empty record.

  - `acFormEdit`: Opens the form with the ability to edit records contained within the table.

  - `acFormReadOnly`: Opens the form in read-only mode, so that the user can view, but not change, the data.

- ✦ `WindowMode`: Specifies the appearance of the form window upon opening, using any of the following options:

  - `acWindowNormal`: Opens the form in its normal view. If you omit this argument, `acWindowNormal` is the setting that's applied automatically.

- **acDialog:** Opens the form by using a fixed-size, dialog box-style border.

- **acHidden:** Opens the form so that the code can have access to the form's controls and data but doesn't make the form visible on-screen.

- **acIcon:** Opens the form minimized to an icon in the Access program window.

✦ **OpenArgs:** Can be used to pass data to the form's class module, where other code can use it.

Methods of DoCmd   Help for DoCmd method

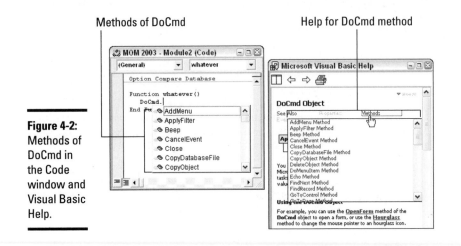

Figure 4-2:
Methods of
DoCmd in
the Code
window and
Visual Basic
Help.

When you type a `DoCmd.OpenForm` statement into the Code window, the mini-syntax chart keeps you posted on which argument you're currently typing (by showing that argument in boldface). When you get to an argument that requires a constant, the Code window displays a drop-down list of acceptable constants. You can just double-click, rather than type, the constant that you want to use.

Look at some examples of using the `OpenForm` method of the `DoCmd` object. The following line

```
DoCmd.OpenForm "Products Form"
```

opens the `Products Form` form. Because no optional arguments are specified, no filter is applied, and all other optional settings take on their default values. Opening the form by double-clicking its name in the Database window accomplished the same thing.

Macros and the DoCmd object

Access macros (Book VI) use the DoCmd object to carry out most of their actions. Often, you can use macros to write a series of DoCmd statements without the complexities of manually typing each statement by hand. Create a macro to do whatever you want your code to do. Then convert the macro to VBA code, as we discuss in Chapter 1 of this book. When you open the converted macro in VBA Editor, you see that most, if not all, of its actions are converted to DoCmd statements. You can then cut and paste those statements into some other procedure that you're writing. Or just add any necessary code to the converted macro.

The following statement opens the Products Form form, displaying only those records where the Selling Price field contains a number greater than 100:

```
DoCmd.OpenForm "Products Form", , , "[Selling Price] > 100"
```

The commas with nothing after them represent required arguments that the command isn't using. If you need to review what that's about, see Chapter 2 of this book.

The following statement opens a Sales Tax Calcs form with the Window Mode property set to the dialog box style:

```
DoCmd.OpenForm "Sales Tax Calcs", , , , , acDialog
```

As you can see, the DoCmd object offers a lot of flexibility in specifying how you want to open a form. The same is true of many other methods of the DoCmd object. These few examples don't even come close to showing all the variations. The important thing is knowing that the DoCmd object exists and that you can perform many Access actions on objects within your database.

Closing a form with DoCmd

Just like you can open a form with DoCmd, you can also close it. The syntax to close an object using DoCmd is

```
DoCmd.Close(ObjectType, ObjectName, Save)
```

Each argument in the syntax represents the following:

✦ ObjectType: The type of object that you want to close expressed using one of the available constants, such as acForm, acReport, acTable, acQuery.

✦ `ObjectName`: A string expression that identifies a currently open object.

✦ `Save`: One of the following constants:

- `acSaveNo`: Closes the object without saving any changes.
- `acSavePrompt`: (Default) Displays the standard "Do you want to save . . ." message so the user can choose whether to save or not.
- `acSaveYes`: Saves all changes to the form and then closes it.

If you want to close a form, from code, without saving any design changes made to the form and without asking the user to decide whether to save those changes, use the following statement:

```
DoCmd.Close acForm, formName, acSaveNo
```

where *formName* is the name of the form that you want to close. If you want a line of code to close the `Products Form` form, the syntax would be

```
DoCmd.Close acForm, "Products Form", acSaveNo
```

Changing Form Controls with VBA

When a form is open, you can use VBA code to change the contents and even the appearance of the form — from the big picture down to the individual controls on the form. Suppose you have a form that includes a control for choosing a payment method. You're thinking that you may want other controls to be enabled or disabled based on the selected payment method. To do this, you want the Paid field to be marked True if Cash, Check, or Credit Card is selected, and marked False if Purchase Order is selected. You may even want to make a control, like the Expiration Date label, visible or invisible, depending on the selected payment method, as in Figure 4-3.

Within VBA, use the following syntax to change a control's property:

```
ControlName.PropertyName = Value
```

where *ControlName* is the complete name of a control on an open form, *PropertyName* is the name of the property that you want to change, and *Value* is the new value for the property. A dot separates the control name from the property name. The *complete name* means that the name has to contain both the name of the form and the name of the control. However, in a class module, you can use the keyword `Me` to stand for the form name. The keyword `Me` means "the form to which this class module is attached."

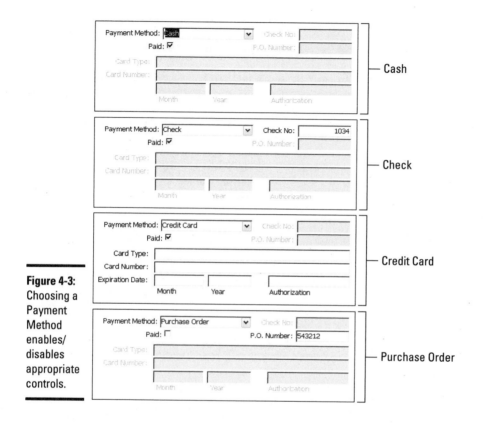

Cash

Check

Credit Card

Purchase Order

Figure 4-3:
Choosing a
Payment
Method
enables/
disables
appropriate
controls.

Some cool control properties

If you want to make a control named `ExpireLabel` invisible, use the
statement

```
Me.ExpireLabel.Visible = False
```

To make the control visible, use the statement

```
Me.ExpireLabel.Visible = True
```

To *disable* a control (so that it is dimmed and doesn't respond to mouse clicks
or the keyboard), set the control's `Enabled` property to a `False` value. For
example, to disable a control named `PONumber`, use this statement:

```
Me.PONumber.Enabled = False
```

To set the control back to its normal `Enabled` status, use this statement:

```
Me.PONumber.Enabled = True
```

**Book VIII
Chapter 4**

**Controlling Forms
with VBA**

Why not just show everything?

In case you're wondering why we don't show all the methods of the DoCmd object, or all the objects, properties, and methods available in all the object libraries, the truth of the matter is this: It's too many words. And not in the sense that we're too lazy to type that many words. Rather, there aren't enough pages in this entire book to fit that many words.

The sheer quantity of information makes remembering every detail of every VBA statement and object nearly impossible, so it wouldn't do much good to print that information here anyway. Even professional programmers spend a lot of time looking up the syntax of keywords and objects in the Help system (or the Object Browser). The sooner you become fluent in using the VBA Editor's Help, or the Object Browser (or both), the better off you are. See Chapters 1 and 2 of this book for more information on the Object Browser and VBA Help.

The Enabled property doesn't apply to Label controls. The property only works on controls that display data from the underlying table or query. But you can use the Visible property to make a label visible or invisible.

To change the value (contents) of a control, use the Value property. For example, to put a check mark in the Yes/No field named Paid, use the statement

```
Me.Paid.Value = True
```

To clear that check mark, use

```
Me.Paid.Value = False
```

Although the next few examples don't pertain to the Payment Method example, knowing that you can change the contents of any control is useful. To insert new text into a text box, use the standard syntax but enclose the new text in quotation marks, as in the following example (where ProductName is the text box control on the current form):

```
Me.ProductName.Value = "9-Passenger Lear Jet"
```

To increase or decrease a value in a numeric field, set the Value property of its control to an expression that does the appropriate math. Suppose that a form contains a UnitPrice control that's a Currency field. The following statement increases that control's current value by 10 percent:

```
Me.UnitPrice.Value = 1.10 * Me.UnitPrice.Value
```

Controlling properties with your program

You can see how you actually write the code within a class module by looking at the Payment Methods example that we mention earlier in the chapter. Take a look at Figure 4-4 where you can see the name of each control in its text box. The one control in that form that is just a label — and not attached to any control — is ExpireLabel. Because you can't see its name, the figure points out its location.

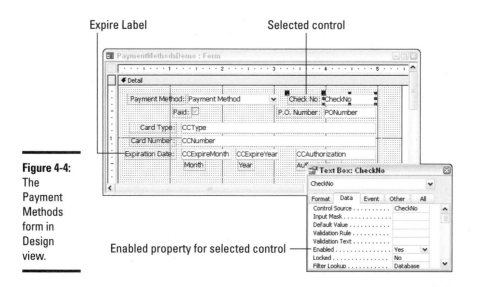

Expire Label   Selected control

Figure 4-4:
The
Payment
Methods
form in
Design
view.

Enabled property for selected control

Figure 4-4 also shows the Properties sheet for the currently selected control CheckNo. Note that on the Data tab of the Properties sheet, you set the Enabled property to a Yes or No value. If you set a control's Enabled property to the No value, the control disables automatically when the form first opens. But you can then use code to enable or disable controls in response to events, as you do in a moment.

The first thing that you need to think about is, "What event is going to trigger all this enabling and disabling of controls?" In this case, when a user chooses a payment method, you want the controls to be enabled or disabled whenever the contents of the Payment Methods control change.

The After Update event is the best event for this situation because that event occurs after a new value is selected, and any validation criteria for the field have already been met. So in this case, you click the Payment Method control (in Design view) to select it. If the Properties sheet isn't already open, right-click that control and choose Properties. Click the Event tab in the Properties sheet. Click the After Update event, click its Build button, and then choose the Code Builder from the dialog box that appears, as illustrated in Figure 4-5.

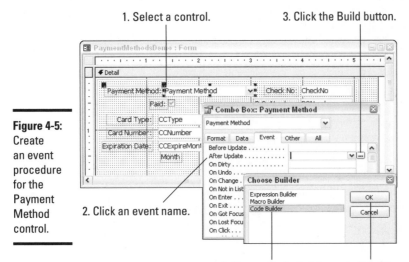

1. Select a control. 3. Click the Build button.

Figure 4-5: Create an event procedure for the Payment Method control.

2. Click an event name.

4. Choose Code Builder and click OK.

After you click the OK button in the Choose Builder dialog box, the class module for the form opens up. The first and last lines of the procedure are already typed in for you. In this example, the lines look like this in the module:

```
Private Sub Payment_Method_AfterUpdate()

End Sub
```

When writing the procedure, be sure to put all the lines between the `Private Sub` and `End Sub` statements. We typed in the necessary code in the following block. Just to make things even fancier, we threw in a few `DoCmd.GoToControl` statements to position the cursor to the next control that the user would likely type in next. For example, the statement `DoCmd.GoToControl "CCType"` means "move the blinking cursor into the control named `CCType`."

```
Private Sub Payment_Method_AfterUpdate()

    'First, disable controls and hide the label,
    'to create a simple starting point.
    Me.CheckNo.Enabled = False
```

```
    Me.PONumber.Enabled = False
    Me.CCType.Enabled = False
    Me.CCNumber.Enabled = False
    Me.CCExpireMonth.Enabled = False
    Me.CCExpireYear.Enabled = False
    Me.CCAuthorization.Enabled = False

    Me.ExpireLabel.Visible = False

    'Now selectively show and enable controls,
    'and fill the Paid field, based on the
    'contents of the Payment Method control

    Select Case Me.[Payment Method].Value

        'If selection is Cash...
        Case "Cash"
            Me.Paid.Value = True

        'If selection is Check...
        Case "Check"
            Me.CheckNo.Enabled = True
            Me.Paid.Value = True

            'Move cursor to CheckNo control
            DoCmd.GoToControl "CheckNo"

        'If selection is Credit Card...
        Case "Credit Card"
            Me.CCType.Enabled = True
            Me.CCNumber.Enabled = True
            Me.CCExpireMonth.Enabled = True
            Me.CCExpireYear.Enabled = True
            Me.CCAuthorization.Enabled = True

            Me.ExpireLabel.Visible = True
            Me.Paid.Value = True

            'Move cursor to CCType control
            DoCmd.GoToControl "CCType"

        'If selection is Purchase Order...
        Case "Purchase Order"
            Me.PONumber.Enabled = True
            Me.Paid.Value = False

            'Move cursor to PONumber control
            DoCmd.GoToControl "PONumber"

    End Select
End Sub
```

**Book VIII
Chapter 4**

**Controlling Forms
with VBA**

Looks can be deceiving

When you create a lookup field, what you see in that field may not match what Access has actually stored in the field. For example, you may have a ContactID field that shows a customer name in the format *Jones, Hank.* But Access actually *stores* that person's ContactID as a number (perhaps 39 or whatever).

VBA sees what Access sees — the ContactID *number* in the preceding example, not the name. Any code that you write needs to take that into consideration. To create an `If` statement that makes a decision based on the contents of the ContactID field, use something like this:

```
If Me.ContactID.Value = 39
```

If you use the following statement instead, the code either generates an error message or perhaps doesn't give the result that you think it should:

```
If Me.ContactID.Value =
"Jones. Hank"
```

You can add a `Debug.Print` statement to your code and run it from the Immediate window to see what type of data is stored in a control. For example:

```
Debug.Print
Me.ContactID,Value
```

displays the contents of the `ContactID` control. If that's a number, you know that the ContactID field in every record contains a number.

In a class module, adding code to open the form is not necessary because the form is already open by the time that any procedures in its class module are called.

The code and comments should be fairly easy to read. For starters, the `Sub` procedure name, `Payment_Method_AfterUpdate()`, tells you that this code executes after a user makes a selection from the `Payment Method` control, and Access accepts that change.

The first lines under the `Sub` statement disable most controls and hide the expiration label, just so that we know the status of each control before the `Select Case` statement executes.

The `Select Case Me.[Payment Method].Value` statement uses the value (contents) of the `Payment Methods` control to make a decision about which controls to enable and make visible. When the `Cash` option is selected, only this code is executed, filling the Paid check box with a check mark:

```
Case "Cash"
     Me.Paid.Value = True
```

When the `Check` option is selected, the following lines execute to enable the `CheckNo` control, place a check mark in the `Paid` control, and move the cursor to the `CheckNo` control:

```
Case "Check"
    Me.CheckNo.Enabled = True
    Me.Paid.Value = True

    'Move cursor to CheckNo control
    DoCmd.GoToControl "CheckNo"
```

And so it goes, each `Case` statement modifying certain controls and positioning the cursor based on the current value of the `Payment Method` control.

After typing in the code, close the Code window and Visual Basic Editor to return to your form. There you can save the form, open it in Form view, and try out your code.

If you have difficulty with our own code, you may find some of the debugging techniques described in Chapter 6 of this book useful for diagnosing and fixing problems.

Understanding Objects and Collections

Working with controls on a form or report from within a class module is greatly simplified by the `Me` keyword, which refers to the form or report to which the class module is attached. Things become more complicated when you write code in standard modules, where the keyword `Me` doesn't refer to anything because a standard module isn't attached to any particular form or report. When you step outside a class module, you need to think more in terms of the object models.

As you (hopefully) know, just about everything you work with in Access is an object — tables, queries, and forms are all objects. Some objects are very much alike; tables are alike in that they all contain data. Forms are alike in that they all present data from tables in a certain format. A group of like objects forms a *collection.* For example, all the tables within your database represent that database's tables collection.

In some cases, a single object may be a collection as well. A single form is one object in the collection of forms. But a single form is also a collection in its own right — a collection of controls. Each control on a form is also an object in its own right. But even a single control is a collection. A control has lots of properties, as you can see on any control's Properties sheet in Design view. Figure 4-6 shows how a collection is a bunch of objects that have something in common, and how any given object can also be a collection.

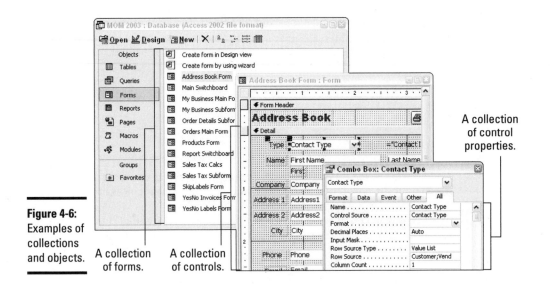

Figure 4-6:
Examples of
collections
and objects.

Properties, methods, and events

All objects have some combination of properties, methods, and events.
Objects in the real world as well as objects in Access have properties, methods, and events. You can describe a car in terms of its properties (make,
model, size, color, and so forth), methods (you drive a car), and events (you
press the brake pedal, which causes a series of actions that slow the car
down). But getting back to Access, we define those terms as follows:

✦ **Property:** A *property* of an object (or collection) is some characteristic
of that object, such as size, color, font, and so forth.

✦ **Method:** A *method* is something that you can do to the object. Every
form has an Open method and a Close method because you can open
and close forms. (The DoCmd object that we mention earlier in this chapter provides access to the methods provided by most Access objects.)

✦ **Event:** An *event* is something that happens to an object. When you click
a button on a form, you trigger its On Click event (or Click event).

If you open a form in Design view, you can right-click the gray area behind
the design grid and choose Properties to get to the form's properties. There
you can see the form's properties and events, as illustrated in Figure 4-7.

Many of the methods that an object supports are displayed when you right-
click the object's icon in the database window, as in Figure 4-8.

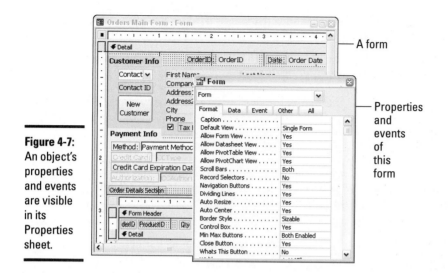

Figure 4-7:
An object's
properties
and events
are visible
in its
Properties
sheet.

— A form

— Properties
and
events
of
this
form

Of course, when you're working in VBA, the visual interactive tools that
Access offers — tools such as shortcut menus and Properties sheets —
aren't visible. In VBA, you write code to access collections, objects, properties, methods, and events.

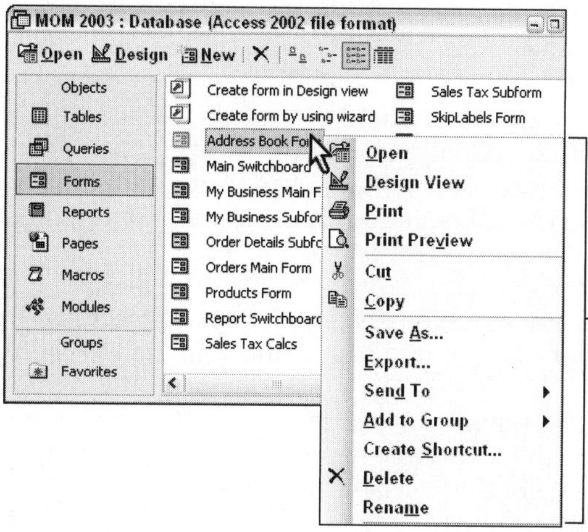

Figure 4-8:
Methods of
a form
object are
on its
shortcut
menu.

— Form methods

Book VIII
Chapter 4

Controlling Forms
with VBA

Referring to objects and collections

Manipulating an object through VBA code starts with a two-step process:

1. **Declare an object variable (by using** Dim**) as the appropriate object or collection type.**

2. **Set the object variable (by using the** Set **keyword) to a specific object or collection within your database.**

The syntax of the statements for performing those two steps looks like this:

```
Dim anyName As objectType
Set anyName = specificObject
```

where *anyName* is a variable name of your choosing, the *objectType* is one of the keywords shown in the first column of Table 4-3, and *specificObject* represents a specific named object.

Table 4-3	Common Types for Object Variables
Object Type	*Use to Declare*
AccessObject	Any type of Access object in AllForms, AllReports, and other collections
Form	A form
Report	A report
Control	A control on a form or report
Property	A property of an object
RecordSet	A group of records (see Chapter 5 of this book)

At the highest level of the object model, you can use the AllForms, AllReports, and other collections contained within the CurrentProject object to refer to any form or report — even forms and reports that aren't open. Each object in those collections has a general type called AccessObject.

For a detailed explanation of the CurrentProject object and the collections it supports, look up the CurrentProject object in the VBA Editor's Help.

If you want to create a reference to a form named Products Form, in code, and give that form a short variable name, like myForm, declare myForm as an AccessObject. Then set that variable's value to the form by using the syntax Set myForm = CurrentProject.AllForms("*FormName*"), as the following shows:

```
Dim myForm As AccessObject
Set myForm = CurrentProject.AllForms("Products Form")
```

After the code runs, the variable named myForm refers to the form named Products Form.

Naming conventions for object variables

In this chapter, we use the letters `my` at the start of variables names, just to provide some consistency. Some programmers, however, follow certain naming conventions, replacing the letters `my` with a tag that represents the object type that the variable refers to. If an object variable refers to an `AccessObject`, programmers may use `obj` as the first letters of an object variable name, as in `Dim objForm as AccessObject`. Some may use `ctl` as the first letters of an object variable that refers to a control, as in `Dim ctlProductID as Control`.

Naming conventions are especially useful in large projects where many different programmers work with code. They help identify the object type each variable refers to. But naming conventions are also entirely optional. Don't feel that you must use them in your own code.

An example: Seeing whether a form is open

You can create a custom VBA function that uses a collection and an object variable. You can prevent your code and macros from opening multiple copies of a form. The name of this custom function is `isOpen()` and is shown in Figure 4-9.

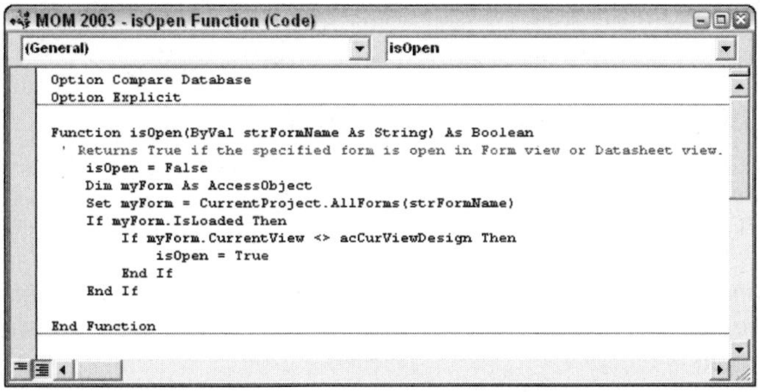

Figure 4-9:
The isOpen() function determines whether a form is open.

```
MOM 2003 - isOpen Function (Code)

(General)                              isOpen

Option Compare Database
Option Explicit

Function isOpen(ByVal strFormName As String) As Boolean
' Returns True if the specified form is open in Form view or Datasheet view.
    isOpen = False
    Dim myForm As AccessObject
    Set myForm = CurrentProject.AllForms(strFormName)
    If myForm.IsLoaded Then
        If myForm.CurrentView <> acCurViewDesign Then
            isOpen = True
        End If
    End If

End Function
```

The `isOpen()` function is stored in a standard module, rather than a class module, so you can access it freely from anywhere in your database.

You use the `isOpen()` custom function, just like you would a built-in function, by passing a form name to the function, as the following shows:

```
isOpen("Products Form")
```

**Book VIII
Chapter 4**

**Controlling Forms
with VBA**

When called, the isOpen() function returns True if the specified form is open, or returns False if the specified form is closed. The first statement of the isOpen is the following:

```
Function IsOpen(FormName As String) As Boolean
```

which defines the name of the function as isOpen, accepting a single string value that is referred to as FormName within the procedure. This custom function returns either True or False (a Boolean value).

The ByVal keyword, used in front of an argument name in a Sub or Function statement, passes the value directly instead of as a reference to the object. ByVal, although optional, can speed the processing.

The next line sets the initial value to be returned by the function to False. Later code in the procedure turns that to True if the form is open in Form or Datasheet view:

```
isOpen = False
```

The next line in the code declares an object variable named myForm and sets its type to AccessObject:

```
Dim myForm As AccessObject
```

The next line then makes the myForm object variable refer to the specific form, based on the name that passes to the function:

```
Set myForm = CurrentProject.AllForms(strFormName)
```

If you call the function by using isOpen("Products Form"), the variable name myForm refers to the Products Form after the line is executed.

The next statement uses the built-in IsLoaded property to determine whether the form is open. If the form is open, isLoaded returns True. If the form is closed, isLoaded returns False:

```
If myForm.IsLoaded Then
```

If (and only if) the form is indeed open, the next statement uses the CurrentView property to see whether the form is currently open in Design view. (CurrentView is a property of all form objects; acCurViewDesign is a constant that means "currently open in Design view"):

```
If myForm.CurrentView <> acCurViewDesign Then
```

If, and only if, the form is open — but not open in Design view — the following statement sets isOpen to True. If the form isn't open, or is open in Design view, the next line doesn't execute, so isOpen retains its original value of False:

```
isOpen = True
```

The rest of the procedure just contains an End If statement for each If block, and the End Function statement to mark the end of the procedure.

To see some practical uses of the custom isOpen() function, imagine that you already added that custom function to a standard module in your database. Now you want to use the function to see whether a form is open before you execute code to open that form. In particular, you want the code to see whether Products Form is open and, if it isn't, to go ahead and open the form. Use the following code to open a form:

```
'Open Products Form, but only if it isn't open already.
If Not isOpen("Products Form") Then
   DoCmd.OpenForm "Products Form"

End If
```

Suppose you want a procedure to close the form. But you want to make sure the form is, indeed, open before using DoCmd.Close to close the form. In that case, use these statements:

```
'Close Products Form if it is currently open.
If isOpen("Products Form") Then
   DoCmd.Close acForm, "Products Form", acSaveNo

End If
```

In a macro, you can use isOpen() in the Condition column to ensure that the macro doesn't try to open a form that's already open. You can also use isOpen() to make sure that a form is open before you close it, as shown in Figure 4-10.

Looping through collections

Access provides a slight variation on the For...Next loop, known as the For Each...Next loop, that's designed to specifically repeat once for each item within a collection. With each pass through the loop, the object variable used in the For Each...Next loop refers to the next object in the collection. The syntax of the For Each...Next loop is

```
For Each element In collection
    [statements]
[Exit For]
    [statements]
Next [element]
```

where *element* is an object variable of the appropriate type for the collection, *collection* is the name of a collection, and *statements* are any number of statements to be executed within the loop.

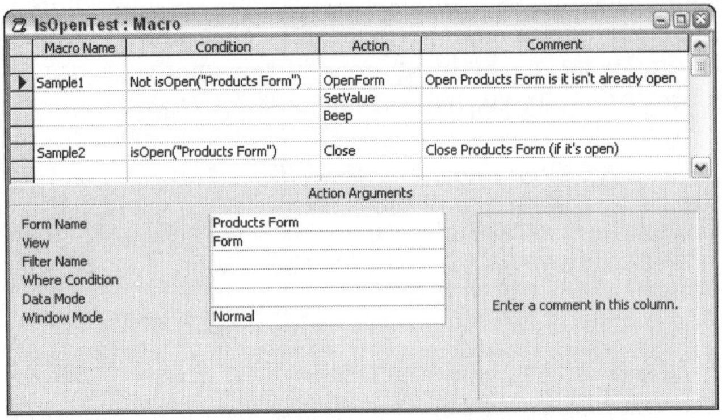

Figure 4-10:
Using
isOpen()
in the
Condition
column of a
macro
group.

	Macro Name	Condition	Action	Comment
▶	Sample1	Not isOpen("Products Form")	OpenForm	Open Products Form is it isn't already open
			SetValue	
			Beep	
	Sample2	isOpen("Products Form")	Close	Close Products Form (if it's open)

IsOpenTest : Macro

Action Arguments

Form Name	Products Form
View	Form
Filter Name	
Where Condition	
Data Mode	
Window Mode	Normal

Enter a comment in this column.

Whether you ever need a `For Each...Next` loop in your own code depends on how fancy things get. But if you use other peoples' code, you may come across an occasional `For Each...Next` loop, so you need to have an idea of what that loop does.

For example, recall that the `AllForms` collection in the `CurrentProject` object contains all the forms in the current database. Each form in the collection is a type of `AccessObject`.

The `Forms` collection contains only the forms that are currently open. The `AllForms` collection includes both closed and open forms.

In the following example , we use the `Dim` statement to declare an object variable named `myForm` as an `AccessObject`. Then we use a `For Each...Next` loop to loop through the `AllForms` collection and print the `Name` property of every form in the database:

```
Dim myForm as AccessObject
For Each myForm In CurrentProject.AllForms
    'Code to be performed on every form.
    Debug.Print myForm.Name

Next
```

Running the code prints the name of each form in the current database to the Immediate window.

Recall, too, that a form is a collection in its own right — a collection of controls. To set up a loop that looks at each control on a form, you first need to make sure that the form is open. Then, define an object variable as the `Control` element type. The collection name used in the `For Each...Next` loop needs to be a specific open form.

The following code snippet opens a form named `Products Form`. The `Dim` statement creates an object variable, named `myCtl`, as the generic `Control` type of object. The `For Each...Next` loop specifies all the controls on the current form as the collection. With each pass through the loop, the `Debug.Print` statement prints the name of the current control:

```
DoCmd.OpenForm "Products Form"
Dim myCtl as Control
For Each myCtl In Forms![Products Form]
    'Code to be performed on every control goes below.
    Debug.Print myCtl.Name

Next
```

A *control,* as you may recall, is also a collection: A *collection* of properties defines the control's name, contents, appearance, type, and behavior. If you want to set up a loop that accesses each property that a control supports, you need to ensure that the form is open. With that accomplished, define an object variable of the `Property` type and use the specific control's name as the collection name in the `For Each...Next` loop, as the following shows:

```
DoCmd.OpenForm "Products Form"

Dim myProp as Property
For Each myProp In Forms![Products Form].[Product Name]
    'Code to be performed on every control goes below.
    Debug.Print myProp.Name & " = " & myProp.Value

Next
```

The first line opens a form named `Products Form`. The next line defines an object variable named `myProp` as the `Property` type. Then the `For Each...Next` loop displays the name and value of every property for the Product Name field.

Using With...End With

If you need to change a whole bunch of properties associated with an object, you can save a little typing by using a `With...End With` block. The syntax for the block is:

```
With objectName
.property = value
End With
```

where *objectName* is the name of an open object, or the object variable name that points to the object, *.property* is a valid property for that object, and *value* is the value you want to assign to that object. Assuming that myCtl refers to a control on an open form, as in the following example, you can use a With myCtl...End With block to change several properties of that control:

```
Dim myCtl As Control
Set myCtl = myForm.[Selling Price]
With myCtl
    .Visible = True
    .SpecialEffect = Flat
    .FontBold = True
    .Value = 1.1 * myCtl
End With
```

The With...End With block changes the Visible property of the Selling Price control to True, sets its Special Effect property to Flat, sets its font to bold, and increases the value stored in that field by 10 percent.

As in the case of the For Each...Next loop, the With...End With statement is optional and not something you *must* use in any code you write. Our main purpose is to take the mystery out of it, in case you should ever come across With...End With in someone else's code.

Chapter 5: Using SQL and Recordsets

Working with data in tables and queries through Visual Basic for Applications (VBA) is — in a word — weird. You don't exactly work with a table or query directly in VBA. Instead, you work with a *recordset*. As the name implies, a *recordset* is a set of records. A recordset can be all the records in a given table, all the records in the results of a query involving two or more tables, or a subset of particular records from any table or query. In other words, a recordset can contain any records from any tables you want.

Recordsets and Object Models

Because Access offers two different object models for the purpose of working with recordsets, you may find recordsets confusing. One is *DAO* (Data Access Objects), the other is *ADO* (ActiveX Data Objects). The DAO model is the older of the two. DAO works only with Access tables. ADO, the newer of the two, works either with Access tables or external data sources, such as Oracle and Microsoft SQL Server.

Working with external data sources, such as Microsoft SQL Server, is a major topic of Book IX. This chapter focuses on using ADO with tables and queries inside your Access database.

At first glance you may think, "Well, I'll never use external data sources, so I'll stick with the DAO object model." But picking an object model isn't that easy. The newer ADO model is currently favored by Microsoft, meaning that ADO will continue to grow and get better while DAO remains in maintenance mode, which generally spells doom for a technology. If a technology is in maintenance mode today, that pretty much guarantees that it won't exist at all in the not-too-distant future.

Given the bias of Microsoft, we stick with ADO in this book. To make sure the stuff that we do in this chapter works on your computer, make sure the ADO object model is loaded in your copy of Access. To do so, open the Visual Basic Editor, choose Tools⇨References from the VBA Editor menu, and select the Microsoft ActiveX Data Objects 2.7 Library option, as in Figure 5-1. (You may need to scroll down the list to find it.)

Figure 5-1:
The
Microsoft
ActiveX
Data
Objects
Library
selected
in the
References
dialog box.

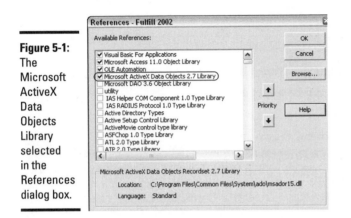

Because ADO is evolving quickly, you'll likely find several versions of the ActiveX Data Objects library in your References dialog box. Select only the most recent one — the one with the highest version number. Then click OK.

Quick and easy recordsets

If your goal is to create a recordset that contains all the fields and records from a single table in your database, the job is fairly straightforward. Just type the following code, exactly as shown, into a procedure but replace *tableName* with the name of the table that you want to open:

If you don't yet know how to type code into a procedure, see Chapter 2 of this book.

```
Dim myConnection as ADODB.Connection
Set myConnection = CurrentProject.Connection
Dim myRecordset as New ADODB.Recordset
myRecordSet.activeConnection = myConnection
myRecordset.Open "tableName", , adOpenStatic,
    adLockOptimistic
```

After all the lines execute, the myRecordSet object variable refers to all the fields and records in whatever table you specified as *tableName* in the last line of code.

ADO recordset properties and methods

Most ADO recordsets support the following methods, which allow you to manipulate the data in the recordset with VBA code:

✦ `.AddNew:` Adds a new, blank record to the recordset.

✦ `.MoveFirst:` Moves the cursor to the first record in the recordset.

✦ `.MoveNext:` Moves the cursor to the next record in the recordset.

✦ `.MovePrevious:` Moves the cursor to the previous record in the recordset.

✦ `.MoveLast:` Moves the cursor to the last record in the recordset.

✦ `.Move numrecords, start:` Specifies the number of records to move through and the starting point.

✦ `.Open:` Opens a new recordset.

✦ `.Close:` Closes a recordset.

✦ `.Update:` Saves any changes made to the current row of a recordset.

✦ `.UpdateBatch:` Saves all changes made to the current recordset.

Some properties that you can use to determine the number of records in a recordset, as well as the current position of the cursor within the recordset, are the following:

✦ `.RecordCount:` Returns the total number of records in the recordset.

✦ `.AbsolutePosition:` Returns a number indicating which row the cursor is in. (1 is the first record, 2 is the second record, and so forth.)

✦ `.BOF:` Beginning Of File; returns `True` when the cursor is above the first record in the recordset.

✦ `.EOF:` End Of File; returns `True` when the cursor is past the last record in the recordset.

Looping through a recordset

When a recordset is open, you can use a loop to step through each record within the recordset. As an example, Figure 5-2 shows some code that creates a recordset named `myRecordSet`. The `While...Wend` loop steps through each record in the recordset — one record at a time — and prints the record's position and the contents of the first couple of fields in each record.

Needless to say, the code in Figure 5-2 isn't exactly simple. The sections that follow, however, shed some light on some of its meaning.

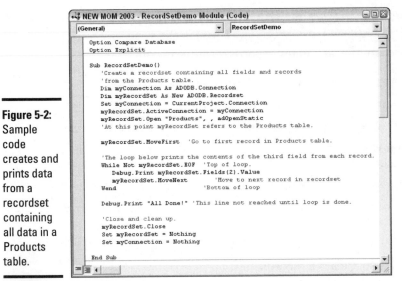

Figure 5-2:
Sample code creates and prints data from a recordset containing all data in a Products table.

```
NEW MOM 2003 - RecordSetDemo Module (Code)
(General)                              RecordSetDemo

Option Compare Database
Option Explicit

Sub RecordSetDemo()
    'Create a recordset containing all fields and records
    'from the Products table.
    Dim myConnection As ADODB.Connection
    Dim myRecordSet As New ADODB.Recordset
    Set myConnection = CurrentProject.Connection
    myRecordSet.ActiveConnection = myConnection
    myRecordSet.Open "Products", , adOpenStatic
    'At this point myRecordSet refers to the Products table.

    myRecordSet.MoveFirst   'Go to first record in Products table.

    'The loop below prints the contents of the third field from each record.
    While Not myRecordSet.EOF  'Top of loop.
        Debug.Print myRecordSet.Fields(2).Value
        myRecordSet.MoveNext          'Move to next record in recordset
    Wend                          'Bottom of loop

    Debug.Print "All Done!" 'This line not reached until loop is done.

    'Close and clean up.
    myRecordSet.Close
    Set myRecordSet = Nothing
    Set myConnection = Nothing

End Sub
```

Chapter 3 of this book to review `While...Wend` loops.

Defining a recordset's cursor type

When you open a table in Datasheet or Form view, you see the blinking cursor and move it around freely using your mouse or keyboard. With recordsets, you can choose from different types of cursors. These types of cursors have nothing to do with how the cursor looks because in a recordset, you can't see the cursor (or the data)! Rather, the cursor type in a recordset defines how the cursor behaves within the recordset. You can define a recordset's cursor type two separate ways: One is by changing the recordset's `CursorType` property by using the following syntax:

`recordsetName.CursorType = constant`

where *recordsetName* is the name of the recordset, and *constant* is one of the constants listed in the first column of Table 5-1. You must define the recordset's cursor type before opening a recordset.

You can also specify the cursor type when opening the recordset by using this syntax:

`myRecordset.Open "tableName/SQL", , CursorType`

where *tableName/SQL* is the name of the table in the current database or a valid SQL statement (which we discuss in a moment), and *CursorType* is one of the constants listed in Table 5-1.

Many of the cursor type options are only relevant to multi-user databases. When working with a single-user database, the adOpenStatic setting is the easiest to work with.

Table 5-1	Recordset Cursor Types	
Constant	*Name*	*Description*
adOpenDynamic	Dynamic Cursor	Allows unrestricted cursor movement. You can modify data in the recordset. Changes made by other users in a multi-user setting reflect in the recordset.
adOpenStatic	Static Cursor	Recordset is a nonchanging version of the table. Changes made by other users have no effect on the recordset.
adOpenForwardOnly	Forward-Only Cursor	Same as Static Cursor, but the cursor only moves forward through the table. This setting is the default if you don't specify a cursor type.
adOpenKeyset	Keyset Cursor	Like a Dynamic Cursor, but records added by other users aren't added to the recordset. Records deleted by other users are inaccessible to your recordset.

The .RecordCount and .AbsolutePosition properties only return correct values when you're using a static cursor type, which is another reason why we use adOpenStatic as the cursor type in our examples. When using a dynamic cursor, .RecordCount and .AbsolutePosition always return -1. because of the fact that the number and position of records in the recordset may change.

Field names in recordsets

In a recordset, each record is a collection of fields. You can refer to fields by their position in the record. myRecordSet.Fields(0) refers to the first field in the record, myRecordset.Fields(1) refers to the second field, and so forth. You can also refer to fields by their names. The syntax is

```
myRecordSet.Fields("fieldname")
```

where *fieldname* is the name of the field as defined in the table. To print the Product Name and Selling Price fields from the Products table in Figure 5-2, change the `Debug.Print myRecordSet.Fields(2).Value` statement to `Debug.Print myRecordSet.Fields("Product Name") & " " & myRecordSet.Fields("Selling Price")`.

SQL and Recordsets

You don't have to base a recordset on a single table. You can base it on a query if you wish. But you can't use the query's name in the `myRecordset.Open` statement because only table names are allowed there. If you want to base a recordset on a query, you need to use the query's *SQL statement* to create the query.

SQL (pronounced *see*-quel), stands for Structured Query Language. You can't get very far in database management without hearing some reference to SQL, because SQL is "the" standard language for extracting information from data stored in Access tables, Microsoft SQL Server, Oracle, and a whole bunch of other database products.

As a language, SQL is pretty simple. The syntax of a SQL statement looks something like this:

```
SELECT fields1 FROM table(s) [WHERE criterion] [ORDER BY
     fields2]
```

where *fields1* represents a list of fields from the table (or * for all fields), *table(s)* represents the name of the table (or tables) where the data are stored, *criterion* represents an expression that filters records (for example, `State="CA"`), and *fields2* represents fields to use for sorting the records. The `WHERE` and `ORDER BY` portions are optional.

Writing SQL statements is fairly easy; you rarely need to write them by hand. Every time that you create a query using Design view, you actually write a SQL statement. The fields that you choose for the query become the fields included in the recordset, although only those fields that have a check mark in the Show box are actually included. The `FROM` table that you select records from is plainly visible at the top of the grid. The Sort row defines the `ORDER BY` clause. The Criteria row specifies the `WHERE` clause, as illustrated in Figure 5-3.

To see the SQL statement for any query you create, right-click the title bar of your query (in Design view) and choose the SQL option from the shortcut menu. Or, choose View⇨SQL View from the Access menu. You see the SQL statement the query uses to get the data specified, as shown in Figure 5-4. The SQL statement may already be selected (highlighted); copy it, if you wish, by pressing Ctrl+C.

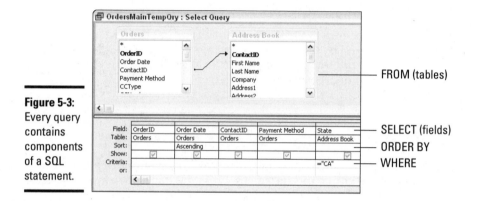

Figure 5-3:
Every query contains components of a SQL statement.

FROM (tables)

SELECT (fields)
ORDER BY
WHERE

If the SQL statement isn't already selected, drag the mouse pointer through the entire SQL statement to select it, and then press Ctrl+C. After you copy the SQL statement to the Clipboard, you can paste it into a myRecordSet.Open statement in VBA code where indicated by *SQL statement here*:

```
myRecordset.Open "SQL statement here", , cursorType
```

Unfortunately, just pasting the SQL statement isn't quite enough to get the job done. You have to change some things in the VBA code, namely:

✦ You must remove the semicolon (;) from the end of the SQL statement.

✦ If the pasted SQL statement breaks across multiple lines, gather the lines together into one long line. (Or break up the line by using the continuation character, as we discuss in a moment.)

✦ If the SQL statement contains any double-quotation marks ("), replace them with single quotation marks.

**Book VIII
Chapter 5**

Using SQL and Recordsets

Figure 5-4:
A SQL statement produced by a sample query.

OrdersMainTempQry : Select Query

```
SELECT Orders.OrderID, Orders.[Order Date], Orders.ContactID, Orders.[Payment Method],
[Address Book].State, Orders.CCType, Orders.CCNumber, Orders.CCExpireMonth,
Orders.CCExpireYear, Orders.CCAuthorization, Orders.PONumber, Orders.Paid, Orders.[Sales
Tax Rate Applied], Orders.[Ship Via], Orders.[Shipping Charge], Orders.InvRecPrinted,
Orders.LabelPrinted, [Address Book].[First Name], [Address Book].[Last Name], [Address
Book].Company, [Address Book].Address1, [Address Book].Address2, [Address Book].City,
[Address Book].ZIP, [Address Book].Phone, [Address Book].Fax, [Address Book].Email,
[Address Book].[Tax Exempt], [Address Book].[Tax Exempt ID]
FROM Orders LEFT JOIN [Address Book] ON Orders.ContactID = [Address Book].ContactID
WHERE ((([Address Book].State)="CA"))
ORDER BY Orders.[Order Date];
```

Take a look at Figure 5-4 (earlier in this chapter) for an example of a big SQL statement. The first step is to select the SQL statement by dragging the mouse pointer through it until you highlight all the text. Then press Ctrl+C or choose Edit⇨Copy from the Access menu to put a copy of the SQL statement on the Clipboard.

Within your procedure in the Code window, type out the `recordset.Open` statement, followed by two sets of double quotation marks. Place the cursor between the two quotation marks, as in the following example(where the | character represents the cursor):

```
myRecordSet.Open "|"
```

Press Ctrl+V to paste the SQL statement between the quotation marks.

The cursor lands at the end of the SQL statement, just to the right of the semicolon at the end of the statement. Press the Backspace key to delete the semicolon.

If the SQL statement breaks into multiple lines, you need to unbreak it. Move the cursor to the end of the first line. If a quotation mark is at the end of the first line, delete it. Then press the Delete (Del) key to delete the line break and bring the next line up to the current line. Leave a blank space between any whole words. Repeat this process until the entire SQL statement is one, big, long line in the Code window.

Finally, look through the SQL statement for any double quotation marks. Don't disturb the quotation marks surrounding the whole SQL statement. Just change any double quotation marks within the statement, as in the following example:

```
WHERE (((Address Book].State="CA" ORDER BY
```

to single quotation marks as the following shows:

```
WHERE (((Address Book].State='CA' ORDER BY
```

When everything is clean, the Code window accepts the statement without showing any red lines or Compile Error messages.

Breaking up long SQL statements

In the previous section, we said that in order for a copied SQL statement to work in your code, you have to treat it as one extremely long line. An alternative to the one-extremely-long-line approach is to store the SQL statement as a string variable. Then use that variable name in your *myRecordset*.Open statement. Within the code, build the lengthy SQL statement by joining short chunks of text together.

The first step is to declare a string variable, perhaps named mySQL, to store the SQL statement, as the following variable shows:

```
Dim mySQL As String
```

Assign the SQL statement to the string. Use the following rules to assign the SQL statement:

✦ Each chunk is fully enclosed in quotation marks.

✦ If a blank space is after a word, leave that blank space in the line.

✦ Follow each line with an *ampersand* (&) character (the join strings operator), a blank space, and the continuation character (_).

✦ Use the variable name in the recordset.Open statement.

Don't forget that you still need to convert any embedded double quotation marks to single quotation marks and remove the ending semicolon.

The following example shows an original SQL statement. (Just imagine that the code stretches out as one long line, which the margins of this book prevents us from actually showing.)

```
SELECT Orders.*, [Address Book].* FROM [Address Book] INNER JOIN Orders ON
    [Address Book].ContactID = Orders.ContactID WHERE (((([Address
    Book].State)="NY")) ORDER BY Orders.[Order Date];
```

The following statements show some VBA code to store that SQL statement in a mySQL string variable. The myRecordSet.Open statement creates the recordset from the SQL statement:

```
'Form a SQL statement from "chunks".
Dim mySQL As String
mySQL = "SELECT Orders.*, [Address Book].* FROM [Address Book] " & _
    "INNER JOIN Orders ON [Address Book].ContactID = Orders.ContactID " & _
    "WHERE (((([Address Book].State)='NY')) " & _
    "ORDER BY Orders.[Order Date]"
'Fill the recordset with data defined by the SQL statement.
myRecordSet.Open mySQL
```

Notice how each chunk of the SQL string is enclosed in double quotation marks, the blank space after a word is included at the end of the line, the ampersand and continuation character, separated by a blank space, end each line. The myRecordSet.Open statement then uses the mySQL variable name in place of the lengthy SQL statement. Figure 5-5 shows how that all looks in the Code window.

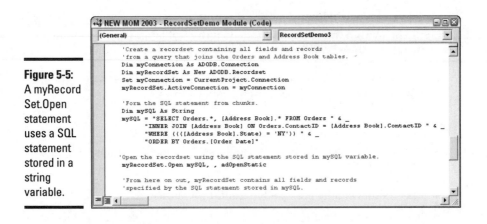

Figure 5-5:
A myRecord
Set.Open
statement
uses a SQL
statement
stored in a
string
variable.

Running Action Queries from VBA

Everything we discussed about SQL so far in this chapter is about *select queries* — queries that select data from tables to display but don't in any way alter the data from the tables. *Action queries* actually change the contents of tables.

Book III, Chapter 3 introduces the update and append form of action queries.

To execute an action query from VBA, you don't need to define a recordset or use a `RecordSet.Open` statement. Instead, use the `RunSQL` method of the `DoCmd` object as follows:

```
DoCmd.RunSQL SQLstatement
```

Follow the same rules for executing an action query as you do a select query, as described in the "SQL and Recordsets" section. Figure 5-6 shows a sample action query to update records in Design view and SQL view.

Figure 5-6:
An update
query in
Design and
SQL views.

In the VBA Code window, store the SQL statement in a string variable and follow the `DoCmd.RunSQL` statement with that variable name — as in the following example, where `mySQL` is the name of the variable that stores the SQL statement:

```
Sub RunUpdateQry()
    'Declare a string variable named mySQL
    Dim mySQL As String
    'Store an action SQL statement in the mySQL variable.
    mySQL = "UPDATE Orders SET Orders.LabelPrinted = True " & _
            "WHERE (((Orders.LabelPrinted)=False))"
    'Run the action query.
    DoCmd.RunSQL mySQL
End Sub
```

Normally when you run an action query — whether from Access or from VBA — Access displays a warning before the query actually runs stating that you're about to change records in a table, which gives you a chance to change your mind. But in many cases, you won't want that warning to appear. For example, if you know the query does what it purports to do and you're writing code for other people to use, presenting them with a warning message that they may not know how to respond to is pointless.

To prevent that warning from appearing when your code executes and in order for the query to run without asking for permission, use the `SetWarnings` method of the `DoCmd` object to disable the warnings. In Figure 5-7, the code includes a `DoCmd.SetWarnings False` to turn off permission-asking just before executing a `RunSQL` statement. The code then turns the normal warning messages back on (`DoCmd.SetWarnings True`) after the query runs.

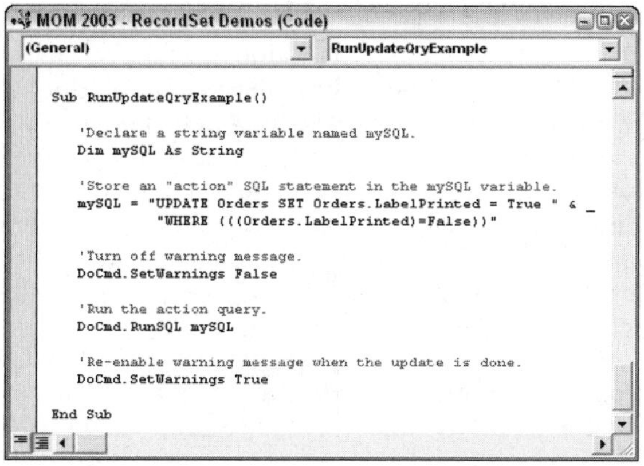

Figure 5-7:
Code that executes an action query without displaying a warning message.

```
MOM 2003 - RecordSet Demos (Code)

(General)                          RunUpdateQryExample

Sub RunUpdateQryExample()

    'Declare a string variable named mySQL.
    Dim mySQL As String

    'Store an "action" SQL statement in the mySQL variable.
    mySQL = "UPDATE Orders SET Orders.LabelPrinted = True " & _
            "WHERE (((Orders.LabelPrinted)=False))"

    'Turn off warning message.
    DoCmd.SetWarnings False

    'Run the action query.
    DoCmd.RunSQL mySQL

    'Re-enable warning message when the update is done.
    DoCmd.SetWarnings True

End Sub
```

When you run an update, append, make-table, or delete query from within a VBA procedure, use the query's SQL statement as the argument to a `RunSQL` statement in your code.

Cleaning up connections

Before your procedure ends, you may want to close both the recordset and the active connection to the local tables. Doing so prevents these objects from remaining open after your code moves on to other tasks. To close a recordset, follow the recordset's name with a `.Close` method, as in the following example:

```
myRecordSet.Close
```

To terminate the connection to the local tables in the database, set the object variables to `Nothing`. The following code creates a database connection named `myConnection` and bases the recordset on that connection. To close both connections, set the object variable names each to `Nothing`, as the following shows:

```
Set myRecordSet = Nothing
Set myConnection = Nothing
```

You're probably wondering why you'd ever want to write all this ridiculous-looking code to open a table or recordset that you can't even see on-screen. After all, you can open a table or query by just double-clicking the name in the database. The rest of this chapter details putting recordsets and SQL to practical use to solve a common problem.

Using Recordsets to Skip Over Blank Labels on Sheets

If you print mailing labels on sheets of paper, you are no doubt aware of this problem: You print a few labels on the sheet and — because you kind of need them here and now — you remove them. Now, however, you have a sheet of labels with some of the labels missing. When you try to print on that sheet, the first labels print in the place where you already removed the label. Neither your computer nor your printer can see that page in the printer and doesn't know labels are missing from the sheet. Every sheet prints as though it were completely new and filled with labels.

Nothing in Access allows you to say "Print these records on mailing labels but skip over the places on the sheet where I already used the label." When you want to do something that isn't built into Access, VBA is usually the solution.

Why SkipLabels won't work outside of MOM 2003

The `SkipLabels()` function shown here is specifically written for tables and fields in the MOM 2003 database. You can't just cut and paste this function from one database to the next. The Web site for this book, however, has a more generic version of `SkipLabels()` that's relatively easy to adapt to other databases.

In this chapter, we focus on those elements of `SkipLabels()` that use SQL and action queries to do the real work. For a more detailed description of how `SkipLabels()` works, see the book's Web page at `www.dummies.com /go/access03_allinone`.

As an example, we created a `SkipLabels` function in the MOM 2003 database, which you can download from this book's Web site (`www.dummies.com/go/ access03_allinone`). As its name implies, `SkipLabels` is designed to handle this problem of missing labels on a sheet. The syntax for calling the custom `SkipLabels` function is

```
SkipLabels(BlanksToSkip , ReportName [,filterCondtion])
```

where *BlanksToSkip* is the number of blank labels to skip over, *ReportName* is the name of the report that prints mailing labels, and *filterCondition* is an optional expression that defines records to be printed. For example, the Orders table in the MOM 2003 database maintains a LabelPrinted field that's `False` if the mailing label for an order has never been printed or `True` if that label has been printed.

If you want `SkipLabels()` to print all records currently waiting to be printed by a report named "Avery 9462 Labels Report" and also skip over the first five (used) labels on your sheet, use the expression =`SkipLabels(5,"Avery 8462 Labels Report")`. If you want `SkipLabels()` to print only records that have `False` in the LabelPrinted field, you pass that condition on as an expression enclosed in quotation marks, like this: =`SkipLabels(1,"Avery 8462 Labels Report","Not [LabelPrinted]")`.

How SkipLabels ( ) works

The solution to the problem of skipping over empty labels is tricky because the table from which the labels print needs to have one blank record at the top for each label to skip over when printing. If four empty label slots on the label sheet need to be skipped, the table needs four blank records at the top. Adding the appropriate number of blank records manually is a pain. `SkipLabels()` uses behind-the-scenes recordsets and action queries to do the job automatically.

**Book VIII
Chapter 5**

**Using SQL and
Recordsets**

Creating the empty TempLabelsTable

In MOM 2003, SkipLabels () knows that labels print from the Orders Main Qry query. A SQL statement, derived from an append query, selects fields needed for filtering and printing labels from that table. From those fields, a new, empty table named LabelsTempTable is created that eventually contains all records to print on labels. The WHERE False condition at the end of the following SQL statement ensures that no records from the query copy to the empty table.

```
'Create an empty table with fields needed to print labels,
'and filter by OrderID, ContactID, InvRecPrinted, and LabelPrinted.
mySQL = "SELECT CLng([Orders.OrderID]) AS OrderID, " & _
    "CLng([Orders.ContactID]) AS ContactID, " & _
    "[Address Book].[First Name], [Address Book].[Last Name], " & _
    "[Address Book].Company, [Address Book].Address1, " & _
    "[Address Book].Address2, [Address Book].City, " & _
    "[Address Book].StateProv, [Address Book].ZIPPostalCode, " & _
    "[Address Book].Country, Orders.InvRecPrinted, " & _
    "Orders.LabelPrinted INTO LabelsTempTable " & _
    "FROM [Address Book] INNER JOIN Orders ON " & _
    "[Address Book].ContactID = Orders.ContactID " & _
    "WHERE False"
DoCmd.RunSQL mySQL
```

The CLng() function used in the SQL statement converts AutoNumber fields to regular Long Integer fields in the temporary table. Trying to insert blank records into a table that contains AutoNumber fields is fraught with potential problems. Converting the AutoNumber fields to Long Integer fields in the temporary table eliminates all those potential problems.

After the DoCmd.RunSQL mySQL statement runs, the LabelsTempTable table contains all the fields specified by the query, but no records, as in Figure 5-8.

Figure 5-8:
An empty LabelsTemp-Table table after the first SQL action executes.

OrderID	ContactID	First Name	Last Name	Company	Address1	Address2	City	StateProv	ZIPPostalCode

LabelsTempTable : Table

Record: |◄ ◄| 1 |► ►| |►*| of 1

Adding blank records to LabelsTempTable

The following code uses a recordset to add some blank records to the LabelsTempTable table. The howMany variable contains the number of blank labels to skip over. This code also uses a For...Next loop to add enough blank records to the LabelsTempTable table to skip over the appropriate number of labels. If SkipLabels() is called with SkipLabels(5,"Avery 8462 Labels Report"), then howMany equals 5. The loop adds five empty records to the LabelsTempTable table.

```
'Now we add howMany blank records to empty LabelsTempTable.
mySQL = "SELECT * FROM LabelsTempTable"
myRecordSet.Open mySQL, , adOpenDynamic, adLockOptimistic

For myCounter = 1 To howMany
    myRecordSet.AddNew
    myRecordSet.Update
Next

'Now LabelsTempTable has howMany empty records in it.
myRecordSet.Close
```

After the code runs, the LabelsTempTable table contains a blank record for each empty label on the label sheet, as shown in Figure 5-9. (The last blank record is just the one that always appears in a table and is replaced by actual data to be printed next in the procedure.)

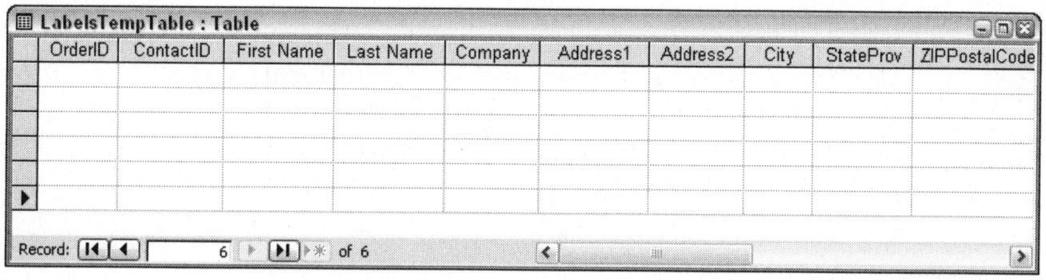

Figure 5-9:
The
LabelsTemp-
Table table
with blank
records at
the top.

Adding records to print to LabelsTempTable

The procedure adds appropriate records from the report's original table or query to the LabelsTempTable table. The following code creates the necessary SQL statement (the SQL comes from an append query in Access):

```
mySQL = "INSERT INTO LabelsTempTable ( OrderID, ContactID, " & _
    "[First Name], [Last Name], Company, Address1, Address2, " & _
    "City, StateProv, ZIPPostalCode, Country, " & _
    "InvRecPrinted, LabelPrinted ) " & _
    "SELECT CLng([Orders.OrderID]) AS OrderID, " & _
    "CLng([Orders.ContactID]) AS ContactID, [Address Book].[First Name], " & _
    "[Address Book].[Last Name], [Address Book].Company, " & _
    "[Address Book].Address1, [Address Book].Address2, " & _
    "[Address Book].City, [Address Book].StateProv, " & _
    "[Address Book].ZIPPostalCode, [Address Book].Country, " & _
    "Orders.InvRecPrinted, Orders.LabelPrinted FROM [Address Book] " & _
    "RIGHT JOIN Orders ON [Address Book].ContactID = Orders.ContactID "
'If a filter condition was passed to this function,
'tack that on to mySQL string as a WHERE condition.
If Len(passedFilter) > 2 Then
```

```
    mySQL = mySQL & " WHERE " & passedFilter
End If

DoCmd.RunSQL mySQL
```

Note the If Len(passedFilter) > 2 Then statement in the code, which says "If a filter condition is passed to this function, tack that filter onto the SQL statement to copy only appropriate records to LabelsTempTable." If SkipLabels()is called with SkipLabels(5,"Avery 8462 Labels","Not [LabelPrinted]"), then passedFilter contains Not [LabelPrinted]. When tacked onto MySQL as WHERE Not [LabelPrinted], only records that have False in the LabelPrinted field copy to the LabelsTempTable table.

After all the code runs, the LabelsTempTable table contains enough blank records to skip over the missing labels, followed by each record to print on the labels, as in Figure 5-10.

Figure 5-10:
The LabelsTemp Table table now contains blank records and records to print.

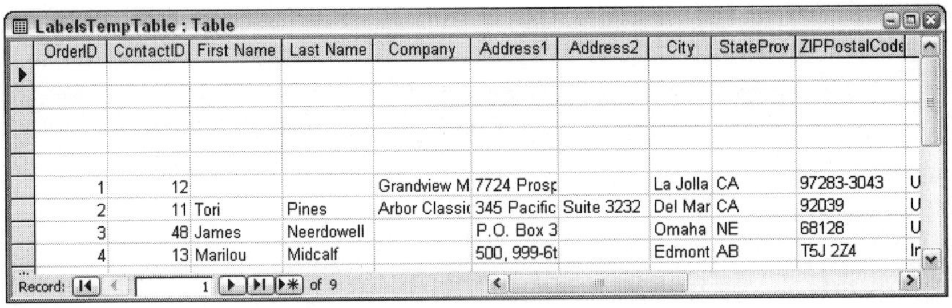

Binding LabelsTempTable to the mailing tables report

Recall that the name of the report that SkipLabels() uses to print labels is passed to the function as its second argument, ReportName. To avoid changing that original report format, the following lines copy that report to a new report named LabelsTempReport:

```
'Now LabelsTempTable has the empty records and the records to print.
'Make a copy of the labels report to work with.
DoCmd.CopyObject , "LabelsTempReport", acReport, ReportName
```

The code changes the Record Source property of the LabelsTempReport report to all records in the LabelsTempTable table and then closes the LabelsTempReport report as the following code shows:

```
'Next make LabelsTempTable the Record Source for LabelsTempReport.
DoCmd.OpenReport "LabelsTempReport", acViewDesign, , , acWindowNormal
Set myReport = Reports![LabelsTempReport]
myReport.RecordSource = "SELECT * FROM LabelsTempTable"
DoCmd.Close acReport, "LabelsTempReport", acSaveYes
```

At this point, the `LabelsTempReport` report and the `LabelsTempTable` table are all ready to go. The function then just prints the report by using this statement:

```
'Now we can finally print the labels.
DoCmd.OpenReport "LabelsTempReport"
```

This may seem like an awful lot of code and work to do something as simple as skipping over blank labels on label sheets. But to go back to what we've been saying throughout this book: If you need to do something that Access can't do on its own, writing custom code is usually the solution.

Remember: `SkipLabels()` isn't a generic function that you can just drop into any database and use right off the bat. A version that works, or at least easy to adapt, to a wide variety of databases is on this book's Web page at `www.dummies.com/go/access03_allinone`.

Chapter 6: Debugging Your Code

In This Chapter

✔ **Identifying types of errors (bugs)**

✔ **How to solve compiler errors**

✔ **Trapping and fixing runtime errors**

✔ **Digging out logical errors**

*I*nstant gratification is rare in the world of programming. Nobody writes perfect code every time. Usually it takes some trial and error; you write a little code, test it, find and fix any *bugs* (errors), write a little more, test a little more, and so on until the code is fully *debugged* (free of errors) and runs smoothly every time. With the help of some debugging tools built into Visual Basic for Applications (VBA) and the VBA Editor, you can usually track down, and fix, any problems that are causing your code to fail.

Considering Types of Program Errors

Many things can go wrong while writing code, especially for a beginner. The ability to identify what type of error you're dealing with is helpful. The three types of errors that all programmers have to contend with are

- ✦ **Compiler errors:** These indicate a problem with the code that prevents the procedure from running at all. Messages alerting you to compile errors often appear right in the Code window, such as when you type a faulty VBA statement and press Enter.

- ✦ **Runtime errors:** The code compiles okay but fails to run properly in practice, often because of a problem in the environment. For example, if a procedure assumes that a certain form is already open in Form view, but the form is not, and the code *crashes* — stops running — before the procedure completes its task.

- ✦ **Logical errors:** The code compiles and runs without displaying any error messages, but the code doesn't do what it's supposed to do.

Fortunately, the VBA Editor contains tools that help you track down, catch, and fix all these different errors. We start with compiler errors because you have to fix them before the code can do anything at all.

Fixing Compiler Errors

When you write code, the stuff that you're writing is referred to as *source code*. Before your code executes, VBA *compiles* your source code to an even stranger language that the computer executes very rapidly. You never actually see that compiled code — humans only work with source code. But if a problem in the source code prevents compilation, you definitely see the error message.

Most compiler errors happen immediately. For example, if you type just **DoCmd.** and press Enter, you get a compiler error. The DoCmd. statement alone on a line isn't enough for VBA to compile the line. You need to follow DoCmd. with some method of the DoCmd object.

If you happen to be familiar with other languages, VBA code doesn't get compiled to native code (.exe files), nor p-code for the Common Language Runtime of .NET. Compiled VBA code in Access is just a tokenized version of the source code.

Not all compiler errors are caught the moment that you press the Enter key. Furthermore, code may be in your database (or project) that's never been compiled. When you call the code, it compiles on the spot and then executes. That extra step slows performance. To compile all the code in a database (or project) — both to check for errors and to improve performance — follow these steps:

1. **If you're currently in the Microsoft Access window, go to the VBA Editor.**

   When you're in the Microsoft Access window, you can press Alt+F11 to quickly switch to the VBA Editor.

2. **Choose Debug⇨Compile *name* (where *name* is the name of the current database or project) from the VBA Editor menu.**

   Doing so compiles all the code in all standard and class modules. If any errors lurk anywhere, you see a Compile Error message box. The message provides a brief, general description of the problem, as in the example shown in Figure 6-1.

   The location of the error is highlighted in gray. The Compile Error message box in Figure 6-1 shows that the compiler was expecting an End Sub statement at the gray highlight. You can click the Help button for more information about the error, although in this example, the fix is pretty easy. Every Sub procedure needs an End Sub statement, and one of the procedures in this module has no End Sub statement. Click the OK button to close the error message box. Then type in the missing End Sub statement at the gray highlight.

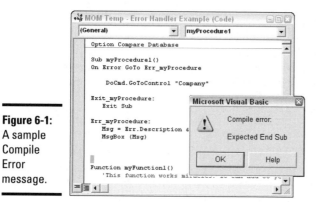

Figure 6-1:
A sample
Compile
Error
message.

When you can choose Debug⊅Compile *name* without seeing any error messages, you know that all your code is compiled and free of compiler errors. The `Compile` command on the Debug menu is also disabled (dimmed) because no uncompiled code is left to compile. Any remaining errors are runtime or logical errors.

Trapping Runtime Errors

Some VBA errors may be caused by events in the environment rather than in the code. Suppose your code performs some operation on data in an open form. If the form isn't open when the code executes, code execution stops, a runtime error occurs, and an error message pops up on-screen. Another example may be when an expression performs division using data from a table, and the divisor ends up being zero. Because dividing a number by zero doesn't make sense, code execution stops, a runtime error occurs, and an error message appears.

If people who know nothing about Access use the database that you create, the error messages that pop up on-screen won't likely help those users much. What you want to do is anticipate what kinds of errors may occur, *trap* them (tell Access to let you know when they happen) and fix them when they occur. To do this, you add an error handler to your code. The *error handler* is just a chunk of code within the procedure that intercepts the error and fixes the problem without stopping code execution or displaying an error message.

To create an error handler, you first need to add an `On Error` statement to your code, preferably just after the `Sub` or `Function` statement that marks the beginning of the procedure. Use one of the following three different ways to create an `On Error` statement:

✦ `On Error Goto label`: When an error occurs as a statement runs, code execution jumps to the section of code identified by *label* within the same procedure.

✦ `On Error Resume Next`: If an error occurs as a statement runs, that statement is ignored, and processing just continues with the next line of code in the procedure.

✦ `On Error GoTo 0`: This disables any previous `OnError Goto` or `On Error Resume Next` statements, so VBA handles future runtime errors rather than your own code.

You can use the `Resume` statement in any error-handling code to tell VBA exactly where to resume code execution after the runtime error occurs. The syntax for the `Resume` statement can take any of the following forms:

✦ `Resume`: Causes VBA to re-execute the statement that caused the error. You only want to use this statement if the error-handling code fixed the problem that caused the error in the first place. Otherwise, executing the same statement again just causes the same error again.

✦ `Resume Next`: Causes execution to resume at the first statement after the statement that caused the error. The statement that caused the error does not execute at all.

✦ `Resume label`: Causes execution to resume at the label specified.

In addition to the `On Error` statements, VBA includes a helpful object known as an `ErrObject`, which stores the error message that pops up on-screen when an error occurs. Each of those built-in error messages has its own number and text. The `ErrObject` stores that number and text, so you can write code to identify the error and work around it. The `ErrObject` has several properties. The two main ones that you need to understand first are as follows:

✦ `Err.Number`: Returns either the number (integer) of the error that occurred or 0 for no error.

✦ `Err.Description`: Returns the textual description of the error that occurred as a string.

The `ErrObject` also supports a couple of methods, whose jobs are summarized in the following list:

✦ `Err.Raise(errNo)`: Causes the error specified by `errNo` to occur. Generally used for testing error-handling code. (No practical reason exists to intentionally cause an error in actual working code.)

✦ `Err.Clear()`: Clears all current properties of the `ErrObject`. (`Err.Number` returns to zero, `Err.Description` returns to a null string, and so forth.)

Code created by Control Wizards and macro conversions may already have error-handling code written into it. You can easily enter such code into any procedure that you write. As a rule, you want the On Error Goto label: statement to execute early in the procedure. That way, no matter where an error occurs in the procedure, execution passes to the error handler.

The label text can be any text at all, provided that it starts with a letter and contains no blank spaces. Using the word Err and an underscore, followed by the procedure name and a colon, is customary. (The colon is mandatory.)

Place the error-handling code at the bottom of the procedure, just before the End function or End Sub statement. You need to place an Exit Sub statement, as well, before the error handler. That prevents code execution from reaching the error handler code when no runtime error occurs.

Because you can't always anticipate every conceivable runtime error, having the error handler display the error number and error description is best, so at least you know what caused the error. The following example shows an error message, where *[main body of code]* stands for all the code that makes up the actual procedure.

```
Sub myProcedure()

On Error GoTo Err_myProcedure

    [main body of code]

Exit_MyProcedure:

    Exit Sub 'Returns control to whomever called procedure.

'Error handler starts below.
Err_MyProcedure:
    Msg = Err.Description & " - " & Err.Number
    MsgBox Msg

    Resume Exit_MyProcedure

End Sub
```

The following list details what happens when a runtime error occurs while code in *[main body of code]* executes:

✦ **On Error GoTo Err_myProcedure:** Because this statement told VBA to transfer execution to the Err_myProcedure label, execution does not stop cold. Instead, execution continues at the first line after the Err_myProcedure label.

✦ `Msg = Err.Description & " - " & Err.Number:` Creates a string of text that contains the description of the error and the error number.

✦ `MsgBox Msg:` Displays the error message text and number in a message box with an OK button. Code execution stops until the user clicks the OK button in the message box.

✦ `Resume Exit_MyProcedure:` Causes execution to resume at the first line after the `Exit_MyProcedure` label.

✦ `Exit Sub:` Causes the procedure to exit without any further error messages.

Error-handling code, by itself, doesn't fix the error or allow the procedure to continue its job. However, if an error does occur, you see the message (text) and the number that identifies that message. So then you can have the error handler fix the problem, and then go back and continue executing the code.

Suppose that the main body of the code is just trying to move the cursor into a control named `Company` on the current form, using the statement `DoCmd.GoToControl "Company"`. If you run the procedure when the form that contains the Company field isn't open, a runtime error occurs. The error handler displays the message box, shown in Figure 6-2. Code execution stops because nothing in the error handler takes care of the problem.

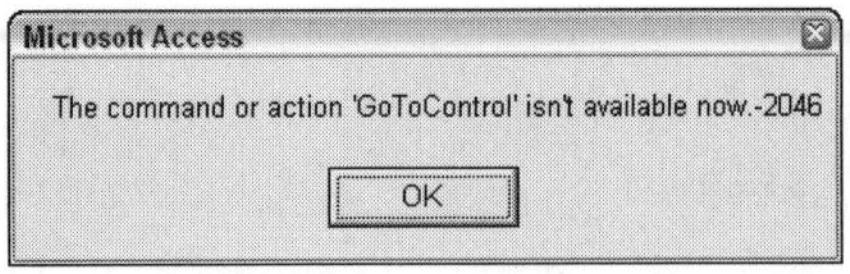

Figure 6-2:
A sample error message returned by an error handler.

The error description and number (2046) display in the error message. In this particular example, the `GoToControl` action isn't available because the form that the code expects to be open isn't open. The solution is to come up with a means of making sure the appropriate form is open before the code executes.

Fixing the runtime error

One way to handle the problem is to use an `If...End If` block (or `Select Case...End Select` block) to provide a solution to error 2046. Because error 2046 is telling us that a form the code expects to be open is in fact closed, the solution is to open the appropriate form, as in the following example:

```
[code above handler]

Err_MyProcedure:

    'Trap and fix error 2046.
    If Err.Number = 2046 Then
        DoCmd.OpenForm ("Address Book Form")
        Resume    'Try again now that form is open.
    End If

    'Errors other than 2046 still just show info and exit.
    Msg = Err.Description & " - " & Err.Number
    MsgBox Msg
    Resume Exit_MyProcedure

End Sub
```

Eliminating the runtime error

A cleaner, more elegant solution to the problem, though, is to rewrite the procedure so that the runtime error can't possibly occur. In the following example, the procedure starts by checking to see whether the required form is already open. If it's not, the procedure opens the form before the `DoCmd.GoToControl` statement executes:

```
Sub myProcedure1()
    On Error GoTo Err_myProcedure

    'Make sure Address Book form is open.
    If Not isOpen("Address Book Form") Then
        DoCmd.OpenForm "Address Book Form", acNormal
    End If

    'Now move the cursor to the Company field.
    DoCmd.GoToControl "Company"

Exit_myProcedure:
    Exit Sub

Err_myProcedure:
    Msg = Err.Description & "-" & Err.Number
    MsgBox (Msg)

End Sub
```

**Book VIII
Chapter 6**

Debugging Your Code

The IsOpen() function used in the preceding example isn't built into Access. See Chapter 4 of this book for a description of the IsOpen() function.

Dealing with Logical Errors

After your code is free of compile and runtime errors, Access executes every statement perfectly. But that doesn't necessarily mean that the code does exactly what you *intended*. If you were thinking one thing but wrote code that does something else, an error in the logic of the code occurs — a logical error.

Logical errors can be tough to pinpoint because when you run a procedure, everything happens so fast. You'll find slowing things down and watching what happens while the procedure runs helpful. Several tools in Access can help with that.

Watching things happen

You can use the Debug.Print statement anywhere in your code to print the value of a variable, a constant, or anything else. Because all output from the Debug.Print statement goes to the Immediate window, those statements don't disrupt the normal execution of your procedure.

Suppose that you write a procedure that's supposed to make some changes to all the records in a table with the help of a loop embedded in your code. But when you run the procedure, the expected result doesn't happen. You can put a Debug.Print statement inside the loop to display the current value of some counting variable within the loop, as in this example:

```
Function Whatever()
    [code]

    For intCounter = LBound(myArray) To UBound(myArray)

       'Show value of inCounter with each pass through loop
       Debug.Print "intCounter = " & intCounter

    [Code]
    Next

    [maybe more code]

End Function
```

If you run the procedure with the Immediate window open, the Immediate window displays something like this:

```
intCounter = 0

intCounter = 1

intCounter = 2

etc..
```

If some problem with the loop's conditional expression exists (the logic that makes the loop repeat *x* number of times), you may just see something like the following:

```
intCounter = 0
```

The preceding output tells you the loop repeats only once, with a value of zero. You need to go back into the code, figure out why the loop isn't repeating as many times as you expect, fix that problem, and then try again.

After you solve the problem, remove the `Debug.Print` statements from the code because they serve no purpose after the debugging phase is done. Optionally, you can *comment out* the `Debug.Print` statement by adding an apostrophe to the beginning of its line, thereby making it appear as a comment to VBA. After you comment out a statement, it is not longer executed in the code. To reactivate the `Debug.Print` statement in the future, uncomment it by removing the leading apostrophe.

Slowing down procedures

Another way to check for logical errors in code is to slow things way down to see exactly what's happening, step by step, while the procedure runs. To do this, you set a breakpoint at the line of code where you want to start slowing things down.

If you want the entire procedure to run slowly, you can set the breakpoint in the first line of the procedure (the `Sub` or `Function` statement). To set a breakpoint, right-click the line where you want to set the breakpoint and then choose Toggle⇨Breakpoint from the shortcut menu. The line where you set the breakpoint is highlighted in yellow and has a large dot to the left, as in Figure 6-3.

You can also open the Locals window to watch the values of variables change as the code is running in *break mode*. (After you set a breakpoint, the code runs in break mode, or one line at a time.) To open the Locals window, choose View⇨Locals Window from the VBA Editor main menu. Like other windows in the VBA Editor, you can dock the Locals window to the VBA Editor program window or drag it away from the window border to make it free-floating.

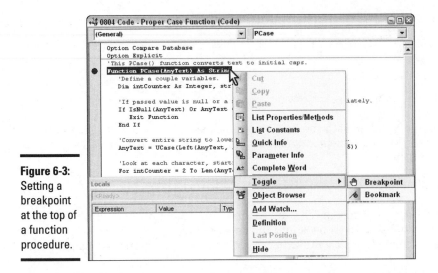

Figure 6-3:
Setting a
breakpoint
at the top of
a function
procedure.

After you set a breakpoint, just run the code normally. Before executing a line of code, VBA highlights the line that's about to execute and shows an error to the left of that line. You have three choices at that point:

✦ To execute the one line (only), press F8 or choose Debug⇨Step Into.

✦ To skip the currently selected line without executing it, press Shift+F8 or choose Debug⇨Step Over.

✦ To bail out of break mode, press Ctrl+Shift+F8 or choose Debug⇨ Step Out.

Some types of runtime errors cause VBA to go into break mode automatically. You see the yellow highlight line when that happens.

While your code executes, the highlight moves from line to line. Each time that an executed statement changes the value of a variable, the Locals window updates to reflect that change, as in Figure 6-4.

Cleaning up

When you finish debugging or just want to start over with a clean slate, do one of the following:

✦ To clear the Locals window, right-click any text within the window and then choose the Reset option from the shortcut menu that appears.

✦ To clear all breakpoints from your code, choose Debug⇨Clear All Breakpoints.

Locals window

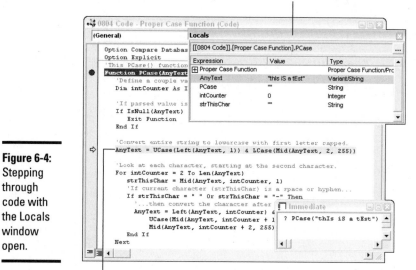

Figure 6-4:
Stepping
through
code with
the Locals
window
open.

Next line executed

Of course, you can also close the Locals window by clicking the Close
button in its upper-right corner.

Chapter 7: Integrating Office Applications

In This Chapter

✔ What is Automation, anyway?

✔ Exchanging information without programming

✔ Loading object libraries for other Office programs

✔ Referring to information in other programs

✔ Sending e-mail to the customers in a table

*V*isual Basic for Applications (VBA) isn't a programming language for Microsoft Access alone. It's a programming language for all application programs that support Automation. *Automation* (with a capital *A*) refers to the ability of a program to be manipulated programmatically, or controlled automatically using a programming language such as VBA. All the major applications in Microsoft Office, including Access, Excel, Outlook, PowerPoint, and Word, support Automation. You can write code to automatically share data among them.

The terms *Component Object Model (COM)* and *OLE automation* are older terms for — but basically synonymous with — what's currently called Automation.

Before You Start Writing Code

Before you exchange data between Access and other programs in the Microsoft Office Suite, please be aware that writing code to do the job is rarely required. You can do plenty of importing and exporting data between Microsoft Office applications without writing any code at all. For example, you can do the following things:

✦ Import and export data by using options on the Access File menu (see Book II, Chapter 4.)

✦ E-mail Access objects, such as reports, by choosing Send To➪Mail Recipient.

✦ Use the OfficeLinks feature to send objects to other programs.

✦ Use basic Windows cut-and-paste techniques and OLE (Object Linking and Embedding) to copy and link data between programs.

✦ Merge data from Access tables to Microsoft Word letters, labels, envelopes, or other reports, using the Word Mail Merge feature. (Search the Word Help system for *merge*.)

If you're just looking to get data from Access to another program (or vice versa), writing code is probably not the easiest approach. Any of the previous approaches are easier than writing custom VBA code to do the job.

Of course, once in a proverbial blue moon, you come across a situation where writing VBA code is the only, or perhaps just the best, way to get the job done. This chapter provides some sample code that sends e-mails to people from an Access table automatically. But before we get to the specific code, we cover some basic concepts that you need to understand.

Loading the Appropriate Object Models

As you find out in Chapter 1 of this book, the Access object model provides a means of referring to objects by name so that you can manipulate those objects by using VBA code. Every Office application program that exposes itself to VBA has an object model, just like Access does. After an application program's object library is available, you can use VBA to control that application, as illustrated in Figure 7-1.

An *object model* defines the names and organization of objects in the application. An object library is the actual file, stored on your hard disk, that defines that conceptual object model.

Before you write code to control an external application from Access, you need to load the appropriate object library into the References dialog box in Access. Follow these steps:

1. **Make sure that you're in the Visual Basic Editor.**

Press Alt+F11 if you're in the Access program window.

2. **Choose Tools⇨References from the Visual Basic Editor menu.**

The References dialog box opens.

3. **Scroll through the Available References list and select the object libraries for the programs that you want to control.**

In Figure 7-2, we select object libraries for Access, Excel, Outlook, PowerPoint, and Word (among others).

4. **Click OK.**

All the selected object libraries open, and you have access to all their object models from this point on.

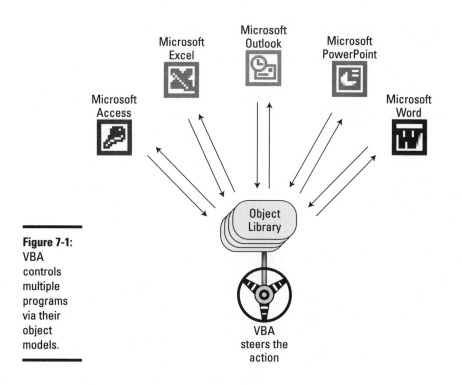

Figure 7-1:
VBA
controls
multiple
programs
via their
object
models.

Unloading object libraries

Loading more object libraries than necessary is wasteful because VBA programs run slower. In real life, you rarely need to select all the object libraries available (see Figure 7-2) unless you really intend to interact with all those programs from the current database.

You can unload libraries as easily as you load them. Open the References dialog box and clear the check mark next to any object library that you don't really intend to use.

Exploring a program's object model

The Object Browser in the Visual Basic Editor provides access to all the object models currently selected in the References dialog box. Each loaded object model contains many objects, classes, properties, and such. But for Automation, you mainly want to look at each program's Application Object. The Access Application Object exposes Access to other programs that support Automation. The Excel Application Object (contained within the Excel object library) exposes Excel to other Automation programs, and so on.

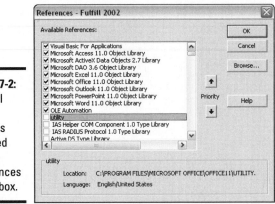

Figure 7-2:
Several
object
libraries
selected
in the
References
dialog box.

To open the Object Browser in the VBA Editor, choose View⇨Object Browser
or press F2. To get help with an item in the Object Browser, click its name,
and then click the Help (?) button on the Object Browser toolbar.

When you choose <All Libraries> from the Project/Library list in the Object
Brower and scroll down the Classes list in the left column, you see several
Application objects. When you click one of the Application objects, the
name of the application appears down near the bottom of the dialog box.
Members of that application object appear in the pane to the right, as
shown in Figure 7-3.

Project/Library list

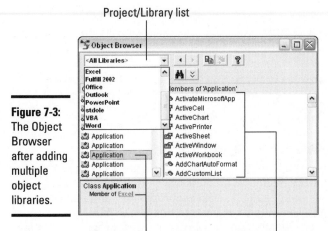

Figure 7-3:
The Object
Browser
after adding
multiple
object
libraries.

Selected Application object   Members of Excel's
is the one for Microsoft Excel   Application object

Setting References to Other Programs

After you load the object models, you're ready to start setting up references to available programs in VBA code. The first step is to use a `Dim` statement to create an object variable that refers to the application to which you want to connect, using the following syntax:

```
Dim anyName As [New] program.Application
```

In the syntax, *anyName* is any name you like to use within your code to refer to the application. The *program* argument is the official name of the Automation program. The `New` keyword is optional. If included, the `New` keyword opens a copy of the application in the background (not necessarily visible on-screen) before the code runs. Some examples of `Dim` statements are the following:

```
Dim appExcel As New Excel.Application
Dim appOutlook As New Outlook.Application
Dim appPowerPoint As New PowerPoint.Application
Dim appWord As New Word.Application
```

A `Dim` statement is only valid if the appropriate object library is loaded. For example, the `Dim appWord As New Word.Application` statement fails if the object library for Microsoft Word isn't selected in the References dialog box.

Starting other programs

The `Dim` statements described in the previous section merely create object variables that refer to the application from within your code. To actually make the connection to an application's Application object, you need to set the object variable name to the application. The syntax is

```
Set objectVariable As CreateObject("appName.Application")
```

where *objectVariable* is the same as the name you specify in the `Dim` statement, and *appName* is the name of the application program. Referring to the earlier `Dim` statements, the `Set` statements that you use for each defined object variable are the following:

```
Set appExcel = CreateObject("Excel.Application")
Set appOutlook = CreateObject("Outlook.Application")
Set appPowerPoint = CreateObject("PowerPoint.Application")
Set appWord = CreateObject("Word.Application")
```

Although there isn't nearly enough space in this book to discuss every application program's object model in depth, we present a useful example: using Microsoft Outlook as a program for sending e-mail messages to e-mail addresses stored in an Access table.

**Book VIII
Chapter 7**

**Integrating Office
Applications**

Automating Outlook E-Mail

As an example of using VBA and Automation in the real world, the MOM 2003 sample database (available from the book's Web page at www.dummies.com/go/access03_allinone), offers the Email Messages Form, shown in Figure 7-4. The form allows you to type and save any number of e-mail messages. Each message has a name to uniquely identify it. The Subject, Body, and optional Attachment sections in the form become the subject, main body, and attachment for one e-mail message, which may be sent to any number of recipients.

At the bottom of the form, you can choose to whom you want to send the message: New Customers (customers to whom you haven't sent any messages yet), All Customers, or Just (an individual customer or vendor in that database's Address Book table). Clicking the Send button creates and sends the e-mail message to the specified customers or individual.

The code that we present here works *only* if you already use Microsoft Outlook as your e-mail client or you set up Outlook as an e-mail client. You cannot use this code, or Outlook, with America Online or most HTTP or Web-based mail systems. As far as we know, you can't automate those other e-mail clients from Microsoft Access. Sorry. . . .

A recent security patch to Outlook displays a message whenever any program tries to send e-mail programmatically. You have to click the Yes button and wait five seconds for each message to be sent. Although not too terribly inconvenient when dealing with relatively few messages, you wouldn't want to do it with hundreds, or thousands, of records.

Figure 7-4: A form for sending e-mail messages from Access.

Message subject

Message body

Message attachment

Message recipients

The entire procedure used by the Email Messages Form is described at the book's Web page at `www.dummies.com/go/access03_allinone`. In this chapter, we focus on the VBA code that manipulates Microsoft Outlook from within Access. The code is stored in an event procedure that's attached to the `On Click` event of the Send button on the form. If the MOM 2003 sample database is open in Access on your screen right now, you can view all the code you like. Open the Email Messages Form in Design view, right-click the Send button, and choose the Build Event option from the shortcut menu to get to the code.

Defining Outlook object variables

The first step to interacting with another application programmatically is to define the necessary object variables so that you can set up references to the other program. Within the sample procedure we describe in this chapter, the following `Dim` statements create the object variables required to automate Microsoft Outlook. The comment after each statement describes what each object variable refers to:

```
'Define some object variables for Outlook
Dim appOutlook As Outlook.Application
'Refers to Outlook's Application object.

Dim appOutlookMsg As Outlook.MailItem
'Refers to an Outlook e-mail message.

Dim appOutlookRecip As Outlook.Recipient
'Refers to an Outlook e-mail recipient.
```

After the code executes, the type of object that each object variable name refers to, stated in plain English, is as follows:

- ✦ `appOutlook`: Refers to Microsoft Outlook

- ✦ `appOutlookMsg`: Refers to a single e-mail message in Microsoft Outlook

- ✦ `appOutlookRecip`: Refers to the recipient of the current e-mail message (specifically, the recipient's e-mail address)

At this point, the object variables only refer to some *type* of Outlook object. They don't refer to any *specific* objects. But keep their names in mind because code later in this chapter assigns specific objects to those variables. For example, the `appOutlook` object variable gets its value from this next line of code:

```
'Create an Outlook session in the background.
 Set appOutlook = CreateObject("Outlook.Application")
```

After the statement runs, `appOutlook` refers to an open instance of Microsoft Outlook.

When you look at the actual procedure in the MOM 2003 sample database, you see a bunch of code that defines a recordset containing the names and e-mail addresses of all recipients for the message. We won't confuse matters by describing that code here. The same type of code is described in the previous chapter of this book. Just keep in mind that the name myRecordSet in upcoming VBA statements refers to a recordset that contains the e-mail address of every person to whom the e-mail message needs to be sent.

Creating and filling the e-mail messages

The code that creates and fills an Outlook e-mail message in our example starts with this statement:

```
'Create a new, empty e-mail message.
Set appOutlookMsg = appOutlook.CreateItem(olMailItem)
```

After the statement executes, the object variable appOutlookMsg refers to a brand new, empty e-mail message in Microsoft Outlook. appOutlook.CreateItem(olMailItem) tells Access to create a new message in Outlook, and appOutlookMsg is already defined as an object variable of the Outlook.MailItem type. That olMailItem thing in the code is a constant in the Outlook object model that means the same as MailItem.

Moving down the code, the following With appOutlookMsg statement ensures that all standalone property names to follow in the code (for example, .Recipients, .Subject, .Body, and .Attachments) refer to the current blank e-mail message named appOutlookMsg.

```
With appOutlookMsg  'Using the new, empty message...
```

The next statement types the e-mail address of the recipient (taken from the recordset that contains all recipients' addresses) into the To section of the blank e-mail message:

```
'Use eMailAddress from Recordset as recipient's address
Set appOutlookRecip = .Recipients.Add(eMailAddress)
appOutlookRecip.Type = olTo
```

The next lines copy text from the subject and main body portions of the Email Messages Form to the subject and body of the blank e-mail message:

```
' Fill in the Subject line and main body of message.
.Subject = Me![Subject]     'Fill in the subject line.
.Body = Me![MessageBody]    'Fill in the message body.
```

When working in a class module, the word Me! refers to the form or report to which the class module is attached.

In other words, `.Subject = Me![Subject]` is short for
`appOutlookMsg.Subject = Forms![Email Messages Form].[Subject]`.
In English, it means "Make the subject of the current e-mail message equal to
whatever's typed into the Subject control on the Email Messages Form." The
`.Body = Me![MessageBody]` statement does the same thing for the main
body of the e-mail message.

The next chunk of code looks at the Attachments box on the Email Messages
Form (referred to as `Me![Attachment]`) in code). If that control isn't empty,
`Attachments.Add(Me![Attachment])` adds the attachment to the current
e-mail message:

```
'Add attachments, if any, to the e-mail message.
If Len(Me![Attachment]) > 0 Then
    .Attachments.Add (Me![Attachment])

End If
```

The attachment typed into the Email Messages Form must be the path to
an available file. For example, `C:\Documents and Settings\Susan\My
Documents\MyZipFile.Zip`, shown in Figure 7-4, refers to a file named
`MyZipFile.zip` in the My Documents folder of a user named Susan.

After all the statements execute, the once new, blank e-mail message now
has a recipient, subject, body, and possibly an attachment. The message
is ready to send. The following statement (still enclosed within the
`With...End With` statement) sends the message now (the comment is
optional):

```
    .Send    'Send the completed message.
End With
```

That completes the process of creating and sending one e-mail message.
In the Email Messages Form, the process repeats once for each record in
`myRecordSet`.

What about the dumb warnings?

As mentioned, the current security model for Outlook requires that each
e-mail message sent from Access be approved for sending, which is a pain.
But as of this writing, we haven't found a way around the problem. When you
first run the procedure, the message shown in Figure 7-5 appears on-screen.

When that message appears, enable the Allow Access For check box and
choose a time limit (10 minutes is the maximum). Then click the Yes button.

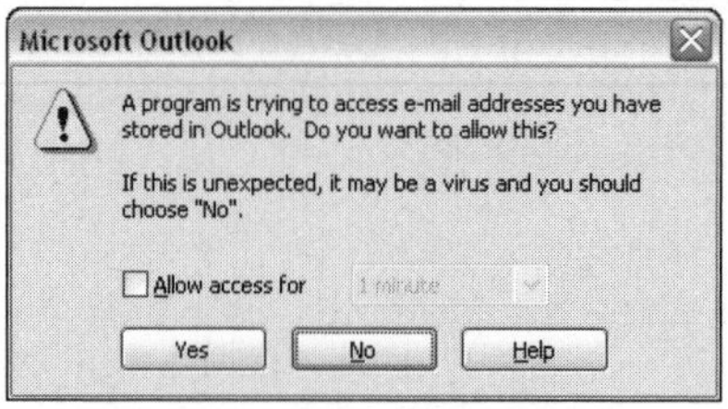

Figure 7-5:
The first
message
to appear
when
sending
e-mail
program-
matically.

As though to add insult to injury, you then have to wait five seconds and click the Yes button for each e-mail message being sent in response to the nearly identical dialog box shown in Figure 7-6.

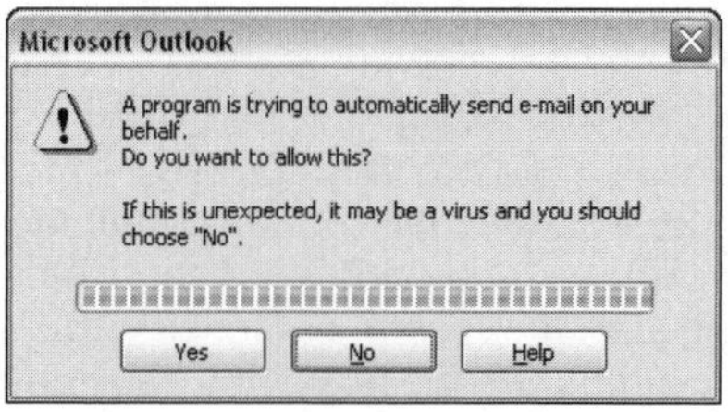

Figure 7-6:
This dialog
box appears
for every
message
being sent
from
Outlook
(ugh!).

In Outlook, messages are sent automatically if the Send Immediately When Connected option in the Outlook Options dialog box is selected. (Choose Tools⇨Options from the Outlook menu and then click the Mail Setup tab.) If that option is not selected or if Outlook wasn't online when you ran the procedure, the new messages wait in the Outlook Outbox. You can open Outlook and open its Outbox to see the messages waiting, as in Figure 7-7. Double-click any message to open and review it. Click the Send/Receive button on the Outlook toolbar to send the messages on their way.

Of course, this is just one tiny example of using VBA to automate interaction between Office applications. Each application in the suite has its own object model with its own objects and properties, but the basic ideas are the same regardless of which program and object model you use.

Figure 7-7:
Auto-
created
e-mail
messages in
the Outlook
Outbox.

One of the best resources for finding more information on Office
Automation and examples of code is the Microsoft Web site. Go to
search.microsoft.com and search for something like *Office+Automation.*
Or better yet, include the name of the program that you're interested in.
For example, search for *Word+Automation, Excel+Automation*, or
Outlook+Automation, depending on which program you want to
control through VBA.

Book IX

Access on the Web

The 5th Wave   By Rich Tennant

"Sometimes I feel behind the times.
I asked my 11-year old to build a web
site for my business, and he said he
would, only after he finishes the one
he's building for his ant farm."

Contents at a Glance

Chapter 1: Creating Data Access Pages

In This Chapter

✔ Finding out about data access pages

✔ Where to store data access pages

✔ How to create data access pages

✔ Designing custom data access pages without wizards

✔ Managing and troubleshooting data access pages

*B*uying a copy of Microsoft Access for each computer in a small business network, or home network, is an expensive proposition. As an alternative, you can first store Access on one computer in the network and then provide other computers access to your database through *data access pages* (DAP).

What's a Data Access Page?

A data access page is like an Access form on a Web page on the Internet. However, data access pages aren't like "pure," generic Web pages: They contain Microsoft-specific code. To use a data access page without having Access installed, the computer must be running Microsoft Internet Explorer (5.0 or later), as illustrated in Figure 1-1. People who use older versions of Internet Explorer can download and install the latest version, for free, at www.microsoft.com/ie.

A data access page can look like a table, a form, a pivot table, or a chart. It all depends on how you design it. The important point is, though, that it allows people who don't have Microsoft Access installed on their computers to view and manipulate data using a simple Web browser.

Because data access pages only work with relatively recent versions of Internet Explorer, they aren't good candidates for publishing on the public World Wide Web. Data access pages are best used in intranets (small networks found in private homes and small businesses) where you have control over shared resources and the Web browser that people are using.

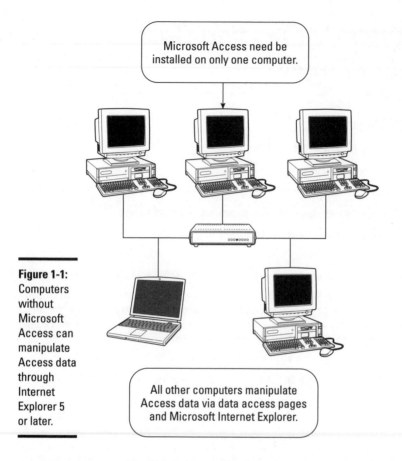

Microsoft Access need be
installed on only one computer.

Figure 1-1:
Computers
without
Microsoft
Access can
manipulate
Access data
through
Internet
Explorer 5
or later.

All other computers manipulate
Access data via data access pages
and Microsoft Internet Explorer.

Storing Data Access Pages

Data access pages are different from Access forms and reports in many
ways. For one thing, unlike other types of Access objects, data access pages
aren't stored in your Access .mdb file. Instead, each data access page you
create is stored as its own separate .htm file.

If you're familiar with creating Web pages, you'll recognize the .htm file
extension as being typical of Web pages. The .htm is short for HTML
(Hypertext Markup Language). And HTML, in turn, is the markup language
used to create all Web pages.

Unlike your standard Web page on the Internet, data access pages don't use
pure HTML. Instead, data access pages use DHTML (Dynamic HTML), a

markup language that includes Microsoft-specific programming only Internet Explorer deals with. Furthermore, only Internet Explorer provides the capability to make the connection between the data access page and the database. Don't let the .htm extension fool you into thinking that any old Web browser can open and use a data access page.

Before you create data access pages, you need to create a folder for them. Because you presumably want to give multiple users access to these Web pages, share that folder on the network after you create it.

Exactly how you go about creating a shared folder varies slightly from one version of Windows to the next. But in general, the process is similar to the following steps (using Windows XP as our sample operating system):

1. **Close Microsoft Access if it's open.**

    You don't need Access open while creating the folder.

2. **Open the folder that will act as the parent folder in Windows Explorer.**

    For example, open your Shared Documents folder in Windows XP.

3. **Choose File⇨New⇨Folder from the menu in Windows Explorer.**

    A new folder appears with its temporary name highlighted.

4. **Type in a new name for the folder (say, Data Access Pages), and press Enter.**

5. **If you didn't open an already-shared folder in Step 2, you need to share the new folder you just created. Right-click that folder and choose the Sharing and Security option from the shortcut menu that appears. Then choose the Share This Folder option and give the folder a share name. Then click OK.**

    You can tell that a folder is shared because its icon includes a little hand.

For more information on creating and managing shared folders in your version of Windows, open Windows Help and search for *share folder*.

Creating Data Access Pages

Just as you can create a form or report in many ways, you have lots of options when creating a data access page. We look at all those options in the sections to follow. We start with the simplest example of taking an existing table or query and copying it straight to a data access page.

Creating a page from a table or query

Data access pages display information in a tabular view similar to what you see in Datasheet view. Such pages are also the easiest to create, because you just have to save a copy of the table or query as a data access page. Follow these steps to do so:

1. Click the Tables or Queries button in the Objects list of the Database window.

If the Database window isn't visible, press F11.

The list of tables or queries appears on the right side of the Database window.

2. Right-click the name of the table or query you want to copy to a page and then choose the Save As option from the shortcut menu that appears.

The Save As dialog box opens.

3. Enter a name for the page.

We recommend entering names that end in DAP — short for data access page — as shown in Figure 1-2. Such a naming strategy just makes keeping track of data access pages easier.

4. Click the As drop-down menu, choose the Data Access Page option, and click OK.

The New Data Access Page dialog box appears.

5. Navigate to the folder in which you want to store the data access page, and then click OK.

Data access pages are stored outside the .mdb file, so they can be accessed from a Web browser. In Step 5, be sure to choose a shared folder to which appropriate users have access.

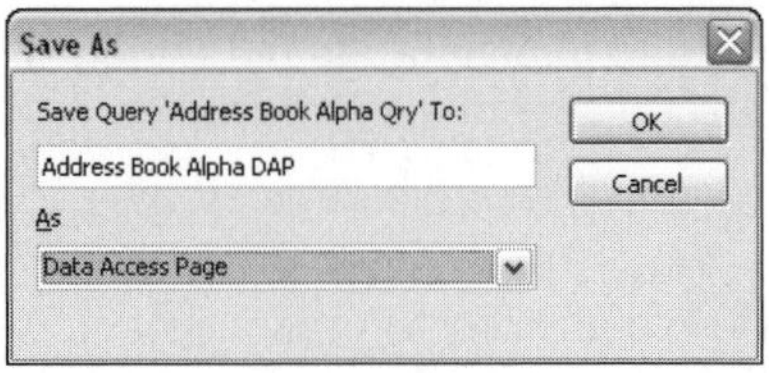

Figure 1-2:
Save a
query as a
data access
page.

Save As	
Save Query 'Address Book Alpha Qry' To:	OK
Address Book Alpha DAP	Cancel
As	
Data Access Page	

Access generates the page, and then displays it in Page view as shown in Figure 1-3. Note the navigation bar at the bottom of the page, and how its buttons resemble those found on the Datasheet and Form view toolbars. You can point to any button in the bar to see its name.

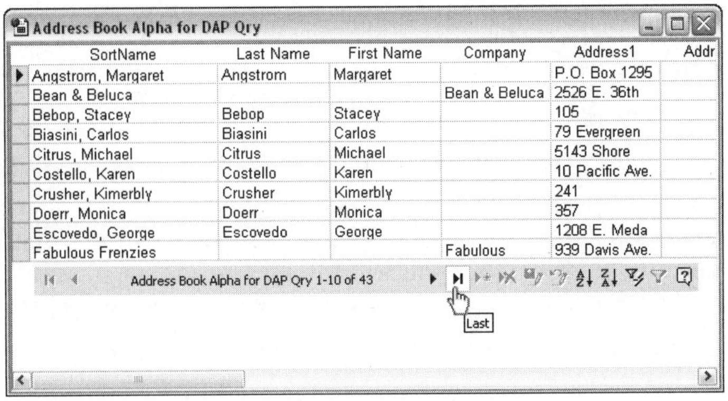

Figure 1-3:
A data
access
page from
a query,
currently in
Page view.

With the page open in Page view, you can right-click the page's title bar, or click the View button on the Access toolbar, to switch to Design view or Web Page Preview. (Right-clicking the title bar with data access pages doesn't offer Design view as an option in pages.) We talk about the other views in more detail throughout the chapter. To close the page, just click its Close button (the X at the upper-right corner of the data access page).

Copying a form or report to a data access page

Creating a data access page from a form or report is virtually identical to creating a data access page from a table or query. However, you need to be aware of an important "gotcha." If your form or report contains subforms or subreports, those do not copy to a data access page. We talk about how you can create rough equivalents of subforms and subreports in the section, "Designing a data access page from scratch," later in this chapter. Take a look at the following steps for copying a simple form or report to a data access page.

1. **Click the Forms or Reports button in the Objects list of the Database window, depending on which type of object you want to copy.**

The list of forms or reports appears on the right side of the Database window.

2. **Right-click the name of the form or report that you want to copy and then choose the Save As option from the shortcut menu that appears.**

The Save As dialog box opens.

3. **Type in any name you like for the data access page.**

We still recommend that the name end in DAP — short for Data Access Page — but all other parts are fair game.

4. **Click the As drop-down list and choose the Data Access Page option.**

5. **Click OK.**

   The New Data Access Page dialog box opens.

6. **Navigate to the folder in which you want to store the data access page.**

7. **Make sure the File Name option at the bottom of the dialog box reflects the file name you want to give to the page, and that the Save As Type option is set to the Microsoft Data Access Pages option.**

8. **Click OK in the New Data Access Page dialog box.**

Access creates the data access page and shows it in Page view, as shown in Figure 1-4. (This process may take a minute or two.) You can right-click the page's title bar, or click the View button on the Access toolbar to switch to one of the other views: Design view or Web Page Preview.

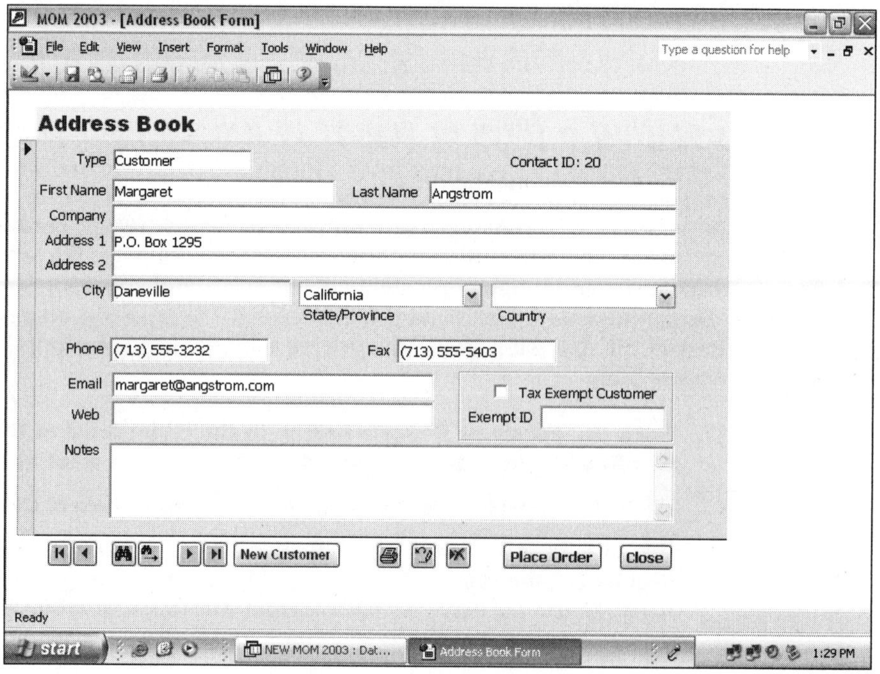

Figure 1-4: An Access form converted to a data access page.

Using the Page Wizard

As an alternative to using an existing form as the basis for a data access page, you can create one by using the Page Wizard, which is similar to the Form Wizard described in Book IV, Chapter 1. The wizard probably won't create the perfect page for you, but you can modify it later. Follow these steps:

1. **In Access, with your database open, click the Pages button in the Objects list of the Database window.**

As with most other types of objects, a list of wizards and any data access pages you already created appear on the right side of the Database window.

2. **Double-click the Create Data Access Page by Using Wizard option.**

The Page Wizard starts.

3. **Select the table or query from which the page gets its data from the Tables/Queries drop-down menu. Then move the fields you want into the Select Fields list from the Available Fields list and click Next.**

In the Available Fields list, use the > or >> button to copy fields that you want on the page to the Selected Fields list. Use the < or << button if you change your mind about a field. If you want fields from several tables or queries, change the Tables/Queries box to a different table or query and select additional fields.

4. **If you want to add any grouping levels, click the name of any field on which you want to group, and then click the > button and then click Next.**

If you select fields for grouping, you can click the Grouping Options button in the Page Wizard to specify how you want records grouped.

5. **Optionally, you can define a sort order for records in the data access page, as instructed by the wizard. Click Next after making your selection(s) (if any).**

6. **On the final wizard page, type in a title for the data access page.**

The default title matches the name of the table or query on which the form is based.

7. **Click the Finish button.**

The new page opens in Design view. We talk about how you design a page in the section, "Designing Data Access Pages," later in this chapter.

Viewing sample pages

The Northwind sample database that comes with Microsoft Access includes some sample data access pages. To view them, first open the Northwind database by choosing Help⇨Sample Databases⇨Northwind Sample Database. Click OK in the first form that opens. Then in the Main Switchboard, click the Display Database Window button.

In the Database window, click the Pages button in the Objects list. To view a sample page, right-click its name after it appears in the list on the right side of the database window and then choose the Open, Design View, or Web Page Preview option from the shortcut menu, depending on how you want to view the page.

Editing an existing Web page

Suppose you already created a Web page, either from scratch or by using an HTML editor, such as Microsoft FrontPage or Macromedia Dreamweaver. Now you want to add some controls to that page that link to your Access database, turning the regular Web page into a data access page. To use that existing Web page as your starting point, follow these steps:

1. **In Access, with your database open, click the Pages button in the Objects list of the Database window.**

   The list of data access pages appears on the right side of the Database window.

2. **Double-click the Edit Web Page that Already Exists option.**

   The Locate Web Page dialog box opens.

3. **Navigate to the folder in which the Web page is stored.**

4. **Click the name of your existing Web page, and then click the Open button.**

The page opens in Access. This type of page won't show the same grid lines that data access pages you create with Access show, but you can edit the page and add controls, as described in the section, "Designing Data Access Pages," later in this chapter.

Designing a data access page from scratch

You can design a data access page completely from scratch, if you like. This approach isn't the easiest in the world, but it is an option. Here's how to create a new, empty data access page from scratch:

1. **In Access, with your database open, click the Pages button in the Objects list of the Database window.**

The list of pages appears on the right side of the Database window.

2. **Double-click the Create Data Access Page in Design View option.**

A new, blank data access page opens in Design view. You're ready to start designing the page as we describe in the section, "Designing Data Access Pages," later in this chapter.

Saving data access pages

When you save a data access page, you may see a message explaining that the *connection string* that defines the location of the database is currently defined as an absolute path. For now, you can ignore that message and just click its OK button, so long as you remember to store all your data access pages in the shared folder you set up for that purpose. The absolute path that the message refers to becomes a problem only if you later move a page, or the database file, to a different folder or computer.

We talk about potential problems with connection strings, and their solutions, in the "Managing Data Access Pages" section, near the end of this chapter.

Designing Data Access Pages

Even though data access pages are stored outside of your .mdb file, you can still see them in the Access Database window. Just click the Pages button in the Objects list, and you see any pages you already created. If you right-click the name of an existing data access page, you see options for opening the page, as in Figure 1-5. The view options are also available from the View menu as well as the View button on the Access toolbar.

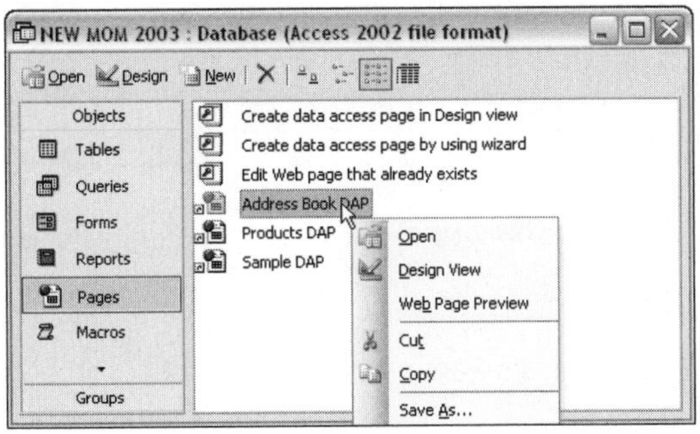

Figure 1-5:
Right-
clicking a
data access
page's icon
displays the
shortcut
menu.

+ **Open:** Opens the page in Page view, which shows roughly how the page looks in a browser. Page view is similar to Form view and Report view for forms and reports.

+ **Design View:** Opens the page for editing. You see the design grid, which looks like a sheet of graph paper in the page editor. (It looks like Design view of a form or report, actually.)

Web pages created outside of Access don't show the design grid. But you can still edit the page using other available tools.

+ **Web Page Preview:** Opens the page in your Web browser. You can see exactly how the page looks in a browser.

Figure 1-6 points out the major components of Design view for data access pages. As you can see, the Field list and Toolbox look different from their counterparts in Design views for forms and reports. Choose View➪Toolbars from the Access menu to decide which toolbars you want to see.

Toolbox   Field list

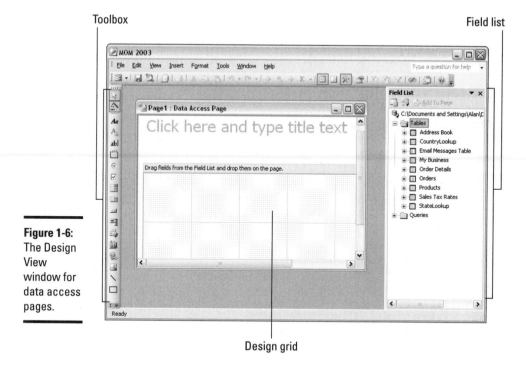

Figure 1-6: The Design View window for data access pages.

Design grid

The Field list, rather than showing only fields from a single table or query, lists the names of all tables and queries in the database. As in all such lists, you can use the + and - signs next to names to expand and contract lists. For example, in Figure 1-7, we expanded the Tables and Address Book lists, and you can see the names of fields from the Address Book table.

When you first open Design view, the Toolbox may be anchored to the left side of the window. You can use the dragging handle (a series of dots) near the top or left of that toolbar to drag the bar away and allow it to float freely. As in all Windows programs, you can point to any button in the Toolbox to see its name, as shown in Figure 1-7.

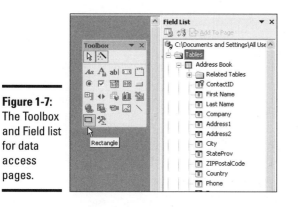

Figure 1-7:
The Toolbox and Field list for data access pages.

Adding controls to data access pages

The Field list that appears in Design view for data access pages is definitely different from its counterpart in forms and reports. For starters, the Field list lists all tables and queries from the current database. Unlike Access forms and reports, a data access page is not bound to a specific table or query. Instead, a data access page is bound to any field in any table or query.

If the Field list isn't visible in Design view, choose View➪Field List from the Access menu to make it visible. Choose View➪Toolbox from the menu to show or hide the Toolbox.

Because the Field list in Design view is so extensive, it's presented as a collapsible "tree" type list, where you can click the + sign next to any name to expand that heading and see its details. Click the – sign next to any item to hide the details. If the list you expand represents a table, you see a Related Tables folder before the list of fields. The Related Tables folder lists the tables and fields related to the table you expanded in the Field list. To add any field from the Field list to your form, click the field's name, and then click the Add to Page button on the toolbar at the top of the Field list. Or, just drag the desired field name onto the design grid.

Creating sections on data access pages

Data access pages don't support the use of subforms and subreports. If you want to show some data in columnar format, and other data in tabular format, then you need to break the report into sections, as shown in Figure 1-8.

Columnar section

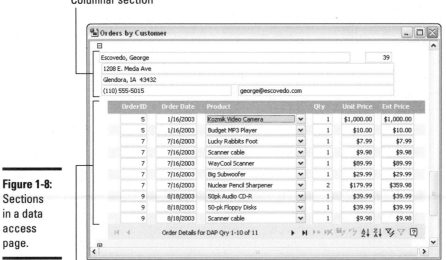

Figure 1-8:
Sections
in a data
access
page.

Tabular section

To create a new section, just drag a table name from the Field list into the design grid. In the Layout Wizard that appears, choose either the Columnar (if you want to arrange fields in a column format) option, or the Tabular option (if you want to arrange fields in a tabular datasheet format).

In Design view, each section has a header at the top and a navigation bar at the bottom. When you click within the section, the entire section gains sizing handles, as shown in Figure 1-9. So you can size a report section as you do any other type of control. Click within that section to display the sizing handles. Then drag any handle to size the section.

Section header

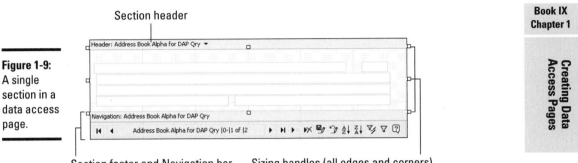

Figure 1-9:
A single
section in a
data access
page.

Section footer and Navigation bar   Sizing handles (all edges and corners)

You can actually create report sections, on the fly, as you drag field names
from the Field list onto the page. It's a little trickier this way than dragging
an entire table name onto the grid. If you're not observant you may not even
notice that the option exists. Here's how it works: Say you drag some fields
from one table, the Address Book table, onto the form. Then you drag a field
from some other table to the same report. When you do, the dragged field is
currently hovering over the report section with the blue border.

Above and below the existing section, you see Create New Section placeholder areas followed by the name of the previous section, as shown in
Figure 1-10. That new section disappears if you don't use it. But if you drag
a field name into that placeholder area, the placeholder area has the bright
bold border. If you drop the field into that new section, Access then converts the placeholder to an actual report section. The Layout Wizard,
described in the upcoming section, then appears asking how you want
the new section laid out.

Placeholder for optional new section

Figure 1-10:
The Create
New
Section
place-
holders in
a data
access
page.

| Create new section above **Address Book Alpha for DAP Qry** |
| Header: Address Book Alpha for DAP Qry ▼ |

| Create new section below **Address Book Alpha for DAP Qry** |
| Navigation: Address Book Alpha for DAP Qry |
| ◄◄ ◄   Address Book Alpha for DAP Qry |0-|1 of |2   ► ►◄ ► |

Placeholder for optional new section   Existing section

Using the Layout and Relationship Wizards

Whenever you create a new section on a report, the Layout Wizard shown in Figure 1-11 appears. Choose how you want to display the related data in the Layout Wizard. Specifics of the various formats are described in more detail in later sections in this chapter.

+ **Columnar:** The field displays in a regular control, as in a standard form.

+ **Tabular:** The field displays in a datasheet-style tabular format.

+ **PivotTable:** The field constructs a PivotTable.

+ **PivotChart:** The field plots a chart of data on the page.

   See "Adding PivotTables and PivotCharts Pages," later in this chapter, for more information on those layouts.

+ **Office Spreadsheet:** The field is used as a field in an Excel-style spreadsheet that's displayed on the page.

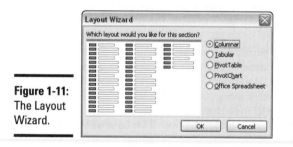

Figure 1-11:
The Layout
Wizard.

After choosing an option from the Layout Wizard, click OK. Depending on the option you select, and whether or not relationships among tables are already defined, you may be presented with the Relationship Wizard next, shown in Figure 1-12.

Your job in the Relationship Wizard is an easy one: Just follow the instructions presented by the wizard. *Note:* All questions concern the field (and the table the field comes from) that you just added to the page. Click OK after making your selections, and you're done adding the field (or fields) to the page.

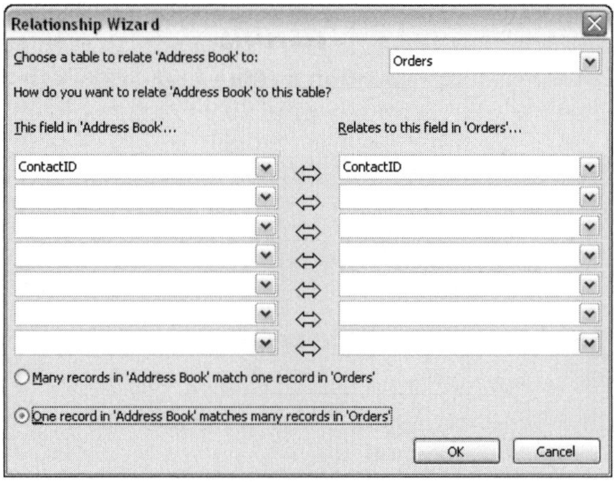

Figure 1-12:
The
Relationship
Wizard.

Aligning and sizing page controls

You can size and align controls on data access pages in much the same way you do with regular forms and reports — by choosing options from the Format menu in Design view. First, you need to select two or more controls to size or align to each other, which is slightly different in data access pages.

See Book IV, Chapter 2 for more information on sizing and aligning controls in forms and reports.

As with forms and reports, you can select multiple controls by dragging the mouse pointer through them. Optionally, you can select one control by clicking it, and then select additional controls using Ctrl+Click or Shift+Click.

When sizing and aligning, whichever control you select last acts as the model to which other selected controls are sized or aligned. The model control has white sizing handles, as opposed to black. We selected the left-most control in Figure 1-13 last; you'll notice the white sizing handles. Choosing Format⇨Align⇨Top causes the tops of all selected controls to align with the top of that model control.

Figure 1-13:
Selecting
multiple
controls in a
data access
page.

Selected controls

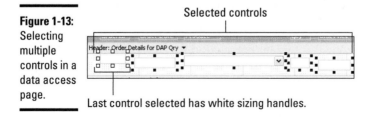

Last control selected has white sizing handles.

After you select multiple controls in a data access page, you can use the following commands from the Access menu to size and align the controls. Just remember that in the descriptions that follow, *model* refers to the last-selected control — the one with the white sizing handles:

✦ **Format⇨Align⇨Left:** Aligns the left edge of each selected control to the left edge of the model.

✦ **Format⇨Align⇨Right:** Aligns the right edge of each selected control to the right edge of the model.

✦ **Format⇨Align⇨Top:** Aligns the top of each selected control to the top of the model.

✦ **Format⇨Align⇨Bottom:** Aligns the bottom edge of each selected control to the bottom edge of the model.

✦ **Format⇨Align⇨Align Middle:** Aligns the vertical center of each selected control to the vertical center of the model.

✦ **Format⇨Align⇨Align Center:** Aligns the horizontal center of each selected control to the horizontal center of the model.

✦ **Format⇨Size⇨Height:** Changes the height of each selected control to match the height of the model.

✦ **Format⇨Size⇨Width:** Changes the width of each selected control to match the width of the model.

✦ **Format⇨Size⇨Both:** Changes the height and width of each selected control to match the height and width of the model.

Other options available on the Format menu, such as Format⇨Vertical Spacing⇨Make Equal, work the same in data access pages as they do in forms and reports. With those options, no selected control acts as a model. All the selected controls are just spaced equally.

Expanding and collapsing page sections

When you first view a data access page in Page view or through your Web browser, you may be surprised to see that subsections don't appear by default. If you look closely, however, you see a little + sign (an Expand control or button) in a box near the top of each section. When you can click the Expand button, the hidden section expands and the + sign in the Expand button turns to a - sign, as in Figure 1-14. Clicking the - sign collapses the section again, hiding the data in that section.

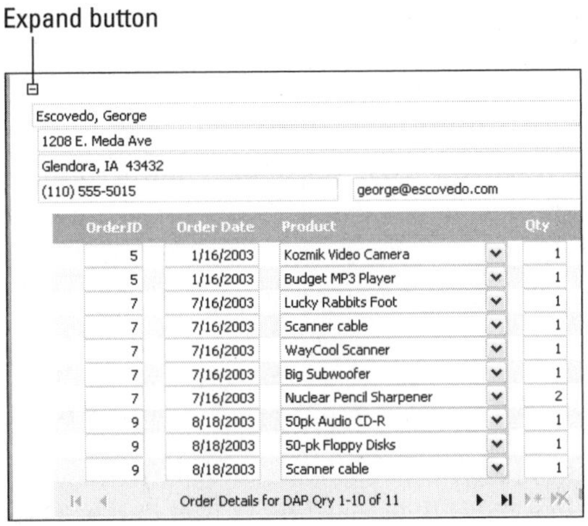

Expand button

Figure 1-14:
In Page
view or
a Web
browser,
use the
Expand
button to
hide/show
sections.

OrderID	Order Date	Product		Qty
	Escovedo, George			
	1208 E. Meda Ave			
	Glendora, IA 43432			
	(110) 555-5015	george@escovedo.com		
5	1/16/2003	Kozmik Video Camera	∨	1
5	1/16/2003	Budget MP3 Player	∨	1
7	7/16/2003	Lucky Rabbits Foot	∨	1
7	7/16/2003	Scanner cable	∨	1
7	7/16/2003	WayCool Scanner	∨	1
7	7/16/2003	Big Subwoofer	∨	1
7	7/16/2003	Nuclear Pencil Sharpener	∨	2
9	8/18/2003	50pk Audio CD-R	∨	1
9	8/18/2003	50-pk Floppy Disks	∨	1
9	8/18/2003	Scanner cable	∨	1

Order Details for DAP Qry 1-10 of 11

You can control whether a section automatically expands or collapses when someone first opens a report by following these steps:

1. **Open the data access page in Design view if it's not already open.**

2. **Click the header above the Expand button for the section you want to show or hide by default.**

3. **Right-click that same header and choose the Group Level Properties option from the shortcut menu that appears.**

   The Properties sheet appears, showing the properties of the group.

4. **On the All tab of the Properties sheet, set the `ExpandedByDefault` property to `True` if you want the section to expand automatically. Otherwise, select `False` to have the section collapsed by default.**

A data access page that contains collapsible sections is sometimes referred to as a *banded* data access page.

Adding PivotTables and PivotCharts Pages

As discussed in Book III, Chapter 4 and Book IV, Chapter 3, PivotTables and PivotCharts allow users of a database to analyze data from many different angles — sometimes referred to as *slicing and dicing data*. From the standpoint of the database developer (you), they allow you to create a single dynamic form — rather than many separate forms — that allows you to view data from many perspectives. Creating and using PivotTables and PivotCharts in data access pages is similar to creating their counterparts in regular forms.

PivotTables and PivotCharts are interdependent in the sense that after you create a PivotTable, you've done most of the legwork for a PivotChart.

Creating a query for a PivotTable or PivotChart

You can make life easier by creating a query that contains all the fields required for your page *before* you create the actual page. PivotTables and PivotCharts are best used in larger databases with lots of records, and lots of categories and subcategories. The Northwind sample database that comes with Microsoft Access provides enough data to allow you to practice creating pages that use those features. We use that database as a working example in this section.

The easiest way to open the sample Northwind database is to choose Help⇨Sample Databases⇨Northwind Sample Database.

The query, of course, needs to contain all the tables and fields from which the PivotTable gets its data. Because, typically, people in sales and marketing departments like to look at data grouped by timeframes (such as quarterly), by category, and by salesperson — we use those fields in this example. We also need some numbers to work with in order for the sample query we use to contain some order totals. Figure 1-15 shows the sample query we created. The following list details the calculated fields the columns are too narrow in the grid to show.

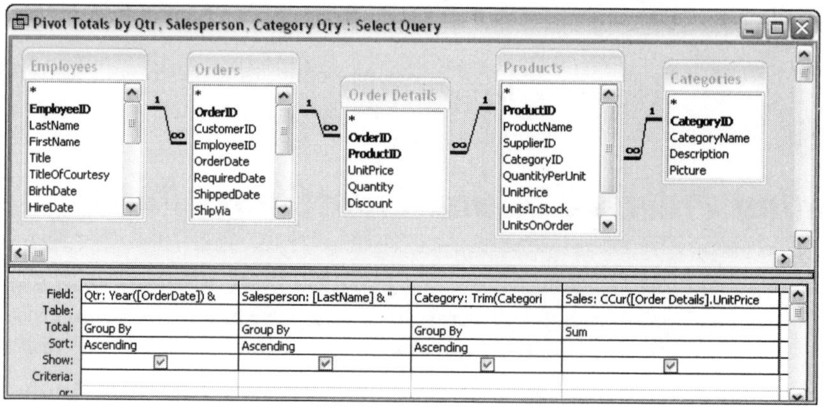

Figure 1-15:
A sample query used for PivotChart and PivotTable data access pages.

◆ Qtr: Year([OrderDate]) & " Q" & DatePart("q",[OrderDate])

◆ SalesPerson: [LastName] & ", " & [FirstName]

◆ Category: Trim([Categories].[CategoryName])

◆ Subtotal: CCur([Order Details].UnitPrice*[Quantity]*(1-[Discount])/100)*100

After the query completes, save it as you do any other. In this example, we name the query "Pivot Totals by Qtr, Salesperson, Category Qry" though you can name your query as you see fit.

Creating a PivotTable data access page

With your query in place, you're ready to create a new, blank data access page, and add a PivotTable control to it. Here's how:

1. **In the Database window, click the Pages button in the Objects list, and then click the New button on the toolbar.**

The New Data Access Page dialog box opens.

2. **Click the Design View option, and then click OK.**

A new, blank data access page opens. You can click the text at the top of the page and enter a new title for the page.

3. **In the Toolbox, click the Office PivotTable button, and then click wherever you want to place the upper-left corner of the table in your page.**

You may want to make the PivotTable control quite large for starters, as in Figure 1-16 (which also points out the locations of various drop zones within the control). Just click the control and drag its sizing handles to the size you wish.

4. **Expand the Queries list in the Field list, and then the query you designed for the PivotTable.**

If the Field list isn't visible, choose View⇨Field List from the Access menu.

5. **Drag field names from the query to the various drop zones based on the instructions in the PivotTable and the following list.**

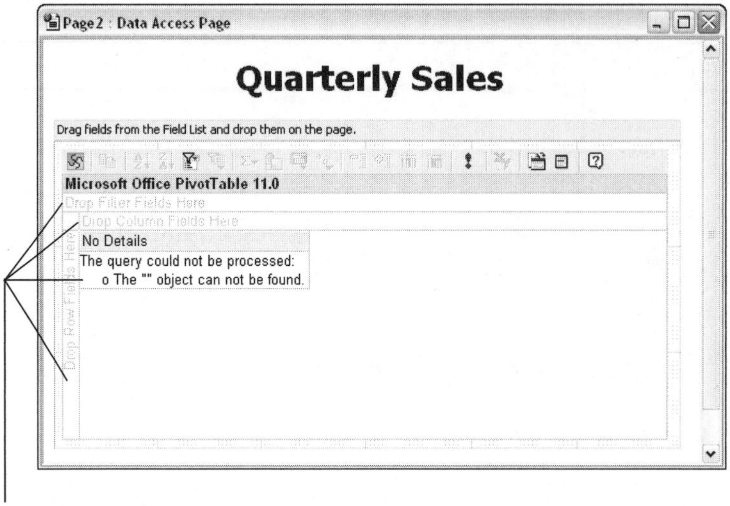

> **Page2 : Data Access Page**
>
> # Quarterly Sales
>
> Drag fields from the Field List and drop them on the page.
>
> **Microsoft Office PivotTable 11.0**
> Drop Filter Fields Here
> Drop Column Fields Here
> No Details
> The query could not be processed:
> o The "" object can not be found.

Figure 1-16:
An empty PivotTable control added to a data access page.

Drop areas

If the drop areas aren't visible in your PivotTable control, right-click the control and choose the Drop Zones option from the shortcut menu that appears. Add the field names for the query to these drop areas:

✦ **Drop Column Fields Here:** Drag the name of the field you want to show in columns to this area. To avoid making the control exceptionally wide, choose the field that has the fewest different values — such as the Category field.

✦ **Drop Row Fields Here:** Drag the names of up to two fields to show in rows to this area — such as the Salesperson field.

✦ **Drop Filter Fields Here:** Drag the names of any fields you want to use for filtering to this area — such as the Qtr field to filter by quarter.

✦ **Drop Totals or Detail Fields Here** (or No Details): Drag the name of the field that contains the value to be shown by the main body of the PivotTable to this area — such as the Sales field, which contains numeric totals.

Changing the number format

You may want to consider changing some options to make things look better. You may want the numeric values in the details area to appear as currency numbers rather than as plain numbers. To accomplish that, open the Properties sheet (choose View➪Properties from the Access menu). Then click a column heading in the Details area (the Sales title in this example). Scroll through the Properties sheet until you get to the `NumberFormat` property, and then change that to the Currency formatting.

Adding grand totals

To add grand totals to the PivotTable, scroll to the far right column of the PivotTable control until you get to the Grand Total column. Drag the name of the field you want totaled (the Sales field in this example) to the Grand Total column, and drop it there. The empty Grand Total column (and row at the bottom of the control) fills with totals of sales.

Showing/Hiding Details

The PivotTable shows an awful lot of detail when first opened, because most categories automatically expand when you first open a PivotTable. You may be interested only in summary data, such as totals. To change the default so that the details are collapsed, change the `Expanded` property for the category to `False`.

To show only totals per salesperson by default, make sure the Properties sheet is open (choose View➪Properties from the Access menu if the Properties sheet is closed). Then click the Salesperson category heading to display its properties. At first glance, changing the property won't seem to have any effect. But when you open the completed page in a Web browser later, the details collapse out of view automatically.

Figure 1-17 shows the complete sample PivotTable. You can close and save it when you finish your work. Speaking of saving data access pages, when you do so, you see a message about the connection string of the page specifying an absolute path to the data source. See the "Saving data access pages" section, earlier in this chapter. For now, you can just ignore the message and click OK.

Creating a PivotChart

If you're looking for an easy way to create a PivotChart to go with a PivotTable on a data access page, your best bet is to put the chart on the same page as the PivotTable. Follow these steps:

1. **Open the page that contains the PivotTable in Design view.**

2. **Click the Office Chart button in the Toolbox.**

3. **Click wherever you want to place the upper-left corner of the chart in your page (most likely beneath the PivotTable control).**

   A Chartspace appears (a placeholder with the words "Microsoft Office Web Components" inside).

4. **Size the Chartspace to your liking with the sizing handles.**

5. **Right-click the Chartspace and choose the Data option from the shortcut menu that appears.**

   The Commands and Options dialog box opens, shown in Figure 1-18.

6. **Choose the third option — Data From the Following Web Page Item — in the Select Where the Chart Data Comes From section and choose the PivotTable option.**

7. **Optionally, click the Type tab in the Commands and Options dialog box and choose a chart type.**

Figure 1-19 shows an example of a Stacked Area graph that we created using data from the preceding PivotTable.

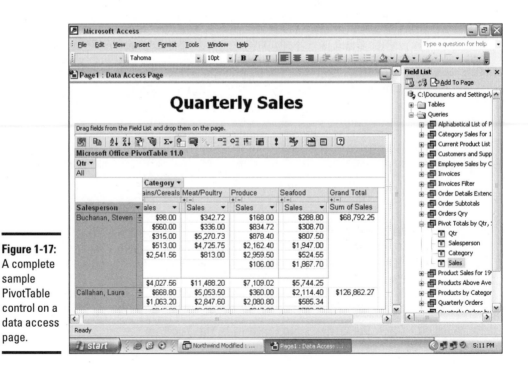

Figure 1-17:
A complete sample PivotTable control on a data access page.

Figure 1-18:
The
Commands
and Options
dialog box
for an Office
PivotChart
control.

Figure 1-19:
The sample
Office
PivotChart
on a data
access
page.

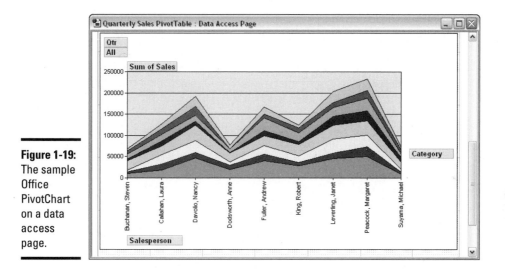

After the chart contains data, you can right-click it and choose the
Commands and Options option from the shortcut menu to return to the
major options for formatting the chart. With the Commands and Options
dialog box open, you can click a specific area of the chart to format just that
section. Figure 1-20 shows the results of converting the Sales totals to
Currency format down the left axis of the chart.

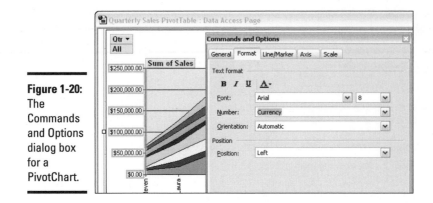

Figure 1-20:
The
Commands
and Options
dialog box
for a
PivotChart.

Other Data Access Page Controls

The Toolbox in Design view for data access pages offers several controls that don't appear for forms or reports. Though they offer features unique to pages, they work in much the same way as they do in forms and reports. For example, you can click a tool, and then click in the design grid to place that control on the page. Or, in many cases, you can click a tool, click a control name in the Field list, and then click the page to add the control, already bound to the field.

To get help with a control, first add it to your page. Then click the control to make sure it's selected, and press the Help key (F1) for more information. To change the properties of a control on the page, right-click the control and choose the Element Properties option from the shortcut menu. You can change the following properties:

✦ **Select Objects:** Returns the mouse pointer to normal operation after clicking a tool.

✦ **Control Wizards:** Enables the control wizards for those controls that provide a wizard.

✦ **Label:** Places unbound text anywhere on the page, just like in regular forms and reports.

✦ **Bound Span:** Creates a bound control that shows data, or the results of an expression, from the underlying table or query. People viewing the page can see, but not change, the contents of a bound span control.

✦ **Text Box:** Creates a standard text box control that's bound to a field in the underlying table or query.

✦ **Scrolling Text:** Displays text in a scrolling marquee format. If you add this as an unbound control, you can then type the text to display by the control directly into the control itself. Or, right-click the control on the page, choose the Element Properties option from the shortcut menu, click the Data tab in the Properties sheet, and type the text to display, enclosed in quotation marks, in the `AlternateDataSource` property.

✦ **Option Group:** Creates a single control for storing multiple option buttons.

✦ **Option Button:** Adds an option button to an Option Group control already placed on the page.

✦ **Check Box:** Creates a standard check box, which can be bound to a Yes/No field in the underlying table or query.

✦ **Drop-Down List:** Creates a drop-down menu for a user to select an option, which is similar to a combo box. But unlike a combo box, you can't type data into a Drop-Down List control.

✦ **List Box:** Creates a standard bound List Box control on the page.

✦ **Command Button:** Creates a standard button on the page.

✦ **Expand:** Emulates subforms and subdatasheets on a data access page when used with record navigation tools.

✦ **Record Navigation:** Inserts a record navigation toolbar into the data access page.

✦ **Office PivotTable:** Adds a Microsoft Office PivotTable control to the page. (See the section, "Creating a PivotTable data access page," earlier in this chapter for details.)

✦ **Office Chart:** Adds a Microsoft Office Chart control to the page. See the "Creating a PivotChart" section, earlier in this chapter, for an example of creating a PivotChart.

✦ **Office Spreadsheet:** Adds a Microsoft Office Spreadsheet control to the page. This control can be bound to any table or query. But the data is presented as a mini-Excel worksheet rather than as a standard Access table.

Probably the easiest way to add an Office Spreadsheet control to a data access page is to simply drag the name of any table or query from the Field list onto the page. When the Layout Wizard opens, choose the Office Spreadsheet option and then click OK.

✦ **Hyperlink:** Creates a hyperlink to another resource, such as a Web page.

✦ **Image Hyperlink:** Inserts an image that also acts like a hyperlink.

✦ **Movie:** Inserts a control for displaying video on the page.

✦ **Image:** Creates an unbound control for displaying a picture on the page.

✦ **Line:** Draws a line on the form.

✦ **Rectangle:** Draws a rectangle on the form.

✦ **More Controls:** Provides a list of additional, more advanced controls for use on data access pages.

Managing Data Access Pages

As mentioned earlier in the chapter, whenever you save a data access page, you see the message shown in Figure 1-21. You don't need to be concerned right away — the page works just fine on your current computer if you simply ignore the message and click OK. But, if you move the database file (the .mdb file), the *connection string* that tells the data access page where to look for the database file no longer works. When you, or any other users, try to open the data access page using a Web browser, or when you try to edit the page from within Access, you get an error message.

Figure 1-21: This message appears when you save a data access page.

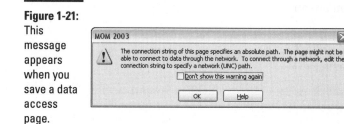

The exact message you get depends on whether you moved the page (the .htm file), the database (the Access .mdb database file), or both. We look at all the potential problems, and their solutions, in the sections that follow.

You move the data access page

Recall that when you create a data access page, you actually create a Web page (.htm file) that exists outside the database. When you click the Pages button in the Objects list of the Database window, the icons for the pages include the little shortcut arrow, which tells Access where to find the Web page. If you move or rename the page, and then try to edit it by double-clicking its name in the database window, you see the error message shown in Figure 1-22.

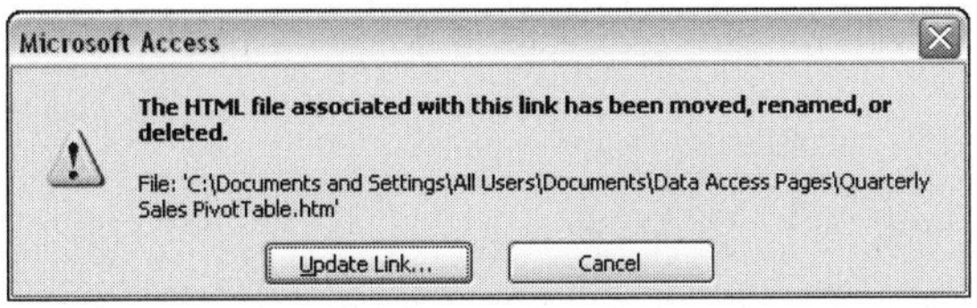

Figure 1-22:
This message appears when you try to edit a moved or missing data access page.

> **Microsoft Access**
>
> ⚠ The HTML file associated with this link has been moved, renamed, or deleted.
>
> File: 'C:\Documents and Settings\All Users\Documents\Data Access Pages\Quarterly Sales PivotTable.htm'
>
> [Update Link...]   [Cancel]

The error message in this case also provides the solution to the problem. Just click the Update Link button to get to the Locate Data Access Page dialog box, which looks just like a typical Open dialog box. In that dialog box, navigate to the folder where the page is now located, and then click the name of the page and click OK. Access corrects the link; the icon now points to the page, and you are able to edit the page normally.

You move the database file

If you move or rename the database (.mdb) file after creating a data access page, attempting to open the page using your Web browser may not generate an error message per se. However, the page won't show any data because it can't find the database .mdb file where the data resides.

To fix the connection string to a Web page using Access, go ahead and open Access and your database normally. Click the Pages button in the Objects list of the Database window, right-click the name of your page in the list that appears, and choose the Design View option from the shortcut menu, as you do normally. You may see a message indicating that all or some components of the page are missing. But you can still click OK and get to the page (minus its data) anyway. After the page opens in Design view, follow these steps to fix the connection string:

1. **Right-click the page and choose the Page Properties option from the shortcut menu.**

   The Properties sheet for the entire page opens.

2. **Click the Data tab.**

3. **Click in the** ConnectionString **property, and then click the Build (...) button that appears to the right of the property.**

   The Data Link Properties dialog box opens, shown in Figure 1-23.

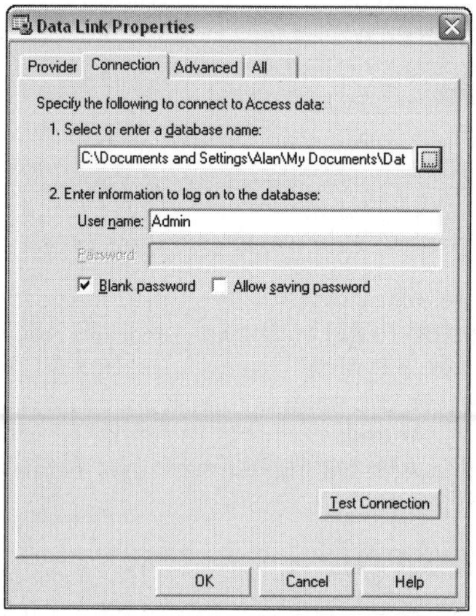

Figure 1-23: The Data Link Properties dialog box.

4. **Click the Build button next to the Select or Enter a Database Name field.**

   The Select Access Database dialog box opens. This dialog box is identical to the standard Open dialog box that appears when you choose File⇨Open from any program's menu.

5. **Navigate to the folder that contains the .mdb file from which the page gets its data, and then click the name of the database that contains the page's data.**

UNC connection strings

For network administrators, if your Access .mdb file and data access pages are on separate computers, you can use Universal Naming Convention (UNC) syntax to specify connection strings. You need to create shares for the database and data access pages, and then point to those shares with UNC. For example, say you put the .mdb file in a shared folder named SharedDB on a server named Server01. The name of the database is OurData.mdb (for lack of a better name). The UNC connection string that points to that database is:

```
//Server01/SharedDB/OurData.mdb
```

You can also use UNC to point from a database file to a data access page. For example, suppose you put a data access page named myDAP.htm in a network share named DAPs on a computer named Max. The UNC path to that data access page is:

```
//Max/DAPs/myDAP.htm
```

6. **Click the Open button in the dialog box.**

   You return to the Data Link Properties dialog box.

7. **To verify that the new connection string works, click the Test Connection button.**

   You should see a `Test Connection Succeeded` message indicating that you chose the right database.

8. **Click the OK button in the Data Link Properties dialog box.**

   You can also close the Properties sheet in Access at this point, if you wish.

If the page doesn't show data immediately, try closing the page and clicking the Yes button when asked if you want to save your changes. Then re-open the page normally from the Database window.

Obtaining OWC components

Data access pages require that users of the pages be using Internet Explorer 5.0 or later. Many components also require that the user's computer have the Office Web Components (OWC) installed. If a user opens a data access page on a page that doesn't have those components installed, he or she sees the message shown in Figure 1-24.

Figure 1-24:
This message appears when you try to open a page that requires OWC.

Data Access Page Notification

This page requires the Microsoft Office Web Components.

See the Microsoft Office Web site for more information.

Lucky for you, you don't have to do a darn thing to fix this problem. The person attempting to view the page just needs to click the Microsoft Office Web site link, and follow the instructions on the Web page to download and install the necessary components.

Chapter 2: Creating Access Projects

In This Chapter

✓ **What is an Access project?**

✓ **Installing Microsoft SQL Server Desktop Edition**

✓ **Upsizing an Access database to SQL Server**

✓ **Creating an Access project from scratch**

✓ **How to create SQL tables, queries, and database diagrams**

*Y*ou probably think that anything you do with Access is a "project," because creating the tables, queries, forms, reports and whatnot for a given database always involves a zillion steps. But the term *Access project* actually refers to something different from the topics we describe in other chapters of this book. Project, in this context, refers to using Access to create the *front end* for a large database, while using another product, such as Microsoft SQL Server, for the *back end*.

What all that means, and why you'd want to do that, takes some explaining. This chapter starts with a bird's-eye view of what Access projects are all about and goes into details later.

Why Access Projects?

When you create an Access database, the objects that make up that database (tables, queries, forms, reports, and such) all end up in a single database file with the .mdb extension. Those objects get, and store, their data using what's known as the Microsoft Jet *database engine*. A database engine, in turn, is that component of a database that stores and manages the raw data you find in the Access tables.

The Jet database engine used by Access is fine for personal and small business use. But it's not really designed to handle the enormous amount of traffic that large corporations and large online businesses, such as Amazon and eBay, handle. Those large business databases need to handle thousands of users who are all adding, viewing, and changing data simultaneously. While Access is relatively easy to use, it simply doesn't have the horsepower to handle something similar to all the thousands of branch offices that make up, say, Bank of America.

Large corporations use huge (and hugely expensive) products, such as Microsoft SQL Server and Oracle, to handle their data processing needs. They have to, because at any given time, the database may need to handle thousands — if not tens or hundreds of thousands — of requests for data from as many people.

SQL, often pronounced like the word *sequel,* stands for Structured Query Language, and is an industry standard for large-scale databases.

Expense and *scalablity* (the ability to handle huge amounts of traffic) aren't the only things that separate the big corporate databases from Microsoft Access. The big boys tend to be hugely complex, and offer little in the way of user friendliness. The corporate database administrators that manage enormous databases tend to have a lot of technical training and advanced degrees in computer science. Also, many people take years to design and develop these enormous databases — certainly much more training and time than an average PC user wants to invest in developing a personal or small business database. And that's where Access projects come into play.

An Access project tries to simplify the development of large-scale databases by using the enormous database engine as a back end only. You can use the big corporate database program to store and manage the back-end database, but you use Access to develop all the front-end stuff, such as forms and reports. In other words, an Access project gives you the convenience of Access for developing the forms and reports and such, while at the same time keeping the enormous horsepower on the back end to manage the huge traffic flow. Figure 2-1 shows the relationship between a back-end database and the front-end components you create with Access.

Book VII, Chapter 2 talks about how to split an Access application into two files, a front end and a back end. This is the same idea, except that the back-end database is stored in a file maintained by a more powerful database program. If you already have an Access application that's split into front-end and back-end databases, read on to find out how to migrate the back end to a SQL server.

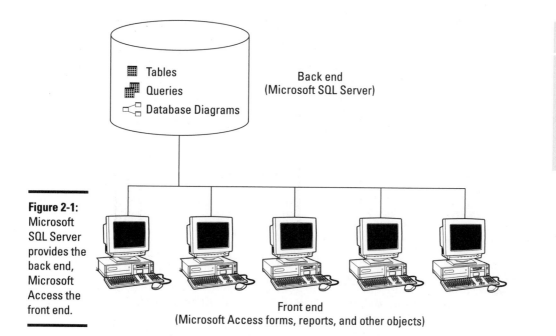

Figure 2-1:
Microsoft
SQL Server
provides the
back end,
Microsoft
Access the
front end.

Does that mean you need to go out and spend thousands of dollars on
Microsoft SQL Server or some other large database product *before* you can
start developing a large-scale project, or even before you can even find out
the skills required to design and develop large-scale databases? Fortunately,
no. When you bought Microsoft Access, you also got the Microsoft SQL
Server 2000 Desktop Engine. Technically, it *is* Microsoft SQL Server 2000.
However, it can't handle the huge amount of traffic that the expensive full-
blown SQL Server products can. To use the SQL Server 2000 Desktop
Engine, you just need to install it from your Microsoft Office CD-ROM.

If you happen to be a network administrator, you can think of SQL Server
2000 Desktop Engine as the client/server equivalent of the Access Jet database engine. For more details and specific limitations, search for *Desktop
Engine* or *MSDE* in Access Help, or at the Microsoft Search page (search.
microsoft.com).

Installing the SQL Server Desktop Engine

If you want to start building a large-scale database project, but don't have a
copy of SQL Server installed to work with, you can just follow the upcoming
steps to install the freebie Desktop Engine from your Microsoft Office CD.

In the (unlikely) event that you previously installed Microsoft SQL Desktop Edition (MSDE) from an earlier version of Access, uninstall that previous version prior to completing the following steps.

1. **Close and save any open Access objects. Then close all open program windows to get to your Windows desktop.**

2. **Insert your Office 2003 CD into your computer's CD-ROM drive.**

3. **If the Installation procedure starts automatically, click the Exit or Cancel button to close it.**

4. **Open your My Computer folder.**

   In Windows XP, you can click the Start button and choose My Computer.

5. **Right-click the icon for your CD-ROM drive and choose the Open option from the shortcut menu.**

   The contents of the CD appear in a folder window.

6. **Open the MSDE2000 folder.**

7. **Double-click the SETUP (or SETUP.EXE) program icon (*not* the Setup folder icon).**

8. **Follow the instructions on-screen.**

   If you're not sure how to answer any question on the screen, just accept the default (suggested) response by clicking the Yes, OK, or Continue button.

9. **When the installation completes, remove the CD from your CD-ROM drive.**

10. **Restart your computer.**

The only difference you'll notice, after you restart your computer, is a new little icon down in the Notification Area (or system tray) in your Windows taskbar, as shown in Figure 2-2. When you see the green right-pointing triangle on that icon, that means the desktop engine is running and ready for use. When you point to the icon, you should see a ToolTip that reads "Running..." followed by your computer's name and MSSQLServer. Double-clicking, or right-clicking, the icon provides options for pausing and stopping the service. But you do no harm in just leaving it running all the time.

Figure 2-2:
Microsoft
SQL Server
Desktop
Edition is
installed,
running, and
ready to
use.

SQL Server Desktop Edition icon

Upsizing a Database to a Project

After you install SQL Desktop Edition, you can create a new project from
scratch. Or, you can upsize an existing Jet database (.mdb file) to a project
(.adp file). If you already invested a lot of time in creating an Access database, this is the preferred approach. You won't have to re-create all the
tables, queries, forms, reports, and so forth. Plus, it's a relatively easy thing
to do, thanks to the built-in Upsizing Wizard. Follow the upcoming steps to
use the wizard to convert an existing Access database to a project.

The Upsizing Wizard actually copies a .mdb file to an .adp project file. You
don't have to worry about losing your original .mdb database when you use
the Upsizing Wizard.

1. **Make sure SQL Server Desktop Edition is installed and running.**

2. **Open Access and your database in the usual manner.**

   If your Access database is already open, close any open objects (tables,
   forms, and so forth, so that only the Database window remains open).

3. **From the Access menu, choose Tools➪Database Utilities➪Upsizing
   Wizard.**

   The first page of the Upsizing Wizard opens. The wizard wants to know
   whether you have an existing SQL Server database or if you want to
   make one.

4. **Choose the Create New Database option to create a new database and
   then click the Next button.**

5. **On the second wizard page, you can just accept the defaults by clicking the Next button.**

6. **On the third wizard page, click the >> button to export all the tables
   you want to store in SQL Server, and then click the Next button.**

7. **To convert all objects with minimal fuss, just click the Next button on each remaining wizard page, and then click the Finish button.**

Now you just wait. (This may take a while.) When the conversion is complete, the original .mdb file closes, the new .adp version of your database opens, and you see the Print Preview version of a report titled Upsizing Wizard Report.

8. **If you like, you can print a copy of the report by right-clicking it and choosing the Print option from the shortcut menu. Then close the report by clicking its Close button.**

Your original .mdb database closes, and the new project equivalent of that database opens. The new copy has the same name as the original database followed by the letters CS, short for "Client/Server."

At first glance, you'll not likely notice any major changes in your database, other than a new object titled Database Diagrams in the Objects list of the Database window. But as you explore table designs, query designs, and other objects, you'll start to see some differences. The changes have to do with the differences between Access projects and Access databases, as we discuss in the sections that follow.

Unfortunately, the Upsizing Wizard may not be able to convert all the objects in a database with 100 percent accuracy; expecting perfection here may be unrealistic. But still, if you already invested time in creating an Access database, then converting it to a project and working out the kinks is a lot easier than starting the whole thing over from scratch!

When you browse through the Windows folders, you see two icons for your database. The original database icon and name are the same. The project version of your database has a slightly different icon, with the letters CS (short for "Client/Server") tacked on. If the file name extensions are visible, as shown in Figure 2-3, you see the .adp extension on the project version of your database.

Figure 2-3: MOM2003.mdb is the original database. MOM2003 CD.adp is the new project version.

Creating an Access Project from Scratch

No rule says you have to create an Access database first, and then upsize it to a project. You can create a new Access project, from scratch, and start building your database from there. Assuming you install the SQL Server Desktop Edition and it's currently running, you can follow these steps to create a new Access project from scratch:

1. **Open Microsoft Access in the usual manner.**

2. **Choose File⇨New from the Access menu.**

3. **Click the Project Using New Data option in the task pane on the right.**

   The File New Database dialog box opens.

4. **Navigate to the folder in which you want to store the new project.**

5. **Type in a file name where indicated. (The default name, adp1, isn't very descriptive!)**

   Make sure the Save as Type option reads "Microsoft Access Project."

6. **Click the Create button and wait a few seconds.**

   The Microsoft SQL Server Database Wizard, shown in Figure 2-4, opens.

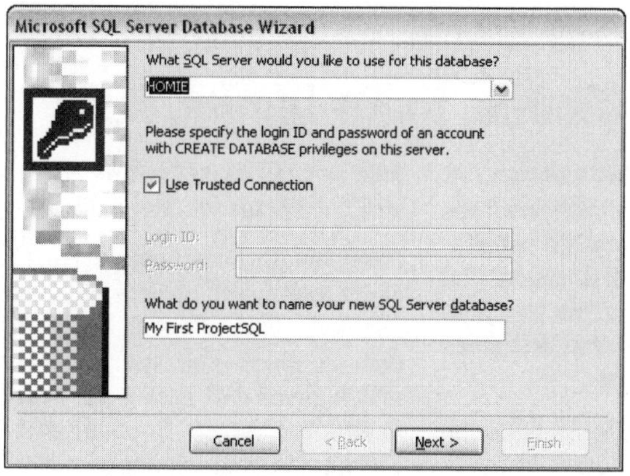

Figure 2-4: The Microsoft SQL Server Database Wizard.

7. **You can accept the default (suggested) options by clicking the Next button, and then click the Finish button.**

After another brief delay, you are presented with the Database window. It's not too different from the regular Access Database window. You see a new object type, named Database Diagrams, in the Objects list, and not quite as many wizards to choose from in the main window. But other than that, things work pretty much the same way they do in regular Access databases.

A couple of not-so-obvious differences occur behind the scenes, though. The front-end objects are stored in a file that has the .adp (Access Database Project) extension, rather than the usual .mdb (Microsoft Database) extension. The back-end objects — tables, queries, and database diagrams — are stored in a separate file that has the .sql extension. But the splitting of objects into back-end and front-end files isn't at all apparent while you work in Access, so you don't have to worry about that.

Creating Tables in a Project

As in any database, the first step in creating a new Access project is to design your tables. We refer to these as *SQL Server tables,* to distinguish them from tables you create in regular Access. (Besides, they are SQL Server tables!) Anyway, to create a SQL Server table, just click the Tables button in the Objects list of the Database window. Then double-click the Create Table in Design View option from the list that appears on the right side of the Database window.

ANSI, Unicode, fixed-length, huh?

The reason so many data types exist in SQL Server is because when you deal with hundreds of thousands of records, and multiple simultaneous users, every little bit of disk space, and every little sliver of time, counts. The idea is to choose the smallest data type that still gives you the range of values you need.

Many text fields give you a choice between ANSI and Unicode. ANSI characters take one byte (eight bits) each, but only store characters from the English language alphabet. Unicode characters take two bytes (16 bits each), but can store characters from all written languages, not just English. Field names that start with *n*, such as nchar and ntext, use Unicode (the "n" stands for "national").

Fixed-length data types store all data at the same length, which wastes a little disk space but saves time. Variable-length data types use only as much disk space as a value needs, which saves disk space, but costs a little more in time to manage. Because disk space is dirt cheap, and time expensive, it's usually preferable to go with a fixed-length, rather than variable-length, data type when given the choice. The names of variable-length data types contain the letters *var*, as in varchar and nvarchar.

The Design view for tables looks a little different from the Design view for creating Access Jet tables. SQL uses the term *Column* where Jet uses the term *Field*. Where the Jet table shows Field Properties, the SQL table displays a long list of properties. So long, in fact, that you have to use the scroll bar to get through the whole list. But aside from that, things aren't too unfamiliar. Use these columns in the Design view for tables when working with an Access project:

+ **Column Name:** Enter a field name of your own choosing. Though for maximum compatibility with large SQL databases, avoid using blank spaces in field names.

+ **Data Type:** Choose a data type from the drop-down list (shown in Figure 2-5). You have more types to choose from. Table 2-1 lists the data types, the range of values each type stores, and the Jet (Access .mdb) equivalent (where applicable).

+ **Length:** If you choose a data type with a variable length, you can type in a length of your choosing in this column. Many data types have fixed lengths, in which case the length appears in this column, but you can't change it.

+ **Allow Nulls:** If selected (checked), users who enter data into the table can leave the field empty. If the Allow Nulls property is not checked, the field cannot be left blank during data entry (the equivalent of a required field in a Jet database).

+ **Description:** Enter a plain-English description of the field here. You can leave it blank if you prefer because this field is optional.

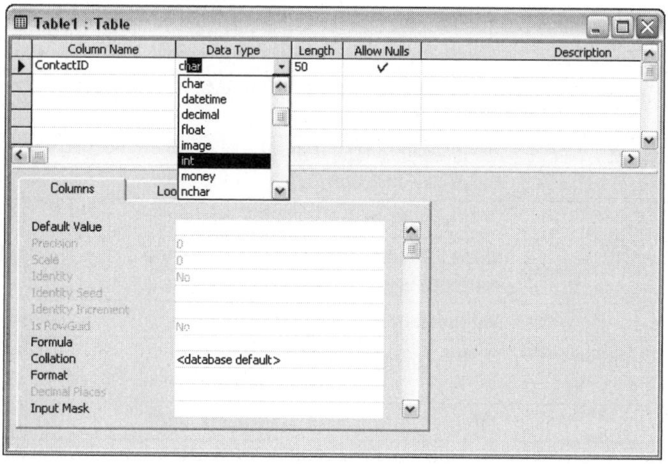

Figure 2-5:
Choosing a field's data type when designing a SQL table.

Table 2-1   **SQL Server Data Types and Closest Jet Equivalents**

SQL Server Data Type	Description/ Values	Jet Equivalent
bigint	Whole numbers from -2^{63} to 2^{63}-1	n/a
binary	Fixed-length binary data up to 8,000 bits long	n/a
bit	A single bit that can only be either 0 or 1	Yes/No
char	Text up to 8,000 ANSI characters	Text
datetime	Dates from January 1, 1753 to December 31, 9999	Date/Time
decimal	Numbers from -10^{38}-1 to 10^{38}-1	n/a
float	Numbers from $-2.23E-308$ to $-1.79 E+308$	Number (Double)
image	Any large object (picture, sound) up to 2,147,483,647 bytes	OLE Object
int	Whole numbers from -2,147,483,648 to 2,147,483,647	Number (Long Integer)
money	Dollar values from $-\$922,337,203,685,477.5707$ to $\$922,337,203,685,477.5807$	Currency
nchar	Fixed-length text up to 4,000 Unicode characters	Text
ntext	Variable-length Unicode text from 16 to 2,147,483,647 characters	Memo
numeric	Numbers from -10^{38}-1 to 10^{38}-1	Number (Double)
nvarchar	Text up to 4,000 Unicode characters	Text
real	Numbers from $-1.18E-38$ to $3.40E+38$	Number (Single)
smalldatetime	Dates from January 1, 1900 to June 6, 2079	Date/Time
smallint	Whole numbers from -32,768 to 32,767	Number (Integer)
smallmoney	Dollar values from $-\$214,748.3648$ to $\$214,748.3647$	Currency
sql_variant	Variable data type that returns the value of a function	n/a
text	Text from 16 to 2,147,483,647 characters	Memo
timestamp	Code that updates automatically when a record is added or changed	n/a
tinyint	Whole numbers from 0 to 255	Number (Byte)
uniqueidentifier	A 16-bit globally unique identifier	Number (Replication ID)
varbinary	Variable data type of 8,000 bytes long	n/a
varchar	Variable length text up to 8,000 ANSI characters	Text

To view the design of a table converted from a .mdb file, just right-click the table name and choose the Design View option from the shortcut menu, as you do in a .mdb database.

Field properties in SQL Server tables

After you create a field, you can use the Columns and Lookup tabs at the bottom of the Design View window to define properties for that field. On the Columns tab, use the scroll bar to scroll through all of the available properties for the field. Don't be alarmed if many of the options are disabled (dimmed). A disabled property is simply one that doesn't apply to the data type for the field you're currently defining.

Primary key fields in SQL Server tables

You can mark any field, or any combination of fields, in a SQL table as a primary key using the same techniques you use in Jet tables. Select the field names that act as the table's primary key, and then click the Primary Key button on the toolbar. Or, right-click the selected field name(s) and choose the Primary Key option from the shortcut menu that appears. Note that fields for which you select the Allow Nulls property cannot be defined as a primary key, because each record must have a unique value in the Primary Key field.

Unlike Access, where a primary key is optional, you must define a primary key in a SQL Server table if you want to add and edit data. When you try to change the contents of a table that has no primary key defined, the keyboard seems to be dead when you type new data into a field, and the This Recordset Is Not Updatable message appears in the status bar.

Creating AutoNumber fields in projects

While SQL tables don't offer an AutoNumber data type, creating an AutoNumber field in a SQL Server table is easy. Just follow these steps:

1. **Type a field name of your own choosing into the Column Name box.**

2. **Choose the int Data Type for the field.**

3. **Leave the Length setting at four, and leave the Allow Nulls option unchecked.**

   Whether or not you type in a description is up to you.

4. **On the Columns tab — in the Properties sheet below the grid — set the Identity property to the Yes setting.**

   Setting the Identity property to the Yes setting ensures that each new record you add to the table automatically gets a new, unique number.

5. **Optionally, set the** `Identity Seed` **property to the first number to be assigned.**

   The `Identity Seed` property defines the number assigned to the first new record in the table.

6. **Set the** `Identity Increment` **property to whatever increment you want each new number by.**

As an example, Figure 2-6 shows a new ContactID field set up as an auto-numbered primary key. The first customer entered into the table is automatically assigned the number 1001 as his or her ContactID (because of the `Identity Seed` property of `1001`). Each new customer added to the table gets the next number in sequence assigned as his or her ContactID. The second customer is 1002, then 1003, 1004, and so forth, because the `Identity Increment` property is set to 1.

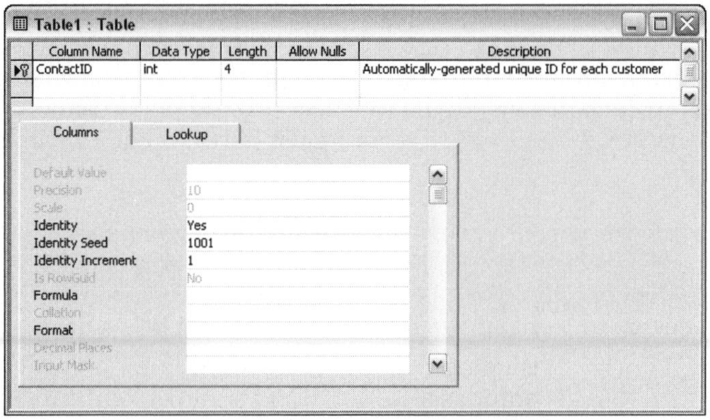

Figure 2-6: The ContactID field acts as an autonumbered primary key.

Creating hyperlink fields in projects

When you design a table in an Access project, you can't choose the Hyperlink data type. But you can easily create a hyperlink field by following these steps:

1. **Type the field name into the Column Name box.**

2. **Choose the char Data Type for the field.**

   Optionally, you can choose the nchar, varchar, nvarchar, ntext, or text data type, but char works just fine. You can set the Length, Allow Nulls, and Description columns however you want.

3. **On the Columns tab in the Properties sheet, scroll down to the** Hyperlink **property and choose the** Yes **setting.**

Figure 2-7 shows an example where the URL field name is currently selected in the list of field names. You can see we set the Hyperlink property to the Yes setting in the lower part of the window.

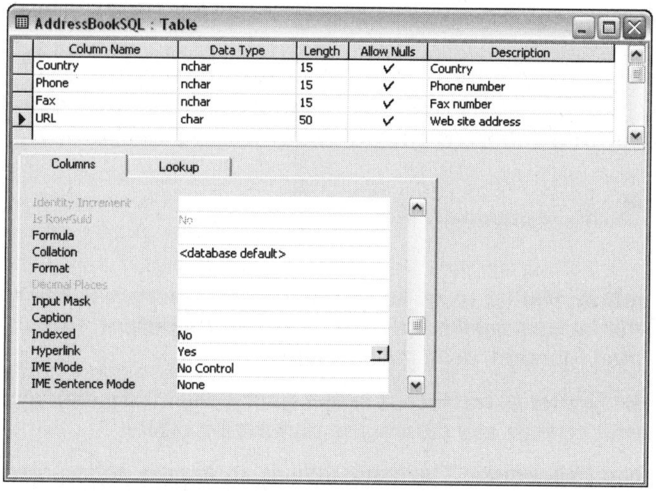

Figure 2-7:
The URL field in this SQL table is like a Hyperlink field in a Jet table.

Saving a SQL Server table

When you finish designing your table, just close the Design View window as usual. You see a prompt asking if you want to save the table. Click the Yes button. The Choose Name dialog box opens. Type in a name of your own choosing for the table, but don't use any blank spaces. (Technically, you can use blank spaces, but not all SQL-related programs handle blanks well, so your best bet is to just avoid using blank spaces in table and field names when working on a project). Click OK, and you're done. The name of the table appears in the Database window whenever you click the Tables button in the Objects list of the Database window.

Creating Queries in Projects

Queries in projects use a whole different vocabulary than queries in a regular Access database, as is readily apparent when you click the Queries button in the Database window's Objects list (see Figure 2-8). The options in the main pane allow you to create a *function, view,* or *stored procedure.* As intimidating as those options may seem, you can reduce the fear factor by relating each to its (roughly) equivalent Access query type:

Figure 2-8:
The Queries
button
selected
in the
Database
window's
Objects list.

MOM 2003CS : Project - MOM 2003 SubsetSQL...

🔲 Open 🔧 Design 📄 New | ✕ | ᵃₒ ✲ ▦ ▥

Objects

▦ Tables

🗐 Queries

🗗 Database Diagrams

🖹 Forms

🖺 Reports

🗋 Pages

▾

Groups

▣ Create function in designer

▣ Create view in designer

▣ Create stored procedure in designer

✦ **Function:** Similar to an Access parameter query, you can supply criteria on the fly, just before the query displays its output. (Also called a User-Defined function, or inline function.)

✦ **View:** Similar to an Access select query, the query displays data, but doesn't change any data in the underlying table.

✦ **Stored Procedure:** The same idea as an Access action query (update query, append query, make-table query, delete query) in that the query actually *changes* data in tables — not just *displays* data.

The Design View window for queries is a little different, too, in that what once were columns now are rows, and vice versa, as you see in the sections that follow. But other than that, the differences aren't *too* dramatic. Annoying, yes. But not too dramatic.

Creating a SQL Server view

Creating a view in a project is almost identical to creating a select query in an Access database. Follow these steps to create a SQL Server view:

If you long since forgotten what a select query is, see Book III, Chapter 1.

1. **In the Database window, click the Queries button in the Objects list on the left side of the window.**

The list of queries appears on the right side of the Database window.

2. **Double-click the Create View in Designer option.**

The Design View window appears and the Add Table dialog box opens.

3. **Click the name of any table you want to add to the query, and then click the Add button.**

Repeat Step 3 to add as many tables as you wish.

4. **Click the Close button in the Add Table dialog box.**

The Add Table dialog box closes, and the Field lists of the selected tables appear in the top of the grid. You can move and size those Field lists by dragging their title bars or borders, as usual. You can join two tables by dragging the primary key from one table to the corresponding field in the related table. And, if need be, you can change the type of relationship between two tables by right-clicking the join line and choosing an option from the shortcut menu that appears.

To add a field to the query grid, just click that field's name. The names of all fields displayed by the view have a check mark, and also appear in the grid in the bottom half of the window. Note that the row/column arrangement of the Query by Example grid is transposed as compared to regular Access databases. Field names are listed down the left column. Options for each selected field appear in column headings across the top of the grid, as shown in Figure 2-9.

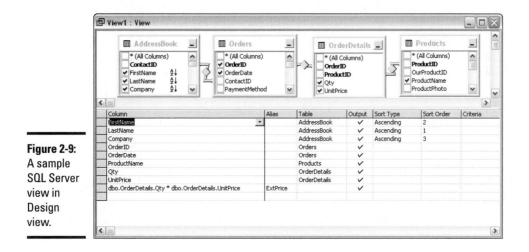

Figure 2-9:
A sample
SQL Server
view in
Design
view.

Project panes

The Design window in a project is slightly different from that in an Access database. You can pick and choose from three different panes to display, using the buttons described in the following list from the toolbar. Just click any button to show, or to hide, a pane:

✦ **Diagram:** Shows or hides the field lists in the top pane.

✦ **Grid:** Shows or hides the grid (middle pane).

✦ **SQL:** Shows or hides the SQL statement generated by the query in a third pane at the bottom of the window.

SQL Server sorting

Sorting the output of a view is only slightly different from doing so in an Access query. For any field you can choose both a sort type (ascending or descending) as well as a sort order. The sort order is probably better referred to as the *sort precedence,* because that's what it really means. The sort order in the sample QBE grid shown in Figure 2-9 looks like this:

FirstName	Ascending	2
LastName	Ascending	1
Company	Ascending	3

Records in the view's output are sorted by LastName, then by FirstName within identical last names, and then by Company name within identical last name, first name pairs. You don't need to put fields into the grid in a certain order to define a sort order precedence; you use the Sort Order column instead.

SQL Server calculated controls

The last field in the example shown in Figure 2-9 is a sample calculated control. When defining a calculated control in a view, you don't use the *fieldname:expression* syntax you see in a regular Access database. You just type the expression into the first column, and then type the field's name into the Alias column. And you don't have to type the complete expression as shown in the figure. To create the calculated control shown, we just typed the expression using the regular `[Qty]*[UnitPrice]` syntax. The query itself then converted the regular syntax, automatically, to the more complex SQL Server syntax:

```
dbo.Orders.Qty * dbo.OrderDetails.UnitPrice
```

When the grid adds a dbo. prefix to a name, just leave it as is. It stands for *database owner*, and is just part of the SQL Server syntax.

You can use the Alias column in the grid to give any field an alternative name in the query's output. Say you have a LastName field, but you want Last Name to appear (with the blank space) in the column heading of the query's results. In that case, you just select the LastName field to display, and then type Last Name (with the blank space) into the Alias column of that row in the grid. Whatever you type into the Alias column automatically appears as the field name in the query's output.

When creating calculated fields that contain strings (text), you have to use a slightly different syntax in the expression. The differences are:

✦ Always enclose field names in square brackets ([])

✦ Use single quotation marks (') rather than double (") to enclose literal text.

✦ Use + rather than & to concatenate (join) strings.

✦ If you want to trim trailing blanks off the end of fields, use the RTRIM( ), rather than TRIM( ) function.

To display a customer name in the format *LastName, FirstName* without any trailing blanks, type the expression as:

```
rtrim([LastName] + ', ' + rtrim([FirstName])
```

The grid changes your expression to proper SQL Server syntax, which is considerably more complicated looking:

```
RTRIM(dbo.AddressBook.LastName) + ', ' + RTRIM(dbo.AddressBook.FirstName)
```

But as long as you follow the syntax rules we describe, you can get away with typing the expression without typing in the dbo.*tablename* portion yourself.

SQL Server view criteria

You can enter filter criteria in a SQL Server query using syntax similar to the syntax used in Jet queries. One exception is that you don't use the # character to delimit literal dates. Use the single quotation mark instead. Or, if you don't use any delimiter, the quotation marks are filled in for you. Figure 2-10 shows a criterion added to the QBE grid to limit output from the query to records that have a date between January 1, 2003 and December 31, 2003.

SQL Server tends to capitalize these things as well. If you type in, say, **between 1/1/2003 and 12/31/2003**, the criterion ends up displayed as BETWEEN '1/1/2003' AND '12/31/2003'.

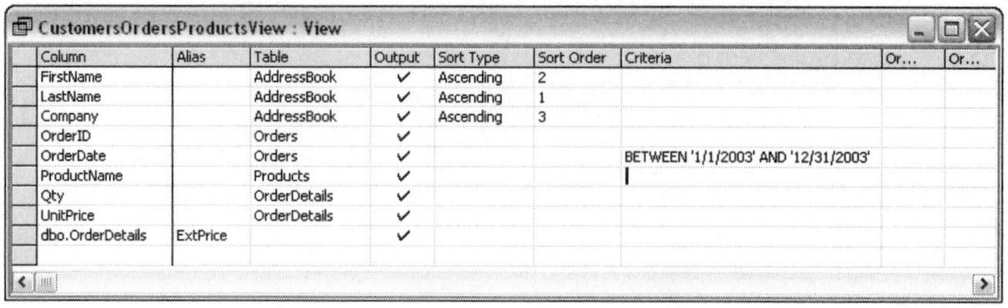

Figure 2-10:
A filter criterion added to a SQL Server view.

You can use the Or columns to the right of the criterion to provide additional criteria, just as you use the extra blank rows at the bottom of the Jet QBE grid to specify additional criteria for a field.

Totaling SQL Server views

In Access Jet queries, you can total values by clicking the Sum button, and then by choosing options from the Totals row in the QBE grid. In SQL Server view, you click the Group By button on the toolbar. When you do, a new Group By column is added to the QBE grid.

Initially, each field in the Group By column is set to the Group By setting. To total a numeric column, just click the Group By column and change it to the Sum setting. In Figure 2-11, the [Order Total] alias (calculated field) multiplies the Qty and UnitPrice fields to come up with a total. The Sum setting in the Group By column ensures that for each record the query displays, the Order Total field shows the total of each entire order.

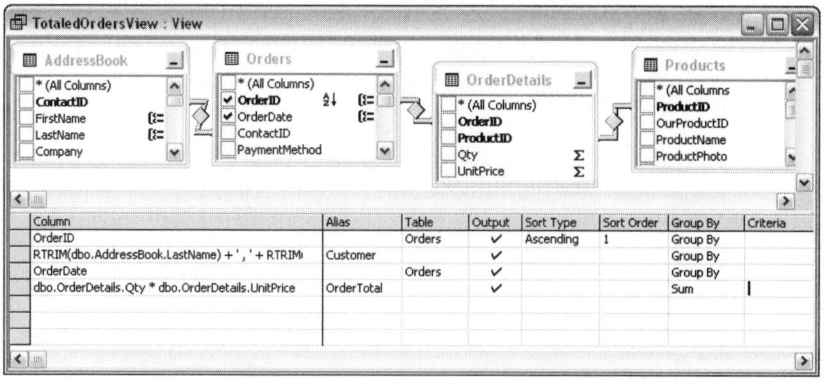

Figure 2-11:
This query displays order totals, due to the Sum setting in the Group By column.

Seeing a view's results

In a project, you can't just right-click a view's title bar to see its output. You need to actually save the query, and run it by clicking the Run button on the toolbar — even if the query is a view that doesn't alter data. If you click the Run button before saving the query, you are prompted to save the query, and then the query runs. Figure 2-12 shows the results of the query shown in Design view in Figure 2-11.

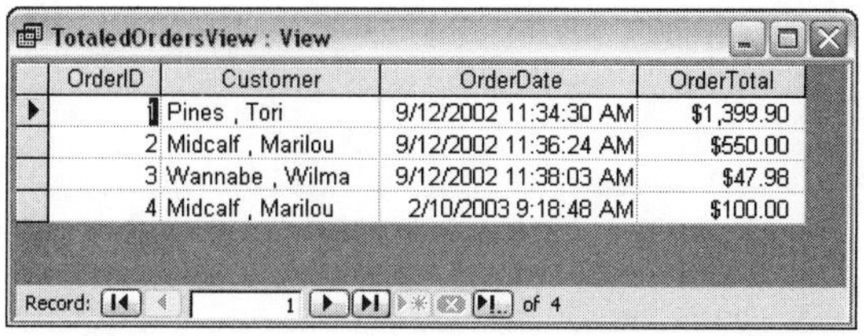

Figure 2-12:
The results
of the query
shown in
Design
view in
Figure 2-11.

	OrderID	Customer	OrderDate	OrderTotal
▶	1	Pines , Tori	9/12/2002 11:34:30 AM	$1,399.90
	2	Midcalf , Marilou	9/12/2002 11:36:24 AM	$550.00
	3	Wannabe , Wilma	9/12/2002 11:38:03 AM	$47.98
	4	Midcalf , Marilou	2/10/2003 9:18:48 AM	$100.00

TotaledOrdersView : View

Record: 1 of 4

Creating SQL Server functions

A SQL Server function is basically the same idea as an Access parameter query. A function offers all the capabilities of a view, and follows the same basic rules. After you have the hang of creating views, you only need to find out how to define parameters in functions — which is pretty easy.

See Book III, Chapter 3 for more information on Access parameter queries.

To create the query, make sure you double-click the Create Function in Designer option in the Database window (not the Create View in Designer option). The Design View window appears, with its Add Table dialog box. Choose your tables and create the query normally.

To define parameters, type a criterion expression into the Criteria column of the field(s) you're interested in. But don't type literal values into the criterion expression. Instead, make up a new name for each parameter, and enclose that name in square brackets. Make sure the names you enter into the criterion don't match the names of any fields in the query.

Suppose you want a query to filter records by a range of dates, but you want the user to specify those dates when using the query. Because the names *startdate* and *enddate* aren't field names in the query, you can use those in the criterion expression, like this:

```
Between [startdate] and [enddate]
```

The Design View window replaces the square brackets with a single leading @ character, like this:

```
BETWEEN @startdate AND @enddate
```

In Figure 2-13, we used the exact preceding expression to define a couple of parameters in the Criteria column of the OrderDate field.

Figure 2-13:
The criterion for the OrderDate field contains two parameters named @startdate and @enddate.

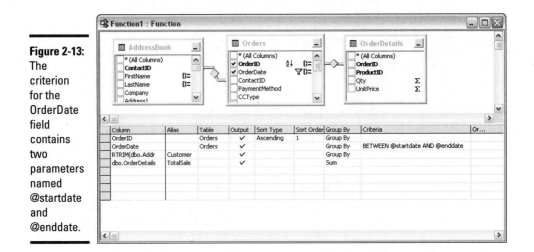

When you run a function, you see an Enter Parameter Value dialog box for each parameter before the function displays its output. In each dialog box that appears, type in a valid value, as shown in Figure 2-14, and then click OK. Do the same for each parameter. Say you type **1/1/04** for the startdate parameter and **12/31/04** as the enddate parameter, and click OK. The query displays only those records whose OrderDate field contains a date from the year 2004.

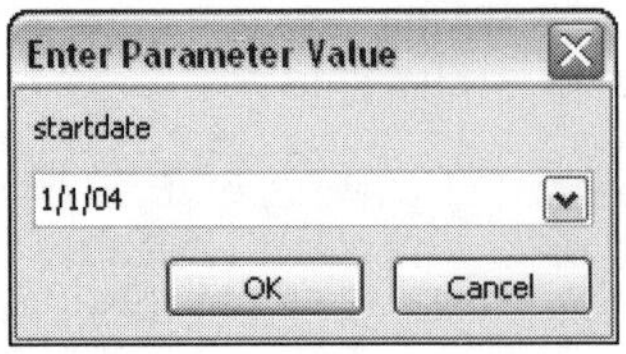

Figure 2-14:
The Enter Parameter Value dialog box from a SQL Server function.

You can set defaults for parameters in SQL Server functions, so that the Enter Parameter Value dialog box comes up with a suggested value already typed in, rather than empty. If you think, in most cases, people want to see orders for the year 2004, you can make 1/1/04 the default value for the start-date and 12/31/04 the default for enddate. Follow these steps:

1. **Make sure you're viewing the function in Design view.**

If you're in Datasheet view, right-click the title bar and choose the Function Design option from the shortcut menu.

 2. **Click the Properties button on the toolbar, or choose View⇨Properties from the Access menu, or right-click the QBE grid and choose the Properties option from the shortcut menu.**

The Properties dialog box for the query opens.

3. **Click the Function Parameters tab.**

The names of existing parameters appear (disabled, because you can't rename them here), followed by each one's data type and an empty box for entering default values.

4. **Type in a default value for each parameter.**

In Figure 2-15, we entered **1/1/04** as the default value for the startdate parameter, and **12/31/04** as the default for the enddate parameter.

5. **Close the Properties dialog box.**

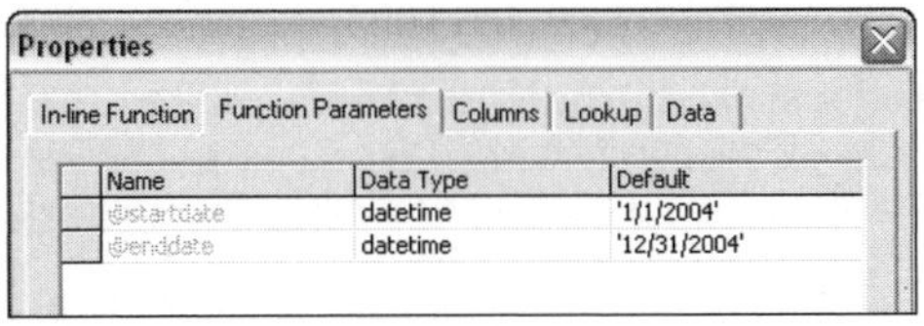

Figure 2-15:
Default values for the sample startdate and enddate parameters.

Name	Data Type	Default
startdate	datetime	'1/1/2004'
enddate	datetime	'12/31/2004'

6. **Save the function, and then run it.**

The Enter Parameter Value dialog box opens. But rather than typing in a value for each parameter, you can just choose the default setting from the drop-down list in the dialog box, and then click OK.

Creating a SQL Server stored procedure

A SQL Server stored procedure is basically the same thing as an Access Jet action query. The methods you use for views in this chapter apply directly to stored procedures. But the column heads vary slightly depending on the type of action query you create. Follow these steps to create a SQL Server stored procedure:

1. **In the Database window, click the Queries button in the Objects list and then double-click the Create Stored Procedure in Designer option in the list that appears in the right pane of the Database window.**

The Design View window and Add Table dialog box open as usual.

2. **Choose the table(s) you want to include in the stored procedure, and then click the Close button in the Add Table dialog box.**

3. **Click the Query drop-down menu on the Access menu, and then click the type of action query you want to create (Make-Table Query, Update Query, Append Query, or Delete Query).**

If you choose the make-table or append query, you are prompted to enter the name of a table to receive the query's output. Go ahead and specify a table name. Column heads in the QBE grid adjust to support the type of action query you select.

4. **Add fields from the Field lists to the QBE grid in the usual manner.**

5. **Enter new values to be placed into fields if you're creating an update query.**

Access action queries are covered in Book III, Chapter 3.

In Figure 2-16, we created a stored procedure that updates the contents of the InvRecPrinted and LabelPrinted fields to true (-1 in the New Value column), where those fields are currently false (0 in the Criteria column).

InvRecPrinted and LabelPrinted field values in the Orders table are each the bit data type, equivalent to a Yes/No field in a Jet table. When using bit fields, enter **0** (a zero) to specify false, a **-1** to specify true.

Save and run the query just as you do a view or function. Don't be alarmed if you see a message indicating that the stored procedure executes successfully but did not return any records. The phrase "did not return records" in this context means "didn't show any records on-screen." Because most action queries change, but don't display data on-screen, you don't see the results. To see the results of the stored procedure, you need to open and scroll through the table that the stored procedure created or modified.

Figure 2-16:
This stored
procedure
changes
the contents
of the
InvRec
Printed and
LabelPrinted
field values
from false
(0) to true
(-1).

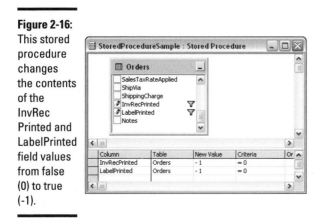

Creating Database Diagrams

In Access, you can use the Relationships window to define default relation-ships between tables, and to enable referential integrity between joined tables. In SQL Server, you use database diagrams to perform similar tasks. But because SQL Server is often used for very large databases, perhaps con-taining hundreds of tables, you're not limited to the one Relationships window found in a Jet database. You can create as many database diagrams as you wish, with each focusing on the tables that make up one component of the overall database.

Creating database diagrams is easy. Follow these steps:

1. **Click the Database Diagrams button in the Objects list of the Database window.**

The list of diagrams appears on the right.

2. **Double-click the Create Database Diagram in Designer option.**

An empty diagram and the Add Table dialog box open.

3. **Click the name of any table you want to add to the diagram, and then click the Add button.**

Repeat Step 3 to add as many tables as you wish to the diagram.

4. **Click the Close button in the Add Table dialog box when you finish adding tables to the diagram.**

A Field list for each selected table appears in the diagram.

The diagram may be larger than the screen, in which case you need to use the scroll bars to move around and see them all. You can move Field lists around by dragging their title bars and size them by dragging their borders. You can also change the magnification of the diagram with the Zoom Modes drop-down menu, allowing you to see as much — or as little — as you wish. Speaking of toolbars, you can use the buttons in the toolbar to view, change, print, and save a diagram.

✦ **Save:** Click to save the diagram and give it a name.

✦ **Print:** Click to print the diagram.

✦ **Add Table:** Click to reopen the Add Table dialog box and add more tables to the diagram.

✦ **Hide Table:** Select any tables you want to hide, and then click this button to hide them.

You can actually edit your database — even delete tables from your database — through the Database Diagram window. To avoid deleting an entire table by accident, make sure you use the Hide Table button on the toolbar to remove a Field list from the diagram only.

✦ **Zoom Modes:** Change the magnification of the diagram to see more or fewer Field lists.

You can also click the four-headed arrow in the lower-right corner of the Database Diagram window to scroll to a specific place in the diagram.

✦ **Table Modes:** Click to choose the level of detail you want to see in the selected table, ranging from minimal detail (table name only) to properties (table name, field names, and field properties).

To select tables to work with in a diagram, use the same techniques you use to select icons in a folder. To select a single table, click it. To select multiple tables, first select one, and then use Ctrl+click or Shift+click to select others. Optionally, you can lasso a group of tables by dragging the mouse pointer. To select all the tables in a diagram, choose Edit⇨Select All or press Ctrl+A.

Joining tables in a diagram

Unlike a query, where you define relationships between tables by dragging field names around, you define relationships between tables in a database diagram by using the Properties dialog box. Click any single table name in the diagram to select it. Then right-click it and choose the Properties option from the shortcut menu. The Properties dialog box for the table opens. Click the Relationships tab in the Properties dialog box, and then click the New button to define a new relationship.

You don't need to change the relationship name that appears after you click the New button. However, you do need to define which table is the primary table (the table on the "one side" of the one-to-many relationship) and the foreign table (the table on the "many side" of the relationship), using the two drop-down list options. Then choose the field name from each table that defines the link. In Figure 2-17, we linked the AddressBook table to the Orders table via a ContactID field.

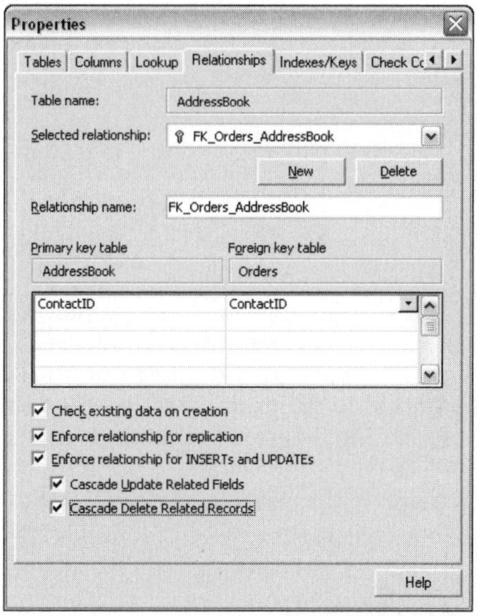

Figure 2-17:
Joining the
Address
Book table
to the
Orders table
in the
Properties
dialog box
for a
database
diagram.

Enforcing referential integrity in database diagrams

After you define a relationship between two tables, you can use the check boxes near the bottom of the Relationships tab of the Properties dialog box to enforce referential integrity. You can also cascade updated and deleted records across tables, just as you can in the Relationships window of a Jet database. In Figure 2-17, we enforced all of the referential integrity options, including the options to cascade updated and deleted records.

For more information on referential integrity, see Book II, Chapter 6.

When you finish defining a relationship, just close the Properties dialog box by clicking its Close (X) button.

In database diagrams, the lines joining tables just go from table to table, not necessarily to specific fields within the tables. But you can drag the lines, and their edges, to lay out the lines however you wish. In Figure 2-18, we set up relationships among four tables, and customized the join lines a bit to resemble the format used in queries and the Relationships window in the Jet database.

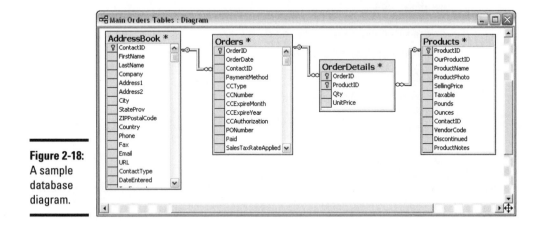

Figure 2-18:
A sample database diagram.

When you finish creating a database diagram, just close its window and save it in the usual manner. To reopen the diagram in the future, click the Database Diagrams button in the Objects list of the Database window, and then double-click the diagram's name in the list that appears in the main pane.

More on Projects and SQL Server

We don't cover every nook and cranny of creating projects and using Microsoft SQL Server in this chapter. To cover everything down to the smallest detail would require a chapter that's at least as large as this entire book!

If you're interested in discovering more about projects and SQL Server, the Access Help feature provides much information. Just search for appropriate buzzwords like *project* or *ADP*. For detailed information on Microsoft SQL Server, the free SQL Server Books Online from Microsoft provide an exhaustive resource. Last we checked, you can download these from www. microsoft.com/sql/techinfo/productdoc/2000/books.asp. But if they're no longer there when you look, just go to search.microsoft.com and search for *SQL+Server+Books+Online*, and you should be able to find the download page in short order.

Chapter 3: Introducing XML

In This Chapter

✔ Discovering XML

✔ Exporting Access data to XML

✔ Importing XML data to Access

✔ Creating live Web reports from projects

XML is a major buzzword (or buzzacronym) that's bandied about by industry pundits. The importance of XML as a technology centers around its development as an Internet standard. Historically, moving information from databases across the Internet has been a "catch-as-catch-can" affair. Businesses had to write custom software to do the job (which is expensive).

XML solves the incompatibility by providing both a single set of rules and a specified language for defining, formatting, and transmitting data. A program merely needs to support XML. XML, in turn, takes care of all the headaches posed by the diversity of the platforms and programs used in today's businesses.

What Is XML?

To understand what XML does, you really need to know a bit about Web page development. *XML* (Extensible Markup Language) is an Internet standard that allows different programs on disparate platforms to exchange information automatically. It fills the gap left by other Web technologies for using database data on the Internet. The broader range of technologies for Web development, whose names you're likely to come across often, is summarized in the following list:

✦ **HTML (Hypertext Markup Language):** The industry standard for formatting text and pictures in Web pages.

✦ **DHTML (Dynamic Hypertext Markup Language):** A fancier version of HTML that allows you to create fancier Web pages. But not all Web browsers can handle DHTML. DHTML isn't considered as much an Internet standard as plain old HTML.

✦ **CSS (Cascading Style Sheets):** An addition to HTML and DHTML that allows for more flexible formatting of text and figures as well as the ability to create generic styles similar to custom styles used in word processing programs, such as Microsoft Word.

✦ **JavaScript:** A programming language that you can write right into a Web page to provide some basic automation that goes beyond the text and picture formatting provided by the other technologies.

✦ **JScript:** The Microsoft implementation of JavaScript, JScript provides all the capabilities of JavaScript plus additional commands and functions supported only by Microsoft Internet Explorer.

✦ **VBScript:** Similar to JScript, but VBScript uses a syntax more like Microsoft Visual Basic than JavaScript (which, in turn, uses a syntax similar to the Java programming language's syntax).

✦ **Java:** An advanced programming language that is used to create any sort of program and creates *applets* (small applications that run inside of Web pages).

As illustrated in Figure 3-1, these particular technologies really focus on the presentation of information on Web pages. XML's role is unique in that it transfers data to and from databases.

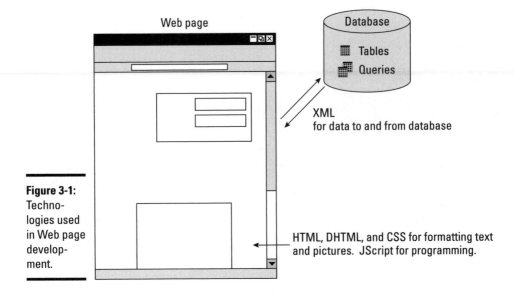

Figure 3-1:
Technologies used in Web page development.

Web page

Database

Tables

Queries

XML
for data to and from database

HTML, DHTML, and CSS for formatting text and pictures. JScript for programming.

Figure 3-1 doesn't tell the complete story, though. Data access pages don't use pure XML to transfer data between pages and tables. Data access pages use Microsoft Office Web components instead. But as XML evolves, more and more Web pages using pure XML to manage data in databases will be possible. For now, you're probably more likely to use XML as a means of transferring data between otherwise incompatible programs.

The group that defines the standards for HTML, CSS, and XML is the World Wide Web Consortium (W3C). For more information on these technologies, you can visit its XML Web site at `www.w3c.org/xml`.

Although you don't need to be an XML expert to use XML with Access, knowing what XML looks like isn't going to hurt you. If you're familiar with HTML, you know that you type the HTML tags inside of angle brackets (< >) to separate the HTML from the regular text. XML uses the same basic approach — tags are written inside of angle brackets. An XML document may look something like this:

```
<?xml version="1.0"?>
<ORDER>
    <CUSTOMER>Tori Pines</CUSTOMER>
    <PRODUCT>
        <ITEM>Lawn Flamingo</ITEM>
        <PRICE>$29.99</PRICE>
        <QUANTITY>1 </QUANTITY>
    </PRODUCT>
</ORDER>
```

Many tags come in pairs to form an *element* — a single chunk of data. The ending tag contains the same name as the starting tag, but includes a slash. For example, `<QUANTITY>` is the starting tag, and `</QUANTITY>` is the ending tag for an element named `QUANTITY`. The text between the tags is the value of the element. The following list looks at the preceding sample XML document in a little more detail:

✦ `<?xml version="1.0"?>` is a *declaration* that states the document contains XML that follows the standards defined for XML Version 1.0.

✦ `<ORDER>` marks the start of the XML document and `</ORDER>` marks the end of the XML document. The name is arbitrary. You can name your document anything you wish by using a different word in the start and end tags.

✦ `<CUSTOMER>Tori Pines</CUSTOMER>` describes a single element of data named CUSTOMER. Think of CUSTOMER as the name of a field in a table, and Tori Pines as the content of that field from one record in the table. Or, in this case, the name of the person who placed the order being described by the document.

✦ `<PRODUCT>` and `</PRODUCT>` mark the beginning and end of an element named PRODUCT. The product element is further broken down into facts about the item ordered, including its name between the `<ITEM>`. . . `</ITEM>` tags, its price between the `<PRICE>`. . .`</PRICE>` tags, and the quantity ordered between the `<QUANTITY>` . . . `</QUANTITY>` tags.

HTML writers beware! Unlike HTML, XML is case-sensitive. If you define an element named CUSTOMER (all uppercase) in the start tag, the end tag must also contain CUSTOMER in all uppercase letters.

XML would almost be easy to learn if that were all there was. The preceding sample XML document, though, really just shows XML *base* tags. An entirely separate component, called XSL, is used to format, manage, and transform data among documents.

XSL: Formatting and transforming data

XSL is roughly the equivalent of CSS (Cascading Style Sheets), which is used to format text and pictures on Web pages. *XSL* (Extensible Stylesheet Language) is the language for defining XML style sheets, which in turn, defines how to display a given XML document. While XML defines what the data is, XSL defines how it looks. XSL actually consists of three separate technologies:

✦ **XSLT (XML Transformations):** A language for transforming XML data to other formats and for transmitting data between different programs. You can use XSLT to take raw XML data and transform it into a Web page, or to transmit data from one organization's database to another organization's database. A file that defines how data is transmitted is called an *XML transform.*

✦ **XPath (XML Path Language):** A language for accessing pieces of XML documents and for providing tools for isolating and manipulating strings (text), numbers, and Boolean (Yes/No) data.

✦ **XSL-FO (XSL Formatting Objects):** As the name implies, a set of tools for defining the exact format of data. Especially used for printing data on paper with page numbers, specific margins, and so forth.

Like HTML and XML, XSL contains code within angle brackets (< >). The contents of XSL tags show the prefix xsl: or fo: (for *format*), which helps to make them easily recognizable:

```
<xsl:template match="/">
<fo:root>
    <fo:layout-master-set>
        <fo:simple-page-master master-name="my-page">
            <fo:region-body margin="1cm" />
        </fo:simple-page-master>
    </fo:layout-master-set>
    <fo:page-sequence master-reference="my-page">
        <fo:flow flow-name="xsl-region-body">
            <xsl:apply-templates />
        </fo:flow>
    </fo:page-sequence>
</fo:root>
</xsl:template>
```

XML Schemas (XSD)

Another component of XML is the XML Schema. A *schema* describes the structure of XML data in a format that all XML-enabled programs can read and use. More specifically, the schema tells programs the data types, rules, and limitations for using the data. Using a schema to clearly define the data ensures that any program that attempts to read or write XML data doesn't break any rules along the way.

Like other components of XML, define XML Schemas using tags enclosed in angle brackets. The prefix for schema tags is *xsd: (XML Schema Definition)* as in this chunk of code:

```
<xsd:complexType name="USAaddress">
    <xsd:sequence>
        <xsd:element name="name" type="xsd:string"/>
        <xsd:element name="address" type="xsd:string"/>
        <xsd:element name="city" type="xsd:string"/>
        <xsd:element name="state" type="xsd:string"/>
        <xsd:element name="zip" type="xsd:decimal"/>
    </xsd:sequence>
</xsd:complexType>
```

So what?

You don't have to sit down and learn XML — or XSL or XSD — right now, because Access automatically creates everything you need. Picturing something in your mind when you hear those oft-used acronyms is helpful, though. Also, when you look behind the scenes at XML files created by Access, the code won't look like totally meaningless gobbledygook. (Just mostly meaningless gobbledygook.) But that's enough about XML, XST, and XML Schema details.

Exporting Access Data to XML

For those of you already familiar with XML in Access 2002 (all two of you), let us first point out that the enhanced XML support in Access 2003 allows you to specify XSL transform files when importing data from, or exporting data to, XML. When importing, the transform applies to data as soon as importation starts, before a new table is created or an existing table is appended to.

When exporting data to XML, you can include any predefined filters or sort order when exporting data to XML. You can export just the data, just the schema, or both. Also, if a table contains lookup values stored in a separate database, you can include that data in the exportation.

You can easily export any table, query, form, or report to XML files from a regular Access database (.mdb file) or an Access project and Microsoft SQL Server database (.adp file). When you export a form or report, you actually export the data behind the form or report (you export the data from the form or report's underlying table or query). Regardless of which type of object you export, though, the procedure is the same.

The first step is to click the Tables, Queries, Forms, or Reports button in the Objects list in the Database window and select the item you want to export from the list that appears in the right pane of the window. If you want to export all the data that the object stores, you can just right-click the object's name and choose the Export option from the shortcut menu. Then skip the next paragraph.

If you don't want to export a complete table or query, you need to export data from a table or query. Open the table or query, and then do any of the following:

✦ If you want to export a single record only, select that record.

✦ If you want to filter records for export, apply a filter to the records now.

✦ If you want to specify a sort order for the records, arrange the records into that order now.

After you select the records, choose File⇨Export from the Access menu.

The Export dialog box opens. Navigate to the folder in which you want to store the exported data. Choose the XML (*.xml) option from the Save As Type drop-down menu, as shown in Figure 3-2.

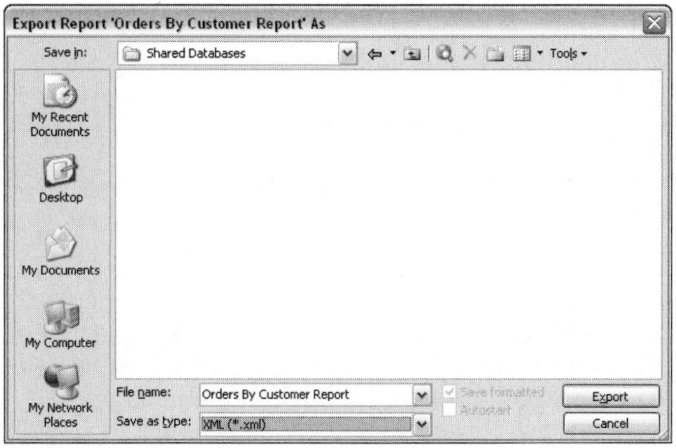

Figure 3-2:
Setting up
the Export
dialog box
to export a
report to
XML.

Click the Export (or Export All) button in the dialog box, and the Export XML dialog box opens, as shown in Figure 3-3. You have a choice of exporting only data to an XML file, exporting a schema of your data to an XSD file, exporting the presentation of your data to an XSL file, or any combination thereof.

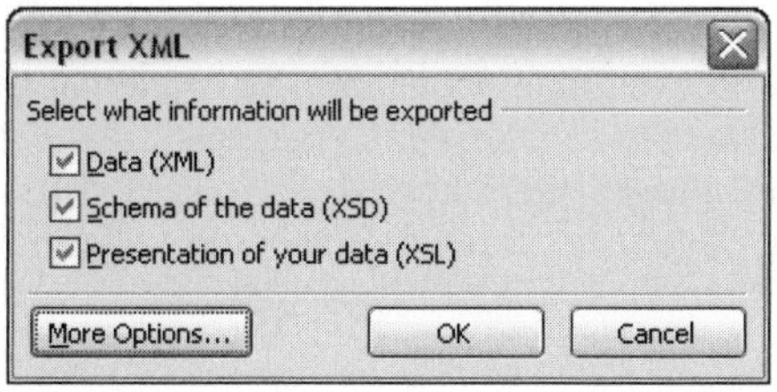

Figure 3-3:
The Export
XML dialog
box.

Optionally, you can further refine your selections by clicking the More Options button. Clicking the More Options button expands the Export XML dialog box to . . . show more options! Note the three tabs across the top of the dialog box: Data (shown in Figure 3-4), Schema, and Presentation.

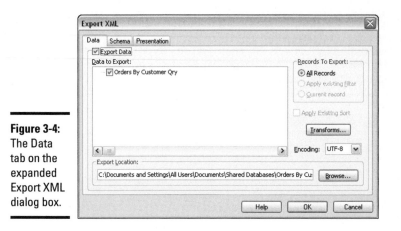

Figure 3-4:
The Data
tab on the
expanded
Export XML
dialog box.

Choosing XML data options

On the Data tab, you can choose to export all records, filtered records, or the current record. Also, you can opt to apply the sort order that's currently applied to the object. (However, those options are dimmed if you export something to which those options don't apply, such as an entire report.)

If you previously defined relationships between tables in the Relationships window in Access or the Database Diagram window in SQL Server, you can choose whether or not to export data from related tables as well. Click the + sign next to any table name to see the name of any related table. Select the check mark that appears next to any table name to include that table's data in your export.

The Transforms button allows you to choose from any custom XML transforms that you may have written or acquired. If you export data that is imported into some esoteric database program, the owner of that database may supply you with a transform file. You can then click the Transforms button and choose that transform file. Likewise, if you need to use a special encoding for that esoteric database, you can choose one from the Encoding drop-down list.

Choosing XML Schema options

The Schema tab, shown in Figure 3-5, allows you to choose options for exporting a schema file for your object. You can choose to include or ignore primary key and index information. You can also choose whether you want the schema information to be embedded in the XML data document, or stored as a separate file. How you choose options here depends on the program to which the exported data is later imported.

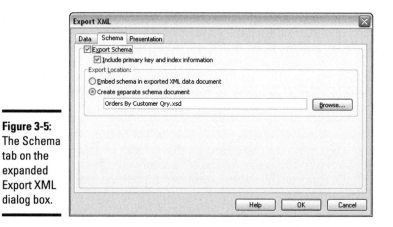

Figure 3-5:
The Schema
tab on the
expanded
Export XML
dialog box.

Choosing XML presentation options

The Presentation tab, shown in Figure 3-6, provides options for defining an
XSL file. You can choose to export to Client (HTML), which can be read by
any Web browser. If you plan to put the XSL file on a Web server that supports Active Server Pages, you can choose the Server (ASP) option instead.

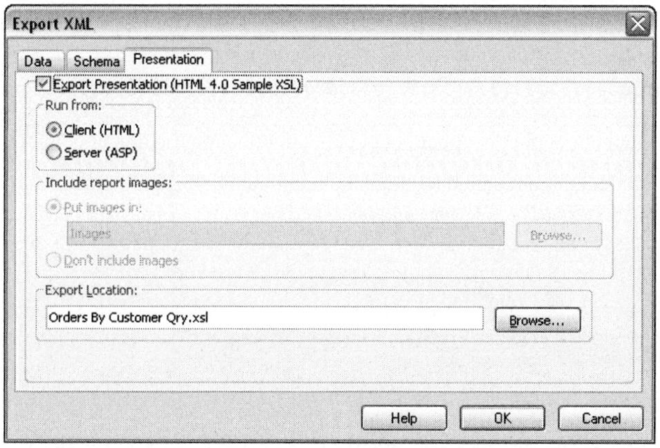

Figure 3-6:
The
Presenta-
tion tab
on the
expanded
Export XML
dialog box.

If the data you export includes pictures, you can choose to export those
pictures or just ignore them. If you opt to include images, you can specify
the name of the folder in which the images are placed.

Choosing to export a presentation file actually generates two files. One is an .xsl file, which includes all the XSLT code needed to define how the data is presented. The second file is an .htm file — a relatively plain and simple Web page. That Web page is a "snapshot" of the data at the moment of exportation, not live data that's connected to the database. However, the .htm file opens in Internet Explorer to reveal the actual data from the table or query, not just a bunch of XML tags and raw data.

When you finish making your selections, click the OK button. The exportation may only take a few seconds, depending on the amount of data you export. When done, you return to Access. You won't see any changes in your Access database, but the exported files are in whatever folder you specified during the exportation process.

Viewing the XML files

To view the XML files that Access created, you need to browse to the folder, via Windows, to which you exported those files. You see an icon for each file, as shown in Figure 3-7.

Figure 3-7:
Files created by exporting an Access object to XML.

If you don't see file name extensions in your Explorer window, but want to, choose Tools➪Folder Options from the Explorer menu. On the View tab, clear the check mark next to the Hide Extensions For Known File Types option and then click OK.

You can open any file by double-clicking its icon. Most files open in Internet Explorer, which shows a color-coded version of the file. (To open the .xsd file in Internet Explorer, right-click its icon and choose Open With⇨Internet Explorer from the shortcut menu.) Optionally, you can right-click any icon and choose the Open With option to open the file in a text editor, such as NotePad. Figure 3-8 shows an XML data document (the .xml file). If you scroll through the document, you see why writing XML when you use Access to manage your data is not important. Every bit of XML is written into the document for you!

The %20 and _x0020_ characters you see sprinkled throughout a file are just the XML codes for a blank space.

None of the files created provide the interactive capabilities that data access pages offer. But anyone with an XML-enabled program can import the data in those XML files by following the appropriate procedures for that particular program.

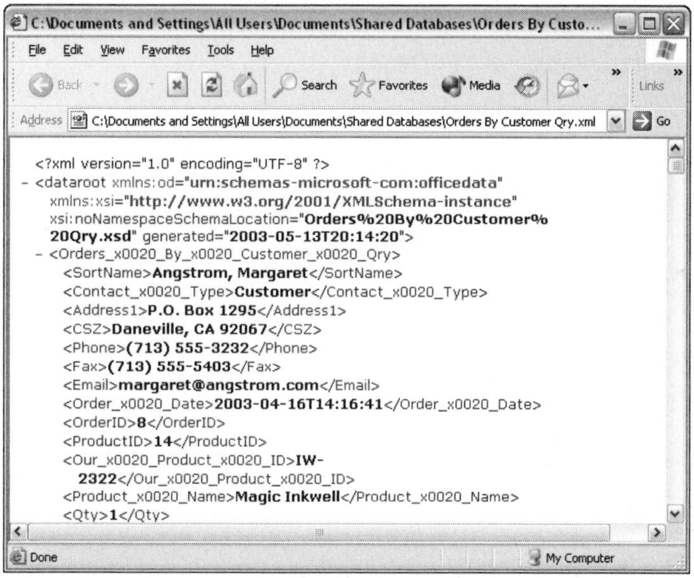

Figure 3-8:
An XML document created by Microsoft Access 2003.

```
C:\Documents and Settings\All Users\Documents\Shared Databases\Orders By Custo...
File   Edit   View   Favorites   Tools   Help

Back              x   Search   Favorites   Media              Links

Address   C:\Documents and Settings\All Users\Documents\Shared Databases\Orders By Customer Qry.xml        Go

  <?xml version="1.0" encoding="UTF-8" ?>
- <dataroot xmlns:od="urn:schemas-microsoft-com:officedata"
    xmlns:xsi="http://www.w3.org/2001/XMLSchema-instance"
    xsi:noNamespaceSchemaLocation="Orders%20By%20Customer%
    20Qry.xsd" generated="2003-05-13T20:14:20">
-   <Orders_x0020_By_x0020_Customer_x0020_Qry>
      <SortName>Angstrom, Margaret</SortName>
      <Contact_x0020_Type>Customer</Contact_x0020_Type>
      <Address1>P.O. Box 1295</Address1>
      <CSZ>Daneville, CA 92067</CSZ>
      <Phone>(713) 555-3232</Phone>
      <Fax>(713) 555-5403</Fax>
      <Email>margaret@angstrom.com</Email>
      <Order_x0020_Date>2003-04-16T14:16:41</Order_x0020_Date>
      <OrderID>8</OrderID>
      <ProductID>14</ProductID>
      <Our_x0020_Product_x0020_ID>IW-
        2322</Our_x0020_Product_x0020_ID>
      <Product_x0020_Name>Magic Inkwell</Product_x0020_Name>
      <Qty>1</Qty>

Done                                                      My Computer
```

Importing XML Data to Access

If you have an XML-enabled program that contains data you need to export to Access, you can follow whatever procedures that program provides to create some XML files. Then you can import those files to a regular Access database (.mdb file) or project and SQL Server database (.adp file). Follow these steps:

1. **Open the Access database (or project) into which you want to import data or create a new, blank database.**

2. **Choose File⇨Get External Data⇨Import from the Access menu.**

   The Import dialog box opens.

3. **Choose XML (*.xml;*.xsd) from the Files of Type drop-down list.**

4. **Navigate to the folder in which you placed the XML file(s).**

5. **Click the name of the .xml file that contains the data you want to import, and then click the Import button.**

   The Import XML dialog box, as shown in Figure 3-9, opens. Now you have some choices to make:

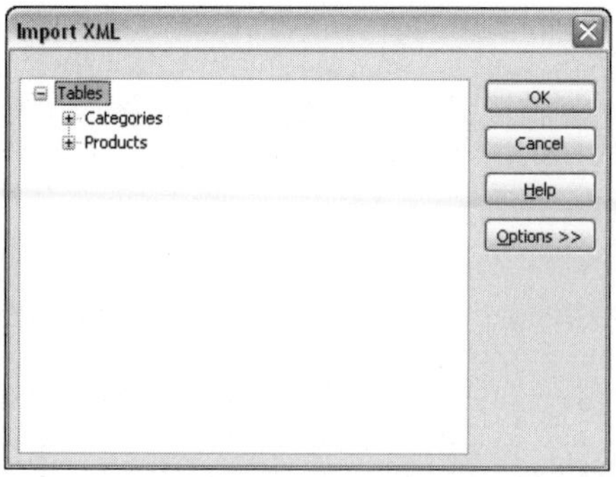

Figure 3-9:
The Import
XML dialog
box.

- If you want to import all the data from the tables shown in the dialog box to new tables, skip to Step 6 now.

- If you want to append imported data to existing tables in your database, or if you want to import the table structures only, click the Options button and make your selections from the options at the bottom of the dialog box.

- If the data provider included a transform file (.xsl file), click the Options button and then click the Transform button. Click the Add button, click the name of the .xsl file to use, and click the Add button. Then click OK.

6. **Click the OK button in the Import XML dialog box.**

   You see a message on-screen indicating when the import completes. Click the OK button to close the message.

To view the imported tables, click the Tables button in the Objects list of the Database window. Then double-click any imported table name in the list that appears in the main pane to view its contents.

Creating Live Web Reports from ADPs

If you have access to an Internet Information Services Web server, and your data is stored in an Access project (.adp), you can use XML export to create live reports. A *live report* is one that gets its data on the fly, the moment a user downloads the report — a very handy way to ensure that users always get up-to-the-minute data from your SQL Server tables.

This approach works only with project files, and only when SQL Server is accessible to the Web server. Also, SQL Server 7 and earlier versions don't support this approach. To provide live Web reports or interaction with your data via the Web using an Access Jet database, create data access pages instead. You must have access to a Web server that supports Microsoft Access. Some Web Presence Providers, such as WinSave (www.winsave.com) provide such Web server space.

See Chapter 1 of this book for the goods on creating data access pages.

Exactly how you organize folders and upload data to your company's Web server, or your Web Presence Provider's server, is up to the administrators of those networks. If in doubt, your best bet is to contact the people who administrate the server for assistance. But, assuming you know how to get things to your server and you have an Access project (.adp) file to work with, you create a live Web report with the following steps:

1. **Open your project in the usual manner.**

2. **Click the View or Report button in the Objects list of the Database window, right-click the name of the view or report you wish to export to the Web, and then choose the Export option from the shortcut menu.**

   The Export Report dialog box opens (refer to Figure 3-2).

3. **Navigate to the folder on the Web server in which you want to place the report.**

4. **Choose the XML (*.xml) option from the Save As Type drop-down list.**

   Optionally, you can enter a new file name for the data to be exported. Because users may have to type this name, and spaces don't work well in URLs, try to think up a short but meaningful name that doesn't contain any blank spaces.

5. **Click the Export button.**

   The Export XML dialog box opens (refer to Figure 3-3).

6. **Click the More Options button.**

   The Export XML dialog box expands, shown in Figure 3-10.

7. **On the Data tab, select the Live Data option, and enter the path to the Web server virtual directory and the Export path.**

   If you don't know the exact paths to use, be sure to ask your network administrator or Web Presence Provider. Simply copying the paths shown in Figure 3-10 won't work.

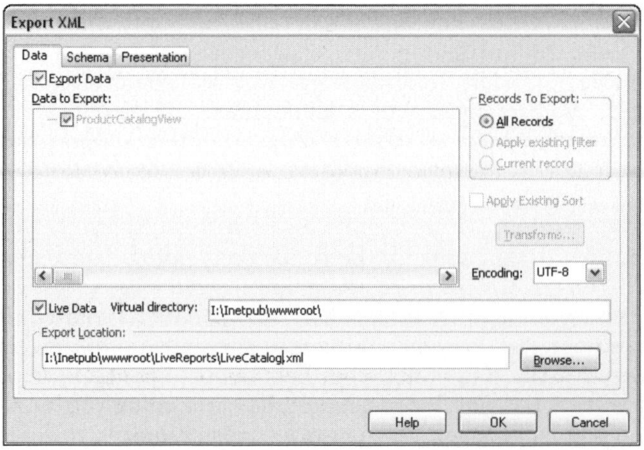

Figure 3-10:
Specifying the live data for a project report exported to a Web server.

8. **Click the Presentation tab, and choose the Export Presentation (HTML 4.0 Sample XSL) option.**

9. **In the Run From section, select the Server (ASP) option, as in Figure 3-11.**

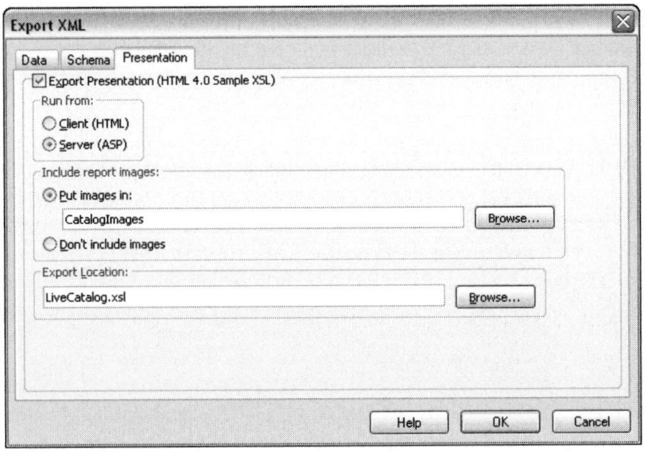

Figure 3-11:
The
Presenta-
tion tab for
exporting a
live Web
report to a
Web server.

10. **If your report includes images, choose whether to include images in the exported report.**

If you opt to export images, enter a folder name in the Put Images In text box.

11. **Click OK.**

To view the live Web report from your Web browser, enter the path to the Web server's virtual directory and the name of the page, using the syntax `http://WebServerName/virtualDirectoryName/pageName.asp`.

XML Web Services

If you have any exposure to the computer industry press at all, you probably have come across the term *Web services* at least once. Web services has been talked about incessantly in the trade press for years, but is only now coming to fruition. In fact, as we write this book, the whole Web services concept is just starting to show up in the real world, though it hasn't quite reached a point where it's truly ready for prime time.

The idea behind Web services is this: Rather than buying a program to do some little job, you just connect to some service on the World Wide Web that can do that job for you. For example, you can get current stock quotes, find zip codes, verify e-mail addresses, get up-to-the-minute weather reports, compare prices for an item from multiple Web sites, and translate text from one language to another through Web services. You can rig things so all these things take place automatically as you work with data in your Access databases.

By the time you read this book, chances are that Web services will be much further along in their evolution, and ready to use in your Access database. Web services use XML as a means of moving data around on the Internet. You may have to wrangle with some XML to use a Web service in your database. For current information on using Web services in Access, consider visiting `search.microsoft.com` and searching for *Access+XML+Web+Services*.

Appendix: Installing Microsoft Access

You need your Microsoft Office or Microsoft Access CD, and the 25-character Product Key that came with it. You find the Product Key on the yellow sticker, included with the rest of the packaging that came with your product. To get started with the installation, follow these steps:

1. **If you're currently using any programs, close them and save your work.**

2. **Insert your Microsoft Office or Microsoft Access CD into your computer's CD or DVD drive.**

   Wait a minute for the installation program to start. If no program starts automatically, choose Start⇨My Computer, right-click the icon for your CD or DVD drive, and choose the AutoPlay option from the shortcut menu.

3. **After a brief delay, the installation program prompts you to enter your Product Key (see Figure A-1). Go ahead and type in that information, and then click Next.**

Figure A-1:
Type in your Product Key to install Office or Access.

In the boxes below, type your 25-character Product Key. You will find this number on the sticker on the back of the CD case or on your Certificate of Authenticity.

Product Key: ▢-▢-▢-▢-▢

4. **On the next page, type in your name, initials, and the name of your company (these are optional). Then click Next.**

5. **The End-User License Agreement (EULA) appears next, containing the usual legalese about licensing. Read the agreement (yeah, sure), choose "I accept the terms in the License Agreement" and click Next.**

6. **The next page asks how you want to install the program. For simplicity, you can choose the Complete Install option, click the Next button, and skip to Step 7.**

If you're installing Office and choose the Custom Install option, you are prompted to choose which programs you want to install. Make sure you choose Microsoft Access. You can then select the Choose Advanced Customization options check box and click Next.

If you opt for the advanced customization options, click the + sign next to Microsoft Access For Windows to expand that list. To make life simple, click any option and choose the Run from My Computer option, as illustrated in Figure A-2. You don't need to install Database Replication though, unless you plan in replicating a database across multiple computers in a network (not recommended).

Figure A-2:
Advanced
installation
options
allow you
to pick and
choose
optional
components.

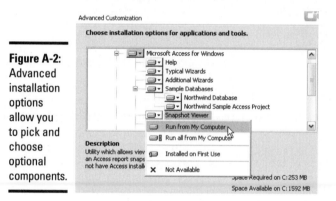

7. **Click the Install button and wait.**

You may be waiting a while. When the installation finishes, you see a message telling you so, and you have a couple of last options.

8. **If you have Internet access and are online, choose the Check the Web for Updates and Additional Downloads option, as shown in Figure A-3.**

It's not vital, but making sure you get anything new that's come out since Access was first released is worth checking.

9. **Leave the Delete Installation Files option unselected.**

Don't select it unless your hard disk is getting very near full, and you want to hang on to the small amount of disk space that otherwise is used by the installation and maintenance files.

10. **Click the Finish button.**

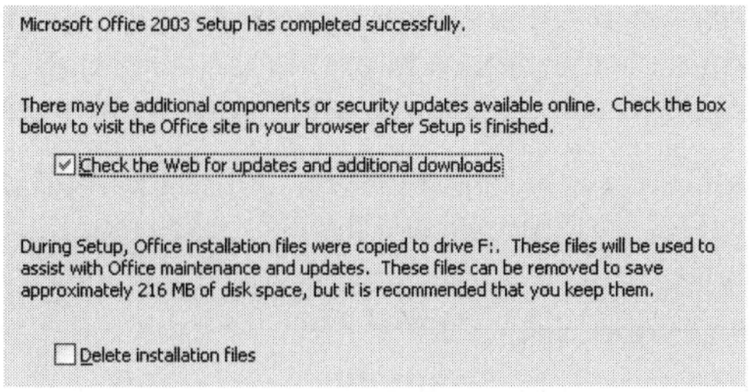

Microsoft Office 2003 Setup has completed successfully.

There may be additional components or security updates available online. Check the box below to visit the Office site in your browser after Setup is finished.

☑ Check the Web for updates and additional downloads

During Setup, Office installation files were copied to drive F:. These files will be used to assist with Office maintenance and updates. These files can be removed to save approximately 216 MB of disk space, but it is recommended that you keep them.

☐ Delete installation files

Figure A-3:
Two last options at the end of installation.

Note that if you did choose the option to check the Web for updates and additional downloads, your Web browser runs and you see the Office Update Web site. If any new or updated files are available when you get there, you can choose which ones you want to download and install.

Be sure to store your original CD and Product Key in a safe place where you can easily find them in the future. You just never know when a bad disk crash or nasty virus will force you to reinstall Access from scratch!

Activating Access

Microsoft now requires product activation, which is a process designed to prevent people from installing their products on multiple computers. The first time you start Access (or some other Office application program), you are prompted to activate the product. Just go ahead and follow the instructions on-screen to activate.

When Microsoft came out with product activation, many people were alarmed that Microsoft would spy on them, correlating their Access usage with their personal information, and other appalling privacy invasions. As it turns out, product activation doesn't do any of those things. Product activation is unconnected with product registration, which is when you give Microsoft your name and address. Activation just connects your Office Product Key with your specific computer, so that no one else can install your Office license on his or her computer. Go ahead and activate Office with no worries!

Repair, Reinstall, or Uninstall Access

If something bad happens to your hard disk and you can't start Access on your computer, you may have to reinstall or repair it. Or, if you opted to do a minimal or custom installation of Access, you may later change your mind and want to install some component you previously declined. No matter what the issue, you need to reinstall some stuff from your original CD.

If you chose the Not Installed option for a component, you are not prompted to install it on the spot. You need to install that component manually. Here's how, using Windows XP as the sample operating system. (The procedure is similar in all versions of Windows.)

1. **Close any open programs and save your work.**

2. **Click the Windows Start button and choose Control Panel.**

   The Control Panel window appears.

3. **Open the Add Or Remove Programs icon.**

4. **Click the Microsoft Office or Microsoft Access installed program.**

5. **Click the Change button.**

You see the options shown in Figure A-4. Just choose whichever option best describes what you want to do, and then follow the instructions on-screen.

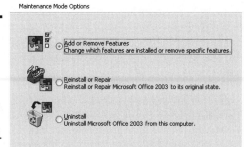

Figure A-4:
Options to repair, reinstall, uninstall, or add/remove Office components.

Index

Numbers & Symbols

3-D bar chart, 427
3-D Column chart, 427
3-D cone bar chart, 427
3-D cylinder bar chart, 427
3-D effects
  charts, 438
3-D pyramid bar chart, 427

A

abbreviations, 46–47
Access
  activating, 765
  applications compatible
    with, 129–130
  compatible versions, 129
  function procedures, 593
  installing, 763–765
  menus, 20–24
  opening databases from
    previous versions, 26
  reinstalling, 765–766
  repairing, 765–766
  running, 19
  running sub procedures
    from, 590–592
  sample databases, 26–28
  turning down security
    setting, 461
  uninstalling, 765–766
  versions, 1
Access 2.0, 26
Access 95, 26
Access 97, 26
  supporting users, 502
Access 97 file format, 61
Access 2000, 26
Access 2000 file format,
  60–61
Access 2002, 26

Access 2002 file format,
  60–61
Access 2003 All-in-One Web
  site, 7
Access object library, 559
(The) Access Web site, 31
Access window
  task pane, 20–24
  toolbar, 20–24
  windows, 25
AccessObject type, 640, 644
acCurViewDesign constant,
  642
action queries, 14, 25, 175,
  618
  append query, 241
  backups before running,
    242
  creation of, 241–244
  delete query, 241
  executing action, 243
  make-table query, 242
  opening, 243
  recognizing, 243
  records matching criteria,
    243
  Run button, 242–243
  running from VBA,
    656–658
  safely creating, 243–244
  selecting type, 242
  update query, 242
  View button, 242–243
  viewing records, 244
actions
  arguments for, 451,
    453–454
  changing properties of
    form control, 471–473
  macros, 451, 452–453
Active Server Pages, 141
Add Procedure dialog box,
  575–576
Add Table dialog box, 735
Add to Group option, 508

Add to Group⇨New Group
  command, 509
Add-in Manager, 494
add-ins, 494
  application-specific add-
    ins, 495
  builders, 495
  COM (Component Object
    Model) add-in, 495
  creation of, 495–496
  deleting, 494
  installing, 494
  managing, 494
  menu add-in, 495
  wizards, 495
addition, 209
Addition (+) operator, 155,
  208, 222
Admin user, 527, 537
Admins group, 527–528, 533
ADO (ActiveX Data
  Objects) object model,
  647–648
ADODB (ActiveX Data
  Objects) library, 559
.adp extension, 726
.adp files, 163
advanced filter, 123
Advanced Filter Sort
  window, 121
Advanced Filter/Sort
  feature, 120–123
Advanced Filter/Sort filter,
  115
Advanced Filter/Sort
  queries, 174
After Update event, 464,
  633
After Update property, 473
aggregate functions,
  365–367, 396
aggregating data, 264–273
All Programs⇨Microsoft
  Office Access 2003
  command, 19

B

U

Notes

FOR DUMMIES®

The easy way to get more done and have more fun

PERSONAL FINANCE & BUSINESS

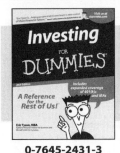

Investing
0-7645-2431-3

Home Buying
0-7645-5331-3

Grant Writing
0-7645-5307-0

Also available:

Accounting For Dummies
(0-7645-5314-3)

Business Plans Kit For Dummies
(0-7645-5365-8)

Managing For Dummies
(1-5688-4858-7)

Mutual Funds For Dummies
(0-7645-5329-1)

QuickBooks All-in-One Desk Reference For Dummies
(0-7645-1963-8)

Resumes For Dummies
(0-7645-5471-9)

Small Business Kit For Dummies
(0-7645-5093-4)

Starting an eBay Business For Dummies
(0-7645-1547-0)

Taxes For Dummies 2003
(0-7645-5475-1)

HOME, GARDEN, FOOD & WINE

Feng Shui
0-7645-5295-3

Gardening
0-7645-5130-2

Cooking
0-7645-5250-3

Also available:

Bartending For Dummies
(0-7645-5051-9)

Christmas Cooking For Dummies
(0-7645-5407-7)

Cookies For Dummies
(0-7645-5390-9)

Diabetes Cookbook For Dummies
(0-7645-5230-9)

Grilling For Dummies
(0-7645-5076-4)

Home Maintenance For Dummies
(0-7645-5215-5)

Slow Cookers For Dummies
(0-7645-5240-6)

Wine For Dummies
(0-7645-5114-0)

FITNESS, SPORTS, HOBBIES & PETS

Fitness
0-7645-5167-1

Golf
0-7645-5146-9

Guitar
0-7645-5106-X

Also available:

Cats For Dummies
(0-7645-5275-9)

Chess For Dummies
(0-7645-5003-9)

Dog Training For Dummies
(0-7645-5286-4)

Labrador Retrievers For Dummies
(0-7645-5281-3)

Martial Arts For Dummies
(0-7645-5358-5)

Piano For Dummies
(0-7645-5105-1)

Pilates For Dummies
(0-7645-5397-6)

Power Yoga For Dummies
(0-7645-5342-9)

Puppies For Dummies
(0-7645-5255-4)

Quilting For Dummies
(0-7645-5118-3)

Rock Guitar For Dummies
(0-7645-5356-9)

Weight Training For Dummies
(0-7645-5168-X)

Available wherever books are sold.
Go to www.dummies.com or call 1-877-762-2974 to order direct

 WILEY

FOR DUMMIES®

A world of resources to help you grow

TRAVEL

Italy FOR DUMMIES
0-7645-5453-0

Hawaii FOR DUMMIES
0-7645-5438-7

Walt Disney World & Orlando FOR DUMMIES
0-7645-5444-1

Also available:

America's National Parks For Dummies
(0-7645-6204-5)

Caribbean For Dummies
(0-7645-5445-X)

Cruise Vacations For Dummies 2003
(0-7645-5459-X)

Europe For Dummies
(0-7645-5456-5)

Ireland For Dummies
(0-7645-6199-5)

France For Dummies
(0-7645-6292-4)

Las Vegas For Dummies
(0-7645-5448-4)

London For Dummies
(0-7645-5416-6)

Mexico's Beach Resorts For Dummies
(0-7645-6262-2)

Paris For Dummies
(0-7645-5494-8)

RV Vacations For Dummies
(0-7645-5443-3)

EDUCATION & TEST PREPARATION

Spanish FOR DUMMIES
0-7645-5194-9

Algebra FOR DUMMIES
0-7645-5325-9

U.S. History FOR DUMMIES
0-7645-5249-X

Also available:

The ACT For Dummies
(0-7645-5210-4)

Chemistry For Dummies
(0-7645-5430-1)

English Grammar For Dummies
(0-7645-5322-4)

French For Dummies
(0-7645-5193-0)

GMAT For Dummies
(0-7645-5251-1)

Inglés Para Dummies
(0-7645-5427-1)

Italian For Dummies
(0-7645-5196-5)

Research Papers For Dummies
(0-7645-5426-3)

SAT I For Dummies
(0-7645-5472-7)

U.S. History For Dummies
(0-7645-5249-X)

World History For Dummies
(0-7645-5242-2)

HEALTH, SELF-HELP & SPIRITUALITY

Diabetes FOR DUMMIES
0-7645-5154-X

Sex FOR DUMMIES
0-7645-5302-X

Parenting FOR DUMMIES
0-7645-5418-2

Also available:

The Bible For Dummies
(0-7645-5296-1)

Controlling Cholesterol For Dummies
(0-7645-5440-9)

Dating For Dummies
(0-7645-5072-1)

Dieting For Dummies
(0-7645-5126-4)

High Blood Pressure For Dummies
(0-7645-5424-7)

Judaism For Dummies
(0-7645-5299-6)

Menopause For Dummies
(0-7645-5458-1)

Nutrition For Dummies
(0-7645-5180-9)

Potty Training For Dummies
(0-7645-5417-4)

Pregnancy For Dummies
(0-7645-5074-8)

Rekindling Romance For Dummies
(0-7645-5303-8)

Religion For Dummies
(0-7645-5264-3)

Available wherever books are sold. Go to www.dummies.com or call 1-877-762-2974 to order direct

FOR DUMMIES®

Plain-English solutions for everyday challenges

HOME & BUSINESS COMPUTER BASICS

0-7645-0838-5

0-7645-1663-9

0-7645-1548-9

Also available:

Excel 2002 All-in-One Desk Reference For Dummies (0-7645-1794-5)

Office XP 9-in-1 Desk Reference For Dummies (0-7645-0819-9)

PCs All-in-One Desk Reference For Dummies (0-7645-0791-5)

Troubleshooting Your PC For Dummies (0-7645-1669-8)

Upgrading & Fixing PCs For Dummies (0-7645-1665-5)

Windows XP For Dummies (0-7645-0893-8)

Windows XP For Dummies Quick Reference (0-7645-0897-0)

Word 2002 For Dummies (0-7645-0839-3)

INTERNET & DIGITAL MEDIA

0-7645-0894-6

0-7645-1642-6

0-7645-1664-7

Also available:

CD and DVD Recording For Dummies (0-7645-1627-2)

Digital Photography All-in-One Desk Reference For Dummies (0-7645-1800-3)

eBay For Dummies (0-7645-1642-6)

Genealogy Online For Dummies (0-7645-0807-5)

Internet All-in-One Desk Reference For Dummies (0-7645-1659-0)

Internet For Dummies Quick Reference (0-7645-1645-0)

Internet Privacy For Dummies (0-7645-0846-6)

Paint Shop Pro For Dummies (0-7645-2440-2)

Photo Retouching & Restoration For Dummies (0-7645-1662-0)

Photoshop Elements For Dummies (0-7645-1675-2)

Scanners For Dummies (0-7645-0783-4)

Get smart! Visit www.dummies.com

- **Find listings of even more Dummies titles**

- **Browse online articles, excerpts, and how-to's**

- **Sign up for daily or weekly e-mail tips**

- **Check out Dummies fitness videos and other products**

- **Order from our online bookstore**

Available wherever books are sold. Go to www.dummies.com or call 1-877-762-2974 to order direct

FOR DUMMIES

Helping you expand your horizons and realize your potential

GRAPHICS & WEB SITE DEVELOPMENT

Photoshop 7 For Dummies
0-7645-1651-5

Creating Web Pages For Dummies
0-7645-1643-4

Macromedia Flash MX For Dummies
0-7645-0895-4

Also available:

Adobe Acrobat 5 PDF
For Dummies
(0-7645-1652-3)
ASP.NET For Dummies
(0-7645-0866-0)
ColdFusion MX For Dummies
(0-7645-1672-8)
Dreamweaver MX For
Dummies
(0-7645-1630-2)
FrontPage 2002 For Dummies
(0-7645-0821-0)

HTML 4 For Dummies
(0-7645-0723-0)
Illustrator 10 For Dummies
(0-7645-3636-2)
PowerPoint 2002 For
Dummies
(0-7645-0817-2)
Web Design For Dummies
(0-7645-0823-7)

PROGRAMMING & DATABASES

C++ For Dummies
0-7645-0746-X

Visual Studio .NET All-in-One Desk Reference For Dummies
0-7645-1626-4

XML For Dummies
0-7645-1657-4

Also available:

Access 2002 For Dummies
(0-7645-0818-0)
Beginning Programming
For Dummies
(0-7645-0835-0)
Crystal Reports 9 For
Dummies
(0-7645-1641-8)
Java & XML For Dummies
(0-7645-1658-2)
Java 2 For Dummies
(0-7645-0765-6)

JavaScript For Dummies
(0-7645-0633-1)
Oracle9i For Dummies
(0-7645-0880-6)
Perl For Dummies
(0-7645-0776-1)
PHP and MySQL For
Dummies
(0-7645-1650-7)
SQL For Dummies
(0-7645-0737-0)
Visual Basic .NET For
Dummies
(0-7645-0867-9)

LINUX, NETWORKING & CERTIFICATION

Red Hat Linux 7.3 For Dummies
0-7645-1545-4

TCP/IP For Dummies
0-7645-1760-0

Networking For Dummies
0-7645-0772-9

Also available:

A+ Certification For Dummies
(0-7645-0812-1)
CCNP All-in-One Certification
For Dummies
(0-7645-1648-5)
Cisco Networking For
Dummies
(0-7645-1668-X)
CISSP For Dummies
(0-7645-1670-1)
CIW Foundations For
Dummies
(0-7645-1635-3)

Firewalls For Dummies
(0-7645-0884-9)
Home Networking For
Dummies
(0-7645-0857-1)
Red Hat Linux All-in-One
Desk Reference For Dummies
(0-7645-2442-9)
UNIX For Dummies
(0-7645-0419-3)

Available wherever books are sold.
Go to www.dummies.com or call 1-877-762-2974 to order direct

WILEY